KT-526-138

Brief Contents

iii

Preface . . . . **xiv**

CHAPTER 1   Introduction to Computer User Support. **1**

CHAPTER 2   Customer Service Skills for User
Support Agents **55**

CHAPTER 3   Skills for Troubleshooting
Computer Problems **102**

CHAPTER 4   Common Support Problems **151**

CHAPTER 5   Help Desk Operation **196**

CHAPTER 6   User Support Management **250**

CHAPTER 7   Product Evaluation Strategies
and Support Standards. **288**

CHAPTER 8   End-User Needs Assessment Projects . . . **330**

CHAPTER 9   Installing and Managing End-User Computers **384**

CHAPTER 10   Training Computer Users **444**

CHAPTER 11   Writing for End Users **491**

CHAPTER 12   A User Support Utility Tool Kit **537**

APPENDIX A   Answers to Check Your Understanding
Questions **602**

APPENDIX B   HelpSTAR® 2008 Student Edition **607**

APPENDIX C   User Support Presentations and Meetings . **639**

Index **661**

Contents

iv

Preface . . . . **xiv**

CHAPTER 1   Introduction to Computer User Support. **1**

Historical Changes in Computer Use. 2
    The 1950s and 1960s: Early Computers 4
    The 1970s: The First Steps Toward
    Decentralized Computing 4
    The 1980s and 1990s: The Growth of
    Decentralized Computing 4
    The Late 1990s and 2000s: The Era of
    Distributed and Network Computing 7
Classifying End Users 7
    Environment. 8
    Skill Level 8
    Frequency of Use 8
    Software Used. 8
    Features Used 9
    Relationship 9
Resources End Users Need. 9
    Basic Hardware .10
    Add-on Peripherals. 10
    Hardware Maintenance and Upgrades 10
    Software and Software Upgrades 11
    Supplies 11
    Data and Information 11
    Technical Support 12
    Facilities, Administration, and Overhead 12
End-User Applications Software 13
Problems End-Users Experience. 16
    Waste of Resources 17
    User Mistakes 17
    Computer Crime .17
    Theft of Resources. 18

FOURTH EDITION

A GUIDE TO COMPUTER USER SUPPORT FOR HELP DESK & SUPPORT SPECIALISTS

FRED BEISSE

Lane Community College

COURSE TECHNOLOGY
CENGAGE Learning™

Australia • Brazil • Japan • Korea • Mexico • Singapore • Spain • United Kingdom • United States

COURSE TECHNOLOGY
CENGAGE Learning™

A Guide to Computer User Support for Help Desk & Support Specialists, Fourth Edition
Fred Beisse

Executive Editor: Marie Lee

Acquisitions Editor: Amy Jollymore

Managing Editor: Tricia Coia

Developmental Editor: Mary Pat Shaffer

Content Project Manager: Matthew Hutchinson

Editorial Assistant: Zina Kresin

Marketing Manager: Bryant Chrzan

Art Director: Marissa Falco

Text Designer: Shawn Girsberger

Cover Designer: Cabbage Design Company

Cover Image: © JupiterImages

Manufacturing Coordinator: Julio Esperas

Copyeditor: Andrew Therriault

Proofreader: Christine Clark

Indexer: Elizabeth Cunningham

Compositor: International Typesetting and Composition

Photo credits: Figure 1-7 Courtesy of Sapphire Technologies; Figure 2-1(a) Image copyright MalibuBooks, 2009. Used under license from Shutterstock.com; Figure 2-1(b) Image copyright vgstudio, 2009. Used under license from Shutterstock.com; Figure 3-7 Image copyright Monkey Business Images, 2009. Used under license from Shutterstock.com; Figure 3-9 Image copyright Christina Richards, 2009. Used under license from Shutterstock.com; Figure 4-2 Image copyright Chris Hellyar, 2009. Used under license from Shutterstock.com; Figure 5-10 David Hanover/Getty Images; Figure 7-2 Image copyright Monkey Business Images, 2009. Used under license from Shutterstock.com; Figures 7-4, 7-5, and 7-6 Courtesy of Honolulu Community College; Figure 9-5 Image copyright Natalia Siverina, 2009. Used under license from Shutterstock.com

International Student Edition:
ISBN-13: 978-1-4390-4205-2

ISBN-10: 1-4390-4205-5

Course Technology
20 Channel Center Street
Boston, MA 02210
USA

Cengage Learning is a leading provider of customized learning solutions with office locations around the globe, including Singapore, the United Kingdom, Australia, Mexico, Brazil, and Japan. Locate your local office at: **www.cengage.com/global**

Cengage Learning products are represented in Canada by Nelson Education, Ltd.

To learn more about Course Technology, visit **www.cengage.com/coursetechnology**

Purchase any of our products at your local college store or at our preferred online store **www.ichapters.com**

Some of the product names and company names used in this book have been used for identification purposes only and may be trademarks or registered trademarks of their respective manufacturers and sellers.

Course Technology, a part of Cengage Learning, reserves the right to revise this publication and make changes from time to time in its content without notice.

Printed in Canada
1 2 3 4 5 6 16 15 13 12 11 10

Invasion of Privacy. .18
Abusive Users 18
Computer Viruses 18
Health Problems 19
Addressing the Need for User Support Workers 19
How Organizations Provide a User Support Function 21
    Peer Support 22
    Part Time User Support 23
    User Support Worker or Work Team 24
    Help Desk Support. 24
    User Support Center 25
    User Support as an IT Responsibility. 25
    User Support Outsourced to a Vendor 26
User Support Services. 27
    Staff a Help Desk, Hotline, or Chat Service to
        Provide Information. 28
    Provide Technical Troubleshooting Assistance 29
    Locate Information to Assist Users 29
    Evaluate Hardware, Software, and Network Products 29
    Coordinate Organization-Wide Support Standards 30
    Perform Needs Assessment and Provide
        Purchase Assistance for Users 30
    Provide Installation Assistance 30
    Provide Training on Computer Systems
        and Procedures 31
    Prepare Documentation on Computer Use 31
    Assist Users with Software Development Projects. 31
    Position Descriptions for User Support Staff 32
    Knowledge, Skills, and Abilities 35
Alternative Career Paths for User Support Workers 39
    Programmer/Developer. 39
    Network Technician 39
    Web Site Maintainer 39
    Support Manager .39
    Project Manager .40
    Trainer/Technical Writer 40
    Security Specialist. 40
Chapter Summary 41
Key Terms 42
Check Your Understanding 45
Discussion Questions .48
Hands-On Activities 49
Case Projects 52

CHAPTER 2   Customer Service Skills for User
Support Agents **55**

Communication and Customer Service Skills 56
    Listen Carefully 59
    Build Understanding 61
    Respond Effectively 63
Develop an Effective Personal Communication Style. 67
Special Challenges of Telephone Communication 68
Develop an Incident Management Strategy 70
    Ask Goal-Directed Diagnostic Questions 72
    Be Honest. 72
    Say "I Don't Know" When You Don't 72
    Apologize 72
    Say "Thank You" 73
    Use Incident Management, not User-Management,
      Techniques 73
    Teach Self-Reliance 73
Customer Service and Personality Types. 74
Strategies for Difficult Clients and Incidents 77
    Users Who Complain 78
    Contacts by "Power Users" 79
    Incidents That Get Off Track 79
    Users Who Are Upset or Angry 80
    Users Who Are Abusive. 81
    Users Who Are Reluctant to Respond 81
    Users Who Won't Stop Responding 82
Client-Friendly Web Sites and Web 2.0 83
    Content. 85
    Organization. .85
    Format 86
    Mechanics. 86
Comprehensive Client Services 87
Chapter Summary .88
Key Terms 90
Check Your Understanding 91
Discussion Questions 94
Hands-On Activities 94
Case Projects 97

CHAPTER 3   Skills for Troubleshooting Computer Problems. . **102**

What Is Troubleshooting? 103
    Problem-Solving Skills 105
    Critical-Thinking Skills 106
    Decision-Making Skills 108

Tools Troubleshooters Use 108
   Communication Skills. 109
   Information Resources 113
   Diagnostic and Repair Tools. 122
   Problem-Solving Strategies 124
   Personal Characteristics of Successful Troubleshooters . . 133
Developing Your Own Approach to Problem Solving 135
Chapter Summary 136
Key Terms 138
Check Your Understanding 140
Discussion Questions 143
Hands-On Activities 144
Case Projects 147

CHAPTER 4   **Common Support Problems** **151**

Common End-User Problems 152
   Hardware Problems 152
   Software Problems. 158
   User Problems. 166
   Documentation Problems 170
   Vendor Problems. 171
   Operating Environment Problems 172
   Network Problems 172
Problem-Solving Processes Applied to
   Typical End-User Problems 175
   Problem 1: Sounds Like Trouble. 175
   Problem 2: The Problem with Modems 177
   Problem 3: Give Credit Where It Is Due. 178
   Problem 4: Antivirus Protection Worth
     Every Cent You Pay for It 180
   Problem 5: The Path Not Taken 180
   Problem 6: The Nonresponsive Network 181
   Problem 7: The Big, Red X 183
Chapter Summary 184
Key Terms 185
Check Your Understanding 187
Discussion Questions 190
Hands-On Activities 190
Case Projects 194

CHAPTER 5   **Help Desk Operation** **196**

What Is a Help Desk?. 197
The Incident Management Process 199
   Receive the Incident 200

Prescreen the Incident 200
Authenticate the User 201
Log the Incident 201
Screen the Incident 203
Prioritize the Incident 203
Assign the Incident 204
Track the Incident 205
Escalate the Incident 205
Resolve the Incident 206
Close the Incident 206
Archive the Incident 207
Help Desk Service Best Practices 208
Physical Layout of Help Desk Work Areas 209
Job Stress in Help Desk Work 210
Help Desk Technology and Tools 213
Help Desk Software 213
HelpSTAR^{2008} Software 221
Computer Telephony Systems 226
Web-Based Support 228
Trends in Help Desk Operations 230
Technology Trends 231
Workplace Trends 233
Chapter Summary 236
Key Terms 237
Check Your Understanding 240
Discussion Questions 242
Hands-On Activities 243
Case Projects 247

CHAPTER 6   User Support Management 250

Managerial Concerns: Mission, Performance,
Staffing, and Training 251
User Support Mission 252
User Support Performance and Justification 253
Staffing the Help Desk 257
User Support Staff Training 262
User Support Certification 265
Formal Education Certification 265
Vendor-Specific Certification 266
Industry-Standard Certification 267
User Support and Help Desk Certification 268
User Support Center Certification Programs 268
The Benefits of Certification 269
Certification Exam Preparation 270

User Support as a Profession. 272
Chapter Summary 276
Key Terms 277
Check Your Understanding 279
Discussion Questions 282
Hands-On Activities 282
Case Projects 285

CHAPTER 7   Product Evaluation Strategies and
Support Standards **288**

How Product Standards Emerged 289
Methods for Evaluating and Selecting Computer Products . . 291
    Information Resources 293
    Decision-Making Tools 296
Product Support Standards. 308
    How Organizations Develop Computer Product and
        Support Standards 313
    How Organizations Implement Computer Product and
        Support Standards 316
Chapter Summary 318
Key Terms 319
Check Your Understanding 321
Discussion Questions 323
Hands-On Activities 324
Case Projects 326

CHAPTER 8   End-User Needs Assessment Projects . . . **330**

Overview of User Needs Analysis and Assessment 331
End-User Needs Analysis Steps and Tasks 333
    Step 1: Understand the End User's and
        the Organization's Goals 334
    Step 2: Understand the Decision Criteria and Constraints. . 336
    Step 3: Define the Problem Clearly 338
    Step 4: Identify the Roles of Stakeholders 339
    Step 5: Identify Sources of Information 341
    Step 6: Develop an Understanding of the Existing System. . 342
    Step 7: Investigate Alternatives to the Existing System . . 344
    Step 8: Develop a Model of the Proposed Solution 346
    Step 9: Make a Build-Versus-Buy Decision 347
Needs Analysis and Assessment Tools 349
    Project Charter 350
    Cost-Benefit Analysis 352
    Data-Collection Instruments 353

      Charts and Diagrams. 356
      Prototyping Software. 357
    Managing a User Support Project 358
      Project Management Steps 359
      Project Management Tools 364
      Other Needs Assessment and Project
        Management Tools 367
    Chapter Summary 368
    Key Terms 368
    Check Your Understanding 371
    Discussion Questions 374
    Hands-On Activities 375
    Case Projects 377

CHAPTER 9   **Installing and Managing End-User Computers. . 384**

    System Installation Overview 385
    Pre-Installation Site Preparation 386
      Location 387
      Ergonomics 390
      Power Requirements 396
      Network and Telephone Access 399
      Air Conditioning 400
      Lighting 400
      Fire Suppression. 401
    Site Management Documentation 403
    Hardware Installation Tools 408
    Common Hardware Installation Steps 410
    Typical Operating System and Network
      Installation Steps. 413
      Operating System Installation 413
      Network Installation 415
    Typical Steps to Install Application Software 417
    Typical Installation Wrap-Up Tasks. 420
    Ongoing Site Management Responsibilities 422
      Media Backup 422
      Security Problems and Challenges. 423
      Disaster and Contingency Planning 425
    Other Site Management Activities 426
      Preventive Maintenance. 426
      Computer Supplies. 428
      Managing the Recycling of Computers, Peripherals,
        and Supplies. 429
    Chapter Summary 430

Key Terms 431
Check Your Understanding 434
Discussion Questions 436
Hands-On Activities 437
Case Projects 440

CHAPTER 10   Training Computer Users **444**

What Is Training?. 445
The Training Process. 446
Step 1: Plan the Training 447
    Determine the Trainees' Backgrounds 447
    Determine the Trainees' Content Needs 447
    Determine the Skill Levels Trainees Need 448
    Determine What Trainees Already Know 449
    Define the Training Objectives. 450
Step 2: Prepare for the Training. 454
    Specify Which Topics Will Be Covered 454
    Organize the Topics 455
    Select an Effective Training Format 456
    How Learners Learn 458
    Select Delivery Methods for the Training Materials 461
    Develop Specific Training Materials 471
    Design Training Evaluation Methods 471
Step 3: Present the Training 473
    Practice the Presentation. 473
    Arrive Early to Check Out the Facility 474
    Don't Read Notes or PowerPoint Slides 474
    Don't Try to Cover Too Much Material 474
    Teach the Most Important Skills 475
    Use Humor Sparingly. 475
    Pause for Comprehension Checks 475
    Monitor the Training Environment 475
    Provide Frequent Breaks 476
    Obtain Professional Feedback. 476
Step 4: Progress Toward Higher-Quality
    User Training 476
Chapter Summary 479
Key Terms 480
Check Your Understanding 481
Discussion Questions 484
Hands-On Activities 484
Case Projects 487

CHAPTER 11   Writing for End Users **491**

Types of User Documentation. 492
   Brochures and Flyers. 492
   Newsletters 493
   Handouts and Training Aids 493
   User Guides, Handbooks, and Manuals. 494
   Online Help Systems 494
   E-Mail and Chat Messages 495
   Web Pages 496
   Proposals, Letters, and Memos 497
   Procedural and Operational Documentation. 497
   Troubleshooting Guides. 498
How Technical Writing Differs from Other Writing 498
   Technical Writing Style 498
   How Technical Documents Are Organized. 500
Document Planning 501
   Who Is the Target Audience? 502
   What Does the Audience Already Know? 503
   What Does the Audience Need to Know? 503
   What Do You Want the Audience to Be Able to Do? . . . 503
   What Medium Will Be Used to Transmit the Document
     to Its Audience? 503
The Technical Writing Process 504
   Step 1: Generate an Idea List. 504
   Step 2: Organize the List into an Outline 505
   Step 3: Expand the Outline into a First Draft 505
   Step 4: Edit the Draft 507
   Step 5: Get an Outside Review 508
   Step 6: Revise the Draft 508
   Step 7: Proofread the Document 509
Technical Writing Strategies 510
   Analogies 510
   Repetition. 510
   Consistent Word Use 510
   Parallel Structure 512
   Consistent Verb Tense 512
Common Technical Writing Problems. 513
   Clutter 513
   Inappropriate Typefaces 514
   Gender References. 515
   Unclear Referents 515
   Passive Voice 515
   Nominalization. 516

Wordiness. 517
Jargon 517
Undefined Acronyms 518
Dangling Modifiers 518
Technical Writing Tools 520
Documentation Evaluation Criteria. 521
Chapter Summary 522
Key Terms 523
Check Your Understanding 525
Discussion Questions 527
Hands-On Activities 528
Case Projects 533

CHAPTER 12   **A User Support Utility Tool Kit** **537**

Introduction to Utility Software and Information Resources. . 538
Categories of Utility Software Tools 541
Hardware Support 541
System Information 546
Software Support – Operating Systems 549
Software Support – Applications. 556
System Problem Diagnosis 559
Network Support. 562
Internet Support 565
File Management Tasks 567
Performance Enhancements 572
Security Solutions 577
User Support Tools 585
Chapter Summary 589
Key Terms 589
Check Your Understanding 592
Discussion Questions 595
Hands-On Activities 595
Case Projects 599

APPENDIX A   Answers to Check Your Understanding
Questions **602**

APPENDIX B   HelpSTAR® 2008 Student Edition **607**

APPENDIX C   User Support Presentations and Meetings . **639**

Index **661**

Preface

As in previous editions of this book, my goal for the fourth edition is to address the needs of readers who want to learn about the user support field and who need resources to help them learn. This fourth edition is designed as an introduction to the broad range of topics that an entry-level user support specialist is expected to know about. The responsibilities of support positions vary widely; however, armed with the foundation of topics and activities covered in this book, workers entering the support industry will be better prepared to meet employer's expectations.

I continue to believe that learning about user support requires exposure to trade books, vendor manuals, and Web sites, but these materials are often not designed for students or for entry-level support staff. First-time learners also need textbooks with aids to learning such as key term definitions, discussion questions, hand-on activities, and case projects that help them practice and apply their new knowledge. Since the earlier editions of this book, many aspects of user support have remained the same; however, a surprising number of changes have occurred. I am grateful that Course Technology gave me the opportunity to update the book to reflect recent changes in the user support field.

The Intended Audience

This book is primarily intended for three kinds of readers:

- Readers who are considering career opportunities in computer user support and who want an introduction to the field. This book describes the kinds of knowledge, skills, and abilities they need to be employable in the support industry.

- Readers who work in another field, but find themselves in a position with growing user support responsibilities. They will be able to use this book to acquire additional breadth and depth in the support field. This audience includes programmers, computer operators, network administrators, customer support representatives, and computer applications specialists.

- Readers who are taking a course in a user support or related degree program. They can use this book to tie together knowledge and skills introduced in other courses. These readers will especially benefit from the end-of-chapter activities that provide practice skills and experiences they will use on the job.

The Approach

A Guide to Computer User Support is designed as an introduction to each of the topics covered. I believe that a user support textbook can do little more than introduce basic concepts and a beginning perspective, lead readers into the field, and point readers toward appropriate knowledge, skills, and resource materials. To derive maximum benefit from this book, each reader must be an active participant in the learning process.

The end-of-chapter discussion questions and hands-on activities are specifically designed to develop knowledge and skills, a significant percentage of which are gained through interactions with school or work colleagues. Learning to work with others in project groups or teams is important preparation for the team-oriented work environment of the 21st century. Many of the end-of-chapter activities are designed to acquaint readers with information resources and technical tools that are essential to function effectively in many support positions.

Assumed Knowledge

This textbook assumes that its readers have a background in the following areas, either through course work, independent study, or work experience:

- Basic computer concepts or computer literacy

- Word processor, spreadsheet, and database applications

- Internet and Web access

Overview of This Book

The organization of this book is based on the knowledge, skills, and abilities commonly found in user support position descriptions and on the tasks employers expect entry-level support staff to be able to perform.

CHAPTER 1: INTRODUCTION TO COMPUTER USER SUPPORT briefly discusses the historical context of end-user computing, how users increase their productivity using computer systems, the resources they need, and common problems end users encounter.

It also covers the kinds of help that support groups provide and the various ways organizations have found to support end users. It concludes with a description of the knowledge, skills, and abilities a successful applicant for a support position needs. The fourth edition also includes information about career paths for support workers.

CHAPTER 2: CUSTOMER SERVICE SKILLS FOR USER SUPPORT AGENTS describes the communication and customer service skills user support staff need. It also outlines ways to develop an incident management strategy and handle difficult support situations. The fourth edition includes new material on communicating with users through support Web sites.

CHAPTER 3: SKILLS FOR TROUBLESHOOTING COMPUTER PROBLEMS discusses common tools and methods troubleshooters use to solve computer problems. It also describes eight problem-solving strategies that a user support specialist can apply to a troubleshooting situation. The fourth edition includes new material on root cause analysis.

CHAPTER 4: COMMON SUPPORT PROBLEMS approaches computer problems from a practical perspective. It describes the types of common computer problems and shows how to apply problem-solving strategies to several real-life problems pulled from the experiences of support workers. The fourth edition includes several new end-of-chapter activities and problems that can make an important contribution to building problem solving skills and abilities.

CHAPTER 5: HELP DESK OPERATION introduces a multi-level support model and the incident management process, and provides an overview of the features of help desk software packages. The fourth edition includes coverage of industry best practices in help desk operation, expanded information about help desk job stress, and features HelpSTAR®2008 software to illustrate typical features of help desk software.

CHAPTER 6: USER SUPPORT MANAGEMENT discusses responsibilities and perspectives of support managers and supervisors that support workers need to understand. It describes the mission of support groups, and how to staff and train them. The fourth edition updates coverage of computer industry certification, professional associations for support workers, and standards of ethical conduct.

CHAPTER 7: PRODUCT EVALUATION STRATEGIES AND SUPPORT STANDARDS describes strategies to evaluate computer products and define product standards for an organization. It includes pointers to information resources and decision-making tools for evaluating and selecting computer products. The fourth edition includes an extended example of technology product standards in use at Honolulu Community College.

CHAPTER 8: END-USER NEEDS ASSESSMENT PROJECTS provides tools to help user support staff analyze and assess user needs for computer hardware, software, and network products and services. An extended case study illustrates the steps in assessment projects throughout the chapter. The fourth edition includes Microsoft® Office Project 2007 to illustrate the use of project management software tools in assessment projects. Some activities in the chapter are based on a 180-day version of the software, which is included on a CD bundled with the book.

CHAPTER 9: INSTALLING AND MANAGING END-USER COMPUTERS covers the steps to prepare an end user's site and install hardware, operating systems, and applications software. It described the role and contents of a site management notebook as well as tasks support workers often perform to help users manage their computers. The fourth edition updates many of the installation checklists from previous editions.

CHAPTER 10: TRAINING COMPUTER USERS explains how to plan training activities; how to prepare training materials; and how to present, evaluate, and improve training for end users. The fourth edition emphasizes role-playing as a training activity. (Each chapter includes a role-playing scenario designed to give readers an opportunity to apply what they learn to a work situation.)

CHAPTER 11: WRITING FOR END USERS briefly examines the many types of documents a support specialist may be assigned to prepare, and explains how to plan, write, and evaluate end-user documentation. It covers the common strategies and tools technical writers use and discusses how to avoid common writing problems. The fourth edition updates the online resources for technical writers.

CHAPTER 12: A USER SUPPORT UTILITY TOOL KIT is a new chapter in the fourth edition that addresses the growing importance of utility software to diagnose, resolve, and repair the variety of problems support specialists encounter. The chapter provides suggestions for over 30 software utilities that can be used as a starting point for building a support resource tool kit. Many of the utilities described can be downloaded, installed, and used without cost in order to get experience with the use of utility software. The chapter includes an extended case study to illustrate how several of the utilities can be used in support situations.

APPENDIX A: ANSWERS TO CHECK YOUR UNDERSTANDING QUESTIONS provides answers to end-of-chapter self-check questions.

APPENDIX B: HELPSTAR®²⁰⁰⁸ STUDENT EDITION provides a step-by-step tutorial and hands-on activities to help readers get experience with help desk software. A 180-day version of HelpSTAR®²⁰⁰⁸

Student Edition, developed by Help Desk Technology International Corporation, with access to their Web site resources, is included on a CD bundled with this book.

APPENDIX C: USER SUPPORT PRESENTATIONS AND MEETINGS is a new appendix in the fourth edition which recognizes the expectation that support workers need to be able to prepare effective presentations to users, managers and work colleagues as part of their job responsibilities. This appendix responds to requests from several instructors for coverage of presentation skills. The appendix concludes with strategies for making support worker meetings more productive.

Features

Several features in this book are designed to aid readers' understanding of user support concepts and improve its value to learners.

CHAPTER OBJECTIVES Each chapter begins with a list of the important concepts presented. This list orients readers with a quick reference to the contents of the chapter and is a useful study aid.

FIGURES AND TABLES Figures and illustrations in each chapter help readers visualize concepts and examples. Tables list conceptual items and examples in a visual and readable format.

BULLETED FIGURES Selected figures contain bullets that summarize important points. They provide an overview of upcoming discussion points and help you review material when you need to recall chapter topics.

ON THE WEB These features point readers to the Web for more information about a topic, an example related to what was learned in the chapter, or to additional information resources.

 TIPS These marginal features point readers to practical tips and other comments from the author to supplement the information in a nearby paragraph.

 NOTES These marginal features point readers to where they can find additional material on a topic elsewhere in the book.

 INFORMATION RESOURCES These marginal features point readers to additional information resources on the book's companion Web site.

ROLE-PLAYING SCENARIOS Each chapter features a role-playing scenario designed to give readers an opportunity to apply what they learn. These scenarios are based on the experiences of actual support workers and are included to give readers an opportunity to gain insight into real-world applications of the topics and build support skills.

CHAPTER SUMMARIES Each chapter's text is followed by a summary of chapter concepts. These summaries provide a helpful way to recap and revisit the main ideas covered in each chapter and help readers review chapter contents to prepare for quizzes and hands-on activities.

KEY TERMS Each chapter contains a list of the terms introduced in the chapter and a short definition of each. This list is a convenient way to review the user support vocabulary you have learned.

CHECK YOUR UNDERSTANDING End-of-chapter assessment begins with a set of approximately 20 review questions that reinforce the main ideas introduced in each chapter. These questions, which are expanded in the fourth edition, gauge whether you have mastered the concepts and provide examples of questions you might encounter on a quiz or exam. Answers to these questions are provided in Appendix A.

DISCUSSION QUESTIONS Discussion questions, a feature expanded in the fourth edition, are designed to supplement and extend the chapter topics and provide an opportunity for readers to formulate and discuss positions on issues they are likely to encounter in the support field.

HANDS-ON ACTIVITIES Although the vocabulary and concepts in user support topics are important, no amount of vocabulary can substitute for real-world experience. To supplement conceptual explanations, each chapter provides approximately ten Hands-On Activities to help readers build experience with user support tasks. Some activities involve researching information from people in the support industry, printed resources, and the Web. Others let readers work with software used by support agents in the workplace. Because Hands-On Activities ask readers to go beyond the boundaries of the text itself, they provide practice in the real-world research like that performed in a user support position.

CASE PROJECTS The end of each chapter includes several Case Projects. The projects are somewhat longer and more open-ended than Hands-On Activities and are designed to help readers apply what they have learned to business situations. They provide an opportunity to independently analyze, synthesize, and evaluate information, examine potential solutions, and make recommendations—much as one would in an actual business situation.

HELP DESK SOFTWARE A CD included with this edition includes a 180-day version of HelpSTAR®2008 Student Edition. The student edition can be used to get experience with help desk software and operational procedures such as those described in Chapter 5.

PROJECT MANAGEMENT SOFTWARE A CD included with this edition includes a 180-day version of Microsoft® Office Project Professional 2007. The trial edition can be used to plan user needs assessment and other special projects such as those in Chapter 8.

Instructor Resources

The following supplemental materials are available to instructors when this book is used in a classroom setting. All of the instructor resources available with this book are provided to the instructor on a CD.

ELECTRONIC INSTRUCTOR'S MANUAL The Instructor's Manual that accompanies this textbook includes additional instructional material to assist in class preparation, including items such as Sample Syllabi, Chapter Outlines, Technical Notes, Lecture Notes, Teaching Tips, Discussion Topics, and Additional Case Projects.

EXAMVIEW® ExamView is a powerful testing software package that allows instructors to create and administer printed, computer (LAN-based), and Web-based exams. ExamView includes hundreds of questions that correspond to the topics covered in this text, enabling students to generate detailed study guides that include page references for further review. The computer-based and Internet testing components allow students to take exams at their computers, and saves instructor time by grading each exam automatically.

POWERPOINT® PRESENTATIONS These are included as a teaching aid for classroom presentation, to make available to students on a network for chapter review, or to be printed for classroom distribution. Instructors can add their own slides for additional topics they introduce to the class.

DISTANCE LEARNING Course Technology offers WebCT and Blackboard courses for this text to provide the most complete and dynamic learning experience possible. When you add online content to one of your courses, you're adding a lot: automated tests, topic reviews, quick quizzes, and additional case projects with solutions. For more information on how to bring distance learning to your course, contact your Course Technology sales representative.

Visit this Book's Web Site

In order to extend the information contained on the pages in this book, references to many sites on the Web are used throughout the book. Sooner or later, these sites will change or be replaced with newer information. In some cases, a URL in the book may result in a "Web address not found" message. As a way to reduce the amount of typing to enter lengthy URLs and to provide alternate Web resources for obsolete links, a Web site is available to readers at **www.CUS4e. com**. The following features can be found on the book's Web site:

- Links to Web resource URLs in each chapter
- Replacement URLs for obsolete links
- Additional Web site links and information to supplement topics within the chapters
- Errata for the book and Instructor's Resources
- An e-mail link for readers and faculty to provide feedback and report broken links

Acknowledgments

I want to express my heartfelt thanks to the staff at Course Technology who played vital roles on the team of people who guided the development of the fourth edition. Amy Jollymore, Acquisitions Editor, got the project started, and Tricia Coia, Managing Editor, and Ekta Dixit, Project Manager, kept the project on track. So many other people worked on the production of the book. Several of them are listed on the copyright page, and each of them made important contributions to the result you are reading.

I want to single out the many contributions of Mary Pat Shaffer. She was the Developmental Editor for the fourth edition, and the improvements she introduced are visible in every sentence on every page. Mary Pat has the eye of a professional editor and an ability to deal with minute details. But she never loses sight of the big-picture, overall objectives we shared. I am very grateful for her ability to ask pointed questions, her on-target advice, and voluminous contributions to this book, but especially for her patience when I got stuck or missed a deadline.

I want to express my appreciation to the faculty members who reviewed a preliminary outline of the revision proposal and provided valuable feedback and insights into the organization and contents of the fourth edition.

Gerlinde Brady, Cabrillo College; Kenneth J Dreistadt, Lincoln Technical Institute; Judi Elmer, Ogden-Weber Applied Technology College; Dawn Fread, Western Technical College; Harold Grabemeyer, Southwestern Michigan College; Ronald Koci, Madison Area Technical College; and Dawn Lewis, Community College of Rhode Island.

The software bundled with this book has the potential to materially aid the understanding and job preparation skills of readers, and

I want to thank Microsoft Corporation and Help Desk Technology International Corporation for making academic versions of their products available. Thanks, too, to the staff at Honolulu Community College for their willingness to share the product standards in effect at the college as an example of an industry best practice.

I am also indebted to four professional educators who read each chapter draft and willingly shared their expertise in the support industry and in teaching user support courses. Their many suggestions for revisions and resources that will be useful to readers added significantly to the value of the book. The reviewers are Gerlinde Brady, Cabrillo College; Judi Elmer, Ogden-Weber Applied Technology College; Harold Grabemeyer, Southwestern Michigan College; and Ronald Koci, Madison Area Technical College.

I want to dedicate this fourth edition to my brother and sisters, Mark A. Beisse, Mary Ann Shaffer, and Kay E. Beisse to applaud their passion for education, information resources, and community service.

Fred Beisse
Eugene, Oregon

About the Inside Front Cover

Check out our interviews with recent graduates who are now working in the IT field. One is featured on the inside front cover of this book. If someone you know recently landed a job in IT, we'd like to interview that person too! Send your suggestions via e-mail to Amy Jollymore, Acquisitions Editor, at Amy.Jollymore@Cengage.com.

CHAPTER 1

Introduction to Computer User Support

In this chapter, you will learn about:

◎ How historical changes in computer technology have affected computer use

◎ Ways to classify end users

◎ Resources computer users need and major categories of end-user software

◎ Common problems users encounter

◎ The job market demand for user support workers

◎ Common ways to organize and provide support services

◎ Typical position descriptions for user support staff

◎ The knowledge, skills, and abilities for an entry-level support position

◎ Career paths for user support workers

The computer industry has been changing continuously since it began in the middle of the 1900s, and it will undoubtedly continue to change in the future. One result of this constant change is that computer industry professionals rarely work with the same hardware, software, networks, operational procedures, and job descriptions that they learned about in school or in training courses. In order to prepare for future positions in the computer industry, students today must learn more than just the current technology. Today's students need to learn how to keep up with constant change and must know how to make learning new technologies a part of their day-to-day work routine.

The purpose of this book is to help you learn about and prepare for information technology jobs that focus on the problems and needs that your coworkers or clients will encounter when they attempt to make effective use of computer technology. The book includes information on what you need to know and what you need to be able to do in order to work in the field of computer user support. This chapter gives you an overview of information technology from two perspectives. First, we will look at computer use from the perspective of end users—your coworkers and clients who use computers in their work or for personal activities. Second, we will introduce computer user support as a career field, and how you may prepare to work in the field as a computer support professional. In order to understand the context of end-user computing within the computer industry and the need for computer user support workers, we will begin with a brief overview of the past 60 years of development of computer technology.

Historical Changes in Computer Use

End-user computing refers to the use of computers for both business and personal use. At every level, workers today use personal computers (PCs) to accomplish their work. Furthermore, most people also have computers in their homes or use computers in public places such as libraries, schools, and government offices. However, when computers were first used in business, most workers did not have computers on their desks, nor did they use computers themselves—at least not directly. The highlights of changes in computer technology and the developments that led to end-user computing and user support are summarized in Table 1-1.

Decade	Primary Types and Uses of Computer Systems
1940s	• Invention of central processing units and peripherals
1950s	• Early use of large computers in large corporations
1960s	• Widespread use of large-scale computers
	• Early use of smaller, workgroup computers
1970s	• Widespread use of workgroup computers
	• Terminal access by workers to large-scale and workgroup computers
	• Early use of personal computers
1980s	• Widespread use of home and business personal computers
	• Availability of mass-market applications software and GUI personal computer operating systems
	• Early use of data communications and networks to connect personal computers to each other and PCs to larger systems
1990s	• Widespread use of data communications and local area and wide area computer networks
	• Distributed computing
	• Rapid growth of the Internet as a global network
2000s	• Increased use of the Internet for electronic business and business-to-business transactions
	• Availability of very low-cost PCs
	• Development of wireless communication technologies

Table 1-1   Milestones in the adoption of computer technology

3

ON THE WEB

A detailed time line of events in the history of computers is available at The History of Computing Project Web site: **www.thocp.net**. For a history of the Internet, view a slide show (requires Microsoft PowerPoint, or a viewer): **www.isoc.org/internet/history/2002_0918_Internet_History_and_Growth.ppt**.

Instead of entering the lengthy Web site addresses in the On the Web features in this book, use the book's companion Web site at **www.cus4e.com** *to link to the address of each resource described in the book.*

The 1950s and 1960s: Early Computers

In the 1950s and 1960s, computer systems in business and government were highly centralized. Early computer systems were physically very large, very expensive to buy and operate, and were therefore installed in secure central locations. These systems were programmed and operated not by users, but by computer professionals. The primary goal of early computer use was to increase worker and business productivity by automating manual tasks. However, workers used these early, large-scale systems by transporting trays of punched cards that recorded business transactions to a central site for processing.

The 1970s: The First Steps Toward Decentralized Computing

During the 1970s, computer use in many organizations gradually became decentralized. Two developments occurred to encourage the transition:

● The development of terminals (keyboards and display screens) that were located on worker's desks and could be connected directly to large computer systems.

● The development of smaller, less expensive computer systems that reduced the cost of ownership to businesses and government agencies. These systems were used by smaller businesses or departments or workgroups in larger organizations.

The 1980s and 1990s: The Growth of Decentralized Computing

It was not until the 1980s and 1990s that large numbers of workers in many companies began to use computers directly on a daily basis—a trend that ushered in the era of end-user computing. Several trends converged in the 1980s to make the widespread transition to decentralized end-user computing possible. These trends are summarized in Figure 1-1.

● The backlog of requests for new computer applications

● An increase in the number of knowledge workers

● The availability of inexpensive personal computers

● The availability of inexpensive productivity software

● The development of user-friendly graphical user interfaces

Figure 1-1   Major reasons for the growth of decentralized computing

Applications Backlog

The **applications development backlog** refers to the excess demand for new computer applications that could not be met by the supply of computer professionals available to develop them. The backlog problem—widespread and well known during this period—was a source of frustration for both the professional data-processing staffs and the business departments that demanded new applications.

More Knowledge Workers

Knowledge workers are employees whose primary job is to collect, prepare, process, and distribute information. The growth in the number of knowledge workers has corresponded with shifts in the U.S. economy from agricultural and industrial to automated work tasks that rely on computer technology in the information age.

ON THE WEB

The demand for more knowledge workers continues today. An examination of the number and kinds of jobs advertised in the Help Wanted classified ads in a Sunday newspaper attests to the unmet demand for knowledge workers in many industries. To learn more about knowledge workers, read the article "The Age of Social Transformation" by Peter Drucker (who invented the term in 1959) on the *Atlantic Monthly* Web site at **www.theatlantic.com/issues/95dec/chilearn/drucker.htm**.

Declining Personal Computer Costs

Another reason for the growth of end-user computing during the 1980s and 1990s was a dramatic drop in the cost of providing computer technology to workers. As computer costs decreased, technology capabilities (especially semiconductor power and capacity) doubled every 18 to 24 months due to advances in microcomputer technology. A **microcomputer** is a complete computer (often called a personal computer, or PC) built on a smaller scale than large-scale or workgroup systems, with a microprocessor as the central processing unit (CPU). During the 1980s, the first micro-computers in an organization were often acquired by individual workers who made unauthorized purchases, despite warnings by computer professionals that money should not be wasted on these "toy" computers.

ON THE WEB

Moore's Law is a popular rule of thumb in the computer industry. Intel co-founder Gordon Moore predicted in 1975 that the capabilities of the technology (CPU speed, for example) would double every two years. Read a 2005 interview with Gordon Moore at **news.cnet.com/Gordon-Moore-on-40-years-of-his-processor-law/2008-1006_3-5657677**.

Inexpensive Productivity Software

While early computer hardware was expensive, programming applications software was even more costly. Many organizations reported that they actually spent more on programming custom software applications than on hardware. The development of inex-pensive mass-market applications software (such as WordStar, VisiCalc, Lotus 1-2-3, and dBASE) meant that many organizations, and sometimes even individual workers, could afford not only per-sonal computer hardware but also the software that would make workers more productive computer users. As a consequence, many end users were no longer dependent on computer professionals (and the related applications development backlog) to automate their work tasks.

User Friendly Graphical User Interfaces

Early computer systems executed commands that a user typed at a terminal to communicate with the computer's operating system. During the 1980s and 1990s, many of the programs written for per-sonal computers incorporated menus and **graphical user interfaces (GUIs)** or screen images that enable users to access the program features and functions intuitively. GUIs and point-and-click mouse-pointing devices made programs much easier to use than command-oriented software.

ON THE WEB

For more information about the development of the graphical user interface, including a time line of development highlights, see **toastytech.com/guis/index.html**.

The Late 1990s and 2000s: The Era of Distributed and Network Computing

Innovations in the way computers are used continue to develop. Large-scale and workgroup computers have not been replaced by end-user personal computers in many organizations; rather, the two have been joined through the technology of computer networks. **Distributed computing** describes an environment in which the needs of the organization and its workers determine the location of its computer resources. Organizations frequently require large-scale and workgroup computers, acting as network servers, to perform enterprise-wide transaction processing and information storage, as well as desktop tools to increase personal productivity at each worker's workstation. Distributed computing relies on server, wired, wireless, and Internet network technology to link workers and clients in a small business or throughout an entire enterprise.

Changes in computer technology over the past 60 years have been accompanied by organizational changes. What was formerly known as the Data Processing Department in the 1960s and 70s has been renamed **Information Systems** or **Information Services (IS)**, or **Information Technology (IT).** The name change reflects a broader role for technology in organizations and an increased emphasis on providing services to knowledge workers. The IS or IT Department now operates distributed corporate networks that can include large-scale workgroup, desktop, notebook, and wireless systems, as well as individual communications devices, such as cellular technology.

Classifying End Users

To understand the variety of environments and situations in which organizations provide technical support to their information workers, it is helpful to recognize the different types of end users. Who are end users? Where are they located? Do they use computers in a business or home environment? How do they use computers? There are many useful ways to classify end users. Figure 1-2 lists some common ways to classify end users.

- **Environment**: personal (home) user or worker (corporate, organizational, enterprise) user
- **Skill level**: novice, semiskilled, or expert
- **Frequency of use**: occasional, frequent, or extensive
- **Software Use**: word processing, e-mail, accounting, or others (see "End-User Applications Software" in this chapter)
- **Features used**: basic, intermediate, or advanced (power users)
- **Relationship**: internal user (co-worker) or external user (client)

Figure 1-2   Common categories of end users

Environment

It can be helpful to distinguish between people whose primary use of computers occurs at home with non-business-related applications and those whose primary use occurs at work with business-related applications. Of course, many users fall into both groups at different times.

Skill Level

End users span a range from novice users (who have little or no computer experience, difficulty with basic computer vocabulary, and many questions) to highly skilled users who may be largely self-sufficient. Even users who are highly skilled in one application program may be novices in another application program or operating system.

Frequency of Use

Some people use computers only occasionally; they may not use a computer every day, or even every week. Other users make frequent, possibly daily, use of a computer. Some users make almost continual use of the computer.

Software Used

Users can be classified by which software applications they use. For example, some home users primarily work with word-processing and e-mail programs and play computer games for entertainment. Business users often work with spreadsheet and database applications or software designed for specific business use, such as a specialized medical accounting system.

Features Used

Some users may use only basic software features. They may know only how to perform a limited set of simple tasks using common features of a program. Others may use more features, including several that are intermediate in their power and complexity. Users who are comfortable with advanced software features have learned to use the full power of the software in order to be very productive, and are sometimes called power users.

Relationship

Another way to classify end users is by their relationship to the support provider. Some users are **internal users** who are coworkers in the organization that provides support services. They are sometimes called in-house clients from a support perspective. In this context, a coworker who telecommutes from home is an internal end user. Others are **external users** who are clients or customers of an organization. They are located outside the organization, which is usually seen by an external user as a vendor of hardware or services. Some external users are individual retail customers, such as users who purchase hardware, software, or technical services from a retail vendor. Other external users are enterprise users, such as those who work for a company that purchases hardware, software, or services from a vendor. As you will learn, internal and external users can make very different demands on the support services they require to be productive.

Any user may, of course, fall into several of these categories. For example, a specific end user may be a semiskilled, internal user in the Accounting Department who makes frequent use of intermediate features of QuickBooks accounting software. No matter how they are categorized, all end users need some common resources to make their use of computer technology as effective as possible.

Resources End Users Need

People who want to use computers at home, on the job, or in school often purchase their first computer on the basis of media advertising. Ads for computers may tout complete systems for less than $500. These are usable, but fairly basic, hardware configurations that may or may not include the full range of hardware a user needs to be productive at a specific task. First-time purchasers are often surprised that the full cost of owning a personal computer system is often much more than just the purchase price of the initial hardware. What kinds of resources do end users need, and what costs are they likely to encounter?

Basic Hardware

Hardware refers to the electrical and mechanical components that are part of a computer system. In addition to the system unit with a central processing unit (CPU), users need memory, storage space, a keyboard and a mouse, a monitor, and usually a printer for even basic tasks such as word processing or e-mail. The cost of the hardware is only a starting point in the cost of a complete system.

Add-on Peripherals

In addition to basic hardware, users frequently need **peripheral devices**, or hardware add-ons that plug into the computer's system unit, either internally (inside the case) or externally. For example, anyone who wants to connect to the Internet needs a dial-up or broadband modem or a wired or wireless connection to a local area network. Users who work with graphic images usually purchase a scanner or a digital camera, or both. Anyone who wants to make convenient media backups might invest in a removable disk. The list of available peripheral devices is long and can add considerable expense to a basic system.

Hardware Maintenance and Upgrades

Most PCs are sold with a basic warranty and perhaps some technical assistance to cover initial installation or operational problems. Warranties of 90 days to a year are common. During a warranty period, hardware problems are repaired or replaced without charge. A few companies also offer next-day on-site repair services. Other companies offer a warranty that specifies that the user must pay shipping to return a defective device to the manufacturer or to a repair depot. Some companies offer extended warranties on hardware components. Because most computer components that fail do so early, during the standard warranty period, the cost of extended warranties is often very high relative to their value. In any case, computer purchasers should know the features of the warranty that comes with a new PC and whether technical assistance is available locally or via a long-distance call.

Even after the initial purchase of a system and peripherals, additional costs may arise. During the two- to four-year life of a typical computer system, users might need to upgrade the amount of memory, the CPU speed, the size of the hard disk drive, the speed of a peripheral (such as a modem or a printer), or other system components. As technological improvements are introduced, users may want to take advantage of new devices such as an improved graphics or sound system or a removable hard drive. Hardware upgrades help keep systems fully functional as more complex software packages with higher memory and disk space requirements become available, and as hardware devices with more capabilities are developed.

Although the hardware components in most PCs are generally reliable, hardware service organizations stay busy diagnosing and repairing a multitude of malfunctions. Most organizations and even individual users with a sizable investment in computer equipment should budget for occasional hardware repairs. Although individual home users may beat the odds and never need hardware repairs, the probability is that at some point, a user will experience a burned-out power supply or a crashed hard drive, and have to pay the cost of a replacement.

Software and Software Upgrades

Most hardware packages are bundled (sold) with a preconfigured operating system. However, some users need an alternate operating system such as Linux, instead of, or in addition to, Windows. For these users, the alternate operating system often represents an added cost.

Users should anticipate their application software needs and budget accordingly, especially if they need to purchase one or more special-purpose packages. Examples of specialized software include a computer-aided design (CAD) program, or a software package tailored to a specific business, such as a patient-billing system. Although mass-market software is often fairly inexpensive, specialized software can add thousands of dollars to the cost of a system. The significant cost of software is a reason users are attracted to open source software, which is distributed free of charge.

Besides the initial purchase of an operating system and applications software, users need to budget for software upgrades. Although some software upgrades are free when downloaded from the Internet, many software upgrades must be purchased. Common examples include annual fees for many virus-protection programs and annual updates to a tax-preparation program.

Supplies

When estimating the total cost of a computer system, users should be sure to include consumables, such as printer paper, mailing labels, ink-jet or laser printer cartridges, cleaning supplies, media (recordable CDs and DVDs or tape cartridges), cables, and other supplies they will need to operate their system.

Data and Information

As end users communicate more with other users and obtain information from outside sources, they can incur costs for information services. The monthly cost of an Internet service provider falls into this category, as do the costs of downloading stock market, financial, or economic data from an online service. Although many information

11

vendors initially offer free access to data to attract customers, providers of specialized and proprietary information and expert knowledge will typically charge for this access after an introductory period.

Technical Support

As end users buy and learn new programs and discover new uses for programs they already own, they often need technical support. Support costs can include installation assistance, training courses, books, and magazines. Users may want to contract with a vendor to perform the initial system installation tasks, or may need to contact a help desk to solve an installation or operational problem. When they do, they might have to pay for long-distance telephone charges in addition to the cost of the support call itself. Some computer vendors sell installation assistance and user support by the hour or for a fixed fee. In a large organization, personal computer support for its workers is a major budget item.

Training is a good example of a technical support service that can add substantially to the cost of a computer system. Training for end users is available in a variety of formats, as described in Chapter 10. Some users try to avoid the cost of training by using a trial-and-error learning method, which would appear to be free. However, when you factor in the cost of reduced productivity and the errors made by a poorly trained user, the hidden costs of this approach to training are significant. While the purchase of a $40 tutorial, book, or online course for a software product may seem inexpensive, a worker's time must be included as a hidden cost.

Facilities, Administration, and Overhead

Both home users and businesses should budget for the cost of the facilities needed to house and operate a computer system. Facilities include furniture, ergonomic devices (such as keyboard wrist rests and antiglare screens), electricity, air conditioning, power conditioners, space, and other workplace components that are necessary to operate a computer system.

In many organizations, overhead and supervisory costs are related to the management of end-user computing systems. These costs include acquisition assistance, purchase-order processing, shipping, inventory control, insurance, security, and related costs of doing business. The cost of end-user computing must include a proportional share of overhead costs.

The list of cost categories for an end-user computing system is long. Of course, not all costs apply to each user or to every system. But what does it all cost, bottom line? The **total cost of ownership (TCO)**, or the total expenditures necessary to purchase, maintain, upgrade, and support an end user's personal computer over its expected useful lifetime, provides this figure. Gartner, a technology consulting company that researches trends in the computer industry, estimates that the total cost of ownership to an organization for a personal computer system over a four-year period averages over $23,000, or approximately $5800 per year. Hardware costs accounted for only about 20% of the total cost of ownership; software, maintenance, and support made up the remainder.

As you can see from this overview, end users need many types of resources to make their computers true productivity tools. End users who are attracted to an ad for a $500 computer should be aware that other ownership costs must be included in the total package.

ON THE WEB

To learn more about total cost of ownership and the factors users should consider in a computer budget, see **www. jaekel.com/white3.html**.

End-User Applications Software

Among the computer resources end users need, applications software is a resource that has a significant impact on user productivity. Tasks that formerly required considerable manual effort, such as preparing a budget report or maintaining a mailing list, can be done faster and more accurately with a well-designed applications software program. End users run a variety of software applications, which are grouped into several broad categories:

Chapter 9 lists some of the popular packages in each category.

- **Electronic Mail and Instant Messaging**—Electronic mail (e-mail) enables users to communicate with other users. It is one of the most common business and personal uses of computers today. A popular feature of e-mail is the ability to send attachments to a message (an attachment is separate file transmitted with the e-mail message that contains a document, worksheet, graphic image, or other output from an application program). Instant messaging (or "chat") is communication between two or more users who are online (connected to the Internet) at the same time.

- **Web Browser**—A Web browser is a software tool that enables users to find and display information on the Internet and to perform tasks such as banking and shopping from a home computer. Pages of information in a format called Hypertext Markup Language (HTML) are stored and transmitted via Internet servers. A Web browser retrieves each page and displays it on the user's PC.

- **Word Processing**—Word-processing software enables users to prepare and change text and to easily integrate graphics, numeric data, and footnotes into a document that can be printed or e-mailed as an attachment. Word processors are usually part of an office suite of software tools.

- **Spreadsheets**—Because office workers frequently prepare numeric reports in addition to narrative text, electronic spreadsheets are close to the top of many users' software shopping lists. Spreadsheets are used to prepare budgets, sales reports and forecasts, financial statements, and management analyses. Spreadsheet software is also commonly a part of an office suite of software tools.

- **Database Management**—End users frequently need to track information that relates to business activities and projects. A database manager is used to maintain client lists, mailing lists, personnel records, office supply inventories, and class rosters. Database software runs the gamut from easy-to-use packages that are often included in office suites to sophisticated enterprise-wide data-management packages.

- **Graphics**—Users often need to summarize and present information in the form of pictures, charts, maps, or drawings. Graphics software lets a user create illustrations and charts that analyze trends, show relationships, and summarize large amounts of data. Many word-processor, spreadsheet, and database packages include some limited graphics capabilities.

- **Planning and Scheduling**—Office workers spend considerable time planning and scheduling their individual tasks as well as collaborating on team projects. Software packages for planning and scheduling include personal information managers, which help business or home users maintain an electronic calendar, a to-do list, and an electronic address book. For collaborative projects, scheduling and calendar software can help users arrange meetings at an available time for all team members. In addition, project-management programs allow managers to plan, schedule, and monitor the status of tasks in a project team, as you will see in Chapter 6.

- **Desktop Publishing**—Desktop publishing software combines the features of a word processor and a graphics program. Desktop publishing software enables users to design, lay out, and prepare—at a relatively low cost—high-quality brochures, newsletters, posters, manuals, and other printed material that would otherwise need to be designed and typeset by a printing professional.

- **Web Site Development—Web site development software** is popular with professional and home users who design and maintain a business or personal Web site. Web developer tools enable users to create, maintain, and update Web pages that include a mixture of text and graphics and incorporate features such as e-mail links, blogs, chat rooms, File Transfer Protocol (FTP), and restricted access for security.

- **Educational and Entertainment Software**—Educational software provides learners with hands-on experience to supplement an instructor's lectures or distributed materials. Educational software can simulate real-world activities, test learner understanding, and provide feedback on a learner's progress. Computer games are, of course, a significant portion of the entertainment industry.

- **Enterprise Applications**—Corporations and business enterprises continue to run many of the same applications on their large-scale systems as they did decades ago: payroll, accounting, inventory and asset control, manufacturing, and human resource management. Newer categories of applications software for large-scale systems include customer relationship management (CRM) and enterprise resource planning (ERP).

- **Industry-Specific Application**—In addition to the general categories of applications software listed earlier, many businesses and professionals use computer applications that are specific to their specialized businesses. Examples include:

  - Patient care and billing software used in medical, dental, optometric, veterinary, and other health-care occupations for recordkeeping and billing

  - Geographic Information Systems (GIS) software used by governmental, urban planning, and engineering organizations to analyze geographic data and prepare maps

  - Brokerage transaction systems that allow financial institutions and individual investors to submit buy and sell orders for stocks and commodities directly to a stock exchange

  - Automated design software used by engineering and construction firms to plan structural steel and concrete bridges and buildings and manage the details of infrastructure construction projects

The preceding categories describe some common personal computer applications and include many of the primary applications workers

16

use in business, government, education, and other organizations. New categories of applications continue to emerge as needs develop. Whether for home or business use, almost all software applications are designed to increase users' productivity. In fact, most organizations justify their computer purchases on the basis that they help make workers more efficient. Computers can either increase the amount of output (product or service) a worker can produce based on a given amount of input (effort), or reduce the amount of input required to produce a given amount of output. In general, end-user computing has accomplished this ambitious goal, but not without problems along the way.

ON THE WEB

For some examples of how productivity of knowledge workers is measured and improved, read an industry white paper prepared by Microsoft that measures productivity gains due to using an office suite: **download.microsoft.com/download/ c/6/c/c6c4093f-851d-4ddb-9a0f-d27f0567321f/ Office-System-Business-Value.doc**.

Problems End-Users Experience

The productivity gains from end-user computing are often accompanied by a new set of problems that organizations must address. Although not necessarily unique to end-user computing, the problems listed in Figure 1-3 can result from an environment in which powerful hardware and software tools are used (can be easily misused) by a large number of workers.

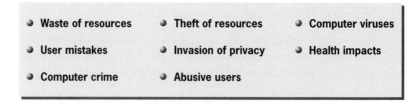

● Waste of resources	● Theft of resources	● Computer viruses
● User mistakes	● Invasion of privacy	● Health impacts
● Computer crime	● Abusive users	

Figure 1-3   Common problems related to end-user computing

There is a good chance that every end user will either encounter or even cause one or more of these problems in the course of their work or home computing experience.

Waste of Resources

Waste occurs when money, time, or other resources are spent in ways that do not contribute directly to increased user productivity, or that result in lower productivity. Examples include:

- A user who does not have the expertise and experience to make cost-effective purchasing decisions about hardware, peripherals, software, and networks. For example, an inexperienced end user might purchase software that is incompatible with existing hardware.

- A user who spends excessive time trying to solve a problem with hardware or software that could be solved quickly with a phone call to a support person.

- A worker who spends time searching for information on the Internet or reading and sending e-mail messages that are not directly job related.

User Mistakes

Users who are careless or not properly trained can easily make mistakes as they use sophisticated software. Examples include:

- A user who prepares a spreadsheet to estimate a project's cost may inadvertently enter the wrong formula or data for critical calculations.

- A user who attempts to clean up disk space deletes or uninstalls important software or data because he or she does not understand its purpose.

- A user who fails to make a backup copy of important information and loses the data due to a hardware failure.

Computer Crime

Computers are also used to commit intentional crimes. Examples include:

- A worker who has access to sensitive company information that would be potentially valuable to a competitor may try to profit from the sale of the information.

- A new user who is not familiar with fraudulent requests for information receives an e-mail message and reveals bank account information. The user becomes a victim of identity theft.

Theft of resources

Another form of computer crime is theft of computer equipment, software, or services. Examples include:

- A user who illegally copies, distributes, or uses computer programs or information (proprietary data, videos, or music), commonly called software **piracy**.

- A worker who uses the Internet at work (contrary to company policy) to sell items on eBay.

- A user who finds a removable USB drive in a machine in a school's teaching lab and pockets the device instead of turning it in to lost and found.

- A worker who removes a software installation CD from his/her place of employment and takes it home to install on a home computer. Legal or illegal? The answer depends on the software vendor's license agreement (which may or may not permit home use), and on the employer's policies.

Invasion of Privacy

Another form of computer crime is invasion of privacy, where unauthorized parties exploit personal information. Examples include:

- A user who has access to confidential medical information at work searches the files of friends and relatives.

- A user who is unaware of the risks of spyware inadvertently downloads software that secretly records information about purchases made on Web sites. The spyware periodically sends a history of the user's purchases to a company that resells profiles of users.

Abusive Users

Worker abuse is not unique to the information age, however, workers who use computer technology in an abusive way present difficult challenges to managers. Examples include:

- A user who continues to send unwanted, personal e-mail messages to a coworker despite repeated requests to not send personal messages.

- A user who displays offensive, off-color material on an office display screen that is visible to coworkers.

Computer Viruses

A **computer virus** is a piece of software created with malicious intent that can destroy information, erase or corrupt software, or adversely affect the operation of a computer that is infected by the virus software. Examples include:

- A user who downloads software that contains a virus, which attacks services throughout an office network.

- A user who forwards e-mails to colleagues with an attachment that contains a virus.

- A user who sends information to e-mail contacts about a suspected new virus attack. The virus is a well-documented hoax, but the message results in lost time as coworkers investigate the potential problem.

Health Problems

Every tool that can be used can also be misused. A common source of misuse that may not even be apparent to end users is the physical environment in which a computer is operated. Without proper lighting, space, furniture, and environmental safeguards, physical injury to end users can result. Examples include:

- A user who doesn't take adequate breaks loses work time due to **carpal tunnel syndrome**, which is severe hand or wrist pain due to an inflammation of the tendons in a user's hand and wrist, and back and neck aches.

- A user who experiences extreme stress due to the frustrations of working with technology is forced into early retirement due to health problems.

- An employer who refuses to purchase ergonomic office furniture despite requests from workers risks injury to workers, lower productivity, and disability claims. **Ergonomics** is a field that studies how to design a workspace that promotes worker health, safety, and productivity. Many common ailments can be avoided by paying attention to office ergonomics.

 Chapter 9 discusses ergonomic concerns and workspace design in more detail.

Professionals who provide technical support to end users often confront these problems. A user support worker's responsibilities may include consulting with users about possible solutions to problems that arise due to the use of technology.

Addressing the Need for User Support Workers

Most manufacturing, service, or consulting organizations provide computers to their knowledge workers to help them be more productive. But an organization's commitment usually does not end with the initial purchase. Most organizations understand that they must also provide some form of ongoing assistance to their workers so that the computers become tools that increase worker productivity instead of stumbling blocks and sources of frustration. To meet the demand for computer support, many organizations have recognized an increasing need for user support workers. With the growth of end-user computing, along with the growth of the Internet as a way to obtain information, organizations often find themselves unable to meet the demand for user support and support workers. The U.S. Bureau of Labor Statistics (BLS) estimates that the number of computer support and network specialists will grow from about 800,000 to over 1 million over the next 10 years, a growth rate (25%) that is somewhat faster than job growth in the U.S. economy.

ON THE WEB

If you would like to know more about the BLS outlook for employment in computer and network support occupations, see their updated reports at **www.bls.gov/oes/current/oes151041.htm** for Computer Support Specialists and at **www.bls.gov/oes/current/oes151071.htm** for Network Support occupations.

During the first decade of the twenty-first century, several trends have influenced the demand for user support workers.

1. The economic recession from 2001–2003 caused a gradual increase in the overall U.S. unemployment rate to about 6%. As a result, hiring in all information technology fields, including user support, decreased from the rapid growth years of the 1990s.

2. The transfer of some technical support jobs overseas (especially to India and East Asian countries), where well-trained workers are available and wages are comparably lower has reduced the demand somewhat for IT and technical support workers in the United States.

3. Some organizations that need technical support services now contract with temporary employment agencies for the workers they need. Some of these temporary work opportunities evolve into permanent positions, so that the temporary assignment is effectively a trial period for both the employee and the employer.

ON THE WEB

To learn about temporary employment agencies in your area that seek computer professionals, see the Web site of the American Staffing Association at **www.staffingtoday.net**.

4. Some organizations have experienced an increased demand for support workers due to the expansion of mobile technologies and the increased need for computer security specialists.

ON THE WEB

ComputerWorld, a computer industry magazine, provides an interactive salary estimator on its Web site at: **www.computerworld.com/action/usertools.do?command=getSalaryInformation&yr=2007**. Enter the job title in which you are interested (for example, Help Desk/Technical Support Specialist), select an industry, and then select a region of the country. Note that the estimates in *ComputerWorld*'s survey are often based on small numbers of respondents and are reported as averages. Salaries for entry-level, starting positions are much lower than average salaries.

How Organizations Provide a User Support Function

Computer user support (or simply user support) provides information and services to workers or clients to help them use computers more productively in their jobs or at home. Computer user support includes a broad spectrum of services provided to computer users to help them resolve problems that arise and to help them be more productive when they use computer technology. The user support function is known by a variety of names in various organizations. Common names for user support include customer service, help desk, technology support services, client support services, computer assistance, computer help hotline, call center, information center, or the word "support" with any modifier, such as "user," "product," "hardware," "software," or "network." **Technical support** is usually a level of user support that focuses on high-level troubleshooting and problem solving.

In some organizations, user support is called technical support, especially if the support staff consists of workers who are technicians or who have high-level technical skills. No matter what name is used, what is important are the tasks that user support performs in an organization.

Organizations provide support to their workers or clients in a variety of ways. Figure 1-4 lists the most common methods of organizing the user support function. These methods are described in more detail in the following sections.

- Peer support
- Part-time user support
- User support worker or work team
- Help desk support
- User support center
- User support as an IT function
- User support outsourced to a vendor

Figure 1-4   Common ways that organizations provide a user support function

The strategy that a specific organization selects to provide user support often depends on the organization's size, type, location, financial situation, and goals for computer support services, as well as the skill level and the support needs of workers and clients. In fact, an organization may use different support strategies at different times as the needs of its workers and clients change, and it may use more than one strategy at the same time.

Peer Support

Many small organizations and even individual departments in larger organizations provide support services with a peer support model. One or more workers, whose job titles usually have little to do directly with computers (for example, they are office managers, administrative specialists, or accounting department heads), are generally recognized as *the* person to turn to when a computer user has a question. This form of support is called **peer support**, and is often informal, because workers look to their colleagues, or peers, when they need computer assistance. For example, a sales representative with a special interest in computer technology may become the "guru" for computer problems that arise in the sales department.

ON THE WEB

Microsoft has extended the strategy of peer support to the Web in the form of virtual user groups of peers who share common interests. To learn more about Microsoft user groups, go to **www.microsoft.com/communities/usergroups/default.mspx**. Click the **Find a Community** link to see a list of peer user groups. A vendor-neutral Web site that offers a technical support forum is: **www.techsupportforum.com**.

An informal network of peers who provide user support to their work colleagues often precedes the formation of a more formal organizational structure. Informal peer support also occurs in colleges and vocational schools, where students quickly learn who among their classmates is a good source of information and assistance. You may have provided informal peer support in a computer or training lab when the person next to you asked for your help in solving a hardware or software problem.

Part Time User Support

Often the first step an organization takes toward a formal computer support function occurs when some user support responsibilities are written into an existing worker's position description. This step may formalize a responsibility that existed informally for some time. The combination of user support with other responsibilities is a good way for very small organizations to meet the need for computer support when they cannot justify the cost of a full-time support position. Workers who are assigned user support responsibilities in conjunction with other duties often see the designation as a positive career step because their expertise is recognized formally and perhaps rewarded financially. On the downside, these workers can become overloaded and stressed because computer support tasks can make significant demands on their time and can interrupt or compete with other assigned tasks.

Small organizations that sell computer hardware or software often provide informal client support during the early stages of product development and sales. When the volume of sales is small, client support may be assigned to a product development engineer or a programmer along with their other duties. As sales increase, the need to provide support to a growing client base becomes greater. At that point, the support function usually becomes more formal, in the form of a full-time support position or a user support group.

User Support Worker or Work Team

When organizations find that part-time or peer workers can no longer handle the volume or variety of requests for computer support or that the hidden costs of peer support are growing, they have several options. One alternative is to devote a full-time position to provide support. Some organizations recognize that they have reached this point when a number of workers are engaged in informal peer support roles or when several workers provide computer support as one of their official responsibilities. Organizations that devote a full-time position to user support tasks may seek the expertise of a support worker who has a greater breadth and depth of technical skills and an ability to communicate effectively with users.

A second alternative is to organize the part-time support workers into a **user support team**, a formal workgroup that is organized to provide computer support services. Depending on the needs of the organization, a user support team can consist of workers who provide support in addition to other job responsibilities. The advantage of these split positions is that the support workers can be very familiar with the day-to-day business operation of the organization. A user support team can also combine full- and part-time staff into a support group.

Another alternative open to companies that experience a growing demand for computer support is to outsource their support needs, a strategy that is discussed in an upcoming section.

Help Desk Support

When individual workers need assistance, they may turn to the staff of a user support team or they may contact a help desk facility. A **help desk** provides a single point of contact for users in need of technical support, whether they are internal workers or external clients. A help desk manages client problems and requests and provides solutions-oriented support services. A help desk may be part of a larger user support group, or it may stand alone as the primary source of user support. In a large organization with many internal users, a help desk may be one of many support services offered. In a computer products vendor organization, a help desk may be the only support service provided to customers.

A help desk facility often includes one or more of these options:

- A physical location where internal workers or external clients can go when they have a question or problem, or want to request an office visit or a field service call

- A telephone number (sometimes called a **hotline**) that external clients or internal workers can call for assistance with a hardware or software product

- An e-mail address, Web site, or online **chat service** that workers or clients can contact for technical assistance

Help desk staff attempt to resolve problems as soon as possible. If they cannot, they may refer the problem to someone else for resolution. For example, a help desk staff member may serve as an interface between an internal user with a problem and an external vendor who can solve the problem.

User Support Center

Another organizational model for user support services is a user support center. A **user support center** (also called an **information center**) provides a wider range of services than a help desk to an organization's computer users who are primarily internal users. These services can include consultation on computer purchases (it may even sell computer products to workers); a training center or training program to provide learning experiences, manuals, and other documentation on supported hardware and software products; and a help desk for information, troubleshooting, and assistance. The user support center in some organizations may provide facilities management and hardware repair services as well.

User Support as an IT Responsibility

Although some organizations view computer user support as a separate, independent function, other organizations assign this responsibility to the IT department. Technical support as part of the IT department has advantages and disadvantages. On the one hand, because the IT department's primary responsibility is to design and develop application programs and operate the organization's large-scale systems and telecommunications networks, some organizations have found that the IT department is not an effective location for the end-user support function. The IT staff is often busy working on its own priorities, and may have little time to devote to work with end-users. On the other hand, other organizations believe that all corporate computing activities should be organized under one umbrella (the IT department) in order to provide a single point of contact for all network, personal computer and telecommunications users. Whether end-user support is organized separately or combined with other computer activities in an IT department depends on an organization's history, its experience with computer support, its organizational culture, and its users' needs.

The operation of a help desk is described in greater detail in Chapter 5.

Telephone help desk support is a small part of a much larger industry. The call center industry includes incoming, outbound, and blended telephone centers that respond to clients in the travel, telecommunications, and financial services industries. A user support hotline or telephone help desk is technically an incoming call center. Telemarketing and political surveys are examples of activities in outbound call centers. Blended call centers combine both incoming and outbound telephone operations.

25

ON THE WEB

Chaim Yudkowsky, a CPA writing about how organizations provide user support services to its workers, discusses the pros and cons of locating the help desk function inside and outside IT. Read his perspective at **accounting.smartpros.com/x33607.xml**.

User Support Outsourced to a Vendor

Outsourcing is another alternative for organizations that need to provide support services to their workers and clients. To **outsource** its user support services, an organization contracts with a vendor that specializes in user support functions to handle problem incidents. Organizations can outsource support services for both internal and external users. For example, workers may contact a support provider via a dedicated telephone line or e-mail. Alternately, an organization's internal help desk operation may handle some incidents itself and refer difficult technical problems to an external support provider. Outsourcing can be an attractive option for an organization that wants to control its costs or take advantage of expertise it does not have among its existing support staff.

ON THE WEB

To learn more about the advantages of outsourcing help desk and user support services, visit the Web site of Convergys, a company that provides outsourced support for other organizations and vendors, at **www.convergys.com/industries/technology/technical-support.php**.

Several disadvantages of outsourcing user support include:

1. Outsourced support usually occurs by telephone or e-mail because on-site assistance can be prohibitively expensive and is rarely included in an outsourcing agreement.

2. Outsourced support costs are predictable, but not necessarily lower than internal support.

3. When an organization outsources support, it relies on a vendor's staff for an important organizational function. It does not develop its own in-house technical support expertise.

4. When support is outsourced, the support staff rarely develops a personal relationship with an organization's end users. A personal relationship between end users and support staff often encourages users to report problems and request help.

ON THE WEB

Client Outsource is an example of a technical support vendor that reflects the trend for support providers to locate in India and East Asian countries. Visit their Web site at **www. clientoutsource.com**.

No single, one-size-fits-all organizational structure for end-user support works well in every situation. More often than not, an organization's approach to user support evolves over time, and is influenced by its history, goals, resources, corporate culture, expertise, and needs.

User Support Services

The user support function in an organization frequently provides a variety of services. The range of services provided depends on the goals of the organization, the specific needs of the workers or clients, and the resources the organization decides to devote to the support function. Figure 1-5 lists some common user support services.

- Staff a help desk, hotline, or chat session to provide information
- Provide technical troubleshooting assistance for hardware, software, and network problems
- Locate information to assist users
- Evaluate hardware, software, and network products
- Coordinate organization-wide support standards
- Perform needs assessment and provide purchase assistance for users
- Provide system installation assistance
- Provide training on computer systems and procedures
- Prepare documentation on computer use
- Perform computer facilities management tasks
- Assist users with software development projects

Figure 1-5   Common user support services

Figure 1-6 illustrates the wide variety of support services users need. User support, as a field within information technology, includes all of these functions. Not every organization provides all these services to its workers or clients, but organizations that provide user support offer at least some of these services to respond to worker or client needs.

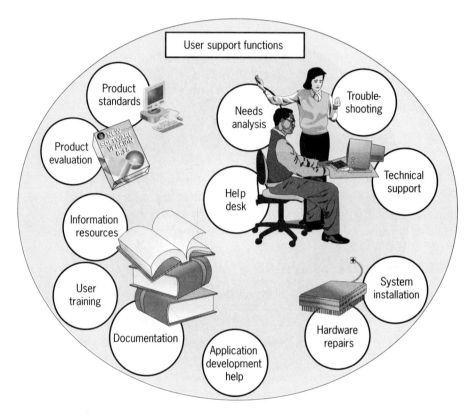

Figure 1-6 Common user support functions in organizations

Staff a Help Desk, Hotline, or Chat Service to Provide Information

Chapter 2 discusses the client service and communication skills that support staff need in a help desk environment. Chapter 5 describes the operation of a help desk from the perspective of a help desk agent.

Users who encounter problems with their computer system need a place to turn for information. A help desk, hotline, or chat service often meets this need for information. Providing information is one of the most common types of services provided by a user support organization. A help desk, hotline, or online chat service can provide a variety of information services, such as:

- Responding to requests for product information

- Providing solutions to common problems

- Marketing and selling products and services

- Receiving and logging user complaints about product features
- Handling warranty claims and authorizing product returns or exchanges

Provide Technical Troubleshooting Assistance

Although a help desk, hotline, or chat service can handle common user problems and questions, some problems fall outside a help desk's expertise. Most organizations recognize the need for a level of technical troubleshooting provided by people who have the expertise to resolve intractable problems that occur. These problems can include hardware diagnosis, repairs, or upgrades, fixes or workarounds for difficult applications software problems, and troubleshooting network crashes or poor performance.

Chapter 3 presents some strategies for troubleshooting difficult technical problems. Chapter 4 provides examples of common user support problems. Chapter 5 describes how problem incidents are managed.

Locate Information to Assist Users

A challenge that continually confronts user support staff is the need to locate information to resolve a user's question or problem. Although organizations provide their workers with computers and software, they often do not supply manuals or documentation about computer operation. In other cases, manuals get misplaced or thrown away by users, or become obsolete. Users can sometimes use online help, which is can be excellent in commercial software products. But online help is often neither in-depth enough nor technical enough to help users solve every problem, especially difficult ones. And sometimes vendor documentation is just not very good. For their information needs, users often turn to the support staff.

Information can be found in a variety of places: printed vendor manuals, trade books and textbooks, online help, CD-ROM databases, Web sites, and automated telephone voice-response units. User support workers need to understand the characteristics of each of these information resources and be able to use them effectively.

Check the **Information Resources** section on the companion Web site (**www. CUS4e.com**) for pointers to information resources that user support staff have found helpful.

Evaluate Hardware, Software, and Network Products

Most organizations are on the lookout for new technologies that will help their workers enhance productivity. Consequently, the user support staff must research, compare, and evaluate new technology products and services, including hardware, software, and network products, against existing products. The user support staff must find answers to such questions as:

- Will a new product make workers more productive?
- Will a specific product meet user needs better than another product?

29

- Should some or all users upgrade from one version of an application to a newer one, or wait until the next version is released?

- What features are important to evaluate in the purchase of a new computer?

- Will a particular hardware configuration or software package be cost effective?

Chapter 7 provides examples of tools to help support staff with product-evaluation tasks.

Individual workers do not always have the information and expertise they need to make these decisions wisely. When users make individual purchasing decisions, organizations can encounter incompatibilities, excessive costs, unusable products, and productivity problems that can be difficult to resolve. The evaluation of new hardware and software products is an important, challenging, and ongoing task for user support staffs.

Coordinate Organization-Wide Support Standards

Chapter 7 describes the role of support standards in organizations.

A task closely related to product evaluation is the definition of product support standards. **Support standards** are lists of computer products that an organization allows its workers to use and that it will support. Support standards help limit the hardware, software, and network products that a support staff must be able to support. Therefore, standards reduce support costs. Support standards are important because it is impossible for an organization to support every hardware configuration or software package that an individual user or department might choose to purchase.

Perform Needs Assessment and Provide Purchase Assistance for Users

Chapter 8 explains how to perform a needs analysis for an end user.

In addition to evaluating computer products and defining support standards, the support staff tries to match supported products with the needs of each user. Occasionally, the match between a user's needs and specific products is obvious. In other cases, support staff may perform a user **needs analysis** (or needs assessment), which is an investigation to determine the features and configuration of hardware and software (from among those supported or available) that will best match a user's specific needs. Most support teams that offer this service also assist users with the paperwork required to purchase a system, such as forms to justify the purchase, place an order, and pay for the system.

Provide Installation Assistance

Once an organization or individual user has purchased a system or upgrade, the support staff may offer to unpack, set up, install, and configure the system for an end user. The purpose of this service is efficiency; the support staff often has the tools and expertise to make sure the installation is done correctly and can identify and solve many common installation problems that might frustrate an inexperienced user. Where applicable, the support staff can ensure that the appropriate network software is installed and configured to connect a computer to the organization's network. They can also install peripheral devices such as printers and scanners, and install and configure driver software for these devices. While some users might be able to perform these tasks, user support staff can often do the work faster and with fewer errors because they tend to have more experience with system installations than end users.

31

In addition to installation assistance, user support teams often help users with **computer facilities management** tasks such as network security, media backups, virus detection and prevention, ergonomic analyses, supplies management, preventive maintenance and repairs on hardware and peripherals, and other related tasks.

Chapter 9 details the system installation process.

Provide Training on Computer Systems and Procedures

Users who have new hardware or software, or new job responsibilities, may require training to use their new or upgraded system effectively, or to use their existing system more effectively. With proper training, users can become productive more rapidly than if they learn by trial and error. User support teams in many organizations provide end-user training. The support team may have periodic group training sessions, provide one-on-one training, or suggest ways to learn a new system that match a user's personal learning needs and style.

Chapter 10 presents some guidelines on how to prepare effective user training materials and conduct training sessions.

Prepare Documentation on Computer Use

Although user training is a necessary and often efficient way to teach users how to effectively use the features of a system, documentation is equally important. Whereas a training session is generally a one-time event, documentation can be retained by a user to answer questions or as a reminder of how to perform a task they may perform only occasionally.

Documentation includes introductory manuals for new users, explanations of organizational computer use procedures and guidelines, as well as "how to" tutorials and reference manuals on specific software products. It also includes online documentation in the form of help files, answers to frequently asked questions (FAQs), and e-mail responses to remote users.

Chapter 11 provides pointers on how to write documentation and other materials targeted to end users.

Assist Users with Software Development Projects

Most user support teams do not provide software development or programming as part of their regular services to users. However, in some organizations, the support staff may *help* users develop

Because software development is an extensive topic, no chapter in this book is devoted specifically to software development tasks for support staffs. The ability to provide assistance with software development projects requires additional training or education in applications software and programming languages.

software applications to solve specific problems or meet specialized requirements for information. For example, support staff may consult with users on the most effective way to program a difficult task in a spreadsheet.

Software development has long been considered the domain of the IT department. However, with today's powerful application development tools, such as scripting languages, spreadsheets, database-management packages, and Web-page development tools, end users can often develop some applications independent of the IT department.

Although the mission of user support groups in organizations differs considerably, the tasks they perform define their service profile in an organization. Whereas most support groups provide help desk services and troubleshooting assistance, a smaller percentage provide documentation or product training. Few provide applications development assistance.

Position Descriptions for User Support Staff

Positions in the user support industry frequently include some combination of the tasks outlined in the previous section. A **position description** is a written description of the qualifications and responsibilities for a job in an organization. It is a tool that reflects how an organization structures its user support function. For example, when describing a user support position, an organization with a full-fledged support group is more likely to include the ability to analyze worker computer needs and recommend hardware and software purchases. On the other hand, an organization that primarily provides telephone support usually emphasizes problem-solving and communication skills, and is much less likely to expect applicants to assess user needs or to be able to train end users, for example.

To understand more about the specific job of a user support staff member, let's look in detail at two position descriptions of actual support positions. The first position description, shown in Figure 1-7, describes the duties and responsibilities of a Help Desk Support Representative. Sapphire Technologies, a company that provides IT staffing recruitment for other companies, prepared the position description to recruit applicants for the position described. The position description in Figure 1-7 provides a good picture of the wide range of activities you might encounter in user support positions in today's job market. If you are a prospective user support worker, you should be aware that managers will probably look for these kinds of capabilities.

Company: Sapphire Technologies

Location: New York, NY

Job Title: Help Desk Support Representative

The Opportunity: The Help Desk Support Representative is an integral member of the Information Technology team and is involved in resolving technical issues and troubleshooting. This is an excellent opportunity to join IT and support the needs of our internal clients.

The Role:

- The IT Help Desk Representative responds to telephone calls and e-mail messages and provides first-level support to in-house and remote users.
- The IT Help Desk Representative is responsible for many related IT support activities, including
  - recording technical issues in the IT Help Desk database system (Track-It!)
  - testing and troubleshooting desktop computer hardware and laptops
  - testing and troubleshooting new and upgraded end-user applications
  - troubleshooting printers
  - submitting requests for network account maintenance
  - submitting requests for replacement PC hardware following IT Department procedures
  - advising users on best practices in word processing, electronic spreadsheet development, and graphical presentations
- This position writes documentation in plain English for end users and IT contacts for common computing tasks and schedules the use of loaner laptops, LCD projectors, and other computer-related resources.

Key Requirements:

- A college degree is preferable or technical institute diploma as well as some prior help desk support experience in a professional services environment.
- The Help Desk Support Representative will have a strong working knowledge of Microsoft Windows XP Professional, Microsoft Office 2003, with an emphasis on Outlook, Word, Excel, and PowerPoint. Familiarity with Citrix Client for Windows, VPN, Microsoft Project, Visual Basic for Applications, DOCS Open or Interwoven WorkSite (or similar document-management system), Internet protocols, and client-side virus scan utilities.
- Candidates should have excellent personal organization, time-management, and follow-up skills in order to perform well within a fast-paced and busy working environment, and clear spoken English and excellent listening skills (particularly over the telephone) for communication of technical information with non-technical users.

Sapphire Technologies, a Randstad company, is an Affirmative Action Employer, EOE, and M/F/D/V.

Figure 1-7   Position description for Help Desk Support Representative

The second user support position description, shown in Figure 1-8, is from the U.S. Federal government. The position description describes a network support position to support users who work in the U.S. Department of Agriculture (USDA) and other federal agencies. Compare the responsibilities in this position, which emphasizes network support, with those listed in the Sapphire Technologies position description, which provides primarily desktop support of applications software.

Organization: U.S. government (USDA and other agencies)

Location: Various in United States

Job Title: Information Technology Specialist (Network)

Nature of work:

This position is in Information Technology Services (ITS). Its mission is to meet the business needs of service center agencies within the USDA by providing outstanding customer service in the form of infrastructure support, as well as assistance in the field of information technology. This position:

- Maintains workstation operating systems to include the troubleshooting and installation of upgrades, patches, and security files.
- Performs workstation maintenance to include troubleshooting hardware failure, resolving workstation issues and problems, and replacing workstation components.
- Implements and carries out inventory disposition and deployment and keeps inventory database up to date. Coordinates the sanitization and disposal of excess equipment according to property policy.
- Performs server software installations. Performs server system administration and support, including monitoring and restoring backups, Dynamic Host Configuration Protocol leases, manages user accounts on domain to include adding, removing, and moving users on servers.
- Provides data network support to users by troubleshooting network issues, isolating problems with network components, performing setup and maintenance, and supports cable installations as needed.
- Provides user account support to include setup and configuration (e.g. user profile, e-mail, printer access), and troubleshoot user account problems.
- Provides user support, training, and troubleshooting on a variety of workstation, software applications, hardware, and hardware accessories (e.g., digital camera, PDA, scanners, etc.) issues.
- Independently addresses, investigates, and resolves workstation security issues, such as viruses, worms, and/or spyware. Performs security reviews and audits for customer agencies, and performs workstation security scans.
- Works with senior specialists, customer agency managers, and staff in the selection, testing, and implementation of hardware and software based on user requirements and procurement policies.
- Creates backup files for users on workstations and servers. Recovers files as needed.

Figure 1-8 Position description for an information technology specialist for the U.S. government (*continues*)

Minimum requirements:

- Experience: 3 years of experience, 52 weeks of which is equivalent to at least the GS-04 level, and includes the following: Accomplishment of computer project assignments that required a basic knowledge of IT requirements and techniques. Such experience may have been gained in work such as computer operator or assistant, computer sales representative, program analyst, or other positions that required the use or adaptation of computer programs and systems.

  OR

- Education: Bachelor's degree required.
- **Additional evaluation of qualifications is based on**:
    - Ability to provide IT technical support
    - Ability to work on multiple projects concurrently
    - Ability to provide quality customer service to end users to resolve IT-related issues
    - Ability to communicate orally in order to effectively represent a group of IT specialists at conferences, meetings, and symposiums
    - Ability to work in a team environment

All applicants are considered without regard to race, religion, color, national origin, gender, political affiliation, age (with authorized exceptions), labor organization, marital status, nondisqualifying disabling condition, or any other nonmerit factor.

Figure 1-8 Position description for an information technology specialist for the U.S. government (*continued*)

Knowledge, Skills, and Abilities

One way to better understand the requirements for a specific position is to analyze them in terms of **KSAs**—the knowledge, skills, and abilities needed to perform the job. Human Resources personnel often analyze a position description and prepare a checklist of KSAs to use to screen applicants.

Knowledge

Each position includes a description of what a worker needs to know in order to do the job. The knowledge component may be stated in terms of a specific number of years of education, a degree in a specified field, a specific industry certification (such as an A+ certificate), or a list of topics a worker is expected to know.

Examples of knowledge required for the Help Desk Support Representative position in Figure 1-7 include:

- Knowledge of Windows XP Professional operating system

- Knowledge of applications software such as Word, Excel, and PowerPoint

Skills

Each position requires specific job skills or tasks that a support specialist must be able to perform well. User support positions may require advanced skills in one or more areas. In general, a skill is a task that a support specialist can perform better (at a higher level of effectiveness or efficiency) with practice and experience.

Examples of skills required for the Help Desk Support Representative position in Figure 1-7 include:

- Skill in troubleshooting hardware and software problems

- Personal organization, time management, and follow-up skills

Abilities

Each position requires special tasks that a support specialist must be able to perform. Abilities are functions that an applicant either can or cannot do. For example, some positions may specify abilities such as being able to lift 50-pound boxes or communicate in Spanish.

Examples of abilities required for the Help Desk Support Representative position in Figure 1-7 include:

- Ability to schedule the use of computer-related equipment and resources.

- Ability to write documentation in English

If you have difficulty with the precise differences between skills and abilities, don't worry. People often use the terms interchangeably.

ON THE WEB

If you want to learn more about the KSAs required for entry-level positions for computer support specialists, visit America's Career InfoNet Web site at: **www.acinet.org/acinet/tools/tools_tech. aspx?onetcode=15-1041.00**. Click View Occupation Profile and select the state you are interested in. The Web site includes a short video on computer support specialists. You can also find information on the employment outlook and typical wages for computer support specialists for your state.

How does one person ever learn to do all the tasks and acquire all the KSAs noted in these position descriptions? Actually, very few workers start in an entry-level position on day one with all the knowledge, skills, and abilities they need to perform every task listed in the job description. Most user support positions include a training program before a support worker ever answers a live telephone call or installs and configures a piece of network hardware. Most user support positions also include a significant amount of continuing education or on-the-job learning. So don't get discouraged if you can't do everything in these job descriptions today.

If you compare the services offered by user support groups and the job duties listed in the preceding position descriptions with the table of contents of this book, you will find that this textbook is organized around these job duties—many of the primary tasks of a support staff member are described in this book.

ON THE WEB

For more information about help desk careers, use these resources:

- To view a short video on jobs in information technology, visit **jobs.collegegrad.com/JS/CareerResources/ CareerVideos/**. Select the category Information Technology and view the videos for Help Desk Technician and any others you are interested in. (RealPlayer, a free download, is required to view the videos.)

- To read more about the Help Desk Technician field, visit **www.collegegrad.com/careers/proft45.shtml**.

- To assess your interests in an IT career, take a short inventory at the NWCET Web site: **www.nwcet.org/programs/ cybercareers/students/test/default.asp**.

- To assess some of your skills with software tools, you can try a simple assessment activity at the ACE Training Web site: **www.ace.co.nz/Pages.aspx?id=161&sectionid=96**. (Registration is required, but the skill assessment is a free service.)

A ROLE-PLAYING SCENARIO

This is a transcript of a conversation between two colleagues in a user support group, Chris and Lee. If possible, have fellow students or coworkers play the parts of Chris and Lee, and then discuss your feeling about their conversation.

CHRIS: I have been working on a position description for the new help desk specialist we plan to hire. Would you like to look it over for typos?

LEE: Hmm! I see that you have listed almost all technical qualifications for the position. Everything is hardware and software and networks.

CHRIS: That isn't true! Look at item 8. I listed problem-solving ability there.

LEE: Yes, but there is nothing on the list of qualifications that mentions any people skills. You know, listening skills, communication skills, ability to explain information to users in nontechnical language, ability to work as a member of a team. That sort of thing.

CHRIS: Well, I've always felt that you can teach someone to use good communication skills, but you can't teach them the technical and problem-solving parts of a help desk job. So I emphasized technical qualifications in the position description.

LEE: I'm sorry, Chris, but I don't buy that! Given a choice between technical skills and soft skills, I'd prefer the new person come into the job with good interpersonal skills. I don't think you can teach that. But I can teach someone to use and troubleshoot the specific software features our users call us about.

CHRIS: I guess it's a question of whether you really believe you can teach someone to be a good communicator. I think I can!

LEE: Well, obviously, we'd prefer to find someone with both technical and people skills. But given a choice, I'd take the people skills as a given and teach the technical skills.

CHRIS: I think we just disagree about that.

LEE: For purposes of the position description qualifications, I think we should agree to list both, and then see if we can find applicants who have both.

CHRIS: Okay, but I want to emphasize the technical skills as being definitely more important than the interpersonal skills. Okay?

Alternative Career Paths for User Support Workers

Many user support workers select this field as an entry into other, more advanced positions. Into which careers can an entry-level position in user support lead?

Programmer/Developer

User support workers who are technically oriented may want to work toward a position as a computer programmer or Web applications developer. Workers in these positions write code (instructions) in a computer language such as C++, Java, or Visual Basic, or in a scripting language such as JavaScript, VBScript, Perl, or PHP. Advancement into a programmer/developer position usually requires coursework in programming languages and a four-year degree.

Network Technician

Another career path for user support workers is into technical network positions. These positions often involve tasks such as installing and configuring network servers and client systems, network cabling, troubleshooting, performance analysis and configuration, security, facilities management, and related tasks. Although many user support workers perform simple network administration and monitoring tasks, a career as a technical network support worker usually requires a two- or four-year degree that specializes in advanced network topics.

Web Site Maintainer

A Web site maintainer is a worker who uses software packages, such as Dreamweaver, FrontPage, and ColdFusion, to build and maintain Web sites. These positions are less technically demanding than Web applications developers described earlier, but require someone who has a good eye for visually pleasing layouts and understands Web navigational tools to make Web sites usable.

Support Manager

Support workers who enjoy the challenge of user support can aspire to a lead worker or supervisory position in a support group. These workers often plan and schedule the work of other support staff as well as prepare budgets, hire and evaluate staff members, and work with user departments or groups to better understand their support needs. Many colleges and vocational/technical schools offer courses aimed at workers who want to become supervisors or managers. Courses that are designed for beginning supervisors or managers of technical and professional workers are especially useful for those who aspire to a support management position.

Project Manager

Chapter 6 describes some project management tools you should understand if you have an interest in project management as a career. Some schools and colleges offer coursework on project management and how to use project management software tools.

A career path that many entry-level support workers do not consider, but perhaps should, is project management. IT projects in both business and government often require leaders who can successfully manage other workers, as well as budgets, schedules, and deadlines.

Trainer/Technical Writer

Many entry-level support positions include some percentage of time devoted to end-user training and technical writing, which are described in detail in Chapters 10 and 11. Support workers who enjoy these tasks may want to specialize in either of these areas, which are described in the following:

- A full-time trainer designs, prepares, presents, and evaluates training materials not only for computer users, but also for other workers. Training topics can include company orientations for new employees, introductory supervisory training, time and project management, stress management, conflict resolution, and other subjects. A support worker who is interested in training as a career should take some "train-the-trainer" courses or courses in adult education.

- A full-time technical writer designs, writes, and edits a variety of technical documentation, such as brochures, newsletters, user guides, management reports, Web-based materials, and other printed and online documents. Those who aspire to technical writing careers can take additional coursework in a college or vocational/technical school to prepare.

Security Specialist

A growing job category after the attacks on the United States on September 11, 2001, is computer security specialist. Workers in these positions develop and implement plans to protect computer systems and networks from various sources of internal and external threat that could result in destroyed, lost, or stolen information. These positions generally require additional study and specialization beyond a basic user support degree.

ON THE WEB

To learn more about the job duties, knowledge, skills, and abilities associated with the jobs described in this chapter, visit the Occupational Information Network (O*NET) Web page at **online.onetcenter.org/gen_search_page**. Enter a keyword from the following list:

- User support specialist
- Network support specialist
- Computer security specialist
- Computer programmer
- Training specialist
- Technical writer
- Web developer
- Web administrator

Chapter Summary

- Early computer systems were primarily large, centralized corporate or government systems. They were used to automate manual tasks. The first steps toward decentralized computing were the use of terminals to connect workers to a central system, and the introduction of less powerful but less expensive workgroup computers.

- The development of end-user computing was spurred by several industry trends during the 1970s and 1980s: (1) the backlog of requests for new software applications; (2) an increase in the number of knowledge workers who work primarily with information; (3) the availability of inexpensive personal computers; (4) the availability of inexpensive productivity software; and (5) the development of user-friendly graphical user interfaces.

- End users can be categorized according to environment (personal use or business use), skill level (novice, semiskilled, or expert), frequency of use (occasional, frequent, or extensive), software used, features used (basic, intermediate, or advanced), and relationship (internal coworker or external client).

- Resources that users need to be productive include hardware, peripherals, hardware upgrades and maintenance, operating system and applications software, software upgrades, supplies, data and information, facilities, and technical support. These resources significantly affect the total cost of end-user computing for an individual or a company.

- End users operate a variety of software packages on their personal computers, including e-mail and instant messaging, Web browsers, word processors, spreadsheets, database management, graphics, planning and scheduling, desktop publishing, Web page development, educational and entertainment software, as well as enterprise and industry-specific business applications.

- A primary goal of end-user computing is to make workers more productive in their jobs. However, productivity is not without costs, because personal computers can pose many challenges. Common problems include waste of resources, user mistakes, computer crime, piracy, invasion of privacy, abusive use, computer viruses, and health problems.

- End user assistance can be organized in several ways, including peer support from a coworker, support from a user support group, a help desk/hotline/chat session operation, a user support center, directly from the technical staff in the IT department, or from a vendor who contracts to provide outsourced support services.

- Users need a variety of support services, depending on how they use their computers, and their level of expertise. User support centers frequently provide help that includes: operating a help desk, hotline, or chat session; troubleshooting difficult problems; locating information; evaluating new hardware, software, and network products; establishing organization-wide product support standards; analyzing and assessing user needs; installing systems; training users; writing user documentation; managing computer facilities; and assisting with software development projects.

- The job descriptions for support staff members reflect the variety of services a support function may offer. Many jobs require a combination of knowledge, skills, and abilities in hardware, operating systems, applications software, networks, interpersonal communication, problem solving and analysis, and supervision or leadership.

Key Terms

applications development backlog—The excess demand for new computer applications that outstripped the existing supply of computer professionals to develop them.

carpal tunnel syndrome—Severe hand or wrist pain due to an inflammation of the tendons in a user's hand and wrist; often a result of overuse in combination with an improper physical environment.

chat service—A Web-based interactive service that allows two or more users who are both online to communicate by alternately typing and viewing messages; also called instant messaging.

computer facilities management—Support services to help users with information and questions about security, media backups, viruses, ergonomics, purchase of supplies, preventive maintenance, and other tasks required to keep a computer system operational.

computer user support—A job function or department in an organization that provides information and services to workers or clients to help them use computers more productively in their employment or at home.

computer virus—A piece of software created with malicious intent that can destroy information, erase or corrupt other software or data, or adversely affect the operation of a computer that is infected by the virus.

distributed computing—A computing environment in which the needs of the organization and its workers determine the location of computer resources; this often includes a centralized system, such as a network server, and decentralized systems, such as individual PCs on worker desks.

end-user computing—The use of computer technology for both business and personal use; it is designed to increase the productivity of workers, managers, students, and home users of computers.

ergonomics—The study of how to design a workspace that promotes user health, safety, and productivity.

external user—An end user who is a client or customer of an organization, such as retail customers of hardware and software vendors, or corporate users who have purchased products or services from a vendor.

graphical user interface (GUI)—Screen images that enable users to access program features and functions intuitively, using a mouse or other pointing device.

help desk—A single point of contact for users in need of support services, whether in-house employees or external clients; a help desk may provide information and problem-solving services face to face, by telephone, by e-mail, or by an online chat session.

hotline—A telephone number that an internal or external user can call to reach a help desk service.

information center—An older name for a user support center.

Information Technology (IT), Information Systems, Information Services (IS)—The modern names of the earlier Data Processing department; this department also may be responsible for network and distributed systems, such as user PCs and support services.

internal user—An in-house worker located inside an organization who uses computers to do his or her work.

knowledge worker—An employee whose primary job function is to collect, prepare, process, and distribute information.

KSAs—The knowledge, skills, and abilities required to perform the tasks in a job.

microcomputer—A complete computer (often called a personal computer, or PC) built on a smaller scale than a large-scale or a workgroup system, with a microprocessor as the CPU.

needs analysis—An investigation to determine the features and configuration of hardware and software that will best match a user's specific needs; also called needs assessment.

outsource—An agreement in which an organization contracts with a vendor that specializes in user support functions to handle support incidents for internal and external users.

peer support—An informal level of user support whereby colleagues in an organization or department exchange information and provide assistance about computer use and problems encountered.

peripheral device—A hardware add-on that plugs into a computer's system unit, either externally or internally; peripheral devices include input devices (keyboard, scanner), output devices (monitor, printer), input and output (modem, network interface card, touch display screen), and storage (magnetic media such as tapes and disks, and optical media such as CDs and DVDs).

piracy—Theft of computer resources such as software, services, or data; often involves illegal copying, distribution, or use of computer programs or information.

position description—A written description of the qualifications and responsibilities of a job in an organization.

support standards—A list of computer products that an organization allows its employees to use and that it will support; product support standards limit the hardware, software, and network components that a staff supports in order to reduce support costs.

technical support—A level of user support that focuses on high-level troubleshooting and problem solving; whereas computer user support deals with a broad spectrum of support issues, technical support usually deals with more advanced and difficult problems that users encounter.

total cost of ownership (TCO)—The total expenditures necessary to purchase, maintain, upgrade, and support an end user's personal computer system over its expected useful lifetime; TCO includes hardware, software, network connectivity, information, training, and technical support costs.

user support center—A group or department in an organization that provides a wide range of services to an organization's computer users who are primarily internal; services may include a help desk, consulting on product purchases, training, documentation, and facilities management.

user support team—A formal workgroup that is organized to provide computer user support services; the team may include combinations of full- and part-time and peer support.

Web site development software—Software that enables users to create, maintain, and update Web pages that include a mixture of text and graphics and incorporate features such as e-mail links, downloadable files, chat rooms, File Transfer Protocol (FTP), and restricted access for security.

Check Your Understanding

Answers to Check Your Understanding questions are in Appendix A.

1. True or False? The goal of early large-scale computers was to automate as much manual processing of business information as possible.

2. Which of these developments account for the trend to decentralized computers in the 1980s and 1990s?

    a. increase in the number of knowledge workers

    b. availability of inexpensive microcomputers

    c. availability of inexpensive productivity software

    d. all of these

3. Computer users can be classified by characteristics such as skill level, frequency of use, and _____ and _____.

4. A modern name for the Data-Processing (DP) department is _____.

5. Widespread use of the Internet among business and home computer users first occurred during which decade?

   a. 1960s

   b. 1970s

   c. 1980s

   d. 1990s

   e. 2000s

6. An internal user is a(n):

   a. end user

   b. worker in an organization

   c. retail customer

   d. client who buys over the Internet

7. True or False? Technical support costs are generally included in the purchase price of a computer product, and are therefore free to users.

8. _____ is a field that studies how to design a work environment that promotes worker health, safety, and productivity.

9. Use of a computer to obtain unauthorized access to information about a customer, student, or patient is:

   a. a waste of resources

   b. an ergonomic problem

   c. an invasion of privacy

   d. piracy

10. A(n) _____ uses pull-down menus and screen images that are easier to use than systems that require users to memorize and type lengthy commands.

11. True or False? Small companies often meet their need for computer support by combining user support with another position description.

12. True or False? A help desk provides a single point of contact for computer users in need of support.

13. Help desk services can be provided via:

    a. a physical location where users can get help

    b. a telephone hotline users can call for help

    c. an e-mail address where users can send a message

    d. any of the above

14. Which of the following statements is an advantage of out-sourcing as a way to provide user support?

    a. Outsourcing is a low-cost support method.

    b. Outsourcing develops in-house support expertise.

    c. Outsourcing uses expertise a company may not have.

    d. Outsourcing provides on-site assistance.

15. True or False? The purpose of product standards is to limit the hardware and software configurations a support staff must support and, therefore, product standards reduce support costs.

16. The process of matching a user's needs with supported computer products is called a(n) _____.

17. _____ are lists of approved and recommended computer products that an organization is committed to support.

18. Which of the following job responsibilities would you least expect to find in a position description for a user support specialist?

    a. troubleshoots problems

    b. recommends product standards

    c. operates a large-scale computer

    d. installs hardware and software

19. Printed or online tutorial or reference materials for computer users are called _____.

20. What you need to know or be able to do to perform a job is called _____.

21. A Web-based communication between two Internet users who are online at the same time and alternately type and view messages is called:

   a. peer support

   b. e-mail

   c. a hotline

   d. a chat session

Discussion Questions

1. Why do you think that so much of the software that ran on large-scale computers was custom-written by programmers, whereas today most personal computer software is purchased off-the-shelf?

2. Do you think the changes in the way computers are used are due primarily to advances in computer technology over the past 50 years or due primarily to demand for improvements among end users?

3. Based on your knowledge and studies of the computer industry, what other information would you add to Table 1-1 that would help someone understand important changes in computer technology? Add a row to Table 1-1 labeled 2010s. What do you think will be the significant new developments in computer technology in the next decade?

4. Are the end-user problems described in this chapter inevitable or can they be resolved?

5. Do you agree or disagree with the following statement? "Facilities management is more of a concern with large-scale computer systems than in an end-user computing environment." Explain your position.

6. Is it more important for a user support staff member to have the ability to solve difficult technical problems or the ability to communicate with a difficult user? Why?

7. How do you think the knowledge, skills, and abilities needed for telephone support are different from the KSAs needed to provide e-mail or online chat support? Compare these to the KSAs needed for face-to-face support.

Hands-On Activities

Activity 1-1

Interview a technical support person. Locate a technical support worker at your school, your work, or a local company. Find out the following information:

1. Ask the technical support worker to use the categories of end users in Figure 1-2 in the chapter to describe the users he or she supports.

2. What types of software applications does the support worker need to know in order to support users?

3. Do any users or applications present particularly difficult problems for him or her as a technical support worker? Ask for a description of some typical problems.

4. Does the organization that employs the worker have policies on software piracy, invasion of privacy, and virus protection?

5. Ask the technical support worker if he or she can provide you with a copy of their position description.

Write a one-page summary of the information you collect.

Activity 1-2

Predict future computing trends. Based on your knowledge of current trends in the computer industry, add more information to the decade milestones shown in Table 1-1 for the 2000s decade. What do you think the significant events and trends in the next decade (2010s) will be? Make predictions about computer size, cost, ease of use, and primary functions in business and home during the next decade.

Activity 1-3

Identify software packages. Find a mail-order computer catalog (in your computer room or library) or an Internet site that sells applications software packages like those described in this chapter. For each category—electronic mail and messaging, Web browser, word processing, spreadsheets, database management, graphics, planning and scheduling, desktop publishing, Web site software, and educational and entertainment software—list the names of two or three representative packages. Include the price range for a typical package in each category.

Activity 1-4

Identify computer users' health concerns. Interview three classmates, coworkers, or family members about their health, safety, and productivity concerns related to their use of computers. Make a list of their concerns. What similarities in concerns did you find? Did any of their concerns surprise you? Write a brief summary of your conclusions.

Activity 1-5

Evaluate TCO. A Houston, Texas consulting company, JDA Professional Services, provides an online worksheet for calculating the TCO of computer technology. Read about the factors the company thinks contribute to the TCO at its Web site: **www.jdapsi.com/client/ Articles/Default.php?Article=tco**. Write a one-page report that describes how the factors JDA considers significant are different from those in this chapter.

Click the **JDA's Online TCO Worksheet** link. Enter the data for the following scenario: An instructional computer lab manager wants to purchase 10 computers for a new lab at a cost of $1200 per machine. The cost of a network server, laser printer, and related hardware and software is expected to be $5000. The lab will require two part-time support staff, expected to cost $15,000 each. Use the Gartner Group's recommended percentage for hidden costs. Answer the following questions:

1. What is the total cost of ownership per machine?

2. Is this a one-time cost or an annual cost?

Activity 1-6

Evaluate user support position descriptions. Use the Internet to locate a position description for a user support job in government and other organizations. If possible, find information about a position in your state or local employment area, and a job that might be of interest to you. How do the duties and responsibilities you found compare with those described in this chapter? What are some similarities? What are some differences?

Some Internet sites you could visit are listed in Table 1-2.

Web site	Description
www.dop.wa.gov/NR/rdonlyres/26AC7209-C99D-4099-BF87-F2A19F0FA0F7/0/479I.doc	State of Washington job description for an Information Technology Specialist 1
agency.governmentjobs.com/desmoines/default.cfm?SearchLetter=H&action=agencyspecs&AgencyID=1219 Click U for User Support Technician	City of Des Moines, Iowa job description for a user support technician
www.computerjobs.com Click the link for a region in which you are interested, and then click the **Help Desk** link.	IT employment Web site
www.dice.com Click Advanced Search. Enter a keyword, such as **Help Desk** or **Computer** Support; use the location menu to specify a state or local area, and then click the **Search** button.	Job search Web site for computer professionals
www.JustTechJobs.com Click Search Jobs; enter the keyword Help Desk and select the geographic area in which you are interested.	Site specializes in technology industry positions
jobsearch.monster.com Click Find Jobs; in the keyword box, enter **Help Desk**; and then in the Occupations pull-down menu, click the + in front of **IT/ Software Development**, and check the box in front of **Desktop Service and Support**. Use the location menu to narrow the search to your state or local area.	Global online network for careers

Table 1-2   Internet sites with information about user support positions

Activity 1-7

Evaluate user support positions. Select a position description for a user support position in this chapter or one you found in Activity 1-6. Answer the following questions:

1. Would you classify the job described in the position description as primarily a technical position or a people-oriented position? Explain your answer.

2. Do you think the position description requires a person who is a specialist (one with depth of knowledge) or a generalist (one with breadth of knowledge)? Explain why.

3. What personal qualities do you think will be necessary for someone to be successful in the position?

If you are a member of a class or project group, meet with the other members and discuss your answers to these questions. Write a one-page summary of your conclusions.

Activity 1-8

Compare your KSAs to a user support position. Select a position description for a user support position in this chapter or one you found in an earlier activity. Make a list of the knowledge, skills, and abilities (KSAs) you would need to perform the duties in the position description. Don't worry too much about the differences between skills and abilities. Compare your own knowledge, skills, and abilities with those for the position description. Analyze your strengths and areas where you need additional KSAs for the position. How do the KSAs you listed correspond to courses you are taking now or have taken in the past? What additional courses could you take to satisfy some of the KSAs on your list?

Activity 1-9

Analyze your personal skills for a support position. Compare your personal skills, with those of some basic job categories. Visit the Occupational Information Network (O*NET) Web site at **online. onetcenter.org/gen_skills_page**. Check the skills you have or are working on in the list of skills and learn which job categories best match your skills. Is Computer Support Specialist on your list? Click the **Skills Matched** column to learn why or why not.

Case Projects

1. TCO of a $500 Computer

Your friend Ron has asked for your help in buying a home computer. He is skeptical of ads for computers that cost less than $500. He intends to use the computer for word processing, e-mail, entertainment, and Internet access, and he wants your advice about how much he should budget for a home personal computer system. What is a realistic amount your friend might expect to spend, both at the time of initial purchase and over the next four years of ownership? Use catalogs, computer magazines, or the Internet to obtain current price information. Use a spreadsheet to draw up a sample budget, showing your recommended initial expenditure and the annual cost for the next four years. Break down the costs by the categories described in this chapter. Show the total cost of ownership over the four years that Ron plans to own the computer.

2. Training Facility Problems at Cascade University

Mary Ann Lacy is the coordinator of Cascade University's computer training facility. The facility offers courses in computer applications software to Cascade's regular students and faculty, and to employees of local organizations that send their workers to Cascade's Continuing Education Division to upgrade their computer skills.

The computer training facility consists of two rooms: a training room where scheduled classes are conducted and an open lab where students can work on assignments outside class time. The entire training facility is open from 8 a.m. to 5 p.m., Monday through Friday. Each room is equipped with 24 PCs. Mary Ann operates a Windows 2008 server operating system so that students can access software on the network server, store data files, and access e-mail and the Internet. She also teaches some of the continuing education classes in the training room. Cascade University's computer faculty members teach in the training room when it is not in use for continuing education classes.

Mary Ann recently conducted a user satisfaction survey to learn how Cascade students, faculty, and continuing education students rated the entire training facility. She was pleased that users were very satisfied with the equipment because she tries to keep the systems properly maintained and gets PCs repaired as soon as a problem arises. The Electronics Shop at Cascade maintains the hardware. The users also expressed satisfaction with the operation of the network server and with the selection of software that is available to them. However, Mary Ann was less pleased about some of the comments users wrote on their survey forms. Here is a sample of some comments:

- "I am an advanced user of the open lab. Some of the inexperienced students have discovered that I know quite a bit about the hardware and the network. They ask me a lot of questions. I don't mind answering them, but when I have a class assignment due, I can't take time out to help everyone who has a question. After a while, some of the questions get pretty repetitious."

- "The open lab runs smoothly when the coordinator is in the room. But when she is next door teaching a class in the training room, there is no one to ask for help. I feel badly when students have to interrupt her training session to report a problem like a server crash or even to get a new ink cartridge put in the printer."

- "The software manuals are in a locked cabinet. When I need one, I have to track down Mary Ann to get the key. Why can't the documentation cabinet be left unlocked?"

- "Last year, there was seldom a wait to get a computer in the open lab. This year, with more classes in the training room, the wait is longer. It would be nice if the lab were open more than 8 to 5. Some evening and weekend hours would be great."

Mary Ann has decided to ask a small group of training facility users, consisting of students, faculty, and continuing education students, to meet to discuss the responses to her survey. If you were a member of the group, what advice would you give Mary Ann that would address the concerns described about the operation of the training facility? What user support issues have users raised? What are some other ways Mary Ann could address these issues? Are some alternatives more expensive than others?

3. Computer User Satisfaction at Indiana University Bloomington

Indiana University Bloomington (IUB) is a public university in Bloomington, Indiana. University Information Technology Services (UITS) conducts a survey of its students, staff, and faculty to measure their satisfaction with computer use on campus. A summary of the results of their survey for the most recent year is available at **www.iu.edu/~uitssur**. Most questions are answered on a scale of 1 to 5, where 5 is very favorable. Analyze the results of the survey and answer these questions.

1. Use responses in the section Computing and Computer Networking to write a short narrative description of a typical (average) computer user at IUB.

2. Based on the responses to the Computing and Computer Networking section, which kinds of computers should be supported by UITS staff? Which should not be supported? Explain your decision.

3. Based on responses in the User Support Services section of the survey, which service provided by UITS needs the most improvement? Why?

4. Based on the section General Assessment, which of the three groups, teaching faculty, researchers, or student learners, are the most satisfied with their computer support at IUB? Which are the least satisfied? Are the differences between the groups significant?

5. Over all, are computer users at IUB satisfied with the computer services they experience? Explain your answer.

CHAPTER 2

Customer Service Skills for User Support Agents

In this chapter, you will learn about:

- ◎ The importance of communication skills and customer service relationships for support agents
- ◎ Reasons support agents listen and read carefully
- ◎ How agents build and communicate understanding
- ◎ Aspects of effective speaking and nonverbal communication for user support
- ◎ How support agents develop a personal communication style
- ◎ Strategies support agents use for telephone communications
- ◎ How support agents develop an incident management strategy
- ◎ How developing an understanding of different personality types and work styles can help an agent
- ◎ Strategies support agents use to handle difficult clients
- ◎ Guidelines for client-friendly communications on user support Web sites
- ◎ How to build excellent customer service

As you learned in Chapter 1, communication and interpersonal skills are very important for help desk and user support agents. Whether they supply help to end users face to face, via telephone, in e-mail messages, through a Web site, in chat sessions, via remote access, or in blog articles, all successful support staff must be able to listen, understand, communicate, and work effectively with users to solve end-user problems.

Excellent communication and interpersonal skills are often more challenging for new user support workers to learn than technical or business skills. Communication and interpersonal skills are also more difficult to measure and evaluate. Practice is the key to learning how to use communication skills effectively. Experienced user support agents and their managers know that client satisfaction is directly related to how well agents listen to, understand, and communicate with users. Support agents who concentrate solely on finding the correct technical answers may be frustrated and surprised to learn that clients can be less than satisfied with their support interactions.

In this chapter, you'll learn some practical listening, understanding, speaking, and client-relationship skills. User support staff can apply these skills to almost any support situation to help solve problems and achieve two important goals of every support request: client satisfaction and excellent customer service. Although many of the skills discussed in this chapter apply directly to telephone and face-to-face support, these skills also apply to written communication, such as e-mail, online chats, and communication with end users on support Web sites. In fact, written communication is often trickier than oral communication because the tone and voice intonations are missing. The point is that strong communication and interpersonal skills are essential in any support environment.

Communication and Customer Service Skills

Communication skills are essential to providing high-quality customer service. Communication is a process that involves both listening and responding. Some communications, notably face to face, telephone, e-mail, and chat sessions, are two-way interactions between a support agent and an end user. Other communications, including support Web sites and blogs, are primarily one-way. To effectively solve end user problems, agents must be able to hear or read and understand a user's problem or question, and then reflect their understanding of the problem or question in their spoken or written response. Listening, understanding, and responding are essential to solving user problems. A support organization that can solve user problems effectively and efficiently, and does so using good interpersonal skills, creates client satisfaction and demonstrates its commitment to providing excellent customer service.

Help desks and user support organizations frequently incorporate a customer-service ethic into their mission statements. A **customer-service ethic** is an organization-wide commitment—shared by everyone from top management to operational staff—that client relationships and client satisfaction are the most important aspect of a business. Many organizations aim for a target of 100% client satisfaction 100% of the time. This means that the user support staff aims to satisfy every client in every support incident.

Chapter 6 discusses mission statements in detail.

57

How important is customer service to organizations? In a classic article in *Harvard Business Review* (*HBR*), Thomas O. Jones and W. Earl Sasser, Jr. discuss "Why Satisfied Customers Defect" (*HBR*, Nov–Dec, 1995). They describe a study of Xerox company customers in which "totally satisfied" customers were six times more likely to purchase other Xerox products than customers who were just "satisfied." The authors conclude: "Merely satisfying customers who have the freedom to make choices is not enough to keep them loyal. The only truly loyal customers are totally satisfied customers." Another author, Frederick Reichheld, writes in a March 1996 *HBR* article, "Learning from Customer Defections," that "on average, the CEOs of the U.S. corporations lose half of their customers every five years." Although these articles were written several years ago, they are classic works in customer satisfaction literature, and the conclusions still apply.

Support organizations place a greater emphasis on customer-service excellence than they did in the past. Why? First, totally satisfied clients are more likely to be repeat customers. A frequent reason that clients leave a hardware or software vendor for another is the poor service they receive. In fact, excellent service may be more important to clients than product features, price, convenience, or any other aspect of a business transaction. Second, it usually takes more support resources to handle incidents from dissatisfied clients than from satisfied ones. Dissatisfied clients are more likely to generate:

- Lengthy support incidents
- Repeated callbacks or help desk contacts
- Complaints and ill-will that are shared with potential clients, which can translate into a poor business image and lost sales
- Incidents that need to be rerouted to a higher-level support agent or a manager
- Product returns and requests for a refund

Because dissatisfied clients consume more support resources, any of these results reduce support staff productivity and may lead to a reputation for poor support service.

ON THE WEB

Jeff Davis, a frequent contributor to *Tech Republic*, shares tips on the importance of communication skills for support professionals in his article "Improve Your Communication Skills with these Techniques" at **articles.techrepublic.com. com/5100-10878_11-1052198.html**.

MindTools, a Web site focused on career skills, offers several short articles on improving communication and listening skills at **www.mindtools.com/page8.html**.

What are the characteristics of a support organization that is devoted to a customer-service ethic? A customer-service ethic means that, in the pursuit of excellent customer service, support staff members:

- Provide clients with the information, service, or solutions they need, if there is any reasonable way to do so.

- Explain to the client what they *can* do for him or her if the client's problem cannot be resolved immediately.

- Treat clients and potential clients with respect and courtesy.

- Communicate to clients how long they are likely to be on hold, how long it will be before they receive a return call or e-mail, and how long it may take to provide information or solve a problem.

- Return phone calls or e-mails when promised, even if just to report that no progress has yet been made.

Think of each user as a valued client. Always remember that user support is essentially a customer service business and that the goal is to create totally satisfied clients. If users are not treated as valued clients, they may not remain clients for long. If clients have a choice of vendors, where do you think they will choose to make their next purchase? Usually, they will buy where customer service is taken seriously. Even in telephone support, users observe your attitude and react to the way you communicate and handle an incident. Support agents communicate by their voice or written responses whether they consider an incident interesting or boring and whether they value the user or view the incident as an intrusion on their time.

Treat each incident as an opportunity to build total client satisfaction. To create client satisfaction and help attain an organization's customer service goals, support agents must master the essential communication skills: listening, understanding, and responding. These three skills are the foundations of the communication process between a support agent and a user, as illustrated in Figure 2-1.

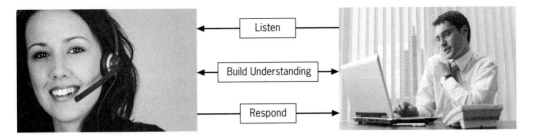

Figure 2-1 Foundations of the communication process between a support agent and a user

Listen Carefully

In any support conversation, learn to listen before you speak. Listen initially to a caller's description of the question or problem to develop a thorough understanding of it. Interrupting a caller is one indication to a customer that you are not listening carefully. In any written communication, read all of the text and try to fully understand the user's problem before you initiate a response.

 In Chapter 3, you'll learn about a technique called active listening, which is a way to restate and clarify what you heard to reach a common understanding of a user's problem.

Experts in listening skills have identified six different types or purposes of listening. These six types are shown in Table 2-1.

Listening Type	Purpose
Discriminative	Learn about the user • What is the knowledge level of the user? What level of technical language do they use? • What is the tone and style of the user's communication? Are they upset or angry?
Comprehensive	Understand the user's message • Do I have a complete and accurate understanding of the information the user provided?
Critical	Analyze and evaluate the user's message • Does the information the user provides make sense? • Do I need additional information from the user?
Therapeutic	Identify opportunities to provide positive support to the user • Can I find opportunities to empathize with the user's situation? • Am I listening to the user without prejudging the message?
Appreciative	Find enjoyment • Am I treating the user as a real person, not just a voice? • Does my communication treat the user with dignity and respect? • Do I have empathy for the user?
Relational	Develop rapport with user • Am I taking advantage of opportunities to use "small talk" with the user to develop an effective working relationship?

Table 2-1   Six types of listening

ON THE WEB

To learn more about the six purposes of listening, read a paper by John A. Kline, an author who has written widely on listening and speaking skills, at **www.au.af.mil/au/awc/awcgate/kline-listen/b10ch4.htm**.

When a user begins to describe a problem, be sure to make effective use of these discriminative listening skills:

- Listen to or observe the *language* the user uses to describe the problem. A user's language frequently provides important clues as to whether the user is a novice or an experienced user. Support agents can then adjust the language in their response so as to avoid language that is too complex or too technical for the user to understand.

- Listen to *how* the user describes the problem, which can provide further insight into the problem and the user. What tone of voice does the user use? Does the user sound angry or frustrated? Does he hesitate or struggle or apologize about the misuse of technical terms? Does he sound distracted or in a hurry? Subtle cues like these can provide valuable information about how to handle an incident.

Although detecting a user's "tone of voice" is more difficult in written communication, support agents can look for statements that indicate frustration. For example, a user who writes, "This is my third chat session to try to resolve this problem," is undoubtedly making more than a simple factual statement.

ON THE WEB

A short online article by author Lillian D. Bjorseth, "Shhh! Listen, Don't Just Hear," offers some useful strategies for becoming a better listener. Read the article at **www.selfgrowth.com/articles/bjorseth4.html**.

To view a guide to developing better listening habits, read a summary sheet at **www.scribd.com/doc/1095379/Active-Listening-A-Guide.**

While many support workers focus on comprehensive and critical listening skills, therapeutic and relational listening skills are probably more important in satisfying the goal of an effective customer service ethic. Figure 2-2 lists some suggestions to help you listen effectively and some obstacles that can hinder effective listening.

Tips for effective listening	Barriers to effective listening
● Avoid distractions	● Focusing on your own concerns instead of the user's
● Give the user plenty of time to explain, think, and communicate	● Allocating insufficient time to a user's problem
● Summarize what the user says	● Talking too much instead of listening
● Probe for more details	● Talking to avoid silences
● Use attentive body language (face the user, maintain an open stance, establish eye contact)	● Avoiding eye contact
● View the problem from the user's perspective	● Taking user complaints or criticism personally or responding defensively
● Be positive and encouraging	● Lecturing the user
● Speak clearly and concisely	● Speaking rapidly
● Match your speech to the user's proficiency level	● Using overly technical language or jargon

Figure 2-2 Tips for and barriers to effective listening

To build listening skills, look for courses in small group or interpersonal communication, which often place equal weight on listening and speaking skills. Many vocational-technical training programs and professional development seminars in customer service skills also include opportunities to work on listening and speaking skills. To develop your written communication skills, look for opportunities to study e-mail messages from friends or colleagues. Practice analyzing each message to examine the language used and look for clues about how the sender feels. Ask yourself whether you can accurately restate the sender's message. If possible, ask the author of the message if your restatement is accurate.

Build Understanding

Once you have heard or read a user's problem description, try to develop an understanding of the user's situation. Ideally, you will develop some level of empathy with the user. **Empathy** is an understanding of and identification with another person's situation, thoughts, and feelings. Support agents who can empathize with a user understand the problem or question from the user's point of view. One measure of empathy is whether you can express a user's problem in your own words. Another measure of empathy is whether a user agrees with your expression of their problem; in other words, have the two of you reached a consensus understanding? Empathy does not mean that you take complete ownership of and responsibility for a problem, but that you understand it and can relate effectively to the user, who does own the problem. Try to understand, for example, why the problem is important to a user, why a user might want to know a piece of information, or why a user is frustrated, upset, or angry. The following are examples of empathetic responses:

"Clearly, we need to get this program running again so you can create the report you need. Here's where we'll start . . ."

"It sounds like you've had a very frustrating morning, but I think I can help you with this . . ."

"To help you close your accounting month on time, I can give you a workaround for this problem. Then, later, we can diagnose the problem you're having, so it doesn't happen again."

"I will be here if you need any additional help with this problem."

ON THE WEB

To view an article on empathy and trust in customer relations, visit the Web site **www.businessballs.com/empathy.htm**. Another short introduction to empathy can be found at **www. live.ac.uk/documents/intro_to_empathy.pdf** (requires a PDF viewer).

As you develop an understanding of the user and the problem, communicate to the user that you view him or her as a person, rather than as a support incident. One technique that experienced support agents use is to visualize the user. Even if you don't know the user personally, think of someone in your own experience who sounds like or is similar to the user and then communicate with that image rather than with a voice at the other end of the phone line or a chat message on your display screen. A second technique is to use inclusive language, such as "we" rather than "I" and "you." A telephone technique you can use effectively is to smile while you are talking with a user. Even though a conversation is on the telephone, many users can tell whether you are smiling.

Respond Effectively

In a support interaction, all aspects of your speech or writing communicate your understanding of a situation, lead to successful incident resolution, and influence the user's level of satisfaction with the incident. Four important aspects of your response are your greeting, how you use scripts, your tone and style, and your nonverbal communication.

Use a Sincere Greeting

If every journey begins with a single step, all support communications begin with a **greeting**, which can affect the course of the entire interaction with the user. The greeting is the icebreaker. Based on your greeting, users form their first impressions of the support staff person, the support service, and ultimately the entire organization that provides support. The greeting also sets the tone for the remainder of the incident. A sincere, positive greeting can be the first step toward calming a frustrated user and channeling an incident in a fruitful direction. Most support organizations train their staff members to use a standard greeting, which often includes the agent's first name and the name of the organization or other identification. A common greeting is:

(phone) *"This is Joel in Computer Support. Thanks very much for your call. How can I help you?"*

(e-mail) *"I'm Kana at the Help Desk. Thank you very much for contacting us with the problem you encountered. Here is how I understand the problem . . ."*

Practice using a sincere greeting with a tone that communicates interest and enthusiasm and avoids sounding stiff, overly rehearsed, insincere, or bored. A sound recorder or colleague can help provide feedback on your telephone greeting style. By the way, the immediate "thank you" in these examples communicates to the user that you appreciate and value the contact. Also, a sincere "thank you" contributes to a positive first impression, even if the user is upset or frustrated. If a user gives his or her name after your telephone greeting, write it down so you can use it during the incident. Many support organizations prefer the use of Mr. or Ms. and a user's last name in preference to a first name, unless the user specifically invites first name use.

Use Scripts Appropriately

Many support groups provide their agents with a script to help handle routine aspects of an incident. A **script** is a prepared sequence of questions and statements that covers the several important parts of an incident. A script can include branches and decision points so that a support agent follows a path through the script that matches a user's answers. Scripts can be useful training aids for new support agents as well as helpful tools for handling complex technical problems and difficult users. However, a user should never suspect that you are simply reading a script or any other information unless you communicate beforehand that you are reading a piece of technical information to ensure accuracy. Furthermore, experienced support agents recognize situations in which they should deviate from the script, such as when the user demonstrates expert knowledge of the problem situation. Scripts can be very useful if an incident evolves into an argument or other inappropriate communication. Reverting to a script can help you get an interaction back on track and make sure that the incident is handled according to organizational policy.

Some help desks maintain a database of frequently asked questions (FAQs) and prepared responses to them. When using prepared responses, use them like scripts. Don't read lengthy responses, unless you make it clear that is what you are doing. Instead, restate the responses in your own words.

ON THE WEB

As part of a training program, a support agent may be asked to learn or develop model answers to questions. Experienced support staff and supervisors are useful sources of information about what constitutes a "good" response to an FAQ. For an example of an online FAQ database, visit a FAQ for Microsoft PowerPoint at **www.pptfaq.com/index.html**.

Use Tone and Style Effectively

How you communicate with a user is often more important than the content of the communication. Your tone and style have a direct impact on a user's satisfaction with a support incident. Which of these user statements best illustrates the desired outcome of a support incident?

"The help desk agent provided me with adequate information, but I felt through the whole conversation that I was intruding on his time. He spoke rapidly and curtly, and wasn't very pleasant. I felt like he had 'been there, done that', and wasn't interested in my problem."

"The help desk agent couldn't tell me what I needed to know, but explained why the information wasn't available yet, when it would be, and invited me to call back. I felt like a valued client and that my call was important to her."

Note that the first user received the information he sought, but was dissatisfied with the interaction; whereas the second user was fully satisfied even though her question was not answered.

Often, as part of help desk or user support training for a new agent, support organizations describe in detail the kind of communication style they want their agents to use—whether formal or informal, casual or professional, or somewhere in between. They realize that style is important because it communicates the organization's image. In reality, support staff members often modify the organization's desired standard somewhat, depending on their experience, user feedback, and their own personalities.

Recognize the Importance of Nonverbal Communication

Researcher Albert Mehrabian emphasizes the importance of **nonverbal behaviors** in the communication process. He found that facial expression, body language, and use of words (style and tone) are often more important than the specific words and the meanings of words in a communication. These nonverbal behaviors are described in Table 2-2.

Nonverbal Behavior	Use These Behaviors	Avoid These Behaviors
Posture	Use an open stance	Folding arms
	Face the user	Crossing legs
		Bowing head
		Looking at a distant object or a clock
Facial expression	Smile	Frown
	Use a facial expression that indicates interest	A facial expression that indicates boredom, disbelief, or impatience
Eye contact	Establish frequent, but not excessive, eye contact	Looking off into the distance or down at your feet
		Staring at the user
Gestures	Use head, hand, and arm movements to communicate your active involvement and to help with explanations	Limited gestures and animation
		Overly stiff gestures
		Shifting weight from one leg to the other
Distance	Stand or sit at a comfortable distance from the user	Standing so close that you make a person uncomfortable
		Standing at too great a distance so as to communicate disinterest
Voice quality	Speak at a comfortable level of loudness	Shouting (especially if the user is not a native English speaker)
	Use voice inflection to add interest	Whispering
		Speaking in a monotone voice
	Speak at a normal pitch	Speaking in a sing-song voice
	Speak in a tone of voice that is upbeat and warm	Speaking in a voice pitch that is too high or too low
		Speaking in a tone of voice that sounds negative, cold, unfriendly, or bored

Table 2-2   Nonverbal behaviors in communication

ON THE WEB

Vicki Ritts and James Stein offer several suggestions for improving nonverbal behaviors in the communication process. Although aimed at classroom teachers, their suggestions apply equally to support workers. View their ideas at **honolulu.hawaii.edu/intranet/committees/ FacDevCom/guidebk/teachtip/commun-1.htm**.

Develop an Effective Personal Communication Style

Every person's **personal communication style** is the result of decisions an individual makes about how he or she wants to communicate; that style can be polished with some practice in effective communication.

Use clear, succinct speech and match your speed to the user's proficiency level. Many inexperienced support agents have a tendency to speak too fast, which is often a natural reaction to job stress and a pressure to be productive. Practice speaking slowly, but not so slowly as to sound condescending. Remember, too, that shorter sentences are easier for a user to follow than long ones. Avoid a rising inflection at the end of sentences, which sounds like you are asking a question or are unsure. Many of the suggestions about writing for end users in Chapter 11 also apply to verbal communication style, including the use of gender-neutral language and avoiding wordiness, long words (when shorter ones will communicate the same meaning), overly technical terms, acronyms, and jargon.

Avoid using empty phrases in support incidents. Inexperienced support agents, in particular, sometimes continue to talk when they don't have anything to say, just to fill the pauses. Avoid empty phrases, such as "Now let me see . . .," "I think I've seen that problem before . . .," or "I'm sure I must have that information somewhere here . . ." These phrases do not convey useful information and do not instill confidence that you are on top of the problem, although they may give the appearance that communication is occurring. Instead of empty phrases, learn to be comfortable with pauses.

Phrase communications with end users positively, rather than negatively. For example, instead of saying or writing "The problem with your document occurred because you didn't follow the procedure described in Chapter 2 of the manual," use a positive statement, such as "I think the procedure on saving a document in Chapter 2 describes a way to avoid the problem with the document you experienced. Let me find the page for you."

Although technically correct solutions to user problems are critical, they will not by themselves guarantee satisfied clients. Successful support agents use greetings, scripts, and their tone and style to communicate their willingness to help, their regard for the client's value, and their organization's concern for the client's satisfaction.

ON THE WEB

A vendor that offers online courses in communication and listening skills aimed at customer support workers is LearnCustomerServiceOnline.com. View a list of available courses at **www.learncustomerserviceonline. com/CustServiceModules.htm**. You can try a free preview of one of their courses on active listening skills at **www.learncustomerserviceonline.com/Preview/ ActiveListeningCS/FrameMaster1.htm**.

Special Challenges of Telephone Communication

While all support communication with clients is important, the challenges posed by telephone communication are unique. Many support agents use the telephone as a communication medium for both external and internal clients. All the suggestions in this chapter about the importance of the customer service ethic and the role of communication to meet that ethic apply equally, or probably more so, to phone interactions with end users.

Even before an agent answers a telephone support call, a client evaluates whether the telephone menu system to connect to an agent is well designed and offers meaningful choices. The client also evaluates the length of time it takes for an agent to answer the call. The initial greeting is also part of the first impression. It is worth practicing a sincere greeting until you get it down without sounding like you are reading a script.

Since a caller cannot see the agent on the other end of the phone, you might think that nonverbal aspects of communication are unimportant in a telephone support call. While there is no direct way for a caller to measure visual cues such as body language or facial expression, new support agents are always surprised to learn how much nonverbal behavior contributes to the success of a call. Support agents need to develop effective ways to perform these standard parts of a telephone support call. Table 2-3 lists some suggested dialog for a variety of common user support telephone activities.

Telephone Activity	Example Dialog
Call greeting	"This is the Help Desk and I am Amy. Thanks very much for calling us. How can I help you today?"
Put a call on hold	"I need to research this problem to make sure I give you accurate information. Would you like me to put you on hold, or call you back when I have the answer?" • When a return call is promised, be sure to call back promptly!
Transfer a call	"Since you are asking about a billing question, I am going to transfer you to the billing department, where Ms. Chang will help you with your question. She will be on the line in a moment."
Terminate a call	"It appears that rebooting your computer has reestablished your connection to the Internet. Thanks for calling us about the problem. Is there anything else I can help you with today?"

Table 2-3   Suggested telephone dialog

ON THE WEB

For additional information about telephone communication, download a one-page Telephone Ready Reference at **www.businesstrainingworks.com/Onsite%20Training%20Web/Free%20Articles/PDFs/Telephone%20Ready%20Reference.pdf**.

To increase your skills with telephone communication, try the tutorials and exercises in a book by Jeannie Davis, *Beyond "Hello": A Practical Guide for Excellent Telephone Communication and Quality Customer Service* (Now Hear This, Inc., 2000).

A ROLE-PLAYING SCENARIO

This is a transcript of a telephone support call between Wes, an end user in the Accounting Department, and Gene, a relatively new worker in a support group. If possible, have fellow students or coworkers play the parts of Gene and Wes, then discuss your reactions to this support call.

GENE: This is the problem hotline. What's your problem please?

WES: This is Wes in Accounting.

GENE: Oh, yes, I remember you. I've talked with you several times before. What's the problem this time?

WES: I'm having trouble printing a report this morning.

GENE: Your printer is probably out of paper.

WES: I've clicked the Print button three times and gone down the hall to get the printout, but each time there is just a stack of about 50 sheets in the printer with a line or two of junk characters on each one. But my report is not there.

GENE: Oh, we've been hoping whoever was wasting those reams of paper would call. I should send you a bill for the paper you wasted.

WES: I'm sorry, but I've never had this problem before. What am I doing wrong?

GENE: It is probably a user error. Did you reboot your computer?

WES: No. Do you think that would help?

GENE: Probably not.

WES: Can you suggest something else I should try?

GENE: What are you trying to print?

WES: The report is in a file named REPORT2008.EXE.

GENE: Well, there's your problem right there. Didn't the training course you took cover printing .EXE files? .EXE files are programs, not reports. You can't print an .EXE file, you can only run them.

WES: Oh, I see. I guess I forgot about that. I feel like an idiot.

GENE: Yes, well, see if you can find a file on your hard drive named REPORT2008 with a different extension and call me back.

Case project 5 at the end of this chapter is designed to provide readers with an opportunity to build interpersonal communication skills in an end-user support environment.

Develop an Incident Management Strategy

Support agents who provide telephone, e-mail, chat session, remote access, and even face-to-face support often have many incidents waiting in their queue. At the same time that they provide correct technical answers and excellent customer service, they must also handle incidents efficiently. An **incident management strategy** is a collection of tools, techniques, and strategies that successful support agents use to move through an incident effectively and efficiently, from the initial greeting to the end of the incident. The four goals of incident management are to:

1. Provide the user with the information he or she needs.

2. Manage stress levels for both the user and the support agent.

3. Ensure that the incident progresses from start to finish in an effective and efficient way.

4. Make the user more self-reliant.

All support agents develop and refine their own incident management strategy. However, new help desk agents do not have to invent an incident management strategy from scratch. Resources you can build on and incorporate in your personal strategy include:

- Organizational policies on incident management and expectations

- Incident management strategies covered in support agent training programs

- Observation and imitation of respected and experienced support agents

- Your personal communication experience and style

- Feedback from users, coworkers, and supervisors on your incident-management strengths and areas for improvement.

An incident management strategy begins with knowledge of the support organization's policies and guidelines, an understanding of the operation of automated help desk and user support tools such as the telephone and e-mail systems and help desk software package (described in Chapter 5), and guidelines that experienced support agents have found useful. Figure 2-3 lists some examples of incident management guidelines.

- Ask goal-directed questions
- Be honest
- Say "I don't know" when you don't
- Apologize when appropriate
- Say "Thank you"
- Use incident management, not user management techniques
- Teach self-reliance

Figure 2-3   Incident management guidelines

Ask Goal-Directed Diagnostic Questions

Chapter 3 suggests several critical questions to ask in a troubleshooting situation.

Each question a support agent asks should be designed to move an incident toward a successful resolution. Diagnostic questions can be embedded in a script or they can be based on a support agent's experience.

Be Honest

It is better to be honest and forthcoming with users about product features, limitations, known bugs, and future product releases than to try to hide or cover up product problems and limitations. However, you must also abide by organizational policies on what information you are authorized to provide to users. For example, some vendors, as a matter of policy, will not disclose future product features or availability dates. So you may encounter situations in which you have the information a user requests, but cannot divulge it yet because your employer asks you not to. Many organizations also have a policy that discourages communicating negative comments about a competitor's products, even though you may have an honestly negative opinion about them.

Say "I Don't Know" When You Don't

It is often more productive to admit that you don't know an answer than to waste both your time and the user's time trying to suggest possibilities you aren't sure of. A user rarely expects a support agent to know everything. However, never use a tone that conveys, "I don't know, and therefore your question is stupid," "I don't know, and I don't think anybody else does," or "I don't know, and I don't care." If you honestly don't know an answer, refer the user to a colleague or other information resource where she or he can get the needed information. You can also promise to research the question and get back to the user with the needed information.

Apologize

A sincere apology to a user who feels that they have been done an injustice is never a sign of weakness. One way to defuse a potentially difficult situation is to empathize with a user's situation and offer an apology for the perceived injustice, whether a user has spent a long time on hold, been the victim of a runaround (however unintentional), or purchased a product ill-suited to his or her needs. A corollary to this guideline is to avoid being overly apologetic to the point of being patronizing.

Say "Thank You"

Thank the user for contacting the user support group at both the beginning and end of the interaction. "Thanks for contacting the Help Desk" is a simple but effective way to communicate that the user and the contact are important. A "thank you" ends the incident on a positive note, even if the problem has been a difficult one.

Use Incident Management, not User-Management, Techniques

Be sure to distinguish between *incident* management and *user* management: manage the incident, not the user. Do not attempt to manipulate users by, for example, judging how well they communicate their needs, by criticizing how they organize their files and folders, or by lecturing them on their computer use. The relationship between a support agent and a user is not a boss-to-worker relationship and should not be based on different levels of power. Although you can recommend that a user read a particular chapter in a manual or suggest a different way to organize their documents, you should not make accepting your suggestion a condition for helping the user. Do not communicate that you are upset or be defensive if a user chooses not to take your advice. Users who feel that a support agent is trying to manage them or their work habits will rightfully feel resentful or manipulated and are more likely to be dissatisfied with a support incident.

Teach Self-Reliance

An immediate goal of each support incident is to provide information or to solve a user's problem. A secondary, longer-term goal is to make each user more self-reliant when possible. To create **self-reliance**, support agents explain a solution so that the user understands the reasons they encountered a problem and how to fix it. Agents also help create self-reliance when they refer to relevant printed or online documentation where a user can locate additional information about a problem or a question. To some extent, user support has a built-in contradiction: the support staff would like every user to call back (because their jobs depend on a flow of support incidents), but the staff hopes to resolve each user's problem so that he or she does not have to call back.

In reality, users will never become completely self-reliant. As computer use becomes even more widespread and computers become increasingly complex, both new and experienced users will continue to need an increased array of support services. Even expert users and computer gurus occasionally need assistance. In addition, some users don't want to become self-reliant; they feel that it is the support staff's job to solve their problems. Recognize that you cannot force users to change their behavior. However, start with an assumption that each user is interested in understanding a problem and your solution to it until the user indicates clearly that they are not interested. Though complete user self-reliance may never be achieved, it is an important long-term goal for a support staff.

Successful incident management is rarely a skill or ability that comes easily to support workers. It takes practice to develop your own incident management strategy, and even then, some incidents still go awry. As you will see in the next section, even the best incident management approach can sometimes be derailed by the personalities or work styles of the participants.

Customer Service and Personality Types

A personality analysis commonly used in business and industry is the **Myers-Briggs Type Indicator (MBTI)**. The answers to a series of questions about work styles and preferences determine where a worker falls on four basic personality dimensions. The four dimensions of personality measured by the MBTI are:

- **Where do you direct your energy? Introvert (I) versus Extrovert (E)** This dimension measures whether you focus your energy externally, to people, activities, and words (extroversion) or internally, to thoughts and ideas (introversion). An Extrovert is more social and expressive, whereas an Introvert is more private and quiet.

- **How do you process information? Sensing (S) versus Intuition (N)** Sensing people work more with facts and experiences that they obtain through their senses, whereas Intuitive people tend to emphasize personal insights and reflection. A Sensing person tends to prefer direct communication, while an Intuitive person often acts on hunches and seeks creative or novel ways to process information.

- **How do you make decisions? Thinking (T) versus Feeling (F)** Thinking people base decisions on logic, analysis, guiding principles, and objective factors, whereas Feeling people base decisions on personal values and subjective factors. Thinkers try to clarify decisions by detaching themselves from a problem, whereas Feelers are more likely to view themselves as inside a problem situation.

- **How do you organize your life? Judging (J) versus Perceiving (P)** Judging people prefer a structured lifestyle in which they are well-organized and make structured decisions. Perceiving people are more open, flexible, and explore their options. Judging people like to be in control, whereas perceiving people like spontaneity.

Each person is not a pure type of any of these descriptions, but falls along a continuum within each of the four dimensions. Furthermore, these four personality dimensions can be combined into any of 16 types. For example, one personality type is an ISTJ, while another is an ENFP. There is obviously no one, correct personality type. Most people are a mixture of these types.

One use of the Myers-Briggs personality types is to help workers understand how users and coworkers—either as individuals or in work groups—view the work world and behave differently in it. This understanding can help work groups avoid or work through conflicts and help support agents understand different approaches taken by end users.

ON THE WEB

For a thumbnail sketch of each of these types, visit the MBTI Club's Web site at **www.mbticlub.com/info_center. asp**. To learn more about the MBTI personality test and the 16 personality types it measures, consult one of these resources:

- Jean M. Kummerow, Nancy J. Barger, and Linda K. Kirby, *Work Types*. New York: Warner Books, 1997.

- Otto Kroeger, Janet M. Thuesen, and Hile Rutledge, *Type Talk at Work (Revised)*. New York: Delta, 2002.

- David Kiersey, *Please Understand Me II*. Delmar, CA: Prometheus Nemesis Books, 1998.

- The Team Technology Web site at **www.teamtechnology. co.uk/tt/t-articl/mb-simpl.htm**. This Web site includes several pointers to additional information about the MBTI personality types, including articles you can download for an in-depth discussion of personality types.

As part of a larger study of the role of personality in information technology work teams, the Department of Defense studied the MBTI personality types in IT work groups compared with the general population. The results of the study apply to all workers in information technology and not exclusively to support workers. They found that:

- The two most common personality types among information technology (IT) workers they studied were ISTJ and ESTJ. Thirty-nine percent of the IT workers they studied were one of these two types, compared with 19% in the general population.

- Female IT workers were somewhat more likely to be ESTJ, whereas male IT workers were somewhat more likely to be ISTJ.

- Personality types that were less likely to be found among Information Technology workers included the Sensing, Feeling, and Perceiving types.

ON THE WEB

To read more results from this study, download **www.sstc-online.org/Proceedings/2002/SpkrPDFS/ThrTracs/p567.pdf**.

Some communication difficulties that arise between a support agent and an end user may be traced to differences in basic personality type. For example, imagine the differences in communication style that may arise when a support agent, George, works on a problem with an end user, Hamida.

George, a support agent, is an ISTJ personality type on the Myers-Briggs scale. He is a very quiet, private person who prefers to work alone on problems by collecting data. He usually bases decisions on evidence he has carefully evaluated and analyzed. George prefers e-mail communication with users so that he has a written record of each incident.

Hamida, an internal end user, is an ENFP personality type. She is a warm, outgoing person who enjoys a collaborative, teamwork approach to problems. Hamida prefers to work on problems in person so that she can see a help desk agent's facial expression and read his or her body language. She likes the challenge of problem solving by trial and error and is often willing to make guesses and take risks to try to find a solution.

George thinks Hamida is overly aggressive and disorganized. Her approach to problems seems illogical. He finds working on a problem using her hit-and-miss approach to be stressful and a waste of time. Hamida thinks George fits the stereotype of a typical computer nerd who can't see over his pocket protector. She is frustrated that he seems unwilling to engage in give-and-take about a problem. She doesn't understand why he isn't willing to work on a problem together, but instead prefers short meetings and then quickly returns to his office to work.

As a support professional, George works hard to accommodate Hamida's work style. He understands that personality type differences can help explain communication problems between himself and Hamida, but are not an excuse for a lack of cooperation or communications that aren't civil.

George and Hamida are very different personality types based on the Myers-Briggs classification scheme, but even small differences in basic personality can affect work and communication styles. In this section, we have focused on personality types as a way to help explain behavioral differences between support agents and end users. However, the application of the MBTI personality types can also help us anticipate problems that can occur when teams of support agents work on a project together and when support workers and other workers in the IT department work together. For example, the user support field often attracts workers whose basic personality type includes a comfort level in working with groups of people (extroversion), whereas other information technology workers who are primarily technical professionals may be more comfortable working alone (introversion). IT managers often express concern about the ability of their professionals to function in work teams that include user support and end users. The more you know about basic personality types and their different work styles, the better you will be able to understand the dynamics of any work team.

Apart from differences in basic personality types, other barriers to effective communication between user support and end users occur because of difficult situations with which support agents must learn to deal. The next section describes some strategies for dealing with difficult clients and difficult incidents, whether they arise from differences in basic personality types, or from situational factors.

Strategies for Difficult Clients and Incidents

Although most users are rational and courteous, support agents may encounter several kinds of difficult users. A **difficult client** is one who requires special handling strategies because the user is angry, not communicative, rude or abusive, or exhibits a variety of other challenging attitudes or behaviors. The goal for a support agent is to steer a difficult situation to a successful conclusion. You will never be able to change a user's personality. Instead, focus on the specific problem, on getting the user the needed information, on providing excellent customer service in a respectful manner, and on moving to the next incident. To deal with difficult situations that might interfere with these goals, consider the strategies that experienced agents use. Table 2-4 summarizes the characteristics of difficult clients.

Difficulty	Characteristics
Users who complain	User is unhappy with features of products and services
	User is rarely satisfied with an apology or an explanation
Power users	User is technically knowledgeable, or at least thinks they are
	User indicates they should receive special treatment based on what or whom they know
Incidents that get off track	User is confused or provides contradictory or inaccurate information
	User is dissatisfied with lack of progress or problem resolution despite several attempts to solve the problem
Users who are upset or angry	User expresses real or perceived grievances about product or support services
	User evidences verbal and nonverbal communication that indicates dissatisfaction
	User loses the ability to communicate in a professional or productive manner
	User continually returns the communication to the source of the perceived grievance
Users who are abusive	User employs inappropriate language or behavior
	User engages in personal attacks on a company or its representatives
Users who are reluctant to respond	User talks slowly, very little, or not at all
	User does not answer direct questions
Users who won't stop responding	User continues to talk well after a problem has been resolved
	User changes the topic or relates personal experiences

Table 2-4   Characteristics of difficult clients

Users Who Complain

Instead of simply describing a problem, some users want to gripe about an organization's products or services. Complaint handling and management is often an important function of a help desk staff. Give a user with a gripe ample opportunity to voice their complaints or concerns. Don't transition into problem-solving mode too early in an incident when a user wants to complain. Instead, use empathy:

"I can certainly understand why someone who has experienced this problem would be upset . . ."

"Let me take down the information about your experiences with this product so I can pass it along to the project manager."

"Our company is willing to refund your purchase price if we can't help you make the product meet your needs."

Many support organizations treat reasonable complaints as a valuable source of feedback and suggestions for future product and service enhancements. Try to understand that most complaints are not directed at you personally, and learn (with practice!) not to be defensive about complaints.

Contacts by "Power Users"

In this context, **power users** are those who are technically very knowledgeable, or at least think they are, or who believe they warrant special attention or treatment because they have personal connections with significant people in an organization. These users often describe their powerful position early in an incident in an attempt to communicate their importance or expert knowledge (and occasionally to mask their actual lack of knowledge). They may, for example, try to impress a support agent with jargon to direct attention away from their lack of actual experience. One strategy for handling these users is to use inclusive language that makes them feel like a member of a team. Use pronouns like "we" to refer to the problem-solving process, such as:

"I think we can solve this problem if we work on it together . . ."

"The problem you called about is an interesting one. Will you give me some additional information so that we can work on it?"

"I appreciate your calling us about this problem and I would like to work with you on it."

Use an authoritative tone or speaking style because users who feel that they are important users like to communicate with important, knowledgeable agents. Remember that an agent's role is not to diminish the end user's sense of self-importance, but to solve the problem they contacted you about.

Incidents That Get Off Track

Occasionally in the course of resolving an incident, it becomes apparent to an agent that the process has taken a wrong turn and needs to get back on track. For example, a user might make a statement that contradicts an earlier statement. Or perhaps repeated attempts to isolate a problem have not succeeded. An incident during which a user becomes confused or one that results in lengthy, but unfruitful problem-solving approaches, indicates the process is off track. When this happens, try to refocus the process. Apologize to the user for the lack of a prompt resolution, summarize the basic incident information, and offer to continue to work toward a solution. Express confidence that, together, you will find a solution to the problem if you continue to work on it and that perhaps a different approach will achieve the results you both want.

"I'm sorry we haven't been able to resolve the problem yet. I think we have eliminated a hardware problem as the cause of the trouble you're seeing. I believe if we work for a while longer on why the software won't work, we'll be able to resolve this."

"We haven't made any progress on this problem yet. I'd like to take a fresh approach and see if a different perspective will identify the cause of the problem you're seeing."

Users Who Are Upset or Angry

Angry users are the most common kind of challenge. Angry users may be upset because of the way they have been treated. They may have been on hold too long, sent or received too many e-mails, worked with too many different support agents with contradictory suggestions, or explained the problem too many times. Or they may be upset because of real or perceived inadequacies in a product. They may also be angry due to circumstances that are totally unrelated to the incident at hand, such as a negative encounter with a coworker or family member.

The first principle for handling angry users is to let them vent their anger. Say little during the venting period, except to offer occasional agreement, and don't offer an explanation or switch to problem solving too early. Explanations to an angry person may sound defensive, or like an invitation to argue. The second principle is to reassure an angry user that the problem is an important one, and that you are willing to work with them resolve it. The third principle to remember is that angry users may continue to vent several times before they work through their anger. A polite question that refocuses the angry user may be effective:

"What would you like me to do to help solve the problem at this point?"

"How can we work together to resolve this situation to your satisfaction?"

"This is an important problem and I'm open to suggestions about how you think we can work together to resolve it."

Remember to avoid defensiveness and don't sound patronizing. An angry user is rarely upset with you personally. As with all incidents, continue to follow up on promises made to an angry user to build trust and confidence.

Users Who Are Abusive

Abusive users are rude, use inappropriate language, or make personal attacks on a support agent. A support agent's goal is to transform an incident with an abusive user: first, into an incident where the user is just angry (and no longer abusive), and ultimately to transform the incident into one with a satisfied user. This goal is not always achievable. Some support groups assign experienced staff members with special training and skills to handle abusive users; these workers pride themselves on their ability to defuse difficult situations. In general, handle abusive users according to the support organization's policies and procedures for this type of user. For example, some support organizations instruct their agents to terminate an incident when abusive language is used. In other organizations, support agents are trained to invite the user to use more appropriate and professional language:

"We would like to work with you on this problem. But we need to communicate about it in an appropriate and professional way. Is that agreeable with you?"

"Our company tries to use appropriate language in support calls. I'd like to continue to talk with you about the problem, but first, I need your commitment to use respectful language."

"If we can't use more appropriate language, I don't believe we are going to be able to make any progress on this problem."

Users Who Are Reluctant to Respond

Users who are slow or reluctant to provide information are often confused, lack confidence, or don't understand the questions. Many are inexperienced computer users. To obtain the information you need from these users, use very simple language and avoid technical jargon. Try different kinds of questions. For example, if open-ended questions fail to initiate a fruitful conversation, switch to questions that can be answered with yes or no. Begin with very simple questions, such as:

"Is there a Start button in the lower-left corner of the screen?"

"Can you read to me what it says in the box in the center of the screen?"

Or, temporarily switch to discussing the problem-solving process, such as:

"I'll ask you some questions about what you see on the screen and you answer them, or tell me that you're not sure. Any information you can give me will help us solve the problem."

Also give positive feedback when a reluctant user does provide useful information, such as:

"Thank you. I think the information you just provided will be helpful to us."

Finally, if a user continues to be reluctant to respond, suggest exchanging information in another mode (e-mail, chat session, telephone, remote access, or face to face) as a way to facilitate the problem-solving process.

Users Who Won't Stop Responding

Some users have a hard time letting go of a problem. Even after a problem is solved, they may continue to explain how bad it was or how similar it was to another problem they encountered. To deal with excessive communicators, use behavior that indicates the incident is over. For example, briefly summarize the incident and describe the conclusion. Thank the user for contacting the support group. Express your conviction that the problem is solved. Use very short answers that don't provide the user with lead-ins to additional responses. In face-to-face interactions, stand up and pack your briefcase.

"Thank you for calling about the problem today. Please call back if you encounter any further problems."

"I think that solves the problem you called about. Thanks for contacting us about this problem."

"I enjoyed working with you on this problem and hope it doesn't give you any more trouble. Have a good one . . ."

ON THE WEB

The Help Desk Institute has published a document on "How to Handle Difficult Customers". View the paper online at **www.thinkhdi.com/library/deliverfile.aspx?filecontentid=28**.

Jeff Dray, a help desk professional, has provided suggestions for dealing with abusive users at the TechRepublic Web site, **www.techrepublic.com/article.jhtml?id=r00320000726det02.htm**.

He also published an article that describes 10 types of difficult users at **blogs.techrepublic.com.com/10things/?p=343**. Access to the TechRepublic site requires a free membership.

Lisa DiCarlo, describes "The 5 Users from Hell" on *Computerworld*'s Web site at **www.computerworld.com/action/article.do?command=printArticleBasic&articleId=9050878**.

Handling difficult users is never an easy task, but over time you can improve your skills with practice and patience. Inexperienced help desk and support staff can learn a great deal about difficult users from experienced support agents. Veteran agents are a good resource for organization-approved and time-tested techniques for dealing with difficult situations. Training sessions for new help desk and support agents often cover organizational guidelines for dealing with these situations.

Client-Friendly Web Sites and Web 2.0

Use of **support Web sites** to communicate with end users has increased dramatically in the last decade. Although customer service skills are obviously important in face-to-face and telephone interactions, these skills apply equally to written communication, such as e-mail, online chat, and communication with users on a support Web site. The first generation of support Web sites provided primarily one-way communication between support providers and end users. Support Web sites are useful because users can get answers from frequently asked questions (FAQs) and problem solution knowledge databases quickly, at any time, and from anywhere Internet access is available. Because user support Web sites are cost-effective and popular with end users, these sites are increasingly popular and used in the support industry to augment other modes of user support.

ON THE WEB

CIOinsight, an industry trade magazine, has published the results of a survey that documents the extent to which support Web sites have become a dominant method of providing support services. Of the companies surveyed, 88% use Web support to communicate with clients, compared with 74% telephone and 65% field service (face-to-face). View an article with additional data at **www.cioinsight.com/c/a/ Research/Trend-3-The-Web-Becomes-the-Front-Line-For-Customer-Service**.

As the Web has evolved in recent years to include more interactivity and two-way communication, new methods of support are also emerging. **Web 2.0** is the recent development of technologies and Web applications that emphasize interactions among communities of users and the social networking aspects of collaboration and communication among users. Online social communities such as MySpace and Facebook and the online collaborative encyclopedia, Wikipedia, are examples of Web 2.0 applications. Web 2.0 trends have also impacted the way support services are delivered to users. For example, many vendors that formerly offered only support FAQs and knowledge bases, now sponsor forums and blogs where users who share common interests or have purchased similar products can interact, share information and opinions, collaborate on mutual problems, and offer their expertise to a user community. A **user forum** is a feature of a Web site where various discussions are organized as to which members of a user community may contribute. A **blog** is a feature of a Web site where an individual (the blogger) posts messages about which interested members of a user community are invited to comment.

User support Web sites are a cost-effective way to communicate with and among end users, whether internal or external. To the extent that users can locate information about problems, either from an FAQ or a knowledge base, or from another user in a forum discussion or blog, the cost of customer support is reduced. Hardware manufacturer Intel sponsors an interactive online user community, shown in Figure 2-4.

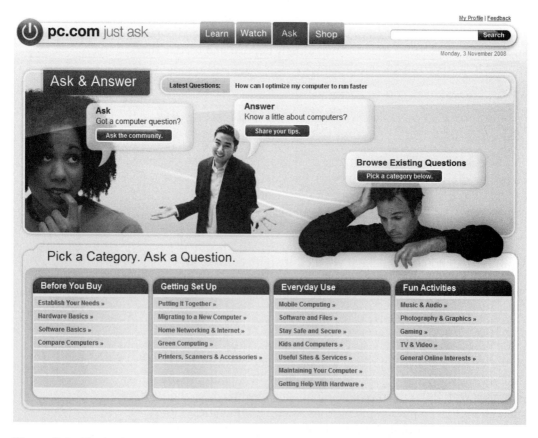

Figure 2-4   The Intel-sponsored interactive user support forum **www.pc.com/ask**

Customer service concerns and a customer-service ethic also apply to the design and construction of support Web sites. You have probably visited Web sites that were well organized and simple to use with information and features you could locate easily. But you've probably also visited some that failed the ease-of-use test. An organization that spends the resources to build a support Web site should build a client-friendly one that builds on the customer-service ethic described in this chapter. An organization's support Web site is as much a reflection of the business or agency as support phone contacts, e-mail exchanges, chat sessions, and face-to-face contacts with clients.

Because a support Web site is an important extension of an organization, a support specialist who has the responsibility to maintain the site needs a heightened awareness of customer-service concerns, and additional job skills to implement a successful site. The first issue in support Web site design is a clear definition of the purposes of the site. Common purposes of support Web sites include:

- Provide product information

- Take sale orders

- Access technical support

- Provide software updates and downloads

- Communicate with end users

- Encourage communication and collaboration among users

- Provide user forums and blogs as communication media

- Provide links to related sites

Four general criteria apply to written communication with end users, including Web site design. These four criteria are content, organization, format, and mechanics. A support Web site implementer uses these criteria as tools to evaluate how a Web site measures up to the customer-service ethic.

Simple support Web sites can be built and maintained with popular word processors as well as with more powerful Web-site-development tools such as Adobe Dreamweaver, Microsoft FrontPage or Publisher, Avanquest Web Easy, Six Apart TypePad, NetObject's Fusion Essentials, and WordPress.com. Several of these development tools are open source or offer basic, free Web-authoring tools, including blogs.

85

Content

Keep all product, support, and contact information accurate and up-to-date. Present a smaller amount of information that can be maintained and kept current rather than a larger amount of information that is out-of-date. Make the content relevant to what users need to know.

Organization

The design of the home page is critical. An effective home page is appealing and well organized, but avoids information overload and too many special graphic effects. Extensive graphics can affect download time for users with slower Internet connections. Some sites offer a text-only option to accommodate users with slow connections. The best support Web sites have menus, icons, and information "teasers" (summaries) on the home page, with navigational links to more detailed information if a user desires.

Support Web sites can be organized by product, by function, or in other ways. Sites organized by product should include search capabilities in case a user cannot find a specific product by model number. Sites organized by function may include separate pages for product features and information, an FAQ knowledge base, software downloads, a shopping cart, support contact information, a site map, and a site feedback mechanism.

Format

Information should be formatted into small units. A document that takes more than two-to-three PgUp or PgDn keystrokes to access should be segmented into multiple pages or easy-to-find sections.

Navigation aids expand the usability of a Web site. A well-formatted Web site includes multiple ways of accessing information, including navigation aids (to return to the top of a long page, jump to the next or previous page, or return to the home page), a search engine to help locate specific information, and menu icons to access main topics. The pages, navigation aids, and menu bars should be consistent across the site. Fonts and format features should maintain a consistent style and feel.

Mechanics

Chapter 11 discusses these four criteria—content, organization, format, and mechanics—in more detail.

Check spelling and grammar on all Web documents as well as FAQ databases. For most Web sites, it is best to use a writing style that is straightforward and easy to read.

ON THE WEB

A good example of a support Web site that illustrates many of these design criteria is Cisco's site that was established to support their network products. You can visit the site at **www.cisco.com/en/US/support/index.html**. What Web sites have you discovered that you think are easy to use and contain useful support information?

A Web site devoted to user support is useless unless users know about it and visit it. A support site can be registered with popular search engines so that Web surfers who enter relevant keywords will locate the site. A support Web site can be prominently displayed in user manuals and in online documentation (for example, a link on the toolbar of a software product). A reference to the Web site can also be included in product literature, organizational newsletters and brochures, as well as business cards. Pointers to a support Web site can be publicized in support phone calls, e-mails, and chat sessions.

ON THE WEB

To learn more about the features of Web sites that increase their usability for clients, visit **www.usabilityfirst.com**.

Many colleges and professional-technical schools offer coursework in Web site design, implementation, and maintenance. These courses are a good way to add value to a user support worker's resume.

Comprehensive Client Services

User support communication and interpersonal skills are essential to provide excellent client services. Yet, a comprehensive approach to excellent client service is also based on specific organizational values, attitudes, and actions.

Excellent client services start when every employee, from high-level managers to the newest support agents, recognizes that its clients are the primary reason for the organization's existence. Each employee's job depends directly on client satisfaction. Most support organizations' mission statements express the commitment that each end user's enhanced productivity is a primary objective of the support staff. In a user support environment, client productivity and satisfaction are directly related to the extent to which each user is treated as a valued client.

Customer service excellence depends on whether a support staff is willing to take extra steps to make sure clients are satisfied. For example, an excellent support organization keeps its clients apprised of the progress or lack of progress toward a problem solution. It actively promotes win-win outcomes for each incident. It seeks agreement that problems have been adequately addressed, and then conducts follow-up client surveys to measure the extent of client satisfaction and identify areas where client relationships can be improved.

 Excellent customer service does not necessarily mean that the client is always right. Sometimes requests by even the most valued clients cannot be met for a variety of sound business reasons. In those situations, stress what you *can* do for a user, and look for alternate ways to meet user needs.

Outstanding customer service requires adequate support resources. Customer service excellence rarely happens by accident, but is based on advanced planning, adequate staffing, and a sufficient budget for help desk tools and information resources that encourage excellence. A sufficient support budget is not always easy to achieve because support expenses are sometimes difficult to justify, as you will learn in Chapter 6.

A comprehensive client service orientation among a support staff must apply not only to every staff member in an organization, but also to every mode of communication with users. Although most of this book covers technical problem solving and operational details associated with the day-to-day operation of a help desk or support group, this chapter on communication and customer service is really the most important one in the book. Why? Because you can perform all the technical and operational duties of a support job adequately and still fail if you don't provide excellent service to your clients.

This chapter introduced customer service skills and interpersonal communication tools that support agents need to learn about and use in order to be effective in their jobs. However, reading a chapter about customer service skills or listening to a lecture on the subject, while a good beginning, is a very limited way to develop your own skills. The "On the Web" notes in this chapter contain pointers to additional information that you can use to learn more and build your own customer service and interpersonal skills. The discussion questions, hands-on activities, and case projects at the end of this chapter are especially important because they give you additional opportunities to get practical experience that will serve you well on the job.

Chapter Summary

- Communication and interpersonal relationships are the foundations of excellent customer service, which is a goal expressed in many support organizations' mission statements. Communication is a process that involves listening and reading, understanding, and speaking and writing skills.

- The most important communication skill for help desk and user support staff is the ability to listen to or read information provided by clients. In addition to a description of a user's problem, help desk staff need to evaluate a user's language level so the staff can target their responses to a similar level. Help desk staff need to listen or read for cues that indicate whether a user is frustrated, confused, or angry.

- Understanding a client involves being able to restate their problem, but it also means an ability to empathize with the user's situation and feelings and to understand why the problem is an important one for the client.

- The ability to respond effectively includes skill with a greeting, the use of scripts as aids, and the ability to use a tone and style that help rather than hinder. Nonverbal aspects of communication, such as posture, facial expression, eye contact, gestures, and voice quality may impact the success of a communication more than the meanings of words.

- Practice is the key to developing a personal communication style that adds to user satisfaction, perhaps even more than technically correct answers. Experienced agents learn to use clear, succinct speech or writing that is positive and avoids empty phrases that contribute little meaning.

- Support workers who communicate on the telephone learn effective ways to greet a user, put a call on hold, transfer a call, and terminate a call.

- Support agents should develop a personal incident management strategy. Goal-directed diagnostic questions, honesty, as well as the ability to say "I don't know," to apologize, to create user self-reliance, and to thank a user for contacting a support group are all components of a personal incident management strategy.

- Some barriers to communication between a support agent and a user may be related to differences in basic personality types and work styles which can be better understood by using the Myers-Briggs classification scheme.

- Difficult support incidents include user complaints, incidents with power users, incidents that get off track, incidents with angry or abusive users, and incidents from users who are either reluctant to respond or who won't stop responding. Skilled support agents develop specific strategies to channel difficult users into satisfied ones.

- A user support Web site is a cost-effective way to communicate with users and to encourage communication among communities of users to collaborate and share information. Web site developers need additional skills and tools to manage information content, site organization, a client-friendly format, and writing mechanics to build a support Web site that meets the goals of a customer-service ethic.

- A comprehensive approach to client services includes not only communication skills but also an organization-wide recognition of the importance of each client, a willingness to take extra measures to satisfy users, and adequate support resources to provide client satisfaction. Comprehensive customer service applies equally to telephone, face-to-face, remote access, and written interactions with users, such as e-mail messages, chat sessions, FAQs, and blogs.

Key Terms

blog—A feature of a Web site where a writer posts messages to which members of a user community are invited to comment.

customer-service ethic—An organization-wide commitment, shared by everyone from top management to operational staff, that client relations and client satisfaction are the most important aspects of a business.

difficult client—A user who requires special handling strategies because they are angry, uncommunicative, rude or abusive, or exhibit other hard-to-handle behaviors.

empathy—An understanding of and identification with a user's problem situation, thoughts, and feelings. A support agent who can empathize with a user understands the problem or question from the client's perspective and why it is important to the client.

greeting—The first few sentences in a support incident that introduce an agent form the basis for the first impression of the support service by the user, and get the incident-resolution process started on a positive note.

incident management strategy—A collection of tools, techniques, and strategies that support agents use during an incident to move effectively and efficiently from the initial greeting to the conclusion of the incident.

Myers-Briggs Type Indicator (MBTI)—A personality analysis commonly used in business and industry to identify worker personality and work style preferences.

nonverbal behavior—Facial expression, body language, and the tone and style of communication. Nonverbal communication behavior may be more important than the specific words used in a communication.

personal communication style—The result of a series of decisions each support agent makes about how they communicate with end users.

power user—A user who is technically knowledgeable (or believes that they are), or who may have a relationship with an organization that they feel warrants special attention to their incident.

script—A prepared sequence of questions and statements that support agents can use to handle parts of an incident; a script may include decision points and branches to handle different situations.

self-reliance—A goal of support service providers that seeks to increase user self-sufficiency and reduce a user's dependence on support services.

support Web site—A Web site devoted to providing clients with product information, software downloads, support staff contacts, and a sales channel. Support Web sites are a cost-effective method to communicate with users, but should be designed to be client-friendly.

user forums—A feature of a Web site where various discussions are posted to which members of a user community may contribute. User forums emphasize the collaborative nature of the Web as a way to encourage interaction and collaboration among users.

Web 2.0—The recent development of technologies and Web applications that emphasize the social networking aspects of collaboration and communication among users. Web 2.0 emphasizes interactive use of the Web.

Check Your Understanding

Answers to Check Your Understanding Questions are found in Appendix A.

1. True or False? Communication skills are often more difficult for a new help desk agent to learn than technical skills or business skills.

2. A(n) _____ is a choice each support agent makes about how professional or casual, how respectful or condescending, how formal or informal, or how terse or verbose they will be in their interactions with users.

3. A user's first impression of a support agent usually comes from the:

   a. incident greeting

   b. solution to the problem

   c. incident script used

   d. agent's tone and style

4. Which listening type focuses on opportunities to empathize with the user and provide positive support?

    a. Discriminative

    b. Comprehensive

    c. Critical

    d. Therapeutic

    e. Relational

5. Which listening type focuses on learning about the knowledge level and emotional state of the user?

    a. Discriminative

    b. Comprehensive

    c. Critical

    d. Therapeutic

    e. Relational

6. Which of these is not a tool for effective listening?

    a. avoid distractions

    b. view the problem from the user's perspective

    c. talk to fill awkward silences

    d. probe for details

7. Nonverbal communication behaviors include posture, facial expression, _____, and _____.

8. True or False? Nonverbal behaviors are almost as important as the meaning of words in a communication.

9. True or False? Empathy means a user support agent takes ownership and responsibility for a user's problem.

10. A support agent should make liberal use of the word:

    a. I

    b. You

    c. We

    d. Oops

11. One measure of whether a support agent understands a user's problem is whether they can express the problem in:

    a. the user's actual words

    b. the support agent's own words

    c. industry standard vocabulary

    d. the wording of the script for the problem

12. True or False? Of the three essential communication skills, listening or reading comes before understanding and responding.

13. True or False? Scripts designed to guide a user support agent through an incident should be memorized or read verbatim to a user to avoid mistakes.

14. A support worker who uses a telephone extensively is likely to need to know how to put a call on hold and _____.

15. True or False? One of the goals of incident management is to help users be more self-reliant.

16. Which of the following is not a primary strategy for a support organization that aims for customer service excellence?

    a. Treat clients with respect.

    b. Explain to clients what you can do for them.

    c. Agree to any demand a client makes.

    d. Return calls to clients when promised.

17. Which of these is not a recommended incident management strategy for support agents?

    a. Ask goal-directed diagnostic questions.

    b. Say thanks.

    c. Teach the user self-reliance.

    d. Never admit that you are not sure.

18. True or False? A successful support worker is one who has learned from experience how to manipulate a user's behavior to make the user more productive.

19. True or False? A customer-service ethic is an organization-wide commitment that the client is always right.

20. A support Web site implementer uses four criteria to evaluate a client-friendly site: content, _____, _____, and mechanics.

Discussion Questions

1. Why are communication skills often more challenging for inexperienced support agents to learn than technical or business skills?

2. Should a support agent ever just hang up on a caller who is rude or uses abusive language? Describe some pros and cons to this approach, and explain your position.

3. Are providing excellent user support and teaching users to be more self-reliant contradictory strategies? Explain why or why not.

4. Will different work styles and communication differences among workers who have different MBTI personality types inevitably lead to conflict? Explain your position.

5. Describe some pros and cons to Web 2.0 interactive tools that allow users to post messages on a blog or user forum support Web site that other users can view and respond to. Do the pros outweigh the cons?

6. A sales manager made the following comment at a vendor conference: "Good customer relationships are a worthwhile goal for us, but we usually find that it is just too expensive to provide really excellent customer service. The costs always outweigh the benefits." Do you agree or disagree with her statement?

Hands-On Activities

Activity 2-1

Evaluate a help desk mission statement. California Polytechnic State University in San Luis Obispo (Cal Poly) operates a help desk for its campus users. Read the mission statement of Cal Poly's service desk operation at **www.servicedesk.calpoly.edu/computing_support/about_us/goals_mission.html**.

Identify at least five ways in which the Cal Poly help desk mission statement includes a customer-service ethic as described in this chapter.

Activity 2-2

Practice effective listening skills. The Web page **workhelp.org/content/view/174/46/** describes an exercise where you listen to the radio to practice focused listening skills. Read the article and follow the steps the author suggests to improve your ability to focus on the message of users.

Activity 2-3

Interview a support agent about difficult users. Invite a help desk agent in your school or company to talk with you and your classmates. Use the following questions as a guide for your interview:

- Please tell me about some of your experiences with difficult users.
- What techniques do you use to handle these situations?
- In your experience, what is the most common kind of difficult incident?
- What kinds of incidents do you personally find the most difficult to handle?
- What policies does your support organization have to deal with difficult users?

Write a brief report that summarizes the main points of the interview.

Activity 2-4

Explore ways to improve client service. Read an article about customer service available on the Internet at **techupdate.zdnet.com/techupdate/stories/main/0,14179,2804648,00.html** ("Improve Customer Service—And Cut Costs" by George Lawton). Write a short summary of the article that answers the following questions:

1. Who should read this article (who is the intended audience)?

2. What trends in customer service does the author describe?

3. What will readers of this article learn? (List the main points.)

Be sure your summary includes information about the source of the article.

Activity 2-5

Evaluate your qualities as a help desk agent. Read an article on the desirable qualities of a help desk agent by Paul Chin, at www.paulchinonline.com/portfolio/ij/ij20061024.htm. Make a list of the qualities of a good help desk worker described by the author. Then use Chin's criteria to evaluate your own strengths and areas where you could improve your skills. Which of the qualities will you need to improve the most in a job as a help desk agent?

Activity 2-6

Evaluate your communication skills. Take a 25-question quiz on your personal communication skills at **www.optimalthinking.com/ quiz-communication-skills.asp**. Be as honest with your responses as you can. Briefly describe any of the 25 items for which you checked *sometimes* or *rarely*. Then describe any patterns or themes that you can identify in the items you checked as *sometimes* or *rarely*. Finally, what resources are available to you to address the patterns of skill improvement that you have identified?

Activity 2-7

Learn more about effective Web site design. Read an article on effective Web site design elements by Jennifer Stewart, a professional writer who maintains a Web site devoted to improving writing skills: **www.write101.com/101web.htm**. Make a list of five design ideas or suggestions for support Web site developers that add to the guidelines provided in the chapter.

Activity 2-8

Solve a customer service crossword puzzle. Customer service week is celebrated each year in October. The Customer Service Week Web site includes a variety of puzzles to challenge customer service workers at **www.csweek.com/customer_service_week_puzzles.php**. As a measure of your understanding of customer service vocabulary and concepts, try out the crossword puzzle. How many words did you need to look up in the solution?

Activity 2-9

Listen in on a support call. A user of America Online (AOL) services, Vincent Ferrari, called the vendor's hotline to cancel his account. Since he had heard rumors about the difficulty of cancelling an AOL account, Vincent recorded the call. A television interview with Vincent that includes an edited version of the call is available on YouTube at **www.youtube.com/watch?v=xmpDSBAh6RY**. View the video and answer these questions:

- List the mistakes that John, the help desk representative, made during the call.

- Describe three steps you would recommend to avoid an incident like this.

- How do you think the easy availability of this video on YouTube will impact AOL's business?

Activity 2-10

Working with Personality Types. In this chapter, you read about George and Hamida in the section on MBTIs. Recall that George, a user support agent, is an ISTJ personality type and Hamida, an end user, is an ENFP type. Learn more about these personality types at **www.mbticlub.com/info_center.asp**.

1. Briefly describe the ISTJ and ENFP personality types in the Myers-Briggs categories.

2. If George and Hamida are assigned to work on a project team together, describe any problems you anticipate they might encounter working together, based on differences in work styles.

3. Describe some ways George and Hamida could function successfully working together.

4. If you joined the project team with George and Hamida, whose work style would you be least comfortable with? Explain your answer.

Case Projects

1. An E-mail Reply for Bug-Free Software Limited

You are a support agent for Bug-Free Software Limited, which develops customized software for businesses on a contract basis. You receive the following e-mail message from a large client:

We received the custom Visual Basic programs from your new programmer and installed them on our system last week. It was obvious from the first time we ran the programs that the programmer was new to your organization. It was not clear the programmer had much prior experience with programming or with Visual Basic. The new programs we received converted the information from our old COBOL programs to our report formatter fairly well, according to the specifications we provided her. But we discovered that she built the specific data-conversion instructions into the Visual Basic programs. The programs lack the flexibility we need to handle all of the different data formats we have to convert. The programs should have been written with the conversion information in tables that are easily modified. The way they were written means we have to modify the programs every time we run them.

Write a reply to this e-mail that shows empathy for the problem and a good customer-service ethic.

2. User Support Personality Types

Based on your understanding of the 16 personality types in the Myers-Briggs classification and on your knowledge of help desk communication and customer service skills described in this chapter, work with a team of three classmates or coworkers to identify which of the 16 MBTI types you think is best suited to providing excellent customer service. Would more than one of the 16 types be effective?

If you have never taken the Myers-Briggs test or have not taken it recently, you may be able to take the test at your school's counseling department or at your organization's human resources office. If you would like to take a shorter, online version, go to The Keirsey Temperament Sorter II Web site at **www.advisorteam.com/user/kts. asp**, or the HumanMetrics Web site at **www.humanmetrics.com/ cgi-win/JTypes2.asp**. While neither of these online tests are a substitute for the full Myers-Briggs test, they will give you an indication of your type.

If the results indicate that your personality type is not as well suited for help desk or user support work as other personality types, understand that the 16 MBTI personality types are not absolutes. Each person is actually a mixture of the eight pure categories in the test. The MBTI test simply measures tendencies. Most people are more adaptive than the test often indicates.

Write a summary of your research into the MBTI personality types and customer service orientation among help desk staff.

3. A Complaint-Handling Script for Max Modem

Molly Jeavsey, who works in the administrative group at Max Modem, is the person to whom complaints about company products are directed. Molly has kept a running tally of which modem products generate the most complaints. She periodically passes the complaint tallies to the product design engineers and assembly line managers in the manufacturing division as feedback on problems end users or retail stores encounter with Max Modem's products.

Recently, the engineers became aware of a large volume of complaints about a new model of DSL modem, D-700i. They have asked Molly to collect more information from users and retailers about the problems with the new D-700i modems.

Help Molly by writing a draft of a simple script help desk agents could use to collect some basic information for Molly about the problems users and retailers are encountering with the D-700i modems. The script you write should respond to two goals: (1) to collect basic product information that would be useful to Max Modem's engineers and managers; and (2) to exhibit a diplomatic way of asking for information that reflects an excellent customer-service ethic.

Compare your script with that of others in your class or work group to look for ideas on how to improve your script.

4. Evaluate Vendor Support Web Sites

Select three or more support Web sites from among the following hardware vendors:

- Apple: **www.apple.com/support/hardware**
- Dell: **support.dell.com**
- eMachines: **www.emachines.com/support/product_support. html**
- Gateway: **support.gateway.com/support/default.asp**
- Hewlett-Packard (HP): **welcome.hp.com/country/us/en/ support.html**
- Lenovo: **consumersupport.lenovo.com/lenovo/drivers/ index.html**
- Toshiba: **www.csd.toshiba.com/cgi-bin/tais/su/su_sc_home.jsp**

You may substitute other hardware manufacturers you are familiar with if you wish. Compare and evaluate each vendor's support Web site using the customer support criteria discussed in this chapter. Limit your evaluation to the support home page and perhaps one level below the home page.

Address questions such as:

1. How easy or difficult is it to find information about a specific model?

2. Does the site provide the kind of information that a user support specialist would need to know?

3. Is the information in a format that is usable?

4. What tools are available on the Web site to allow someone to contact the vendor with a question?

5. Is it easy to navigate the Web site?

6. Based on its support Web site, how do you rate each vendor's commitment to excellent customer service?

5. Practice Interpersonal Communication Skills

The purpose of this case project is to learn about a useful spyware utility program, Spybot Search and Destroy, and to develop good interpersonal communications in a support situation. First, download and install the free spyware program from the Web site **www.safer-networking.org/en/download/index.html**. (You may substitute a different utility program if you wish.) Second, spend some time learning about the features of the program.

Then, team up with your work or school colleagues to practice your interpersonal skills in a variety of support roles. Take turns with the roles of 1) end user, 2) support provider, and 3) observer/evaluator. In each role-playing session, the end user can take on a role such as:

• A novice user in a face-to-face support environment with little previous experience installing and using spyware.

• An experienced user in a face-to-face support environment with a good understanding of spyware technology.

• A novice user in a telephone support environment with little previous experience installing and using spyware. If a telephone setup is not available, you may be able to simulate one using separate rooms or a barrier between the user and support provider.

• A difficult to handle user, such as an angry or reluctant communicator (this is a difficult user role which may require some acting ability). The role of the end user in this situation is to challenge the interpersonal skills and abilities of the support specialist, but not to overact and provide an impossible situation for the support agent.

The goals of the support provider in each role playing activity are:

1. Explain the problem that spyware is designed to address.

2. Explain how to download and install Spybot Search and Destroy.

3. Use excellent interpersonal communication skills as described in this chapter.

The role of the observer/evaluator is to provide feedback to the person playing the support provider role. If available, use a device to record the interaction so that the support provider can use the recording for a self-evaluation.

Finally, when you have completed several different role-playing sessions, discuss how interactions with end users vary depending on the experience level of the user and whether the interaction is face-to-face or on the telephone.

CHAPTER 3

Skills for Troubleshooting Computer Problems

In this chapter, you will learn about:

◎ The troubleshooting process and the thinking skills required for successful troubleshooting

◎ Communication skills for troubleshooting

◎ Information resources to help solve computer problems

◎ Diagnostic and repair tools used to troubleshoot computer problems

◎ Strategies for troubleshooting

◎ How to develop your own approach to problem solving

Solving computer problems is one of the most critical and frequent tasks user support agents perform. Concerns that end users bring to user support agents are varied, including requests for information, questions about how to perform a task, complaints about a product or feature, and problems that prevent end users from operating hardware or software. Many problems are relatively easy for support agents to solve quickly. The problem may be one they have seen before and, therefore, already know the solution; or they may be able to find the solution quickly in a database of problem solutions.

Some problems are more challenging and difficult to solve. These include problems that support agents have never encountered or those for which the solutions are not obvious. Despite attempts to find a quick solution, the problem-solving effort may not succeed at first. On occasion, a seemingly straightforward problem report may turn out to be the first in a long series of separate incidents about a significant problem with a new or recently modified product.

This chapter describes the tools, methods, and strategies that support agents use to work on user problems, especially difficult ones. After examining these strategies, you will be encouraged to use these tools to develop your own problem-solving skills.

What Is Troubleshooting?

Troubleshooting is the process of defining, diagnosing, and solving computer problems. Some people think of the process of solving computer problems as a fixed sequence of steps that can be followed to diagnose and repair any malfunction with computer hardware, software, or networks. The ability to follow a sequence of steps, such as would be necessary to complete installation of a software package, is an important job skill for support agents. However, no single sequence of steps is likely to diagnose every computer problem. Troubleshooting computer problems is often more complex than that.

Troubleshooting is often an **iterative process**, a process that involves several paths or approaches to problem solving. This means that a troubleshooter follows one sequence of steps for a while and then loops back and performs other, perhaps similar, steps down a different path. The process can include many false starts and temporary pauses as a troubleshooter pursues an approach, hits a dead end, switches to an alternate approach, makes some progress, only to hit a snag and starts down another path. Figure 3-1 graphically compares a sequential process with an iterative process.

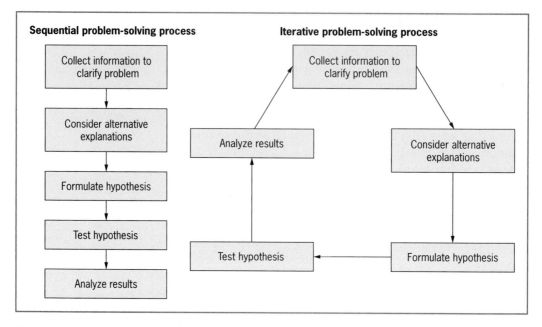

Sequential problem-solving process

Collect information to clarify problem

Consider alternative explanations

Formulate hypothesis

Test hypothesis

Analyze results

Iterative problem-solving process

Collect information to clarify problem

Analyze results

Consider alternative explanations

Test hypothesis

Formulate hypothesis

Figure 3-1   Sequential versus iterative problem-solving processes

An iterative process may seem repetitious, and in a way it is. Troubleshooting is not always a neat, linear, and orderly process. It is often both a logically structured and a creative process that requires flexibility, thinking skills, and patience. It is partly a scientific process that follows rules of logic and partly an artistic process that relies on insight and creativity.

The approach to troubleshooting advocated in this chapter differs from two alternate approaches, the first of which treats troubleshooting as a fixed sequence of steps one follows (1, 2, 3, etc.) until a problem is solved. Sometimes a predefined sequence of steps moves troubleshooters toward resolution, and sometimes it doesn't. A second alternative might be described as a hit-or-miss approach (sometimes called trial-and-error) to troubleshooting. It consists of randomly trying various things in hopes of eventually hitting on something that works. "I'll poke around and see what I can find" is a common way to describe the hit-or-miss approach. Occasionally, a hit-or-miss approach stumbles across a solution and resolves a problem, but often it doesn't. And sometimes troubleshooters using the hit-or-miss approach try things that actually make matters worse.

Like woodworkers, computer troubleshooters use a variety of tools and skills as they try to solve a difficult problem. They may pick up one tool, work on an aspect of a problem, set that tool aside for a while, and pick up another tool, only to turn back to a tool or skill used previously. The tools user support agents employ in troubleshooting can be physical tools, such as a diagnostic program or a database of information, or they can be thinking skills, such as problem solving, critical thinking, and decision making.

ON THE WEB

To get practice with general troubleshooting methods, complete one or more of the activities detailed in this PDF file: **www.ibiblio.org/kuphaldt/socratic/output/trouble2. pdf**. Although the problems are not all computer related, this worksheet illustrates several problem-solving strategies. Note that suggested answers are at the end of the PDF.

Problem-Solving Skills

The term **problem solving** is often used in business and mathematics to describe a process of moving from the current state of events X (the problem state) to a future, desired state of events Y, sometimes called the **goal state**. Figure 3-2 illustrates this problem-solving model applied to a malfunctioning printer.

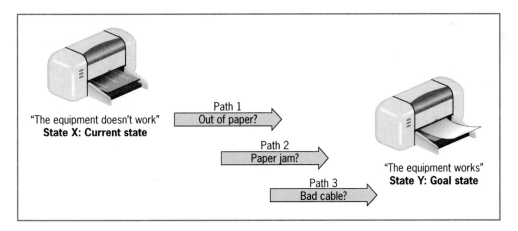

Figure 3-2 Problem-solving model

In Figure 3-2, the objective is to move from the problem state (the printer doesn't work) to the goal state (the printer works again). A problem solver is looking for a path from the problem state to the goal state that locates the correct answer. Good problem solvers are skilled at getting from problem to goal quickly, accurately, and efficiently.

ON THE WEB

To get another perspective on approaches to problem solving, read a paper by Fred Nickols, "Choosing the Right Problem Solving Approach," at **home.att.net/~OPSINC/ choosing.pdf**.

Problem solvers use a variety of thinking skills. For example, a problem solver may analyze a problem on the basis of:

- **Analogies**—Ways in which the current problem is similar to other problems that have been solved; for example, "This problem with the address book in Microsoft Live Mail is very similar to a problem with the address book I've seen in Outlook Express."

- **Contradictions**—Situations in which a fact established through investigation rules out, or contradicts, a potential solution; for example, "If this network card doesn't operate in one computer, but works in another one, the problem is unlikely to be a defective network card."

Analyzing analogies and contradictions may lead a problem solver to a possible solution.

Critical-Thinking Skills

Critical thinking describes the cognitive skills a problem solver uses to analyze a situation, search for the underlying logic or rationale for it, and seek out alternate ways to explain it. To think critically is to use personal experience, the power of logical thinking, "mental models" of how things work, and various analytic tools to examine and understand a situation. Computer problem solvers rely on critical-thinking skills such as those listed in Figure 3-3 in many situations to try to understand the possible causes for the observed behavior (or misbehavior) of a computer system.

- Mental models
- Hypothesis testing
- Creativity
- Metacognition

Figure 3-3   Critical-thinking skills

Each of these critical-thinking skills is described in the following.

- **Mental models**—A mental model is a conceptual picture that a problem solver builds in order to understand how things work. Mental models are often based on education and experience. For example, a user support agent, when confronted with a software program that does not operate, may construct a mental model of the sequence of steps a computer takes to find, load, and execute a program. Based on the model, the problem solver may formulate some hypotheses about which steps in the sequence could fail.

- **Hypothesis testing**—Hypothesis testing involves formulating a **hypothesis**—a guess or prediction based on experience—about the cause of a problem and then designing a test that will prove or disprove the hypothesis. Troubleshooters usually formulate a hypothesis based on their mental model or prior experience with other problems. For example, a problem solver may make an initial guess that garbage characters output on a printer are due to a faulty signal cable from the computer to the printer, and then use critical-thinking skills to devise a series of tests to determine whether the signal cable is indeed the cause of the problem. A critical thinker may then look for another operational printer cable nearby to use in place of the original signal cable as a test.

- **Creativity**—Creativity in problem solving is the ability to find a novel or innovative solution to a problem. Creative troubleshooters have an ability to see a problem from new or different perspectives. For example, a computer problem solver may discover a unique solution to a problem he or she has never seen before by thinking about how a similar piece of hardware or software operates. Some troubleshooters refer to the search for a novel approach as thinking outside the mental model, or "thinking outside the box."

- **Metacognition**—The ability to think about thinking is called metacognition. Successful troubleshooters have the ability to step back from a problem-solving situation and analyze their thought processes. Using metacognition, for example, a troubleshooter may realize that he or she is assuming that a problem is hardware related, when, in fact, it may be software related. Metacognition is a critical-thinking skill that can help good troubleshooters become better ones, because it involves self-analysis and challenging one's assumptions.

    Examples of metacognitive questions that troubleshooters can ask themselves include:

    - What assumptions did I make that led me in the wrong direction?

    - Where did I go wrong solving this problem?

- Why did one problem-solving approach work well in this situation when another one didn't?

- How could I have thought differently about this problem to solve it more effectively or efficiently?

Decision-Making Skills

Decision making is the ability to select one alternative from among a number of alternatives, based on some evaluation criteria. For example, business decisions are often based on criteria such as lower cost, greater output volume, higher profit margin, improved quality, superior customer service, or better employee morale. Good decision makers often define several effective alternatives, weigh the pros and cons of each alternative against some predefined criteria, and reach a decision.

Decision making in computer problem solving is particularly important when support agents are confronted with several explanations for a problem. For example, when a number of diagnostic tests can be used to gather information, a problem solver must decide which test is most likely to produce useful and informative results. Selecting the wrong test could delay progress toward the correct solution and reduce the efficiency of the problem-solving process.

Troubleshooters routinely use skills such as problem solving, critical thinking, and decision making in their work, whether they are computer support agents, auto mechanics, clock repairers, or medical doctors. Several of the problem-solving scenarios in this and the next chapter illustrate problem-solving methods that use these thinking skills.

Tools Troubleshooters Use

Most successful troubleshooters use tools that fall into one of five broad categories, which are listed in Figure 3-4. Think about the tools you have used to work on computer problems in your own experience and try to determine how the tools fit into one of these categories.

- Communication skills
- Information resources
- Diagnostic and repair tools
- Problem-solving strategies
- Personal characteristics

Figure 3-4 Categories of problem-solving tools

Communication Skills

Communication and interpersonal skills are important troubleshooting tools, because most computer problem situations require at least some interaction with an end user, and sometimes with a vendor. Troubleshooters use communication skills to get a basic description of a problem, to learn the user's perspectives on the problem, and to probe for additional information. After a problem has been solved, troubleshooters also need to communicate the solution effectively to the user. The six principal types of communication skills used to troubleshoot computer problems are: basic listening skills, active listening, probes, critical questions, explanations, and verification skills. Successful support agents are adept at using these skills in almost every user support situation.

Basic Listening Skills

To start a troubleshooting challenge on the right foot, support agents try to obtain as accurate a description of the problem as possible from the user's perspective. Therefore, the foremost communication skills every troubleshooter needs are listening skills.

Listen to the words the end user chooses to describe a problem. The danger of a support agent not listening carefully, or of not giving the user enough time to explain the problem, is that the agent may jump ahead of the user and begin to work on a solution before they really understand the problem. When troubleshooters turn their attention away from what a user is saying to focus on the solution to a problem, they can miss critical pieces of information. The result is a troubleshooting process that is less efficient and perhaps frustrating for the end user, who feels that he or she has to repeat information unnecessarily.

Listen to the user describe the problem's symptoms. Some support agents take notes about the symptoms. Listen for causal, "If . . . Then" statements of the form, "If I do X, then the result is Y." For example, "If I try to adjust the monitor, then the screen goes blank," or, "When I click Cancel, my system freezes." User reports of computer behavior in this "If . . . Then" form often provide clues that lead to a possible path toward a solution more quickly than simple statements such as, "My LCD display doesn't work."

Active Listening

If basic listening skills are the most important communication skill, active listening skills rate a close second place. In **active listening**, the listener is as engaged in the communication process as the speaker—rather than being a passive receiver of information. An active

Avoid describing a problem using the identical words that a user uses. Parroting is not a useful feedback technique and is unlikely to lead to clarifications.

listening skill that is often extremely helpful to user support agents is **paraphrasing**, restating in your own words what you heard the user say. The user can then verify that you understood him or her. Paraphrasing is especially helpful to clarify a problem description and often leads to resolving misunderstandings about the nature of the problem. In describing a problem, a user might include unclear, unnecessary, or even contradictory information. As a troubleshooter paraphrases a problem statement, the user may correct the words to clarify the meaning.

The following examples show how paraphrasing can help clarify the problem definition.

End-user description: *I don't know what happened, but the program doesn't work. I wonder if it is a defective program or if I am doing something wrong.*

Support agent paraphrase: *Let me make sure I understand. The program used to work, but now it doesn't?*

End-user description: *No, I just got the program installed, and it doesn't start up right. You would think they wouldn't sell this stuff until it operates correctly.*

Support agent paraphrase: *So you installed the program following the instructions in the manual, and when you double-click the program icon, the program doesn't run at all?*

End-user description: *Well, the box on the screen asks me for a file to open, but there are no files listed. Can't the program find its own files?*

Support agent paraphrase: *So the program opens a window and starts to run, but when the Open Files dialog box appears, the file list is empty?*

ON THE WEB

Executive Blueprints has developed an eBook and a PowerPoint presentation (both media cover the same material) titled *Active Listening: Hear and Understand Content and Feeling in Communication*. If you would like to learn more about active listening skills, you can review their materials at **www.executiveblueprints.com/agenda/0306activelistening.htm**.

Probes

Follow-up questions intended to elicit more information from a user about a problem are called **probes**. Successful troubleshooters learn to ask effective follow-up questions to clarify their understanding of a problem situation. Consider the role-playing scenario that follows. See if you can identify the points at which the troubleshooter uses effective probes.

A ROLE-PLAYING SCENARIO

This is a transcript of a conversation between a user, Randy, and a support agent, Lou. If possible, have fellow students or coworkers play the parts of Randy and Lou, and then discuss Lou's use of probes.

RANDY: When I am in the middle of working on a spreadsheet or a text document, my computer frequently starts running another program automatically. Something just pops up in the middle of the screen and takes over my computer. Is there something wrong with the CPU or a short in the circuitry?

LOU: Maybe, but maybe not. When a program pops up in the middle of the screen, is it always the same program, or a different one each time?

RANDY: Usually it is my e-mail program.

LOU: Does it ever automatically run any program other than e-mail that you can remember?

RANDY: No, I guess not. Do I need to reinstall my e-mail program?

LOU: How often does this problem happen?

RANDY: Every once in a while.

LOU: Like, once a week, once a day, or more often?

RANDY: It seems like several times a day.

LOU: Does the e-mail program seem to pop up on a regular basis or at random times?

RANDY: Now that you mention it, it is probably about every half hour, or so.

LOU: Okay. Some e-mail programs have a feature to automatically check to see if you have any new messages. That feature may be turned on in your e-mail program. You can check the preferences to see if it is on, and if it is, either turn it off or set the time interval to a longer period, like one or more hours.

Notice the importance of probes as follow-ups in this scenario. Through a series of probing questions and careful listening, the troubleshooter was able to determine that what the user originally thought was a hardware problem probably wasn't, and to suggest a course of action to try to solve the problem for the user.

Critical Questions

Another helpful troubleshooting tool is a list of **critical questions**— questions designed to elicit important information from a user. These questions also serve to challenge common assumptions support agents may make (sometimes incorrectly) about a problem situation. Five examples of critical questions are:

1. Has the problem system or component or feature *ever* worked?

2. Have you ever had this problem before? When?

3. Can this problem be replicated?

4. What were you doing on your computer just before you first noticed the problem?

5. Have you made any recent hardware or software changes to your system?

In their responses to critical questions, users often reveal information they perhaps wouldn't have thought to mention to a support agent. Consider several examples:

*   A user might forget to say that her inability to print a specific Corel Draw document is because she has *never* been able to print from Corel Draw.

*   A user may neglect to say that he encountered the same problem burning recordable DVDs the last time he bought a particular brand of inexpensive discs.

*   A user may omit the information that a problem logging on to a network occurs in only one computer lab on campus and not in any other lab.

*   A user might fail to mention that a power outage occurred immediately before she reported that her display screen no longer works correctly.

*   A user may not tell a troubleshooter that his system became sluggish when he installed a new version of the Microsoft Office suite of software.

In each of these examples, responses to one of the five sample critical questions could provide important additional information, or force a support agent to challenge some assumptions he or she may have made intentionally or unintentionally about a problem situation.

Critical questions often enable a support agent to move beyond a situation in which a problem investigation has reached a dead end.

All successful support agents have a checklist of favorite critical questions, such as those suggested earlier. These questions are especially useful in breaking new ground after an agent has asked every other question or probe he or she can think of, but still hasn't arrived at a solution, and is momentarily stuck.

Explanations

Communication skills are also important at the end of a troubleshooting session. Effective troubleshooters explain a problem's solution to the end user. **Explanations** involve a support agent describing the solution to a problem, so the user understands why the problem occurred and what steps are required to resolve it.

For many users, a word of explanation is helpful and is more satisfying than merely concluding, "Click the Cancel button to fix the problem." One way help desks and support groups can reduce repeated callbacks is to explain a problem solution at a level the user can understand. The user will then have some insight into the cause of the problem and into how the given solution fixes the problem. Otherwise, a user in the preceding example may incorrectly assume that the solution to every problem is to press the Cancel button.

Verification

Communication at the end of a troubleshooting process also provides important closure to the process. **Verification** is a communication skill that permits troubleshooters to confirm their perception that a problem is fixed. If the user's perception and troubleshooter's perspective are different, verification can help resolve the differences. Verification can be as simple as, "I believe rebooting the router has restored your network connection. As a test, can you list the files in the folder on the server?"

Information Resources

Support agents can't possibly have had prior experience with every problem situation they come across, so they must have access to information resources when they need to research solutions to problems that they have not yet encountered. Because new products and versions of software are released every day, support agents' prior experience and the information they can recall instantly are less important than their ability to use information resources effectively to locate what they need to know.

Technical information about how computer systems work—and an understanding of some reasons they don't—are invaluable for support agents to bring to a troubleshooting situation. The more information support agents know from experience (the better their mental models), the more likely they will be able to find a quick solution to a problem. However, all troubleshooters encounter problems they have never seen or problems with hardware or software they have never worked with. Examples of common information resources include: personal experience, scripts and checklists, knowledge bases, coworkers and professional contacts, support vendors and contractors, and escalation and team problem solving.

Personal Experience

Most support agents have a personal store of knowledge, based on their education, career background, and previous experiences that they bring to each problem-solving event. One of the first steps in any troubleshooting situation is to search your personal knowledge for information about the problem or related problems: "Have I seen this problem before?" "How is this problem similar to or different from the problem I worked on last week?" "What did I do last time the printer beeped three times and quit printing?" "Do I have a good mental model of this problem situation?" This type of personal knowledge search usually happens almost automatically.

An alternative to an informal paper and pencil notebook or a more formal company-wide problem database is a personal database maintained by a support agent using Microsoft Access or another database product.

Successful troubleshooters often make notes after they have solved a problem. Notes can be informally organized in a loose-leaf binder or notebook or formally entered into a problem-solution database. Written troubleshooting notes can help avoid a situation in which troubleshooters too often find themselves: "I know I've seen this problem before, but I don't remember what we did to fix it." A notebook with reminders of past problems solved becomes an important personal resource for troubleshooters and can be used even if a help desk or support center doesn't have a formal record-keeping procedure. A troubleshooting notebook can be organized by symptoms, equipment or software category, date, or in any other logical way that makes the information easy to find.

Scripts and Checklists

Organizations that provide computer support on a contract basis or that provide telephone help desk support often develop scripts and checklists to aid in the troubleshooting process. Among other benefits, these tools ensure that a standard set of questions gets asked and that agents provide a uniform response to user questions. A **script** is a document that lists questions to ask, along with appropriate follow-up probes, depending on the user's response to each question. Often organized in the form of a flowchart or a decision tree, scripts are arranged in a logical sequence and cover many of the possible (known) paths to solve a problem. Although scripts tend to be oriented toward common problems, they can also contain valuable pointers to unusual problems, such as problems that occur very

See Chapter 8 for an example of a troubleshooting flowchart.

infrequently or only in a few relatively rare configurations. Figure 3-5 shows an example of a script to diagnose problems with a hypothetical printer model based on the control panel LED lights.

Script: SpeedJet Model 5 Printer Diagnostics (revised March 8, 2009)

A SpeedJet Model 5 printer has several LEDs on its control panel that indicate its status: 1) ONLINE, 2) BUSY, and 3) OTHER LEDs. When a printer problem occurs, the behavior of the LEDs often provides important diagnostic information. Use the following script when a user calls about a problem with the SpeedJet Model 5 printer.

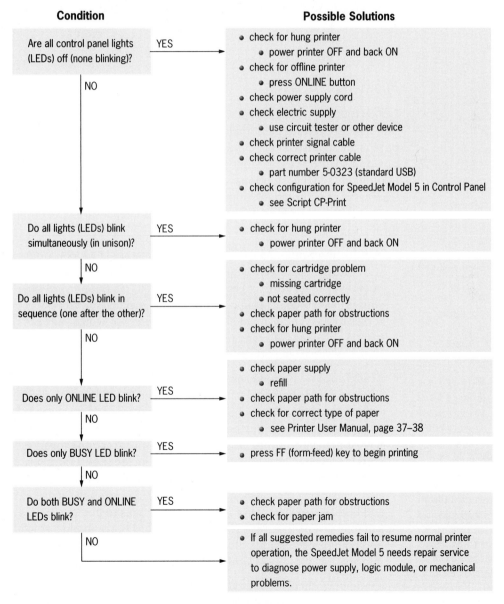

Condition

Possible Solutions

Are all control panel lights (LEDs) off (none blinking)? — YES

- check for hung printer
  - power printer OFF and back ON
- check for offline printer
  - press ONLINE button
- check power supply cord
- check electric supply
  - use circuit tester or other device
- check printer signal cable
- check correct printer cable
  - part number 5-0323 (standard USB)
- check configuration for SpeedJet Model 5 in Control Panel
  - see Script CP-Print

NO

Do all lights (LEDs) blink simultaneously (in unison)? — YES

- check for hung printer
  - power printer OFF and back ON

NO

Do all lights (LEDs) blink in sequence (one after the other)? — YES

- check for cartridge problem
  - missing cartridge
  - not seated correctly
- check paper path for obstructions
- check for hung printer
  - power printer OFF and back ON

NO

Does only ONLINE LED blink? — YES

- check paper supply
  - refill
- check paper path for obstructions
- check for correct type of paper
  - see Printer User Manual, page 37–38

NO

Does only BUSY LED blink? — YES

- press FF (form-feed) key to begin printing

NO

Do both BUSY and ONLINE LEDs blink? — YES

- check paper path for obstructions
- check for paper jam

NO

- If all suggested remedies fail to resume normal printer operation, the SpeedJet Model 5 needs repair service to diagnose power supply, logic module, or mechanical problems.

Figure 3-5 Example script to diagnose printer problems

ON THE WEB

For more information about the use of scripts in a call center environment, visit the Digisoft Web site at **www.digisoft.com/ faqs/ss-qa.htm**. Digisoft is a vendor of Telescript, a call center script-development tool. For examples of scripts implemented as a flowchart or a decision tree, see **www.extremetech. com/article2/0,3973,16621,00.asp** or **support.mfm. com/support/troubleshooting/copyprot.html**.

Knowledge Bases

Good troubleshooters have at their fingertips a variety of information resources to augment their personal experience. A **knowledge base** is an organized collection of information, articles, procedures, tips, and solutions to previous problems that can serve as a resource in problem-solving situations. In effect, a support agent's personal troubleshooting notebook of previous problems and their solutions is a simple knowledge base. Knowledge bases come in a variety of other forms from several sources.

Microsoft Press publishes books on troubleshooting for several popular Microsoft products. To see a list of the titles in the troubleshooting series, see **learning.microsoft. com/Manager/catalog. aspx**. In the search box, enter the keyword "troubleshoot" and the name of the Microsoft product of interest.

- **Vendor manuals**—Most hardware and software products come with tutorial or reference manuals, sometimes in print, but frequently in an electronic format, such as on a CD. Support agents who provide technical support for specific products need easy access to the vendor manuals for the products for which they are responsible. Vendor manuals often contain chapters on troubleshooting and frequently asked questions.

- **Trade books**—Because some vendor manuals are poorly written, a thriving trade book industry has developed to fill the vacuum for well-written information about popular hardware and software products. Web sites for online booksellers such as **www.amazon.com**, **www.barnesandnoble.com**, and **www.computerbooksonline. com** have search capabilities to help users locate trade books for specific hardware or software products. Computer trade books are also available at most general bookstores, large computer stores, and libraries—where you can browse the books to find one that is suitable. Over time, most successful troubleshooters build a small personal or professional library that is a convenient source of information about problems with products they support.

- **Trade periodicals**—Computer industry trade magazines and journals publish regular features on problems and solutions. These publications are available on a subscription basis, or in large book and computer stores. Examples include *Smart Computing, PC World, MacWorld, PC Today, Redmond Magazine*, and *PC Magazine*.

- **Online help**—Most software products, and some hardware products, have an online help feature. Sometimes the online help is no more than a convenient way to access the same information covered in the vendor manual. However, online help may include interactive troubleshooting wizards that provide useful insights into problem situations. Wizards are a form of online script or flowchart that guides a user or support agent through a series of steps to diagnose a problem. Windows incorporates several online troubleshooters into the operating system. To access them In Windows XP, press **F1** and search help for the keyword "troubleshooting". In Windows Vista, click the Windows Start button, select **Help and Support** from the menu, and then click the **Troubleshooting** icon (**?**).

- **Web sites**—Web sites maintained by product and service vendors are popular and widely available support information resources. Most sites provide product information and problem-solving suggestions; some sites include interactive troubleshooting assistance. Microsoft offers an extensive Web knowledge base for its products at **support.microsoft.com/default.aspx**, shown in Figure 3-6. Microsoft's knowledge base contains articles, problem reports, and other support resources.

Figure 3-6 Microsoft's Help and Support Web site

117

- **Search engines**—When looking for information resources on a specific problem, don't forget to try a general-purpose search engine, such as **www.google.com** or **www.ask.com**. These search engines are likely to turn up reports, suggestions, and forum discussions from other users who have encountered a similar problem to the one you're researching. Follow these suggestions to narrow a search for information in a search engine:

  1. Use noun keyword descriptors of a problem, including the exact wording or number of any error messages, such as "DVD drive write error."

  2. Use the present tense of verbs; avoid "-ing" and "-ed" verbs, use "write error" instead of "writing error."

  3. Include the manufacturer or vendor's name, model number of hardware, and software version numbers, such as "HP 640 Lightscribe DVD."

  4. Include the operating system name and version, such as "Windows Vista."

  5. Put quotation marks around phrases, such as "Apple iBook."

  6. Put + in front of essential keywords, such as "DVD +burner."

  7. Use the Boolean operator "and" to narrow a search; "or" can be used to expand a search, such as "Vista OR XP."

ON THE WEB

For a tutorial on Google search engine operation, visit **www. googleguide.com**.

Coworkers and Other Professional Contacts

Access to other computer professionals is an important resource for problem solving. The term "professional contacts" can mean work colleagues, but it also refers to other experts in the computer industry. Contact with these computer professionals can take place through discussion forums on Web sites, ListServs, newsgroups, and RSS feeds.

COWORKERS Coworkers are an important resource for many troubleshooters. When a troubleshooter experiences a block trying to solve a problem, a different perspective or "another set of eyes" can often help break through the block. On occasion, just the process of describing a problem to a colleague may trigger new insights into a problem. When a problem is especially complex or of high priority, a meeting of the team members in a support organization may be convened to address a problem, as illustrated in Figure 3-7. Although a team approach to problem solving may be expensive because it involves several staff members, it is sometimes the only way to solve really difficult problems. Team members often bring different personal experiences and creative energies to finding a solution.

Many support agents report that informal relationships with other user support students or trainees have served them well later in their careers. It is never too early to begin networking and developing professional relationships.

119

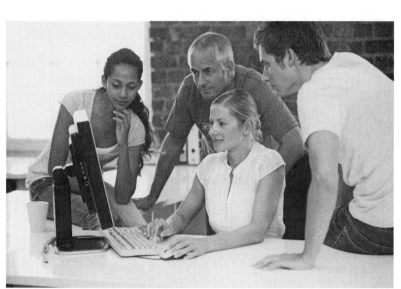

Figure 3-7   A team of support agents provides varying perspectives on a complex problem

DISCUSSION FORUMS   Many Web sites have discussion forums that provide access to industry professionals and experts, including these examples:

- Tech Support Guy (**www.techguy.org**)

- 5 Star Support (**www.5starsupport.com**)

- TechRepublic (**www.TechRepublic.com**); click the **Forums** tab, and then click **Ask a Question** (registration required)

- Cyber Tech Help (**www.cybertechhelp.com/forums/index.php**)

- Computer Hope (**www.computerhope.com**)

- PC Guide (**www.pcguide.com**); click **Discussion Forums** or **Live Chat Channel**

120

LISTSERVS A **ListServ** is an automated e-mail service that distributes all (or selected) e-mail messages posted to the ListServ to every member who has subscribed to the ListServ. Some computer vendors operate ListServs to provide their distributors, retail resellers, and customers with information and a communication channel for technical problems. An active ListServ can be an excellent information resource but can also result in a high volume of mail in your inbox.

ON THE WEB

A list of ListServs can be found at **www.lsoft.com/lists/ list_q.html**. Enter keywords to describe a topic that interests you. For example, to find ListServs that address topics of interest to Macintosh computer owners, enter "Macintosh" as a keyword. Similarly, support agents interested in Microsoft Access could join a ListServ that discusses use and problems associated with the database software.

Many ListServs maintain archives of e-mail messages that were distributed to their membership. ListServ archives can be used by a prospective member to get a feeling for the kinds of topics discussed on a ListServ prior to joining. You can also search the archives for answers to specific problems that were previously posted.

NEWSGROUPS **Newsgroups** are Internet discussion groups in which participants with common interests in a topic post messages. They are like an electronic bulletin board. Participation is open to anyone who has an interest in a topic, and access is through a newsreader, which is built into most Web browsers or search engines, such as Google. Many support agents find newsgroups an effective way to ask questions and to obtain and provide information. Many newsgroups offer new participants an FAQ archive that can be a valuable resource for troubleshooters.

ON THE WEB

Tens of thousands of active newsgroups are in operation. Some are very general; others are highly specialized. Professionals with interests in a specific field are often regular contributors to newsgroups. Many Web browsers and search engines maintain lists of current newsgroups. For example, go to **groups.google.com**. Enter a topic of interest in the search box. If you are interested in accommodations for users with various disabilities, enter "adaptive technology" to find a newsgroup of professionals in that field. To locate popular newsgroups in the computer field, visit the site **www.managementhelp.org/infomgnt/newsgrps/ newsgrps.htm**.

RSS FEEDS An information service that simplifies access to Web resources is **RSS (Really Simple Syndication)**. A support worker may subscribe to an RSS feed that aggregates information from several newsgroups, blogs, forums, news, and other Web sites whose content changes rapidly. The RSS feed delivers information selected by a user to his or her desktop in a convenient, single point of access, easy-to-use format.

Support Vendors and Contractors

Product vendors are often an extremely useful information resource. A vendor may have seen a baffling problem before and be able to offer suggestions on how to resolve it. Some vendors provide e-mail access to their technical support staff or open access to their proprietary troubleshooting knowledge bases.

Alternative troubleshooting resources include companies that provide outsourcing of support services. As you learned in Chapter 1, outsourcing companies provide problem-solving assistance for a fee. These companies can provide a useful resource to augment the internal support services in an organization. For example, an organization might contract with a support service provider to handle incidents for products that are beyond the expertise of its help desk staff or to provide backup to the internal help desk when the volume of problem reports is greater than the support staff can handle.

ON THE WEB

Stream International is an example of an external technical support provider. You can learn more about the company's services at its Web site: **www.stream.com**. Another technical support service provider is LiveTeam, **www.liveteam.com**.

Escalation and Team Problem Solving

When all other problem-solving attempts fail, a referral to a higher support level, called an **escalation**, is often an option. Escalation usually involves referring a problem from a level 1 or level 2 support agent to a higher level of technical support. However, some support organizations de-emphasize staff levels and organize their support agents into teams where mutual assistance and group problem solving is encouraged; in these organizations, an entire team is responsible for solving problems, not just individual staff members.

Diagnostic and Repair Tools

Support agents often use a variety of diagnostic tools to detect and repair hardware, software, and network problems. Many of these tools correspond to the carpenter's hammer and saw, the auto mechanic's wrench and test equipment, and the physician's x-ray machine. Hardware repair and network technicians and engineers use hardware diagnostic tools, such as circuit testers, signal loop-back tools, and network protocol analyzers. The purpose of diagnostic software tools, sometimes called utility software, is to provide troubleshooters with information, problem diagnosis, and even repairs for common computer problems.

General-Purpose and Remote Diagnostic Tools

These tools include software utilities that aid troubleshooters with the diagnosis of computer problems. One type of software utility permits support agents to control the operation of a user's computer remotely over a network or telephone connection. **Remote access** tools are an economical way to provide support for users in distant locations, because a support agent does not have to be in the same physical location as the user. When a remote access connection is established, a help desk staff member can see a remote user's desktop and control the operation of the user's PC directly from a help desk system. Examples of remote control software include:

- Expertcity's GoToAssist product (**www.gotoassist.com**; click the Quick Tour button to see how this technology works)

- RapidAssist (**www.rapidassist.com/index.asp**)

- pcAnywhere from Symantec (**www.symantec.com/norton/ symantec-pcanywhere**).

For a review of several remote access products, visit **www. remotepcaccess.net**.

Organizations that are concerned about the security of remote access to a user's PC via the Internet can adopt **virtual private network (VPN)** technology. A VPN uses the Internet to connect remote users to corporate servers, but it employs sophisticated user authentication and encryption technologies to provide heightened security when a remote user connects to a corporate server. The level of security in a VPN rivals the security in a hard-wired network, and the VPN software may include remote access tools for help desk connection to a user's desktop.

Hardware Problem Diagnosis

These tools include software utilities that help diagnose common hardware problems. Many desktop and laptop systems are bundled with preinstalled hardware diagnostic utilities. Diagnostic software can detect some defective hardware components, identify performance enhancements, recover some kinds of lost data, fix problems with defective media, document hardware-configuration information and common configuration problems, and monitor the operation of a system. Examples of hardware diagnosis software include:

- Norton SystemWorks, which contains Norton Utilities (**www. symantec.com/norton/systemworks-basic-edition**)

- PC Diagnostics (**www.pc-diagnostics.com**)

- PC-Doctor, which provides a variety of hardware diagnosis utilities (**www.pc-doctor.com**)

Software Problem Diagnosis

These tools include utilities that can identify the software configuration of desktops, laptops, and servers as well as identify and repair various kinds of software installation and configuration problems. They can detect authorized and unauthorized software installations, identify incorrect or incompatible software versions, and repair some

123

In addition to the software tools described in this chapter, help desk agents also use problem incident-tracking software to help record, prioritize, assign, monitor, and document problem incidents. Software tools that help agents track problem incidents are described in Chapter 5.

kinds of problems with the Windows registry. Both experienced troubleshooters and novice support agents who need assistance with basic problem identification can use software diagnostic tools. Examples of problem diagnosis software include:

- PC-Tools Registry Mechanic (**www.pctools.com/registry-mechanic**)
- iolo technologies System Mechanic (**www.iolo.com/system-mechanic/standard**)
- Belarc Advisor (**www.belarc.com/free_download.html**)
- Dean Software Design's PC Surgeon (**www.winutils.com/pcsurg.htm**)

Network Problem Diagnosis

These tools include network monitoring, remote management, and performance management utilities. Network monitoring software runs on a local area network to search for network connectivity problems, configuration problems, unauthorized access, and performance problems. Remote management software can help manage the distribution and configuration of software to a few or hundreds of networked PCs, as well as restore software and configurations on PCs that have failed for a variety of reasons. Performance management utilities track the uptime, responsiveness, and throughput of a network and identify problems as well as performance enhancement opportunities. Examples of network diagnostic tools include:

- EMC's SMARTS networking products (**www.smarts.com/products/family/smarts-family.htm**)
- SolarWinds network management tools (**www.solarwinds.net/Tools/Standard/index.htm**)
- PacketTrap's Network and Traffic Analyzer (**www.packettrap.com/product/network_traffic.aspx**)
- Manage Engine's OP Manager (**manageengine.adventnet.com/products/opmanager/index.html**)

 This chapter introduces several utilities to help with problem diagnosis. Chapter 12 expands the coverage of user support tools and resources.

Successful troubleshooters keep several of their favorite diagnostic utilities at their fingertips to aid in solving hardware, software, and network problems.

Problem-Solving Strategies

Troubleshooters often apply one or more common strategies to solve problems. Figure 3-8 summarizes eight commonly used logical approaches to problem solving that are often effective in a variety of troubleshooting situations, even difficult ones.

- Look for a simple, obvious solution
- Attempt to replicate the problem
- Examine the configuration
- Initiate a root cause analysis
- View a system as a group of subsystems
- Use a module replacement strategy
- Apply a hypothesis-testing approach
- Restore a basic configuration

Figure 3-8   Eight common problem-solving strategies

Look For a Simple, Obvious Solution

Because most computer problems are not difficult to solve, the first problem-solving strategy in any situation should probably be to look for a simple, obvious solution to a problem. For example, if a monitor does not work, and you've tried to fix it without success, consider the possibility that it may have become unplugged. But remember that there are four possible ways for a display screen to become unplugged, as shown in Table 3-1.

	At the Display Screen	At the Other End
Power cord	Is the power cord plugged into the back of the display?	Is the power cord plugged into the wall outlet? Is the wall outlet working?
Signal cable	Is the signal cable plugged into the back of the display?	Is the signal cable plugged into the video card on the back of the system unit?

Table 3-1   Ways for a display screen to become unplugged

Furthermore, a power or signal cable that looks like it is securely plugged in may not be. Where possible, unplug and replug a cable to verify it is connected. Experienced troubleshooters sometimes find it amazing how often a nonoperational system is caused by a custodian who accidentally unplugged equipment while moving furniture to clean the floor. Table 3-1 illustrates that even a simple problem-solving incident requires some logical thinking skills. The example also illustrates another simple problem-solving tool: a diagram or checklist of possible alternatives, which reduces the chance that a potential source of the problem will be overlooked.

Checklists as a problem-solving tool are illustrated in Chapter 9.

Another "old standard" in every support worker's toolkit is, "If every other obvious fix fails, try rebooting the system." This advice falls into the category of looking for a simple, obvious solution, because rebooting a system can eliminate a number of stubborn problems (low memory resources, device conflicts, applications software freezes, or inoperative peripheral devices, for example). However, sometimes old standbys, such as rebooting a system to clear a problem, actually mask the real cause of the problem and will eventually result in a callback when the problem recur.

ON THE WEB

Faithe Wempen wrote an article on troubleshooting entitled "Top 10 Tips for Troubleshooting PC Problems" (**certcities. com/editorial/tips/story.asp?EditorialsID=17**). Many of her suggestions fall into the category of quick and simple things to try.

If a simple, obvious fix solves a problem, that may be the end point. After all, many technology problems are so-called "n=1" problems because they never or rarely reoccur. And if a simple reboot or replugging a cable solves a problem, why spend more time on it? However, some problems that appear to be solved with a simple fix return, as we will see in the next chapter.

Attempt to Replicate the Problem

Replication is the process of trying to repeat a problem, either in the same or a different situation or environment, to see if the problem reoccurs. A user may report that a problem occurs every time she performs a specific activity or series of steps. Although most users do not intentionally try to mislead a help desk agent, their problem description may omit important pieces of information. First, support agents should try to replicate a problem on the user's computer if possible. Second, they should try to perform the same task or reproduce the same situation on another user system or on their own support system. If they can't get a problem to reoccur on the user's system, it may be traceable to a mistake the user is making. If the problem won't reoccur on another system, a difference in the configuration of the two systems may account for the problem. Then a troubleshooter can begin to look at differences between the two systems (hardware and operating system configuration differences, different software versions, and so on) to get to the root of the problem.

Examine the Configuration

Some problems with computer systems occur because a particular combination of hardware, operating system, and applications software doesn't work well together. In technical jargon, they don't interoperate well. Examining and verifying the ways hardware and software are configured may lead to an understanding of the problem or a solution. For example, failure of an image scanner to work on a user's system may be traceable to one or more of the following configuration problems:

- The scanner device is not supported by the operating system.

- The scanner was not configured to work correctly with the operating system.

- An up-to-date device driver may not have been installed and configured to support the device.

- The applications software that inputs scanned images may not have been correctly configured for the specific model of scanner.

- Another device may conflict with the scanner's use of system resources.

- Software has recently been installed that conflicts with the scanner or its software.

The documentation for most hardware and software packages includes a description of the configuration requirements (for example, amount of memory, type of processor, disk space, or type of video card) needed to operate correctly. A comparison of the configuration requirements with the actual installation configuration can often resolve incompatibilities.

Initiate a Root Cause Analysis

We began this list of strategies with looking for a simple, obvious solution to a problem. Many, if not most, problems benefit from that approach as a first strategy. However, some problems cannot be solved by rebooting a system, reinstalling and configuring a software package, or rechecking the cables. In some cases, a simple, quick fix may get rid of the symptoms of a problem, but fail to get to the underlying cause of the problem. **Root cause analysis** is a strategy that applies primarily to problems that reoccur (and can be replicated). In these cases, a troubleshooter should look beyond the visible symptoms of a problem to search for its root cause (the real cause). In most cases, root cause analysis is an iterative process that asks a series of *Why?* questions about an observable event (problem), until the root cause is identified.

The first step in root cause analysis is to identify what the problem is. Many root cause analysts insist that writing a clear, complete statement of the problem helps to clarify their thinking. The second step is to ask why the problem you described occurs, and to write down the answer. If the second step doesn't identify the root cause of the problem, the next step is to ask why again, and write down the answer. This process continues until the root cause (the real cause) is identified. Root cause analysis may take five or more iterations to find the root cause.

ON THE WEB

To learn more about root cause analysis, read an article on TechRepublic's Web site at **blogs.techrepublic.com/ security/?p=579**. The article illustrates the use of a fishbone diagram, which is a tool used frequently in root cause analysis.

Several of the strategies described in the following section are useful in a search for an underlying cause to a problem that can be replicated.

View a System as a Group of Subsystems

A computer system is actually a group of subsystems linked together to form a complete system. One problem-solving strategy is to consider the subsystems as a sequence of linked components, some hardware and some software. For example, consider the problem of a user who wants to print a memo in the Courier font. However, when printed, the memo is in Arial font. Where does the problem lie? Several subsystems are involved in the process of printing the memo in the correct font. These include:

- The applications software module that prepares the output
- The printer driver in the operating system that adds printer control codes
- The operating system software that transmits the output to the hardware
- The BIOS operating system component that sends data to the printer
- The parallel or USB port where the printer is connected
- The cable from the port to the printer

- The firmware in the printer that translates data received from the computer into formatted characters

- The circuitry in the printer, including the print head, that transfers the formatted characters onto the paper

Some of these subsystems, such as the printer cable and the print head, may be less likely culprits in this problem situation. However, a short in one of the signal lines in the printer cable may turn out to be at fault. There is not enough evidence yet to eliminate this possibility.

One strategy in this situation is to break the sequence in the chain of subsystems at some point (the midpoint is often a good place to start), and determine on which side of the midpoint the problem occurs. In this example, you might select the point at which the printer cable connects to the parallel or USB port as the midpoint. A support agent could observe, perhaps with a different printer, whether the font problem is on the printer side or the system unit side of the midpoint. Another strategy is to start at one end of the sequence of subsystems and trace the problem either forward or backward. Used with the module replacement strategy described next, treating a system as a group of subsystems can serve as a strategy to help isolate a problem.

Use a Module Replacement Strategy

Hardware technicians frequently use module replacement as a tool to diagnose computer hardware problems, as shown in Figure 3-9.

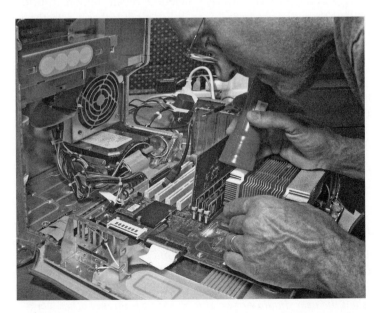

Figure 3-9   A hardware technician performs module replacement to evaluate a problem

Experienced troubleshooters take precautionary steps before they do a module replacement on an internal device. Hardware technicians routinely draw a sketch and label cable connections before they unplug any hardware components. Support agents back up any software prior to reinstallation in case a problem arises during the reinstallation process. Prior to reinstalling a software package, support agents also uninstall the package to avoid possible contamination between the inoperable image and the fresh installation.

Module replacement is a problem-solving strategy that involves replacing a hardware or software component whose operational status is unknown with a component that is known to be operational. For example, if a DVD drive fails to work correctly, the problem may be the DVD drive itself or a piece of hardware or software related to its operation. One way to determine whether the problem really is the DVD drive is to disconnect it from the computer where it is malfunctioning and connect it to a second system. If the DVD drive works correctly in the second system, then the problem is not with the drive itself, and the technician can consider other options, such as the DVD driver software or the signal cables that connect the drive. Many organizations troubleshoot hardware modules only to a field replaceable unit (FRU) level such as an expansion card, a circuit board, the motherboard, the power supply, a disk drive, and so forth, and replace the entire FRU, if necessary. It is usually not cost effective to go further to identify a defective component below the board level.

The module replacement strategy also works for software. In the case of malfunctioning software that has worked, but now fails, the equivalent of rebooting a computer is to reinstall the software package. Occasionally, the image of a software package stored on a hard disk becomes corrupted when some of the bits in the instructions are accidentally overwritten. The faulty software image loads into memory when the program runs, but the software fails to perform as it did previously. Reinstalling the software package replaces the copy of the program (module) on the disk with a fresh image. Some software packages include a "repair" option. Instead of reinstalling the entire program image, only a module that is defective is reinstalled, which takes less time.

Apply a Hypothesis-Testing Approach

In hypothesis testing, a troubleshooter formulates a hypothesis about the cause of a problem. Then the troubleshooter carries out an experiment to determine whether the hypothesis is true or false. For example, a user may report that he is unable to log on to a network server:

User: *I type my username and password, just as I usually do. The network gives me an error message that the username and password are invalid.*

The troubleshooter listens to the problem description and may formulate some hypotheses that would explain the problem:

Troubleshooter (to herself): *This problem may be a hardware, software, or network problem. Where should I start? It is unlikely a hardware problem, so I'll assume (hypothesis) that it is a network problem. If it is, then the user should not be able to log on from any other workstation on the network. So I'll try an experiment to see if the problem is specific to a particular workstation.*

In this case, suppose the user can, in fact, log on from another workstation.

Troubleshooter: *If it's a network problem, it must not be on the server side. I'll look at* (hypothesis) *the client side. If there is a problem with the client software, then no one else should be able to log on from the user's workstation. Let me try* (experiment) *to log on to my own account from the user's workstation.*

In this scenario, suppose the troubleshooter was indeed able to log on to the server from the user's workstation using her own username and password.

Troubleshooter: *Interesting! We've apparently eliminated the network as a culprit. Maybe* (hypothesis) *the user is the culprit. Maybe he's mistyped his password. Let me try* (experiment) *to log on to the user's account from his workstation.*

In this case, the troubleshooter's attempt to log on was unsuccessful, too. She was able to replicate the user's problem.

Troubleshooter: *Okay! What now? Perhaps* (hypothesis) *the user's record in the database of user accounts does not have access rights defined appropriately for this user from his workstation.*

A call to the network administrator determines that the user database record for the user does include the correct username, password, and access rights for the user.

Troubleshooter: *Hmmm! I assumed* (hypothesis) *that the problem was unlikely to be hardware. Maybe I should reconsider that assumption. Suppose I plug a different keyboard* (experiment) *into the user's system and try again. Ah, ha! Success. The problem is a defective key on the keyboard, and it is a key that happened to be in the user's password.*

Although this scenario is oversimplified, it illustrates the hypothesis-testing and experimental method that is at the heart of many problem-solving efforts. The ability to formulate a series of hypotheses and carry out experiments to test them is a valuable skill for any troubleshooter to build. This skill is based in large part on a troubleshooter's experience with a number of different problem situations, the ability to devise a successful experiment to test a hypothesis, and the ability to think clearly and carefully about a problem situation. An important ingredient in hypothesis testing is critical thinking. The hypothesis-testing strategy works best when a support agent can think of several alternate explanations for a situation. Sometimes it helps to make a list of possible causes for a problem and to brainstorm alternatives with other agents in a team environment.

ON THE WEB

To learn more about hypothesis testing, also called the scientific method, read an article at **www.inetdaemon.com/tutorials/ troubleshooting/scientific_method.shtml**.

Restore a Basic Configuration

Some problems occur when hardware or software interacts with other parts of a system. If a problem cannot be traced to a configuration problem, another problem-solving strategy is to remove components (hardware or software) to "pare back" a system to a basic configuration. This approach is suggested at the end of the list of strategies intentionally, because modifying a configuration by de-installing components can have side effects that are unpredictable and cause other problems. The strength of this strategy is that it eliminates **variables**, or factors in a problem-solving situation. The presence of extra variables can make a problem too complex to solve easily, especially when more than one problem is present.

For example, if a piece of hardware such as an external DVD burner will not operate correctly when added to a system, a support technician may try removing one or more other components to see if the new hardware component will operate correctly in a stripped-down system configuration. If a technician finds that the DVD burner works fine when another component is removed, but fails when that component is reconnected, then incompatibility between the two devices can be researched.

In another common scenario, a software package may fail to run when installed on a computer connected to a network. One approach is to disconnect the computer from the network and observe whether the program runs on the computer in standalone mode. This experiment removes a variable (the network connection) to see whether that factor makes a difference. If the software runs on a standalone PC, but not on a networked system, then the technician can examine the network configuration requirements for the software.

The problem-solving strategies just described are critical tools in a troubleshooter's repertoire. They involve logical, organized, and critical-thinking skills that are designed to lead to a satisfactory solution. Problem solving is a skill that can be learned, but practice and experience really build problem-solving expertise. Other factors that contribute to successful problem solving include several personal characteristics.

Personal Characteristics of Successful Troubleshooters

Personal characteristics play an important role in the troubleshooting process. Some personal characteristics can contribute directly to one's success as a troubleshooter. These are listed in Figure 3-10.

- They are patient and persistent
- They enjoy the problem-solving process
- They like working with people
- They enjoy continuous learning

Figure 3-10   Characteristics of successful troubleshooters

To some degree, these characteristics are part of a support agent's basic personality. However, personal experience, feedback from users, and coaching by other support staff can affect the degree to which a support agent makes effective use of these characteristics.

Patience and Persistence

Problem solving is often difficult work. It is frustrating to follow a strategy, reach a dead end, admit you've hit a wall, and start over with a different approach. A certain amount of stress and frustration over an especially difficult problem is inevitable. But successful troubleshooters find ways to deal with stress and frustration. One useful strategy to regain patience and perspective is to take a break from a problem. Go for a walk or work on another task where progress is possible, and then return later to the problem for which progress seemed impossible. When you return, you can take a fresh look at the problem and can perhaps see other alternative solutions you overlooked earlier.

Patience is important in two respects. Troubleshooters not only need to be persistent and patient with themselves, but they also need to be patient with users. Successful support agents are able to shield users from their own frustrations. Expressing impatience with a client or a problem only impairs communication with the client, a situation that will not help resolve the problem. Users may also lack persistence. They may be too willing to give up on a difficult problem ("Oh, it's not that important."), and may need to be reassured that a problem is not insurmountable—that possible approaches and resources have not yet been exhausted.

Enjoy the Problem-Solving Process

Successful support agents get enjoyment from the problem-solving process. Where users may see the computer world as a never-ending sequence of technical problems and frustrations, support agents tend to see challenges and opportunities. They enjoy finding the sometimes-obscure relationship between a problem and its cause. Like physicians, who only see sick people, user support staff members are hired to solve problems for end users. If you don't enjoy the challenge of solving problems and the satisfaction when an apparently difficult problem gets solved, you should perhaps consider a career in a field other than user support.

Like Working with People

The ability to work with all types of people is critical in the user support industry. User support agents don't have to like every user they encounter, and they don't have to treat each user as a personal friend in order to solve problems successfully. But they do need to communicate with users and to interact with them in a professional manner. If you don't enjoy working at a professional level with users, user support is not a field you'll likely enjoy for very long.

Enjoy Continuous Learning

Change is one of the constant features of the computer industry and the user support field. The hardware or software package you learn in school is not the one you will likely get assigned to support on the job. Last year's products you knew inside and out will become obsolete. Anyone with a serious commitment to the user support field must enjoy learning about new products.

Continual learning is an important job skill in a support position, whether it is written into a formal position description or not. Most user support agents subscribe to one or more computer industry periodicals to keep up to date with changes in the computer field and with industry trends. Support agents regularly attend training sessions and teach themselves new software packages. They look for opportunities to learn from other support agents. Some support organizations sponsor formal professional development opportunities, such as training sessions and informal sessions over lunch to encourage support staff to exchange information about products and the computer industry.

ON THE WEB

Trade publications that offer a broad perspective on trends in the computer industry include:

Computer Industry Periodical	Web Address
ComputerWorld	**www.computerworld.com**
InformationWeek	**www.informationweek.com**
InfoWorld	**www.infoworld.com**

Developing Your Own Approach to Problem Solving

The problem-solving approach in this chapter treats troubleshooting computer problems as a process, but not a process with a fixed sequence of one-size-fits-all steps that are guaranteed to work every time. You have learned about several problem-solving tools that you can apply to many troubleshooting situations. Like a carpenter or auto mechanic, support agents reach into a tool bag, grab a tool, use it, and then pick up another tool, use it, and so on. Either a problem gets resolved, or the troubleshooter recognizes that he or she doesn't have the tools needed to solve it and begins to search for other resources.

All support agents are eventually confronted with problems they cannot solve easily. At these times, they need a personal approach to problem solving. A personal problem-solving perspective includes an understanding of the strengths a support agent brings to each problem. It is based on the experience that selected tools and skills have been successful in solving past problems. It relies on information resources that have proved useful in past situations. It is improved by the metacognition process described in this chapter, whereby problem solvers carefully examine their own thought processes. Without a personal problem-solving approach, support agents are more likely to use a random, hit-or-miss, trial-and-error strategy instead of a logical, well-organized problem-solving approach. They are more likely to get frustrated by difficult problems or become overly reliant on others when they encounter a dead end. Successful troubleshooters recognize a dead end not as a stopping point but as an opportunity to get a fresh start, question assumptions, and try another approach with perhaps a different tool.

How do you develop your approach to problem solving?

1. Use your own experience, knowledge, skills, thought processes, access to information, and communication skills as the basis for your personal strategy.

2. Improve your troubleshooting skills and learn to use the problem-solving tools described in this chapter.

3. Analyze your troubleshooting approach. Recognize your personal strengths and areas where you need to improve. For example, some support agents develop extremely good skills at finding information about a problem on the Internet. They learn to use search engines effectively and bookmark Web sites on their browser's favorites list that have been useful in the past. They pride themselves on their ability to find information quickly. Other support agents develop a network of colleagues with whom they regularly exchange e-mail or phone calls about difficult problems. They are proud of the fact that if they don't know an answer, they know someone who does.

Chapter 4 and the hands-on activities and case projects in this chapter provide examples of common problems you can use to help develop your own problem-solving skills.

Of course, no one support agent is equally adept at all the strategies in this chapter. Successful troubleshooters develop a sense of what works for them (a plan of attack) and what doesn't, and they try to take maximum advantage of their strengths. A problem-solving perspective is not necessarily something a support agent writes down. However, a personal approach to problem solving is something a successful support agent thinks about a lot and works to improve.

Chapter Summary

- Most computer problems are not difficult to handle. They are requests for information, complaints, or problems with which a support staff member has previous experience.

- Troubleshooting is the process of solving more difficult computer problems. Rather than a series of sequential steps, troubleshooting is an iterative process—a creative process in which a support agent tries an approach, and if one approach doesn't work, he or she tries another.

- Troubleshooters use an assortment of skills in their work, including problem solving, critical thinking, and decision making. They also use several kinds of troubleshooting tools, including communication skills, information resources, problem-solving strategies, and personal characteristics. Troubleshooters select from among these tools, skills, and resources to tackle various aspects of a problem.

- Communication skills include listening to a user's description of problem symptoms, active listening (or paraphrasing) to verify understanding of a problem, and using critical questions to obtain information from a user and to challenge a support agent's own assumptions that may block the path to a solution. Helpful communication skills also include the ability to ask probing questions, explain a problem resolution to a user, and verify that a problem is solved.

- Information resources include a troubleshooter's personal experience with similar or related problems, prepared scripts and checklists that follow a logical path to a solution, and various knowledge bases. Vendor manuals, trade books, online help, ListServs, newsgroups, Web sites, and search engines are rich sources of information about problems. Coworkers, industry professionals, friends, and vendors are other information resources that may move a problem toward resolution.

- Computer troubleshooters use a variety of diagnostic and repair tools to solve problems. Remote access utilities let a support agent view and control events on a user's computer from a remote location. Other utility software is designed to diagnose and help repair hardware, software, and network problems and improve system performance.

- Problem-solving strategies include eight logical-thinking processes that are often useful to troubleshooters:

  1. Look for a simple, obvious fix.

  2. Attempt to replicate a problem.

  3. Examine the configuration.

  4. Initiate a root case analysis.

  5. View a system as a group of subsystems.

  6. Use a module replacement strategy.

  7. Apply a hypothesis-testing approach.

  8. Restore a basic configuration.

- Personal characteristics that aid successful troubleshooters include patience and persistence, enjoyment of the problem-solving process, satisfaction in working with people, and the ability to continually learn new materials.

- All support agents need to develop their problem-solving skills, to think about the problem-solving process, and to develop their own approach to problem solving. The perspective should include an awareness of their strengths and areas for improvement when working with the problem-solving tools and resources described in this chapter.

Key Terms

active listening—A communication skill that results in a listener being as involved and engaged in the communication process as the speaker; paraphrasing is an example of active listening.

analogy—A way in which a current problem is similar to other problems that have been solved; an analogy between similar problems may suggest a possible problem solution.

contradiction—Situations in which a fact established through investigation rules out, or contradicts, a potential solution.

creativity—The critical-thinking ability to find a novel or innovative solution to a problem; the ability to see a problem from new and different perspectives.

critical question—A question designed to elicit important information from a user that may force a support agent to challenge some basic assumptions about a problem.

critical thinking—Cognitive skills a problem solver uses to analyze a problem, search for the underlying logic or rationale, or strive for alternate ways to explain an event or situation.

decision making—The ability to select one alternative from among a number of alternatives, based on some evaluation criteria; an important skill for troubleshooters.

escalation—A problem-solving tool whereby a difficult or complex problem is referred to a higher-level support person or team for resolution.

explanation—A communication skill that involves a support agent describing the solution to a problem so the user understands *why* the problem occurred and the steps required to resolve it.

goal state—A desired outcome or objective; in troubleshooting, a common goal state is to diagnose or repair a computer subsystem to return it to a normal operational state.

hypothesis—An initial guess, hunch, or prediction based on experience.

hypothesis testing—Formulating a hypothesis about the cause of a problem and designing an experiment that will prove or disprove the hypothesis.

iterative process—A process that involves several paths or approaches to problem solving; steps are repeated in a loop until a fruitful path is found; troubleshooting is an iterative process in that it uses and reuses a variety of tools and skills.

knowledge base—An organized collection of information, articles, procedures, tips, and solutions to existing problems that can serve as a resource in a problem-solving situation.

ListServ—An automated e-mail service that distributes all (or selected) e-mail messages posted to the ListServ to every member who has subscribed to the ListServ; organized around a topic of special interest to its members.

mental model—A perceptual picture that a problem solver builds to help understand how a system works; mental models are based on education and experience.

metacognition—The ability to think about thinking; the ability of a troubleshooter to step back from a problem-solving situation and analyze his or her thought processes.

module replacement—A problem-solving strategy that involves replacing a hardware or software component whose operational status is unknown with a component that is known to be operational.

newsgroup—An Internet discussion group in which participants with common interests in a topic post messages; similar to an electronic bulletin board.

paraphrasing—A communication skill that involves you restating in your own words what you think you heard the speaker say.

probe—A follow-up question designed to elicit additional information from a user about a problem; a sequence of probes often clarifies a problem situation.

problem solving—A process of moving from a current state of events X (the problem state) to a future desired state of events Y; the objective of problem solving is to get from X to Y quickly, accurately, effectively, and efficiently.

remote access—Utility software that lets a support agent view and control events on an external user's computer.

replication—The process of trying to repeat a problem in a different situation or environment to reproduce a problem.

root cause analysis—A troubleshooting strategy that requires a support worker to look beyond the visible symptoms of a recurring problem to search for its underlying cause.

RSS (Really Simple Syndication)—A Web service that aggregates selected information from various Web resources, including newsgroups, blogs, forums, and other news and information services and delivers it to a user's desktop in a convenient, easy-to-use format.

script—A document that lists questions to ask, along with appropriate follow-up probes, depending on the user's response to each question; a script is often organized as a checklist, flowchart, or decision tree that describes many of the possible (known) paths to a problem solution.

troubleshooting—The process of defining, diagnosing, and solving computer problems; involves the use of several thinking and communications skills, information resources, strategies, and methods.

variable—A factor or aspect in a problem-solving situation that can change or be changed; eliminating variables by removing components simplifies a complex problem so it is more manageable and can be solved.

verification—A communication skill that permits a troubleshooter to confirm their perception that a problem is solved.

virtual private network (VPN)—A computer network that uses the Internet to connect remote users to a corporate network; a VPN uses authentication and encryption to enhance security on a network.

Check Your Understanding

Answers to Check Your Understanding questions are in Appendix A.

1. Which of these is not an example of a difficult support problem?

   a. a problem a support worker has not seen before

   b. a problem involving an angry caller

    c. a problem for which the solution is not obvious

    d. All of these are difficult problems.

2. True or False? Troubleshooting computer problems is a fixed sequence of steps a support agent follows from the initial problem description to the resolved problem.

3. True or False? Problem solving, critical thinking, and decision making are different names for the same skill.

4. The strategy in which the listener is as engaged as the speaker in a communication is called:

    a. probing

    b. active listening

    c. paraphrasing

    d. replicating

5. A mental model to help a computer troubleshooter understand and explain a problem situation is based on:

    a. metacognition

    b. critical thinking

    c. decision making

    d. problem solving

6. A troubleshooting process that involves selecting one alternative from among a number of possible alternatives based on some evaluation criteria is called _____.

7. True or False? To restate a problem description using the user's exact words is called paraphrasing.

8. _____ is a problem-solving tool that involves a difficult or complex problem being referred to a higher-level support person for resolution.

9. The ability to step back from a troubleshooting situation and analyze one's own thinking process is called _____.

10. A follow-up question a troubleshooter asks to get additional information about a problem situation is called a(n) _____.

11. An organized collection of information, articles, procedures, tips, and problem solutions is called a:

   a. script

   b. flowchart

   c. knowledge base

   d. newsgroup

12. True or False? A troubleshooting strategy that involves swapping a hardware or software component whose status is unknown with one that is known to be operational is called module replacement.

13. Rebooting a system in an attempt to fix a problem is an example of which of these problem-solving strategies?

   a. Look for a simple, obvious fix.

   b. Attempt to replicate a problem.

   c. Use a module-replacement strategy.

   d. View a system as a group of subsystems.

14. A successful troubleshooter recognizes a dead end (or block in progress) as:

   a. a frustration

   b. the end of the troubleshooting process

   c. a stopping point

   d. an opportunity to look at other alternatives

15. Show that you understand the concept of paraphrasing by writing a paraphrase for the following problem statement: "The screen on my PC is blank."

16. A troubleshooter who observes that a suspected faulty modem does not work in computer A, but operates correctly in computer B is confronted with a _____.

17. A communication skill that confirms a troubleshooter's perception that a problem is fixed is:

   a. authentication

   b. verification

   c. explanation

   d. metacognition

18. True or False? Root cause analysis is a troubleshooting strategy designed to eliminate the symptoms of a problem.

19. A network technology that uses authentication and encryption to connect remote users to a company server over the Internet is a _____.

20. Simplifying a problem situation by removing components from a configuration is a strategy to eliminate or reduce the number of _____ in a problem.

Discussion Questions

1. Suggest some additional critical questions that you would add to the list of five described in the chapter to help a support agent and a user who have reached a roadblock in their search for a problem solution. Are some questions more useful than others?

2. Which of the personal characteristics in this chapter is the single most important trait for a successful troubleshooter? Describe some attributes of successful troubleshooters that were not discussed in the chapter.

3. Which are more important to a successful computer troubleshooter: good technical skills or good people skills? Why?

4. Which are more important to a successful computer troubleshooter: good listening skills or good speaking skills? Why?

5. Which is more important to a successful computer troubleshooter: what they know or what they can find out? Why?

6. If you were a user support specialist who supported internal users, which tool or information resource described in this chapter would you want to have available to you if you could pick only one? Defend your answer.

7. Discuss the pros and cons of contracting with a support services vendor to provide help desk services to an organization versus in-house support. Do the advantages of outsourcing outweigh the disadvantages?

8. Are the personal traits of successful problem solvers discussed in this chapter hardwired parts of a support specialist's basic personality, or can they be learned and improved upon?

Hands-On Activities

Activity 3-1

Listen actively. Team up with another student or coworker and practice listening and paraphrasing skills. One person takes the role of the user; the other takes the role of a support person. The user describes a common problem with a computer system to the support person, who then paraphrases the problem description back to the user.

The user's role is important because he or she needs to listen for important parts of the problem that the support person omitted, that didn't exist in the original problem description, or that the support person modified. Continue the paraphrasing activity until the person in the support role can correctly paraphrase the original problem description. Then change roles and repeat the process. (Note that the purpose of this activity is to practice paraphrasing, not solve the problem.)

Activity 3-2

Ask questions. Study the following problem description. Then determine what additional information you, as a support agent, would want from this user. Develop several questions you could ask to obtain the information you would need to resolve this problem.

"My computer is hung up. I don't know what I did wrong. The screen is frozen. Nothing I try does any good. I press keys on the keyboard, and nothing happens. The mouse pointer won't move."

Activity 3-3

Provide explanations. Write an explanation to a user who wants to know why the Office 2007 software suite will not operate on a PC he purchased in 2001. The user has a PC with a 133 MHz processor, 128 MB of RAM, a VGA monitor, and runs the Windows 2000 operating system. Use the Internet search skills described in this chapter to prepare your explanation.

Activity 3-4

Examine the configuration. A software package runs correctly on computer A, but the same package does not operate correctly on computer B. Make a list of basic computer system configuration information you would like to know to diagnose this problem further.

Activity 3-5

Use information resources. A user of Quattro Pro X3, which is part of the WordPerfect Office suite, installed Quattro Pro on a new

Windows Vista PC. When he runs Quattro Pro, he immediately gets an error message, "Program c:\Program files\wordperfect office x3\QPW.exe abnormal program termination." Write a brief problem report that answers these questions:

1. Describe the approach you would take to solve this problem.

2. Based on your research, what solution would you recommend to the user?

3. Will the solution you recommend in Step 2 fix the root cause of the problem?

Activity 3-6

Develop a printer troubleshooting script. Use the Windows help system to locate the troubleshooting tools in your current version of Windows. (*Hint:* Go to **Help and Support** from the Start menu, and then click the **Troubleshooting** icon (**?**).) Write a script with a minimum of five steps that documents how to diagnose and fix several common printing problems users might encounter. Don't worry about rare printer problems.

Activity 3-7

Evaluate a troubleshooting event. Think about the most difficult troubleshooting problem you've encountered in your recent experience—one where the solution was not straightforward and where the problem was not a simple request for information. The problem you pick might be one you experienced personally, one you encountered at work or while helping in a lab, or one you encountered while helping a friend. Write a description of the troubleshooting event that answers the following questions:

1. What troubleshooting tools, methods, and strategies did you use? Describe them using the concepts in this chapter.

2. What subsystems were involved in the problem?

3. What communications tools, information resources, and problem analysis/diagnosis tools did you use?

4. Were the troubleshooting methods you used effective? Why or why not?

5. How could you have improved the effectiveness of your troubleshooting strategy?

Activity 3-8

Learn about Windows system utilities. The Windows operating system includes several diagnostic utility programs that are useful to troubleshooters. Use the Windows Help system to learn the purpose of each of these utilities:

- System Information

- Performance Information and Tools

- Windows Easy Transfer

- Disk Cleanup

- Disk Defragmenter

- System Restore

Write a brief description of the purpose of each of these utilities. Include in your description in what situation a troubleshooter might need to use each tool. Finally, briefly explain the difference between Disk Cleanup and Disk Defragmenter.

Activity 3-9

Alternative system utilities. Use Google or another search engine to locate examples of software utilities that are alternatives to the utilities supplied with Windows listed in Activity 3-8. In each case, briefly describe features of the utilities you found that differ from the comparable Windows utility. Also note whether the utilities you find are commercial products, shareware, freeware, or open source software.

Activity 3-10

Create and solve a practice problem. Based on your personal experience, write up a problem statement similar to the examples in Case Project 1, which follows the hands-on activities. Then, exchange problem statements with another student or coworker and see if you can solve the problem he or she described. Try to make your problem a common one you've encountered, and don't make the problem you write too difficult. Remember, they are writing a problem for you to work on, too!

Activity 3-11

Adjust small print. A user complained that printed output from her Web browser and e-mail client was very tiny. Write an explanation that could be included in an e-mail to the user that describes how to increase the size of the print from these programs. (Assume she uses the same Web browser and e-mail programs that you use.)

Case Projects

1. Problem Solving: Your Turn

See how many of these problems you can solve working by yourself. Use books, manuals, online help, the Internet, and other resources, as necessary. Some of these problems are easier than others, so don't work too long on a problem that seems difficult; ask your work colleagues or your instructor for help. As you work on these tasks, make some brief notes that describe your experience. Do some metacognition about your problem-solving approach.

1. A user running Internet Explorer reports a message, "Internet Explorer cannot display the webpage." What information about this problem can you provide the user?

2. A user gets an error message: "Error Loading Kernel. You must reinstall Windows." What is the likely cause of this message? Do you really have to reinstall Windows to fix the problem?

3. A Microsoft Excel user often selects the Shrink-to-Fit feature in Microsoft Word to force a memo that is a little too long to fit on a single page. He wants to know if a similar feature is available in Excel to force a worksheet to fit on a single page without overlapping to a second page. Is there a Shrink-to-Fit feature in Excel? If so, how is it used?

4. If you have a desktop computer, unplug the keyboard from your computer while it is turned off. Then power up your system. During the power on self test (POST) boot up diagnostic tests, one of the devices tested is the keyboard. What message appears to alert the user to the keyboard problem? If you plug the keyboard back in, will the system recover without rebooting? If necessary, plug your keyboard back in and reboot.

5. Use the operating system utilities on your computer to document the following information about your computer. For each question, indicate what tool you used to find the information.

   a. What model of processor is in your system?

   b. What type of bus architecture is used?

   c. How much total memory does your system have?

   d. Is the subdirectory C:\NET in the search path?

   e. How is the environment variable TEMP defined?

    f. For the mouse on your system, what is the IRQ address and the device driver version?

    g. What is the size of the hard drive? How much free space is available on it?

6. Find a utility program in Windows that will scan your hard drive for errors (such as ScanDisk). (*Hint:* Use Windows help and search for "disk errors.") Run the error scan utility on your computer's hard drive. What problems, if any, did the error scan find? If problems exist, what is the procedure you would follow to eliminate them? What precautions should a user take before taking action to eliminate lost disk clusters?

7. A user received a floppy disk from a friend in another organization, but can't read it on her system. The user says she has never had a problem reading a floppy disk before and doesn't understand why she can't read the disk now. Make a list of the questions you would ask the user to help determine the solution to this problem.

8. A user reports that she has a program named ERU.exe on her hard disk. She doesn't know its purpose, doesn't want to try running it for fear it will damage her system, and doesn't want to erase it for fear it is necessary for Windows to operate correctly. What can you tell her about the function of ERU.exe and who should run it?

9. A user in engineering says he has a very old program on a floppy disk that he used to run 25 years ago to perform a special analysis on steel structures. He now has a client for which he needs to run the program. The program ran previously on an operating system named CP/M. The program could be rewritten to run on a modern system, but the rewrite would take several weeks. Is there any way to run a CP/M program on today's computers?

10. A user reports that when he runs a program on his hard drive, he gets an error message about a missing VBRUN600.dll file. He has searched the hard drive and cannot find the missing file. How can he get a copy of the missing VBRUN600.dll? He mentions that his computer does have a file named VBRUN500.dll. Can he use it instead? If so, how?

11. A user who has recently changed departments from manufacturing to product design says that all the e-mail messages

he sends have two lines appended automatically to the end of each message:

GRIGORY VLADNIK
MANUFACTURING DEPT, XT 555

He wants to change the department name to PRODUCT DESIGN, but does not know how the automatic lines get there because he doesn't type them. How can he make the change in his e-mail program? (Use Microsoft Outlook or another e-mail program with which you are familiar to answer this question.)

12. A Microsoft Word user noticed that another user in her department has more than four files listed in the recently used files list in the Files pull-down menu. How can she increase the number of files listed on her computer?

13. A panicked user writes the following e-mail: "I just accidentally deleted a Microsoft Project .mpp file from my hard drive, and I really need to get it back. My job may depend on it. Can you help me get the deleted file back?" Describe the strategies you would use to help this user.

14. A Microsoft Excel user has a spreadsheet with a cell that contains #REF! What does this cell entry mean? Research and prepare a list of other messages that Excel can display in a cell that indicates a possible problem with the cell contents.

15. A user discovered a program Win32.exe on his hard drive. He would like to know if it is a program required by the Windows operating system, and what its function is. What advice would you give him?

2. Dale Andrew's Macintosh Disk

Dale Andrews, a hardware repair technician, walked into the support center late one afternoon after a busy day repairing PCs. He called out to anyone who was listening, "Help!" Dale explained to the support agents who were in the office that he has a machine-readable copy of the manual for a hardware component on a floppy disk that he couldn't read on the PC in his shop. He said, "The box says the manual on the floppy is in Word format, but I suspect the disk was created on a Macintosh because that manufacturer used to do a lot of work with Macs. I am stuck until I can find a way to read the manual on this disk. I don't think there is a Mac in the entire organization! I would ask the manufacturer for a manual in PC format, but the manufacturer doesn't support this product anymore." One of the support staff jokingly said, "Go out and buy a Mac!"

List as many ways you can think of that the support center staff could help Dale solve this problem. Describe each alternative you listed in terms of its approximate cost and speed. Are some of the alternatives more feasible than others, given that Dale needs the manual now and doesn't want to spend a lot of money to get it? What approach would you recommend to Dale?

3. Diagnostic Software for Pre-Fab Engineering

Tamara Harold received the e-mail message shown below from Fred Long, president of Pre-Fab Engineering. Tamara is busy working on another project now, and asks you to help with this assignment.

To: TamaraHarold@Pre-Fab.biz
From: FredLong@Pre-Fab.biz

I would like to help our engineering users at Pre-Fab become more self-reliant when they encounter computer problems.

Since you are one of the most knowledgeable computer users at Pre-Fab, I wonder if you would look into whether a diagnostic utility program would be useful. I am especially interested in the kinds of problems these utility programs can detect and whether the software would make our employees more productive when they have problems. Could you pull together some information about the capabilities a diagnostic program might offer us so that we can make a decision about whether to purchase one for each of our workers' use?

I will very much appreciate your advice on this one.

Download a trial or evaluation copy of a diagnostic utility such as one described in this chapter, or use another similar program with which you are familiar. Install it and try it out. Write a short description of the capabilities of the program that Tamara can send to Fred.

Common Support Problems

In this chapter, you will learn about:

◎ Several categories of common end-user computer problems

◎ Problem-solving processes that can be applied to typical support problems

As you learned in Chapter 3, many problems that a user support agent handles are not particularly difficult or complex. In that chapter, you learned about effective problem solving and troubleshooting processes as well as some of the tools support agents use to solve more difficult problems. In this chapter, you will examine some actual problem-solving situations and how user support agents resolved them.

This chapter is not a comprehensive catalog of every kind of problem a user support agent might encounter; that would be an impossible task. However, experienced support agents see some problem types frequently, and in this chapter, you will look at examples of some of the most common types of problems. The examples detail how the user described the problem, what problem-solving strategies the support agent employed to solve the problem, and the agent's conclusions about the process. All of the examples are based on actual support situations.

Common End-User Problems

Although computer problems come in a variety of forms, most problems fall into one of seven categories. Figure 4-1 lists these common problem categories. The following sections discuss each category in more detail, with examples presented to illustrate problems support specialists may encounter. The details about specific problems are less important than the categories they illustrate.

- Hardware problems
- Software problems
- User problems
- Documentation problems
- Vendor problems
- Operating environment problems
- Network problems

Figure 4-1   Seven common problem categories

Hardware Problems

Many hardware problems stem from one or more of four sources: improper installation, incompatibilities, configuration problems, and malfunctions.

Hardware Installation and Compatibility Problems

End users encounter a large percentage of hardware problems when they install a new hardware product or upgrade an old one. A problem may arise because a product is incompatible with existing hardware or because the end user did not install it correctly. **Incompatible** computer components are those that cannot operate together in the same system. The following example illustrates the discovery of hardware incompatibility during installation and the user support agent's solution.

PROBLEM A user purchased a new desktop computer, which included one 512 MB memory module. The user decided to upgrade his RAM to speed up the computer. He researched the type of memory that was used in the motherboard of his desktop model and purchased a 1 GB memory module as an upgrade. However, after he installed the memory upgrade, the computer beeped several times and failed to boot up. When he removed the 1GB memory module, the computer booted up correctly. The user also tried removing the 512 MB memory module and using just the new 1GB module, and the computer again booted up correctly.

SOLUTION An e-mail to the desktop vendor's technical support staff confirmed that 512 MB and 1GB memory modules do not always function correctly together on the motherboard of the user's computer model. The hardware vendor suggested that if the user needed over 1 GB of RAM that he exchange the 1 GB module for a 2 GB module.

ON THE WEB

Hardware compatibility problems are common when a new version of an operating system is released. An article on the following Web site describes hardware compatibility problems relating to the release of Windows Vista: **www.articlesbase. com/operating-systems-articles/windows-vista-hardware-compatibility-issues-121465.html**.

Some vendors provide information about compatible hardware devices. Microsoft provides a list of devices certified to be compatible with Windows XP and Vista at **winqual.microsoft. com/hcl**.

Hardware Configuration Problems

Configuration problems occur when hardware (or software) options are set incorrectly for the computer environment in which a component must operate. Hardware settings may be changed by adjusting small jumper pins or DIP switches, as shown in Figure 4-2. For example, a hard disk drive may serve as a master drive or a slave drive depending on how jumper pins are set. Hardware settings can also be modified by using a software utility program that selects among various hardware configuration options. A serial port on a communication adapter card can be addressed as COM1, COM2, COM3, or COM4, depending on how the COM address is set when the configuration software is run during installation. In some cases, a computer's startup files must be modified by installing a vendor's software driver to get a hardware component to operate.

Figure 4-2　Dip switches can be used to set configuration options on a motherboard

ON THE WEB

To learn more about the role that jumper pins and DIP switches play in hardware configurations, read about these terms in the Webopedia at **webopedia.internet.com/ TERM/j/jumper.html** and **webopedia.internet.com/ TERM/D/DIP_switch.html**.

Hardware configuration problems were much more common before the widespread adoption of **Plug and Play standards**, which are a set of protocols followed by hardware and operating system vendors relating to hardware installation. These standards specify the communication methods and rules that an operating system uses to recognize and incorporate hardware components into an operational system. With Plug and Play, an operating system can often recognize the existence of a new hardware component and select configuration options that permit the component to communicate successfully with the operating system.

ON THE WEB

To learn more about Plug and Play standards, visit the Web site of the UPnP Forum, the industry organization that works to establish standards to reduce configuration problems, at **www.upnp.org/resources/default.asp**.

Although Plug and Play standards can help a user load the appropriate device drivers, it does not always automatically adjust software settings to take maximum advantage of the new hardware's capabilities, as shown in the following example.

PROBLEM   A user purchased a new video graphics adapter card to increase her computer's display screen resolution from 1024 × 768 pixels to 1280 × 1024 pixels. The card installed easily, and the operating system recognized on startup that a new piece of hardware had been added to the system. The Windows Add New Hardware Wizard went through the process of installing an updated software driver to support the new video card. However, when the user restarted the computer after installation, the video image was the same resolution as before.

SOLUTION   A PC repair technician suggested that the new video graphics adapter card actually supported several different display screen resolutions, including the older 1024 × 768 and the newer 1280 × 1024 settings. The technician pointed out that the default resolution for the operating system was probably still set at 1024 × 768. The technician then instructed the user to open the Display Properties in the Control Panel and change the default settings for the display to 1280 × 1024. Once the user changed the operating system's settings to match the new video card's capabilities, the screen image appeared at the higher resolution.

Hardware Malfunctions

Some hardware problems result from components that have either never worked or no longer work. To cut down on this type of problem, an organization's support staff may "burn in" a new system

Electromechanical devices that have moving parts (such as hard disks, scanners, CD and DVD drives, and printers) are much more likely to develop hardware problems than components that are entirely electronic (such as CPUs, memory, bus slots, USB drives, and expansion cards).

before installing it at a user's workstation. During a **burn-in test**, a new computer or component is operated continuously over a 48- to 72-hour period in an attempt to discover obvious operational problems and to identify any marginal or temperature-sensitive components. A burn-in test gives the support staff the opportunity to identify hardware malfunctions before they become a source of frustration to a user. A burn-in test is effective because a defective component often fails during its first few hours of operation. If a component successfully completes the burn-in test, it is much less likely to fail in the future.

ON THE WEB

Passmark sells utility software that performs hardware burn-in tests at **www.passmark.com**.

Vendors that sell hardware components often include a diagnostic utility to help users and support agents detect possible problem components. Many software vendors also sell hardware diagnostic software, which helps user support agents identify common hardware malfunctions. These software programs can detect problems such as a device that is not getting power, a device that is not communicating correctly with other hardware devices, or a device that has a defective logic circuit on its controller card. Although some hardware components that malfunction can be repaired after a problem is identified, the hourly charge for electronic shop labor often makes it more cost-effective to replace rather than repair faulty devices. Support specialists who work with a large population of computers often keep a small supply of spare parts on hand to use when a device needs to be replaced. Others rely on overnight shipping from hardware vendors when a replacement part is needed quickly.

PROBLEM A user called a help desk regarding a problem with his PC's keyboard. The problem was an inoperative S key. The user wondered if the S keycap could have broken and asked if he could bring the keyboard in to the service department to get it repaired. He also asked about the cost to repair the S key.

SOLUTION The user support agent at the help desk said that physical damage to a keycap is rare and that, more frequently, the contacts located underneath the keycap wear out or get sticky. The support agent explained that hardware technicians rarely try to repair a keyboard malfunction because the cost of a replacement keyboard is usually much less than a technician's time to diagnose and repair a broken keyboard.

ON THE WEB

Companies that offer software utilities to help diagnose hardware malfunctions include PC-Diag Inc (**www.pc-diagnostics.com**), DIAG (**www.diagnoseprogramm.de**), and AnswersThatWork.com (**www.answersthatwork.com**).

Effective Hardware Problem-Solving Steps

To solve hardware problems, support agents should be sure to do the following:

1. Check the hardware vendor's Web site for updated drivers or reports of hardware problems for the specific model that has encountered a problem.

2. Use the Windows troubleshooters to identify common problems. To access the troubleshooters in Vista, click **Help and Support** on the Start menu, click the **Troubleshooting** icon, and then select an appropriate troubleshooter.

3. Look in the Device Manager for possible interaction problems between hardware devices and software drivers. To access the Device Manager from the Start menu, click **Control Panel**, and then select **Device Manager**. (On some systems, the Device Manager is a tab on the System icon in the Control Panel.)

4. Examine any applicable README files on the distribution media that accompany the hardware component for updated compatibility information.

5. Use an Internet search engine to locate reports of hardware problems and possible fixes in forums, blogs, and technical support sites.

 These resources often lead to solutions to hardware installation and incompatibility problems. Chapter 3 described several general diagnostic utility programs that also provide useful tools for diagnosing common hardware problems.

ON THE WEB

For a list of hardware vendors and their contact information, visit **support.microsoft.com/gp/vendors**.

Software Problems

Many software problems stem from one of five common sources: improper installation, incompatibility, configuration problems, bugs, and poor performance.

Software Installation and Compatibility Problems

Software problems occur more frequently during the installation (or setup) process than they do after software is operational. However, installation of new software products and upgrades to existing products are generally easier today than in the past. During the 1970s and 1980s, a user manually created a subdirectory (or folder) for the new software, copied files from the distribution media to a system's hard drive, and then configured software drivers and system startup files to set software options to match the hardware configuration. Because command strings were lengthy and the probability of a typing error was great, the potential for mistakes during this manual procedure was substantial.

Today, the software installation process is usually automated, and users who install software can avoid common problems that once plagued both users and support agents. **Installation software** is special-purpose utility software used by software vendors to help users install software packages. A software vendor writes a script with the steps to perform an installation. The script can perform steps such as checking on hardware compatibility, creating folders, copying files, updating the system registry, configuring the software based on the hardware configuration, and other related tasks. The goal of the script is to automate as many installation tasks as possible. In many cases, the user has only to choose the kind of installation she or he wants, as shown in Figure 4-3. Most steps in the installation offer defaults that a typical user can accept, or an advanced user can override. When a vendor has completed the script, it uses the installation software to create a package that includes the software to be installed, the software installation utility, documentation (such as a user's guide), device drivers, and anything else needed to perform the installation. When a user downloads the vendor's installation package or uses a distribution CD, the user runs the installation utility provided by the vendor. The utility automatically examines the hardware configuration to determine whether the software and hardware are compatible, creates folders with correct pathnames, and sets configuration options in the software and the operating system to match the hardware.

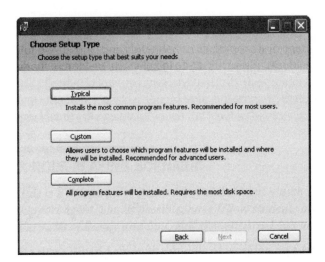

Chapter 9 contains additional information about software installations.

159

Figure 4-3   This installation utility provides users with setup options

ON THE WEB

Many vendors use InstallShield (see **www.acresso.com/ products/is/installshield-overview.htm**); however, if you need to purchase a product for your use, many shareware vendors sell lower-cost alternatives, such as wItem Software's Installer2Go (see **www.witemsoft.com/togo**).

ON THE WEB

Information about many software compatibility problems can be found in vendor manuals, in README files on distribution media, and on vendor Web sites. For example, see Microsoft's Web site that addresses application software compatibility problems with Windows and offers a compatibility toolkit at **technet.microsoft.com/en-us/desktopdeployment/ bb414773.aspx**.

Despite installation programs that solve many common hardware and software configuration issues, support agents still deal with installation problems. Not all software installs automatically, and end users frequently do not understand the implications of various options provided during the installation process. In addition, support agents are occasionally asked to install older software, as in the following example.

PROBLEM   A support agent installed a software package, which was originally programmed to run in a Windows 2000 environment on a Windows Vista system. Unfortunately, the Windows 2000 application did not operate correctly in Windows Vista because it was programmed to use features of Windows 2000 that are no longer supported in Windows Vista. Specifically, it sent information to the display screen in ways that are incompatible with Vista's methods.

In some circumstances, a computer may be set up as a dual-boot system so that it can run both a newer operating system and an older one. This solution sometimes permits legacy versions of software to operate on newer computers using an older operating system. A utility that helps set up and manage a dual-boot system is ProNetwork's Vista Boot Pro at **www.vistabootpro.org**.

SOLUTION   The support agent attempted to contact the software vendor but learned that the company had been sold to another vendor, and the product was no longer supported. However, a technical support representative at the new company suggested that the support agent investigate Windows Vista compatibility mode, which allows programs designed to run on older versions of operating systems to run under Vista in compatibility mode. The support agent typed "Windows Vista compatibility mode" into a search engine and found several useful articles about setting an application to operate in compatibility mode. Fortunately, the software that was originally designed to run in Windows 2000 worked correctly in Windows Vista under compatibility mode.

Shareware software downloaded from the Internet can be another source of compatibility problems. **Shareware** is commercial software that users can try out with the vendor's permission during an evaluation period (usually 10 to 45 days; 30 is most common) prior to making a purchase decision. Although many shareware programs are written to industry programming standards and are designed to be compatible with operating systems and other applications, some shareware programs may produce conflicts with hardware or other software. A **conflict** is a condition in which a computer component uses systems resources (CPU, memory, or peripheral devices) in a way that is incompatible with another component. Conflicts often make systems inoperable or prevent them from operating normally (for example, by slowing down performance).

Another category of software that can sometimes cause compatibility problems is **freeware**, which, as the name implies, is distributed without cost or a licensing fee. Although a donation is sometimes solicited (donationware), users are free to use, but not sell, the software. Some freeware runs trouble-free, but users are advised to take precautions, such as making a backup copy of the system Registry (described below), prior to the installation of freeware programs. Those who write and distribute freeware do not intend to provide software that is incompatible. However, some shareware and freeware may not be tested for compatibility to the same extent that commercial software is.

ON THE WEB

Distributors of shareware programs include **www.tucows. com**, **www.jumbo.com**, **www.shareware.com**, and **www. download.com**.

A distributor of freeware programs is **www.freewarebox.com**.

Freeware and shareware are not the same as open source software. **Open source software** is developed collaboratively by a loose-knit group of programmers who agree to share their efforts to improve and debug a software product and make the source code (and the program) available to anyone. Open source software may carry a certification called Open Source Initiative (OSI). The certification means that the software has been developed under specific design principles and guidelines. Open source software is often comparable in quality to commercial software.

ON THE WEB

To learn more about the development of open source software, visit **www.opensource.org**. A collection of some of the most popular open source software is maintained at **www.opensourcewindows.org**.

162

Software Configuration Problems

Some software problems are related to the way the software is configured to run on a system. Configuration problems result when software options are not set correctly for the specific operating environment or hardware. These problems may occur when end users install or upgrade new hardware or software or attempt to use a software feature for the first time, as in the following example.

PROBLEM   A Windows user installed a new software application that uses a utility program called WordViewer. After the installation, the end user could not open any Microsoft Word document by double-clicking it. When the user double-clicked a Word (.doc) file, WordViewer opened the document rather than Word itself. However, the user reported that if he started Word and used the File menu's Open command, he could successfully open a document in Word. For convenience, he would like to be able to double-click a Word file and have it open in Word.

SOLUTION   A support worker researched the problem on the Web and found that WordViewer is a free Microsoft utility. It is designed to let a user who does not have the Word program view, but not modify, any Word file. The support agent suggested that perhaps when the new application that uses WordViewer was installed, it configured WordViewer as the default application for all Word (.doc) files. The support agent advised the user to perform the following steps: Right-click any Word file to select it, and then click the Open With command. In the Open With dialog box, select Word, and then click the check box in front of the option to "Always use this program to open this kind of file."

Warning!
Modification of the Windows system Registry should never be attempted by anyone who is not entirely familiar with the purpose of a Registry, how it is organized, and how to back up, restore, modify, and save it. A damaged Registry can cause serious problems. Support agents who need to learn about the role of the Registry should consult one of the many trade books that describe its use and proper procedures for modification.

Another source of problems related to software compatibility and configuration in the Windows operating system is the system Registry. Much of the information that the operating system needs about hardware and software components is collected in one large Registry file. During normal system operation, the Registry is frequently read from and written to by applications and system software. The Registry file can also be edited with a software utility, regedit.exe or regedit32.exe (depending on operating system version). However, end users and support agents who are unfamiliar with the Registry, its entries, and how to modify the configuration information, should avoid making or modifying entries in the Registry. Improper Registry information can result in an inoperable system. Due to the frequency of Registry problems, Windows includes a feature to restore a prior version of the Registry on a computer that fails to operate because of invalid changes to Registry information.

ON THE WEB

To take a tutorial on Registry basics, visit: **www.pctools. com/guides/article/id/1**. A list of utility tools to modify and repair a Registry can be found at **www.winsite.com/ tech/reg**. Any tool that works with the Registry should be used with care and appropriate precautions.

To guard against an inoperable system due to Registry corruption, many support specialists advise users to create an emergency system recovery CD, DVD, or USB drive for each system, and to learn to use automated Registry recovery utilities when an operating system offers these tools. For more information, use an operating system's help feature to search for detailed procedures.

Software Bugs

Bugs are errors in a computer program that occur when a programmer writes incorrectly coded instructions during program development. A bug causes the software to either not do what it is expected to do or to do other things that it is not intended to do. Some bugs occur because a programmer just made a mistake, but more often they occur because the programmer could not anticipate every possible situation that might arise when the program is used on various hardware platforms or with other software. Bugs are more likely to occur in freeware, shareware, and custom-developed programs than in mass-market commercial programs; they are also more likely to occur in the first version of any software than in subsequent versions. In all software, bugs are more likely to be encountered in infrequently used features of a program. Many bugs are eliminated during the testing period that occurs before a software product is released for sale. However, even the most popular software products have known bugs several years after their initial release.

In order to fix bugs and provide new features, software vendors often distribute patches, updates, service packs, new releases, new versions, and upgrades:

- A **patch** is a replacement for one or a few modules of a software package to fix known bugs.

- An **update** is a bug-fix distribution that repairs known problems in a previous version or release of a software package; some vendors now include an **automatic update** feature that periodically checks the vendor's Web site for updates that are recommended to solve specific problems.

- A **service pack** (or **service release**) contains both updates and patches to fix documented problems with a version of a program.

- A new **release** of a program is a distribution that contains some new features not found in the original program.

- A new **version** of a software package contains significant new features and is usually the result of a substantially rewritten program.

- An **upgrade** is a new version of an existing program that is sold at a reduced cost to owners of a previous version of the program.

Although no industry standards dictate how vendors should number software distributions, some software vendors use the version number to indicate the release type. For example, version 2.0 is the first distribution of a new version, and version 2.1 is an update with new features. Version 2.11 (or 2.1.1) is a bug-fix release or an update of version 2.1 that does not necessarily include major new features. Other vendors add a service pack/release letter to a version number. For example, version 2.5A is the first (A-level) patch of release 2.5. Some software vendors also use the year of release to number their software versions. For example, Office 2007 is the release of the Office Suite issued in the year 2007. Although there is usually no direct correspondence between competing vendors' version-numbering schemes, vendors may intentionally skip a version number in order to maintain parity with the version number of a competitor's product.

The following example illustrates how one end user obtained a patch.

PROBLEM   An end user experienced a formatting problem in an accounting program that occurred only with very large dollar amounts.

SOLUTION   When the end user contacted the software vendor's help desk, the user learned that the problem was a known bug, that it had been repaired, and that a patch could be downloaded from the vendor's Web site or requested on a CD. The vendor's help desk staff provided the user with instructions on how to download the patch and explained that it would self-install when the user double-clicked the downloaded file.

Before a user or support agent installs any patch, he or she should verify that the patch is for the software version that is actually installed on the user's system. A cautious user or support agent may choose to back up the original copy of a program before updates are installed. In addition, any software updates, service packs, or patches that are installed on a computer should be documented in the site installation notebook, as described in Chapter 9. If a patch is installed, it must be reinstalled if it becomes necessary to reinstall the original software from the distribution media. Therefore, support agents should maintain a record of all updates and patches installed on a system as a reinstallation reminder. In general, new software releases or versions incorporate all bug fixes that have been reported and fixed prior to the new release. For example, software version 3.1 contains all patches released for version 3.0. However, the documentation for some patches may include a note, for example, that patch 3.4A must be installed before patch 3.4B can be installed.

In cases where no patch exists for a software bug, a support agent or software vendor may be able to suggest a workaround for a problem. A **workaround** is a procedure or operation that accomplishes the same result as the original feature that currently does not work due to a bug or other malfunction. Workarounds are used when it is impossible or impractical for a support agent to correct an underlying problem. For example, a command in a GUI environment can often be entered in several ways: keyboard commands, menu commands, toolbar icons, or shortcut keys. If a menu option does not work correctly, a keyboard shortcut may provide a successful workaround.

Software Performance Problems

Performance problems occur when a computer is operational but is not operating as efficiently as it should. Performance problems often result from poor interaction between hardware and software. For example, a user may report that a PC's hard disk drive light comes on more frequently and stays on longer than it used to and that the system seems sluggish. Or the response time from when a Save command is selected to the completion of the Save task has become increasingly longer. The user may suspect that the problem is due to hardware—perhaps the hard disk drive is beginning to fail. However, performance problems are usually related to how the software—the operating system, in this case—is managing the hardware. Before concluding that a hard drive failure is the likely problem, a support agent might investigate alternate explanations, such as those in the following list:

- The hard disk drive may be nearly full; the operating system may not have adequate unused space to write temporary files to the hard drive during its file management tasks. The user may need to back up and then delete infrequently used programs and data files, or install a second hard drive in the system.

- The hard disk may be fragmented; files written on the disk in small chunks may take longer to read and write than files in contiguous

Performance problems may also occur in a system that is not properly maintained. Users should take advantage of automatic update features in operating systems, software utilities, and application programs. Performance is usually maintained or enhanced when a system's software is kept up-to-date on a regular schedule by downloading updated modules from a vendor's Web site.

sectors on the disk. A defragmentation (or defrag, for short) utility can often fix this problem.

- The hard drive may contain wasted space because links to free space are lost. Scandisk or a similar Windows utility program can often locate and reclaim lost space resulting from improperly linked allocation units on a disk.

- The system may not have enough RAM to run the software and may be using the hard disk as an extension of RAM (called virtual memory or swap file space) to accommodate large amounts of data. The virtual memory may need to be enlarged, or the computer may just need additional internal memory to run the software efficiently. Hardware experts often emphasize that the most effective way to improve software performance is to add RAM.

- The system may be infected with one or more kinds of malware, such as a virus, spyware, or a keystroke logger. Running a utility program to scan the hard drive for malware may improve overall system performance.

Closely related to software problems is a user's ability to operate the software.

User Problems

Workers in the support industry have coined a special acronym to label user problems: PEBSAK is a designation that the "Problem Exists Between Seat And Keyboard."

Users unintentionally cause many support problems. Although most users try to be well informed and do their best to use hardware and software correctly, even the best-intentioned users can introduce problems.

Mistakes

All end users, including computer professionals, make mistakes. During the initial design of a program, systems analysts may not adequately understand all the detailed aspects of a business process and may design a software solution incorrectly. Programmers may make mistakes in the code they write and introduce software bugs. A professionally trained and experienced data-entry operator may type an erroneous keystroke every few thousand characters. Even experienced user support workers make an occasional error. What can be done about user mistakes? Well-designed computer systems anticipate many potential user mistakes, alert the user, and provide corrective action. For example, an accounting program may be able to perform a validity check on input data and detect input errors. A common example is a range validity check on the number of hours each employee worked in a week to identify input that falls outside a predefined range of values. For example, an input of 400 (instead of 40) would trigger a warning.

Despite the best efforts of software developers, users occasionally press a wrong key or click the mouse in an unintended situation and end up in a part of a program where they didn't want to be. Some inadvertent user actions are invalid and have no consequence other than a beep. Other errors can have more drastic consequences. For example, in some word processors, if a passage is selected (highlighted) and the user inadvertently presses a key, the character representing the pressed key replaces the entire selected passage. If a user doesn't know how to recover from this situation, the user can easily lose some work.

Although user mistakes account for a significant percentage of common problems, support agents need to consider carefully how to handle these problems from a client service perspective; some users do not like to be told that they made a mistake. Chapter 2 offered strategies for handling difficult interactions with users.

Misunderstandings

Other end-user problems stem from misunderstandings about product features or limitations. Users may expect a product or service to be able to perform tasks for which it was not intended. Or they may be unaware of a product's features, as shown in the following example.

PROBLEM   A user complained that it took a long time to find a file on his computer. On investigation, a user support worker discovered that the user kept all his user files in the My Documents directory. His My Documents folder had hundreds of files in it, all at the top level. He had never created subfolders for various projects so that his work would be better organized and easier to find. When asked about the practice, he explained that he understood that he could probably create subfolders within folders because he had observed that type of organization in folders created by Windows and other software. However, he had never taken the time to learn about creating folders.

SOLUTION   The user support worker showed the user how easy it is to create folders and subfolders for each project or routine task in Windows, and demonstrated how to drag and drop files into folders. The user support worker explained that it would take some time to reorganize all the files in My Documents, but that the user would be repaid when it was time to locate a file he needed.

Wrong Products

Users may purchase the wrong product to accomplish a task. For example, they may buy a software package or hardware peripheral that is incompatible with their existing system. A common problem occurs when a user of an older model PC hears about a new software product they want to use. They may not understand that the new software requires a more current processor or more memory than

A common keyboarding error is to inadvertently press the CAPS LOCK key instead of the Tab or Shift key. To hear an audible beep to warn whenever the CAPS LOCK key is pressed, go to Vista's control panel and click **Ease of Access Center**. Click the **Change how your keyboard works**, and click on **Turn on Toggle Keys**.

167

User mistakes sometimes provide an opening for a support agent to tactfully point a user toward a training opportunity, whether an in-house session, a trade book, or a computer-based tutorial.

their computer has. Users with Windows computers may inadvertently purchase the Macintosh version of a software package because they have not read the packaging carefully.

Users may also purchase software without understanding its capabilities or without knowledge of alternatives, as in the following example.

PROBLEM   A Macintosh user who wanted to create a newsletter bought a collection of clip art on a CD-ROM from an office supply store because the packaging included an illustration of clip art embedded in a newsletter. The user assumed that the software was capable of producing a newsletter like the one illustrated on the package. When the user installed the clip art on his system, he called the support number in the documentation to complain that the software did not produce the newsletter form he wanted.

SOLUTION   The software vendor's customer support agent provided the user with a Return Merchandise Authorization (RMA) number and suggested that the user return to the store to look for a desktop publishing program with a newsletter template.

A similar problem can arise with the purchase of new hardware, as the next problem illustrates.

PROBLEM   A user purchased an external hard drive to back up data on a computer's internal hard drive. However, the new external drive was designed to connect to a computer's USB port. Unfortunately, the user's computer was an older model that had only two USB ports, which were needed for his keyboard and mouse. Because the user couldn't figure out how to connect the drive to his computer, he put the external drive in his closet, awaiting an opportunity to ask for assistance.

SOLUTION   Unfortunately, the user was unaware that an inexpensive USB port expansion card or hub could easily be added to his system to accommodate other USB devices. Therefore, the external hard drive is still in his closet today. The user occasionally worries about what will happen if he experiences problems with the data on his internal drive.

Inadequate Information or Training

Many computer problems arise because users are inadequately trained or do not read the documentation that came with the hardware or software. A high percentage of calls to support centers can be easily answered by referring to a user manual, a tutorial, or online help. Users often do not know where to find the information they need, or they don't want to take the time to search for information. Users who have not been adequately trained or who do not recall information from a training session pose a challenge for help desk staff. Ideally, training sessions should not only provide users with the information they need, but should also include pointers about where users can locate the information later, without help desk assistance.

Quick start behavior is a tendency among computer users to skip the installation manual and attempt to get new hardware or software installed and operational as rapidly as possible. Their attitude can be summed up as: "If all else fails, I can always read the manual." Many vendors now include a very brief quick start guide, or "Getting Started with…" manual, in an attempt to get users at least to read something before they begin to use a new product. For example, Figure 4-4 shows the first page of a Quick Start tutorial on Yahoo! Mail.

Figure 4-4   Example of Quick Start tutorial for Yahoo! Mail

Lack of adequate information and training ultimately translate into waste and lost user productivity. For example, the Macintosh user described earlier who wanted to produce a newsletter did not realize that his word processor included many of the features he would need to produce a reasonably complex newsletter. He actually had the software he needed but did not realize it. Appropriate training or consulting with user support staff could help him learn how to use an existing program to produce newsletters.

 User problems that result from inadequate training and documentation provide both a challenge and an opportunity for support specialists who enjoy training and writing, as you will learn in Chapters 10 and 11.

Forgotten Information

At times, users simply forget how to perform a task or find the information they need. For example, local area network administrators report that the single most common contact they experience is from users who have forgotten the password to their accounts. Web sites that register users receive many phone calls and e-mails from users who cannot remember the PIN (personal identification number) they

Support agents should caution users against writing their passwords on paper. One of the biggest security problems in many organizations is users who write their password on a Post-It note and attach the reminder to their monitor.

need to log on to the site. Many Web sites that require registration have now automated the password-recovery process via an e-mail reminder so that no support staff time is required to respond to the high volume of requests for passwords.

For users who are forgetful or who infrequently use a password, one strategy is to keep a written note in an obscure location that does not contain their actual password, but contains a word or phrase that serves as a password reminder. Some operating systems and application programs include a feature to store and retrieve passwords for users or ask a prompting question to help refresh a user's recollection of a password. These features should be used with caution in an office or school environment where other users may have access to a system.

Users who make less frequent use of their computers are especially likely to forget information. Reference sheets (formal or informal notes) and scripts or checklists are an effective aid to help users recall how to perform infrequent tasks that are difficult to remember.

Documentation Problems

Another source of end-user support problems can be traced to documentation problems. The readability of computer vendor documentation has generally improved in recent years. However, documentation that is poorly organized, inaccurate, and omits important points is still the direct cause of much misunderstanding and contributes to user frustration as well as the volume of calls a help desk receives.

Complete user documentation includes:

Support staff who prepare user documentation should follow the suggestions offered in Chapter 11 on end-user documentation.

- a quick start guide

- a tutorial that walks a user through the major features of a software package

- a reference manual with information organized by topic

- a troubleshooting guide

- online help, including information that users can search by keyword

- troubleshooting wizards to assist users with common problems

Well-written user documentation takes time to develop. Support staff who write documentation, whether in print or online, should make good use of graphics, because users learn faster and retain information longer when visuals are used to supplement narrative explanations. Support staff should also consider how to address user quick start behavior when they design and develop documentation. Finally, support staff should ask coworkers and end users to review documentation and help identify points that need clarification before publication.

Vendor Problems

Calls to a help desk or hotline may be related to vendor performance. Some vendors consistently oversell their products; they advertise or promise features that may not be delivered as part of the final product. Vendors may also release a beta software version that contains known bugs that can put user data at risk. Some vendors are also notorious for late deliveries of new products, long after they were promised. Help desk agents may find themselves in the uncomfortable position of handling incidents from users who are complaining about their company's performance as a vendor. Or agents may be asked to consult with internal users who have been the victim of vendor performance problems.

Vaporware refers to hardware or software products that appear in ads or press releases but that are not yet available for sale. A vendor may announce a product that doesn't yet exist in order to study market reaction or to confuse its competitors. A help desk that handles incidents for external users usually establishes a policy for its support staff on how to handle clients who have questions about product announcements. Chapter 3 described some client service and communications skills that are useful in handling these incidents.

ON THE WEB

Rebates on hardware and software purchases are often a source of user frustration with vendor performance. The purpose of a vendor rebate is to encourage sales; a price with a rebate subtracted is often attractively low. Failure to provide a rebate during the time period promised in an advertisement is a client service issue, and it can have as much impact as product features or performance on a user's impression of a vendor. Some vendors are very conscientious about rebate deadlines and provide contact information so that clients can check on the status of a rebate. In other cases, rebate fulfillment centers are understaffed and struggle to keep up with the volume of calls and e-mails related to expected client rebates. Questions and complaints about rebates are common to help desk agents in some vendor's support organizations.

To learn more about rebates and how to guard against problems, visit **www.consumeraffairs.com/consumerism/ rebate_madness01.html**.

Operating Environment Problems

Some support calls are about problems in the environment in which computers are operated. The operating environment category includes:

- problems with computing facilities
  - electricity, lighting, and air conditioning
  - office furniture and related office equipment
  - workplace ergonomics and safety
- problems with the computing environment
  - data backup and recovery
  - security threats
  - disaster and contingency planning and preparation

Chapter 9 describes solutions to several problems with computing facilities and the operating environment.

Network Problems

Computer networks are a frequent source of problems that network support agents encounter. However, many network problems are traceable to hardware (including servers, hubs, routers, bridges, switches, and gateways), software, operating systems, or other categories of problems discussed earlier. Network problems are often among those that are most difficult for a support staff to handle because they frequently involve the interaction of hardware, software, and other components.

PROBLEM   A network administrator in a county planning office received several phone calls and e-mails one morning indicating that the office network was running very slowly. The network staff uses a network monitoring and performance utility distributed by ManageEngine called OpManager. This utility tool monitors several aspects of network operation, including servers, network devices, printers, and other aspects of network operation. The administrator checked on OpManager's performance indicators and learned that the server disk space was perilously full. She knew that disk space usage was tight, and that the agency had discussed purchasing additional disk storage for the server. The system had been operating normally the previous day, however.

SOLUTION   Upon further checking, the network administrator discovered that one of the planners had downloaded some very large files of training videos the previous evening; the files had filled up most of the free disk space on the server. She contacted the planner and offered to back up the video files onto a tape cartridge until they were needed. The planner agreed. The network administrator was able to use network monitoring software to help identify the network bottleneck. Then, she was able to troubleshoot the problem and offer a solution that permitted her to free up valuable space on the server's hard drive and return the network to normal operation.

ON THE WEB

If you would like to learn more about the network monitoring tool the administrator used, view a five-minute video overview of OpManager at **manageengine.adventnet.com/ products/opmanager/OpManagerOverview.htm**.

Many print publications serve as a good resource for best practices in troubleshooting common computer problems:

- Morris Rosenthal, *Computer Repair with Diagnostic Flowcharts: Troubleshooting PC Hardware Problems from Boot Failure to Poor Performance*. Foner Books, 2008.

- Jean Andrews, *A+ Troubleshooting Scenarios*. Boston: Course Technology, 2007.

- MSWinVista Team, *Windows Vista Resource Kit*. Redmond, WA: Microsoft Press, 2007.

- John Pierce, *2007 Microsoft Office System Inside Out*. Redmond, WA: Microsoft Press, 2007.

ON THE WEB

Many sites on the Web also provide helpful information for user support staff who work on specific problems or want to know more about the troubleshooting and problem-solving process.

General troubleshooting:

- **pcsupport.about.com**—This About.com site contains a wealth of information on PCs and troubleshooting.

- **www.askdrtech.com/default.asp**—Ask Dr. Tech is a fee-based site that provides 24/7 support services via phone or Web.

(continues)

(continued)

- **www.smartcomputing.com/techsupport**—*Smart Computing* magazine's site offers a variety of services on the Web and via phone, e-mail, or online chat. Some services require a paid subscription to their monthly magazine.

Hardware troubleshooting:

- **www.pcguide.com/ts/index.htm**—The PC Guide is one of the largest Web sites dedicated to information on PC hardware and troubleshooting.

- **www.directron.com/howtobuilyou.html**—Directron. org's site includes troubleshooting tips for several kinds of hardware components.

- **www.tomshardware.com/us**—Tom's Hardware Guide contains a database of searchable articles on common hardware components.

- **www.macintoshos.com/troubleshooting/troubleshooting. html**—This site provides a troubleshooting guide for Mac OS systems.

Software troubleshooting:

- **www.helpwithwindows.com**—HelpWithWindows.com's troubleshooting tips link to articles on a variety of common problems (select your version of Windows in the tabs at the top).

- **support.microsoft.com**—This site is Microsoft's product support center for operating system and applications software. In the search box, enter "troubleshoot" and the name of the product.

- **guides.macrumors.com/Troubleshooting_Software_ Problems**—The Mac Rumors Web site includes several sections for resolving Macintosh software problems.

Other resources:

- **www.google.com**—The Google search engine can locate Web sites for specific problems; use the name of hardware and software products for search keywords, as well as version and model numbers.

(continues)

(continued)

- **www.ask.com**—The Ask search engine provides information in an informal question-and-answer format.

- **www.zdnet.com**—ZDnet is an extensive Web site with product and troubleshooting information and tips. The home page includes a keyword search feature.

- **www.about.com/compute**—About.com is a collection of moderated Web sites with information on a variety of topics. The home page includes an extensive menu and keyword search feature.

Problem-Solving Processes Applied to Typical End-User Problems

As the user support staff in an organization solve the kinds of computer problems described in this chapter, the solutions become common knowledge among members of the staff. They use this ever-expanding bank of knowledge to solve new problems. The greater the variety of problems user support agents are exposed to, the better the knowledge and experience they will have at their command to tackle new problems. User support agents use the problem-solving processes described in Chapter 3 to find appropriate solutions, as shown in the following accounts from support agents about how they resolved some typical support problems.

Problem 1: Sounds Like Trouble

PROBLEM   A user in a remote branch office sent me an e-mail message stating that she had lost the sound in her system. I started the troubleshooting process by asking questions about her basic configuration and some critical questions, such as, "Has this problem ever happened before?" and "What programs were you running when you noticed the sound was lost?" She wrote back that the system is a Pentium 4, running Windows. She indicated that the sound had been working fine, and she couldn't remember exactly which program she was running when she first noticed the sound no longer worked. She also mentioned that two other employees had access to her system.

PROBLEM-SOLVING STRATEGY   My first reaction was to try some quick fixes. I suggested that she:

- Reset the sound card in the expansion slot.

- Try the sound card in a different expansion slot.

- Check all the connections and cables to the sound card.

- Check the Windows device manager to see if there were any IRQ conflicts between the sound card and other devices.

The user responded that she checked these items, but that the sound still didn't work. I discussed the problem with some support colleagues, describing what we had already tried. They came up with a few other suggestions:

- Make sure that the volume is turned up on the speakers.

- Make sure that the volume is turned up in the Windows media player.

- Check that the speakers are connected correctly.

- If the speakers require electrical current, make sure they're plugged in.

The user checked all these possibilities and reported that there was still no sound. I asked her if there were any changes made to her system recently. She wrote back that apparently one of her work colleagues had downloaded a shareware version of an antivirus program from the Internet about the time the sound problem first occurred. The colleague said that, after several attempts, he couldn't get the antivirus program to work correctly on the system, so he uninstalled it. The fact that new software had recently been installed on her system got me thinking in a different direction. I looked on the Internet and found a Web site for her brand of sound card. They listed about 20 different models of cards, one of which was hers. I sent her the Web address where she could download the latest version of the software driver for her particular card. Later that day, I received a message that she had downloaded the sound card driver, installed it in Windows, and her sound worked again.

CONCLUSION   I'm not certain of the diagnosis, but I think the shareware program may have affected the driver software her sound card used. Once she reinstalled the driver, the problem was fixed.

I was pleased that I solved the problem. I used communications skills to get information from the end user, which was not easy using e-mail. I also used critical questions that opened up a different avenue of investigation. I used several information resources, including my support colleagues and the vendor's Web site. I used some troubleshooting strategies, including looking for an obvious fix, some hypothesis testing, and module replacement. *(Based on an incident described by Billie Brendlinger.)*

Problem 2: The Problem with Modems

PROBLEM   I work for an Internet Service Provider (ISP) as an installer/troubleshooter. I was at a client's site in a small, rural town to trouble-shoot an Internet setup on their Macintosh computer. I had previously installed Internet access software and configured the client's machine for Internet access. I had also trained the user to log on and run the software to access the Internet. After the installation, everything appeared to be in working order.

The user called our trouble line about a week later, saying that she had an occasional problem with Internet access from her Mac. Her modem usually dialed our ISP's server successfully, but occasionally it would report than it couldn't get a dial tone.

PROBLEM-SOLVING STRATEGY   On my follow-up visit, I asked a series of questions about her telephone service, including whether she had any features added to her basic phone service, such as caller ID, call waiting, or other services. The end user assured me that her telephone was a standard line with no frills. I checked the modem with the terminal emulation software, and the diagnostic check indicated that the modem was correctly connected. Because the setup had worked after the original installation, I had suspected the modem connection was okay, but I was glad to get the confirmation.

Then I decided to unplug the modem and connect the telephone handset directly to the phone line. My hypothesis was that there was something wrong with the telephone service that was affecting the modem. When I picked up the handset, I heard a "blip-blip-blip-blip" sound, then a long pause, and finally a dial tone. I recalled that I had heard the blip sounds before at a friend's house. I realized that it is the sound that the telephone company's voice mail system makes when the client has a message waiting. If there were no voice mail messages waiting, there were no blip sounds.

CONCLUSION   I advised the user to always to check for voice mail messages before dialing the Internet phone number. I also found a setting in the Internet access software that controls the amount of time the software listens for a dial tone before it gives up. I increased the time to 20 seconds in case the user forgot to check for voice mail messages.

The problem was an interesting one, and I was glad I was able to solve it. I learned that users don't always know the answers to the questions I ask. In this case, the user's answers threw me off track. I also used my personal experience to identify the source of the voice mail tones on the phone line. The rest of the process involved eliminating variables (when I replaced the modem with the telephone handset) and hypothesis testing. *(Based on an incident reported by Jaime Chamoulos.)*

Problem 3: Give Credit Where It Is Due

PROBLEM   I am a support person in an online ticket sales company. A computer operator within our company is responsible for running an electronic data interchange (EDI) software package to process credit card transactions. The program uploads batches of credit card transactions to a credit card processor. The credit card processor then authenticates each transaction and processes it with the financial institution that issued the credit card.

The computer operator was frustrated and unhappy with the EDI software because the program would not process batches of transactions correctly, so she had to enter each transaction individually. She had contacted the EDI software vendor about the problem. The vendor said the problem was likely on the credit card processor's end. When the operator called the credit card processor, they pointed the finger back at the EDI software package. I was assigned the task of finding the cause of the problem.

PROBLEM-SOLVING STRATEGY   Before I contacted the software company, I wanted to make sure I understood how the procedure was supposed to work and what the real problem was. I put together a list of the subsystems in the procedure:

1. Computer operator batches together credit card transactions.

2. EDI software uploads and transmits the batch of transactions to the credit card processor.

3. Credit card processor posts transactions to customer accounts.

4. Credit card processor returns a confirmation report of processed transactions.

5. Computer operator verifies the status of processed transactions.

I considered that the problem could be with the EDI software program, the credit card processor, or the computer operator's procedures. I started at the top of the list and assumed that the problem was with the EDI software. I decided to install it on my own computer, read through the manual, and use the computer operator's notes to learn how to process batches of transactions. Although the software documentation was skimpy, I eventually pieced together enough information so that I understood how the program worked. I put together a few sample transactions to test the system. The test cases that I constructed seemed to work fine. I decided to create better documentation for the computer operator based on the software manual, her notes, and some conversations I had with a representative from the EDI software company about the batch-processing procedure.

Then the computer operator and I went through the process of building a batch of transactions with some actual data. We used my expanded documentation as a guide and a checklist. The batch file we uploaded seemed to process correctly, but we did not receive the expected confirmation that the transactions were received or accepted. According to the software manual, the credit card processor should have downloaded a report file to us to indicate a normal termination of the batch process as well as the status of each transaction. The next day, I called the credit card processor to see if they could verify that the transactions we sent had been received and approved. They had been, so I was fairly confident that the procedure documentation I wrote was accurate. We could upload batches of transactions that were received and processed by the credit card processor.

However, we still did not know why we hadn't received the confirming report file from the credit card processor. I tried to open the confirmation report file from within the EDI software, but nothing happened. It appeared that the report file was missing. I looked around on the hard drive and eventually found the report file, and I used a file-diagnosis utility to examine it. My examination revealed that the report file contained all of the confirmations that successful batches of transactions had been uploaded and received, including the ones we had sent the previous day. For some reason, the EDI program could not display the report file. Then I noticed some corrupted data at the beginning of the report file that was in a different format than the remainder of the file. I made a backup copy of the report file as a precaution and then deleted the original report file. The next day, we ran a batch of about 200 transactions. The credit card processor received the transactions, processed them, and returned the report file successfully.

CONCLUSION   I think the corrupted data in the report file may have been due to an error the computer operator made because she didn't really understand all the steps necessary to transmit batches. When the confirmation for each day's transactions was added to the corrupted file, it could not be displayed. Once I removed the corrupted data, the confirmation report displayed correctly.

I used a list of subsystems and a lot of hypothesis testing on this problem. I also tried to replicate on my own system the problem the operator had experienced. To this day, I'm not sure I understand the exact error the computer operator made. She was very frustrated and obviously needed better documentation. Based on the documentation I prepared, she has been able to process transactions correctly ever since I worked on this problem. *(Based on an incident described by Mark Gauthier.)*

Problem 4: Antivirus Protection Worth Every Cent You Pay for It

PROBLEM A user called the help desk hot line to ask if we had ever heard of a free antivirus program called Vista Antivirus 2008. He had downloaded the program from a Web site, and it had scanned his hard disk for viruses and identified several vulnerabilities. The program listed the problems and indicated the program could remove the infected files if he updated the program by purchasing a full license on the Web. The user asked if our company would pay for a license for the program.

PROBLEM-SOLVING STRATEGY I had never heard of Vista Antivirus 2008 nor the Web site where the user downloaded the program. However, new shareware programs seem to be available daily, so I wasn't surprised—only suspicious. I checked several reputable download sites on the Web and could not find any reference to Vista Antivirus. Upon checking further, I discovered some Web sites that described the program as **malware**, which is a program with harmful or malicious intent that disrupts the normal operation of a computer or network, or attempts to steal information or money as a result of its operation.

I learned that the program is not a Microsoft product, and probably uses the name Vista illegally. Most legitimate antivirus programs will detect and delete Vista Antivirus. I found a Web site with instructions for manual removal (**www.windowsvistaplace.com/antivirus2008-antivirus-2008-removal-instructions/software**). The site also includes links to programs that will detect the malware program.

CONCLUSION I was able to help the user remove the Vista Antivirus program using the instructions I found on the Web. To solve this problem I relied on my experience with popular antivirus software and an ability to locate useful information resources on the Web. I was pleased to be able to save the user from wasting money on a useless piece of software. As a result of this incident, I wrote a short note to warn about the Vista Antivirus program for the next issue of our user support newsletter. I also sent the user a pointer to a Web site where he could download our company's recommended antivirus utility.

Problem 5: The Path Not Taken

PROBLEM The phone call came into the support center late one afternoon. A user said that one of his PCs could no longer access my company's vertical market software. The rest of our support staff was in a training seminar for the afternoon, so I had to solve the problem on my own. As a new member of the support staff, I was a little nervous. The user on the phone said that he had been able to run the software successfully earlier in the day, but the desktop icon to run our software package was no longer visible.

PROBLEM-SOLVING STRATEGY   After asking a few questions and paraphrasing some of his statements, I clarified that the icon for our software was actually still on the desktop but that double-clicking it produced no results. I asked several other questions, including the critical question, "What were you doing on the system when the icon stopped working?" The user responded that he had been deleting some unwanted files.

My first thought was that perhaps the user had accidentally deleted the .exe file associated with the icon. I led him through the steps to see if the .exe program file was still in the correct folder—it was. My next idea was that perhaps the shortcut path from the icon to the .exe file had been destroyed. After checking the shortcut properties, we confirmed that the path was in place. Then I wondered whether the user had somehow deleted the path to some of the files the program needs to operate. I wasn't sure how to check that, but I knew that some of the files were on a server and that each client machine defines the drive mappings to the network drives when it boots up. I explained my reasoning to the user and suggested that he quit all applications and shut down his system, just as if it were the end of the day. We waited a few seconds and then rebooted his system. After the reboot, everything worked fine. Apparently, he had accidentally erased the drive mappings during his system housekeeping.

CONCLUSION   I was pleased to be able to handle the call, which was one of my first as a user support agent. I used several troubleshooting strategies, including communication skills to listen to the user's definition of the problem, paraphrasing, and asking critical questions to give me the information I needed to formulate a hypothesis. I also used a mental image of the sequence from the icon to the disk files to troubleshoot the problem. *(Based on an incident reported by Andra Heath.)*

Problem 6: The Nonresponsive Network

PROBLEM   I am the network support assistant for an economic research think tank. One afternoon I received a call from a staff member who reported that something was wrong with his workstation. He said it was very sluggish. I walked down the hall and looked at his workstation, which was running Excel. The user was in the process of saving a worksheet on the file server, but Excel had not yet responded to the save command.

PROBLEM-SOLVING STRATEGY   I canceled the save operation. Before I investigated the problem further, as a precaution, I tried to save the user's worksheet on the local hard drive instead of on the file server. This time the save operation worked fine, so I thought it was unlikely the user's PC was the problem. My attention immediately turned to the network server.

I went to the computer room where the server is located and found that the console monitor was blank. I noticed that the power lamp indicators were lit on both the server and the monitor, so I eliminated the likelihood of a power supply problem. I tried to log on to the server using a workstation that we have set up in the computer room, but the attempt failed. Then I tried to reboot the server. It did not appear to boot, but I couldn't tell much because the monitor was still blank. I thought that perhaps there was a problem with the monitor, but I wasn't sure. However, I felt that I needed to fix any problem that existed with the monitor first, so that I could diagnose the situation with the server. I disconnected the monitor from the server and borrowed a monitor and cable from a nearby workstation. After I plugged in a different monitor, the server still didn't appear to boot and the monitor was still blank. So the monitor itself was probably not related to the problem.

Because I was focused on the blank monitor screen, my next thought was to replace the video card in the server. So I pulled the video card from the nearby workstation and replaced the one in the server with one I knew was operational. When I rebooted the server, the result was the same blank monitor screen. At this point, I stopped to think about the subsystems that were involved in the display screen problem. I sketched on a notepad the monitor, the cable, the video card, the motherboard, and the power supply. Because the power supply lamp was lit, and because I had replaced everything else, I looked at the motherboard. I could not see any visible problems with it. I decided to set up a substitute server. First I returned the borrowed video card and monitor to the workstation. I then removed the hard drive from the inoperable server and installed it in the workstation. Finally, I crossed my fingers and rebooted the substitute server. It came up okay. The motherboard apparently was the problem.

Only authorized network support personnel should reboot a server.

CONCLUSION   I received a call from the repair shop the next day that confirmed my suspicion that the server motherboard was damaged. It had several burned-out components and needed to be replaced. I obviously relied heavily in this situation on a module replacement strategy and on my knowledge of how the subsystems in a computer are linked together. The incident confirmed for me that users are not always capable of diagnosing the problem, which turned out to be with the server and not with the user's workstation.

Problem 7: The Big, Red X

A ROLE PLAYING SCENARIO

This is a transcript of a conversation between a user, Tracy, and a support agent, Chris. If possible, have fellow students or coworkers play the parts of Tracy and Chris, and then discuss Chris's use of problem-solving tools and skills.

CHRIS: This is Chris in the support center. How can I help you?

TRACY: I am working on a Web site and found some material I want to use in a report. The material includes a graph, but where the graph should appear, all I see is an empty box on the screen with a red X in the left corner.

CHRIS: Which Web browser are you using?

TRACY: Internet Explorer version 7.

CHRIS: What happens if you click inside the box?

TRACY: I tried that. Nothing happens.

CHRIS: Perhaps a server that is transmitting Web pages to you is just slow in loading the graph, or maybe the graph is large and is a slow download. Is the mouse pointer displayed as an hourglass?

TRACY: No.

CHRIS: Does the message on the status bar line underneath the browser window indicate that the browser is waiting or that an image has not completed downloading?

TRACY: The status bar just says, "Done."

CHRIS: Okay, maybe the graphic image is being blocked by your Web browser. Is there a message on the display screen that an image has been blocked?

TRACY: No.

CHRIS: Then let's see if the Web browser you are using can display the graphic image. Right-click inside the box and click Show Picture.

TRACY: Okay, let me try that . . . Well, nothing happens. Same result.

CHRIS: I wonder if the settings in your Web browser are set to display graphic images. Do other images display correctly?

TRACY: As far as I know they do.

CHRIS: Well, let's check the settings just to make sure. Click the Tools menu, and then Internet options. Then click the Advanced tab. Is the box in front of Show Pictures checked?

TRACY: Let me see. Yes, it's checked.

CHRIS: I'm just about out of ideas. But let's try another approach. Right-click inside the empty box, and click properties. What type of image file is the Web browser unable to display? Look on the Address or URL line.

TRACY: The image file is something called a TIFF file.

CHRIS: Ah, I think that your Web browser may not be able to display a TIFF file without a special plug-in.

TRACY: What is a TIFF file?

CHRIS: A TIFF is a common graphic image file, but not one that is supported by all Web browsers. Let me check on that possibility for Internet Explorer. I'll call you back to let you know if a plug-in to display TIFF images is available and how to download it.

TRACY: Thanks, I'll be waiting for your call.

After the role-playing activity, discuss these aspects of this trouble-shooting incident:

1. What strategies did Chris use to determine the cause of the problem?

2. How would you evaluate Chris's use of the communication skills described in Chapter 2 in this incident?

3. Do you think Chris found the cause of the problem?

4. Should Chris consider other potential problems?

5. Is an Internet Explorer plug-in available to display TIFF images? If so, how could Tracy get and install it?

Chapter 3 and the hands-on activities and case projects in this chapter provide examples of common problems you can use to help develop your own problem-solving skills and get experience with common problems support agents encounter.

Chapter Summary

*   Although computer problems vary widely, a few categories of problems account for most user contacts with help desks, hotlines, and support centers. The categories include problems with hardware, software, users, documentation, vendors, operating environments,

and network problems. Network problems are often a combination of several other categories.

- Common hardware problems include difficulties with the installation of hardware components, compatibility of new or upgraded components with other hardware in a system, hardware configuration problems, and actual malfunctions that require repair or replacement of components.

- Common software problems include difficulties with installation (although these problems are less common today than they were with earlier generations of software), incompatibilities with hardware or other software packages, and configuration problems that prevent the software from operating correctly. Other software problems may occur due to bugs or less than optimum system performance.

- User problems are caused by mistakes (which all users make), misunderstandings about how a system operates to perform a task, the purchase of the wrong product, inadequate training, failure to read product documentation, and forgotten procedures or passwords.

- Other problems include difficulties with documentation (such as poor organization and incorrect or incomplete information), vendor problems (such as a tendency of some vendors to oversell their products, misrepresent product features, deliver software with known bugs, or deliver products later than they were promised), operating environment problems (such as problems with electricity, furniture, security, data backup and contingency planning), and network problems (which can often be traced to hardware software, systems, or other categories of problems).

- The greater the variety of problems and solutions user support agents learn about, the better the knowledge and experience they will have at their command when they tackle new problems.

Key Terms

automatic update—A feature of operating systems and applications software that periodically checks a vendor's Web site for updates that the vendor recommends be installed to bring the version of the software up to current specifications.

bug—An error in a computer program that occurs when a programmer writes incorrectly coded instructions during program development.

burn-in test—A hardware test during which a new computer or component is operated continuously over a 48- to 72-hour period in an

185

attempt to discover obvious problems and identify any marginal or temperature-sensitive components.

configuration problem—A difficulty that occurs when the hardware or software options are set incorrectly for the computer environment in which a component must operate.

conflict—A state in which a computer component uses systems resources (CPU, memory, or peripheral devices) in a way that is incompatible with another component.

freeware—Computer software for which no purchase price or licensing fee is charged.

incompatible—A term used to describe computer components that cannot operate together successfully in the same system. *See also* **conflict**.

installation software—Special-purpose utility software that aids in the installation (or setup) of other software packages; it is able to detect and correctly configure software for most hardware and operating environments.

malware—A program with harmful or malicious intent that disrupts the normal operation of a computer or network, or attempts to steal information or money as a result of its operation.

open source software—Software that is developed collaboratively by a loose-knit group of programmers who agree to freely share their efforts to improve and debug a software product; the source code (and the program) is available without cost.

patch—A replacement for one or a few modules in a software package to fix one or more known bugs.

performance problem—A category of computer problems in which a system is minimally operational, but does not operate as efficiently as it should; it often results from poor interaction between hardware and software.

Plug and Play standards—A set of protocols followed by hardware and operating system vendors that specify the communication methods and rules that an operating system uses to recognize and incorporate hardware components into an operational system.

quick start behavior—A tendency among computer users to skip reading an installation manual and attempt to get new hardware or software installed and operational as rapidly as possible.

release—A distribution of a software program that contains some new features not found in the original program.

service pack (or service release)—A software revision that contains both updates and patches to fix documented problems with a version of a program.

shareware—Commercial software that users can try with a vendor's permission during an evaluation period (usually 30 days) prior to making a purchase decision.

update—A bug-fix distribution that repairs known problems in a previous version or release of a software package.

upgrade—A new version of an existing program that is sold at a reduced cost to owners of a previous version of the program.

vaporware—Hardware or software products that appear in ads or press releases but are not yet available for sale.

version—A software package that contains significant new features and is usually the result of a substantially rewritten program.

workaround—A procedure or operation that accomplishes the same result as the original feature that currently does not work due to a bug or other malfunction.

Check Your Understanding

Answers to Check Your Understanding questions are in Appendix A.

1. True or False? Most hardware problems are the result of component failures due to incorrect voltages in a computer system.

2. During _____, a computer system is operated nonstop for a 48- to 72-hour period to give marginal components a chance to fail.

3. Most hardware problems occur:

   a. at the time a component is purchased and installed

   b. when the component becomes obsolete

   c. after the warranty period has expired

   d. hardware problems are almost nonexistent today

4. True or False? Plug and Play-compatible hardware guarantees that users will not experience installation problems with new or upgraded hardware.

5. Which of the following hardware devices is most likely to fail during the operation of a computer system?

    a. CPU

    b. memory

    c. hard disk drive

    d. peripheral adapter card

6. A mismatch between the type of printer connected to a system and the software printer driver installed is an example of a:

    a. design problem

    b. conflict

    c. bug

    d. configuration problem

7. A(n) _____ is a situation in which two software packages use system resources in different and incompatible ways.

8. True or False? By the time a software package has gone through extensive testing and quality assurance, all the bugs have generally been eliminated.

9. A substantially rewritten software package that contains major new features is called a(n):

    a. update

    b. patch

    c. new release

    d. new version

10. A procedure or method to accomplish the same result as a feature that does not work due to a bug or other malfunction is called a(n) _____ .

11. True or False? A computer system that operates at some level, but not as efficiently as it should, is called vaporware.

12. True or False? One difference between end users and computer professionals is that the latter do not make mistakes while using a computer.

13. Performance problems in a computer system are usually due to:

    a. hardware problems

    b. software problems

    c. both hardware and software problems

    d. neither hardware nor software problems

14. True or False? Freeware and shareware may cause compatibility problems when installed because they may not be tested as extensively as commercial software.

15. _____ is a tendency among users to want to get a new hardware or software product operational without reading the installation documentation.

16. List three strategies for dealing with users who forget important information.

17. True or False? Freeware and open source are two words for the same kinds of software.

18. A revision to a software package that contains a collection of patches to fix documented problems with a program is called:

    a. vaporware

    b. a new release

    c. freeware

    d. a service pack

19. Computer components that cannot operate together in the same system are called:

    a. incompatible

    b. a bug

    c. shareware

    d. malware

20. _____ is a feature of an operating system or applications program that periodically checks a vendor's Web site for modifications that can be downloaded and installed in a user's system.

Discussion Questions

1. Why do support staff members rarely know in advance whether a specific problem is hardware-related or software-related?

2. Do you agree or disagree with the statement: "Network problems are not really a unique category of computer problems; all network problems are basically either hardware or software problems, or both"? Explain your reasoning.

3. Why are so many computer problems traceable to user mistakes? Describe a recent mistake you made as a computer user. Do you think it is a common or rare mistake? What could be done in the future, if anything, to prevent the kind of mistake you made?

4. Is freeware or shareware easier or more difficult to support and troubleshoot than commercial software? Explain your answer.

5. A user made the following statement: "With the prices we pay for software today, you would think that vendors would be able to provide programs that work correctly out-of-the-box; instead we get buggy software that requires constant updates." Do you agree or disagree? Explain your position.

6. An engineering company has a policy that its end users should never make changes to the system Registry or perform hardware repairs of any kind on their office systems. Do you think the policy is a good one? Discuss the pros and cons of this policy.

Hands-On Activities

The Hands-On Activities in this chapter provide opportunities to gain additional experience with troubleshooting and problem solving. The activities vary in difficulty from easy to challenging. They require a variety of problem-solving skills and information resources to find the answers. Use them as practice to build your troubleshooting and problem-solving skills. Do not spend too long on any one project. If you run into a roadblock and can't find the answer, ask your instructor or colleagues for assistance.

Activity 4-1

Find Excel's data analysis tools. A user wants to use the advanced statistical functions and features in the Excel spreadsheet program because she does a lot of statistical work in her job. She has a book that explains how to use these features. She clicked the Tools menu in Excel but did not find the Data Analysis menu item that the book had described. She also tried to use some of the built-in statistical functions that are included in Excel according to the book; however, whenever she entered one of the function names, the error message, "#NAME?" appeared. Describe the steps the user would need to take to be able to use the statistical functions.

Activity 4-2

Explore the msconfig program. Find the utility program on a Windows system named msconfig. If you can find it, where is it located? Use the msconfig help system to learn about the features of the program. Write a brief description of its purpose and indicate for whom it would be useful.

Activity 4-3

Evaluate hard drive symptoms. A frantic user called a help desk to report that his hard disk drive did not appear to work. He related that the drive produced neither noise nor any indication of obvious activity. In fact, the drive light on the PC case was not lighting up. The user fears the worst: a hard disk drive failure. List as many alternative explanations you can think of for the behavior he describes.

Activity 4-4

Unresponsive software. A user contacted a help desk with a report that he has an error message on his screen that says, "Program Not Responding." Research possible causes of this error message and suggest one or more ways to fix the problem.

Activity 4-5

Low disk space. A user continually gets a warning message that his disk space is low: "You are running out of disk space on drive C:". He says he knows his disk space is low, but he doesn't have time to deal with the problem. He would like to know if there is a way to disable the message. Can this warning be disabled? If so, how? Is it advisable to do so? Write an e-mail response to the user with your answer.

Activity 4-6

Set up an automatic time log. A user who is away from her office for much of the day wants to keep a simple log of contacts and short notes about client meetings she has throughout the day. She wants to include the current date and time for each entry in the log. She says a work colleague has an icon on her laptop that automatically opens Notepad and inserts an entry in the file that contains the current date and time. Then, it is easy for her colleague to write a short note about a meeting with a client. She wants you to help her set up her laptop with a similar feature. Write a brief piece of documentation listing the steps she should take to accomplish this task.

Activity 4-7

Recover Word's Normal.dot file. A trainer who instructs classes in Microsoft Word reports that one of her students, Robin, accidentally saved a document as Normal.dot. Each time a student at that computer in the training center opens a new Word document, Robin's document appears instead of a new, blank document. She says she has tried to fix the problem, but hasn't hit on a solution yet. What would you suggest to the trainer? Is there more than one solution to this problem?

Activity 4-8

Decipher an Internet error message. An e-mail from a user says: "I have been using Google to search for information on the Web. I received a message, 'Error 403: Forbidden,' when I attempted to access a Web site that interests me. What does this message mean, and how can I view the page?" Research the problem and write a response to the e-mail.

Activity 4-9

Memory errors. A help desk supervisor wrote the following in an e-mail: "As our users' PCs age, we are seeing indications that some of the RAM modules are beginning to experience intermittent failures. Microsoft apparently has a Windows Memory Diagnostic utility program that is available free. Please research the memory utility program and let me know whether it is easy enough to use that we could run it on all our users' PCs." Write a response to the supervisor's request.

Activity 4-10

No volume. A user received a message: "Windows cannot display the volume control on the taskbar because the Volume Control program has not been installed. To install it use Add/Remove Programs in Control Panel." Describe the steps you would take to solve this problem for the user. Is there more than one solution to this problem?

Activity 4-11

What's in a Quick Start guide? Review the Yahoo Quick Start tutorial (shown in Figure 4-4) that is located at **help.yahoo.com/ tutorials/mmail/mmail/mm_basics1.html**, and answer these questions:

1. What are the main topics covered in the Quick Start tutorial?

2. Were the topics covered the minimum required to get started quickly with Yahoo! Mail?

3. What topics were not covered? How did the Quick Start tutorial handle omitted topics?

4. Briefly describe the changes you would make to the Quick Start guide to Yahoo! Mail to make it more useful to users who want a quick way to get started using this service.

Activity 4-12

Improve a troubleshooting strategy. Visit the following Web site, which describes some troubleshooting strategies for common problems users encounter: **www.edgarcaycehouston.org/HALPC-SLC/Troubleshooting/Troubleshooting.htm**. Select a category of problem with which you are familiar. Are the strategies the author recommends effective? Based on your own experience, add two troubleshooting strategies to the category you selected.

Activity 4-13

Edit the Windows Vista Registry

Warning: This activity should not be attempted on a PC for which you do not have permission to edit the Registry. You must have administrator login privileges to perform these tasks.

1. Read a tutorial that covers the basic use of the Registry editor, REGEDIT, at **www.informit.com/articles/article. aspx?p=1151313**.

2. Complete one or more of the brief exercises at **www. computerperformance.co.uk/vista/vista_registry_ tweaks.htm**.

3. Verify that the exercise(s) you completed in Step 2 had the intended effect on the operations of Windows Vista.

Case Projects

1. Document Internet Error Messages

Find out the error messages users are most likely to encounter on the Web. Learn what the messages mean, and what users should do to work around each type of error. Then write a brief document intended for end users that lists the common Internet error messages, provides users with information about each message, and explains how to work around each error, if possible.

2. Disk Space Management at Maps Unlimited

The user support group at Maps Unlimited, a company that makes computerized maps for urban planners, has analyzed the log of support calls it received in the past month to identify the ten most common calls. As part of a project to write model answers for end users' frequently asked questions, the support staff wants you to research and write a short document on disk space management. The support staff finds that many callers with disk space complaints say that they have run out of space on their hard drives. Most of these calls come from active e-mail users and users who frequently download information from the Web. Other calls come from users who have older PCs that were purchased with smaller hard drives than those available today. In many of these cases, the hard drives on their Windows PCs are now full, and they are looking for a solution that doesn't require replacing the hard drive.

Investigate common ways that the space on a hard drive gets filled up. You may want to compare your ideas, experiences, and findings with those of your coworkers or classmates. Then write a document for support staff to provide to end users that briefly describes the reasons that hard drives become full and the procedures you recommend to free up disk space. Organize your document as a checklist, but include any explanations and precautions you feel are necessary before a user embarks on a procedure to reclaim disk space on a hard drive.

3. Problem-Solving Slideshow for Support Staff

Prepare a slideshow presentation that could be used to train new user support staff. The topic of your slideshow should be selected from the following list:

- Common hardware problems and how to solve them
- Common software configuration problems

- Typical user problems and ideas to prevent them

- Tools support staff can use to diagnose common problems

- The most difficult computer problem I have ever solved, and how I solved it

Make your slideshow presentation a professional one that you would be proud to show others as an example of your work. If possible, present your slideshow to your school or work colleagues. Ask for suggestions on how to improve your slideshow.

CHAPTER 5

Help Desk Operation

In this chapter, you will learn about:

◎ Help desk operation procedures

◎ The multilevel support model

◎ The incident management process

◎ Best practices in help desk services

◎ The physical layout of help desk work areas

◎ Job stress in help desk work

◎ Hardware and software tools used by support agents, managers, and end users

◎ Help desk trends

Recall that an organization can choose to provide support to its employees and external clients in several ways. Some organizations opt for informal peer support for workers who use computers. Others choose a more formal structure, such as a user support group or an information center, or they delegate computer support to an Information Technology department. Some organizations outsource all or part of the computer support function. Although the specific structure may differ, many companies organize their user support function internally as a help desk because: (1) the help desk is usually very visible, and its services are well-publicized to employees or clients; and (2) it provides a single point of contact for users who need technical support. To make contact with a help desk, users might visit a physical location, call a hotline, send an e-mail message, or go to a Web site. In each case, users interact with a help desk agent to ask questions or request help with problems.

A help desk operation, like other support methods, can be costly. Therefore, organizations that have a substantial investment in end-user computer systems or a large group of external users continually search for cost-effective ways to provide technical support. This chapter describes a number of strategies and tools that help desks employ to effectively and efficiently support end users.

What Is a Help Desk?

A help desk is an organization that provides a single point of contact for users in need of technical support, whether they are internal workers or external clients. Having a single point of contact streamlines the process for end users and agents. In a user support center with multiple points of contact, a user may not know whom to contact about a specific problem. For example, an end user may not be able to determine whether a problem is hardware related or network related. If hardware repairs are handled by an electronic repair department or a vendor and network problems are handled by a network administrator, an end user could make several calls to the wrong contacts while trying to resolve a problem. Furthermore, an agent who responds to an incident might not have the expertise to answer a particular question. The agent may have to refer the user to a different agent or even a different department for an answer. In extreme cases, multiple points of contact may disagree about the source of a problem or the strategy to resolve it. To avoid situations like these, many organizations have consolidated their user support function into one help desk operation—at least from an end user's perspective.

Although the specifics of the support provided in telephone, face-to-face, e-mail, and Web contacts differ somewhat, there are also similarities in the way help desks organize and provide support and in the kinds of skills they require. Some help desks provide a wide range of support services like those you learned about in Chapter 1. Others focus on limited services. For example, a telephone support hotline for a popular software package will probably limit its services to questions about that specific product. In contrast, the help desk in a large medical center may provide a more extensive array of computer support services to its employees. Whether a help desk includes a hotline, information center, training assistance, support consultant, or any number of other services, its purpose is the same: to keep end users productive by providing them with a single point of contact for resolving computer problems.

Organizations structure their help desks differently, depending on several factors, including whether their users are internal or external, the number of users and products they support, and the organization's goals and objectives for computer support. Organizations frequently structure their help desks into several levels (or tiers) of support, sometimes called a **multilevel support model** or frontline/backline model, shown in Figure 5-1.

Level 1 Support	Level 2 Support	Level 3 Support	Level 4 Support
Customer	Incident Screener	Product Specialists	Technical Support	Support Manager

Figure 5-1   Multilevel support model

In this model, each level is staffed by a worker with different skills. The level 1 incident screener (also called an incident dispatcher or receptionist) is usually an entry-level worker. Higher levels require greater knowledge and experience. A level 2 product specialist is usually a more experienced help desk worker; a level 3 technical support position is often staffed by a programmer, product designer, or engineer; and level 4 support is typically staffed by a supervisor or manager. In small help desk organizations, external vendor support may augment the services provided by the internal help desk staff.

Multilevel help desks and support groups vary in the number of levels they have. In general, help desks try to handle as many incidents at the lowest possible level in the support hierarchy in order to save their higher-level, more experienced staff resources for situations which most require their skills. Lower-level help desk staff members usually have higher-level, more experienced staff members to whom they can refer complex problems and even difficult callers.

Regardless of the help desk structure, all help desks have the same goal: to promote client satisfaction by effectively and efficiently resolving problems and questions. To accomplish this goal, help desk staff use well-defined processes, tools, and strategies.

The Incident Management Process

Incident management is a well-defined, formal process that help desk staff follow to handle problem incidents, obtain the information that end users request or solve an end user's problem, and close the incident. Because it refers to telephone, face-to-face, e-mail, and Web-based forms of support, incident management is a more general term than call management. **Call management** describes the steps in handling primarily telephone contacts between end users and support agents. Figure 5-2 shows the major steps in the incident management process. Each of these steps is described below.

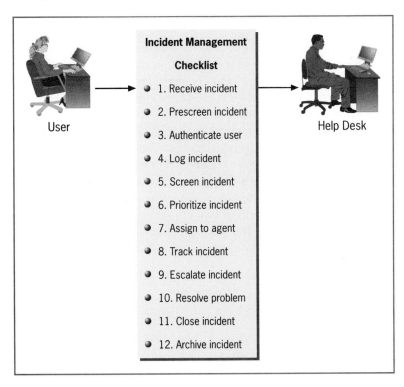

Figure 5-2   Incident management process

Receive the Incident

The incident management process described here applies primarily to telephone calls; however, many of the same steps apply to face-to-face, e-mail, and Web-based contacts with a help desk. Although the specific steps and tools differ somewhat for written and verbal communications, the general flow and communication guidelines described here still apply.

Whether an incident is received in person, via a telephone call, in an e-mail message, or through a Web-based contact, the first step for the agent is to establish a relationship with the end user. Some support groups follow a specific script when contact with a user begins. The script can be in the form of a recommended greeting in a phone conversation or a predefined introductory paragraph that is inserted in a reply to an e-mail message. For example, in a telephone support call, the level 1 help desk agent may confirm the name of the support organization and provide her or his own first name. The agent may ask the name of the person who is calling. Other common early incident management tasks include providing a warning that the incident may be monitored (this is a legal requirement in most states) and an apology for any wait time. If a callback is likely, the support staff may request the caller's phone number or e-mail address. As you will learn later in this chapter, some of these tasks can be automated. In all incident-handling situations, the guidelines for client service, communications, and interpersonal skills described in Chapter 2 apply to each step in the incident management process.

Prescreen the Incident

Incidents may be prescreened manually at support level 1, or by an automated call distribution system, as you will learn later in this chapter.

Prescreening is a filtering process that helps agents identify and respond to simple requests for information quickly, sometimes without even initiating an official incident. Some help desks do not prescreen incidents. If their incident management procedures include prescreening, a level 1 worker asks questions to determine if the incident is a simple request for information that the incident screener can provide. Many help desk incidents fall into this category. For example, a user may want to know when the next version of a software package will be released and whether a known problem will be fixed in the new release. The user may want to receive product information or find out where to buy the product. Information request calls can frequently be handled quickly and easily at support level 1 and then closed without proceeding to the steps below.

Authenticate the User

If an incident is more than a simple request for information, many help desks or hotline services use an **authentication procedure**. In this step, an agent determines whether the help desk is authorized to handle an incident and to provide information or services to a user. Authentication (also called an entitlement verification) may involve asking a user for a product ID number, product serial number, model number, or software license number. In other situations, the screener may ask for the end user's name (and perhaps department or e-mail address) in order to query a database to learn whether the user is a registered owner of a product and which level of help desk support services, if any, the user has purchased. If the user is a client on a pay-per-call basis, the staff member may obtain billing information from the user (usually a credit card or purchase order number). Like prescreening, authentication is a filtering process. The help desk agent determines whether the user has a legitimate claim to support services, and if so, at what service level. Once a staff member has authenticated a user, the incident-handling process can begin.

Log the Incident

In the incident **logging** step, an agent begins documenting the incident. The help desk agent may make an initial entry in a problem log, on a trouble report form, or in an incident tracking database. If user information already exists in a product registration database or user support knowledge base, logging an incident may be a simple matter of clicking a button that opens a new incident record linked to the client's user record. Some incident management software packages automatically fill in the user contact information. Figure 5-3 shows an example of a help desk incident log.

Incident Tracking # [   ]

Incident Tracking Log

User: _____   Dept: _____   Phone: _____

E-mail address: _____

Date opened: [/ /]   Time opened: [   ]   Taken by: [   ]

Problem Category:
- ❏ Request for info   ❏ Question   ❏ Complaint
- ❏ Hardware   ❏ Software   ❏ LAN   ❏ Internet

Priority Code: [   ]

Problem Description: _____

Incident assigned to: _____

Action Taken: _____

Incident escalated to: _____   Incident escalated to: _____

Incident Resolution: _____

Incident closed by: _____ Date closed: [/ /] Time closed: [   ]

Figure 5-3   Incident tracking log

Screen the Incident

During incident **screening**, the help desk agent asks a series of questions to categorize and describe the incident. Incidents are often categorized in one of the following ways:

- Requests for information that could not be handled during pre-screening: "Will the latest release fix my font problem?"

- Questions: "How do I get rid of commas in the numbers on my spreadsheet?"

- Problems: "My printer works with every known software package in the world except yours."

- Complaints: "Your software is so full of bugs it locks up my computer every time I run it."

- Work (or service) orders: "Will you please upgrade the operating system software on my machine so that I can use the latest version of Internet Explorer?"

In addition, the support agent enters a brief written description of the request, question, problem, complaint, or work order into the problem log or incident tracking database. An experienced help desk staff agent learns to capture the essential facts of a problem report in a few key words or phrases. Although lengthy, verbatim details of the problem description are usually not necessary, the support agent should include relevant facts that might be useful in solving the problem. The following is an example of a problem description:

QuickBooks icon missing from Windows Vista desktop after reboot this a.m.

When an incident is contained in an e-mail message or received via a Web-based contact, the user's entire correspondence may be captured in a database or included in the problem log.

Prioritize the Incident

Based on the category and the nature of the problem or request, the support agent assigns the incident a priority code. A **priority code** indicates how serious the problem is, how many users are affected, and the consequence of not addressing the problem immediately. Help desk staff may determine that a problem affects only one user and is therefore a lower priority than an incident in which a malfunction in a network affects an entire department. Examples of priority codes used in some support organizations are: 1 – urgent; 2 – high priority; 3 – medium priority; and 4 – low priority.

204

For example, the network equipment provider Cisco defines these priority levels in its Technical Assistance Center:

- Priority 1—The network is down; no workaround is available; and business processes are at a critical stage.

- Priority 2—The network is badly degraded; business processes are impacted; and no workaround is possible.

- Priority 3—The network is degraded, but most business processes are working.

- Priority 4—Caller needs support for installation or configuration, or information on a Cisco product.

Instead of assigning priority codes, some help desks simply distribute incidents to support staff on a first-in, first-out (FIFO) basis.

During their training, help desk agents are provided with guidelines to help them prioritize incidents. Some organizations use incident management software that automatically assigns a priority code to a problem report. The priority code is frequently based on the type of call, its severity, the number of users affected, and the help desk's policy for handling that type of incident. For users who have purchased a service level agreement, the user's service level may also affect the priority.

When working with an internal user, a support agent may ask the user to help set an incident's priority, or to agree to a priority level. Consensus about an incident's priority ensures that those involved have the same expectations for help desk performance. Some support organizations defer to a user's priority assessment if a user and an agent disagree on the priority level. Furthermore, a priority level may change during the life of an incident. For example, a problem may be defined initially as a priority 1 problem because a network is down. If a quick workaround can be implemented and the network becomes operational, the problem that caused the downtime may be reprioritized to a priority 2 or priority 3.

The type of incident and its priority often determine the queue into which an incident will then be placed. A **queue** is a waiting line, like the line at the cash registers in a grocery store. Just as a grocery store may have separate lines or queues for regular, express, and self checkout, a help desk may have queues for different types and priorities of incidents. The incident queues in a help desk may be defined by product, by priority code, or on any other basis that the help desk uses to allocate and assign incidents to support staff.

Assign the Incident

If the level 1 help desk staff cannot resolve an incident immediately, they may assign the incident to another staff member who has the technical expertise to provide the information, respond to the request, or solve the problem quickly and effectively. Help desks often maintain a list of staff members who specialize in specific products or types of problems. In some automated incident management systems, the process of assigning an incident simply moves it from one queue to another.

New help desk workers sometimes find it difficult to determine the best place to refer an incident they cannot resolve. However, entry-level staff members usually learn quickly who among the experienced technical support staff have good problem-solving skills, give quick and correct answers for a specific type of problem, and can help deal with incidents effectively so that user contacts can be handled at the lowest possible support level in a multilevel structure.

Track the Incident

Whenever the essential facts associated with an incident change, such as when additional problem information is received, a new priority code is assigned, or the incident is assigned to a different staff member, the help desk staff update the incident information record. Incident **tracking** refers to the process of updating the incident record with information about a problem as it progresses. An automated help desk system often records in a database the date and time of each incident tracking entry; this provides a complete record of what happened and when. Incident tracking provides an important history of a problem, how it was handled, and how it was resolved. A record of how an incident was handled can be useful for help desk staff when they encounter a similar problem. Incident tracking information is also important input when measuring the quality of incident management, evaluating the performance of help desk workers, and identifying support staff training needs.

Escalate the Incident

If initial attempts to resolve a user's problem are unsuccessful, most support groups have policies and procedures to escalate an incident. Incident **escalation** is a normal process in which a problem is transferred to a higher level of support that is better able to handle more difficult problems.

In some automated incident management systems, the escalation process is automatic. For example, help desk software can often be programmed to escalate an incident to the next level automatically if a support agent cannot resolve it within a predetermined period of time. If a problem has been active, but unresolved, for more than a defined amount of time (usually a few hours), an incident management system may automatically display it on a support manager's screen, where he or she can monitor it closely to make sure that staff members are progressing toward a solution.

In a small support organization, escalation may be to an external vendor who has the expertise to augment the local help desk's services.

In all escalation situations, whether formal or informal, manual or automated, assigning of ownership of a problem incident is important. A problem incident should not get lost as it moves from agent to agent, or in some cases, as it get referred to an outside vendor for resolution. Help desks need to have mechanisms in place to ensure that the ownership of an incident either stays with the level 1 agent, who is responsible for follow up, or that ownership clearly passes to an upper level staff member or supervisor as the incident is escalated.

Resolve the Incident

Ideally, a help desk staff member will be able to resolve all users' problems and questions. In the incident **resolution** step, a user's problem is solved or a complaint noted or referred to product designers as a suggestion for the next product revision cycle. Alternately, incident resolution may involve giving the client authorization to return a product for replacement or a refund. Incident resolution doesn't necessarily mean the user or client is completely satisfied, however.

A small percentage of all calls, usually those that involve complaints about product bugs or features, may not be satisfactorily resolved during the incident management process. Obviously, one of the goals of a help desk is to minimize the percentage of problems that cannot be resolved satisfactorily, but the percentage is rarely zero. The help desk goal, however, is a situation in which users receive the information or problem resolution they need and feel that the problem has been resolved to their satisfaction.

Close the Incident

In incident **closing**, a support agent may review the steps the help desk took to solve a problem. An agent may also get feedback from the user about her or his satisfaction level. The agent usually terminates an incident by thanking the user for calling or sending an e-mail and inviting the user to contact the help desk if further problems arise or if the recommended solution to the problem does not work. Closing the incident may also involve the agent making additional entries on a problem log or in a database to indicate the disposition of the problem and how it was resolved.

Incident closing can be a challenge, especially in a telephone support environment. Some users either can't accept that their problem cannot be resolved, or don't want to hang up because they enjoy talking about technology with help desk staff. These cases fall into the category of difficult calls, which you learned about in Chapter 2.

Archive the Incident

Closed incidents are often retained in the incident management system for some predefined period in case the user calls back or sends a follow-up e-mail. A help desk's policies usually specify how long a closed incident is retained before it is archived. An incident **archive** is a database or paper file used to store and retain records relating to closed incidents. In an automated system, archived incidents are deleted from the active incident management system. In a manual system that uses written problem logs or trouble reports, the resolved incident archive process may simply involve moving a folder of resolved incidents from one file drawer to another.

Incident archives provide data that can be incorporated into a help desk knowledge base. Recall from Chapter 3 that a knowledge base is an organized collection of information, articles, procedures, tips, and previous problems with known solutions that can serve as a resource for support agents. In some organizations, the closing process may require an agent to enter the incident information into a help desk knowledge base. Support staff members can then search the knowledge base to find previously solved problems with the same or similar characteristics as an active incident. Incident archives may be analyzed to produce statistical reports of the frequency of various categories of incidents.

Reports on the frequency of solved problems are useful to help desk managers in making staffing decisions and analyzing help desk performance trends over time, as you'll learn in Chapter 6.

The incident management steps described here are examples of the kinds of activities that occur during incident processing. Each organization's support policies and procedures may dictate a somewhat different sequence of incident processing events, based on unique business requirements, user expectations, help desk procedures, and an organization's resources. Training for entry-level help desk workers usually includes an orientation and hands-on practice with the specific steps the staff is expected to follow.

ON THE WEB

Mary Baldwin College describes its user support incident management procedures for faculty and staff and explains how priorities for problem resolution are set on its Web site at **academic.mbc.edu/cis/PDF/13.4_User_Support_-_Computer_&_Telephony.pdf**. The University of Connecticut School of Law provides information about its help desk policies and procedures at **www.law.uconn.edu/infosys/sla.htm**.

Help Desk Service Best Practices

Several attempts have been made in recent years to define a set of industry-wide best practices for organizations that provide and manage help desk and computer services. **Best practices** are procedures, tools, and methods that successful support groups employ; these practices often set apart very successful support operations from mediocre ones. One widely followed set of guidelines is the **Information Technology Infrastructure Library (ITIL)**, which is designed to help organizations align and integrate their computer services with their business objectives. The ITIL was initially published in the United Kingdom, based on earlier work on service management objectives initiated by IBM. The ITIL is intended as a "framework" rather than an industry standard in the traditional sense.

The ITIL is an extensive series of publications that document guidelines organizations should consider as they design and manage a help desk or information services function. In a full implementation of the ITIL framework, the guideline documents are often supplemented with purchases of software products and consulting services.

The ITIL best practices describe how successful organizations handle matters such as:

- *Incident management*, which involves any disruption of normal services that affects a user or the business. The goal of incident management is to restore computer services to normal operation as quickly as possible.

- *Problem management*, which are proactive strategies to find and fix the root cause of problem incidents. The goal of problem management is to anticipate, repair, and eliminate the root causes of computer problems.

- *Change management*, which is designed to help organizations plan for the constant changes that occur due to the use of technology. The goal of change management is to develop plans to minimize the impact of technology changes (to hardware, software, networking, and operational procedures) on a business.

- *Release management*, which is the implementation side of change management. The goal of release management is to educate users and provide for a smooth implementation of technology change that minimizes the impact on a business.

- *Configuration management*, which is a database of hardware and software assets used in an organization. The goal of configuration management is to help an organization identify, control, monitor, plan, and audit its investment in technology.

ON THE WEB

For a brief introduction to some basic ITIL guidelines related to help desk operations, read a white paper prepared by ManageEngine, an ITIL software provider, at **manageengine. adventnet.com/products/service-desk/itil-whitepaper.pdf**.

For another perspective on help desk industry best practices, read an industry white paper, *"31 Best Practices for the Service Desk,"* based on research by Forrester Research at **redmondmag.com/techlibrary/resources.asp?id=497** (free registration is required to download the report as a PDF file).

A full enterprise-wide implementation of the ITIL framework is an expensive, ongoing process which includes substantial software and consulting costs. However, the implementation of help desk industry best practices and benchmarks often results in a more effective and efficient help desk operation that is better integrated with an organization's business objectives.

Physical Layout of Help Desk Work Areas

In most large-scale help desk operations, each support agent works in a cubicle that is enclosed on three sides by carpeted wall panels. The wall panels are from four to six feet high, depending on whether visual contact with coworkers is deemed desirable and depending on the need to reduce equipment and background noise. A typical cubicle is eight to ten feet long by six to eight feet wide.

In each cubicle, a support agent sits at a desk that includes space for one or more computer systems. Support agents have their own PCs on which they run incident management software as well as the specific software packages or hardware components they support. Support agents may also have other computer systems in their cubicle with different hardware and operating system platforms, which they can use to replicate a user's problem. In some situations, computers for problem replication may be located in a separate room where they can be shared among support staff. Mainframe computer access (where necessary) may be available through a terminal emulator on a support agent's desktop, or through a separate terminal located in the cubicle. The work cubicle may contain a reference library of manuals and information on the specific products that an agent supports.

Workplace ergonomic issues, important for end users in general, are even more critical for help desk staff members who provide telephone support. Chapter 9 discusses ergonomic concerns that apply to the design of workstations for end users as well as help desk staff.

210

To answer or initiate telephone calls, most support agents prefer a wireless headset rather than a standard telephone handset. The headset helps prevent neck and shoulder ailments and permits considerable freedom of motion when it is necessary to confer with a coworker or supervisor about a problem. Wireless headsets, which often use Bluetooth technology, are an improvement over older model headsets which are connected by a cable to an agent's computer.

ON THE WEB

To view a tutorial by Jim Hanks on how telephone headsets can affect call center productivity, visit **telecom.hellodirect. com/docs/Tutorials/Productivity.1.080701.asp**.

Job Stress in Help Desk Work

Job stress is a common complaint of help desk workers. **Job stress** results from the physical and emotional responses help desk workers experience when there is a mismatch between the personal characteristics and needs of a worker and the requirements of their position. Examples of the mismatch include factors such as the following:

- Inadequate training

- Lack of qualifications or experience for a position

- Inadequate resources (equipment, software, and information) to perform tasks

- Lack of attention to ergonomic issues in the workplace

- Unrealistic management expectations (including workload volume that exceeds resources to handle it, lack of adequate breaks, and long work shifts)

- Abusive callers, or those with unrealistic service or product expectations

- Poor help desk management practices (including inadequate communication within an organization and unclear employee evaluation and promotion criteria)

- Involvement in office politics

Job stress may result in a variety of health-related problems including fatigue and insomnia, head and body aches, inability to concentrate on job tasks, expression of anger, substance abuse, low morale, and low self-esteem. Solutions to reduce the impact of job stress include personal stress management strategies and organizational change.

 Strategies for dealing with workplace stress include getting enough exercise and sleep, eating a healthy diet, reducing alcohol and nicotine consumption, and using time and work management techniques to prioritize work tasks.

211

ON THE WEB

A comprehensive Web site devoted to job-related stress maintained by the National Institute of Occupational Safety and Health is at **www.cdc.gov/niosh/stresswk.html**.

ON THE WEB

To learn more about personal stress management strategies, use the resources at **www.helpguide.org/mental/work_stress_management.htm**. The Web site includes several articles on reducing stress in the workplace.

The working conditions and physical environment of help desk work areas can either contribute to job stress or diminish it. Work areas should be designed to reduce distractions from excessive noise, motion, and other interruptions as much as possible. Frequent and scheduled breaks are useful stress reduction tools. Some support groups provide employee lounges, cafeterias, and break rooms with refreshments, televisions, pool tables, video games, and other diversions.

ON THE WEB

To learn more about organizational changes that can help to reduce workplace stress, read **www.novanthealth.org/eap/tools/Self-Care%20Series%20Stress%20Management%20for%20Managers.pdf**.

A ROLE-PLAYING SCENARIO

This scenario is an excerpt from a meeting between an experienced help desk staff member, Lonnie, and a relatively new help desk agent, Robin. Lonnie has been assigned as a mentor to Robin, and has observed that Robin seems stressed recently. If possible, have fellow students or coworkers play the parts of Lonnie and Robin, and then discuss your feeling about their conversation. In several cases below, Lonnie's responses are blank. Discuss how you would respond if you were Robin's mentor.

LONNIE: I'd like to begin by asking how you feel about your work as a help desk agent after three months on the job.

ROBIN: I like having a job in the help desk, but I don't feel like I fit in very well with the group here.

LONNIE: Why do you feel you don't fit in?

ROBIN: When I can't answer a question and am forced to escalate a trouble report to a tech support person, I feel like I'm not doing my job. And the tech support people I talk to never get back to me on the solution to a problem. So I'm left in the dark about what I did wrong. It is really frustrating to me to be so out-of-the-loop.

LONNIE: (suggest a useful response here)

ROBIN: It seems to me like we get a lot of calls from confused users. I had one last week from a user who has a new PC and couldn't find the icon to run a program he needed because the icon changed slightly and was in a different place on the screen from his old PC. How stupid is that? When I pointed out that he should do a better job of getting to know his PC, he got angry. That was upsetting to me.

LONNIE: (suggest a useful response here)

ROBIN: I don't feel like my training was adequate when I started here. I've been criticized unfairly by some of my coworkers for providing information to users that they say I shouldn't give out. How am I supposed to know what I can and can't say?

LONNIE: Can you give me an example of a situation where you were criticized?

ROBIN: Well, I told one user that I didn't think we would ever upgrade our company PCs to Windows Vista. Someone said I shouldn't make statements like that because it was against company policy. I feel like other members of the help desk team should support each other on things like that.

LONNIE: (suggest a useful response here)

ROBIN: I feel like I am starting to burn out in this job after just three months. At the end of the day, I feel extremely tired and achy. My eyes hurt from staring at my workstation. I feel frustrated that I'm not getting along better. Does this sound like job burnout to you?

Lonnie: (suggest a useful response here)

If you haven't already, as part of Lonnie's responses above, discuss some suggestions Lonnie, as a mentor, could offer based on the comments Robin made during the session.

Help Desk Technology and Tools

Ongoing developments in automation have significantly impacted the help desk industry in recent years. These developments include new and more advanced help desk software packages, computer telephony, and Web support.

Help Desk Software

The incident management process described above often collects, processes, and stores a large volume of incident transactions. Some help desks organize these transactions in a database, in which tables contain detailed information about clients, products, computer configurations, and help desk staff, as well as an archive of solved problems. Transactions occur when links in the database are established between a client and a product (such as a product registration), or between a client, a computer, and a help desk staff member (such as a problem incident report).

A large-scale help desk operation may receive and process hundreds (or even thousands) of incidents every day. A small-scale help desk may handle only a few incidents daily. Commercial software packages are available to help both large- and small-scale help desks manage the volume and processing of support transactions. These packages typically have features and capabilities, described below, that are useful in supporting internal and external clients.

In the paragraphs that follow, you will learn about help desk tools for agents, managers, and end users.

Help Desk Agent Tools

Help desk agents need a variety of tools to be successful. An important tool for agent productivity is often a help desk software package. These tools range from simple, open source packages that small help desks can download and implement (without a cost for the software itself) to enterprise-wide packages with an extensive array of tools for managing help desk activities for internal and external users in a large organization. In the paragraphs that follow, you will learn about features of software packages that serve as important tools for agents.

INCIDENT LOGGING AND TRACKING FEATURES   Help desk software packages include features that allow agents to log and track incidents. They often work in conjunction with a telephone or e-mail system to manage incident queues, set priorities, assign incidents to agents, and escalate incidents when necessary. An incident tracking system is useful even in a very small support center staffed by one or a few workers. No user who needs technical support likes to "get lost in the system." Automated incident management capabilities help support staff keep track of the volume of support incidents, assign incident priorities, and check the status of open incidents. As the size of a help desk staff increases and manual systems become cumbersome, an automated incident management system becomes a requirement.

CLIENT INFORMATION DATABASES   Support incidents invariably involve contacts with people. Help desk packages include capabilities to store, edit, and recall contact and location information about internal clients, external clients, help desk and information systems staff, information resources, and vendors. These packages include a contact database with each contact's name, job title, phone numbers, e-mail addresses, Web site addresses, fax numbers, and other information about clients, staff, and vendors.

LINKS TO PRODUCT INFORMATION   Many users contact a help desk to request product information. A help desk package that contains links to detailed information about hardware, software, networks, and services enables support staff to respond to many common questions regarding product features, limitations, new versions, configuration constraints, known bugs, product availability, and related information. An organization's Web site may provide users with links to product information in order to reduce the level of support staff required to answer requests for information.

ACCESS TO SYSTEM CONFIGURATION INFORMATION   Help desk software typically includes the ability to document hardware, software, and network information about client systems. Although system configuration information about external client systems is useful, it is difficult to collect and keep up to date, unless a service or facilities management contract covers the users' systems. But configuration information is critical to help desk staff members who support internal clients. Some help desk software can scan remote PCs on a network to automatically document their hardware configuration, software licenses, and network connections. A configuration database permits

Much of the configuration checklist information you will learn about in Chapter 9 can be stored in a database.

support agents who must troubleshoot or upgrade a system for an in-house client to easily access basic information about a user's system.

PROBLEM-SOLUTION KNOWLEDGE BASES   A knowledge base (sometimes called a "smart database") used as a support tool contains information about common problems and their solutions. Some knowledge bases are built as user problems are solved and archived. Other knowledge bases with a store of common problems and their solutions can be purchased ready-made. Because a knowledge base of support problems and solutions can be huge and grow daily, the ability to locate relevant information is critical to its effective use. Training for help desk staff often includes practice problems that require them to locate information in a support knowledge base.

The "smart" part of a knowledge base is a set of search tools to help locate past problem situations that are similar to a current problem. Some help desk knowledge bases rely on keyword search strategies to locate problem solutions. Other help desk software incorporates search strategies based on artificial intelligence tools. Expert systems (sequences of IF-THEN rules), neural networks (automated learning systems), case-based reasoning (pattern-matching strategies), and natural language processing (the ability to formulate questions in English) may be incorporated to help support staff quickly locate the specific information in a knowledge base that they need to solve a problem.

DIAGNOSTIC UTILITIES   Some help desk software packages include utility software to assist a support agent in diagnosing a specific problem. Diagnostic software is useful for analyzing the performance of a remote system and identifying potential problem areas. As you learned in Chapter 3, some diagnostic utilities permit support agents to connect directly to a remote client's system, which can facilitate the problem diagnosis and repair process. Using remote access software, support agents can open a window on their system that shows the remote user's PC desktop. When the support agent works in the remote access window, their keystrokes and mouse clicks are performed on the user's system.

COMMUNICATION AND INFORMATION RESOURCE LINKS   Most help desk software packages recognize that connections to communication and information resources are critical for both end users and support agents. These packages frequently include external connections to e-mail and Web resources as well as internal connections to online help files, product documentation, and problem archives.

PRODUCT ORDER ENTRY CAPABILITIES   Marketing is often an important help desk function, because a user's request for information about a product can lead directly to a purchase order for it. Therefore, many help desk software packages include an order-entry capability, which permits a user or a support agent to enter an order online.

Product order entry in a help desk system may be integrated directly with other business systems, such as shipping and invoicing. In this way, a help desk subsystem can be integrated with other enterprise-wide applications.

AGENT TIME MANAGEMENT TOOLS   Help desk software often includes **time management tools**, which are features designed to increase agent productivity. These tools include:

- Calendar management
- Automated reminders
- Meeting and project task scheduling
- Alarms to warn of upcoming events and deadlines
- Collaborative tools (such as the ability to work jointly on a document-writing project)
- To-do lists with priorities
- Project management tools

Help Desk Management Tools

Managers of help desk operations need tools that help them and their team members perform a variety of tasks that fall outside the standard incident management process. This section describes how software packages assist help desks in carrying out management-related functions.

ASSET MANAGEMENT   Many support groups are responsible for technology asset management. They keep track of an organization's inventory of computer hardware, peripherals, software package licenses, network components, spare parts, and related equipment. Many help desk packages offer asset and inventory control features. These capabilities are designed to help the support staff manage an organization's fixed assets (sometimes called capital assets). Computer equipment is often tagged with an asset ID number and recorded in an asset management database, which may be part of the help desk package, or linked to it. The asset management system may also store information about software licenses owned by a company. Because support staff members are often involved in the purchase and installation of computer systems, an automated help desk system is a convenient place to record computer installation information. And because support staff may be involved in moving equipment from one office to another, they can update the asset database at the time of the equipment transfer.

SERVICE MANAGEMENT   Organizations often outsource hardware and peripheral maintenance and repairs to outside vendors. In addition to managing configuration and asset information, some help desk packages include features to manage these hardware service contracts and agreements. These can include the ability to store customers' warranty information and a service history for each product, as well as reminders about when the next preventive maintenance or service is scheduled to be performed and by whom.

SERVICE LEVEL AGREEMENT (SLA) MANAGEMENT Managers of help desk operations are often responsible for service level agreements. A **service level agreement (SLA)** is a contract that defines the expected performance of user support services or external vendor services. Service level agreements may specify that a help desk will respond to internal or external incidents within a defined time period and that incidents will be resolved within another defined time period. For example, an SLA may specify that 90 percent of e-mails will be answered within four hours of their receipt by the help desk. A help desk manager can use the tools in a software package to monitor performance toward meeting the objectives specified in the service level agreement. In turn, a help desk manager may have signed an SLA with one or more of its vendors that specify their performance when the help desk refers a problem for resolution or outsources equipment for repair. In order to manage both internal help desk and external vendor performance expectations, many software packages include service level agreement management tools.

CLIENT FEEDBACK CAPABILITIES Help desks can collect at least two types of user feedback that is useful to an organization. **Client feedback** typically comes in the form of evaluations of the level of user satisfaction with an organization's products or services, as well as satisfaction with specific help desk services.

Measures of satisfaction with products and services can range from complaints about features that don't work as advertised to suggestions for new features. Help desk staff members need a way to capture user feedback and route the information to product designers and engineers. This feedback is often a source of useful ideas for the next round of product planning.

Measures of satisfaction with help desk services can include feedback about the handling of a specific incident, the problem resolution process, or the help desk services in general. Some help desk software packages provide an ability to collect, analyze, and report information from surveys that measure user satisfaction with help desk services. These surveys are an important form of feedback that assists help desk managers and staff to identify strengths and weak points in the quality of services provided.

STATISTICAL REPORTS Help desk software includes built-in statistical reports and dashboards that report on key performance indicators to meet the information needs of help desk staff and management. Reports relating to the abandonment rate (callers who hang up), the number of unresolved incidents by hour and day, the average length

You'll learn more about key performance indicators that are helpful to help desk managers in Chapter 6.

218

of time telephone callers spend on hold, the average length of incident processing (from receipt to closure), the productivity of staff members (incident closure rate), inventory control, performance compared to service level agreement expectations, and statistical summaries of frequently asked questions are examples of predefined reports that are commonly available in help desk software packages. Performance reports may be printed or may be available online at a Web portal, and they may include historical trends and comparisons with performance benchmarks.

CUSTOMIZABLE INTERFACES, FORMS, REPORTS Some help desk software includes features that let a help desk group modify the user interface, toolbars, menus, and data-entry forms the support staff uses. Customization allows a help desk to add or modify fields in the database tables to meet site-specific needs. A report generator that prepares custom reports from database tables is a common feature. Custom reports enable the help desk staff to augment predefined reports with ones designed to address specific staff and management information needs. Some help desk packages include a programming or scripting language that staff can use to write macros or code to support extensions of the basic package.

TELEPHONE SYSTEM INTERFACE Another useful help desk software feature is an ability to interface with a telephone system. Because many help desk support groups deal with a large volume of incoming and outgoing calls, integrated access to an organization's telephone system is important. Automated telephone systems are described later in this chapter.

AUTOMATED INCIDENT MANAGEMENT Some help desk software packages include the ability to define business rules that automate some incident management tasks. For example, in conjunction with an automated telephone answering system or a Web-based trouble report form, business rules within the help desk software may automatically route incidents to a specific agent with special expertise, or to an appropriate problem queue. Other rules may automatically escalate a problem that has been in a queue longer than a predefined amount of time, or has not been resolved and needs focused attention.

Help Desk End User Tools

Although help desk software is intended for agents and their managers, an increasing number of packages include tools that end users can access directly. These tools allow end users to use the Web to locate information about a product or problem, submit an incident, monitor progress on incident resolution, and submit feedback to the help desk on its performance. These tools mean that a user can perform many of the steps related to an incident without direct contact with a help desk agent.

From a user perspective, a help desk incident may be initiated face to face, via a telephone call, or, in an increasing number of cases, via e-mail or Web access. In the latter cases, a user uses an e-mail client or a Web browser to enter and receive incident information. In still other cases, each user installs client software on her or his desktop computer that is used to submit a trouble ticket directly to the help desk software. Web access to a help desk system can provide users with access to information so that simple questions get answered without direct intervention by an agent. Users can also update information about a problem and get an automated status report on the progress toward a problem solution.

The preceding list of help desk software features and capabilities is not in any implied order of importance. Each tool may have greater or lesser importance depending on each help desk group's needs. And although no single help desk package necessarily offers all of these features and capabilities, most packages offer several of them. Selecting a help desk software package from among those on the market (and there are many) is often one of the most important product evaluation decisions a help desk staff makes.

ON THE WEB

The list of companies that sell help desk software packages is long. Some of the most popular packages for large-scale help desk operations are:

- Help Desk Technology HelpSTAR[2008] (**http://edu.helpstar. com/se/software.html**)

- BMC Remedy Service Desk (**documents.bmc.com/ products/documents/27/63/62763/62763.pdf**)

- Epicor IT Service Management (ITSM) (**www.epicor.com/ Products/Pages/ITSM.aspx**)

- HEAT Service & Support (**www.frontrange.com/heat**)

- TechExcel ServiceWise (**www.techexcel.com/products/ servicesuite/servicewise.html**)

Packages targeted primarily at small or mid-scale help desks include:

- Monarch Bay HelpTrac (**www.helptrac.com**)

- Numera Track-It! (**www.numarasoftware.com/Track-It.asp**)

(continues)

220

(continued)

- Manage-IT! (**www.baronsoftware.com**)

- Soffront Customer Helpdesk (**www.soffront.com/crm/ Products/CustomerHelpdesk.asp**)

- ScriptLogic BridgeTrak (**www.helpdesksoftware.com**)

Packages available without charge or at low cost aimed at small help desks:

- Spiceworks (**www.spiceworks.com**)

- Ilient Software's SysAid (**www.ilient.com/web-based- help-desk-software.htm**)

Several of these packages offer downloadable evaluation versions.

Other help desk software vendors are listed at **dir.yahoo.com/ Business_and_Economy/Business_to_Business/Corporate_ Services/Customer_Service/Software/Help_Desk**.

ON THE WEB

For additional information on selecting and implementing a help desk software package, consult these resources:

- BMC Software, a vendor of help desk software tools, provides a white paper on evaluating help desk software packages at **documents.bmc.com/products/ documents/11/29/61129/61129.pdf**.

- TechRepublic offers a call-tracking software evaluation toolkit as a download at **techrepublic.com.com/5129- 6249-10219695.html** (registration required).

- To view a buyer's guide to help desk software, visit **www. helpdesk-guide.com/helpdesk-software-buyers- guide.asp**.

- IssueTrak provides an article that discusses several criteria on how to select a support desk package at **www.issuetrak. com/html/howtoselect.htm**.

HelpSTAR²⁰⁰⁸ Software

The five figures in this section illustrate typical help desk software with a package named HelpSTAR²⁰⁰⁸, which is developed and sold by Help Desk Technology International Corporation (**http://edu. helpstar.com/se/software.html**).

The HelpSTAR²⁰⁰⁸ package is a commercial help desk program, which includes many of the features you just learned about. Like many help desk software packages, HelpSTAR²⁰⁰⁸ has an extensive array of built-in features and is customizable for specific help desk situations.

An academic version of HelpSTAR²⁰⁰⁸ is included on a CD in this book. You can install the academic version to get experience with the features of a help desk software package. HelpSTAR²⁰⁰⁸ is described in more detail in Appendix B, which also includes hands-on activities for HelpSTAR²⁰⁰⁸.

Figure 5-4 shows a sample HelpSTAR²⁰⁰⁸ screen with a new service request (an incident report) from an internal user, Chris Green, an engineer in the design department at Willamette Planning. Chris is unable to connect to Willamette Planning's network, and he called the help desk dispatcher to report the problem. Users with Web access may also submit problem reports via e-mail.

Figure 5-4   HelpSTAR²⁰⁰⁸ service request from user Chris Green

The New Service Request screen shown in Figure 5-4 contains several important elements. The numbers in the feature list below correspond to the numbered bullets shown in the figure:

1. *Ribbon menu*—HelpSTAR[2008]'s user interface is based on Window's ribbon toolbar feature, in which common tasks are represented as menu tabs and icons on the ribbon. For example, a help desk agent can display a user's previous incidents and requests in the History menu tab.

2. *General Information*—This section identifies the request type, the requester, the category, and a request. The incident dispatcher selected the category "Network Support\Server" and gave the request a title to further identify the nature of the problem.

3. *Importance*—These fields allow the agent to identify the priority of the incident from both the user and the dispatcher's perspectives.

4. *Scheduling*—This feature can be used to indicate that an incident or request has a deadline or due date.

5. *Current location*—This field indicates in which queue or status an incident is currently located. Incidents can be reviewed by a dispatcher and assigned to a specific support agent, or entered into a queue according to the category of the incident based on rules the help desk supervisor defines.

6. *Asset/Discovered Item*—This optional field indicates whether a specific piece of equipment is involved in the request.

7. *Memo*—This section allows the agent(s) involved to provide a complete description of the problem, including any notes made by those who work on the problem during its resolution. The Memo window also includes a field showing how much time has been spent on the request.

When help desk agent Beth Markham displays her queue of assigned service requests, she learns that the incident reported by Chris Green has been assigned to her for resolution, as shown in Figure 5-5. Incidents may be assigned to agents manually by a dispatcher, or automatically by application of business rules the help desk supervisors define in HelpSTAR[2008]. Organizations can also specify whether an agent is allowed to manually retrieve a request from HelpSTAR[2008]'s job board, or whether an incident must be assigned to Beth automatically or by a supervisor.

Ref#	Title	Time Logged	Rep
10006	New Employee Setup	5/5/2009 10:42 AM	Beth Markham
10021	Prepare Employee Benefits	5/5/2009 11:08 AM	Beth Markham
10025	Server Crash	5/5/2009 12:01 PM	Beth Markham
10026	Can't connect to Network	5/5/2009 12:34 PM	Beth Markham

My Requests List

Figure 5-5 HelpSTAR²⁰⁰⁸ lists the open requests for help desk agent Beth Markham

If Beth Markham is unfamiliar with the problem reported by Chris Green, she can use HelpSTAR²⁰⁰⁸'s Best Solutions knowledge base to search for a possible solution to the problem, as shown in Figure 5-6.

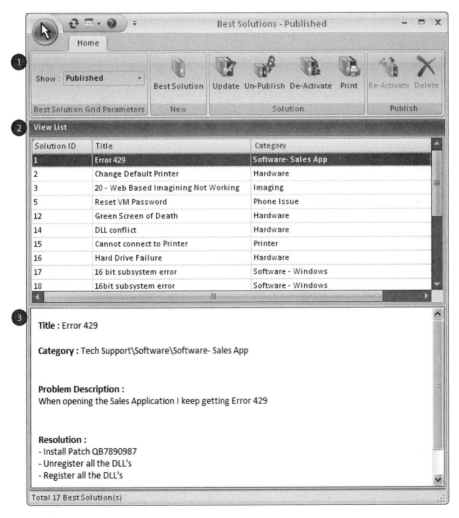

Figure 5-6 HelpSTAR²⁰⁰⁸ includes a knowledge base of Best Solutions that can be searched for problem resolutions

The Best Solutions – Published screen shown in Figure 5-6 is divided into three main sections. The numbers in the feature list below correspond to the numbered bullets shown in the figure:

1. *Ribbon options*—As a help desk agent, Beth can write or edit a draft of a new Best Solution, or update an existing solution.

2. *View List*—This window displays solutions from the knowledge base, which may be searched using text strings, keywords, or by browsing problem categories.

3. *Best Solution details*—This window displays the title and category of the incident that prompted the solution entry into the knowledge base, a description of the problem, and the steps taken to resolve it.

In addition to service requests for assistance, HelpSTAR^{2008} can be used to maintain a database of assets, as shown in Figure 5-7. Assets include hardware and software, but could also include office furniture and other inventory items.

Figure 5-7   HelpSTAR^{2008}'s asset identification screen

The New Asset screen shown in Figure 5-7 has two sections. The numbers in the feature list below correspond to the numbered bullets shown in the figure:

1. *General*—This section contain fields that identify an asset, its type, its identification numbers, the location where it is currently used, and other information.

2. *Memo*—This window provides room for a narrative description of an asset.

Help desk staff may search for an asset with HelpSTAR^{2008}'s Asset Explorer, or perform an audit of networked workstations to determine compliance with software license requirements.

Figure 5-8 is an example of a management dashboard report that is predefined in HelpSTAR^{2008}. A **dashboard** is a visual display of measures based on key performance indicators; it is used to quickly monitor help desk operations and identify aspects that vary from stated goals or require management attention. The dashboard displays are customizable, both with respect to content (which performance indicators are included) and with respect to format (bar chart, pie chart, line graph, etc.).

Figure 5-8   HelpSTAR^{2008}'s management dashboard provides a quick overview of important aspects of help desk operation

The dashboard shown in Figure 5-8 provides information on several different metrics. The numbers in the feature list below correspond to the numbered bullets shown in the figure:

1. *Ribbon option*—Help desk staff can design dashboard reports to display selected key performance indicators to alert management and staff to changes in the performance of the help desk operation. Reports can be created for a user-specified time period.

2. *Throughput*—This bar chart displays the volume of incidents in various categories during the selected time period.

3. *Top Active Categories*—This pie chart shows the request categories with the largest number of unresolved incidents.

Appendix B includes a tutorial for HelpSTAR^{2008} as well as hands-on activities to give you an opportunity to gain experience with HelpSTAR^{2008} help desk software.

To learn more about software packages and tools targeted at the user support industry, consult *A Guide to Help Desk Technology, Tools & Techniques* by Dione McBride (Course Technology, 2000).

4. *SLA Response Time*—This chart provides a quick picture of how effectively the help desk met its response time goals as defined in Service Level Agreements.

5. *SLA Resolution Time*—This shows how effectively the help desk staff met its resolution time goals during the selected time period.

6. *Top Categories by Average Response Time*—This bar graph displays the average response time for several categories of requests.

7. *Top Categories by Average Resolution Time*—This section shows the average time to resolve incidents by category of incident.

Other commercial help desk software packages have similar features and capabilities to those in the HelpSTAR^{2008} package. Many help desk packages can be integrated with telephone systems to provide a powerful suite of tools for help desk staff.

Computer Telephony Systems

Computer telephony is technology designed to increase help desk productivity by providing a seamless interface between the telephone and computer. Computer telephony is popular among support organizations that make heavy use of both technologies to provide help desk services. Whereas many small support centers rely on a help desk receptionist or a call dispatcher to respond to incoming telephone calls, a large number of help desk facilities invest in automated telephone systems.

An **automated call distributor (ACD)** is a computer telephony system that can answer calls, greet callers, provide menus to categorize the type of call, and route the call to a specific support agent or queue. When integrated with a help desk software package, an ACD system can take incident management a step further. When an appropriate support agent becomes available, an ACD system can match the support agent with the highest priority caller, signal the support agent on his or her computer screen, and display information on the agent's monitor about the caller and the problem. The ACD then routes the call to the agent's telephone.

ON THE WEB

One vendor of call center ACD systems is Database Systems. Their call center products are described at **www.call-center-tech.com/call-centers.htm**.

Common features of ACD systems include:

- *Skill set distribution*—routes each call to an agent who has expertise in a problem area

- *Overflow routing*—sends calls to another agent queue when one queue is long or calls have been in a queue longer than a predefined time period

- *Call accounting*—provides statistics on the number of calls received during half-hour periods during the day

- *Lost call reporting*—provides statistics on calls that were abandoned because the caller terminated the call before it was answered by an agent

- *Queue time*—provides statistics on the length of time calls wait in a queue before an agent responds

- *Agent performance*—provides statistics on each agent's call handling, including average length of calls and idle time.

- *Call monitoring*—permit supervisors to listen to or record calls for training and worker evaluation purposes.

The major benefit of an ACD system is that it reduces the amount of time needed to manually respond to and route calls to support staff. Because ACD systems increase the efficiency of help desk staff, they are help desk productivity tools.

Although computer telephony systems are designed to make efficient use of scarce support staff resources, many of these systems have a richly deserved poor reputation among end users. Lengthy hold times, long and complex menu options, repetitious requests for information, and dropped calls are common complaints of users who must navigate ACD systems. The recent emphasis on client relationship management in the support industry may eventually provide users with some relief from poorly designed computer telephony systems.

Another computer telephony product with applications in user support is an interactive voice response system. An **interactive voice response (IVR)** system allows a user to interact with a database of information by pressing keys on a telephone handset or by speaking simple words into the telephone. The IVR unit retrieves information from the database and plays the response for the user. IVRs, which work together with ACD systems, can be programmed with decision tree logic to ask questions to narrow a search for the information the user needs.

ON THE WEB

To learn more about interactive voice response technology, view a tutorial on the International Engineering Consortium's Web site at **www.iec.org/online/tutorials/speech_ enabled/index.html**.

Web-Based Support

As support organizations and their clients search for more efficient and cost-effective ways to provide support to end users, the role of the Web has increased dramatically. Virtually every large hardware component manufacturer, system integrator, software developer, network services supplier, and computer support provider operates a support Web site. Vendor Web sites offer a variety of support services to users, including:

- Product information, specifications, updates, pricing, and licensing

- Product order initiation and order fulfillment status reports

- Product rebate status

- Automated requests for literature, newsletters, and product-related e-mail notifications

- Online manuals and documentation

- Software downloads for drivers, patches, updates, diagnostic tools, templates, product tutorials, and demonstration versions of software

- Troubleshooting wizards

- Knowledge base access to frequently asked questions (FAQs), articles, problem reports, white papers, and technical information

- Bulletin boards and chat rooms to connect knowledgeable users with other users

- E-mail access to technical support staff

- Problem reporting

- Contact information for support staff

- Feedback on client satisfaction with products and support services

- Links to other sites with information about related products and services

Although few vendor Web sites offer all of these services, most vendors now see the Web as an ideal supplement to telephone, face-to-face, and e-mail support services. One of the reasons Web support has become popular, even for small support organizations, is that the cost to provide Web support is often less than that of other methods. Users find that they can frequently locate the information they need on a Web site without a phone conversation or an e-mail exchange with a support agent. When a support organization can respond to a user's needs without involving a support staff member, it saves money. And any time an end user can quickly locate information on a Web site, he or she does not have to spend time in a telephone queue waiting for the next support agent. Web-based support is another tool employed by support centers to meet the objective of making users more self-reliant.

ON THE WEB

Web Help Desk is an incident management system specifically designed for Web-based support. An online demonstration of its features, including the ability to log on as an agent or a user, is available **www.webhelpdesk.com**.

To get experience with an example of a Web-based support site, visit IBM's support site at **www.ibm.com/support/us**. While you are there, take note of the various services IBM provides at its support site.

The potential to abuse a client relationship with canned e-mail responses is enormous. Users who submit a question to a support site sometimes receive several pages of canned response. On occasion, when a user asks a follow-up question, the same canned response is e-mailed back. This problem can occur if a support agent does not read an inquiry carefully or if a support group automatically scans customers' e-mails and sends back canned responses based on keywords in the user's message. Neither of these practices is likely to improve the client relationship.

Even when an e-mail exchange between a user and a support staff member is required, e-mail can be more efficient and less costly than telephone support. First, e-mail is **asynchronous**, which means that the communications between the user and support staff do not have to occur at the same time. A support agent does not have to respond to a user's e-mail request immediately, and does not have to be available to communicate on the client's schedule, as is the case with a telephone call. E-mail support makes more efficient use of support staff resources than telephone support does. Second, e-mail responses to frequently asked questions can be composed in advance, checked for accuracy, stored, and then easily pasted into a response to a user. When appropriate, use of "canned" responses to e-mail requests is a cost-effective use of support staff time.

Increased use of the Web as a user support tool means that some knowledge, skills, and abilities that were important for a support staff member in the past are now less important, whereas other skills are becoming more important. Telephone support emphasizes verbal skills, pleasant voice quality, an ability to recall information quickly, and patience with clients; Web-based and e-mail support require agents who are skilled in written and graphical communications. The ability to recall information quickly is less important in an online environment than the ability to locate information from various resources. The ability to speak is less important than the ability to write clearly. The ability to listen is less important than the ability to read and understand. However, good client service skills and the ability to ask probing questions are important in every support environment.

Web-based and e-mail support are attractive options for small organizations and organizations that provide primarily internal support. Many organizations now use an intranet to deliver information and user support services to their workers. An **intranet** is a network modeled after the Internet, with information organized into Web pages, but accessible primarily or exclusively by workers within an organization. An intranet provides a way to support internal users via tools they are familiar with, such as their Web browser, but it also provides security from access by unauthorized external users. At small organizations and departments within large ones, help desk staff may need skills in Web site layout and design as well as Web applications software and programming languages in order to build pages that provide clients and employees with Web-based user support services.

ON THE WEB

For a short tutorial on intranets and their benefits to an organization, visit the Intranet Road Map at the OpenConsult Web site at **www.intranetroadmap.com/default.cfm**.

Trends in Help Desk Operations

Help desk operation is a field that is changing rapidly. Many of the industry trends that have been described above will continue, and new trends will emerge. Some of these technology and workplace trends are summarized in Figure 5-9 and are discussed in the following sections.

Technology Trends

- Cloud computing

- Further virtualization of software platforms

- Additional demand to support wireless devices

- Increased use of remote diagnosis and voice response technologies

Help Desk Workplace Trends

- Changes in off-shore outsourcing

- Additional employer demand for certified workers

- Acceptance of telecommuting as a work style

- Further development and adoption of industry best practices such as ITIL

- Continued pressure to reduce support costs

- Increased use of Web-based support portals

- Widespread use of quantitative metrics

- Increased resources devoted to computer security

- Help desk software integration

Figure 5-9   Help desk industry trends

Technology Trends

Some trends that will impact the help desk field are due to more general changes in technology, which will affect the services required of help desks as well as the way in which those services are provided.

The Next New Thing: Cloud Computing and Beyond

As this book goes to press, the next new technology on the horizon appears to be cloud computing. **Cloud computing** is a new name for an old idea: providing software as a subscription service over the Internet. The trend toward cloud computing may result in fewer outright purchases of operating system and application software packages. Instead of purchasing, downloading, and installing software on their individual PCs, users will pay a fee to license the use of software on the Internet. Cloud computing is yet another step in reliance on the Internet to provide computer services.

The cloud computing shift in the software delivery paradigm has several advantages, including the instant availability on a software vendor's Web server of the latest version of a software package, complete

232

with up-to-date patches and new features. In addition to software, in cloud computing, user data is stored on Internet servers, which means it is available via any Internet connection. With applications software and data on the cloud (the Internet), collaboration among members of a project team becomes more feasible. While cloud computing may be just the latest paradigm shift that will impact user support workers, it will not be the last. Support workers who do not anticipate and learn about technology changes will find the IT job market a challenge.

Further Virtualization of Software Platforms

Virtualization is a method of partitioning the resources of a computer into multiple execution environments, in which each virtual machine, operating in its own partition, has the capability to run its own operating systems and application software. Each virtual machine shares the hardware resources of the host system, which permits a help desk agent to respond to questions about multiple operating systems and application programs from a single host machine. Virtualization should reduce the equipment and operational costs of help desk groups and increase the resources available to help desk workers to troubleshoot problems.

Additional Demand to Support Wireless Devices

The integration of wireless devices (such as cell phones, MP3 players, PDAs, netbooks (ultra portable notebooks), Bluetooth devices, Wi-Fi networks and GPS units) with computer technology will undoubtedly continue. User support as a field will likely expand its services to include support for integrated wireless technologies.

Increased Use of Remote Diagnosis and Voice Response Technologies

Automation will continue to impact help desk operations. Whereas many help desks in the past were based on walk-in, on-site, or telephone support, future help desks will undoubtedly rely to an increasing extent on e-mail, the Web, self-help, and remote diagnosis to provide help desk services. As mentioned previously, remote diagnosis is the use of a computer system at a help desk site to connect to a client's system, and then test the various components of the user's hardware, examine the user's software configuration, and replicate a problem scenario.

Furthermore, help desk technology in the future will likely incorporate advances in voice recognition and response in products aimed at the user support industry. The key to the successful help desk of the future is to reduce users' reliance on help desk staff by helping them be more self-sufficient, and to increase the productivity (often by decreasing the effort expended) of help desk staff when users cannot be self-sufficient for whatever reason.

Workplace Trends

Other trends that will impact future help desk operations are due to changes in the workplace environment within the help desk industry.

Changes in Off-Shore Outsourcing

As you learned in Chapter 1, an ongoing user support trend is to outsource some help desk jobs to Europe and Asia, especially India, because relative wages there are significantly less than in North America. This trend has reduced the need for workers in the United States to answer help desk telephone calls, respond to e-mails from users, and operate self-help Web sites. Outsourcing has primarily impacted help desk operations that serve external clients. Outsourcing help desk operations overseas raises issues, including the long-range impact on the U.S. workforce, whether quality support standards can be maintained, and the role of help desks in building and maintaining customer relationships.

On a practical level, outsourcing help desk operations overseas means relatively fewer jobs available for entry-level help desk agents in the United States. On the other hand, relatively more entry-level positions will be available in North America for support workers who serve internal clients. This trend will impact academic and training programs for future help desk workers. There are also some recent indications that support organizations that were quick to use off-shore outsourcing are now rethinking that strategy. Complaints from workers and clients about communication difficulties with off-shore agents may result in the return of some user support jobs to North America and Europe.

ON THE WEB

To learn more about trends in off-shore outsourcing, read an article at **www.outsourcing-offshore.com/2007-offshore.html**.

Additional Employer Demand for Certified Workers

Chapter 6 describes the certification process in greater detail.

234

Another computer industry trend that will impact help desk staffing is the certification process. Not only are help desk staff in many organizations expected to pass certification exams for the specific products they support, but certifications are now available for the more general knowledge, skills, and abilities required of help desk agents. Certification is an employment and professional development factor that can enhance a support agent's job marketability, and opportunities for promotion—in combination with the agent's education, training and experience.

Acceptance of Telecommuting as a Work Style

Telecommuting is full or part-time work performed at a home office for an employer. **Voice over Internet Protocol (VoIP)** is a technology that makes telecommuting for help desk work more feasible by transmitting voice communications over the Internet rather than telephone lines. As the quality of VoIP has improved, it has allowed help desk workers to maintain communication with end users and work colleagues from a home office. An increasing number of help desk employers permit or encourage telecommuting as a way to reduce worker turnover, office space and operational costs, and provide workers with greater flexibility in work hours and conditions, as well as reduce the cost of transportation, child care, clothing, food, and other employment-related expenses (see Figure 5-10). Help desk organizations that use telecommuting as an alternate work style must

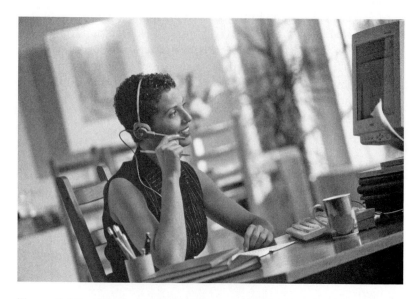

Figure 5-10 Help desk agent telecommutes part-time from home office

address concerns about worker productivity, quality control, confidentiality, as well as the challenges to supervisors of overseeing agents who are located remotely.

Further Development of Industry Best Practices such as ITIL

The Information Technology Infrastructure Library (ITIL) is one of many evolving frameworks, guidelines, and standards that will continue to develop and expand as the help desk industry matures. Adoption of industry best practices should contribute to help desk staff productivity and effectiveness.

Continued Pressure to Reduce Support Costs

Many of the help desk industry trends in this section are the result of pressures to reduce the cost of user support. Increased use of outsourcing, telecommuting, Web-based support portals, and remote diagnosis are obvious examples. The challenge for the user support industry in the next decade will be to further reduce costs while increasing the quality of services provided, which are often contradictory objectives.

Increased Use of Web-Based Support Portals

One response to the need to reduce user support costs is to make increased use of Web sites as a medium for communication with users. Many organizations are developing support **portals**, which provide a single point of Web access for all support services. The development of support portals is both a technical challenge and a customer service challenge, as you learned in Chapter 2. As help desks make increasing use of the Web as a delivery vehicle for support services, the specific skills required of support workers in many organizations will change. Less emphasis on telephone help desk operations will give way to a greater emphasis on more comprehensive training to prepare workers for the broader spectrum of knowledge, skills, and abilities required to support end users

Widespread Use of Quantitative Metrics

As more help desk functions become automated, help desk managers need access to high-quality reports and statistical information that will alert managers and staff to trends in the volume of incidents, the kinds of questions asked, the need for help desk staff with particular skills, and the kinds of problems about which end users are inquiring. Measuring human behavior is never an easy task. However, as help desk managers react to corporate pressures to increase worker productivity and justify the costs of help desk operations, the industry will see expanded reliance on quantitative performance metrics.

Chapter 6 describes some ways help desks organizations and the employees who work in them are measured and evaluated.

Chapter 12 discusses resources help desk staff can use to increase vigilance on client systems.

Increased Resources Devoted to Computer Security

Despite continuing efforts to develop effective tools to fight viruses, spyware, spam, rootkits, keyloggers, phishing, and other malware attacks on servers and user PCs, security threats will never be completely eliminated. Help desk practitioners need to keep up-to-date on trends in security threats and increase their knowledge of tools to manage them. Additional industry efforts at server-based security tools will continue in the future.

Help Desk Software Integration

Help desks of the future will be seen as the front-end of a **client relationship management (CRM)** system. Client relationship management is a relatively new name for an old objective: to meet the needs of clients by providing excellent client service. CRM proponents view each client as the reason an organization exists. CRM is based on findings that the cost to an organization to replace a client is much greater than the cost of managing a successful relationship with an existing client. Going forward, help desk agents will see increasing integration of features in software tools and alignment of their work with other business functions.

The help desk of the future will undoubtedly look very different from today's. The challenge for support workers is to prepare for these operational changes by taking advantage of educational opportunities, professional development, and by learning more about industry trends.

Chapter Summary

- Simply stated, the goal of most help desk operations is to provide clients with a single point of contact for information requests, IT services, and problem resolution.

- Many help desks are organized in a multilevel system. The lowest level is an incident screener. Increasing technical levels include product specialists, technical support, and support managers.

- Many help desk procedures involve the effective management of problem incidents. Incident management addresses the details of how problem incidents are received, prescreened, authenticated to determine the user's right to various types and levels of service, logged for record-keeping purposes, and screened to determine their importance. Incidents are then prioritized, assigned to an appropriate staff member, tracked as they move toward satis-factory resolution, escalated if necessary, resolved, closed, and archived in a database.

- The Information Technology Infrastructure Library (ITIL) is a compendium of best practice guidelines for support organizations that address IT service management, including how to manage incidents and technology changes in organizations.

- The physical environment of a help desk facility includes the workspace, furniture, equipment, and computer systems help desk agents use in their work. Headsets that permit flexibility of movement are an important tool.

- Support workers may be vulnerable to job stress when the expectations of a position do not match the personal characteristics of a worker. The physical layout of a workspace and other work conditions may also contribute to job stress.

- Several tools are available to assist in managing problem incidents. These include help desk software packages with features for agents, managers, and users designed to automate many incident management tasks and procedures; computer telephony systems (including automated call distributors and interactive voice response units) that automate call routing and task assignment; and the Web as a support delivery vehicle.

- Help desks will undoubtedly continue to evolve. Changes in technology demand that workers keep abreast of trends and developments in the computer field, including virtualization, wireless devices, and remote access. Changes in the help desk industry, including outsourcing of help desk services overseas, will impact industry employment trends as well as training programs. Increased use of technology and automation of help desk functions will address the need to improve the productivity of help desk staff as well as the need to be more proactive by anticipating user problems. In a growing number of organizations, help desks will be viewed as an increasingly important component in client relationship management.

Key Terms

archive—An incident archive is a database or paper file used to store and retain records relating to closed incidents.

asynchronous—A method of communication in which the communicators do not have to participate at the same time; e-mail and Web-based communication are examples.

authentication procedure—An incident management step in which an agent determines whether the help desk is authorized to handle a call; authentication usually includes checking product registrations, support services licenses, or contracts.

automated call distributor (ACD)—A computer telephony system that automates many of the first steps in incident management, such as a greeting, menu options, caller authentication, call holding, queue management, and staff notification.

best practices—Procedures, tools, and methods that successful support groups employ; these practices often set apart very successful support operations from mediocre ones.

call management—A process followed by help desk staff when handling telephone contacts between end users and support staff.

client feedback—Evaluations collected from help desk users about their level of satisfaction with a product or service, a specific help desk incident, the problem resolution, or help desk services in general.

client relationship management (CRM)—Business processes that aim to meet the needs of and satisfy clients by providing excellent client service; CRM is based on findings that the cost to an organization to replace a client is much greater than the cost of managing the relationship with an existing client.

closing—An incident management step in which a support agent reviews the steps the help desk took to solve a problem, agrees with the end user that a solution has been reached, invites the user to call back, and makes final entries regarding the incident in a database.

cloud computing—A subscription service in which application software programs are served to a user's computer over the Internet instead of residing on the user's computer.

computer telephony—Technology designed to increase help desk productivity by providing a seamless interface between the telephone and computer.

dashboard—A visual display of measures based on key indicators; it is used to quickly monitor help desk operations and identify performance that varies from stated goals or requires management attention.

escalation—An incident management step in which a problem is transferred to a higher level of support that is better able to handle more difficult problems.

job stress—A physical or emotional response that occurs when the personal characteristics of a help desk worker do not match the requirements of their position.

incident management—A well-defined, formal process that help desk staff follow to handle face-to-face, telephone, e-mail, or Web-based problem incidents, obtain the information that users request or solve an end user's problem, and close an incident; compare to call management.

Information Technology Infrastructure Library (ITIL)—A set of guidelines designed to help organizations align and integrate their computer services with their business objectives.

interactive voice response (IVR)—A computer telephony system that allows a user to interact with a database of information by pressing keys on a telephone handset or by speaking simple words into the telephone.

intranet—A network modeled after the Internet, with information organized into Web pages, but accessible primarily or exclusively by workers within an organization.

logging—An incident management step in which an agent begins documenting the incident and its related problem.

multilevel support model—A help desk structure that organizes support staff and services into several levels, or tiers, of support; sometimes called a frontline/backline model; the goal is to handle calls at the lowest possible support level.

portal—A Web site which provides a single point of entry (or contact) for all support services.

prescreening—An incident management step in which agents identify and respond to simple requests for information, often without initiating an official incident; prescreening is essentially a filtering process.

priority code—A designation assigned to an incident that indicates how serious the problem is for users, how many users are affected, and perhaps the consequence of not addressing the problem immediately; priority codes are often the basis for determining the order in which incidents are assigned to agents.

queue—A waiting line into which incoming calls or incidents are placed when they cannot be addressed immediately; queues are often established for different types and priorities of incidents or specific products, clients, or levels of support.

resolution—An incident management step in which a user's problem is solved, a complaint is noted or referred to product designers, or authorization is given to return a product for replacement or a refund.

screening—An incident management step in which a help desk staff member asks a series of questions to categorize and describe the incident; incidents may be categorized as a request for information, a question, a problem, a complaint, or a work (or service) order.

service level agreement (SLA)—A contract that defines the expected performance of user support services or external vendor services.

telecommuting—Full or part-time work performed at a home office for an employer.

time management tools—Software tools designed to help support agents increase their personal productivity; time management tools include calendaring systems, to-do lists, collaboration, and project management tools.

tracking—An incident management step in which an agent updates the incident record with information about a problem as it progresses.

virtualization—A method of partitioning the resources of a computer into multiple execution environments, in which each virtual machine, operating in its own memory partition, has the capability to run its own operating system and application software.

Voice over Internet Protocol (VoIP)—A technology that transmits voice communications over the Internet rather via than telephone lines.

Check Your Understanding

Answers to Check Your Understanding questions are found in Appendix A.

1. True or False? In a help desk that uses the multilevel support model, the goal is to handle calls at the lowest possible support level.

2. In a help desk patterned on the multilevel support model, what is the common title of workers at each level?

   a. **level 1**: assistant; **level 2**: product specialist; **level 3**: programmer; **level 4**: support manager

   b. **level 1**: incident dispatcher; **level 2**: technical support; **level 3**: product specialist; **level 4**: support supervisor

   c. **level 1**: incident screener; **level 2**: product specialist; **level 3**: technical support; **level 4**: support manager

   d. **level 1**: incident screener; **level 2**: product specialist; **level 3**: support manager; **level 4**: programmer

3. _____ is a well-defined, formal procedure that helps desk staff follow to solve user problems.

4. True or False? Every help desk incident, no matter what kind, goes through all 12 steps of the incident management process described in the chapter, even if some of the steps do not apply.

5. Which of the following sequences lists the order of these steps in the incident management process: (1) authenticate the incident; (2) archive the incident; (3) log the incident; and (4) prioritize the problem?

    a. 4 – 3 – 1 – 2

    b. 3 – 1 – 2 – 4

    c. 1 – 3 – 4 – 2

    d. 1 – 2 – 3 – 4

6. True or False? The percentage of incidents that cannot be resolved during the incident management process is frequently zero.

7. In which category of help desk incidents does the following question fall? "My computer runs slowly when I connect to the Web in the evenings."

    a. a question

    b. a problem

    c. a complaint

    d. a work order

8. A common strategy for assigning a priority to help desk calls is:

    a. first in, first out (FIFO)

    b. last in, first out (LIFO)

    c. in random order

    d. the order the help desk agent prefers

9. An incident management step in which a problem is transferred to a support staff member who has greater experience or resources to handle difficult questions is:

    a. assignment

    b. screening

    c. tracking

    d. escalation

10. A(n) _____ is a waiting line into which incoming calls are placed when they cannot be answered immediately.

11. True or False? An automated incident tracking system is primarily useful in a large help desk operation, but is of very limited use in a small help desk operation.

12. True or False? Knowledge bases that have special search tools and other help desk software features are called smart databases.

13. True or False? The purpose of client feedback features in a help desk software package is to make it easier to terminate support agents with poor customer service skills.

14. A(n) _____ is a telephone system that can answer calls, greet callers, provide menus, and route calls.

15. True or False? Incident management and call management are terms that mean the same thing.

16. True or False? A priority code indicates how easy or difficult a dispatcher thinks an incident will be to resolve.

17. _____ is often the result of the personal characteristics of a worker not matching the requirements of a position.

18. Help desk software packages usually include tools to help _____, _____, and _____ manage problem incidents.

19. An increasing number of help desk incidents are handled:

    a. in face-to-face situations

    b. via a telephone call

    c. on a support Web site

    d. using IVR technology

20. Describe a recent trend in help desk operation and briefly explain how it will impact help desk agents in the future.

21. ITIL is:

    a. a set of industry best practices

    b. a set of industry standards

    c. a set of software programs

    d. an incident management procedure

22. True or False? Telecommuting is working for an employer full- or part-time from a home office.

Discussion Questions

1. Should a help desk organization hire additional agents in order to satisfy 100% of its users 100% of the time? Explain why or why not.

2. Based on your experiences with checkout lines in grocery stores or fast-food restaurants, discuss whether the number of queues makes a difference in the level of service provided. For example, if five clerks are available, is it more effective to have one long queue, where the next customer in the queue gets served next, or five separate queues, one for each clerk, so that a customer has to decide which queue to select. Does either arrangement really make any difference? If so, to whom? Relate your discussion to help desk incident management.

3. Which of the help desk industry trends described in this chapter do you think will have the greatest impact on the work of future help desk agents? Explain your answer. Based on your own experience, what additional trends would you add to the list in the chapter?

4. Is job stress among agents in a help desk operation inevitable? Explain your viewpoint. What characteristics of a help desk operation increase or reduce job stress?

5. Should every help desk operation use an automated incident tracking software, or can some support operations use less formal, paper-and-pencil methods? Explain your position.

6. Is job stress among help desk agents caused more by the characteristics of each worker or by the working conditions in a help desk operation? Is the solution to job stress more the responsibility of each worker or the responsibility of help desk management?

7. Are the steps in the incident management process described in this chapter designed to resolve problem incidents effectively and efficiently? If the objective is effective and efficient problem resolution, what steps would you add, delete, or change?

Hands-On Activities

Activity 5-1

Interview a help desk support agent. Identify a support agent at your organization or school, or one employed in a local business. Interview the agent to find out how his or her help desk is organized and what services it provides. Ask about this person's career path; if possible, obtain his or her current position description. Write a summary of the interview highlights.

Activity 5-2

Visit a local telephone contact center. Arrange a visit to a help desk operation or contact center that provides telephone support, if one is available locally. Study how the physical workspace for contact center workers is organized to facilitate their work. Find out if the organization has a written incident or call management process, if it uses a help desk or call management software, and if it uses a computer telephony system. Write a summary of your findings, including the pros and cons of working in the facility you visited. Include in your summary a sketch of the physical layout of the contact center operation you observed.

Activity 5-3

Assign priority codes to help desk incidents. Use the priority code system shown below to assign codes to various types of situations.

Code	Meaning
U	Urgent
H	High priority
M	Medium priority
L	Low priority

When assigning a priority code to each of the following situations, consider these criteria:

- The severity of the problem

- The number of users affected

- The availability of a reasonable workaround

- Your own judgment

    1. A user calls with a question about how to format a chart in Excel.

    2. The administrative assistant in the manufacturing division calls to report that the server in his building is down.

    3. A user e-mails to report a suspected bug in the way a toolbar works in a software package, but she says the equivalent pull-down menu option does work.

    4. The president of the organization calls to request the latest performance data on the help desk operation.

    5. A bug is reported in the beta release of a software package; the production version is scheduled to ship next week.

6. Several calls are received from irate users who indicate that the accounting software package they purchased 12 months ago does not handle end-of-year processing correctly and the reports prepared contain obvious errors.

7. A user calls to report that your company's Web site is having problems and that the shopping cart feature, among others, no longer works.

Discuss your priority code assignments with two coworkers or classmates. Explore any problem incidents where you differ by more than one priority code. Write a summary of your conclusions, and explain how much difference of opinion you found in how to assign priority codes.

Activity 5-4

Identify information in an incident management database. List the important pieces of information about a typical problem incident that you would expect to find in an incident logging/tracking system. Use a word processor, spreadsheet, or database to design a data-entry form that captures the information you identified. Compare the information you plan to collect with that of others.

Activity 5-5

Evaluate a telephone system user interface. Based on your experience as a user with a help desk or other telephone service that uses an ACD telephone system, write an evaluation of the user interface. Describe the first level of menus and at least one other menu level. Evaluate the menus and menu navigation from a user's perspective. Write at least three suggestions on how the ACD interface could be improved.

Assemble a team of at least three classmates, and compare your suggestions with those of the members in your group. What are some common design principles the members in your group agree on for an ACD system?

Activity 5-6

Learn more about help desk software. Visit HelpSTAR^{2008}'s tutorial Web site **edu.helpstar.com**. Use the icons at the bottom of their home page to view videos that describe their software product. (If your computer doesn't have a sound card, click the caption button (CC) to view the script of each video.) Compare the features of HelpSTAR^{2008} with the list of typical help desk software features described in this chapter. Write a report on whether HelpSTAR^{2008}

has each of the features listed in the chapter. Describe any major features HelpSTAR[2008] has in addition to those described in the chapter.

Activity 5-7

Learn more about the basis for setting incident priorities. Read a short article on Tech Target's Web site, "Use SLAs to assign help desk incident priorities" at **searchwinit.techtarget.com/ tip/0,289483,sid1_gci1273245,00.html#**. Compare the author's description of how incident priorities should be based with the criteria described in this chapter. Write a short report on similarities and differences you found in the two sources.

Activity 5-8

Identify help desk job stressors. Based on your understanding of help desk operations and job stress, make a list of 10 or more different factors in a help desk environment that can increase or decrease the job stress experienced by agents. Use the Web resources listed in the chapter as resources if you need ideas. Then put the stressors into a few categories. Compare your list with those developed by your colleagues. Do you have the same or different categories?

Activity 5-9

Analyze a problem with Web support. Read a help desk manager's report of a problem with a new incident management support site at **www.itsmsolutions.com/newsletters/DITYvol3iss17.pdf**. Then answer these questions about this case.

1.   Why do you think users bypassed the new Service Desk?

2.   Do you think the manager's solution to the problem was an effective one? Why or why not?

3.   Describe alternative steps she might have taken to solve the problem.

Activity 5-10

Take a job stress quiz. Take the job burnout quiz at **stress.about. com/library/burnout/bl_job_burnout_quiz.htm**. Answer the 20 questions about your own situation as best you can and get your result. Do you agree or disagree with the result? Go through the questions a second time and compare each question with the factors that lead to job stress for help desk workers described in this chapter. Do the questions suggest other factors that may be stressors that you would add to those described in the chapter?

Activity 5-11

Research help desk industry trends. Select one of the help desk industry trends described at the end of this chapter. Use a Web search engine to find information about the trend. Write a report or prepare a slideshow presentation on the trend you selected. Include in your report or presentation your ideas about how the trend will impact workers in the help desk industry.

Case Projects

1. A Support Web Site for a Training Facility

You've been hired to design a support Web site for a training facility for end users. Look at examples of existing support Web sites for ideas. Suggested support sites to visit include:

- Gateway Computers support Web site (**support.gateway.com/ support/default.asp**)

- Adobe software support site (**www.adobe.com/support/ main.html**)

- Symantec Web support site (**www.symantec.com/support/ index.jsp**)

- Howard Community College's student support Web site (**www.howardcc.edu/students/helpdesk/index.html**)

Or, visit other product and services support Web sites with which you are familiar. Analyze the features that you like and the features you believe could be improved on the sites you visit. Use a word processor or other tool to lay out your basic ideas for the Home page and for two or three other important pages for the site you design. Your design layout does not have to include the information on the site, but should describe the kind of information you would include on each page. Give special attention to:

- The information users would expect to find on the Web site

- The selection of support features to incorporate in your Web site

- How the support features are organized and presented to users

- The navigation between pages

When you have finished your design, meet with three classmates or coworkers and compare your designs. How did your designs differ? How were they similar? What features of Web site design did you learn from them?

2. An Incident Management Script for the Library

The help desk staff at the library is small, but its responsibilities for providing help desk services are growing. The help desk provides support to library staff who work in multiple offices and also to the public who access e-mail and the Web through workstations in the library building. Most contacts with library staff are on the phone; most contacts with the public, however, are face-to-face.

The current help desk procedures rely primarily on informal communication between help desk staff members:

- Scribbled notes and phone messages about requests for support assistance

- A bulletin board in the help desk office where notes about ongoing problems are posted

- A clipboard that lists pending incidents that need resolution

- The wastebasket as a closed incident archive

The help desk staff would like to transform its current method for handling support problem incidents into a more structured incident management process.

Based on what you learned about incident management in this chapter, write a first draft of a sample script that could be used to train new agents to handle incidents at the help desk in the library. Your script should cover the basic tasks in incident management that you learned about in this chapter. Your script should also cover how to close an incident. Incorporate your own ideas on effective handling of incidents and help desk client relationships.

3. A Help Desk Tool for the Library

Use your experience with a spreadsheet, database package, or programming language to design and develop a prototype for a software tool that could be used by a small help desk, such as the one at the library. A prototype is not necessarily a complete system with every possible useful feature, but one that contains basic functions that could be enhanced and expanded later. The primary purpose of the help desk tool you develop for the library is to keep track of problem incidents. A user of the help desk tool should be able to enter, store, retrieve, update, and close problem reports received from users. The system should also include the ability to create one or more reports from stored data. The report(s) should enable the help desk supervisor in the library to obtain summary information on problem status and to analyze the kinds of problems that arise, including hardware, operating system, applications software, network, user, e-mail, Internet, and other common problem categories.

Assemble a team of three classmates or coworkers and develop design specifications, such as:

- What are the possible features and capabilities of a simple problem-tracking system?

- What information (data elements) needs to be input and stored to meet the primary objectives?

- How will the user interface to the help desk tool be designed to facilitate efficient use by help desk staff?

- How will the data entry screens appear to a help desk agent?

- What query capabilities should the help desk system provide a staff member?

- What reports should be predefined to provide problem-tracking summary and status information?

- What are the highest priority features for development in the first version (prototype) of the help desk tool you are designing?

This project can be a large one. Whether you work alone or with a team, remember to keep the design simple and make decisions about what you can reasonably accomplish in the limited time you have to devote to this project. Remember that additional features can be added later.

CHAPTER 6

User Support Management

In this chapter, you will learn about:

◎ The mission of a support group and the parts of a mission statement

◎ The steps in staffing a support position

◎ The contents of a training program for support staff

◎ Industry certifications that are available to support professionals

◎ Professional help desk and user support associations

◎ Ethical principles that guide the professional behavior of support workers

Some workers in the user support field aspire to become user support or help desk managers; others do not. Whether or not their career plans include a future management position, user support workers can benefit from a basic understanding of the managerial perspective. When applicants interview for a user support position, the interviewer will likely be a user support manager or supervisor. If hired as a user support worker in a very small company, workers may be expected to perform some tasks that require management, supervisory, lead worker, or project coordinator skills.

User support management encompasses a variety of positions. In many organizations, a help desk or user support manager directly manages the user support staff. Managers of large support groups may oversee one or more supervisors or team leaders who in turn supervise a team of support agents. For example, an organization that provides several levels of support, as described in Chapter 5, may have a level 1 team (call screening) supervisor, a level 2 team (product specialist) supervisor, and a level 3 team (technical support) supervisor. Even small support groups may assign some project leader or coordinator responsibilities to user support workers. For example, a user support worker might be assigned a project to learn about a new software or hardware product and disseminate the relevant documentation, training materials, and information on anticipated user problems to other support staff.

Although most of this book focuses on the knowledge, skills, and abilities required for an effective user support worker, this chapter examines some of the particular tasks and issues that user support and help desk managers might face. These tasks include developing a mission statement, staffing and evaluating a user support operation, and training team members. The chapter concludes with information about two emerging help desk industry trends that confront both workers and managers: certification and professionalism.

Managerial Concerns: Mission, Performance, Staffing, and Training

From the moment you decide that you want to pursue a help desk or user support career, you should be aware of the support management's perspectives. Every decision a help desk manager makes affects the people on his or her team. The more support staff members know about their manager's concerns and priorities, the better equipped they will be to understand the need for certain task assignments and to focus their efforts on completing them. Knowing the big picture enables support staff to improve client satisfaction and help the support team succeed. A managerial perspective also helps

When searching for additional information on user support management, be aware that some organizations and authors use alternate terms, such as help desk management, client support management, call center management, and customer support management. These terms are usually interchangeable.

For more information on user support or help desk management, refer to Barbara Czegel's *Running an Effective Help Desk, 2nd edition* (Wiley, 1998). It describes planning, organizing, staffing, and marketing a help desk; procedures that make a help desk more effective; and tools to automate a help desk and measure its performance. An alternate resource is Bob Wooten's book, *Building & Managing a World Class IT Help Desk* (Osborne, 2001).

prepare entry-level staff to advance into positions with more responsibilities and higher salaries.

This chapter is not intended as a comprehensive introduction to user support or help desk management. Instead, this chapter focuses on four areas of user support management that directly affect members of a support staff: the support mission, performance measures, staffing, and training. The objective here is to give you an understanding of some of the issues user support managers face, so that you will be better prepared to obtain and work effectively in a user support position.

User Support Mission

Support groups often develop a **mission statement**, which is used to communicate a set of guiding principles to support team members, users, and management. It says, in effect, "Here is what we think is most important to our support group." Support groups also use their mission statement as a yardstick against which to measure their progress toward their goals. Figure 6-1 shows an example of a user support mission statement. The example addresses primarily support for internal employees, but it could be modified to apply to external clients. The italicized terms highlight important concepts.

User Support Mission Statement

The mission of the user support group is to:

(a) maximize *operational efficiency* among users in the organization by providing timely resolution to *technology use questions*, and

(b) effectively *manage problems* to continuously improve the:

- *quality* of support services to users
- *usability* of information systems
- *effectiveness* of documentation and training
- *users' satisfaction* with support services

Figure 6-1   Example of a user support group mission statement

Several points in the sample mission statement in Figure 6-1 directly address end users' productivity. Increased worker (or client) productivity is usually a primary goal, because every support group or help desk must justify its existence in its organization based on the services it provides to other workers or clients. It must prove to the parent organization that its benefits outweigh its costs. Other mission statements may include goals relating to user self-sufficiency, ethical professional conduct of staff members, increased company profitability, and career path development for user support workers.

A mission statement that includes a laundry list of goals is sometimes less effective than shorter, more focused, guidelines.

253

ON THE WEB

To see an example of a mission statement, visit the Web site of California Polytechnic State University's Service Desk at **servicedesk.calpoly.edu/computing_support/about_us/ goals_mission.html**. Note that the Service Desk expands on its basic mission statement by defining its values and objectives. For guidelines on writing a help desk mission statement, read an article on Tech Republic's Web site at **articles.techrepublic.com.com/5100-10878_ 11-5032967.html**.

User Support Performance and Justification

Performance statistics and measures of client satisfaction are two ways to document and justify the value of user support services.

Performance Statistics

Performance statistics are objective data about the user support or help desk operations. Managers track performance statistics to measure their teams against specific goals, which are often stated in their teams' mission statements. For example, a help desk's mission statement might include a goal of responding to 90 percent of incoming telephone calls within 60 seconds. If the help desk actually responded to 88 percent of the calls in 60 seconds or less last week, then the help desk team fell short of that particular objective. Performance statistics can help a support group measure how effectively and efficiently it responds to incidents. Examples of common help desk performance measures include:

- Average time to respond to incidents (sometimes called **wait time**)

- Percentage of incidents that were abandoned (user hung up or gave up before the support staff responded); also called **abandonment rate**

- Average resolution time for incidents that require problem solving

- Percentage of problems that could not be resolved

- Percentage of closed incidents that had to be reopened

- Number of incidents currently in an unresolved status (perhaps a separate count for each priority code)

254

Many automatic call distributor (ACD) systems collect the raw data from which reports on these and other support performance statistics can be prepared.

These performance statistics can be reported for a point in time, but they are more useful when compared across various times of the day, days of the week, or months. Trends in performance are often more meaningful than isolated measurements. Performance statistics can be reported for an entire support team or for individual workers. These statistics are often used to answer the questions, "Is the help desk operation more (or less) productive or responsive over time?" and, "How does the productivity or accuracy of Emily (for example) compare with other help desk workers?"

HelpSTAR software was introduced in Chapter 5.

Performance measures may be presented in a table of statistical results but are often more useful when presented as a visual graphic, as shown in Figure 6-2. A user support manager used HelpSTAR help desk software to prepare the chart in Figure 6-2 to show the source of incidents opened last week. She learned that the category with the highest number of incidents last week was the PC Support Level 1 category.

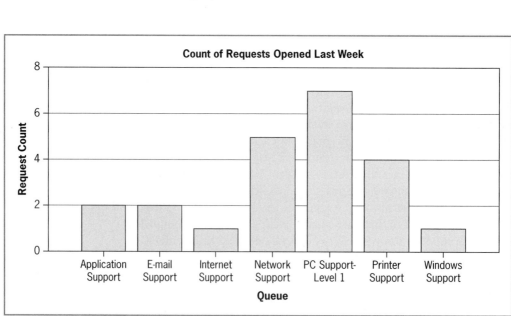

Figure 6-2   A histogram prepared with HelpSTAR software shows the distribution of categories of support incidents

User Satisfaction Surveys

In addition to objective, statistical measures of user support performance, support groups may periodically collect subjective information from its users via a user satisfaction survey. A **user satisfaction survey** is a questionnaire that attempts to measure how satisfied users are with the support services they have experienced. Questions, such as the following examples, are often used to prepare a report card for the user support group:

- *On a scale from 1 (very satisfied) to 5 (very dissatisfied), how would you evaluate the overall user support services you receive as a worker in this organization?*

- *On a scale from 1 (very satisfied) to 5 (very dissatisfied), how would you rate how knowledgeable the help desk staff is?*

User satisfaction surveys may ask users about a wide range of issues, including:

- Availability of help when it was needed

- Responsiveness of support staff

- Ability of support staff to communicate effectively with users

- Usefulness of online information resources

- Technical knowledge of support staff

- Ability of support staff to resolve problems

Satisfaction surveys may also ask users to identify a support staff member who has been especially helpful to them. A help desk that provides external support may ask similar questions of a selected sample of clients. Data from external clients is often collected after an incident has been closed in a follow-up phone call or via a mail or e-mail questionnaire. Organizations that provide Web-based support may include an online feedback mechanism to help evaluate the quality of information and client services their Web site and support team provide. For example, information on a Web page may be accompanied by a question such as, "Did you find this information useful? Click YES or NO."

ON THE WEB

A Web service that offers both free and for-fee questionnaire and survey tools is **www.surveymonkey.com**. The site also offers suggestions on effective ways to ask survey questions.

256

Justifying Support Services

A user support group can be treated as a cost center or a profit center in an organization. In a **cost center operation**, the cost of providing user support services appears as an expense in an organization's budget, without a corresponding revenue source. Typical expenses include staff salaries, benefits, payroll taxes, equipment, software licenses, outsourced services, and overhead (administrative costs). In a **profit center operation**, user support costs are treated as expenses, but those expenses are offset by revenue generated by the user support group. In a profit center operation, a user support group might charge fees to clients or other departments who make use of support services; the fees might be designed to totally or partially offset the expenses of the support group.

Support operations that use the cost center approach can find it difficult to justify support expenses solely on the basis of performance statistics or client satisfaction, because there is no direct revenue stream to offset the costs. One reason many hardware and software manufacturers now charge clients for help desk services is the need to relate the support services they provide to the costs associated with providing the services. Product vendors may offer several levels of user support services, including a free level, a standard (fee-for-service) level, and a premium level, for clients who want immediate service. Although the premium service level may be more responsive to users than the free service or standard service, it also costs more to provide.

 In order to justify user support operations, managers often perform a cost-benefit analysis, a tool you will learn about in Chapter 8.

Support workers at all levels, even in entry-level positions, need to understand the importance of performance measures and the need to justify support services. Performance statistics impact user support management decisions, which directly affect support workers. A support worker who ignores performance and the need to justify support services may end up without a job.

ON THE WEB

Sun Microsystems offers a service to help organizations evaluate the performance of their help desk operations. You can view the criteria they use at **hda.sun.com/ HelpDeskWeb.pdf**. Although many of the criteria are specific to Sun products and services, the document provides additional insight into how help desk performance is evaluated.

Staffing the Help Desk

Help desk managers are responsible for determining the number of agents required, writing position descriptions, and selecting staff members.

Help Desk Staffing Levels

An ongoing challenge for many user support and help desk managers is determining how many support agents are needed to meet the service levels that are expected of the support group. Obviously, support managers want to employ and schedule sufficient staff to meet the performance expectations detailed in the help desk's mission statement. On the other hand, support managers do not want to hire staff beyond the level needed to be responsive to users' needs. If they hire excessive staff, the department's performance statistics when compared to staff expenses will suffer.

So how many support staff workers are required to meet a targeted service level? This problem is similar to determining the number of cashiers a grocery store needs to keep checkout lines from getting too long (which frustrates clients) or too short (which leaves cashiers idle). A calculation tool called an Erlang unit is often used in these situations. An **Erlang** is a unit of traffic (or a user incident, in the case of support groups) processed in a given period of time. The Erlang calculation is used in a variety of situations in which there are queues (such as clients waiting on hold or customers waiting for grocery store cashiers). Managers may also use trial and error, previous experience, or a sophisticated calculator to help make help desk staffing decisions.

ON THE WEB

Westbay Engineers provides an online Erlang calculator to estimate support center staffing needs. See its Web site at **www.erlang.com**, click **Free Calculators**, and then click **Call Centre Calculator**.

Help Desk Position Descriptions

An applicant for a help desk or user support position should be aware of the support manager's staffing priorities. User support staffing decisions often begin with the support group's mission statement. Based on the mission statement, a user support manager writes one

258

or more position descriptions: one if the user support operation is small, several for a help desk operation that has a large staff or a multilevel structure. The position descriptions (like those you examined in Chapter 1) are also based on an analysis of the knowledge and skills that user support staff members need. The mission statement, position descriptions, and a list of the specific knowledge, skills, and abilities (KSAs) required for a user support operation are important resources for managers who must staff a help desk or support group.

A KSA analysis for a user support position begins with a written list of technical, business, and communications qualifications required for a position. These qualifications spell out the position's requirements in terms of:

- Hardware, operating systems, and applications software proficiency

- Technical skills

- Network knowledge and experience

- Internet and Web expertise

- Troubleshooting and problem-solving capabilities

- Communication, listening, writing, and telephone skills

- Work experience as a project team member

- Understanding business information systems and business perspectives

Support managers use categories of qualifications like these as a checklist to develop detailed job-related requirements for specific positions. For example, a support position may require a person to work with Intel-compatible hardware platforms in an office local area network (LAN) environment and to have Windows XP or Vista operating system experience and a working knowledge of Microsoft Office applications software. A help desk manager might emphasize the importance of communication skills and interpersonal relationships for an entry-level position in a help desk that provides primarily telephone support. A manager would probably place greater emphasis on technical knowledge and troubleshooting skills when hiring for a position that provides more advanced technical support.

 Because help desk managers often do not find job candidates who have all of the KSAs they are seeking, job applicants should not rule out positions for which they meet most, but not all, of the qualifications.

After a support manager has developed a detailed list of KSAs, the next step is to develop a position description. Well-written position descriptions, like those in Chapter 1, contain a clear explanation of the staff member's duties and responsibilities. A support manager then uses the position description and KSA checklist to prepare a job posting (for a newspaper classified ad section or a Web-based job board) or position order (for an employment or temporary worker agency). However, the position description and KSA checklist are really wish lists. A manager of support services may or may not find applicants who possess 100 percent of the desired characteristics and skills.

Screening Applicants

The search for a new staff member continues when a support manager receives applications. The next step often involves a selection team who represent the current support staff, user support management, IT Department (if applicable), and Human Resources Department. This team screens resumes and applications to narrow the list of candidates. Applicants whose personal KSAs most closely match the position requirements advance to the next stage in screening—the interview. Some selection teams check applicants' employment and academic references prior to an interview; others check these references after the interview.

Interviewing Applicants

During an interview, managers use a variety of selection tools that may include several kinds of questions:

- Knowledge and skills tests
- Traditional interview questions, including directed and non-directed questions
- Behavioral questions
- Scenario questions
- Stress tolerance assessment
- Illegal questions

A **knowledge and skills test** is a paper and pencil, verbal, or online test that measures a prospective worker's knowledge and problem-solving abilities. These tests may include written, verbal, and/or hands-on components. The tests may be supplied from a vendor that provides testing materials, or they may be developed by a support group specifically for its job applicants.

 An increasing number of user support positions are now advertised on the Web. However, only a fraction of job openings are advertised publicly in any medium. Many job seekers learn about open support positions through informal channels, such as a current employee of an organization or an instructor in a vocational/technical school or community college who has contacts with support employers.

259

ON THE WEB

An example of a vendor that sells help desk aptitude and skills tests is Expert Rating, at **www.expertrating.com/employers/employers.html**.

Employment interviews often include traditional questions about an applicant's resume and qualifications. Some questions are **directed** at specific job requirements and are intended to find out whether an applicant has specific educational or work experiences.

What courses have you taken to prepare yourself to support desktop operating systems?

Other questions are **non-directed**; they are open-ended and are intended to give an applicant an opportunity to talk in general terms about their qualifications for a position.

Tell me about your customer service experience.

ON THE WEB

To view some sample help desk interview questions, visit **www.best-job-interview.com/help-desk-interview-questions.html**. For some examples of general job interview questions and suggested answers, see **jobsearch.about.com/od/interviewquestionsanswers/a/interviewquest.htm**.

Interviews for help desk positions may also include **behavioral questions**, which give an applicant an opportunity to describe the actions she or he took in a specific situation.

Describe the most difficult user you've had to deal with and how you interacted with that person.

ON THE WEB

Examples of behavioral interview questions can be found at **www.emurse.com/blog/2007/05/21/complete-list-of-behavioral-interview-questions**.

Help desk applicants should also be prepared for scenario questions, which help to identify candidates' strengths and weaknesses. A **scenario question** gives applicants a specific problem (or set of problems) representative of the kinds of situations that user support agents actually encounter. A scenario might be a written exercise (sometimes provided as a supplemental questionnaire when an applicant first applies) or a problem-solving exercise during an interview. Interviews for a telephone support position often include an activity that requires an applicant to answer questions in a simulated telephone environment so that the applicant's telephone skills can be evaluated. Scenario questions provide insights into an applicant's problem-solving, conflict-resolution, and communication skills, as well as his or her ability to perform in stressful work situations. When combined with traditional interview questions, the scenario approach is often more effective than traditional interview questions alone in identifying staff who can work well under pressure. Here is a sample scenario:

Suppose a user in the manufacturing division approaches you and wants to bend your ear about the endless network problems that have been affecting the productivity of manufacturing workers. The user relates that manufacturing workers have experienced an increasing volume of network crashes in recent weeks. The user says that it takes forever to get the network restarted when it crashes, and the downtime affects the workers' productivity. The user also mentions that other manufacturing workers feel that they would be better off scrapping the network and working with the manual system they used to have. As a new user support staff member, how would you respond?

Scenario questions can often be answered from a number of perspectives. Some applicants might treat this scenario question as an opportunity to display their technical knowledge about networks. Others might discuss the problem-solving and communication skills they would use to address the problem within the organization.

As if employment interviews are not stressful enough, another interview tactic is a stress tolerance assessment. A **stress tolerance assessment** is an interview environment designed to help employers evaluate how well a job applicant works under pressure. Elements that can add stress to an interview situation include a very noisy interview environment (perhaps with interruptions), interviews by several interviewers, some of whom seem to have different agendas, overly technical questions, and similar tactics.

Finally, both selection teams and job applicants need to be alert to **illegal questions** during an interview, which are designed to obtain information about an applicant's characteristics that are not specifically job-related. Examples of illegal questions may include those that are intended to learn about an applicant's age, ethnicity, marital status, sexual orientation, religion, and some information about disabilities.

ON THE WEB

To learn more about illegal interview questions and how to handle them, visit **www.ehow.com/how_2140042_handle-illegal-intervew-questions.html**.

Many career centers in colleges, universities, and vocational/technical schools offer practice job interviews (as well as résumé preparation) as a part of their services.

For many entry-level job applicants, the employment interview is one of the most anticipated and daunting parts of a job search. However, professionals who have had several job interviews say that the more interviewing experience they have, the more comfortable they are and the more confident they are about their interviewing skills. The following role-playing scenario is designed to help you prepare for job interviews.

A ROLE-PLAYING SCENARIO

The purpose of this role-playing activity is to help prospective job applicants prepare for future employment interviews.

- Select a job description for a typical help desk or user support position. Use a position description from Chapter 1, or find another one that interests you.

- Work with a team of three or four colleagues or fellow students to discuss and prepare some sample interview questions for the position you identified. Limit the number of questions to a few that could be answered in 10–15 minutes.

- Discuss some effective answers to the sample questions with members of the team.

- For some ideas on questions, download a PDF from TechRepublic's Web site at **i.i.com.com/cnwk.1d/i/tr/downloads/home/ 10_questions_help_desk_hires.pdf**.

- Arrange some practice interview situations in which one team member plays the role of the interviewer and another plays the role of a job applicant. Other team members can observe the interview and evaluate how well the job applicant did.

- After each role-playing interview, the interviewer and observers should give the job applicant feedback on what he or she did well, and how his or her interview skills could be improved.

- Remember: the purpose of this activity is to get interviewing experience and help team members improve their interviewing skills. If possible, give each team member more than one opportunity to be interviewed. Participants in similar role-playing activities have said that it often feels like an actual interview, and that they feel more confident about their skills after just one or two practice interviews.

User Support Staff Training

One of the most important aspects of user support and help desk management is staff training. Support **staff training** includes new worker orientation and ongoing training, which allows staff to keep their knowledge and skills current. A well-trained support staff is a critical component of success for a help desk operation. Without a well-trained staff, a help desk can rarely meet its performance objectives. It is important for both management and staff to understand that training is a two-way street. A help desk management team needs to provide training and professional development opportunities for its staff members, including time away from routine responsibilities to participate in training activities. And help desk professionals need to seek out and take advantage of ways to keep their job skills up-to-date in an industry that is constantly changing. As you will see in this section, performance appraisals are often used to identify training needs for help desk staff.

 Many of the end user training methods and strategies you will learn about in Chapter 10 are also effective for training user support staff.

Orientations for New Staff

Some support organizations assume that help desk agents will learn on the job about the organization, the products supported, and the help desk's policies and procedures. However, a more common practice is for an organization to conduct one or more training sessions for new support employees, which often include information relating to:

- Organizational culture, policies, and procedures

- Payroll and employee benefits

- Specific job skill training

- Available help desk tools, including the phone system and incident management software

- Support group policies and procedures

- Performance appraisal criteria and procedures

- Professional development and career path opportunities

Of these training topics, information about support group policies and procedures is especially important. New employees need to have specific job skills to function effectively, but they also need to learn where to find answers to questions such as, "What is the company's policy if a client insists on a refund?" or "What is the recommended procedure if a client demands to speak to a supervisor or the company president?" Although it is not possible to learn about every organizational policy or procedure during an orientation period, it is important that training sessions cover basic information about the organization's general user support philosophy.

ON THE WEB

TechRepublic's Web site frequently carries articles on the training needs of new help desk workers. For example, read Jeff Davis' article *Training Tips Can Jump-Start Your Help Desk Team* at **www.techrepublic.com/article. jhtml?id=r00320010612jed01.htm,** or Jeff Dray, *Create Structured Training for Help Desk Staffers* at **www.techrepublic. com/article.jhtml?id=r00320030415dra01.htm.**

Ongoing Help Desk Training

Often, the biggest challenge in support staff training is scheduling training time for staff members who are in constant demand. To allow support staff members enough time for training, special projects, and paperwork, many managers schedule agents for only a portion of their total work shift (for example, six hours of an eight-hour shift).

Training programs for user support workers should help keep support staff current with changes in computer technology and the way in which the changes affect their client base. However, keeping a team members' knowledge and skills current is a joint obligation. Company training programs for support staff are only half of the solution; personal professional growth is the other half. User support workers are computer professionals who are expected to invest in their own continuing education. They should commit to attending conferences, training sessions, and workshops; reading trade publications and books; and making an investment in their professional growth commensurate with their employer's investment.

Performance Appraisals

Support managers should also communicate with support workers about when and how job performance is evaluated. **Performance appraisal** is the process of evaluating a user support worker according to established achievement criteria. The performance appraisal criteria should be related to the support group's mission, the appropriate position description, and the worker's professional growth objectives. If performance statistics like those described earlier in the chapter are used as part of the performance appraisal process, then managers should communicate to team members the way in which those statistics are collected, interpreted, and used. Support managers often use recordings of monitored support calls to help workers identify areas where performance improvement is needed. In many support groups, performance appraisals are important tools for identifying worker training needs.

If one goal of a support group mission is to provide high-quality service to its users, support workers also need time to learn how to be productive with new technology. Successful user support operations invest in new employee training, ongoing job training, and regular performance appraisals to keep the staff's skills up to date.

User Support Certification

A significant trend in education, training, and employment in the computer field in recent years is certification of knowledge, skills, and abilities. **Certification** is an assessment process to measure and document worker knowledge and skills in a specialized segment of the information technology field. The role that industry certification now plays in the user support field is like one leg of a three-legged stool: education, experience, and certification. Certification offers several benefits to both employers and support workers, as we will see later in this section.

Several kinds of certification are common:

- Formal education that results in a certificate, diploma, or degree

- Vendor-specific product knowledge and skills certification

- Industry-standard knowledge and skills certification in a specific area, such as hardware, networking, or support

- Certification that measures the fitness of a support group against industry-standard criteria

Formal Education Certification

Community colleges and vocational/technical schools have been in the certification business for many years. After a student has successfully completed a well-defined program of courses, the student graduates with a certificate, diploma, or degree. However, certification based on formal education or training from a degree or certificate-granting educational institution may document only general knowledge and skills. Employers are often also interested in a job applicant's specific expertise. For example, a degree in computer user support, or a related field, does not necessarily guarantee that a job applicant has specialized or technical expertise in, say, Windows Vista, although many user support degree programs today include coursework in that operating system. Similarly, coursework in *operating systems* does not guarantee that a graduate can apply what he or she has learned specifically to the Linux operating system.

Some job applicants who excelled at studying a body of material and passing a test discovered that they could study a CNE preparatory book, pass the certification exam, and advertise that they were qualified CNEs. They had a paper to certify their expertise, but no real expertise. Employers coined the term "paper CNE" to describe a person who had passed the CNE test, but did not have any practical knowledge or hands-on networking experience.

Vendor-Specific Certification

Partly in reaction to the industry-wide need to certify product-specific knowledge and skills, vendors in the computer industry offer a variety of certificates that assess knowledge and skills in a specialized product. One of the first vendor-specific certifications was Novell's Certified NetWare Engineer (CNE), created in the early 1990s. The CNE certification process resulted in thousands of network specialists who were certified as specialists on Novell network products. Because the CNE was vendor-specific, however, it did not indicate that a certificate holder necessarily knew anything about the network products of other vendors such as Microsoft or Cisco. As a result, other network vendors began to offer certifications in their specific product lines.

Today, certification is available for many vendor-specific products. Some examples are described in Table 6-1.

Vendor	URL	Certificate/Area of Expertise
Microsoft	**www.microsoft.com/ learning/mcp/msbc/ requirements/default.mspx** For an overview of Microsoft's certification program, visit **www.microsoft.com/ learning/mcp/default.mspx**	• Microsoft Certified Application Specialist (MCAS) offers certifications in Microsoft Office 2007 applications such as Word, Excel, Access, Outlook, and PowerPoint, as well as Windows Vista. The Microsoft Office Specialist certificates (MOS) are for Microsoft Office 2003 versions and Windows XP. • Microsoft Certified Application Professional (MCAP) certifies advanced skills in organizational support, including managing presentations, work teams, and budgets. • Microsoft Certified Technology Specialist (MCTS) certifications document skills with Windows 2008 server and Microsoft network support.
Cisco	**www.cisco.com/web/ learning/le3/learning_ certification_overview.html**	• Cisco Certified Network Associate (CCNA) in network administration
Novell	**www.novell.com/training/ certinfo/cna/index.html**	• Certified Novell Administrator (CNA) in basic networking
	www.novell.com/training/ certinfo/cne/index.html	• Certified Novell Engineer (CNE) in advanced Novell networking projects
Apple	**training.apple.com/ certification/acsp**	• Apple Certified Support Professional (ACSP) covers the Mac OS X operating system and the ability to configure, troubleshoot, and support Macintosh systems.

Table 6-1 Examples of vendor-specific certification programs

ON THE WEB

To see a more complete list of hardware, software, and networking product vendors' certification Web sites, visit **certification.about.com/cs/vendorsites**.

Industry-Standard Certification

An alternate kind of certification is not vendor-specific, but rather aims to measure industry-standard knowledge and skills. Because it is not tied to a specific vendor or product line, this kind of certification is more general and is vendor-neutral. In addition to hardware, operating systems, and troubleshooting skills, industry-standard certifications cover a variety of specialized skills, such as network administration, Web design, and project management. Examples of certification targeted at an industry-wide audience of employers and workers are listed in Table 6-2.

 Project management is covered in Chapter 8, where you will also learn about Microsoft Project 2007, a software tool used to manage special user support projects.

Organization	URL	Certificate/Area of Expertise
Computer Technology Industry Association (CompTIA)	**www.comptia.org**	• A+ certification covers hardware and operating systems, including basic knowledge of configuring, installing, diagnosing, repairing, upgrading, and maintaining computers.
		• Network+ covers network architecture and operating systems, including installing, configuring, and troubleshooting a network client.
		• Security+ certifies skills in organizational security including access controls, authentication, infrastructure, and operational security.
		• Project+ certifies project management skills.
Institute for Certification of Computing Professionals (ICCP)	**www.iccp.org/iccpnew/ acp.html**	• Associate Computer Professional (ACP) certifies knowledge and skills earned primarily through academic or vocational degree programs.
Linux Professional Institute	**www.lpi.org**	• Linux Professional Institute Certification (LPIC) certifies workers who administer the Linux operating system.
Society of Internet Professionals	**www.sipgroup.org/ certification.html**	• Accredited Internet Professional (AIP) covers Web site design, management, and e-business skills.

Table 6-2   Examples of industry-wide certification programs

User Support and Help Desk Certification

In addition to certification in a technical specialty (either vendor-specific or vendor-neutral), user support specialists and help desk staff can also get their support skills certified. Help Desk Institute is a professional organization that certifies support professionals. Microsoft also provides certifications targeted at the technical skills of desktop support workers. User support certifications vary in terms of the topics they cover. Visit the Web sites listed in Table 6-3 for current details on certifications available, topics covered, how to prepare, and costs.

Organization	URL	Certificate/Area of Expertise
Help Desk Institute (HDI)	**www.thinkhdi. com/certification/ individualCertification/**	• Support Center Analyst (SCA) certification targets help desk agents who are the primary contact for customers.
		• Desktop Support Technician (DST) certification is for user support workers who provide face-to-face technical support.
		• Other HDI certifications are for:
		• Customer Service Representatives (CSR)
		• Help Desk Team Leads
		• Help Desk Managers
Microsoft	**www.microsoft.com/ learning/mcp/mcts/ vistaconfig/default.mspx**	• Microsoft Certified Technology Specialist (MCTS) certification covers configuring and supporting Windows Vista.
	www.microsoft.com/ learning/mcp/mcitp/vista/ consumer/default.mspx	• Microsoft Certified IT Professional: Consumer Support Technician (MCITP) covers configuring and supporting Windows Vista and applications software that runs on Vista.
	www.microsoft.com/ learning/mcp/mcdst/ default.mspx	• Microsoft Certified Desktop Support Technician (MCDST) covers supporting users and troubleshooting Windows XP and applications that run on XP.

Table 6-3   Examples of user support and help desk certification programs

User Support Center Certification Programs

Some certification programs are aimed at organizations, rather than individuals. For example, as part of the professional services it provides to its members, the Help Desk Institute offers programs to certify entire help desk groups. Some of these certification programs include consulting services on support industry best practices, such as the Information Technology Infrastructure Library (ITIL). As you learned in Chapter 5, best practices are procedures, tools, and methods employed by very successful support groups.

The Benefits of Certification

For help desk and user support specialists, some of the benefits of certification include:

- A recognized benchmark of minimum-level job skills and expertise in the area covered by certification

- A justification for receiving higher pay, as a new or experienced worker

- Career advancement opportunities because of documented knowledge and skills

- A way for an employer to document an employee's efforts to keep up-to-date in the computer field

- A feeling of pride of accomplishment and increased job satisfaction upon passing a certification milestone

The most common certifications for user support and help desk professionals are the CompTIA A+ and Microsoft MCAS (formerly MOS) certifications. The A+ certification covers hardware, operating systems, and troubleshooting strategies. The MCAS certification documents that a job applicant meets a minimum level of expertise in popular Microsoft applications software packages.

Is certification a requirement for a support position? Some employers specify in job announcements and ads for support positions that they expect applicants to be certified, perhaps in addition to their formal education. However, many employers do not expect or require applicants to be certified. Even these employers, however, may view an applicant's certification as additional evidence of qualification for a support position. Organizations that require prospective support employees to be certified as a help desk professional are not yet common, because the skills required for help desk positions vary between organizations, and certification exams are not yet standardized nor universally recognized.

ON THE WEB

Since the names and details of each certification program change frequently, you can get up-to-date information about industry certifications and exam procedures at **www.certmag.com**. The site also offers a free subscription to an online magazine and newsletter.

Certification Exam Preparation

Many computer industry professionals believe they should be able to pass a certification exam based on their lengthy experience in the industry. However, these exams are not easy to pass, especially for those who do little to prepare. Some exam providers permit exam retakes after additional preparation.

Many college and vocational/technical schools now match the curriculum in their courses with the most common certifications. For example, an introductory spreadsheet course may be targeted at students who wish to prepare for the MCAS Excel exam. An advantage of a preparatory course in a college or vocational/technical school is that assistance is usually available when a student has questions about the course material.

Other common ways to prepare for a certification exam include crash courses, online tutorials, and self-study courses. **Crash courses**, sometimes called boot camps, are intensive classes designed to prepare participants in a short time (usually a week or less) to take a certification exam. Crash courses are expensive, and a student usually must travel to the site where the course is offered. However, for professionals who have experience in a subject area, crash courses are a quick way to review material and prepare to get certified. Several training vendors offer **online tutorial courses** in either computer-based training (CBT) or Web-based training (WBT) formats. CBT and WBT preparatory courses usually cost substantially less than crash courses, but frequently do not include assistance if a student needs help with course materials. Finally, **self-study courses** are preparatory materials, usually in book format, which readers complete at their own pace. The books are often a thousand or more pages. Some are packaged with CBT tutorials and with practice exam questions. Although generally less costly, self-study courses rarely provide student assistance. The market for certification preparatory courses is large, and both product vendors and third-party training vendors offer materials and services to meet the growing interest in industry certification.

ON THE WEB

Organizations that offer certification exam preparation courses include:

- MindLeaders (**link.mindleaders.com/e-learn/courseprice.jsp**)

- Netwind Learning Center (**www.netwind.com**)

- Aaron's Computer Training (**www.aarons-computer-training.com**)

- Learnthat.com (**www.learnthat.com/courses**)

(continues)

(continued)

Many of these training vendors offer a free sample lesson on their Web sites. For other training and certification vendors, see an online list at **dmoz.org/Computers/Education/Certification**.

Prometric is an organization that offers many types of certification tests in testing centers throughout the United States. Prometric's Web site (**www.prometric.com/default.htm**) is a good certification resource because it includes links to Web sites where various certification programs are described. Another organization that offers similar services is Pearson Vue (**www.vue.com**).

Most certification exams are administered on a computer workstation. Some are traditional tests, which ask test takers a fixed-length sequence of questions, similar to the final exam in a college course. In the traditional format, each test taker answers the same set of questions. However, certification exams often use a type of test called an adaptive test. An **adaptive test** asks questions selected from a test database to try to estimate the test taker's ability quickly. The test database for an adaptive test consists of questions that are graded from easy to moderate to difficult. The first question asked in an adaptive test session is of moderate difficulty. As the test taker answers each question, an adaptive test uses a mathematical formula to estimate the test taker's level of ability. Subsequent questions asked are either easier or more difficult, based on the pattern of previous right and wrong answers. An adaptive test continually selects questions from the test database and revises its estimate of the test taker's ability until it is relatively certain that it has an accurate measure. Sometimes the estimation process requires as few as 15 questions. Thus, some test takers may answer more questions than others. Some may respond to easier questions; others may respond to more difficult ones, as an adaptive test hones in on the test taker's ability. Adaptive testing saves time because fewer questions are asked; it reduces boredom from too many easy or repetitive questions; it reduces intimidation from very difficult questions; and ideally, it makes the testing process shorter and less stressful.

 Some certification tests include scenario questions that require the test taker to answer questions using a simulated version of a product. Certification exams also frequently include a hands-on component to eliminate the "paper CNE" phenomenon described earlier.

272

ON THE WEB

For a brief article on computer adaptive testing (CAT), go to **www.appliedskills.com/whitepapers/files/CATs_Item_Banks.pdf**.

ON THE WEB

For information about various certification pre-tests, visit the following vendors' Web sites:

- InformIT's Exam Cram 2 (**www.informit.com/imprint/index.aspx?st=61087**)

- Transcender (**www.transcender.com**)

- Brainbench, which offers a free certification exam for Computer Technical Support agent (**www.brainbench.com/xml/bb/common/testcenter/taketest.xml?testId=68**).

User Support as a Profession

The number of user support and help desk positions in the United States and worldwide increased significantly in the 1990s. However, the recession in the United States that ran from 2001 through 2003 reduced employment in the user support industry, as did the trend to outsource some low-level support positions overseas. The U.S. Bureau of Labor Statistics estimates that over 800,000 workers were employed as computer support specialists and system administrators in 2006, as shown in Table 6-4 below. Most of these were employed as user support workers, help desk agents, and network administrators.

	Employment in 2006	Projected employment in 2016	Net increase in employment	Percent increase in employment
Computer Support Specialists	552,000	624,000	+71,000	+13%
Network and Computer System Administrators	309,000	393,000	+83,000	+27%
Total	862,000	1,016,000	+155,000	+18%

Table 6-4   U.S. employment in user and network support positions (all numbers are rounded)
SOURCE: Bureau of Labor Statistics, "*Occupational Outlook Handbook, 2008–09 edition: Computer Support Specialists and Systems Administrators*," accessed at **www.bls.gov/oco/ocos268. htm#projections_data**.

The recession that began in 2008 may have an impact on these long-term projections; however, the category of Computer Support Specialists is expected to increase at about an average rate compared with most U.S. occupational employment in the next decade. The category of Network and Computer System Administrators is expected to increase at a rate much faster than average.

Examples of related occupations not reported in Table 6-4 include technical writers, trainers, project managers, and Web programmers who may have user support responsibilities.

ON THE WEB

To learn more about these employment categories and employment projections, visit the U.S. Bureau of Labor Statistics (BLS) Web site at **www.bls.gov/oco/ocos268. htm**. A detailed breakdown of employment on the BLS Web site reports on the distribution of workers by industry.

As a result of the large number of people employed in the user support field, several groups have been organized to provide a professional association for these workers. A **professional association** is a formal organization that represents the interests of a group of professionals and provides services to its membership. Professional associations that are targeted to user support and help desk managers and staff are listed in Table 6-5.

274

Association	URL
Help Desk Institute	**www.thinkhdi.com**
Association of Support Professionals	**www.asponline.com**
Network and Systems Professionals Association	**www.naspa.com**
Association of Information Technology Professionals	**www.aitp.org**
Women in Technology	**www.womenintechnology.org**

Table 6-5   User support and help desk professional associations

Professional associations perform a number of functions for their membership. They often publish journals or magazines with articles of interest to the support profession. These associations encourage their members to grow professionally by offering books, seminars, conferences, and other professional growth and development activities. Some associations offer certification programs for their membership. All associations maintain Web sites with links to other sites of interest. Some offer chat rooms, forums, newsgroups, local chapters, and e-mail services with industry news.

One activity a professional association may undertake is to adopt a **code of ethical conduct** or principles to guide its members' professional behavior. Examples of ethical standards to which professional associations expect their members to adhere are shown in Figure 6-3.

ON THE WEB

Web sites where you can view examples and learn more about guidelines for ethical professional conduct include:

- Association of Information Technology Professionals (AITP) (**www.aitp.org/organization/about/ethics/ethics.jsp**)

- Canadian Information Processing Society (CIPS) (**www. cips.ca/about?q=ethics**)

- The SANS Institute (**www.sans.org/resources/ethics.php**)

Example principles of ethical conduct for IT professionals

1. Adhere to federal, state, and local laws, including those that govern information technology, workplace and public health and safety, and the environment.

2. Keep abreast of developments and trends in technology and participate in professional growth and development activities in your area of specialization.

3. Advocate for a better understanding of technology among end users and the public.

4. Act with integrity and honesty in dealing with the public, end users, coworkers, management, and competitors.

5. Avoid conflicts of interest, abuse of power, use of position for personal gain, and exhibit fairness in relationships with others.

6. Avoid workplace discrimination based on gender, ethnicity, sexual orientation, marital status, age, religion, or disability.

7. Respect the intellectual property and copyrights of end users, coworkers, vendors, and competitors, and give credit for others' work.

8. Protect the privacy and reputations of end users.

9. Perform job-related responsibilities in accordance with company policies and industry best practices.

10. Adhere to acceptable technology use policies and do not make unauthorized or personal use of property or resources.

11. Report violations of ethical principles of conduct.

12. Report all security vulnerabilities and work to eliminate harmful uses of technology.

Figure 6-3   Example principles of ethical conduct for IT professionals

The purpose of this chapter has not been to provide a comprehensive primer on user support management, but to discuss selected aspects of support management with an emphasis on information that is likely to be of interest and useful to job applicants and entry-level workers. If you are interested in career advancement into a user support management position, consider taking a community college or vocational/technical school course on business management for a comprehensive look at tasks that challenge managers.

ON THE WEB

Two "hot topic" user support management issues not included in this chapter are salaries and employee retention.

- Each October, *ComputerWorld* conducts an annual salary survey of the information technology field. The survey includes job titles such as help desk/technical support specialist. The survey for 2008 is available online at **www. computerworld.com/action/article.do?command= viewArticleBasic&articleId=9119020**. The survey is nationwide, but it includes some breakdowns that reflect regional differences in salaries.

- For another perspective on salaries, consult **www.salary. com**. In the Salary Wizard box, enter a job title such as help desk, user support, or network support, and your zip code. Then click base salary range.

- Support managers concerned with employee retention should consult a TechRepublic article, "Strategies to boost morale and retention in call center environments," at **techrepublic.com.com/5100-6269-5088913.html**.

Chapter Summary

- People in user support and help desk management positions include those who work as supervisors, lead workers, and project coordinators. Many support groups develop a mission statement to describe the guiding principles and objectives against which the support group can evaluate its performance.

- Performance statistics are used to measure the extent to which a support group and its staff members meet the objectives described in its mission statement. Support groups also use satisfaction surveys to collect data on individual and group performance. Performance measures are often used as part of a periodic performance appraisal of support workers.

- Support managers with an open position analyze the knowledge, skills, and abilities (KSAs) needed for the position and then prepare a position description listing the job qualifications required of applicants.

- The interview process for support positions may include a knowledge and skills test, traditional directed and non-directed interview questions, behavioral and scenario questions, and even stress tolerance questions to gauge an applicant's ability to think under pressure and solve problems. Interviewers and job applicants need to be aware of questions that are illegal to ask during an interview.

- Training programs for support staff include new employee orientation and ongoing professional development. Performance appraisals of user support workers provide important input into professional development for workers.

- Certification in the information technology industry includes college degrees, vendor-specific certification, and industry-standard certification programs. Support professionals can earn certifications in specialized products as well as certifications of their support skills. Adaptive tests are often used in the certification exam process.

- In addition to the industry trend toward certification of skills, associations of support professionals have evolved to meet the needs of workers in IT and the support field. Some professional associations publish codes of ethics and standards of conduct to guide their members.

Key Terms

abandonment rate—The percentage of calls in which the user hangs up before support staff respond.

adaptive test—A certification testing method that asks questions that are graded in difficulty from easy to moderate to difficult to try to quickly estimate a test taker's ability.

behavioral question—An interview question that gives a job applicant an opportunity to describe how she or he behaved in a specific work situation.

certification—An assessment process to measure and document a professional's knowledge and skills in a specialized segment of the information technology field.

code of ethical conduct—Principles to guide a worker's professional behavior; a code of conduct is often distributed by a professional association for its membership.

cost center operation—A user support operation for which the cost of providing services appears as an expense in an organization's budget without an offsetting revenue stream.

crash course—An intensive class, sometimes called a boot camp, designed to prepare participants to take a certification exam in a week or less.

directed question—An interview question about a specific job requirement; directed questions are intended to learn whether an applicant has specific educational or work experiences.

Erlang—A unit of traffic (user incidents, in the case of a support group) processed in a given period of time; it is used to estimate the number of support staff required to respond to an expected volume of incidents in a given time period.

illegal question—An interview question that is intended to obtain information about an applicant's characteristics that are not specifically job related, such as age, ethnicity, marital status, sexual orientation, religion, and some information about disabilities.

knowledge and skills test—A test that measures a job applicant's knowledge and problem-solving abilities.

mission statement—A list of guiding principles that communicate the goals and objectives of a support group to its staff, users, and management.

non-directed question—An interview question that is open-ended and gives an applicant an opportunity to talk in general terms about their qualifications for a position.

online tutorial course—Computer-based training (CBT) or Web-based training (WBT) designed to prepare participants for a certification exam.

performance appraisal—The process of evaluating a user support worker according to established criteria; criteria should be related to the support group's mission, the worker's position description, and the worker's professional development objectives.

performance statistics—Objective data about a user support or help desk operation often directly related to the user support mission statement.

professional association—A formal organization that represents the interests of a group of professionals and provides services to its membership.

profit center operation—A user support operation for which the cost of providing services is treated as an expense that is offset by revenue generated by the group.

scenario question—An interview method that gives a job applicant a specific problem (or set of problems) representative of the kinds of situations user support staff actually encounter; scenario questions are used to measure the applicant's problem-solving skills and ability to work under pressure.

self-study course—Preparatory materials, usually in book format, which readers complete at their own pace prior to taking a certification exam.

staff training—Training designed to orient new support workers to their jobs, as well as ongoing training to update the skills and encourage professional growth of experienced support staff.

stress tolerance assessment—An interview environment designed to evaluate how well a job applicant works under pressure.

user satisfaction survey—A questionnaire that attempts to measure how satisfied users are with the support services they have experienced.

wait time—The average time it takes a help desk to respond to calls.

Check Your Understanding

Answers to Check Your Understanding questions are found in Appendix A.

1. True or False? The employee selection process for a help desk position can be described as an attempt to find applicants with the knowledge, skills, and abilities that most closely match the position's requirements.

2. True or False? Unlike a question in a knowledge and skills test, there is only one correct answer to a scenario question in a job interview.

3. One primary purpose of help desk performance statistics is to:

   a. respond to computer auditors' information requirements

   b. justify the value and expense of help desk services

   c. report to company stockholders

   d. respond to complaints from angry users

4. True or False? Organizations that treat user support as a profit center may have difficulty justifying the cost of support services.

5. Which of the following aspects of help desk operation would you least expect to be covered in a help desk mission statement?

   a. operational efficiency of users

   b. help desk fees for services

   c. customer satisfaction

   d. effectiveness of help desk services

6. A(n) _____ is a process to evaluate a help desk or support worker according to established criteria.

7. A measure of the number of support calls that can be processed in a given time period, often used to determine staffing levels in a help desk operation, is:

   a. a statistical unit

   b. wait time

   c. an MCAS

   d. an Erlang

8. True or False? Support managers often use recordings of monitored support calls to help workers identify areas where performance improvement is needed.

9. True or False? A cost center is a help desk operation that has an expense budget, but no offsetting income budget.

10. True or False? Help desk industry certification is now essentially a requirement for any user support position.

11. Which of the following testing methods is commonly used in industry certification exams?

    a. adaptive test

    b. scenario test

    c. traditional fixed-length test

    d. best practices test

12. Which kind of interview question gives a job applicant an opportunity to describe what he or she did in a specific job situation?

    a. knowledge and skills question

    b. behavioral question

c. scenario question

d. illegal question

13. A(n) _____ is a set of behavior guidelines that a professional organization expects its members to follow.

14. "Tell me about your educational background." is an example of:

a. an illegal interview question

b. a stress tolerance question

c. a directed question

d. a non-directed question

15. Briefly list three examples of an interview situation which can be used to test a job applicant's stress tolerance.

16. In the next decade, the U.S. labor market demand for user support workers is expected to:

a. increase

b. remain about the same

c. decrease somewhat

d. decrease dramatically

17. _____ are recognized procedures, tools, and methods that very successful support groups use.

18. A questionnaire designed to measure the effectiveness of services among a sample of users is called:

a. a user satisfaction survey

b. a statistical analysis

c. a performance appraisal

d. an Erlang assessment

19. The percentage of calls in which a user hangs up before support staff respond is called:

a. wait time

b. frustration index

c. stress statistic

d. abandonment rate

20. A(n) _____ is a formal organization that represents the interest of a group of help desk professionals.

Discussion Questions

1. Is it ethical for a company that operates a telephone help desk to monitor its agents? Under what circumstances should this practice be permitted? Under what circumstances should this practice not be permitted?

2. Will industry certification ever become a minimum job requirement for employment in the user support field? Why, or why not?

3. Is a code of professional ethics, like the examples provided in this chapter, useful for a field as diverse as user support, in which there are so many different kinds of jobs? How would you make the ethical principles more specific to a help desk or user support worker?

4. "A mission statement for a user support group is worthless. It is just a statement of platitudes that are so general that they are almost meaningless." Do you agree or disagree with this statement? Explain your position.

5. What are the pros and cons of using a stress tolerance test as part of a job interview? In what cases should they be used? Not used?

6. Is professional growth and development for a user support worker primarily the worker's responsibility or primarily the responsibility of the organization for which the employee works? Explain your position.

Hands-On Activities

Activity 6-1

Evaluate a user support mission statement. Locate the mission statement for the help desk or user support group at your school or organization, or use the mission statement for California Polytechnic Institute's Service Desk at **www.servicedesk.calpoly.edu/computing_support/about_us/goals_mission.html**. Compare the mission statement with the sample in this chapter. List the similarities and differences you find.

Activity 6-2

Design criteria to evaluate a help desk or support group. Using the mission statement you worked with in Activity 6-1, write three measurable criteria that a manager could use to evaluate the performance of the help desk or support group.

Activity 6-3

Develop a professional growth plan. Write a one-page professional development growth plan for yourself. Base your plan on your personal assessment of your strengths and areas in which you would like to improve, either as a student and future job applicant, or as a current worker. In your development plan, describe the kinds of training, courses, seminars, books, or other learning experiences that would make you a more attractive job applicant or more valuable employee. List any industry certification exams you believe would enhance your employability or promotability. Compare your plan with ones developed by three classmates or coworkers. What useful ideas did you get from them?

Activity 6-4

Write a classified ad for a user support position. Find one or more ads online or in your local paper for information technology and user support positions. (These ads are usually located under "computers" or "information technology" headings.) Note the format and content of a typical help wanted ad in the IT field. Select one of the user support position descriptions in Chapter 1. Write a classified ad that could be used to attract job applicants for the position whose description you selected.

Activity 6-5

Write a scenario question for an interview. Develop a scenario question for a user support or help desk position that measures whether a job applicant is a good problem solver. Start by brainstorming some ideas with three classmates or coworkers. Select a scenario that is feasible for an interview. Remember the objective is to measure problem-solving ability. Work with your team to refine the wording of your scenario question to make it as useful as possible. Exchange your scenario question with another team and write a model response to their question.

Activity 6-6

Online training course evaluation. Use the Web-based resources described in this chapter to locate an online training course that you can try out at low or no cost. After you have worked on the course, answer the following questions:

- Did you finish the course? Why or why not?

- Did you find the course materials easy to use? List examples of any problems you encountered.

- Is an online learning environment effective for your personal learning style? How could the course be improved?

- How could the course be used as part of a training program for end users or support specialists?

Activity 6-7

Take a certification exam. Visit the Brainbench Web site (**www. brainbench.com**), and then click the **Individual Certification** link. Learn about the advantages of online certification. Pick one of the exam areas Brainbench offers and take the exam. Do not worry if you don't pass. The Brainbench tests are not easy, and the passing rate is low for some exams. The purpose of the exercise is to give you experience with a typical certification exam. Was the exam in a traditional format or was it an adaptive test? Write a summary of your experience, and explain how you could improve your performance on the next certification exam you take.

Activity 6-8

Evaluate help desk performance statistics. Read a paper "How to Measure Helpdesk Performance" at **www.techsupportalert. com/pdf/m0165.pdf**. Make a list of at least eight measures the author describes that could be used to evaluate a help desk operation or a help desk worker. From your list, pick the three measures you think are the most important ways to evaluate a help desk operation and three that you think are important measures of a help desk worker's performance. Write a brief description of the measures and explain why the measures you picked are important. Would you want to be evaluated using the measures you selected?

Activity 6-9

Design a short user satisfaction survey. Working with a team of colleagues, design a short questionnaire that could be used to measure user satisfaction with the performance of a help desk or computer teaching/training lab facility. Design at least five questions, one of which should ask about users' overall satisfaction with the help desk services or lab facility. Use the free service at Survey Monkey (**www.surveymonkey.com**) to build a survey that is accessible on the Web. If possible, get a group of typical users to take your survey so you can analyze the results.

Case Projects

1. Help Desk Performance at Virtual-Soft

Beth Goldman, supervisor of Virtual-Soft's Help Desk service, gets weekly data from a help desk software package on her support specialists' performance. She wants to use the data to measure her staff members' productivity. Use a spreadsheet program to enter the data for Beth's staff from last week shown in the table below.

Support Specialist	Calls Handled per Week	Available Hours per Week	Average Minutes per Call
Susan	112	31.5	14.2
Jose	127	31.0	11.3
Sue	0	0.0	0.0
Barbara	87	25.1	15.9
Ekaterina	151	30.0	9.2
Shere-Kahn	63	24.2	13.6
Dennis	77	29.6	11.9
Kristen	63	27.1	10.6

Beth thinks that productivity should be measured as *amount of work accomplished* divided by *effort expended*. Think about this definition of productivity. Then use your spreadsheet to calculate a measure of productivity you think would be appropriate for these workers. Who is the most productive agent on Beth's staff? Is there more than one right way to approach this problem? Print your spreadsheet and explain your results.

2. Help Desk Staffing at Game Shack Software

Game Shack Software develops and sells computer games and related products. Ronald Liew has recently been hired to manage Game Shack's help desk operation. The management at Game Shack is concerned about the best way to schedule help desk agents. They want to employ enough help desk agents to respond to the calls they receive from users, but they cannot afford to have an excess of agents scheduled to work when there are relatively few calls.

Ronald wants your advice about the size of the help desk staff that Game Shack needs as well as the best way to schedule agents during the day. Ron has collected data for a couple of weeks on the number of calls the Game Shack help desk receives. The busiest time of the day is from 9 A.M. to 4 P.M., during which the help desk receives an average of 155 calls. The calls average about 12 minutes, and it takes an agent an average of 2 additional minutes to finish a database entry and terminate the call. The current help desk guidelines at Game Shack state that 85 percent of the calls should be answered in 30 seconds or less. (No more than 1 percent of the calls should be lost because of insufficient available phone lines.)

The 155 calls each day are distributed approximately, as shown in the table below.

Hour	Calls
9 AM	10
10 AM	25
11 AM	25
12 PM	35
1 PM	20
2 PM	15
3 PM	15
4 PM	10

Use the Call Center Erlang calculator at **www.erlang.com** to advise Ronald about the following problems:

1. How many agents does Game Shack need to handle the volume of calls listed above?

2. How many telephone lines are required to meet Game Shack's objectives?

3. When is the peak call volume? How long will an average caller wait during the peak hour?

4. Describe the impact on staffing and number of lines Game Shack needs if the policy guideline on the percentage of calls answered in 30 seconds or less is increased to 95 percent.

3. A Slideshow on Help Desk Employee Retention

Use a variety of online resources to learn about employee retention of help desk and user support workers. You could research questions such as:

1. What are common reasons help desk employees leave their positions?

2. What is the annual turnover among help desk workers?

3. What kinds of programs do successful employers offer to retain help desk workers?

4. What kinds of worker benefits would make help desk workers more likely to stay in an existing position?

5. Are help desk employee retention programs effective?

Prepare a slideshow presentation that you could use to highlight your finding and suggestions. Make your slideshow an example of your best professional work.

CHAPTER 7

Product Evaluation Strategies and Support Standards

In this chapter, you will learn about:

- ◎ How product and support standards emerged
- ◎ Common tools and methods for evaluating and selecting computer products
- ◎ Information resources and decision-making tools for evaluating and selecting computer products
- ◎ Typical product support standards
- ◎ How organizations develop and implement support standards

In addition to the help desk support tasks described in earlier chapters, user support workers are often responsible for evaluating computer products and services and setting product standards for end users in their organization. These tasks are more common for support groups that provide services to internal users; however, some support workers occasionally work on product evaluation and standards for external users, often in the role of a consultant.

User support groups spend time and resources on product evaluations and standards for several reasons. First, support workers often have an expertise in these areas that end users do not have. (Even though a support specialist may have greater expertise than an end user, it is still vital that end users are involved in the process.) Second, assigning support staff the responsibility for product review and evaluation can eliminate duplication of effort. If each end user researches and evaluates products of special interest to him or her, the result can be wasted time as well as deviations from product standards. Third, support groups are often able to play the role of liaison between end users and the IT staff to ensure that all viewpoints are represented when computer products are evaluated and selected.

In this chapter, you will learn about several common methods that support specialists use to evaluate computer products and services and how product evaluations contribute to the definition of support standards. These standards are important for a variety of reasons, not the least of which is to reduce the burden on the support staff. Support staff resources are not unlimited; therefore agreeing to support a specific set of standard products is more realistic than attempting to support any product an end user might choose to use.

 At the end of this chapter, you will examine one organization's product support standards.

How Product Standards Emerged

When the era of end user computing first began, few organizations had established product standards. **Product standards** are lists of hardware, operating system, network, and application software products that have been approved for use within an organization. In the early 1980s, even users within the same department often used several different hardware platforms. Some of the first PC hardware manufacturers included Apple, KayPro, IBM, RadioShack, Commodore, Osborne, AlphaMicro, and Atari—each of whom claimed a share of the PC market. Each PC manufacturer touted the advantages of its system for users in specific application areas where its hardware had competitive strengths. Because manufacturers believed that significant differences between their products and competing products represented a marketing advantage, they felt little pressure to move toward an industry standard in PC hardware.

As widespread as the problem of incompatible and competing hardware platforms was, the problem was even worse in the software market. Owners of identical hardware models of IBM PCs, for example, could select a word processor from a long list that included WordStar, Microsoft Word, DisplayWrite, WordPerfect, PerfectWrite, and PFS Write. Because word processing was the leading application in businesses, many products competed for market share. The list of competing spreadsheet and database software was shorter, but several popular choices were available in those application areas, as well.

It might appear that product incompatibility and competition simply reflected a healthy, competitive market environment. However, from the perspective of an organization purchasing hardware and software products in the 1980s, the lack of product standards caused several problems, which are summarized in Figure 7-1.

Limited opportunities to transfer and share information among users
Incompatible hardware and software products meant that two coworkers might have difficulty sharing data. The primary method of exchanging data files was by transfer on a floppy disk. A floppy disk written on one manufacturer's computer frequently could not be read or modified on another manufacturer's hardware.

Large inventories of parts were required to repair incompatible PCs
To repair the various makes and models of computers its workers had purchased, an organization needed to maintain a large inventory of parts. Hardware incompatibilities substantially increased the cost to make even simple component repairs.

Increased difficulty of training and equipping hardware service technicians to repair different hardware platforms
In addition to large inventories of incompatible parts, technicians had to be trained to understand, diagnose, and repair many different kinds of computers. The architecture of each platform was frequently different.

User skills were difficult to transfer from one system to another
Workers could operate their own desktop system, but often knew little about the computers on their colleagues' desks. The lack of a standard operating system and applications software meant that workers often had difficulty filling in for an absent colleague, which reduced overall worker productivity.

Increased costs as support groups struggled to assist users with many different types of PCs and software
Support groups in large organizations were confronted with the need to provide training, documentation, troubleshooting assistance, hardware problem diagnosis, and software support and upgrades for a large number of incompatible hardware and software products.

Figure 7-1   Problems caused by computer product incompatibility

ON THE WEB

The History of Computing Project (THOCP) presents information about many early hardware and software vendors on its Web site (**www.thocp.net**).

As computer use grew during the 1980s and 1990s, organizations with large investments in computer hardware and software soon realized that a policy (or lack of one) that permitted employees to purchase any desktop computer they chose imposed significant additional support costs on the organization. To help control and reduce costs, many organizations developed product standards. First, they selected a small number of hardware platforms and configurations to meet their users' needs. Second, they adopted standard operating systems and, in the 1990s, network operating systems. Third, they limited the choice of applications software to one or at most a few standard applications packages in each software category.

Organizations handle the responsibility for setting organization-wide support standards in various ways. In many organizations, the head of the IT department, sometimes called the chief information officer (CIO), is ultimately responsible. The CIO may in turn, delegate the responsibility to a committee composed of end users, support staff, and technical IT staff. In other organizations, the task of establishing and enforcing computer product standards is the responsibility of the user support staff.

You will learn more about product standards later in this chapter. But first we will look at how organizations evaluate products so they can set effective standards.

Methods for Evaluating and Selecting Computer Products

To establish standards, the staff evaluates competing products, as shown in Figure 7-2. During **product evaluation**, the staff researches and analyzes computer product features, capabilities, and suitability to meet specific end user needs. In the evaluation process, staff members collect product information, conduct performance tests, compare competing products, make decisions or recommendations, and communicate the results of their work throughout the organization. Recommendations and decisions about which specific products to support are often made with input from end users, the user support staff, technical staff, and the organization's management team.

292

Figure 7-2 User support staff evaluate competing software products to set organizational product standards

The user support staff evaluates new hardware and software products and upgrades to existing products. When the support staff considers a new product, they are guided by questions such as:

1. Does the product or upgrade perform as advertised?

2. Is a competing product significantly better than the one currently in use?

3. Is a new product or upgrade compatible with existing hardware, network, and operating system configurations the organization uses?

4. Does the new product meet the needs of its users?

5. Will the product help increase user productivity?

6. Is the product cost-effective to purchase and support, and will it help reduce the total cost of ownership of technology to the organization?

7. Is the product likely to become an industry standard?

8. Is upgrading to the product now preferable to waiting for a later release?

9. Is the product stable enough that it will solve more problems than it creates?

 If each user in an organization performed his or her own product tests, their efforts would likely be repetitious and not very cost-effective. In addition, an end user who attempted to become knowledgeable about even a few new products could lose focus on his or her primary job.

Members of the user support staff who are familiar with the needs of the end users, computer products, and industry trends can research these and related questions. They can interview end users, observe their work habits, collect relevant product information, and ask critical questions to identify the advantages and disadvantages of competing products. Staff members who evaluate products also conduct product tests, which often take place under controlled conditions.

Information Resources

The user support staff has several tools and information resources at its disposal to help evaluate computer products. These resources include:

- Vendor literature, marketing information, Web sites, and user manuals
- Demonstration and evaluation versions of products
- Product reviews and comparison articles in computer periodicals and on the Web
- Opinions of industry experts published in trade periodicals and Internet newsgroups
- Opinions of colleagues who may have experience with a product

Examples of some of these resources are shown in Table 7-1. Although all are useful resources, independent tests and reviews with side-by-side comparisons of several competing products are often more helpful to evaluators than vendor-supplied information about a single product.

Categories of Product Information Resources	Examples
Vendor literature and marketing information	To download a sample product data sheet on Adobe Acrobat (version 9), go to **www.adobe.com/products/acrobatpro/pdfs/acrobatpro_datasheet.pdf**
Vendor Web sites	To visit the section of Toshiba's Web site that features their laptop computers, go to **explore.toshiba.com/laptops**
User manuals	To download a PDF file of one of several vendor's user manuals, visit Retrevo's Web site at **www.retrevo.com/samples/index.html**
Demonstration and evaluation software	To request a free, 60-day trial copy of ArcGIS (geographical information system) software, visit **www.esri.com/software/arcgis/arcview/eval/evalcd.html**
Product reviews	To read product reviews for several monochrome laser printers, visit **www.consumersearch.com/laser-printers-monochrome**
Product comparisons	To read an About.com product comparison of the Internet Explorer and Firefox Web browsers, visit **browsers.about.com/od/windowsbrowser1/ss/ievsfirefoxwin.htm**
Industry expert opinion	To read editorial opinions on several categories of computer products (hardware and software), visit CNET's Web site at **reviews.cnet.com**
User forums and blogs	To read a forum exchange on alternatives to Adobe products for editing PDF files, visit TechSoup's Web site at **forums.techsoup.org/cs/forums/t/22130.aspx**

Table 7-1   Sources of product information

Several industry trade publications provide comprehensive, up-to-date product comparisons, both in print and **e-zine** (an electronic magazine or Webzine) format on the Web, including those shown in Table 7-2 below.

Publication	URL for Product Information and Reviews
CNET	reviews.cnet.com
Computing.REVIEW.com	www.computingreview.com/reviewcatscrx.aspx
InfoWorld	www.infoworld.com/testcenter/index.html
Macworld	www.macworld.com/browse.html
MaximumPC	www.maximumpc.com/articles/reviews
PC Magazine	www.pcmag.com/category2/0,2806,13,00.asp
PC World	www.pcworld.com/reviews.html
Smart Computing	www.smartcomputing.com/editorial/reviews.asp?atypeid=4 (hardware)
	www.smartcomputing.com/editorial/reviews.asp?atypeid=5 (software)
Tom's Hardware Guide	www.tomshardware.com/us
TopTenREVIEWS	computers.toptenreviews.com
ZDNet	review.zdnet.com

Table 7-2   Computer industry periodicals and Web sites that publish product reviews and comparisons

The product information examples in Table 7-2 are resources primarily within the computer industry. Alternately, many trade publications publish articles that review and evaluate hardware and software products in industries such as accounting, manufacturing, transportation logistics, office administration, marketing, medicine, finance, law, and education. Product comparisons in industry-specific publications are especially useful because they often address issues unique to each application area.

ON THE WEB

For a list of popular computer trade publications, see **dir.yahoo.com/Business_and_Economy/Business_to_Business/Computers/Industry_Information/Trade_Magazines**.

For a list of e-zines targeted at the computer field, visit **www.ezine-dir.com/Computers**.

The following are examples of articles and Web pages that compare and evaluate computer products. For each, note the evaluation criteria used, compare how competing products are rated against the criteria, and look for ways the evaluators highlight the pros and cons of each product. Some articles provide numerical evaluation scores or "best buy" designations for products the evaluators prefer.

- "2009 External DVD Burners Product Comparisons" on TopTenREVIEW's Web site (**external-dvd-burner-review. toptenreviews.com**)

- "What to Consider When Buying an LCD Monitor" on Associated Content's Web site (**www.associatedcontent.com/ article/1383970/what_to_consider_when_buying_an_lcd. html**)

- "Laptop Buying Guide" on CNET's Web site (**reviews.cnet.com/ laptop-buying-guide**)

- "Search Engine Features Chart" is a Web page sponsored by Search Engine Showdown that compares the features of several popular search engines (**www.searchengineshowdown.com/features**)

- "Top Internet Security Suites" on PC World's Web site (**www. pcworld.com/article/158178/top_internet_security_suites. html**)

- "Top 5 Tax Software" on About.com's Web site (**taxes.about.com/ od/taxsoftware/tp/taxsoftware.htm**)

ON THE WEB

For advice about how to read computer product reviews with a critical eye, read an article at **www.techsoup.org/ learningcenter/software/page7379.cfm**.

In addition to studying reviews in periodicals, support staff can frequently request or download demonstration or evaluation copies of software products. A **software evaluation copy** is a limited, trial copy of a software product that permits an end user or support staff to try out a product's features and assess its ability to meet an organization's needs. Evaluation copies are frequently advertised through the mail or on vendor Web sites; they usually are provided on a CD or through a download from a vendor's Web site (when the size of the demo version is not prohibitive). An evaluation copy may not have all the features that would be found in a full commercial version, or it may operate only for a limited trial period (often 30 or 60 days), or for a limited number of launches or file-save operations.

ON THE WEB

Another way to try out commercial software prior to purchase is to use a service that provides evaluation and demonstrations of packages that users can run on a Web server. Visit the Runaware Web site (**www.runaware.com/clients.jsp**) to learn more about this approach.

Although demonstration and evaluation copies of software packages are freely distributed, vendors usually do not offer hardware products for evaluation. Typically a vendor will only provide components for evaluation if a potential sale to an organization is of a substantial dollar value. In those cases, support groups routinely and successfully request evaluation copies of hardware components, or even complete systems, that they are seriously considering.

Decision-Making Tools

When decision makers need to decide which of several products they will select to purchase and support, they can use several tools, methods, and strategies as aids. These decision tools are listed in Figure 7-3 and are described in the upcoming sections.

- Industry standard or bestselling products
- Products used by competitors
- Benchmarks
- Weighted point evaluation method
- Request for proposal (RFP)
- Acknowledged subjective criteria

Figure 7-3   Product evaluation decision-making tools

Industry Standard or Bestselling Products

When user support staff members need to make recommendations for administrative and office automation applications, they often select **industry standard products**—hardware, software, and accessories that are market leaders in sales. Industry standard software products are designed to meet the needs of a broad spectrum of end users across a wide variety of industries and are sometimes called **horizontal market applications**. Few organizations devote much staff time to evaluating popular word processors or spreadsheets, for example, because the best-selling products usually have competitive features and perform most of the functions commonly required by end users. However, when an organization has specialized needs, such as software to prepare a significant volume of legal documents or process medical insurance claims, product evaluators often look beyond mass-market leaders. In these cases, evaluators must often research features available in lesser-known products that are targeted at users with specialized needs. Mass-market products may lack the industry-specific features that some organizations need.

Similarly, the way that accounting software is evaluated depends on the size and scope of an organization. The evaluation process may be a simple task for a small business, because one of the mass-market accounting systems targeted at small businesses will probably meet its needs. Medium- to large-scale businesses often undertake a more extensive evaluation of accounting packages because off-the-shelf products vary considerably in how they handle more complicated circumstances. Most very large businesses develop their own accounting systems or modify a commercial package to obtain the level of customization they need to meet their unique requirements.

Many so-called "standards" in the computer industry are not true standards because no industry-wide group has agreed to the specifications. Often products become standards based on sales leadership and market share.

297

ON THE WEB

During a product evaluation process, some businesses (even small ones) also consider the option of outsourcing selected applications. Payroll processing is a common example. The complexity of and frequent changes in payroll laws and accounting standards mean that small businesses may find it difficult to hire the expertise to operate and maintain an up-to-date payroll system. Service providers such as PayChex (**www.paychex.com**) offer outsource services to provide payroll processing.

Selecting industry standard hardware and software products can reduce an organization's support costs. Popular software products are more likely to be the target of trade books, third-party training courses and materials, and support service vendors. However, market-leading products do not necessarily match the specific and perhaps unique requirements of end users. Furthermore, market leadership changes over time. A product that appears to be a safe purchase today may soon become obsolete, and therefore a poor choice. For example, at one time, WordPerfect was an obvious pick as a word processor, Lotus 1-2-3 was the leading spreadsheet package, and dBASE IV was often the database software of choice. None of these packages is the bestseller in its category today.

Before recommending application software for organization-wide purchase and support, a support group should always get user input. Product evaluators should find out which products end users have experience with, the advantages and disadvantages of competing products for specific tasks, and whether users have preferences among products. Support groups that fail to seek user input during the selection process can make an expensive mistake if the software they select is not a good match with user needs or is too difficult to learn and use.

Products Competitors Use

Trade publications in a specific industry are often a good resource for product ideas and reviews because vendors with targeted products are more likely to advertise and provide feature articles on their products.

In addition to industry standard and bestselling products, support specialists who do product research and evaluation should consider products used by an organization's competitors, especially within a vertical market. A vertical (or niche) market is one that is highly specialized, such as the automobile insurance industry, hair salons, or beer distributors. A **vertical (or niche) market application** is software designed for one of these highly specialized industries. Vertical market software often contains features that would not be useful in other industries. An organization's competitors often have thoroughly researched the market and identified strategic reasons for adopting certain computer products, even if those products are not market leaders. If the information can be obtained legally, a product evaluator should attempt to learn which products are used by competing organizations. Then the support staff can evaluate the strengths and weaknesses of computer products the competitors use. Evaluators who consider products used by the competition are not "copycats"— they simply recognize the fact that organizations in the same industry often have very similar technology needs.

Benchmarks

A **benchmark** is an objective test or measurement used to evaluate the speed, capacity, capabilities, or productivity of competing products. Evaluators use benchmarks to compare two or more rival products. Benchmarks are a popular way to compare hardware products, and they are also useful for software packages or even entire systems. The benchmark method of comparing products begins when an evaluator defines one or more criteria as critical success factors for a specific product. Examples of common benchmark criteria include processing speed, storage capacity, software performance, and user productivity.

Benchmarks are based on **objective evaluation criteria**, or factors used in a product selection procedure that are relatively unbiased. After a benchmark evaluation has been completed, any neutral evaluator should be able to use the same objective criteria to reach the same conclusion because the criteria and measurement methods are less influenced by personal opinions. An evaluator often uses a controlled test environment to measure competing products on the same objective criteria, such as transaction processing speed. In the test, the evaluator attempts to control all variables that do not relate to the product being evaluated. For example, in an evaluation of software performance, the same user operates two or more competing software products on identical hardware, in identical operating environments. **Extraneous variables**, those that could bias the results of a benchmark test in one direction or the other, such as different hardware platforms, have been eliminated. Therefore, observed differences in test results are most likely due to real differences in product capabilities.

 When selecting criteria to use in a benchmark test, an evaluator should pick those criteria that will make a difference in an end user's operating environment. For example, the performance of a graphics display adapter may not be especially important in a word-processing environment, but the performance of a printer might be.

ON THE WEB

To see a bar graph of the results of benchmark tests on the latest models of central processing units, visit **www.cpubenchmark.net**.

An evaluator who wants to use benchmarks to compare the speed of competing printers, for example, may define a constant unit of work, such as printing 100 pages. The pages are selected to represent different examples (text and graphics, color and black-and-white, heavy and light ink coverage) from among those that users frequently print. Then, the evaluator runs a series of tests, using competing vendors' printers that run at comparable speeds, in which the sample of one hundred pages is printed. (Due to product design, performance differences are possible, even among printers that advertise the same relative print speed specifications.) As part of the tests, the evaluator attempts to eliminate other variables that could affect the benchmark results. The evaluator uses the same computer system, the same

Benchmarks are often used to help evaluate computer products, but they are seldom the only factor considered. In the selection of a printer, accounting software, or any other product, factors other than performance should also be considered, as you will see in the next section.

operating environment, the same application software, the same network environment, the same set of test documents, and the same type of paper. The only variable that changes from one trial to the next is the printer itself. In this controlled test environment, an evaluator can determine whether one brand of printer has a significantly faster print speed than competing printers.

An evaluator can also use benchmarking to evaluate software. As with hardware benchmarks, the evaluator defines a constant unit of work—for example, the time it takes a data entry clerk to enter and process 100 typical accounting transactions. Then the evaluator measures the amount of time the data entry operator takes to enter the same 100 transactions using rival accounting packages. Finally, the evaluator compares the benchmarked times for each package.

ON THE WEB

In addition to evaluator-defined benchmarks in product evaluations, vendors and users can utilize several common industry standard benchmarks to evaluate competing products. To learn more about benchmarking computer products, read an article on Wikipedia's Web site at **en.wikipedia.org/wiki/Benchmark_(computing)**.

Companies that provide hardware and software benchmarks include:

- Business Applications Performance Corporation (BAPCO) (**www.bapco.com**—click **Products**)

- PassMark Software (**www.passmark.com**)

- Standard Performance Evaluation Corporation (SPEC) (**www.specbench.org**)

- PC Tech's Web site lists several popular free and shareware benchmark tools (**www.pctechbytes.com/computer/article-51.html**)

Benchmark comparisons are useful because they are designed to use objective criteria and eliminate vendor or user bias in the evaluation of a hardware or software product.

Weighted Point Evaluation Method

Product reviews in computer periodicals sometimes use a weighted point evaluation method, a strategy that support staff can use in their own evaluation projects. The **weighted point evaluation method** is a product comparison tool that uses several key criteria of predetermined importance to evaluate competing products or services and arrive at a numerical score, which is then used as the basis for product selection. This method is also called the Kepner-Tregoe method, after two authors who described methods rational managers can use to make decisions. As with benchmarks, the goal of the weighted point method is to make the evaluation and selection process as objective as possible. It attempts to treat competing products equally, to eliminate possible favoritism or bias among evaluators, and to force evaluators to specify in advance the important factors in the evaluation of competing products. Because weighted point evaluation is an objective procedure that requires the use of well-defined criteria, public agencies are often legally required to use this method or a variant of it.

ON THE WEB

For more information about this method and an example of a weighted point evaluation of software options, see the article "Guide to Selecting a Software and Services Partner" at *Software Magazine*'s Web site (**www.softwaremag. com/L.cfm?Doc=archive/2000aug/Selecting-a-Partner.html**).

Next, you will learn some mechanics of the weighted point evaluation process. You can apply this method to selecting a 1000-user computer network or to selecting a home personal computer. To perform a weighted point evaluation, evaluators follow these steps:

1. Decide on the evaluation criteria.

2. Determine the importance of each criterion.

3. Rate each competing product against all the evaluation criteria.

4. If more than one evaluator rates products, compute the average rating for each criterion for each product.

5. Weight the product ratings for each criterion by importance.

6. Compute the total rating for each product.

7. Compare product ratings.

The evaluation criteria selected for use in the weighted point method are based on several important factors, including:

- The specific type of hardware or software product to be evaluated
- The needs of end users
- Support issues
- Cost

Evaluation articles in periodicals are an excellent source of ideas for criteria to use to evaluate specific products. Table 7-3 provides some examples of criteria in several categories.

Category	Examples of Criteria
Hardware or software	• Processing speed • Storage capacity • Capabilities and features • Transaction volumes • Compatibility with existing systems • Upgradeability (scalability)
End user needs	• Ease of learning • Ease of use • Mandatory features (must have) • Desirable features (nice to have)
Support availability	• Technical support services • Installation assistance • Training • Documentation • Troubleshooting • Maintenance and repair
Cost	• Total cost of ownership (see Chapter 1)

Table 7-3　Examples of criteria used in the weighted point evaluation method

ON THE WEB

To learn about the extensive evaluation criteria used by the Information Technology Planning Board at UCLA, visit **www.itpb.ucla.edu/Documents/2001/Jan/Matrix-ComputerPrinterSrvcsRFP.htm**.

Consider the following example of a simple weighted point evaluation method. Suppose an organization wants three evaluators in the user support group to rate two computer systems for purchase. The evaluators first decide on the comparison criteria to use, as shown in Table 7-4. They also discuss and agree on the relative importance of each criterion. The relative importance of each criterion is usually based on its significance to the organization, the end users, and the support group. For example, a relatively unimportant criterion might receive a weight of 5–10%. The sum of the criteria weights should total 100%.

Criterion	Criterion's Importance (Weight)	System X Evaluation	System Y Evaluation
Hardware configuration	25%		
Software bundled	35%		
Vendor reputation	10%		
Vendor support	30%		
TOTALS	100%		

Table 7-4   Criteria and weights for evaluating two computers

Each evaluator then rates the capabilities of the proposed products and assigns points, usually between 1 and 100, to each product for each criterion. For example, an evaluator could learn from a survey of a vendor's current clients that the vendor is very well regarded and might assign the vendor a score of 95 out of 100 on the vendor reputation criterion. The evaluators work independently to rate each system.

Next, the three evaluators consolidate their results. They could average the points earned for each criterion. Or, the evaluators might discuss their preliminary ratings to identify and negotiate any large discrepancies and arrive at a consensus rating. For example, if one evaluator rated the System X hardware configuration at 60 and the other evaluators rated it at 100, the three evaluators should discuss the discrepancy to determine why there was such a significant difference and to arrive at a mutually acceptable rating of perhaps 80 out of 100. Small discrepancies of a few points are ignored. In this example, after discussion, the evaluators agreed that the hardware configuration for System X was worth 90 points (out of 100), and the competing System Y was worth only 70, as shown in Table 7-5.

Criterion	Criterion's Importance (Weight)	System X Evaluation	System Y Evaluation
Hardware configuration	25%	90	70
Software bundled	35%	70	70
Vendor reputation	10%	50	95
Vendor support	30%	60	90
TOTALS	**100%**		

Table 7-5   Weighted point evaluation method with points assigned to each criterion

In the next step, the number of points assigned to each system is multiplied by the weight of each selection criterion. The resulting points for each system are then summed to arrive at a total number of points, as Table 7-6 shows. The system with the larger number of total points is the system that best meets the selection criteria.

Criterion	Criterion's Importance (Weight)	System X Evaluation	System Y Evaluation
Hardware configuration	25%	$90 \times 25\% = 22.5$	$70 \times 25\% = 17.5$
Software bundled	35%	$70 \times 35\% = 24.5$	$70 \times 35\% = 24.5$
Vender reputation	10%	$50 \times 10\% = 5.0$	$95 \times 10\% = 9.5$
Vendor support	30%	$60 \times 30\% = 18.0$	$90 \times 30\% = 27.0$
TOTALS	**100%**	**70.0/100**	**78.5/100**

Table 7-6   Weighted point method example with evaluation points

In this example, System Y's higher scores on vendor reputation and vendor support offset its lower score on hardware configuration. The weighted point method can be used to evaluate more than two products, and it can accommodate as many criteria as evaluators think are important. For simple product evaluations, a product evaluation worksheet can be prepared using a spreadsheet program.

One advantage of the weighted point evaluation method is that it forces evaluators to address two important questions early in the evaluation process: (1) Which criteria are important to us in the product purchase decision or recommendation? (2) How important to us is each criterion relative to other criteria? Some argue that this method applies numeric values to criteria where numbers have little meaning. However, the weighted point method forces evaluators to look at measurable criteria when they might be tempted to rely on more subjective beliefs. Sometimes the objective results of a weighted point method conflict with an evaluator's subjective feelings. If a product evaluator finishes the process and receives the "wrong" result according to his or her "gut" feelings, the evaluator may be able to reexamine the criteria and the weights and ask why he or she got those results. Sometimes it is the "gut" that is wrong.

Request for Proposal (RFP)

A **request for proposal (RFP)** is a product selection tool or competitive bidding process that uses objective criteria, such as benchmarking and the weighted point evaluation method, to choose among products proposed by competing vendors. By law, many public agencies are required to use an objective evaluation process, such as a bidding process or a request for proposal procedure. A successful RFP process can assure that vendors are evaluated fairly, according to established rules; therefore, it reduces the likelihood of a lawsuit as the result of perceived or real procurement problems.

ON THE WEB

To learn more about the legal aspects of RFPs, read an article by two attorneys who suggest strategies for successful bidding procedures at **www.metrocorpcounsel.com/ pdf/2005/December/06m.pdf.**

Because the RFP process is objective, many businesses also use RFPs or a similar procedure to aid in making purchase decisions. For example, an organization might issue an RFP that invites competing vendors to submit product and price proposals for an office network system. As a result of an RFP process, an organization usually designates the successful bidder as the sole authorized vendor for the office network products covered in the RFP.

To complete the RFP process, an organization follows these eight primary steps:

1. Conduct a user needs analysis (discussed in Chapter 8).

2. Based on the needs analysis, develop a purchase specification for the equipment or software to describe the technical characteristics and features required.

3. Define the decision criteria that will guide the selection process and determine the importance of each criterion. Many criteria are based on mandatory (must have) or desirable (should have) product features; other criteria include technical support, vendor stability, product costs, and compatibility with existing systems.

4. Write an RFP document which describes the user requirements, bidding procedure, and decision criteria.

5. Send the RFP document to prospective vendors (some organizations maintain a list of vendors who are prescreened to meet certain financial stability criteria).

6. Receive vendors' written proposals, which address how their products meet or exceed the user requirements and include a bid price at which each vendor can supply the products or services.

7. Analyze and evaluate the responses to the RFP—using weighted point evaluation or other objective methods.

8. Select a vendor and award the purchase contract.

ON THE WEB

To learn more about the RFP process, read the guidelines for purchasing technology equipment published by the International Foundation for Electoral Systems (**www.ifesbuyersguide.com/resource_center. php?article=cornish#issue**).

Or read an RFP to acquire a computer-aided dispatch system for public safety for the city of Florence, Oregon (**www.ci.florence.or.us/downloads/cad.pdf**). Note the extensive technical evaluation criteria on pages 10 to 21 and the weights the city of Florence uses to select the successful vendor on page 5.

Another RFP resource is an article on software selection on Infotivity's Web site (**www.infotivity.com/selection_steps. html**).

The RFP process is a common and objective decision-making tool. Because RFPs include several lengthy steps and considerable staff time, they are used primarily for purchases of significant dollar value, rather than for purchases of off-the-shelf products.

Acknowledged Subjective Criteria

The evaluation tools and methods described above are primarily based on objective criteria. Using these tools, any neutral observer should be able to reach the same conclusion as the primary evaluator. Either a product performs as well on a benchmark comparison as another product or it doesn't. Although product evaluators base many hardware and software purchase decisions on objective criteria, they sometimes use criteria that are known to be subjective. **Subjective evaluation criteria** are nonobjective factors used in a product selection procedure that are not directly related to the fit between a product's features and end users' needs. Subjective factors include a previous relationship with a vendor, convenience, personal preferences, and reliance on traditional or historical purchasing channels. (A comment such as, "We've always bought network equipment from this vendor" is a good indicator that subjective criteria are in use.) Subjective criteria are neither measurable nor repeatable from one evaluator to another, and two evaluators may well disagree on the result.

Legitimate reasons may lead to a purchase decision based on a personal relationship between an organization and a vendor; an organization and its supplier may have a lengthy business or personal relationship or a partnership agreement that overrides all other evaluation criteria. Occasionally an organization may refuse to consider any products from a particular vendor because it has a low regard for the vendor's product reputation, business ethics, or customer service standards. When an organization has a special relationship with a vendor based on prior experience, reputation, location, or a personal contact, other factors, including price, are often less important.

Large organizations, both public and private, often use an objective evaluation or selection procedure for computer products. Smaller organizations often use more subjective criteria. Support specialists who evaluate and select computer products may use both objective and subjective methods, depending on their employer's guidelines. However, the purpose of all product evaluation and selection strategies is to arrive at the best product choice for each user. Once an organization has researched and selected products and vendors, the next step often is to develop product support standards.

Product Support Standards

As you learned in the first part of this chapter, organizations often try to control support costs by establishing computer product standards to limit the number of hardware and software options users can choose. Although the decision to adopt product support standards may sound like a "one-size-fits-all" approach, it doesn't have to be. Within the standards adopted by an organization, alternatives are often permitted. Most organizations try to strike a reasonable balance between the two extremes of "Select only this product" and "Select anything you want."

Honolulu Community College in Honolulu, Hawaii, is a comprehensive community college that has adopted computer product standards and support policies to minimize the drain on college resources in providing user support to its faculty, staff, and students. Figure 7-4 contains several excerpts from the college's policy that describes the limits it places on hardware and software acquisitions.

Honolulu Community College Policy on Desktop Computing

The intention of this policy is to provide a standard base-line hardware and software configuration for all HCC campus desktop computers. The Supported Products List will include Workstations, Operating Systems and Application Software for use by faculty, staff, classrooms and student labs. The current Supported Products List will include hardware and software specifications for both Windows based computers and Macintosh computers.

The Supported Products List will be published on the ITC web site and updated quarterly. This will allow departments to plan fiscal year budgets based on the published standards.

The Supported Products List will serve to set standards for the campus community for desktop hardware and software as well as network operating systems. Members of the campus community will then follow the published standards or understand that they may not receive support from HCC Technical Desktop Support to solve problems they encounter using non-standard hardware and/or software.

An HCC standardized base configuration will be provided by ITC through HCC Technical Desktop Support, to the faculty and staff of Honolulu Community College. Only fully licensed software and freely distributed software products will be part of the desktop configuration.

In keeping with industry best practices, it is mandatory for all HCC owned desktops to be configured with the HCC configuration. End users of these desktops shall have only operator access to these machines as opposed to administrative access.

All new purchases of computers and desktop workstations must conform to the current Supported Products List. Specifications will be for approved system configurations.

The HCC standardized base configuration is mandatory for all new systems connected to the HCC Campus Internet. Additional software to the base configuration are permitted provided they do not compromise the integrity of the desktop configuration.

The benefits of this policy are:

- Simplify the hardware acquisition and upgrade process
- Provide an HCC customized base configuration for all computer users
- Improve support services by promoting migration to selected technologies and concentrating on these limited products in greater depth;
- Plan effectively for introducing new products and phasing out older products;
- Develop precise goals and objectives for the Technical Desktop Support office to optimize staff training and development in order to offer reliable, high quality services;
- Encourage a more consistent environment through the use of a standard suite of appropriate technologies.

Figure 7-4 Computer product support policies at Honolulu Community College (*continues*)

(*continued*)

If a product is on the Supported Software List, faculty and staff can get assistance with problems related to the use of those products. If a product is not on the list, those who need assistance will receive consultation as resources allow.

The Desktop Computing Policy is accompanied by the following list of responsibilities:

Technical Desktop Support (TDS) Responsibilities with regard to Providing Support for Supported Products

- Maintain expertise for supported products
- Provide or facilitate support
- Work with the Information Technology Center to coordinate support, training and documentation for the supported product
- When appropriate and cost effective, recommend site or volume licensing for supported products.

TDS Responsibilities in Providing Assistance with Unsupported Products

- Limited support is available.
- One hour of courtesy consulting may be provided to help requestor assess options to migrate to supported alternative.
- Referrals to vendors or other sources may be provided, when available.
- Neither training nor documentation will be available.

Customer Responsibilities for Support

- Be familiar with basic desktop skills, attend available training, and read available documentation as appropriate.
- Have valid licenses for supported products (TDS cannot provide support in case of invalid licenses).
- Be able to provide the following information when requesting support: name, campus location, telephone number, e-mail address, type of computer in use, software and version in use, the desired outcome, and a description of the problem encountered.
- Work with TDS staff in troubleshooting problems.
- Run diagnostics provided by TDS or manufacturer.
- Maintain regular backup procedures for their desktop system.

Criteria Used to Evaluate Products for Supported Status

- Industry-wide acceptance and/or standard
- Number of customers who require the software
- Number of departments represented by customers requiring software

*To see updates to these policies, visit **http://itc.honolulu.hawaii.edu/?q=node/9***

Figure 7-4   Computer product support policies at Honolulu Community College

Honolulu Community College's list of supported products includes both PCs and Macintosh computers. The list of approved products specifies selected software packages in several categories. Honolulu Community College's lists of recommended and supported hardware and software products are described in Figures 7-5 and 7-6, respectively.

ITC Windows Based Microcomputer Approved Hardware Specifications
January - March 2009

The following approved systems will meet the needs of Honolulu Community College's faculty and staff for email, MyUH Portal, web browsing, word processing, spreadsheet, graphics, and database functions. HCC approves purchasing the specified systems listed below.

Desktops:

Dell OptiPlex 760 Mini-Tower

Intel Core 2 Duo Processor (2.66GHz, 3M, 1066MHz or higher)
2 GB RAM or higher, but not more that 4 GB
80 GB Hard Drive or higher
DVD+/-RW Drive
10/100 Mbps Ethernet Connection
Windows XP Professional, SP3, x32, with Media, which is the Dell selection; Genuine Windows Vista Business Downgrade, XP Pro Installed, English
4-year On-site Warranty (Recommended)
Surge Protector
Resource CD, which contain Diagnostics and Drivers for the System

Laptops:

Laptops should *not* be purchased as a Desktop replacement

Dell Latitude E6400

Intel Core 2 Duo Processor (2.26GHz, 3M, 1066MHz or higher)
2 GB RAM or higher, but not more that 4GB
80 GB Hard Drive or higher
DVD+/-RW Drive
Wireless LAN (802.11) Mini Card (Compatible with 802.11b and 802.11g networks)
Windows XP Professional, SP3, x32, with Media, which is the Dell selection; Genuine Windows Vista Business Downgrade, XP Pro Installed, English
4-year On-site Warranty (Recommended)
• Warranty does not cover consumables such as batteries
Resource CD, which contain Diagnostics and Drivers for the System
Finger Print (Biometric) Reader is not recommended or supported

Notes:

1. **Antivirus software:** UH Site License Department offers McAfee VirusScan free of charge for UH faculty and students for your home and office computers. Please do not obtain the antivirus software from Dell.

2. **Microsoft Office 2003 Professional:** UH Site License Department offers Microsoft Office 2007 Professional Plus which is downgradable to Microsoft Office 2003 or XP Professional for office use at a volume discount.

To see updates to these specifications, visit ***http://itc.honolulu.hawaii.edu/?q=node/13***

Figure 7-5   Honolulu Community College's list of supported Windows hardware products

Microcomputer Operating Systems and Applications				
	Macintosh Computers		MS Windows Based Computers	
Category	Product	Versions Supported	Product	Versions Supported
Operating System	Mac OS	10.4, 10.5	Windows	2000 Pro, XP Pro
Word Processing	Word	2004, 2008	Word	2000, XP, 2003
Spreadsheets	Excel	2004, 2008	Excel	2000, XP, 2003
Presentation Packages	PowerPoint	2004, 2008	PowerPoint	2000, XP, 2003
Virus Protection	McAfee Virex McAfee VirusScan for Mactel	7.x 8.x	McAfee VirusScan	Ent. 8.5i
Web Browser	Firefox	2.x, 3.x	Firefox	2.x, 3.x
E-Mail Client	Thunderbird	1.x	Thunderbird Pine via SSH Secure Shell	1.x 3.x
Disk Utilities	Norton Utilities		ScanDisk	
Document Browser	Acrobat Reader	8.x, 9.x	Acrobat Reader	8.x, 9.x

To see updates to this list, visit **http://itc.honolulu.hawaii.edu/?q=node/14**

Figure 7-6 Honolulu Community College's list of supported Macintosh and Windows software products

ON THE WEB

Updates to Honolulu Community College's product support policies and supported products lists are posted at **http://itc.honolulu.hawaii.edu**. The online version of these support standards describes the reasons each recommended product was chosen rather than other products.

Not every organization spends the resources to thoroughly research and evaluate products and develop the type of standards described in this chapter. However, larger organizations with a substantial investment in computer technology tend to devote staff time to evaluating products and setting purchase standards because the potential for waste is large. Based on the results of product research and evaluation, user support specialists can prepare lists of approved and supported computer products. Armed with a list of approved products, they can more easily answer questions such as, "Which kind of computer should an employee buy?" and, "Is this printer model compatible with the organization's computer systems?"

How Organizations Develop Computer Product and Support Standards

An organization's computer product and support standards can emerge from a variety of sources. In some organizations, product standards evolve over time as a "computer culture" develops. For example, an organization might have adopted the standard that primarily models of Macintosh computers are supported simply because the early adopters of technology in the organization were predominantly Macintosh users. Alternately, organizations that adopted Netscape as their preferred Web browser during the 1990s may be reluctant to change to a different one, even though Netscape is no longer the most popular browser product.

Although organizational culture and traditions are one source of product standards, some organizations assign the task of developing and maintaining standards to the user support group or to a product standards committee. A **product standards committee** is a group of support specialists, end users, technical support staff, and managers who develop and maintain a list of organization-approved standard products and services. Once established, standards must be effective; that is, they must help end users get their work done. They must be evenly administered and enforced. If end users have to work around the standards to get the equipment, software, and services they need to do their jobs, the organization's computer standards will be widely viewed as ineffective. Some organizations recognize that a "one-size-fits-all" standard is counterproductive in special situations. While standards are generally enforced, a caveat may be added: "Standard products will be purchased and supported, *unless a compelling business reason requires an exception to the standard.*"

A change in standards for supported computer products is often an emotional time for end users who are comfortable with the old standards. Resistance to changes in standards can result in statements such as: "This technology has worked fine for many years, why change it now?" Whenever changes in standards are contemplated, new products should be thoroughly tested, following procedures described earlier in this chapter. The need for a change in standards should be discussed with employees and their feedback should be sought on how new hardware and software products meet, or fail to meet, end users' needs. Changes in product standards tend to

Product and support standards committees usually define software standards before hardware standards. If a standards committee defines a hardware standard first, it may discover later that one or more software packages it wants to select will not run on the hardware standard it defined earlier. Software products determine the minimum hardware requirements in most cases, not vice versa.

be implemented more smoothly when end users are consulted and included in the decision-making and execution processes.

A ROLE-PLAYING SCENARIO

This is a transcript of a conversation between Kerry, a user in the legal research department, and Morgan, a support specialist. If possible, have colleagues play the parts of Kerry and Morgan, and then discuss your reaction to their conversation.

MORGAN: I understand that you are in the market for a new laptop computer.

KERRY: Yes. My Toshiba is starting to have problems. The CD drive no longer works all the time, and the machine is slow by today's standards. I have been thinking about getting a new Toshiba.

MORGAN: The laptop the law firm currently recommends and supports is a Dell Latitude.

KERRY: Well, I like my Toshiba a lot, and I am familiar with Toshiba features, so that is the kind of laptop I'd like to get as a replacement.

MORGAN: The only way the company would permit you to buy a Toshiba is if you could make a business case for why a Dell Latitude would not meet your needs.

KERRY: But I've always had Toshiba laptops since I was in school. In fact, my home computer is a Toshiba laptop. They are very reliable and don't need a lot of repairs.

MORGAN: The problem is the company has standardized on the Dell Latitude running Windows Vista. No Toshiba laptops are on our list of supported computer models.

KERRY: That's another thing. I haven't heard any good things about Windows Vista, so I'd like to stay with XP. I am more productive with XP than I would be with Vista.

MORGAN: Unfortunately the company made the decision to move to Vista on all new computer purchases. I don't think you can even buy a laptop that runs XP today.

KERRY: Yes, I know that Microsoft wants the world to migrate to Vista, but I still have an installation disk for XP, so I would plan to install it on whatever machine I get.

MORGAN: But the firm could not provide tech support for XP. If you had problems with it, you would be on your own.

KERRY: If the company won't buy me a Toshiba laptop and let me run Windows XP on it, then I'll have to go out and get one myself to use here at work.

MORGAN: But if you connect a new Toshiba to the company LAN, we run the risk of you infecting the network with a virus or worm. I doubt we'd let you connect it to the network because we wouldn't want to risk the problems it might cause.

KERRY: Sounds like I am stuck. How did we ever end up with these kinds of policies, anyway?

After the role-playing activity, discuss the following questions:

1. Did Kerry make a strong business case for purchasing a Toshiba running XP instead of the company-supported Dell laptop running Vista?

2. Did Morgan do an effective job of explaining the reason for the product standards to Kerry? If not, continue the conversation with points you would make as an explanation.

Acceptable Use Guidelines

The same committee that sets standards for supported computer products, or a different one, may also address organizational standards in another area: acceptable computer use guidelines. **Acceptable use guidelines** are adopted by organizations and publicized among their employees in an effort to make clear the ways in which end users are permitted and not permitted to use computer systems at school or at work. These use guidelines often describe how users are permitted to use their computers, what they are not allowed to do, and the consequences or penalties for unauthorized or illegal use. The guidelines may cover activities that are illegal according to federal or state law (such as accessing confidential information) or violations of licenses and agreements (such as copying commercial software), and activities that are prohibited by organizational policy (such as use of organizational e-mail for personal messages).

ON THE WEB

For an example, see the University of Oregon's "Acceptable Use of Computing Resources" guidelines (**http://is.uoregon.edu/ cio/acceptable_use.shtml**). A template for an acceptable use policy is available at **www.sans.org/resources/policies/ Acceptable_Use_Policy.pdf**.

How Organizations Implement Computer Product and Support Standards

In many organizations, two forces often influence the adoption and implementation of computer product and support standards. One influence is an organization's existing inventory of hardware and software products. Unless it is very small or has a very large computer budget, an organization could probably not afford to discard its entire investment in computer systems and adopt a new standard overnight. When they define support standards, product support groups often take into account the predominant hardware, software, and network architecture that currently exist in an organization. Support for obsolete computer products may be phased out over time, with ample notice to end users, to minimize inconvenience. To deviate substantially from what employees currently use can result in a large, one-time expense as end users convert to equipment or software that meets a new standard.

A second force that drives changes in product and service standards is the continual introduction of new products, services, and product upgrades. An important task of a user support group is to learn about and evaluate new products that have the potential to replace existing standard products. The decision to modify and update existing product support standards is usually based on criteria such as the following:

- New products offer technical improvements over current products.

- New products have features with the potential to improve employee productivity.

- End user product preferences have changed over time.

- New products and services are available at a lower cost than existing products.

- New products may be compatible with changes in industry standards, unlike older products.

- New products have become more popular than the products they would replace.

However, the decision to replace an existing product or service standard is often difficult to make because organizations may have a sizable investment in the existing standard. Similarly, end users may have invested the time to learn how to use existing products and may be reluctant to change because the conversion means retraining and usually reduced productivity while they are learning the new product. For these reasons, organizations that want to move to a new standard may decide to phase in a new product standard over time.

A transition period occurs when both old and new products are permitted and supported under the standards policy. Of course, transition periods can strain the support staff, because they must provide support for both old and new products. During the transition period, increased support costs are often incurred, as support and maintenance of existing hardware, software, and network products continue for some users, while other users convert to and are trained in the use of new products.

For example, when the Windows Vista operating system first became widely available in 2007, many organizations were reluctant to convert from Windows XP to Windows Vista. They were not convinced that the new features and advantages of the Vista operating system were worth the conversion costs, and they had a substantial existing investment in earlier Windows software and peripherals. Although Vista includes support and updated device drivers for many recent models of peripherals, some vendors of older models of peripherals chose not to provide updated drivers and support, which meant that many older devices could not be used on a Vista system. Consequently, some organizations have stayed with the Windows XP operating system standard. Other organizations included both Windows Vista and earlier Windows versions as standard during an extended transition period, because they had a substantial investment in application software, computers, and peripheral hardware that ran on earlier versions. Many users found their existing hardware and software inventory would not operate correctly under Windows Vista, or required upgraded drivers and new software versions, which increased the cost to convert. However, if versions of new and upgraded software applications that specifically require Windows Vista come on the market, more organizations may feel pressure from their employees to convert to it and purchase new hardware and software when necessary. Reluctance to convert to new industry standards explains why some organizations are still running even older Windows 98/Me/2000 applications.

ON THE WEB

To test a PC for Windows Vista readiness, use PC Pitstop's readiness evaluator (**www.pcpitstop.com/vistaready/ default.asp**), or use Microsoft's upgrade advisor (**www. microsoft.com/windows/windows-vista/get/upgrade- advisor.aspx**).

Product and support standards will continue to change in the future. In the second decade of the 21st century, organizations will face decisions about when to adopt, convert to, and support new peripheral devices based on the Universal Serial Bus 3.0 standard, when to upgrade to 802.1N wireless network devices, and when to adopt voice recognition input technology. Many windows users are still unsure whether to make the move to Windows Vista, or to await Windows 7 (expected in 2010). Users of the Microsoft Office suite are confronted with the choice between learning a new user interface in Office 2007 or staying with the familiar 2003 version. Every decision to modify an existing technology standard or adopt a new one requires analysis and evaluation of products and services by the user support group. It also triggers potential support cost increases for installation, upgrades, training, documentation, troubleshooting, and help desk services.

Chapter Summary

- During the 1980s, organizations with a substantial investment in desktop computer technology recognized the need to evaluate computer products and set product and support standards. Because few widely recognized industry standards existed, incompatible hardware and software increased the cost of computer technology and reduced productivity among users. Today, organizations lower their support services costs by restricting purchases to a limited list of approved products.

- User support workers evaluate computer products and services so they can recommend to end users and organizations the products that will meet their needs. Support workers often help an organization set standards for computer hardware and software products. Standard products help increase the compatibility among various hardware and software components and help to reduce the resources (costs) required to support end user systems.

- Support staff members use a variety of information resources to evaluate hardware and software products, including vendor literature, Web sites, and user manuals; product demonstration and evaluation versions of software; product reviews and comparison articles in computer periodicals; and opinions of industry experts.

- Decision aids can help support specialists make selection choices among competing products and services. These aids include selecting industry standard or bestselling products, analysis of products used by competitors, product benchmarks, the weighted point evaluation method, the request for proposal (RFP) procedure, and acknowledged subjective criteria.

- Many organizations adopt industry standard and bestselling products. These products are in widespread use and make the selection decision appear very simple. However, simply because a product is a bestseller does not mean that it is necessarily the best fit for a user's specialized needs. A less popular product may have unique features that are actually a better match for a specific user's needs.

- Benchmarks are an objective way to compare two or more products by observing them perform a standard, predefined set of tasks. The weighted point evaluation method forces a product evaluator to make a list of important criteria and assign a weight to each criterion that reflects its importance. Competing products are evaluated against the criteria, and the product that best matches the criteria is selected. Common criteria include product features, ease of learning, ease of use, compatibility with existing products, availability of technical support, and total cost of ownership.

- Hardware and software standards are important to organizations because standards help control user support costs. Although some support standards are based on organizational culture and tradition, many standards are the result of systematic analysis and evaluation of new products. The decision to adopt or modify a standard is often made by a group or committee with representatives from the end user group, user support, technical support, and management. Implementation of new standards is influenced by the investment in existing hardware and software and the potential loss of employee productivity during the conversion to the new products.

- Organizations also define acceptable use guidelines for their users, which describe activities users are permitted and not permitted to do with computers in an educational or business environment.

Key Terms

acceptable use guidelines—Standards adopted by an organization and publicized among its employees to communicate policies about activities that end users are permitted and not permitted to do with their computer systems.

benchmark—An objective test or measurement used to evaluate the speed, capacity, capabilities, or productivity of rival products.

extraneous variables—Factors that could bias the results of an objective benchmark test; product evaluators try to eliminate these factors to isolate and measure a product's performance.

e-zine—An electronic magazine organized like a print publication, but distributed via a Web site or e-mail; e-zines (or Webzines) aimed at the computer industry often feature product reviews and comparisons.

horizontal market applications—Software products designed to meet the needs of a broad spectrum of end users across a wide variety of industries (as opposed to *vertical market applications*).

industry standard products—Hardware, software, and peripherals that are market leaders in sales; standards in the computer industry are often not true standards, however, in the sense that typically no industry-wide group participated in the specification.

objective evaluation criteria—Factors used in a product selection procedure that are relatively unbiased; any neutral observer should be able to apply the same objective evaluation criteria and reach the same conclusion.

product evaluation—A process in which staff members research and analyze computer product features, capabilities, and suitability to meet specific end user needs.

product standards—Lists of hardware, operating system, network, and application software products that have been approved for use within an organization; standards are often enforced to reduce the cost of acquiring and supporting computer systems.

product standards committee—A group of user support specialists, end users, technical support staff, and managers who develop and maintain a list of organization-approved standard products and services; these products are recommended for purchase and are supported by the user support staff.

request for proposal (RFP)—A product selection or competitive bidding process that uses objective criteria to choose among products proposed by competing vendors; a request for proposal process is often used as the basis for awarding a contract to provide computer products.

software evaluation copy—A limited, trial copy of a software product that permits end users and support staff to try out a product's features and assess its ability to meet an organization's needs.

subjective evaluation criteria—Nonobjective factors used in a product selection procedure that are not directly related to the fit between a product's features and end users' needs; subjective factors include personal relationships with vendors, convenience, personal preferences, and reliance on traditional or historical purchasing channels.

vertical market application—Software designed for a highly specialized industry; vertical (or niche) market software often contains features that would not be useful in other industries.

weighted point evaluation method—A product comparison method that uses several key criteria of predetermined importance to evaluate competing products and arrive at a numerical summary score as a basis for selection; also called the Kepner-Tregoe method.

Check Your Understanding

Answers to Check Your Understanding questions are found in Appendix A.

1. True or False? By the early 1980s, hardware and software for personal computers were standardized in most organizations.

2. True or False? The larger the number of incompatible software packages an organization owns, the greater the cost to train and retrain workers.

3. _____ are an attempt to strike a reasonable balance between "select only this product" and "buy anything you want."

4. True or False? In order to avoid bias and favoritism, product evaluation and selection decisions are usually made by user support staff working independently of other workers.

5. _____ adopted by organizations often describe how users are permitted to use their computers, what users are not allowed to do, and the consequences or penalties for unauthorized or illegal use.

6. _____ copies of new software packages may have limited features or operate for a limited trial period, and are used to evaluate products.

7. True or False? Industry standard computer products are those selected by a panel of industry experts for use in most organizations.

8. True or False? As a general rule, dominance in the software industry does not change over time; the best-selling products in the early 1980s are still the best-selling products today.

9. A(n) _____ is an objective test or measurement used to evaluate the speed, capacity, capabilities, or productivity of competing computer products.

10. Which of the following product evaluation methods uses several criteria of predefined importance to arrive at a numerical summary score for each competing product?

a. industry standard method

b. benchmark method

c. subjective criteria method

d. weighted point method

11. A(n) _____ is a purchasing procedure that invites competing product vendors to submit product and price proposals for a system a user needs.

12. When support staff select office productivity software such as word processors or spreadsheets, they often use which decision strategy?

a. weighted point evaluations

b. industry standard products

c. request for proposals

d. benchmarks

13. Which of the following letter sequences represents the order of steps in the request for proposal process? (A) send RFP to vendors, (B) develop product specifications, (C) evaluate RFP responses against criteria, (D) define selection criteria

a. A – B – C – D

b. B – D – A – C

c. D – A – C – B

d. A – D – B – C

14. _____ are selection criteria that are neither measurable nor repeatable in an evaluation of competing computer products.

15. True or False? A benchmark test of competing products is designed to use objective evaluation criteria instead of an evaluator's personal opinions.

16. Computer product standards are often defined by:

a. an organization's computer culture

b. early adopters of technology

c. a product standards committee

d. any of these

17. A(n) _____ is a factor that an evaluator tries to eliminate from a side-by-side test of competing products because it could bias the test results.

18. Which of these is not an objective evaluation method for selecting a computer product?

    a. benchmark

    b. request for proposal

    c. user preferences

    d. weighted point evaluation method

19. List three resources a product evaluator might use to locate information about competing products.

20. True or False? Computer product standards originally emerged in order to reduce the cost to provide support for end users.

Discussion Questions

1. Describe a product standard issue or concern you think will confront organizations (perhaps one where you work or attend school) during the next 12 months. How will the issue impact end users? How will the issue impact the user support staff?

2. Based on your personal experience, what do you think about monopolies in the hardware and software industries and their impact on end users? Is it preferable to have a single vendor who has a substantial monopoly in a specific hardware or software product and therefore sets a standard, or is it preferable to have several competing, incompatible products? Why?

3. How would you design an effective benchmark test to evaluate competing brands of document scanners?

4. What is the role of end users when an organization selects new hardware and software products and updates its list of supported products? Describe some strategies for overcoming user resistance to changes in standards.

5. Which do you think are most effective when making a hardware or software purchase decision: objective criteria or subjective criteria? Explain your answer.

6. "The weighted point evaluation method forces evaluators to attach numeric values to criteria that cannot and should not be measured objectively. These numbers are essentially

meaningless as a basis for making purchase decisions." Do you agree or disagree with this statement? Explain your position.

7. "End users should not participate in product evaluations because they cannot be objective about computer products and standards." Explain your reaction to this statement.

Hands-On Activities

Activity 7-1

Investigate product comparison information. Locate a magazine or Web site that contains one or more articles that present a side-by-side comparison of two or more products. (Use resources listed in the chapter, if you like.) Evaluate the effectiveness of the product comparison by considering the questions listed below. Write a summary of your findings.

- What criteria are used to compare the products?

- What additional criteria could have been used?

- Describe the evaluation method used to do the product comparisons.

- Did the method(s) produce an objective or subjective result?

- Do you agree with the results? Why or why not?

Activity 7-2

Compare computer product support standards. Locate the computer product support standards for your workplace or school, or find another organization's computer product support standards online. Write a short comparison between those you find and the support standards at Honolulu Community College described in this chapter. How are they similar and how are they different?

Activity 7-3

Try a benchmark utility program. Several benchmark utility programs are available online, including the ones listed below. Download one of these utilities and run it on one or more different systems to which you have access. Compare your results with those obtained by others. Write a brief summary of your findings.

- System Analyser (**www.sysanalyser.com**)
  System Analyser, developed by Hans Niekus, is a system information utility that measures the speed of a system's CPU, hard drive, and other components.

- Dacris Benchmarks 5.0 (**www.dacris.com/bmarknet**)
  Benchmarks, developed by Dacris Software, is an extensive test
  and evaluation utility.

- Fresh Diagnose (**www.freshdevices.com/benchmark_software.html**)
  Fresh Diagnose is designed to analyze and benchmark various
  computer components.

Activity 7-4

Identify industry standard products. Choose a category of computer
products from among the following: hardware, peripherals, operating
systems, applications software, and local area networks. Make a list of
at least three computer products you think fit the description "industry
standard" in the category you selected. Compare your list with the list of
a team of three classmates or coworkers. Do your team members agree
or disagree about the industry standards? Write a one-page paper that
lists the agreed-upon standards, products over which there are disagreements, and your explanation of the reasons for any disagreements.

Activity 7-5

Compare evaluation criteria for Web browsers. Find two frequent
Web users, one who uses Internet Explorer and another who uses
Firefox. Ask each user why they prefer their browser choice over the
other. What criteria do they use? Are they subjective or objective
criteria? How do their evaluations compare with your own choice?
Write a summary of your findings.

Activity 7-6

Plan a product standards committee meeting. Suppose that you
are the leader of a product standards committee whose assignment
is to develop a product standard for your organization. Write an
agenda for the first committee meeting that lists the highest priority
tasks the committee should undertake. (*Hint*: Think about the information the committee will need, the decisions it will need to make,
and what the end result will look like.)

Activity 7-7

Develop a weighted point evaluation worksheet model. Use
spreadsheet software to develop a worksheet that product evaluators
can use for the weighted point evaluation method. Set up columns
and formulas that will make the worksheet easy to use. To test your
worksheet, enter the data from the example in this chapter. Design
your worksheet to be as general as possible to make it simple to add
more products or evaluation criteria. Save and print your worksheet.

Activity 7-8

Interview a product standards committee participant. Interview a support specialist or other member of a product standards committee in your school or work organization. Learn about the process the committee uses to set and maintain product and service standards. How does the committee ensure that it gets end user input? Ask about difficult decisions to include or exclude products that the committee had to address at recent meetings. Write a short summary of what you learned about product standards and committee meetings from the interview.

Activity 7-9

Evaluate an acceptable use policy. Learn whether the organization where you work or attend school has an acceptable computer use policy for workers or students. Make a list of activities that are permitted and those that are not permitted. Identify on your list those activities that are illegal and those that are not permitted according to organizational policy. Compare your organization's computer use policy with the one in effect at the University of Oregon referenced in the chapter. Describe the similarities and differences.

Case Projects

1. Anti-spyware Utility Evaluation at Les Deux Vaches

You are a user support specialist at Les Deux Vaches, an organization that publishes a trade publication for the dairy industry. Several managers have approached you about a problem they want help with. Each of the managers has a laptop computer they use to connect to the company's intranet and to the Internet. They use their laptops to access e-mail and certain accounting information in the evenings and on weekends. They are concerned about the possibility of accidentally downloading a spyware program that could be used to obtain proprietary corporate information or slow the speed of their laptop computer.

Investigate some free anti-spyware utility programs that are available for download from the Web and make a recommendation to the workers about which program to use. Complete the following tasks:

1. Create an evaluation criteria checklist for an anti-spyware utility. Develop as complete a list as you can, keeping in mind the problem the managers want you to help them solve. You can also consider any software support issues or other factors you think are relevant.

2. Develop evaluation criteria for an anti-spyware utility.

3. Select two or three of the freeware utilities you find online. Download and install the utilities on a computer to which you have access.

4. Read the documentation and try the features of each program you downloaded.

5. Evaluate each of the programs you downloaded in terms of the criteria you established.

6. Write a short summary report for the managers detailing the anti-spyware utilities you evaluated and include your recommendation about which utility you would suggest the managers at Les Deux Vaches use.

2. Evaluate Online User Satisfaction Survey Web Services

The supervisor of the help desk where you work has asked for your help with a small user satisfaction survey project. The supervisor wants to get some experience with online user satisfaction surveys as a way to measure client satisfaction with help desk services. Your task is to evaluate the following two Web services that facilitate collecting survey information:

- SurveyMonkey (**www.surveymonkey.com**)

- Free Online Survey (**freeonlinesurveys.com**)

Each site requires a valid e-mail address to register, but offers a free or evaluation service as an alternate to its fee-based services. Limit your evaluation to the free services.

1. Develop evaluation criteria for an online user satisfaction survey. (You may want to brainstorm criteria with your colleagues.)

2. Read the documentation and view the demo survey to get experience with the features each service offers.

3. Create an evaluation criteria checklist for an online survey tool. Develop as complete a list as you can, keeping in mind the problem the help desk supervisor wants you to help solve. You can also add to your checklist any technical support issues or other factors you think are relevant.

4. Evaluate the two services in terms of the criteria you established.

5. Write a summary report about the survey tools you evaluated. Include your recommendation about which service you would recommend to your supervisor.

3. Invoicing Software for Columbia Sand & Gravel

Mark Allen, owner and operator of Columbia Sand & Gravel, needs some computer advice and wants to hire you as a consultant. Due to several large construction projects and subdivision developments, Columbia has grown in recent years, and needs to replace its soon-to-be-obsolete computer billing system. The existing software runs on an older PC system and was purchased more than 12 years ago. Although Mark is still very pleased with the features of the current billing system, the hardware and software no longer have the capacity and speed to process invoices and record payments for Columbia's client base. Unfortunately, the company that sold the software to Mark is no longer in business, so an upgrade of the existing system is not an option.

Mark is aware of two software companies, Digital Rock and Extractasoft, that sell invoicing applications specifically tailored for use in the sand and gravel industry. Both companies claim to have the best-selling software available for sand and gravel invoice applications. Mark wants you to evaluate these two competing products and make a recommendation on which software invoicing package Columbia should adopt as its new standard.

Mark is also aware that his company will have to purchase new hardware to run the selected software. In recent years, Columbia Sand & Gravel has developed a good working relationship with Modular PC, a local company that sells and services computer hardware products. The owner of Modular PC is a close personal friend of Mark's, but Modular PC does not sell invoicing software as specialized as Mark needs. Although Mark has already decided to purchase the computer hardware from Modular PC, and is ready to cut a purchase order for the new hardware, he wants an outside perspective to help evaluate the software products.

Using what you have learned in this chapter, as well as the information described above, write a letter to Mark in which you:

1. Describe any problems you have identified with the approach Columbia plans to take in the selection of replacement hardware and invoicing software, as described by Mark above.

2. Outline your suggestions for the software and hardware product evaluation approach and methods you would recommend at Columbia Sand & Gravel.

4. An RFP Checklist for Chocoholic Specialties

Reilly Lane at Chocoholic Specialties wants to develop a Web site to sell the company's chocolate candy and cooking products directly to online customers in the United States and Canada. Reilly would like your help with the preparation of a request for proposal (RFP) to local vendors who design and develop commercial Web sites.

Reilly wants you to research what should go into the RFP and to make a list of topics the Web site development RFP should cover. Reilly asked you to submit a checklist of topics or questions that should be included in the written Web site RFP. You do not need to write the RFP, but Reilly will use your list of suggested topics and questions to make assignments to staff members who will pull together the information needed to produce a written RFP.

Begin by doing some research on the content of an RFP. One place you might look is at Web sites that contain guidelines on RFP preparation. These sites often include lists of topics or information that should be included in an RFP. Some sites you might consult are:

- *How to Write a Request for Proposal for a Web Project* by Bruce Morris (**www.webdevelopersjournal.com/columns/writerfp. html**)

- *How to Write a Request for Proposal (RFP)* by Instructional Designs (**www.internettraining.com/6art2.htm**)

- *Client 101: How to Write an RFP* by Sean Carton (**www.clickz. com/933951**)

- *Aristotle's RFP Development Guide* (**www.aristotlewebdesign. com/pdfs/RFP%20Guide.doc**)

This site contains links to several different examples of Web site design RFPs:

- Municipal Research and Services Center of Washington provides examples of municipal government Web site RFPs (**www.mrsc. org/Subjects/InfoServ/webdesignrfp.aspx**).

Or, you may be able to find a book on RFPs, such as:

- Porter-Roth, Bud. *Request for Proposal: A Guide to Effective RFP Development.* Boston: Addison-Wesley Professional, 2001.

End-User Needs Assessment Projects

In this chapter, you will learn about:

◎ Basic strategies for performing end-user needs analysis and assessment

◎ Steps analysts undertake to analyze and assess a user's needs

◎ Common tools that aid support specialists in an end-user needs analysis project

◎ Tasks in managing a user needs assessment project

◎ Project management software tools

User support specialists are often asked to help end users select computer products and services. Sometimes the selection must be made from a limited assortment of products and services, especially if an organization maintains lists of standard, supported products—as you learned in Chapter 7. This chapter describes how to analyze and assess end-user needs and help organizations and users choose the best options among competing products and services. User needs analysis involves thoroughly investigating a situation and problem; assessment involves evaluating the results of the investigation and making a recommendation or a decision.

The chapter applies primarily to user support specialists who work with internal users; it does not apply directly to support specialists who work on help desks or provide telephone support to external users. Support specialists who work with internal users in small organizations are often involved in assessing end-user needs and recommending products for purchase. If the scale of an assessment project is large, it may be conducted by a team that includes a senior support staff member or a supervisor and one or more junior-level support staff. Although the role of an assessment project investigator or manager is usually filled by a more experienced support staff, even entry-level support workers may be assigned to work on a project team.

 In larger organizations, Information Technology staff members are likely to have primary responsibility for needs assessment projects.

If you have taken previous coursework in computer systems analysis and design or information systems, you will probably recognize some of the issues, resources, and tools described in this chapter. In some academic programs, students study systems analysis or information systems before they take courses in end-user computing support. Experience in systems analysis and design provides a good background for end-user needs assessment because the role a support specialist plays in user needs assessment is very similar to the role of a systems analyst in an IT department. However, the tools that support specialists use are not always the same as those used by systems analysts whose primary focus often is to design a new application program for a programmer to code. This chapter focuses on analysis and assessment tools that support specialists use to match an end user's needs to available products and services.

Overview of User Needs Analysis and Assessment

Support staff often analyze and assess user needs to determine which hardware and software products or computer services will best meet an end user's requirements. These tasks may be performed by any support staff member who has special skills, and possibly the title of support analyst. Once a support analyst understands an end user's environment and work situation, the analyst can investigate various products and services to meet the user's needs. The analyst can then also help decide on a solution to meet the user's needs and determine whether to purchase or build the solution.

An end-user needs analysis and assessment project can take many forms. An assessment project can result in the selection of a product, such as a new computer or software package. It may result in selecting a service, such as a training program or a hardware repair vendor. An assessment project can be informal, such as a friend or colleague who asks for help with the purchase of computer hardware or software for home or work use. A project can also be formal, such as when a supervisor assigns a user support specialist the task of working with end users in a department to select a new Internet service provider (ISP), a new printer, or even a new office network. No matter the scale or purpose, most needs assessment projects follow the same sequence of steps, which are summarized in Figure 8-1.

I. Preparation Phase Activities
1. Understand the end user's and the organization's goals
2. Understand the decision criteria and constraints
3. Define the problem clearly
4. Identify the roles of stakeholders
5. Identify sources of information

II. Investigation Phase Activities
6. Develop an understanding of the existing system
7. Investigate alternatives to the existing system

III. Decision Phase Activities
8. Develop a model of the proposed solution
9. Make a build-versus-buy decision

Figure 8-1   Phases and activities in the needs analysis and assessment process

Because each needs assessment project is unique, support analysts don't always perform every step listed in Figure 8-1, and each step is not always of equal importance. But analysts must start with a checklist of activities such as those in Figure 8-1 to guide a needs analysis project to a satisfactory solution. To unintentionally omit one or more of these steps is to risk basing a decision on incomplete or inaccurate information. Similarly, experienced support analysts know that user needs analysis and assessment is neither a perfect process nor one that always results in an obvious solution. End users are rarely certain of their exact needs and may not know how to translate their requirements into words. End users may also have unrealistic expectations about the capabilities of computer technology at an affordable price. However, a support specialist should begin with a list of well-planned questions—even if the answers are sometimes inexact.

End-User Needs Analysis Steps and Tasks

The steps in an end-user needs analysis project can be grouped into three phases: preparation, investigation, and decision. In the **preparation phase**, analysts try to understand the end user's and the organization's goals, as well as the decision criteria and project constraints; they try to define the problem, identify the roles of stakeholders, and identify potential sources of information. In the **investigation phase**, analysts try to understand the present system or situation and identify potential alternatives to it. Finally, in the **decision phase**, analysts develop a model of the proposed solution and decide whether to build it or buy it. Within each phase, analysts take specific steps and use tools that allow them to obtain information and propose a solution. By performing certain tasks for each step, analysts ensure that they have considered relevant sources of information in order to arrive at an appropriate solution for each unique situation. The following sections describe the major tasks of each step of the analysis and assessment process.

CASE STUDY: The Training Team Web Development Project

The case study in this chapter illustrates the steps in a typical needs analysis project. The case is based on The Training Team, a local company that provides custom training solutions to other businesses. After you have read about each step in a user needs assessment project, you will learn how the step applies to solving a current problem at The Training Team.

The Training Team prepares custom training materials and services for other organizations. For years, it provided primarily printed training workbooks, tutorials, and other materials to its clients. However, an increasing number of clients are now requesting Web-based training courses for their workers. The Training Team has responded to these requests by offering Web-based materials as an alternative or a supplement to printed training materials. Let's meet some of the employees of The Training Team.

- **Lindsey Dell** is a training course designer and developer. She is part of a small group of staff at The Training Team who interview clients to learn about their training needs. Lindsey's group also designs training curriculum and materials to address those needs, and prepares workbooks, tutorial material, and some Web-based training for use by its clients.

- **Sara West** provides technical support and some programming services to The Training Team staff. She is responsible for network administration and maintains the company's application software for sales processing, billing, course registration, and accounting transactions.

- **Margaret Rose** is a relatively new employee at The Training Team. Margaret provides desktop support to employees, and she has some experience with project management and user needs assessment from a position at a previous employer.

- **Fred Huntington** is the company president. He has identified a potential problem with the way The Training Team prepares training material for delivery on the Web. Fred assembled an assessment project team of Margaret, Lindsey, and Sara to discuss the Web development problem.

Step 1: Understand the End User's and the Organization's Goals

Before support analysts can recommend new computer products and services, they must develop an understanding of the individual purchaser's objectives as well as the organization's goals. Many medium to large organizations have a strategic business plan or a mission statement that describes the goals and objectives of the organization. Some organizations also have business plans devoted specifically to information technology. If these documents are not available, support analysts can interview managers, supervisors, and individual purchasers to learn about their vision, goals, and future plans.

Regardless of whether support analysts obtain the information through written documents or interviews, they should learn the answers to the following questions:

1. What are the goals of the organization, department, or individual purchaser that will affect the need for computer products or services?

2. Is the organization for-profit or not-for-profit?

3. What plans does the organization have to grow or expand?

4. What is the organization's attitude about technology?

5. Does the organization have a history of successful experiences with adopting changes in technology?

6. What is the organization's budget for computer systems and services?

7. Does the organization's staff or the individual purchaser have the experience and expertise to operate, maintain, and support a computer system?

The purpose of these questions is to understand the big picture—the environment and culture into which the future system or service will fit. Growth or expansion plans are especially important to consider during the assessment process. The solution an analyst might recommend to an organization that is growing 5 to 10 percent per year would probably be very different from the solutions he or she would recommend to an organization that expects to grow 25 to 50 percent per year. Similarly, a smaller organization or an individual purchaser might not be able to operate, maintain, or support a sophisticated system with a lot of features and flexibility; a more straightforward package might be a better choice.

CASE STUDY: The Training Team Web Development Project

In a preliminary meeting with the Web development project team, company president Fred Huntington gave his perspective on the company's problem with developing Web-based training materials. He told the project team that the number of requests for Web-based training materials has been increasing, and he expects that trend to continue in the future. At some point soon, the sales of Web-based materials will exceed those of printed materials. He noted that clients seem to be delighted with Lindsey's work and the results produced by her coworkers on the design and development team.

Fred went on to say that the bottleneck in Web-based projects appears to be getting the training modules programmed and operational on The Training Team's Web site after they are designed. Since Sara West has some experience with HTML and JavaScript, she has done the programming for the Web-based projects. However, her primary responsibilities are network administration and technical support, so the time she has available to develop training materials is limited. As a consequence, a backlog of Web programming projects currently exists. And Sara feels like she is stealing time away from her other responsibilities whenever she is working on a training module programming project.

Fred went into detail about the nature of this problem for Margaret's benefit, since she is a relatively new employee. He asked Margaret to lead a needs assessment project team to analyze the Web development

336

problem because of her previous needs analysis and project management experience. He closed by saying that he did not have any preconceived ideas about how to solve this problem. But he felt that because of the industry trend to Web-based delivery of training, The Training Team needed to become more responsive to client needs in order to remain competitive. The project team spent a few minutes brainstorming various options, including hiring a Web development programmer to work with Sara to implement projects, outsourcing the programming projects to a software development company, using project management software to increase the productivity of development projects, and finding a replacement for Sara so she can devote more of her time to Web development programming

Step 2: Understand the Decision Criteria and Constraints

Support analysts also need to determine early on the criteria the organization will use to make decisions. Analysts usually recommend solutions to end users or managers rather than deciding on a solution themselves. However, the more support analysts understand about the decision criteria, the more they can focus on realistic alternatives.

Support analysts need to clarify what is feasible, or possible, in terms of time, money, and technology. A **feasibility study** is an investigation into the economic, operational, technical, and timeline constraints that will impact a user needs analysis and assessment project. Analysts often consider several kinds of feasibility:

- **Economic feasibility**—What budget constraints will influence the final decision?

- **Operational feasibility**—With what other systems or procedures does this system need to interact? What personnel will be required to operate this system? Do the personnel have the knowledge, skills, and abilities they need?

- **Technological feasibility**—What limitations or constraints does the existing technology impose on possible solutions?

- **Timeline feasibility**—Do time constraints rule out some potential alternatives?

Support analysts also need to understand the business culture factors that will influence the final decision. Does the organization pride itself on doing business with well-known and reputable vendors, so that solutions from established vendors should be considered more seriously than those offered by relatively smaller, unknown vendors?

Does the organization try to stay on the leading edge of technology, or does it take a relatively conservative view of new, and perhaps untried, products? Are users and managers comfortable with the introduction of new technology? What priority does the organization place on vendor support? For example, some organizations rely on their own support staff and don't need extensive vendor support, while others are very dependent on vendor support. The answers to feasibility and business culture questions help define the criteria and constraints that support analysts must consider in order to make a recommendation about an appropriate solution.

ON THE WEB

Geary Rummler has developed a project feasibility guide that lists several kinds of questions an analyst can ask about the feasibility of a project. View this guide at **www.performancexpress.org/0304/images/Project_Feasibility_Guide.pdf**.

CASE STUDY: The Training Team Web Development Project

The user support specialist, Margaret, inquired about the budget to solve the Web development problem. Fred indicated that no budget had been allocated, but that the problem clearly needed to be solved, and the sooner the better. He said there is currently a backlog of promised development projects. He expressed the belief that if The Training Team couldn't respond to requests for Web-based materials in a timely way that it would lose business to its competitors and eventually would probably go out of business. Margaret asked about the time frame for the project. Fred indicated that he would like the project team to make a recommendation to him and the other managers in two to three weeks. Lindsey, the design and development team member, asked whether it would be feasible to hire someone either to do Web development or to replace Sara so she could handle the programming. Fred indicated that if hiring someone was the best solution, he would consider that option, but he expressed concern about finding a new employee who could join the company and be productive in a short period of time.

Sara asked whether the company had ever considered adopting a Web development software package to develop the online training materials. She said the HTML and JavaScript programs she had been writing were probably not the most productive way to develop Web-based training modules. Lindsey said they had discussed Web development software tools in the past, but no one had the time to learn a new software package.

Step 3: Define the Problem Clearly

Project problems come in a variety of forms and sizes. Some are well defined, while others are not. Support analysts who work on user needs assessment projects must dig for details in order to identify the root or underlying problem they are trying to solve. Not all problems are technical; some "computer" problems turn out to be organizational, personnel, workflow, user-training, office politics, management, or resource problems. Experienced analysts look beyond the symptoms of a problem to search for its root causes, whatever they may be.

"Do I really understand the dimensions of the problem I'm trying to solve for this user?" is a question that should guide a needs analysis from beginning to end. For example, an end user may complain that the accounting application he uses does not work and that he wants to replace it with a new one that is more robust. The user may have correctly concluded that he needs new software. However, the problem could also be related to the way the existing program is configured. To recommend replacing expensive hardware or software when the real problem is something else can be a costly mistake. Therefore, clearly defining the root or underlying problem is critical to any user needs analysis.

CASE STUDY: The Training Team Web Development Project

At the next meeting of the needs assessment group, Margaret initiated a discussion that she hoped would lead to a better definition of the problem with Web module development projects. She asked whether the problem was a technical one that could be solved with better technology and more effective software, a staffing problem that could be solved by adding programming resources to the company, or a project management problem that could be solved by adopting better project management methods and perhaps using project management software. The team discussed each of these perspectives on the problem and agreed that the problem was unlikely to be solved by better technology or improved project management methods. However, the other team members suggested that Margaret talk with two other managers at The Training Team to get their perspectives before reaching any conclusions.

- **Zed Langers** is the coordinator of the design and development team, and Lindsey's supervisor. He has extensive curriculum development experience and has a background in corporate training.

- **Naseem Rhea** is the head of the accounting and information technology group at The Training Team; she is Sara and Margaret's supervisor. Naseem's background is in office management, but she has become very knowledgeable about technology during several years of employment at The Training Team.

Step 4: Identify the Roles of Stakeholders

Stakeholders are the participants in an end-user needs analysis and assessment project who might gain or lose from its success or failure. Four kinds of stakeholders are important in a needs analysis project: end users, managers, technical support staff, and the needs assessment analyst. Some stakeholders participate in every step of an assessment project. Others may contribute their expertise and support in only one or a few of the project steps and then leave the project, perhaps to rejoin it at a later step.

End Users

Support analysts should learn which users will work with or be affected by a project. What are their job responsibilities? What computer experience do they have? What training have they received? What is their background? How long have they worked for the organization? What role will they play in the project?

Managers

After identifying end users and their roles, support analysts should identify the manager who will be involved in the decision to purchase a computer system or service, or implement another solution. This manager is sometimes called the project sponsor. The support analysts should determine: Who will make the final decision? What computer knowledge and experience do they bring to the process?

The management perspective is vital for the success of any assessment project. Managers provide important information about the background and priority of the problem, insights into possible solutions, support for a project, as well as financial and decision-making expertise. Experienced support analysts know that one of the biggest mistakes they can make in a needs assessment project is to ignore the management perspective.

 If the final decision makers on a project lack technical expertise, a support analyst may need to spend project time to educate them so that they can make an intelligent decision.

Information Technology or Technical Support Staff

If an organization has an IT or technical support staff, these stakeholders are often important participants in a needs assessment project. IT staff members may be ultimately responsible for installing, configuring, maintaining, and troubleshooting the solution a support analyst recommends. They may have important perspectives on possible alternate solutions and technical feasibility.

Support Analysts

Support analysts who coordinate and conduct needs analysis projects are obviously key participants in the process. As important as it is to understand the roles of other participants, analysts also need to clarify their own role. Is the analysts' role to assist existing company staff with the needs assessment, to perform the analysis and describe the pros and cons of various alternatives, to make a recommendation, or to make the final decision? How much time and resources has the organization allocated to the project, and how do these affect the analysts' work on this project as well as other work responsibilities?

Support analysts who work on a large project that involves several users, managers, and IT or technical support staff may develop a brief written profile that summarizes information about each participant in a project. A profile can include contact information such as phone number and e-mail address, position title, background, primary job functions, and notes on each person's interest in the outcome of the project.

In some needs assessment projects, one or more vendor representatives may be key project participants. Vendor representatives can play a role at various stages in a project if they have perspectives on the problem or will provide part of the eventual solution. Obviously a vendor's role may be limited by a bias toward his or her own products or services.

CASE STUDY: The Training Team Web Development Project

During the initial meeting of the assessment group, Margaret had started making a list of stakeholders in the project. She knew about the roles of Lindsey and Sara in Web development projects. But now she also added Zed, the design and development coordinator, and Naseem, the head of the IT group, to her list of project stakeholders.

Margaret asked Fred whether the assessment team should include one of The Training Team's clients as a representative of its user community. Fred thought the idea was an interesting one, but said that their clients were focused on the end product of a development project and would probably not have much input into how the development work got accomplished. And he observed that a smaller needs assessment group could probably develop a recommendation faster than a larger one. Fred instead suggested that Margaret simply interview a client to get feedback on The Training Team's process and performance. Margaret asked who would eventually make the final decision about the project team's recommendation. Fred said he would make the final decision after discussing it with other managers whose groups would be affected.

Step 5: Identify Sources of Information

Support analysts must also determine the sources of information necessary to complete a project successfully. The following list contains several potentially useful sources of information for a needs assessment project:

- Interviews with end users and managers
- Surveys or questionnaires completed by end users who will be most affected
- Procedure manuals that detail how to operate the current system (if one exists)
- Direct observation of the existing system
- Forms used for input into the existing system
- Reports that are created using the existing system
- Problem-report histories or help desk logs for the existing system
- Diagrams of workflow
- Equipment inventories
- Reports and recommendations from consultants, vendors, or auditors who have studied the existing system

Analysts often start with a checklist of resources, like the one above, to help them gather information about the system or situation they have been asked to analyze. They then add to or subtract from the checklist as needed.

CASE STUDY: The Training Team Web Development Project

Margaret told the assessment team that she would like some time to think about the Web development problem and the possible solutions. On her way back to her desk, she began to compile a list of information-gathering steps she wanted to undertake next.

1. Interview Zed and Naseem to get their perspectives on the problem and possible solutions.
2. Review the results of a recent Web-based training project.
3. Interview a representative client of the company.

Margaret sent an e-mail to Lindsey and Sara to ask for an access code, as well as a copy of the design specifications for a recent project. She also asked Fred if she could interview the client for whom the recent training module was developed. He provided her with the contact information for the client.

342

Step 6: Develop an Understanding of the Existing System

During the investigation phase, support analysts must learn as much as possible about the existing system, whether it is manual or computer-based. In this step, analysts collect and examine important documents (examples of forms, reports, and documentation), interview key participants (users, managers, and technical support staff), observe the operation of the existing system, and develop a clear understanding of what the existing system does and how it works.

One way to organize project information is according to the steps in the analysis process described in this chapter.

Analysts should organize the information they collect so that they can easily locate what they need. Analysts often use a project notebook or file folders to keep records of various forms, reports, meetings, and interviews.

The primary objective of this step is to build a model that describes the existing system. A **model** is a narrative or graphic diagram, or both, that represents a business activity in an organization (such as paper workflow), a computer system, or a network. A model can be a written description or a diagram, such as a flowchart or an organization chart. Analysts can also create a model by using analytic and planning tools, such as software designed specifically for systems analysts.

ON THE WEB

A popular tool support analysts use to diagram a model of an existing business system is Microsoft Visio. To learn more about Visio and take a tour of the product, visit the Visio home page at **office.microsoft.com/en-us/project/default. aspx**.

A shareware product that has similar capabilities is Chartist by Novagraph. Visit its Web site at **www.novagraph.com**, where you can download a trial copy.

After constructing a model, analysts can share it with other project participants to make sure the model accurately represents the existing system. Sharing a model with users, managers, and other project participants often uncovers misunderstandings about the capabilities or features of the existing system.

Support analysts should be able to answer "yes" to the following questions at the end of this step:

1. Do I understand the existing system well enough to explain to other participants how it operates?

2. Do I understand which features of the existing system users like?

3. Do I understand what users think is wrong with the existing system?

Without an understanding of each of these aspects of the existing system or situation, analysts may be unprepared to consider alternatives with which to replace or repair it.

CASE STUDY: The Training Team Web Development Project

During that week, Margaret interviewed Zed and Naseem. They both expressed a need to solve the Web development backlog problem for the future of the company. However, neither ventured an opinion about the best way to solve the problem. Naseem said she could give up a little more of Sara's time to work on the current development backlog. However, she warned that Sara has other responsibilities that, in the long run, would limit the time she could spend on programming projects. Zed indicated that his design and development team members were often frustrated because the programming effort frequently lagged the design and curriculum development work on a module. He said his team wasted time waiting for a Web development module to be programmed so that it could be tested and implemented.

During the week, Margaret had an opportunity to review the sample Web-based training module she had requested, and she studied the design specifications that Sara used to write the HTML code for the module. When she contacted the client for whom the module was developed, the client offered effusive praise for the quality of the training module, but complained that the project had been delivered after the agreed-upon date, and only after several calls to Fred to urge that it be completed.

Step 7: Investigate Alternatives to the Existing System

In previous steps, the analyst's goal was to understand as much as possible about the existing system: its purposes, features, users, advantages, disadvantages, problems, and other important characteristics. In this step, analysts' attention shifts to ways to fix the problems with the current system or situation. Analysts often consider several kinds of alternatives:

- **Additional resources**—In order to operate effectively, the existing system may need additional resources such as personnel, equipment, financial resources, time commitment, or increased priority.

- **Changes to existing resources**—The existing system may continue to meet the needs of the organization if changes are made to it. Common changes to existing systems include reconfiguring software and identifying additional training that may make users more productive.

- **Upgrades**—An organization may need to upgrade hardware or software components to improve processing speed, storage capacity, or compatibility, or offer new features that address identified problems.

- **New hardware**—New hardware may be necessary to address capacity constraints, run software efficiently, or operate new software with features that solve end users' problems.

- **New software**—New software may be necessary to address problems, increase user productivity, or expand business opportunities.

When developing a list of alternatives to consider, analysts often investigate the tools used by users who perform similar tasks successfully in other organizations. These solutions may not solve all the identified problems, but an analyst should investigate them nonetheless, rather than risk spending scarce resources to reinvent a solution someone else has already devised.

A support analyst looking for software for a specific business, such as a video rental store or a veterinary clinic, might find useful leads online.

As you learned in Chapter 7, trade magazines targeted at a specific industry are often a good source of information about products that address specific needs. Articles in trade publications may report on successful computer system implementations in similar organizations. Some trade magazines publish articles that evaluate and compare technology options. Finally, advertisements in trade periodicals often identify vendors that supply hardware, software, and services aimed at a specialized market niche.

___

CASE STUDY: The Training Team Web Development Project

At the next meeting of the assessment team, Margaret shared her recent findings with the other team members. She invited Zed and Naseem to join the group for this meeting to add their management perspective. The expanded group concluded that the development backlog problem was probably not a hardware or project management problem. The discussion turned to staffing as a solution. The staffing alternatives appeared to be:

1. Hire an additional programmer to work on Web module programming projects.

2. Hire a technical support worker to replace Sara, who could then be assigned to work on Web development projects.

3. Outsource Web programming projects to a software developer that specializes in Web-based projects.

As supervisor of information technology, Naseem described the difficulty of hiring an additional programmer in a short time frame and getting them to be productive quickly. She also reported that outsourced programming projects are very expensive and pose difficult timeline and coordination challenges. In response to alternative 2, Sara indicated that she was personally more interested in network administration and technical support than in programming, and would prefer an alternative that reduced her role in programming projects. She added that, for the short term, she would be willing to continue to program training modules to reduce the backlog.

Margaret sensed that the team was about out of options when Naseem and Sara again raised the alternative of purchasing and adopting a Web development software tool. Naseem and Sara reported that they had researched this segment of the software market and found several packages, such as Adobe Dreamweaver, which were designed to develop and maintain Web sites. This kind of tool could serve as a development platform for The Training Team to adopt for future projects. Naseem described Dreamweaver as a higher-level development tool compared with HTML and JavaScript. She said this kind of tool could make a Web developer more productive and potentially reduce both the time to program a training module and the current development backlog. The project team agreed to add a fourth alternative:

4. Acquire and adopt a Web development software tool for future training module projects.

Step 8: Develop a Model of the Proposed Solution

Once analysts have completed the project preparation and investigation phases, they reach the decision phase. With a clear description of the problem, an understanding of the existing system, and a list of possible alternatives, analysts can develop a model of the proposed solution to recommend to users and management.

The model that support analysts build often includes a narrative description of the proposed system or solution and one or more graphic aids to help users and managers understand the proposal. The narrative should include a description of the alternatives the analysts considered, as well as the pros and cons of each alternative. The model should answer the questions, "Why is the proposed solution an improvement over the present system, and why is it the best available alternative?"

A final decision on which of the various alternatives to recommend may be obvious. One solution may be clearly an **optimal solution**, one which is the most feasible, has the lowest cost, and offers the most benefits. However, cost is frequently a major issue, and the best solution may be the most expensive. In this case, the analyst may recommend a **satisficing solution**, one that solves the problem in a reasonable way, but is not necessarily an optimal solution.

A cost-benefit analysis is not an exact science. For a cost-benefit analysis to be most useful, alternatives in the same general category and with the same features should be compared. For most small projects, a detailed cost-benefit analysis may not be necessary, but even an informal analysis will increase the likelihood that analysts have considered the significant costs and benefits of each alternative.

When one solution is not obvious, or when legally required, analysts may do a cost-benefit analysis of several options to help them choose from among the alternatives. A cost-benefit analysis compares the expenses a proposed solution will incur with the solution's payoffs. A cost-benefit analysis often looks like a balance sheet (a sheet of paper divided into two columns) with the costs of a proposed system or solution on one side and the benefits on the other. Later in this chapter, you will look more closely at the factors to consider in a cost-benefit analysis.

When a needs assessment project results in a decision to purchase a new computer, end users' needs should drive the specifications for the new system. End users frequently believe hardware is the most crucial component of a system; however, when users' needs determine the specifications, software solutions should be considered paramount. Software requirements should drive the hardware selection. Only when software is being specified for an already-existing hardware platform should the software selection depend on the hardware configuration.

CASE STUDY: The Training Team Web Development Project

Margaret prepared for the next meeting of the assessment team by researching the capabilities of Dreamweaver and other Web development tools. She found that the acquisition cost for these packages is around $400 per license. When the group reassembled, Margaret reported on her research. However, several issues with this proposed solution remained: Who would use the development tool? How would they learn to use it? What would be the total cost of this solution? And how fast could it happen?

Margaret then related a comment Zed made in their initial interview that his curriculum designers often waste time awaiting the results of a module programming project. She asked if any of his group might be interested in learning Dreamweaver as a development tool. Zed said that he remembered that a couple of his curriculum designers had expressed an interested in learning Dreamweaver or a similar product as a training module prototyping tool. He offered to discuss whether they would be interested in learning Dreamweaver as a professional development opportunity. Lindsey said she might even be interested in learning Dreamweaver.

Margaret reported that her research into Dreamweaver had turned up several tutorials and trade books that could help Zed's staff members learn to use the product at a very reasonable cost.

She concluded that she would write a draft of a report to Fred and the other managers that recommended the use of Dreamweaver by a couple of members of Zed's design and development staff on future Web development projects. The team suggested several items for a proposed budget, including software licenses, training materials, and the cost of staff time to learn the new tool. Margaret felt that a project report was beginning to take shape.

Step 9: Make a Build-Versus-Buy Decision

A significant decision for many organizations is the **build-versus-buy decision**: whether to build a custom solution or purchase one off the shelf. The build-versus-buy decision can apply to building computer hardware, developing software, and providing services. In most cases, however, the build-versus-buy decision applies to software and services. Although many projects result in a decision to purchase off-the-shelf software, the alternative of custom-developed software may better meet an end user's or an organization's exact requirements. For other organizations, acquiring a turnkey system is more appropriate. A **turnkey system** includes an integrated package of hardware, software, and support services purchased from a single vendor, and may include a combination of off-the-shelf and customizable components. Table 8-1 summarizes some of the advantages and disadvantages of building versus buying a system.

Building a Custom Solution	Buying an Off-the-Shelf Solution
• System can be custom designed to meet end-user needs; it can be tailored to exact specifications • System may provide strategic business advantages over competitors	• Lower acquisition cost due to market competition • Faster implementation • Better documentation may be available • Standard user interfaces and components • Fewer bugs due to more exhaustive testing • Ongoing technical support may be available

Table 8-1   Advantages of building versus buying a solution

Developing a complete custom system or solution is prohibitively expensive for many organizations, especially those that do not have an in-house programming staff. Even for organizations with staff members who have programming expertise, the costs of custom software development often outweigh the benefits when reasonable preprogrammed (off-the-shelf) alternatives are available. Some off-the-shelf software also includes features that permit a limited degree of customization to meet a purchaser's specific needs.

Another financial decision in which a support analyst may become involved is buy-versus-lease. Especially where the purchase of equipment of substantial value is involved, an organization may consider leasing as an option to outright purchase. Because the details of buy-versus-lease options (and the pros and cons of each) vary considerably and can be complex, buy-versus-lease is not normally a decision a support analyst makes, but is a decision properly left to an organization's financial officer or advisor.

CASE STUDY: The Training Team Web Development Project

At their next meeting, the needs assessment project group reviewed Margaret's draft proposal. The group agreed with the recommendation to purchase software licenses and to use an in-house resource (designer/developers in Zed's group) to learn to use the new software. However, given the current backlog of Web training module programming, the group suggested that the staff members in Zed's group who expressed an interest in Dreamweaver be sent to an intensive industry seminar at Adobe Software or a third-party training vendor to get them up-to-speed more quickly. Although the cost of this option would add substantially to the total project cost, the future of The Training Team seemed to be riding on the outcome of this project. Margaret said she would revise the draft budget to include the seminars and travel costs before presenting it to Fred.

At the final meeting of the assessment team, Margaret presented the group's recommendations and budget to Fred. He said that he and the other managers would discuss the proposed solution, but that he was inclined to support it since it fit well with the company's culture, mission, and resources. Fred thanked Margaret and the team members for their leadership and service on the assessment team, and they celebrated the successful completion of their project.

Each needs assessment project is unique, which means that the steps in this chapter need to be tailored to each specific situation. In some instances, budget constraints may limit the possible options that can be considered. In other situations, political issues, such as a long-term relationship with a vendor may outweigh other factors.

Needs analysis and assessment projects can be used for purposes other than selecting hardware, software, or network systems. Projects often investigate problems that have organizational, rather than technological, solutions, such as a training program or redesigned position descriptions.

ON THE WEB

To learn more about needs analysis and assessment projects, take a tutorial on the National Oceanic and Atmospheric Administration (NOAA) Web site (**www.csc.noaa.gov/needs**).

Needs Analysis and Assessment Tools

The needs analysis steps mentioned several tools that analysts may use as aids in the assessment process. The next part of this chapter describes some of these tools, which are listed in Figure 8-2, in more detail.

A print resource on needs analysis and assessment is: Kavita Gupta, *A Practical Guide to Needs Assessment*, 2nd edition. San Francisco; Pfeiffer (Wiley), 2007.

- Project charter
- Cost-benefit analysis
- Data-collection instruments
- Charts and diagrams
- Prototyping software
- Project management software

Figure 8-2   Needs assessment tools

Two tools you learned about in Chapter 7 are also useful to analysts who do needs assessments: benchmarks and weighted point comparisons. These tools are especially helpful when analysts need to compare two or more products, services, or approaches to solving a problem.

350

Some of these tools are relatively easy for analysts to create, whereas others require more extensive effort and, in some cases, special software.

Project Charter

All stakeholders should understand basic information about a needs analysis and assessment project. One way to ensure a common understanding is to develop a project charter. A **project charter** is a short narrative that answers basic questions, such as:

1. What are the objectives of the assessment project? What will be achieved if the project is successful?

2. What is the scope of the needs analysis project? What is included in the project and, sometimes more important, what is excluded?

3. What methods will be used to achieve the project's goals? What tools and resources will be used?

4. Who are the key project participants? What are their roles?

5. What are the project deliverables? (A **deliverable** is the end result of an analysis project, such as a written report or a recommendation to purchase, modify, upgrade, or build a system, or to acquire a service.)

6. What are the major steps in the needs assessment project?

7. What is the project timeline? What are the significant project milestones that indicate whether the project is ahead of or behind schedule?

8. How will the project's success be measured?

The form shown in Figure 8-3 is an example of a simple project charter template that you can modify or use as is, depending on the needs of a project. A charter need not be a detailed document, but rather should present a high-level overview of the project. Some organizations use a project request form (more like a work order) instead of a charter, but its contents are similar to a charter, and it serves a similar purpose. An important step in the adoption of a project charter is a sign-off by major shareholders, including the project manager and project sponsor (this is usually the manager with decision-making authority over the project and in whose budget the cost of the project appears).

Project Charter

Project name:

Membership:

Contact person:

Purpose:

Steps:	Deliverables/Success Measures:

Project scope:

Implications for other projects:

Figure 8-3 Project charter

ON THE WEB

To learn more about project charters, read an article, "How to Write a Project Charter," by Michael D. Taylor, who offers courses on project management, available at **www.projectmgt.com/Files/Article-How%20to%20 Write%20a%20Project%20Charter.pdf**.

An alternate project charter template to the one in Figure 8.3 is available at **www.ce.umn.edu/~smith/MOT8221/ charterform.pdf**.

You can also read a project charter prepared by the University of Minnesota's Library to select a help desk software package at **wiki.lib.umn.edu/wupl/Staff. ProjectCharters/hd-charter.pdf**.

Cost-Benefit Analysis

As you learned earlier in this chapter, a **cost-benefit analysis** is a tool to help identify the costs and the corresponding benefits of a proposed solution. A cost-benefit analysis is often prepared in the form of a side-by-side comparison or balance sheet that lists costs on one side of the sheet and benefits on the other.

Table 8-2 lists items that might appear in a cost-benefit balance sheet. It shows that costs can be categorized as **acquisition costs** (whether built or purchased) and **operating costs** (ongoing costs). Benefits can include reduced expenses, increased revenue opportunities, and intangible benefits.

Costs of Alternative	Benefits of Alternative
Acquisition costs	Reduced expenses
• Purchase computer equipment	• Less expensive hardware and software
• Purchase software packages or licenses	• Fewer personnel required to operate system
• Software development costs (programming)	• Lower manufacturing or inventory costs
• Purchase computer services	• More efficient use of staff time or equipment (productivity)
• Purchase supplies and materials	• Faster response to client needs
• Time to implement alternative	
• Administrative costs	
• Unanticipated costs	
Operating costs	Increased revenue opportunities
• Equipment lease or rental	• New projects or services for clients
• Personnel (salaries and benefits)	• Expanded markets (new clients)
• Computer supplies and materials	• Increased volume of business transactions
• Hardware and software maintenance	• Ability to raise prices due to higher quality of products or services
• User training	
	Intangible benefits
	• Ability to take advantage of new technology
	• Improved image of the organization
	• Improved service to clients
	• System easier to learn and use
	• Higher employee morale

Table 8-2   Cost-benefit balance sheet

The goal of a cost-benefit analysis is to weigh the benefits of each alternative against the costs of each alternative. However, cost-benefit analyses are not always easy to do because some benefits may be difficult to quantify. **Intangible benefits** are expected results from a project that are difficult to quantify or measure. Although increased user productivity may be measurable (tangible), increased employee morale is intangible. Analysts should always try to produce a best-guess estimate of intangible benefits of various alternatives, if possible.

Experienced analysts recognize that if most of the benefits of a proposed alternative are intangible, and if few quantifiable benefits will reduce expenses, improve productivity, or increase revenue, then they should seriously consider other alternatives.

353

ON THE WEB

For a more in-depth understanding of cost-benefit analyses, read an article about this tool at the Mind Tools Web site, **www.mindtools.com/pages/article/newTED_08.htm**.

Data-Collection Instruments

Several steps in the needs analysis process depend on analysts' abilities to collect relevant information. When analysts gather information, they often use the sources summarized in Figure 8-4. The sections that follow contain a brief overview of each data-collection instrument.

- Input forms
- Output forms
- Procedure documentation
- Operating or problem logs
- Interviews and questionnaires
- Direct observation

Figure 8-4   Data-collection instruments

Input Forms

An **input form** (sometimes called a **source document**) is a paper document or display screen used to collect information about a business transaction. Because business transaction processing is the purpose of many computer systems, input forms are an important source of information about an organization's business activities. For example, a copy shop might use a form like the sample in Figure 8-5 to collect information about an order for each client. In a project to automate order processing, a support analyst should understand how copy shop workers use the form and what problems occur when they do.

354

ORDER   Date _____

Sold to _____

the print works
1473 Main St.
Stamford, CT 06902
PHONE 555-2697
FAX 555-2698

Paid By ☐ Cash   ☐ Check # _____

FAX Send _____ pgs Receive _____ pgs	
Photocopies	
Taken By:	**TOTAL**

Figure 8-5   Example of an input form for a copy shop order

Output Forms

Output forms contain the results of a business transaction or process. Examples include a sales receipt from a grocery store or restaurant, a paycheck stub, and a report card at the end of a school term. In Figure 8-5, once a copy shop worker fills in the input form and records the prices of each item, the form also serves as an output form, or receipt, for the client.

Procedure Documentation

Procedure documentation is often used to train new workers or to answer questions about how to handle infrequent tasks.

Written instructions about how to perform a business transaction or follow a routine organizational procedure are called **procedure documentation**. Procedure documentation is written for an organization's workers. In the copy shop example, procedure documentation might describe the steps required to fill out the order form accurately for various kinds of copy orders; how to price each item on the form; what to do with the form after it is filled out; and where to file the form when the transaction is completed.

Operating or Problem Logs

A **log** is a list of events or activities recorded in the sequence in which the events occurred. Logs can be used to record routine, periodic information about events that occur normally, such as when the hard drive on a PC was backed up. Logs can also be used to capture unusual events, errors, problems, shortages, or complaints. Analysts can make use of logs as a supplement to direct observation to collect information about business activities.

Interviews and Questionnaires

Analysts often use interviews and questionnaires to collect relevant information from end users about the work they do, the problems they encounter, and how an existing or proposed computer system might affect their work. The advantage of a face-to-face interview is that the interviewer can ask probing questions, where appropriate, to learn the details of issues that are of special interest. The ability to probe is especially useful because it is frequently difficult to anticipate every possible question one might like to ask on a printed question-naire. However, analysts may need to obtain information from many users; therefore, they often use a questionnaire to save time. An alternative when many end users are potentially impacted is a **focus group**, which is a small, representative group of selected users. A focus group often generates ideas that may not occur in a one-on-one interview, as focus group members interact with each other.

 To ensure that they have effective questions, analysts who design interview and survey questions often ask other analysts for help. Questions designed by a team are often better than those written by one investigator. Another strategy is to field-test questions on a small group of users who can give feedback on which questions were confusing or difficult to answer.

ON THE WEB

To learn more about interview and questionnaire methods for user surveys, visit a Georgia Tech Web site that describes in greater detail how to design questionnaires and interview questions at **www.cc.gatech.edu/classes/cs6751_97_winter/Topics/quest-design**.

Direct Observation

Support analysts can often gain critical insights into end-user needs by simply watching users work. Direct observation can be a powerful method of data collection in situations where procedure documenta-tion, questionnaires, interviews, and other forms of data collection aren't possible, or as a supplement to other methods.

Data-collection instruments help analysts find useful, relevant information about an existing system that they can then use not only to evaluate how the system functions, but also to determine its strengths and weaknesses.

Charts and Diagrams

A chart or diagram can illustrate the flow of information within an organization, relationships between workers, or the connection between parts of an information processing system. Because they are visual, charts and diagrams are often easier for users to read and understand than lengthy narratives written in technical language.

Analysts create charts and diagrams either manually or with a variety of graphic design tools. Some of these tools are highly specialized and take training to use effectively; books on systems analysis describe these tools in detail. Other graphic design tools are more accessible and allow analysts with a minimum of experience to create charts and diagrams. Analysts can use relatively simple tools to create two common types of charts: flowcharts and I-P-O charts.

Flowcharts

A **flowchart** is a schematic drawing that uses symbols to represent the parts of a computer system or the steps in a procedure. In a flowchart, rectangular boxes often represent departments in an organization, nodes on a network, or processing tasks that a worker performs. Diamond-shaped symbols usually represent decision points or questions that need to be answered. Lines connect various symbols in a flowchart to illustrate how the parts of the diagram are related or the sequence of processing steps.

ON THE WEB

To view example flowcharts and take a tutorial on flowcharting, visit the Flowcharting Center at **www.smartdraw.com/ resources/centers/flowcharts**, where you can also download a trial version of the SmartDraw flowcharting tool.

I-P-O Charts

Most manual procedures or computer processing tasks can be described as some combination of input, processing, and output steps. An **I-P-O chart** is a diagramming tool that represents the input, processing, and output steps required to perform a task. An I-P-O chart answers three fundamental questions about a procedure that a user or computer performs:

- **Input**—Where do I get the information with which to work?
- **Processing**—What tasks do I perform to process or transform the information?
- **Output**—What happens to the information when I am finished?

Figure 8-6 shows a simple I-P-O chart that describes a procedure in a brokerage firm to prepare a stock portfolio report for a client.

Input	Processing	Output
Download current stock prices from financial Web site	Update total portfolio values in spreadsheet	Prepare report as PDF document and e-mail to client

Figure 8-6   I-P-O chart to prepare a stock portfolio report

ON THE WEB

L. Murray Smith, a CPA, describes several graphic diagramming tools at **acct.tamu.edu/smith/system_tools/systools.htm**. Click the link at the bottom of the page to see an example of each chart.

Prototyping Software

A **prototype** is a working model that support analysts build to let end users experience and evaluate how the finished product of an analysis project will eventually work. The purpose of a prototype is to provide an easy, quick, low-cost way for end users to view the characteristics an operational system will have when one is built.

When an application design project involves software development, prototyping tools can be used to build a working model. For example, programming and database languages such as Microsoft Access, Microsoft Excel, and Visual Basic can be used to build a working prototype of the menus, data input screens, processing steps, output forms and reports, and user interface for a system.

Although prototype systems can give users a realistic preview of how a new system might operate, prototypes usually operate slowly or have limited capacity for data storage. These limitations can be reduced or eliminated when a programmer converts a working prototype into a production system written in a programming language.

ON THE WEB

A group of faculty and students at the University of Washington has developed a prototyping tool for Web page layouts. Learn about their work and download a beta test version of their prototyping tool, DENIM, at **dub.washington. edu/projects/denim**.

Managing a User Support Project

User support work can be divided into routine operational tasks, such as staffing a help desk, and special project work. Much of the work a support group performs falls into the category of routine tasks and everyday activities. A **special project**, on the other hand, is a user support task that does not happen regularly. A special project is often based on less well-defined steps and procedures, usually takes longer to accomplish, and is frequently more complex than routine user support work. Factors that can contribute to a special project's increased complexity include the involvement of several staff members (perhaps along with external vendors or consultants); a time commitment of several days, weeks, or even months; and substantial expenditures in terms of staff time, equipment, software, supplies, and other resources.

In a user support environment, staff members may be assigned to work on special projects such as:

- Performing a user needs analysis or assessment project involving upgrading an organization's PCs

- Selecting and installing a new network server or enterprise-wide application software

- Developing or updating an organization's computer product standards or support policies

- Planning and implementing a new training facility

- Selecting and implementing an automated help desk management system

- Developing end-user documentation or a user training session for new software

Depending on their work responsibilities, some support specialists may receive more special project assignments than others. As organizations rely increasingly on teams rather than individual workers to accomplish tasks, the ability to manage and work as part of a project team have become increasingly important skills.

Project Management Steps

Support specialists who are assigned a special project, such as a user needs assessment, should know the basics of project management, even if they are only a team member. **Project management** is a detailed, step-by-step work plan and process designed to reach a specific goal. Project management usually involves five distinct steps, as shown in Figure 8-7.

Step 1. Project definition

Step 2. Project planning

Step 3. Project implementation

Step 4. Project monitoring

Step 5. Project termination

Figure 8-7   Steps in project management

Step 1: Project Definition

Project definition includes the preliminary work to define the scope of a project, including its goal(s), a tentative project calendar (beginning and ending dates and important due dates), a project budget, and the project participants, including users, support staff, technical staff, management, and a project manager, lead, or coordinator (the specific title varies). A **project goal** is a specific, measurable end result that is the ultimate target or outcome of a project. It is important that the project goal be specific and measurable, even if the calendar and budget are rough estimates at this first step. Compare these two goals:

• Improve user satisfaction with help desk services

• Evaluate, select, install, and implement a help desk management software package and begin operation by the first day of the next fiscal year

The first goal is neither specific nor measurable. It does not specify how user satisfaction will be improved or even measured. Ask yourself, "How will I know that we have achieved this goal?" For the first goal, the answer is not obvious. The second goal is more specific. It describes the scope of the project (evaluation, selection, installation, implementation), and specifies a measurable result by a specific date. A successful project will result in an operational help desk management package. Although the second goal is more specific, it could be further improved by specifying a timeline, budget limit, level of staff participation, and other project specifics.

Step 2: Project Planning

After a project's scope is carefully defined, project planning activities include dividing the project into specific tasks (or objectives), estimating a time (or duration) for each task, identifying available resources and the cost of each, and assigning resources to tasks. Typical project resources are staff time, budget, space, equipment, supplies, support services, overhead, and management support. During the planning step, the project manager defines each project task. A **project task** is a specific activity or objective (outcome) that must be met in order to meet an overall project goal. Examples of tasks include assigning a support staff member to write a handout for a training session, evaluating three help desk software packages for possible purchase, or installing a DSL modem in four office computers. A **project plan** pulls together all project tasks into one document that answers the questions:

- What tasks will be accomplished?

- What is the sequence of tasks?

- Who will perform each task?

- How long will each task take?

- What resources will each task require?

During the project-planning step, the project schedule (calendar) and costs become more definite. Earlier, during project definition, the project manager may receive information from organizational management or users such as, "It would be really great if this training session was ready by the second week of next month" or "Our drop-dead date for installation of Office 2007 in all offices is the end of the year." However, until each project task has been identified in detail, assigned to a staff member, and given a time and cost estimate, the project manager cannot make delivery commitments. After a thorough project planning process, a project manager should be able to make statements such as, "If the staff and budget resources we have identified in the project plan are available, we estimate the project can be completed by the second week of next month." Detailed project planning hones the preliminary estimates of schedule, resources, and costs prepared during the project definition step.

When developing time and cost estimates, experienced project managers know that many things can throw a project off its planned schedule. A project's **risk factors** are the unexpected problems that could arise during the life of a project. Risk factors include poor initial estimates of schedule, costs, or resources, as well as unexpected incidents that may occur during the project. Common risk factors include a sick team member, a task that takes longer to complete than estimated, a team member who lacks the skills required by the project (or who is unreliable), a hardware component that is unavailable when needed or costs more than expected, and a conflict between two team members over the best way to accomplish a task. Do these risk factors mean that it is useless to try to manage a project, or that it is better to "wing it" without a project plan? No. Experienced project managers anticipate risks like these and try to estimate their impact on the project. They set preliminary time estimates to complete a task to reflect a time somewhere between the minimum, best-case scenario and the maximum, worst-case scenario. They factor in time and resources for unexpected incidents that conspire to throw a project off its plan.

Step 3: Project Implementation

The implementation phase of a project is where the real work gets done. During **project implementation,** team members perform the work on each task or objective according to the schedule in the project plan and their task assignments. The project manager's responsibility shifts during Step 3 from project planning to task coordination. When tasks are interrelated, the project manager often spends time resolving conflicts between staff members over how resources are allocated, and dealing with the issues and problems that arise during any moderately complex project. During implementation, project managers must also be able to answer questions such as:

- Will the project get completed on time?
- Will the cost of the project exceed its budget?

During implementation, issues of converting from the previous system to the new system become important. The project team needs to make a decision about whether to perform a direct conversion (the plug is pulled on the existing system when the new system becomes operational), a parallel conversion (both old and new systems are run for a period of time to gain confidence in the new system), a phased implementation (workload is removed from the old system in stages as workload is transferred to the new system), or a pilot project (the replacement system is used in selected situations to gain confidence that it can be implemented organization-wide).

Step 4: Project Monitoring

Project managers need to be able to quickly answer questions such as, "Will this project task, which is behind schedule, benefit from additional staff for some time period?" and "How will adding resources affect the project's completion date?"

Parallel to the implementation step is an important project management task: project monitoring or tracking. **Project monitoring** involves assessing the ongoing status of all project tasks to determine whether they are on target in terms of time and budget estimates. Ideally, if every project task came in on time and under budget, monitoring would not be necessary. Because that seldom happens, project managers need to evaluate each project task regularly to determine:

- How much work has been completed?
- What remains to be done?
- How should staff or other resources be adjusted or reassigned?
- What impact will changes in tasks have on the completion date?

Another management responsibility during project monitoring reflects a reality that experienced project managers understand: projects often change during their implementation to meet new or unexpected demands. In other words, the project's goals or objectives sometimes need to be adjusted. Modifications during a project's implementation are another risk factor that must be managed. **Scope creep** is the tendency for a project to grow or change in unexpected ways, which increases the time frame, resources, and cost required to complete the project. During project monitoring, managers analyze and approve "change orders" and communicate with stakeholders (managers, users, support staff, and vendors) about the impact of changes on schedule and costs. Project managers may periodically prepare project reports to communicate the results of project monitoring and tracking to all stakeholders.

Step 5: Project Termination

The final stage in a project, **project termination**, may include communicating its completion to stakeholders, preparing a final project report, and evaluating the performance of the project and its participants. The project termination activities help project managers to learn from the mistakes of past projects and use their knowledge to improve performance on future projects. During project termination, a manager will answer questions such as:

- What did we learn in the course of this project that will help us better manage future projects?
- How well did the project team members function on their assigned tasks?

Some projects, because of their complexity, lengthy implementation time, sizable resource requirements, team coordination, or large budget, require more project management effort than others. For example, the preparation of a new training session for a software product, such as Windows Live Mail, is a relatively straightforward project. The project plan may be as simple as the example shown in Figure 8-8.

	Project: Windows Live Mail Training Session	
Step	**Task**	**Time Estimate**
1	**Plan training session** Analyze position descriptions for job skills required Interview supervisor and two trainees to learn backgrounds Document skill needs of trainees Define learning and performance objectives (scope) of training	8 hours
2	**Prepare training materials** Develop outline of topics covered Schedule trainees and training facility Locate or develop Windows Live Mail demonstration examples Develop hands-on activities Develop reference sheet of Windows Live Mail features	30 hours
3	**Prepare evaluation materials** Develop hands-on performance test Prepare training session feedback form	4 hours
4	**Beta test training materials** Present training to two support colleagues (2 hours each) Analyze results and revise as needed	12 hours
5	**Present Windows Live Mail training session** Present two-hour session Evaluate and revise as needed	4 hours
	Total:	**58 hours**

Resources Required

Software
   Windows Live Mail (available)
   PowerPoint (available)
Facilities
   Training Room (schedule 2 hours)
Materials
   Position descriptions of trainees (from Human Resources)
Personnel
   Access to supervisor and two trainees for interviews
   Two beta testers (2 hours each)
Miscellaneous supplies (available)

Figure 8-8   Example project plan for Windows Live Mail training session

Based on the time estimates in Figure 8-8, a support manager or training supervisor can quickly determine that about a week and a half of trainer time will be required for this project. In this example, if the cost of a trainer's time is estimated at $46 per hour (including salary, benefits, and overhead costs), then the estimated total cost of the training session is $46 per hour times 58 hours = $2668, which covers the cost of preparing and presenting one training session. This project is not complex, although even a simple project like this one makes some assumptions about the availability of resources, such as the training facility and personnel other than the trainer.

Even a simple project may have risk factors that a project manager needs to evaluate. The project manager may also want to include a contingency factor of, say, 10 to 15 percent ($300–400 in the example) to account for the fact that the completion times in the plan are estimates. In general, the more experience with similar projects a manager has, the more confident in time estimates he or she can be, and the lower the contingency factor can be.

Project Management Tools

Project management software tools are no substitute for careful project planning, good time estimates, accurate budget and resource forecasts, thorough analysis of project risks, and other human inputs to the project planning process.

Projects become more complex when they involve additional staff members (and therefore greater coordination), more resources, a bigger budget, a longer calendar, and additional risk factors. In these situations, a one- or two-page project plan is not sufficient. Fortunately for managers of larger-scale user support projects, or several smaller ones, **project management software** is available to assist with the management tasks described above. For example, project managers who want to automate some project management tasks can use one of several kinds of software tools:

- Microsoft Office Project Professional 2007 is a project management tool, compatible with the Microsoft Office suite (**office.microsoft.com/en-us/project/default.aspx**). A 60-day trial version of Microsoft Office Project Professional 2007 is included on a CD accompanying this book.

To learn more about project management skills, see Kathy Schwalbe, *Information Technology Project Management*, 5th edition. Boston: Course Technology (Cengage Learning), 2008.

- Milestones Simplicity 2008 is a project scheduling tool, one of several sold by Kidasa Software (**www.kidasa.com/Simplicity/index.html**).

-]project-open[is an open source project management tool which is available for free (**www.project-open.com/index.html**).

Figure 8-9 shows a Microsoft Project 2007 plan with required tasks to complete the sample Windows Live Mail Training Session project described above. A **Gantt chart**, in the right pane in Figure 8-9, is a common project planning tool, which shows the basic information about each project task as a horizontal bar on a graph. The Gantt chart identifies each task, its relationship to other tasks, the expected calendar for task and project completion, and task participants. The left pane, in spreadsheet format, shows the input information that produced the Gantt chart. The two leftmost columns list the steps (Task Name) and estimated times (Duration) for each activity listed in Figure 8-9. The Resource Names column lists the four participants: the trainer (TRN1), the users (USR), the training supervisor (SVR), and the beta testers (TST).

Figure 8-9   Steps in the Windows Live Mail Training Session project in Microsoft Project 2007

The Gantt chart reflects the time spent by user support staff on this project, but it does not reflect the time spent by trainees or their supervisor.

Suppose the project team examined the draft Gantt chart in Figure 8-9 and asked some questions, such as, "What if additional support staff is added to this training project?" In other words, "Could we shorten the project if we identified some tasks that other support staff members could accomplish by working simultaneously with the original project trainer?" "What if . . . ?" questions are often easier to answer with a project management or scheduling software tool.

Figure 8-10 shows a modification of the original Microsoft Project 2007 draft plan. The five steps in Figure 8-9 have been expanded into more detailed tasks. In addition, some tasks are listed as predecessor tasks for other tasks (see the new Pred (predecessor tasks) column in the spreadsheet). A **predecessor task** is an activity that must be completed before another task can begin. For example, Step 1 is a predecessor task to Step 2 because the training session must be planned before the training materials can be prepared. In other words, Step 2 cannot begin until Step 1 is completed. Arrows have also been added to the Gantt chart to show the predecessor tasks on the diagram. Finally, instead of assigning one trainer to the entire project, as in the first draft plan, a second trainer (TRN2) is assigned to help with a task (Step 3). In the revised plan, Step 3 can be completed by the second trainer while the first trainer is working on Step 2 tasks. By adding a second trainer to work on tasks that can be performed at the same time as another task, the project completion is moved up from Wednesday morning to Tuesday afternoon.

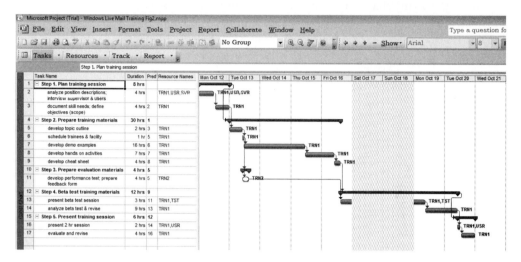

Figure 8-10   A revised Windows Live Mail training project showing the critical path

The dark bars in Figure 8-10 show this project's critical path. A **critical path** is the sequence of project tasks that must be completed on time to meet the project's completion time. The critical path establishes important milestones in a project's calendar. Steps 1, 2, 4, and 5 are critical path steps that are important milestones. If any one of these milestones is missed, the project's completion is in jeopardy. However, the task for the second trainer in Step 3 in Figure 8-10 is not on the critical path. If the expected completion time for Step 3 slips, the completion of the project will not necessarily be affected.

These examples provide a brief introduction to illustrate various aspects of project management, such as project tasks, task time duration, assignments to staff members, what-if analyses, the critical path, and estimated completion time, but they barely scratch the surface of project management tools. Many project management software programs offer features to help a manager with other important project management tasks, including:

- Monitoring partial completion of project tasks and updating the Gantt chart to produce a progress report

- Identifying project tasks that are behind schedule and which might require additional resources

- Assigning personnel, facilities, equipment, supplies, and overhead costs to prepare a project budget

- Defining alternative report formats, including project calendars, budget and variance reports, PERT diagrams (also called network diagrams), and e-mails to staff members regarding project assignments

Many project management software packages now incorporate features that permit project work team members to view not only the overall project plans, but also detailed project task information, each team member's individual assignments, an updated project calendar, and a revised budget. In addition, the software packages enable work team members to communicate online via e-mail or project Web pages.

ON THE WEB

To locate additional information about project management, visit the Web site of Project Management Institute (PMI), a professional organization of project managers (**www.pmi.org**). PMI offers a certification program for professional project managers.

For a brief tutorial on project management, view a slideshow presentation prepared by the Project Management Office at Massey University in New Zealand at **projectoffice.massey. ac.nz/massey/fms//Projects%20office/Documents/ PM%20Tutorial.pps**.

Other Needs Assessment and Project Management Tools

The needs analysis and project management tools discussed in this chapter are among those that support analysts find helpful when they undertake user needs assessment and other projects. However, the tools described here just scratch the surface of the information resources and tools available. New tools, especially automated ones, become available every year.

Not all needs assessment and user support projects require all of the steps described in this chapter; neither do all projects require every resource and tool previously discussed. In an actual project, support analysts choose from among the approaches described here to make the resources and tools fit the task. The most important fact to remember is that end-user needs analysis and assessment is a process, and the process and tools analysts choose to solve one problem will likely be different from the process and tools for another.

Support analysts who spend a significant amount of time on user needs assessment projects may benefit from a course on systems analysis and design. Similarly, those with project management interests and assignments may benefit from a formal course on project management.

Chapter Summary

- User support analysts who undertake a needs assessment for end-users follow a sequence of steps designed to obtain relevant information and help users make an informed decision. In the needs assessment process, support analysts use several tools and information resources described in this chapter to aid them in their task.

- Steps in a user needs assessment follow three distinct phases:

  - **Preparation phase**—Before the detailed work on an assessment project begins, analysts should learn about the project's goals, decision criteria and constraints, stakeholders, and potential information resources.

  - **Investigation phase**—Analysts examine the current system and evaluate possible alternatives that will improve it.

  - **Decision phase**—Analysts create a model of the proposed system and decide how the new system will be obtained.

- Decision and documentation tools are available to support analysts who work on needs assessment projects. Popular tools include project charters; cost-benefit analyses to weigh the cost of alternative solutions against their payoffs; several data-collection instruments (including input and output forms, procedure documentation, interviews and questionnaires, and direct observation); graphic design tools to draw flowcharts, I-P-O charts, and related schematic representations of systems; and prototyping tools to model the operation of software systems.

- Large assessment and other special projects often follow a sequence of steps during which a project team defines, plans, implements, monitors, and terminates the activities and tasks to successfully complete a project.

- Project managers and their team members can benefit from the planning, monitoring, and communication tools included in a project management software package.

Key Terms

acquisition costs—A category of project costs to build or purchase the initial components of a computer system or solution (compare to operating costs).

build-versus-buy decision—The decision an organization makes about whether to build a custom solution or purchase one off the shelf; this can apply to hardware, software, complete systems, or services.

cost-benefit analysis—A comparison of the expenses a project will incur to a project's payoffs; organizations are reluctant to spend resources on projects for which the costs outweigh the benefits.

critical path—The sequence of project tasks that must be completed on time to meet the project's completion time; the critical path defines important milestones in a project's calendar.

decision phase—The third phase of a user needs analysis and assessment project, in which analysts develop a model of the proposed solution and decide whether to build or buy it.

deliverable—The end result of a needs analysis project, such as a written analysis of alternatives, a feasibility report, a recommendation, or a decision to build, buy, or upgrade a system.

feasibility study—An investigation into the economic, operational, technical, and timeline constraints that will impact a user needs analysis and assessment project.

flowchart—A schematic drawing that uses symbols to represent the parts of a computer system or the steps in a procedure.

focus group—A small group of selected users who represent a larger group of users in a needs assessment project; a focus group participates in an interview when including every user is impractical.

Gantt chart—A common project planning tool that shows the expected start and end dates for each task and staff resources assigned as a horizontal bar on a graph.

input form—A paper document or display screen used to collect information about a transaction; also called a *source document.*

intangible benefit—An expected result from a computer or services acquisition that is difficult to quantify or measure.

investigation phase—The second phase of a user needs analysis and assessment project, in which analysts try to understand the present system or situation and specify alternatives to it.

I-P-O chart—A diagramming tool that represents the input, processing, and output steps required to perform a task.

log—A list of events or activities recorded in the sequence that the events occur; a log is used to record information about routine, periodic events or unusual events, such as errors or problems.

model—A narrative or graphic diagram that represents a business activity in an organization (such as paper workflow), a computer system, or a network.

operating costs—A category of project costs which are incurred after the initial acquisition costs to operate a computer system or solution on a continuing basis.

optimal solution—The solution among several alternatives available in a project that is the most feasible, lowest cost, and most beneficial (compare to a *satisficing solution*).

output form—A document that contains the results of a business transaction or process.

predecessor task—A project activity that must be completed before another task can begin.

preparation phase—The first phase of a user needs analysis and assessment project, in which analysts try to understand the end user's and the organization's goals, the decision criteria, and the project constraints; analysts define the problem, identify the roles of stakeholders, and identify potential sources of information.

procedure documentation—Written instructions about how to perform a business transaction or handle a routine organizational procedure.

project charter—A short narrative statement that describes the objectives, scope, methods, participants, deliverables, steps, timeline, and measures of success for a needs assessment project.

project definition—The preliminary work to define the scope of a project, including its goals, a tentative project calendar, a project budget, and the project participants, including users, support staff, technical staff, management, and a project manager.

project goal—A specific, measurable end result that is the ultimate target or outcome of a project.

project implementation—The third step in a project during which team members perform the work on each task or objective.

project management—A detailed, step-by-step work plan and process designed to reach a specific goal; it involves project definition, plan, implementation, monitoring, and termination steps.

project management software—An application software tool to help project leaders and workers organize the steps in a project, set priorities, establish and monitor project tasks and costs, and schedule staff and activities.

project monitoring—An ongoing assessment of the status of all project tasks to determine whether they are on target in terms of time and budget estimates.

project plan—A document that describes all project tasks; it answers questions such as what will be accomplished, by whom, how long each task will take, and what resources will be required.

project task—A specific activity or objective (outcome) that must be met in order to meet an overall project goal.

project termination—The final stage of a project, which includes communicating its completion to stakeholders, preparing a final project report, and evaluating the performance of the project and its participants.

prototype—A working model that analysts build to let users experience and evaluate how the finished product of an analysis project will actually work; a prototype contains enough features of an actual system that users can operate the model to evaluate its ability to meet their needs.

risk factors—The unexpected problems that could arise during the life of a project that would impact the project plan, costs, outcomes, or timeline.

satisficing solution—An alternate solution that solves a problem in a reasonable way, but is not necessarily the optimal solution; satisficing solutions are often adopted when an optimal solution is too expensive.

scope creep—The tendency for a project to grow or change in unexpected ways, which increases the time frame, resources, and cost to complete the project.

source document—Any form used to collect information about a business transaction for input into an organization or computer system; examples include payroll timecards, a problem log, a membership application, and an expense account record.

special project—A user support activity that happens infrequently; a special project is typically based on steps and procedures that are not as well-defined as those in regular support tasks.

stakeholder—A participant in a user needs analysis and assessment project who might gain or lose from its success or failure; stakeholders may be end users, managers, technical support staff, and/or support analysts.

turnkey system—An integrated, packaged solution that provides hardware, software, and support services purchased from a single vendor.

Check Your Understanding

Answers to Check Your Understanding questions are found in Appendix A.

1. True or False? The goals and objectives of an organization are usually long-term and do not normally impact decisions about a user's immediate needs for computer systems and services.

2. Which of the following is not a primary step in the needs analysis and assessment process?

    a. preparation

    b. investigation

    c. decision

    d. purchase

3. True or False? A payroll clerk should make the final decision about whether or not a new payroll software package is needed.

4. In a user needs assessment project, the fact that an organization is uncomfortable with risks due to reliance on a new, untested software package would be considered as part of:

    a. economic feasibility

    b. operational feasibility

    c. technological feasibility

    d. timeline feasibility

5. True or False? Some problems that user support analysts investigate turn out to be organizational problems instead of technology problems.

6. Which sequence of numbers represents the correct order of the following four steps in the user needs analysis process? (1) investigate alternatives to the current system; (2) make a build-versus-buy decision; (3) identify sources of information; (4) understand the organization's goals

    a. 1 - 2 - 3 - 4

    b. 4 - 3 - 2 - 1

    c. 3 - 1 - 4 - 2

    d. 4 - 3 - 1 - 2

7. True or False? When making a decision about a new computer system or service, an organization must consider what is feasible in terms of time, staffing, money, and technology.

8. True or False? In an end-user needs assessment project, software requirements should generally be considered first, followed by hardware needs.

9. A(n) _____ considers whether to purchase a system off-the-shelf or construct one from scratch.

10. A narrative or diagram that explains the structure and operation of a new or existing computer system is called a:

    a. prototype

    b. layout

    c. model

    d. report

11. A(n) _____ is the end result of an analysis project that recommends purchase, modification, upgrade, or construction of a system.

12. True or False? A turnkey system is a package that includes hardware, software, and support services from a single vendor.

13. True or False? The build-versus-buy decision in a needs analysis project applies primarily to computer hardware.

14. True or False? A cost-benefit analysis is often in the form of a side-by-side comparison of the expenses associated with a project and its advantages to the organization.

15. In a cost-benefit analysis, the development or purchase of software is generally considered a(n):

    a. acquisition cost

    b. operating cost

    c. reduction of expenses

    d. intangible cost

16. A(n) _____ is a written narrative that describes the objectives, scope, methods, participants, deliverables, and timeline for a needs assessment project.

17. A(n) _____ is a schematic diagram that uses symbols to represent the parts of a computer system.

18. True or False? A Gantt chart allows a project manager to ask "what-if" questions about how changes in resources impact the timeline of a project.

19. A(n) _____ is a project activity or step that must be completed before another task can begin.

    a. Gantt task

    b. successor task

    c. satisficing task

    d. predecessor task

20. Stakeholders in a needs assessment project are most likely:

    a. end users

    b. managers

    c. support analysts

    d. all of these

Discussion Questions

1. Do you agree or disagree with the following statement: "Because a small dollar amount is involved, a needs assessment to purchase a $600 PC for an employee is overkill." Explain your answer.

2. Why is it important for a support analyst to learn who will make the final decision on a needs assessment project and what decision criteria they will use?

3. In a cost-benefit analysis, which are more difficult to measure, costs or benefits? Explain why.

4. In order to save time and money in a user needs analysis project, if you could choose to omit one of the steps described in the chapter, which step would you omit, and why?

5. How could project management software tools, such as those illustrated in the chapter, be useful to even the smallest project team?

6. What are the advantages and disadvantages of purchasing a turnkey system from a single vendor versus buying components from several vendors?

Hands-On Activities

Activity 8-1

Assess the need for a personal computer. Think about how you would modify the steps described in this chapter if you were asked to recommend a personal computer system to a friend for home use. Which steps would you omit? Which steps would be most important? Write a two-paragraph summary of your conclusions.

Activity 8-2

Avoid needs assessment problems. Some support analysts have expressed the view that the steps in a needs assessment project really should be described as:

1. Unbridled euphoria

2. Questions about the feasibility of the project

3. Growing concern about the project results

4. Unmitigated disaster

5. Search for the guilty

6. Punishment of the innocent

7. Promotion of the uninvolved

Behind each piece of humor may be some grain of truth. Write a two-page report that describes specific steps a support analyst can take to prevent a needs assessment project from turning into the disaster described above.

Activity 8-3

Analyze costs and benefits for a home computer. Study the categories included in the cost-benefit analysis described in Table 8-2. Think about how these categories apply to the purchase of a home computer. What additional categories of costs or benefits would you add to Table 8-2 for a home computer? Which cost categories do you think are most important in the purchase of a PC for home use? Are the benefit categories you listed tangible or intangible benefits? Explain why.

Activity 8-4

Develop a project charter. Think about the last time you purchased a PC, cell phone, MP3 player, or other electronic equipment, or helped a friend or relative purchase one. Write a project charter that describes the purchase process you followed. Use the project charter form in the book as an example or create a project charter form of your own.

Activity 8-5

Develop an I-P-O chart and a flowchart. Select a common sales transaction, such as an automobile gasoline purchase or a grocery store purchase. Analyze the transaction and make a list of the items of information that are input, the processing that takes place as part of the transaction, and the resulting output. Record your analysis in the form of an I-P-O chart as shown in this chapter. Then sketch a flowchart of the transaction. Compare the information communicated in the I-P-O and flow diagrams. Which do you prefer? Explain why.

Activity 8-6

Perform a cost-benefit analysis for DVD burners. Research the relative advantages and disadvantages of internal and external DVD burners using the library or online resources. Although internal DVD burners are generally less expensive, are there reasons why a user would want to pay more for an external DVD burner? Using the format in Table 8-2, develop a simple cost-benefit analysis for internal and external DVD burners.

Activity 8-7

Use project management software to plan a project. Use the Microsoft Project 2007 software included with this book, or download]project-open[or another project management software package. Enter the project steps in Figure 8-8 into the software to prepare a Gantt chart. Print the Gantt chart.

Case Projects

1. Feasibility Analysis of a Computer Facility Problem

Based on your personal experience or on conversations with work or school colleagues, select a current problem in a computer facility at work, in a lab at school, or in a training facility. Meet with a group of your colleagues to perform the first several steps in a needs assessment aimed at solving the problem. First, make sure your group has a clear definition of the root problem. Then identify the stakeholders and sources of information available to you. Brainstorm alternative solutions to the problem. Finally, analyze the feasibility of each alternative.

- Are some alternatives more feasible than others? Explain why.
- What additional information resources would you need to complete the analysis?
- Did your group reach consensus on a recommendation it would make to management?

Write your conclusions in the form of a 2–3-page feasibility report.

2. Needs Assessment for Video and Beyond

Kathleen Marsh is a recent community college graduate who plans to open a video and game rental store in the next couple of months. Kathleen majored in small business management, but also took a number of computer courses as electives in her community college degree program, including:

- Introduction to Business Information Systems
- PC Operating Systems
- Spreadsheets (Excel)
- Database Management (Access)
- Introductory and Advanced Visual Basic
- Systems Analysis and Design
- Introduction to Computer Networks

Kathleen did well in these courses and feels very comfortable with computer technology, but she wants an independent perspective on the feasibility of a computer system for her video and game rental company. That is why she has asked for your advice.

Although this is her first real venture as an entrepreneur, Kathleen has had considerable part-time work experience in video rental stores during high school and college.

Kathleen's store, Video and Beyond, will be in a new shopping center. Kathleen chose the location because a sizable bedroom community is nearby, and because no major competition is located in the area, which is about 15 miles from the nearest large town. She has arranged to rent 1500 square feet of space in the shopping center.

Kathleen has located a distributor who can supply her with a start-up inventory of 3000 to 3500 current releases and popular classic DVDs, Blu-Ray discs, and games. The distributor can also serve as a one-stop supplier for new DVDs and games as they are released to the rental market.

Kathleen has identified her major expenses, both start-up and ongoing, which are shown in Table 8-3.

Start-Up Expenses	Ongoing Expenses
Furniture	Rent & utilities
• Counters	Payroll & taxes
• Video and game racks	New DVD, Blu-Ray, and game releases
• Popcorn machine	Advertising
Initial inventory of DVDs and games	
Computer system (?)	

Table 8-3   Video and Beyond's expenses

Kathleen's initial thinking about a computer system is that she probably cannot afford one in her start-up budget. Instead, she had worked out a simple manual system for keeping track of her video inventory and client rentals. In her system, each DVD or game will have an ID number recorded on the plastic case and on a card she would keep in a *Video* card box on top of the counter. In a separate box on the counter, she would keep a card for each *Client*. The client cards would be filed by telephone number, which she would use as a client ID number. When a client rented one or more videos, she would clip the video card(s) to the client card, and put them together in a third box labeled *Rentals*, which is organized by the due date. When a rental is returned, Kathleen would unclip the video and client cards and return them to their respective card files. At 6 P.M. each day, if there were cards in the rental box for rentals that were past due, Kathleen would contact the client and assess a late charge.

Kathleen thinks this simple manual system would work until her business volume grew and she could afford a computer system. But she wonders whether a computer system would be feasible immediately, when she opens the doors in a couple of months. She even thought that perhaps she could buy a PC and write a simple program in Access, Visual Basic, or Excel to replace the manual card system. Kathleen would appreciate your advice.

1. Prepare a list of interview questions for Kathleen that would help you make a recommendation to her.

2. After you have a list of potential questions to ask in an interview, compare your questions with those of three classmates or coworkers. Merge your questions into a single list from your group. Try to arrange the questions into categories with other similar questions.

3. When you have completed the list of interview questions, your instructor will provide you with Kathleen's responses to several of the questions from an interview with her. Based on her responses, answer these questions:

   • If Video and Beyond decides to purchase a computer system, what major decisions will the owner need to make?

   • Would you recommend that Kathleen Marsh build her own software or purchase one? Explain your reasoning.

   • Make a list of the software Video and Beyond will need to meet the needs Kathleen Marsh described in the interview.

   • In order to build or buy a transaction-processing program to handle rentals and returns, Video and Beyond would probably need a database of DVDs and games as well as a database of clients. List the fields you think Video and Beyond will need to include in either the DVD/games database or the client database.

   • A word processor or a database language such as Access can be used as a tool to build a prototype (model) of a report. Use one of these tools to design a prototype of the video rental agreement that would be printed for clients to sign each time they rent a video.

   • Given what you know of Video and Beyond's business plan and needs and its financial situation, do you think a computer system is feasible? Explain why or why not.

3. Computer Recommendation for Amy Lee

Amy Lee was recently hired as a personnel assistant in the Human Resources department where you work. Because you are the user support specialist, she has contacted you for some help choosing the computer she will use in her job in employee benefits administration.

You want to make sure that she gets the computer tools she will need to be productive.

Amy says that she will need an office suite and that her boss gave her a choice of Microsoft Office 2003 or 2007 or WordPerfect Office X4. Because she has previous work experience with the WordPerfect word processor, which is part of WordPerfect suite, she would like to use it. The WordPerfect suite includes most of the tools Amy needs, so her other software requirements are minimal. In addition to WordPerfect Office, Amy needs the Windows operating system. She also needs a Web browser because an increasing amount of information about benefits and employee compensation is available on the Web.

Amy really needs your help with the decisions on hardware. Amy's boss said that she has very little money left in this year's Human Resources equipment budget for hardware. So she suggested that Amy try to find a basic starter system, but one that could be upgraded next year when there will be more equipment money available. Amy wants you to recommend a hardware configuration that meets her immediate needs, is reasonably priced, and can be upgraded next year. It needs to be able to run the software Amy has selected. Whatever hardware she buys must also be compatible with the local area network in Human Resources. It operates from a Windows server. The network server can provide Amy with access to one of two laser printers, so the hardware system she buys need not include a printer. However, Amy wants to be able to scan documents into her system, and no scanner is available on the network.

Analyze Amy's situation and recommend a specific hardware configuration that will meet her immediate needs. In addition, find equipment for sale in a trade magazine or advertised online or in a local newspaper that you believe is the appropriate configuration for Amy. When you are finished, prepare a recommended list of hardware specifications (and prices, if available) that Amy could take to her boss.

4. LAN Selection for Geo-Habitus

Geo-Habitus is a local company that sells kits used to build vacation cabins shaped like geodesic domes. The company has identified a need for a local area network (LAN) to facilitate communication among workers and permit collaboration on tasks. Bridgette Petrang, the technology supervisor at Geo-Habitus, has asked you to develop a project plan with Microsoft Project 2007. To learn the basic features of project management software, you will input the tasks for a LAN acquisition project at Geo-Habitus, shown in the outline below. The goal of the project is to select a new local area network (LAN) for the company.

Project Plan: Geo-Habitus
LAN Selection Project

Step	Task	Time Estimate
1	Conduct a user needs analysis among Geo-Habitus's managers and employees for a new LAN system	8 days
2	Develop a specification of the required LAN features	4 days
3	Define the selection criteria based on mandatory and desirable features, vendor support, costs, and compatibility with existing equipment; decide on a weight for each criterion	2 days
4	Write a Request For Proposal (RFP) document for vendors that describes LAN operating requirements, bidding procedures, and decision criteria	4 days
5	Send RFP document to LAN vendors	1 day
6	Vendors prepare written responses to RFP	14 days
7	Analyze vendor responses to RFP and evaluate bids	5 days
8	Select a vendor and award the contract for the LAN installation	1 day

Install the 60-day trial version of Microsoft Office Professional Project 2007 from the CD that accompanies this book. Start Microsoft Office Project 2007. Use the interactive Project Guide to help set up a basic project plan for Geo-Habitus. To display the Project Guide, right-click anywhere on the Project 2007 toolbar, and then left-click to turn on the Project Guide icon. The Project Guide icon appears as . Use the icon to toggle the Project Guide on and off in the left pane of the Project 2007 window. For the Geo-Habitus LAN selection project, follow the Project Guide steps described on the next page.

Project Guide task	Step	Activity
Define the project	1	Enter the start date (use the first business day of next month as the start date for the project); then click **Continue to Step 2** at the bottom of the Project Guide pane.
	2	For the question about collaboration on the Web, click **No**, then click **Continue to Step 3**.
	3	Click **Save and Finish**.
Project Working Time	1	Use the default definition of work time based on the standard calendar.
	2	Use the default work week (Monday through Friday).
	3	Enter any holidays your school or company recognizes. Click **Change Working Time . . .**, and follow the instructions in the Project Guide pane.
	4	Use the default time units of 8 hours per day, 40 hours per week, and 20 days per month.
	5	Click **Save and Finish**.
List Tasks		Enter each task in the outline above (task name and duration in days). Project 2007 will number each task for you. Don't worry that each task begins on day 1 of the project at this point. Click *Done* at the bottom of the Project Guide when all tasks are entered.
Organize Tasks		(An optional step)
Schedule Tasks		Use the Schedule Tasks tool to establish links between the project steps. Highlight two adjacent steps with the mouse; then click the **Finish to Start** icon to define a situation in which the first step of the pair must finish before the second step can start. Alternately, you can move the Gantt chart over to the right with the scroll bar at the bottom of the tasks list to display the Predecessor column. Then enter into Predecessor column any step numbers that must precede each step.
		To display the Gantt chart in less space, you can change the time scale displayed on the chart from days to weeks or months. Right-click the time scale column headings at the top of the Gantt chart and modify the time scale settings.
Remaining steps in the Project Guide		The remaining steps in the Project Guide are optional for this project.
		To save your project plan as an .mpp file, click the Project 2007 menu bar: **File, Save As . . .**.

You can get additional information about any step by clicking the **Hint** and **More Information** icons on each Project Guide task screen, or by using the Help system. Remember that Project 2007 is part of the Microsoft Office suite. Many menu commands and icons in Project have the same functions as in other Office programs, including the Undo icon on the Project toolbar.

Your task is to learn enough about Microsoft Project 2007 to prepare a Gantt chart similar to the ones illustrated in the chapter. Experiment with the other features of Project 2007 if you would like, but keep focused on the objective to prepare a project plan so the management at Geo-Habitus can understand the project timeline.

CHAPTER 9

Installing and Managing End-User Computers

In this chapter, you will learn about:

◎ Major site preparation steps for computer installations

◎ Pre-installation site preparation tasks

◎ The purpose and contents of a site management notebook

◎ Tools needed to install hardware

◎ Steps to install and configure hardware, operating systems, networks, and application software

◎ Common installation wrap-up tasks

◎ Ongoing site management tasks

After a support specialist has evaluated computer products, conducted a needs assessment, and perhaps even helped purchase end-user computer products, the next step is to install the system. Installation can include hardware, peripherals, operating systems, utility software, application software, and even office supplies and equipment—either packaged together as a turnkey system or sold individually.

The system installation process can easily intimidate end users, especially less experienced users. Support specialists are often able to set up a system and get it operational in a fraction of the time it would take an end user to figure out the correct procedures and work through any problems that arise. This chapter describes typical tasks that are a part of many personal and office computer installations, although every installation poses different challenges. You will learn about site preparation tasks as well as the tools and steps necessary to install hardware, operating systems, network connections, and application software.

In addition to system installations, support specialists often have responsibility for ongoing user site management tasks including media backup, system security (such as access authorization), disaster preparation (such as creating contingency plans), and related operational tasks.

 During the installation process, a support specialist may also need to handle user training and documentation issues, which you will learn more about in Chapters 10 and 11.

385

System Installation Overview

User support specialists are often responsible for installing computer systems. In an efficient installation, a computer system will be up and running with a minimum of interruption to an end user's work. Adequate preparation, proper tools, and an established process for tracking important details help ensure that system installations run smoothly. Whether an installation is for a single home computer, a small office system, a training lab, or hundreds of networked computers, experienced system installers know that important details can be easily overlooked—whether at the time a system is installed or later when the system needs to be repaired or upgraded. This chapter emphasizes the importance of installation checklists and system documentation as a way of ensuring that all the necessary steps are completed properly.

The major installation tasks are summarized in Figure 9-1 and discussed in detail throughout the chapter.

- Pre-installation site preparation
  - Location
  - Ergonomic planning
  - Power requirements
  - Telephone and network access
  - Air conditioning
  - Lighting
  - Fire suppression
- Site management documentation
- Hardware installation tools
- Hardware installation
- Operating system and network installation
- Application software installation
- Installation wrap-up tasks

Figure 9-1   Overview of system installation tasks

Support specialists may not be involved in all of the tasks listed in Figure 9-1. For example, they might not need to install or configure an operating system if one is preinstalled. Or a specialized network technician may be responsible for connecting a system to a network and configuring it. The checklists in this chapter are generic; you should consider them a starting point and modify them to fit specific situations. In some cases, you may need to add steps; in other cases, some steps may not directly apply. For example, if a new or upgraded software package needs to be installed on an end-user system, the checklists for hardware, operating system, and network connections will not apply.

Pre-Installation Site Preparation

Before installing a complete system, support specialists often visit an end user's location for a pre-installation inspection. The purpose of the site visit is to anticipate problems that may arise so that the installer can address them prior to the installation. Many installers use a written checklist to make sure that they address certain critical questions during the visit. A typical site installation checklist would contain the following queries:

- What space requirements apply to this computer system or workstation?

- What space constraints are potential problems at the user's work site?

- What materials need to be stored for convenient access near the computer?

- What ergonomic issues need to be addressed?

- Do ADA (Americans with Disabilities Act) or OSHA (Occupational Safety and Health Administration) issues or accommodations apply to this installation?

- Is the power supply accessible and adequate for the system?

- Is power conditioning required?

- Where is the nearest network and/or telephone access?

- Is air conditioning required?

- What lighting problems may need to be addressed?

- Is a fire-suppression system installed and operational?

Experienced installers need not carry an actual checklist. Observation of the site may be sufficient to determine what problems exist, if any. However, if they have several installations to perform at different sites, a site installation checklist can help installers keep track of the conditions and special requirements of each location.

Location

When support specialists install a complete computer system, they must determine the best location for the system unit, display screen, printer, keyboard, mouse, and other peripherals and accessories. A system that has properly located components will be easy and efficient to use, will not cause discomfort for the user, and will ensure the physical safety of both the user and the system itself. Each installation site presents unique challenges, and support specialists try to adapt the installation to the space and layout constraints of each site.

System Unit Location

The system unit is usually located within four to five feet of a user's work area—a distance dictated by the length of signal cables between the system unit and the keyboard, mouse, and other peripherals. If a system unit is a desktop model, a table or desk surface is often the most convenient location, especially for users who frequently access the peripherals inside the system unit case (such as the USB ports, removable hard drive, or CD/DVD drive). However, a standard ATX desktop case's **footprint**, which is the number of square inches (length × width) of usable space the computer case occupies, can be large, and may significantly reduce the work area on a desk. Space-saver cases (also called small form factor cases), are popular because

Small form factor (SFF) cases may be designated as MicroATX towers, Slimline, BTX, or DTX cases, depending on the manufacturer.

If a system unit must be located off of a user's desktop, extender cables or wireless devices for the keyboard, mouse, and display screen may be used.

388

System units and older CRT monitors produce heat when they operate. The vent holes in the cases of these units should not be blocked by office or bookcase walls or by shelves. Air should be able to circulate around the cases of all computer peripherals.

The solution to one problem can cause another. In a situation where a chair seat is adjusted high enough to enable wrist comfort, the user's feet may not rest comfortably on the floor, and leg problems can result. An adjustable footrest may help in this situation.

they have a smaller footprint. To save space, a system unit may be located off of the work surface on a bookshelf or even on the floor. Notebook computers (also sometimes referred to as laptops) are increasingly popular as desktop replacements; the location of the system unit is not a primary factor in these installations.

Although installation on an office floor reduces the desk space that a computer occupies, floor installations are not without problems. First, most floors are dusty, and internal fans may pull dust into the case. In order to avoid this problem, arrange for the case to be installed six inches above floor level on a shelf or raised platform. Second, system unit cases located on the floor can be accidentally kicked or may obstruct foot traffic. Cases should be located in such a way as to prevent these problems. Third, for some users, frequent bending to reach a floor unit can cause back strain. Wherever possible, ports and peripherals should be located within arm's reach of a user's normal working position.

Keyboard and Mouse Location

Ideally, a desktop or notebook computer should be installed in a work area where the table or desktop surface is 26 to 28 inches from the floor, which is a comfortable keyboard and mouse height for most users. A typical office desk surface is 30 inches from the floor; a keyboard or mouse used on a regular office desk or table at 30 inches can cause users discomfort because the angle of their wrists at the keyboard is unnatural. To prevent wrist and finger pain, make sure that when a user's hands rest on the keyboard or mouse, they extend in a relatively straight line, or slightly downward, from the forearms. If a 30-inch office desk or table is the only possible keyboard location, one of the following adaptations may be possible:

- Shorten the desk or table legs to get the keyboard to a comfortable height.

- Adjust the chair height so the user's wrists are in a comfortable position.

- Attach an adjustable keyboard shelf to the underside of the desk or table.

As notebook computer models increase in popularity, support specialists need to be aware of the special ergonomic challenges they present. Because notebooks are often transported from one location to another and may be used with docking stations or port replicators, the height of a notebook keyboard varies according to the location where it is used. A notebook should ideally be used on a surface that is at the lower end of the 26- to 28-inch recommended height range because the thickness of the notebook itself can add to the keyboard height.

Display Screen Location

Position the display screen so a user can view it by looking straight ahead or slightly down. The most comfortable display screen position is usually the same position in which a user would hold a book to read at their workspace. A user should not have to look up at the display screen. Tilt the display so the user can view it with a natural head position, without neck strain.

Printer Location

A printer does not have to be placed in the valuable real estate on a user's desktop but can instead be located on a work table or bookshelf or, where available, on a printer stand. A printer should be in a convenient location where users can easily load paper and cartridges and where the case can be opened to remove paper jams. Extender signal cables from the system unit to the printer can be purchased to provide additional flexibility in printer location, but check the printer manual because some printer models will not operate reliably when lengthy extender cables are used. The location of networked printers that will be shared among several users in an office is an important decision. Printers located some distance from frequent users can result in lost productivity.

Supplies

Users frequently want certain supplies located conveniently near their computer equipment. These supplies may include printer paper, mailing labels, ink or toner cartridges, magnetic or optical media, computer manuals, cleaning supplies, tools, and other accessories. Supplies can usually be stored in an office file drawer, bookcase, or closet. Some supplies need to be stored in a special location to avoid certain problems. For example, paper should be stored where it is not exposed to excessive moisture.

Computer Furniture

An end user's desk chair often has more impact on his or her comfort, health, and safety than any other piece of office furniture, the workspace layout, the computer features, or other ergonomic factors. Adjustability is a desirable feature in an office chair: adjustable seat height, seat swivel and tilt, backrest, and arm rests. The seat height should be adjusted so the user's feet rest comfortably on the floor. Seat swivel and tilt features permit a user to vary his or her position with respect to the computer system and work area to avoid the monotony of sitting in a single position for long periods. The seat backrest should be adjusted so it supports the user's lower back. The armrests should be adjusted so the user's elbows rest comfortably on the tops of the armrests when a user is seated in the chair in a comfortable posture. Most ergonomic chairs now have a "waterfall" front edge designed to reduce the pressure on the back of a user's legs. Other chair selection features include a five-leg base (rather than a less stable four-leg base) on rollers, and padding that is supportive and comfortable. In a carpeted office, a plastic floor pad permits a chair to roll smoothly. When possible, a user should have an opportunity to try out an ergonomic chair.

Space Constraint Solutions

Where space permits, a separate computer worktable or an extension to a user's office desk can be used to increase a user's work space.

If a user has an older CRT monitor, a monitor arm can be attached to the desk or wall to move the screen off the desktop. Some newer flat-panel LCD screens can be mounted directly on a wall to free up desk space.

Many ergonomic desks have keyboard shelves attached under the work surface. These shelves can usually be added to standard office desks and worktables. Keyboard shelves are often adjustable. In addition to saving desk space, adjustable keyboard shelves enable a user to position the keyboard at a comfortable height. They are especially useful when multiple users share a work area, such as at a shared desk or in a computer lab or training facility.

With careful planning, desk space can be conserved by locating the system unit, display screen, printer, and other peripherals close to the user's desk area but not actually on it. Several vendors manufacture space-saving furniture specially designed for computer equipment.

In some executive offices, users want systems installed on furniture never intended for computers, such as an antique desk or on a credenza. In these cases, furniture may need to be significantly adapted to avoid ergonomic problems later. Be sure adequate knee room is available, especially if a user is tall.

ON THE WEB

Many office supply and computer vendors carry furniture and other products designed to address the issues discussed in this section. To see examples of products described here, check the online catalogs of K-Log (**www.k-log.com**) or Anthro Technology Furniture (**www.anthro.com**).

Ergonomics

Ergonomics is the study of how to design computer systems (both hardware and software) and lay out workspaces to minimize health problems and maximize worker safety, productivity, comfort, and job satisfaction. Some large organizations employ a safety engineer whose job responsibilities include office and factory floor ergonomics. In smaller organizations, workers may turn to user support specialists for advice about ergonomic issues.

A well-planned computer installation can help users avoid several common ergonomic problems, described in the following sections.

Back or Neck Muscle Pain

Pain in the back or neck muscles can have more than one source. A user may be straining neck muscles to see a display screen that is placed too high. If a user's chair is too low, it can force the user to look up to view the screen. The user's chair may not be designed for computer use. Poorly designed chairs can cut off circulation in legs or force a worker to use back and neck muscles that should be relaxed. The keyboard may be too high, so that the user's arms are angled in an unnatural position. An end user, despite a correctly designed workspace, may work too long without adequate breaks or without shifting body position.

Solutions to back or neck muscle pain can include keyboard height adjustments, a chair with both back and seat adjustment levers, better back support, adequate cushioning, and a "waterfall" seat design that takes pressure off the backs of a user's legs and promotes better circulation. Some users find that a pillow or other support in the curve of their backs helps them sit more comfortably in their chairs. Users should be reminded to take "stretch" breaks at least once an hour. Frequent finger, hand, wrist, and neck stretches during breaks can be effective to prevent and sometimes cure pain, as can isometric exercises.

Software ergonomics deals with usability factors such as legible screen displays that incorporate consistent navigation aids, data-entry processes that eliminate unnecessary keystrokes or mouse clicks, and natural sequences of human-computer interactions.

ON THE WEB

For suggested ergonomic exercises for computer users, visit **www.officefurniture.org/GuideDetail.aspx? GuideID=6&TopicID=5**.

ON THE WEB

Some users report good results with a mesh back support product; view an example at **www.travelonbags.com/ 1918.html**.

Leg Pain

Leg pain can result from an office chair that is too high for the user's feet to touch the floor or one that is improperly designed and impairs leg circulation. Leg pain can also result from a work area with too little knee room or one that forces a user to sit in an uncomfortable position for extended periods.

Solutions to leg pain include ergonomically designed office chairs with back and seat adjustment levers, sufficient back support and adequate cushioning, and a "waterfall" seat design. A footrest placed at a 15-degree angle may be necessary to support the user's legs and reduce strain.

Eyestrain and Headaches

Eyestrain and headaches can result from screen glare. A user's display screen may reflect sunlight or room lights, which is one of the primary causes of eyestrain. (See the Lighting section later in this chapter for more details.) Glasses and contact lenses can also contribute to eyestrain and headaches if they are not appropriate for the distance at which the end user is sitting from the computer screen.

Solutions to eyestrain and headaches include changing the orientation of the computer to the light source, or using window shades to reduce glare. The level of lighting in the computer area may need to be reduced. Antiglare screen filters are available from office and computer supply stores. Users should make an effort to take a break at least once an hour, and they should look away periodically from the display screen at distant objects to minimize eyestrain. End users should also ensure that eyeglass prescriptions are correct for extended computer use.

Wrist and Finger Pain

Wrist and finger pain usually results from a keyboard that is too high or too low. Hand and wrist muscles and tendons should not be tense or strained at a keyboard; a user's arms should be angled slightly downward, and the wrist should have support. Physical problems called **repetitive strain injuries** result from continuous use of joints in a limited range of motion. The symptoms of repetitive strain injuries include swelling, numbness, tingling, and stiffness in joints. The most common form of repetitive strain injury is **carpal tunnel syndrome**, which affects wrists and fingers.

Techniques for reducing the risk of repetitive strain injuries include placing the keyboard at the optimal 26 to 28 inches from the floor; using an adjustable keyboard shelf, wrist rest, and a chair with arms; and taking stretch breaks at least once an hour. An ergonomic keyboard, which splits the right- and left-hand keys in an inverted V shape so that the user's hands, wrists, and forearms are in a more natural and comfortable position, may help reduce strain. Ergonomic keyboards take some time to acclimate to, but those who have used them generally do not want to return to a conventional keyboard.

Figure 9-2 illustrates some of the important workstation dimensions that will help ensure user comfort and eliminate many ergonomic problems. These potential ergonomic problems as well as possible solutions are summarized in Table 9-1.

Ergonomic Problem	Possible Solutions
Back or neck muscle pain or numbness	• Replace office chair with one that is adjustable. • Adjust keyboard height. • Install adjustable keyboard shelf. • Take frequent breaks and perform exercises to reduce repetitive motion and stress.
Leg pain or numbness	• Replace office chair with ergonomic model. • Place footrest on floor.
Eyestrain and headaches	• Reorient computer to reduce screen glare. • Reduce office lighting. • Install display screen antiglare filter. • Check eyeglasses for proper fit and prescription. • Replace display screen with larger size and better resolution. • Take frequent breaks and perform exercises to reduce stress.
Wrist and finger pain or numbness Carpal tunnel syndrome	• Adjust keyboard height. • Install adjustable keyboard shelf. • Use keyboard wrist rest. • Take frequent breaks and perform exercises to reduce stress and repetitive motion strain.

Table 9-1   Ergonomic problems and solutions

Figure 9-2   Workstation ergonomics

With the amount of attention that repetitive strain injuries and other ergonomic problems have received in recent years, it is no surprise that many devices designed to avoid or reduce the impact of extended computer use are on the market. These devices include:

- Adjustable tables and work surfaces
- Adjustable chairs
- Footrests
- Keyboard shelves
- Alternative ergonomic keyboards
- Alternative pointing devices (trackballs and touchpads)
- Wrist rests
- Mouse support rests
- Document holders
- CRT monitor arms
- Task lighting
- Antiglare screen filters
- Assistive devices

Assistive devices are computer peripherals and software that adapt a computer system so that users with various physical limitations can be more productive. For example, users with visual impairments may be able to use special software that displays extra-large type fonts on a screen. Users who cannot see a display screen may be able to use hardware and software devices that "read" the contents of a screen to a user. Users who do not have the motor skills to type may use a keyboard alternative such as a stylus pointer or voice-recognition software.

ON THE WEB

If a support specialist is asked to make a recommendation on the purchase of an ergonomic device, both the support specialist and the end user should understand the advantages and disadvantages of the devices. A Web site that explains the pros and cons of several types of ergonomic devices is **www.office-ergo.com/pros&.htm**.

Or, read an excerpt from *Your Guide to Office Ergonomic Furniture and Accessories*, by Alison Heller, at **www. worksiteinternational.com/downloads/excerpt.PDF**.

Microsoft publishes a free monthly newsletter titled *Accessibility Update*. Subscribe at **www.microsoft.com/ enable/news/subscribe/default.aspx**.

Support specialists should treat end-user ergonomic concerns seriously. Many computer users have experienced painful repetitive strain injuries that require medical treatment. Some repetitive strain injuries can disable a user for an extended period or even permanently, and some end users require a job change to compensate for injuries resulting from ergonomic problems that were not addressed promptly or properly. Employers that have ignored state and federal (OSHA) rules and regulations that cover worksite ergonomics have been the target of legal action by disabled workers.

ON THE WEB

Several Web sites contain useful information about ergonomics, including the latest research findings, specialized products, and treatment options. For example, see the UCLA Ergonomics Web site (**www.ergonomics.ucla.edu**) or the Cornell University Ergonomics Web site (**ergo.human.cornell.edu**).

OSHA also publishes information on computer workstation ergonomics at **www.osha.gov/SLTC/etools/ computerworkstations**.

 Ergonomics is an area in which user support specialists can develop special expertise that adds value to their employment. Extra effort is required to keep up with the latest research and products in ergonomics, but support specialists who devote the time can become recognized as an important resource for office ergonomics issues.

Power Requirements

Most small computer systems do not pose unusual electrical power problems. They plug into standard three-prong outlets. However, before installing a computer, several electrical power situations should be checked.

Electrical Power Checklist

- *Outlets*—If an installation is in an older building with two-pronged outlets (that is, those without the third ground prong), re-wiring or installation of grounds may be necessary. Avoid "cheater" plug adapters, which convert two-pronged plugs to three-prong, because they defeat the ground feature that protects electronic circuits. Instead, recommend upgraded wiring.

- *Outlet wiring*—Test three-prong outlets to make sure the hot, neutral, and ground prongs were correctly wired when the outlet was installed. Incorrect wiring is uncommon, but it can cause problems if a computer system is plugged into an outlet that was improperly wired. A simple, inexpensive outlet tester is available from most electrical suppliers and hardware stores.

During startup, some appliances draw more amps than their stated operational rating.

- *Circuit amperage*—If a computer with a significant number of peripheral devices is installed in an environment with other office equipment (copiers, coffeemakers, radios, refrigerators, fax machines, printing calculators), add up the amperage currently drawing on the circuit to determine whether it can handle the total load. Most appliances, including computers, display screens, and printers, display the number of amps of current they draw on an information plate. If a circuit breaker at the electrical distribution box is 15 amps, the total amperage of devices on the circuit should be less than 15. Otherwise, a separate electrical circuit should be installed for the computer and peripherals.

- *Shared circuits*—A computer should not be installed on an electrical circuit that services a generator, air conditioner, or a device with a heavy motor. These devices can, at times, draw large quantities of power, which may reduce the available amps on a circuit to less than that required for the proper operation of computer devices. For example, hard disk drives rely on electrical current for timing during read and write operations. Inadequate power during one of these operations could cause loss of data on the drive media.

- *Power stability*—In some local areas, the quality of the electric supply varies considerably, even during normal operation. When installing computer equipment in areas with unstable power, consult with the local electric utility to determine whether special equipment is recommended to protect computer hardware. The electric utility may recommend a **power conditioner,** which is an electrical device installed between a computer and its power source that regulates the electrical power to ensure it stays within acceptable limits. A power conditioner draws in electrical power, makes sure that the frequency, voltage, and waveform are within acceptable specifications, and then outputs stable, "clean" power to the computer. Electrical contractors or electricians can test whether or not a power conditioner is required by monitoring a circuit with a special metering device for 24 to 48 hours. Metering devices print a statistical summary of electrical quality and the number of spikes, surges, or brownouts that occurred during the test period.

- *Multiple computers*—If multiple computer systems will be installed in one location, such as an office, training room, or computer lab facility, the total electric power requirements need to be planned in advance, and an electrical contractor should be consulted to verify that the power is adequate and well conditioned. The installation of servers and high-end workstations, whose power requirements can be unusual, may require the help of a qualified electrician.

Electrical power and peripheral signal cables should be installed so they cannot be damaged or stressed by stretching. When computer wires are installed in an existing building, surface-mounted cable conduits (or runways) can be installed along an office or computer lab wall. These conduits provide access to the cables if they need to be upgraded or repaired, but they protect the cables from potential problems due to shorted or broken cables. Avoid running power cables or signal cables over a tile office floor or under a carpet. If power or signal cables must run over or under any kind of flooring, purchase rubber conduits to protect the cables from the wear and tear of traffic. Plastic cable ties can be used to bundle cables and secure them to furniture in order to get them off the floor or out of the way, and to avoid stress on the cable runs.

In work areas where power and signal cable management is a potential problem, wireless devices should be investigated as an alternative.

Specialized Power Devices

In a standard computer installation, electrical power strips are convenient because a user can flip one switch to turn on an entire system. The system unit, display screen, printer, and other peripheral devices can all be plugged into the power strip. However, power strips should not be used as electrical extension cords. Each power strip should be plugged into an electrical outlet and not into another power strip. This requirement is part of the electrical code in many areas and makes good sense even where it is not. The best power strips,

398

Some surge suppressor manufacturers offer a warranty that pays a user if computer equipment is damaged while plugged into their surge suppressors—if the surge suppressor was installed and operated according to the manufacturer's recommendations.

called **surge suppressors** (or surge protectors), include protective circuits that help prevent damage to computer equipment due to power surges and spikes. Surge suppressors may also include filters that protect against radio frequency interference.

ON THE WEB

Not all surge suppressors provide adequate protection from power surges and spikes. Inexpensive models may not have robust circuitry to protect against extremely powerful surges, such as a lightning strike. Electric utilities generally recommend a surge suppressor with the following specifications:

- UL 1449 (second edition) listed
- 40,000 amps or more peak protection
- 330 volts or less clamping voltage level
- 1 nanosecond or less clamping response time
- 750 joules or more energy rating
- Diagnostic LED status lamps

For more information about surge suppressors, visit the Cherryland Electric Cooperative Web site at **www.cherrylandelectric.com/memberprograms/surgeqa.cfm**.

Uptime and downtime measurements may be converted into percentages of time to standardize these measures.

In environments where power problems exist or computer downtime is unacceptable, several tools are available to address specific problems. **Downtime** is a measure of the number of hours (per week or month) that a computer system is unavailable for use because of power failures or other problems; **uptime** measures the number of operational hours. Obviously, uptime for a computer system in a hospital's critical care unit is more important than uptime in a school classroom.

When a power conditioner is used, the device must have the capacity to condition power for the total load it must service. For example, the load on a circuit may include the system unit, display screen, printer, scanner, other computer peripherals, and additional office equipment.

An **uninterruptible power supply (UPS)** is an electrical device that includes power conditioning circuits as well as a battery backup. The battery backup begins operating when the UPS senses that the electrical power supply is interrupted (or reduced during a brownout) and then provides power to the computer equipment for a limited period of time. The battery power rating of a UPS indicates how long a computer system will be able to continue operation after a power failure. A higher-power battery is more expensive; therefore, most UPS devices in use allow for the operation of a computer for a few minutes, up to an hour at most. The battery capacity in a UPS is intended primarily to provide time for users to properly shut down their computer equipment so that application software and operating systems can empty memory buffers, close files, and terminate operation, and hardware can power down normally. Without a UPS, power loss could cause hardware or software to terminate abnormally, which may cause equipment damage or unpredictable problems when the system is powered on later.

 Many modern UPS devices automatically shut down a computer system to protect it from data loss if a user is not available to do it manually.

399

ON THE WEB

To learn more about electrical power problems, conditioning equipment, and UPS devices, visit the NetworkClue.com Web site (**www.networkclue.com/hardware/power**). The site includes pointers to resources for selecting devices to solve various power problems.

Network and Telephone Access

Few computers today are standalone installations. Most office computer systems require connection to a local area network. Home computer systems are usually connected to the Internet. Internet access can be provided by one of the following methods:

- A telephone line for dial-up access to an Internet Service Provider.

- DSL (digital subscriber line) connections in some service areas provide fast data and voice connections over a single telephone line.

- Cable television companies frequently offer broadband Internet service.

- Satellite television providers may offer Internet connection along with television service.

Each of these connection methods requires a modem for data transmission. After establishing the connection requirements for a specific installation, you should locate the nearest telephone, cable, or network access points to determine if extension lines are necessary, or determine whether wireless access is available.

Air Conditioning

Just as many computer installations do not require additional electrical wiring, most do not require air conditioning beyond what is necessary for end-user comfort. However, in locations where a large number of computer systems will be installed in close proximity, such as in a small office, training facility, or computer lab, additional air conditioning may be required. An engineer or consultant who specializes in heating, ventilating, and air conditioning (HVAC) can help determine the requirements. HVAC specialists use a formula that considers the total wattage of electrical devices and the heat generated by people to compute the number of BTUs (British thermal units) of air conditioning capacity required to maintain the temperature within a predetermined range.

Servers and high-end workstations are more likely to require air conditioning than small office computers. However, the total wattage within a space determines air conditioning requirements. Even a few computers in a small office can create a need for air conditioning, especially during summer months.

Lighting

Incorrect office lighting can cause significant ergonomic problems. The lighting level can be too intense, from the wrong source, or the wrong type of lighting. The result can be lower worker productivity due to eyestrain or headaches.

Light Intensity

Many offices are over-lit for computer use. Too much light on a user's work surface can cause glare on a display screen. One solution is to turn off or remove some light fixtures to reduce the amount of glare. In cases where four fluorescent bulbs are housed in a fixture, for example, an electrician may be able to remove two of the four bulbs by making a simple modification to the fixture. If it is not possible to adjust the amount of light in an office, consider an antiglare filter that covers the entire display screen area.

Light Source

In addition to the amount of light, the source of light may cause problems. For example, in an office or training room with windows, computer display screens should be positioned so they are at a 90-degree angle (perpendicular) to the light source. This position is preferable to a light source that hits the screen directly, which can happen when the screen is positioned directly opposite the light source. A user generally should not face a light source, because direct light could cause the user to squint in order to control the amount of light received.

Light Type

Finally, the type of lighting can cause problems with certain types of monitors. Some fluorescent bulbs flicker at the same frequency as the refresh rate on older CRT-type monitors. The result is a noticeable flicker or visible moving horizontal scan line on the screen. In these situations, an electrician or lighting consultant may be able to recommend a fluorescent bulb that flickers less or at a different rate than the monitor.

 Screen flicker is not a problem with LCD flat-panel displays.

Fire Suppression

Fortunately, computer systems rarely burst into flames. However, computer equipment *is* electrical and mechanical, and electromechanical devices can cause fires, primarily due to problems with power supplies. Devices that have moving parts or generate excessive heat, such as disk drives or printers, can also cause fires, although fires from these sources are unusual. While forecasting when a fire may occur is impossible, it is possible to be prepared for one. If an office does not have an existing fire-suppression system, place portable fire extinguishers near the equipment. Choose a fire extinguisher that is rated for electrical fires, because an extinguisher that is designed for wood or paper fires contains a dry chemical that can further damage electronic equipment.

The most effective fire extinguishers for use on and around computer equipment contain halon gas. However, the Environmental Protection Agency (EPA) has made the manufacture of new halon systems illegal because halon depletes ozone gas in the atmosphere. Existing halon systems can continue to be used. Manufacturers have developed effective alternative fire extinguisher gases, such as Halotron, Inergen and FE-36.

ON THE WEB

For additional information about halon, see the EPA Web site at **www.epa.gov/Ozone/snap/fire/qa.html**.

To learn more about alternatives to halon for computer installations, read an article on BFPE International's Web site at **www.bfpe.com/fe_cleanagent.htm**.

Figure 9-3 is a checklist of issues that should be considered during the installation planning stages. As with the other checklists in this chapter, it is a summary of issues, designed as a starting point. Not all issues apply to every installation, nor are all issues of equal importance.

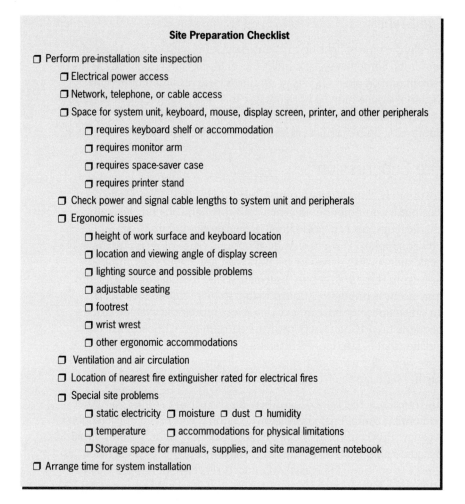

Site Preparation Checklist

☐ Perform pre-installation site inspection

    ☐ Electrical power access

    ☐ Network, telephone, or cable access

    ☐ Space for system unit, keyboard, mouse, display screen, printer, and other peripherals

        ☐ requires keyboard shelf or accommodation

        ☐ requires monitor arm

        ☐ requires space-saver case

        ☐ requires printer stand

    ☐ Check power and signal cable lengths to system unit and peripherals

    ☐ Ergonomic issues

        ☐ height of work surface and keyboard location

        ☐ location and viewing angle of display screen

        ☐ lighting source and possible problems

        ☐ adjustable seating

        ☐ footrest

        ☐ wrist wrest

        ☐ other ergonomic accommodations

    ☐ Ventilation and air circulation

    ☐ Location of nearest fire extinguisher rated for electrical fires

    ☐ Special site problems

        ☐ static electricity ☐ moisture ☐ dust ☐ humidity

        ☐ temperature   ☐ accommodations for physical limitations

        ☐ Storage space for manuals, supplies, and site management notebook

☐ Arrange time for system installation

Figure 9-3 Site preparation checklist

A ROLE-PLAYING SCENARIO

This scenario occurred when Daren, a user support specialist, arrived at the workstation of Sean, a new employee in the human resources department. If possible, have fellow students or coworkers play the parts of Daren and Sean, and then discuss your reaction to their conversation.

DAREN: Good morning. I have a work order to help you install your new computer. I see you have a notebook model.

SEAN: Yes, In my job I will be traveling occasionally and would like to be able to take my computer with me into the field.

DAREN: Good choice. We'll set it up on your desk. Can you move the phone a little, please? By the way, is there a connection to the company network anywhere around here?

SEAN: I don't know. I've just moved in, and I think this is a new carrel. I'm not sure I've seen a connection, come to think of it.

DAREN: Well, I know there is a network drop on that load-bearing wall over there, but that must be 30 feet away, and I don't have any cables that long. I can order one though.

SEAN: How long will that take?

DAREN: Only a couple of days. Until then, we can get the software you requested installed and you can use your computer now, but you won't be able to access the local area network or receive e-mail.

SEAN: Well, if that's the best you can do . . .

DAREN: I did bring along the install CDs for the Office Suite.

SEAN: Is that for Office 2007?

DAREN: Yes, the company converted to 2007 a few weeks back.

SEAN: My manager says my department, HR, is still on 2003. Apparently HR has been busy with end-of-quarter processing and hasn't had the training on 2007 yet. I used Office 2003 at my old job, so I'm not used to the new menus in 2007.

DAREN: Well, I'll install 2007 today, and then you'll be ready when you've had the training. You'll probably be able to pick up the new ribbon menus quickly anyway.

. . .

DAREN: Now I just need to know where you want your printer.

SEAN: Well, I don't have much furniture yet, so I don't really have a place to put it. Could it go on the floor?

DAREN: It probably could. But the cable wouldn't reach then. So we'll just put it on your desk for now. Just until you get something better. Could you move your phone over a little more? Oh, and call me anytime you have any problems with your new notebook.

Describe the problems you identified in this scenario. What suggestions do you have to avoid problems like the ones you identified?

Site Management Documentation

The primary goal of any installation is, of course, to achieve an operational system. However, support specialists may want to accomplish other goals during a system installation. One possible goal is to build a **site management notebook**, a binder that consolidates important information about a system's hardware, operating system, network, and software, as well as facilities management information, in one location.

A site management notebook contains much of the information a support specialist might need in the future to operate, diagnose, troubleshoot, reconfigure, upgrade, and repair the system and its components. A site management notebook is also a useful resource to make sure important steps are not omitted when installing multiple systems.

The site management notebook documents important details about a system, including:

- Hardware configuration
- Operating system configuration
- Network configuration
- Software licenses
- Application software configuration
- Special operating procedures
- Warranty and repair information
- Problem log
- Backup media log

A site management notebook may be overkill for a simple installation of a home or small office computer; however, one is often a necessity for systems installed in larger offices, training facilities, and computer labs. Even some personal computer users have found a site management notebook a useful tool and worth the time it takes to file and maintain the information. A site management notebook is especially critical in locations where a large number of computers are installed, systems are configured differently, and multiple support staff members work on various parts of a system from time to time. The notebook acts as a one-stop source of information to answer questions support specialists may have, such as:

- When was the PC installed and by whom?
- What changes to the standard operating system configuration were made on this machine?
- What software is legally licensed to be installed on this system?
- What are the system's IP and MAC addresses?
- Who should the user contact when the display screen doesn't work?
- Where are the media backups and when were they created?
- Has the printer problem we're seeing today happened before?

Figure 9-4 shows examples of the kind of information often included in a site management notebook, including hardware and software configuration sheets and configuration details.

PC Hardware Configuration Sheet

SYSTEM _____ Serial # _____

Installation Date ___ /___ /___ Installer _____

1. **System Unit**

    ❑ Desktop ❑ Laptop/Notebook Power supply _____ watts

    Manufacturer _____ Model _____

2. **CPU**

    ❑ Intel _____ ❑ AMD _____

    Bus type _____ Motherboard type _____

    BIOS Manufacturer _____ Version _____

3. **Internal memory**

    RAM _____ GB Type _____ Pins _____ Slots _____

    Cache memory L1 _____ KB L2 _____ MB L3 _____ MB

4. **Storage**

    Controller card ❑ IDE ❑ EIDE ❑ ATA ❑ SATA

    Hard drive _____ GB Second drive _____ GB

    External hard drive Manufacturer _____ _____GB

    ❑ Floppy drive

    ❑ Optical CD _____ X ❑ CD±RW _____ X ❑ DVD _____ X ❑ DVD±RW_____ X

5. **Input**

    ❑ Keyboard ❑ Standard ❑ Ergonomic

    ❑ Mouse Type _____

    ❑ Scanner Manufacturer _____ Model _____

6. **Output**

    ❑ Graphics/Video adapter Type _____ Memory _____ MB

    ❑ Display screen Manufacturer _____ Model _____

    Size _____ Resolution _____

    ❑ Printer Manufacturer _____ Model _____

    ❑ Inkjet ❑ B/W _____ ppm _____ dpi ❑ Color _____ ppm _____ dpi

    ❑ Laser ❑ B/W _____ ppm _____ dpi ❑ Color _____ ppm _____ dpi

    Cartridge # _____ Cartridge # _____ Cartridge # _____

7. **Networking**

    ❑ Ethernet _____

    ❑ Modem

    Manufacturer _____ Model _____ Speed _____

    ❑ Workstation ID _____

    IP address _____ . _____ . _____ . _____ MAC address ___-___-___-___-___-___

    ❑ Wireless adapter _____

8. **Expansion**

    ❑ Ports ❑ Serial _____ ❑ Parallel _____ ❑ Mouse

    ❑ USB _____ ❑ 1.1 ❑ 2.0 ❑ 3.0

    ❑ Bus Slots ❑ 8-bit _____ 16-bit _____ 32-bit _____

    ❑ Media adaptor _____

9. **Other**

Figure 9-4 Sample pages from a site management notebook (*continues*)

(continued)

PC Software Configuration Sheet

SYSTEM _____   **Serial #** _____

Installation Date ___ / ___ / ___   **Installer** _____

1. **Application needs analysis**

   ❏ Word Processing   ❏ Desktop Publishing   ❏ Web Authoring   ❏ Spreadsheet

   ❏ Accounting   ❏ Database Management   ❏ Financial   ❏ Project Management

   ❏ Presentation   ❏ Multimedia   ❏ Graphics   ❏ CAD

   ❏ GIS   ❏ Statistics   ❏ Decision Support   ❏ Forecasting

2. **Operating system**   **VERSION**

   ❏ Windows (Service Pack _____)   _____

   ❏ Linux   ❏ Unix   ❏ Mac OS   _____

3. **Tools and Utilities**   **VERSION**

   Programming languages   ❏ Visual BASIC   ❏ C/C++   _____

                                ❏ Java   ❏ Other _____   _____

   Utilities   ❏ Antivirus _____   _____

                                ❏ Firewall _____   _____

                                ❏ Anti-spyware _____   _____

                                ❏ PDF reader _____   _____

                                ❏ Media backup _____   _____

                                ❏ _____   _____

                                ❏ _____   _____

4. **Application software**   **VERSION**

   ❏ Office suite _____   _____

   ❏ Word processor _____   _____

   ❏ Spreadsheet _____   _____

   ❏ Database _____   _____

   ❏ Presentation _____   _____

   ❏ Accounting _____   _____

   ❏ Financial _____   _____

   ❏ PIM _____   _____

   ❏ Desktop publishing _____   _____

   ❏ Web development _____   _____

   ❏ Communications

        ❏ E-mail client _____   _____

        ❏ Web browser _____   _____

        ❏ FTP _____   _____

   ❏ Internet Service Provider _____   _____

   ❏ _____   _____

   ❏ _____   _____

Figure 9-4   Sample pages from a site management notebook (*continues*)

(continued)

Furniture/Supplies/Accessories

❏ desk (26" × 28" height)	❏ chair (ergonomic)	❏ printer forms
❏ printer stand	❏ printer paper	❏ microphone
❏ LCD projector	❏ headset	❏ digital camera
❏ media	❏ media case	❏ extender cables
❏ power strip	❏ surge suppressor	❏ antistatic mat
❏ documentation	❏ bookshelf/rack	
❏ wrist rest	❏ mouse pad	
❏ antiglare screen	❏ footrest	
❏ security lockdown	❏ tool kit	
❏ cleaning supplies:	❏ compressed air ❏ vacuum ❏ wipes ❏ cleaner	

Figure 9-4   Sample pages from a site management notebook

In situations where a complete site management notebook isn't practical for whatever reason, a printout of configuration information from one of these resources is better than nothing when it comes time to reconfigure, upgrade, troubleshoot or repair a PC.

ON THE WEB

For additional details and information on the terms used in the PC Hardware Configuration Sheet, see the Webopedia Web site at **webopedia.internet.com/Hardware** or The PC Guide Web site at **www.pcguide.com**. Follow links on these Web sites to learn more about each hardware option. These sites also include pointers to additional articles and product reviews.

Two free system information utilities can be downloaded to capture and present PC configuration information. Belarc Advisor is available at **www.belarc.com/free_download.html**, and SiSoftware's Sandra is available at **www.sisoftware.net**.

Activity 9-5 at the end of this chapter gives you an opportunity to run one of these system information utilities and learn more about the kind of information they provide.

In Windows Vista, you can explore many of the configuration options for a PC by accessing the System Information Tool (SIT). It is located on the **Start** menu, under **All Programs**. Click **Accessories**, then **System Tools**, and finally, **System Information**. Alternately, click the **Start** button, select **Run**, and enter the command **msinfo32**.

408

Hardware Installation Tools

User support specialists who frequently install and make simple hardware repairs can purchase or assemble a kit with the basic tools needed to perform simple tasks with computer equipment. Computer, electronic supply, and mail order vendors sell tool kits, which start at about $15. Tools for use around computer equipment should be nonmagnetic. Most basic kits contain the following:

- **Screwdriver set**—Used to remove and insert screws; the set should include both a slotted blade and a Phillips-head screwdriver. The heads on the screwdrivers should be smaller than general-use screwdrivers because computer screws are often small. Some hardware repairers prefer a socketed screwdriver with interchangeable heads.

- **Nut driver**—Used to remove the case from a system because the screws on a case are often six-sided nuts. (Nut drivers come in several sizes; get one designed for computer equipment.) Some socketed screwdrivers are the correct size for a nut driver when the screwdriver heads are removed.

- **Pliers**—Used to hold and clamp parts; the kit should include both regular pliers and needle-nose pliers for working with small parts.

- **Parts-picker** (retractable claw)—Used to pick up small screws, nuts, and bolts in a tight work space; some kits contain tweezers and a magnetic parts grabber for small parts.

In addition, support specialists who work frequently on hardware installations or end-user problems may want to augment a basic tool kit with one or more of the following:

- **Pocketknife**—Used for tasks when perhaps no other tool will do the job. (Victorinox makes a version of the Swiss Army Knife, called the CyberTool, that is specifically designed for work with computer hardware.)

- **Small parts container**—Used for keeping track of screws, nuts, washers, and other small parts while working on a computer system.

- **Mirror**—Used to see in tight spaces and behind components that are difficult to move (an angled dental mirror is a good choice).

- **Small flashlight**—Used to illuminate hard-to-see places.

- **Isopropyl alcohol**—Used to clean electrical components, display screens, keyboards, and mouse parts. Isopropyl alcohol should be handled with care, like any chemical; it should not be consumed or inhaled under any circumstances. Alternatives include spray cleaners and packaged wipes.

- **Lint-free cloth or foam-tipped brush**—Used to apply isopropyl alcohol for cleaning; antistatic wipes are also recommended.

- **Microfiber cloth**—Used to clean dust from display screens, keyboards, and computer cases.

- **Antistatic wrist strap**—Used to ground a technician to the computer power supply or case whenever a need arises to handle components inside a computer case. A strap reduces the risk of damaging a component with an accidental static charge. Inexpensive antistatic wrist straps sell for $6 to $10.

- **Cable ties**—Used to bundle together cables to keep them well organized and out of the way.

- **Electrical tape**—Used for simple repairs or in lieu of cable ties.

- **Compressed air**—Used to blow dust out of computer cases, keyboards, printers, and other equipment. An alternative is a small vacuum cleaner designed for electronic equipment, available in many parts supply catalogs.

- **Circuit tester**—Used to determine whether an electric outlet has been properly wired (tests hot, neutral, and ground); inexpensive models are simple plug-in devices.

- **Multimeter**—Used to determine whether an electric circuit is active, whether a cable has a short, or whether a battery still has a charge; a multimeter is sometimes called a VOM (volt-ohm-meter). For many tasks, inexpensive analog multimeters can be purchased for $10 to $15; for work on motherboards, a digital multimeter is recommended.

Some of the small tools recommended for an installer's tool kit can be obtained inexpensively at a dollar store.

409

Figure 9-5 A typical hardware installation tool kit

Once you have inspected the installation site and are sure you have the proper equipment and tools, you can proceed with installing the hardware components.

Common Hardware Installation Steps

For most users in homes and organizations, installing computer hardware includes unpacking, connecting, and testing the basic components. Basic components usually consist of a system unit, display screen, keyboard, mouse, and perhaps a printer. The installation process can also include installing additional memory, expansion cards for peripheral devices, and network connections.

An important first step is to plan the installation. In addition to the pre-installation site checklist and steps described earlier in this chapter, planning also includes a review to make sure you have all the components and tools you will need. An installation time that is convenient for the user should also be arranged in advance. Technicians who install a large volume of systems usually develop a checklist to make sure they bring all the necessary components with them and perform all the steps required. The checklist later becomes a form of documentation that they did so. Figure 9-6 shows a typical hardware installation checklist. The purpose of this sample checklist, and the others in this chapter, is to provide a starting point for support specialists who want to develop their own checklists and procedures specific to each organization and situation.

Support specialists who install systems don't necessarily perform all the steps shown in Figure 9-6 at every installation. To make the checklist more useful, installers can delete steps they never perform or insert additional steps that apply to their installations.

The checklist in Figure 9-6 assumes that a support specialist is installing a preassembled system. Sometimes the installer assembles a system from basic components or installs additional equipment in a preassembled system. Trade books on installing or upgrading a computer system describe in detail the steps involved in assembling a system starting at the individual component level.

Hardware Installation Checklist

BEFORE INSTALLATION:

☐ Review safety checklist

☐ Get tool kit and spare parts container

☐ Unpack hardware components and note any missing or damaged parts

☐ Save boxes and packing material in case components need to be returned

BASIC INSTALLATION:

☐ Connect basic components, power, and signal cables

☐ Perform basic system boot test

☐ Remove case cover and inspect components for proper installation

☐ Fill out hardware configuration sheet in site management notebook

    ☐ Record serial numbers in site management notebook

    ☐ File warranty information

OPTIONAL INSTALLATION:

☐ Install any memory upgrade and expansion cards:

    ☐ Multi-function I/O   ☐ Sound card

    ☐ Graphics adapter   ☐ Network interface

    ☐ Internal modem   ☐ Other: _____

COMPLETE INSTALLATION:

☐ Connect peripherals

    ☐ display screen   ☐ keyboard   ☐ mouse

    ☐ printer   ☐ external modem   ☐ telephone

    ☐ external hard drive   ☐ speakers   ☐ scanner

    ☐ microphone   ☐ digital camera   ☐ _____

☐ Connect power and signal cables

☐ Attach network cable to Ethernet connector

☐ Install power strip, surge suppressor, or UPS power unit

☐ Power up system and adjust display screen

☐ Run diagnostic tests on hardware devices

☐ Install ergonomic devices (screen glare filter, copy holder, wrist rest)

☐ Check cables for excess tension and install tie-wraps to bundle cables

☐ Attach security cables for theft prevention

☐ Record vendor contact numbers and e-mail addresses in site management notebook

Figure 9-6   Hardware installation checklist

Whenever installers remove the case from a computer system, they should follow the basic safety precautions described in Figure 9-7.

Guidelines for Working Inside a System Unit

Before you begin . . .

☐ 1. Understand what tasks you are going to do and how you are going to do them.

☐ 2. Get documentation on how to do each task or step you are going to perform.

☐ 3. Clear an adequate work space. Remove food and beverages from the work area.

☐ 4. Get the hardware components, tools, and software you will need to do each task (include paper and pencil for notes).

☐ 5. Get a collector container for small parts, such as screws.

Before you remove the case . . .

☐ 6. Turn off the power switch (Is there more than one power switch?).

☐ 7. Unplug the power cord (Is there more than one power cord?).

☐ 8. If in doubt, check for electric current with a tester or turn off the power at the breaker box.

☐ 9. Work with at least one other person in the vicinity of where you are working.

☐ 10. Remember: You should not take off the case from a power supply or a CRT monitor, or try to repair those devices.

☐ 11. Avoid loose clothing while working around mechanical parts, such as printers.

After the case is removed . . .

☐ 12. Observe proper handling procedures and warnings for chemicals, such as isopropyl alcohol and printer ink.

☐ 13. Before you begin work, attach an antistatic wrist strap, especially if you are working on memory components, IC chips, the motherboard, or adapter cards.

☐ 14. Before you unplug any component, make notes or a diagram of how it is mounted and how cables are connected to it (or use tape to label cable connections).

Before you restore power to test a component or system . . .

☐ 15. Double-check signal cable connections and power connections to make sure they are secure.

☐ 16. Before you test the system, check inside the system case and around the work area to make sure you can account for all components and tools.

☐ 17. Before you complete installation or troubleshooting, thoroughly test both the components you worked on and other system components.

After you have tested a component or system . . .

☐ 18. If you restored power to the system to test the components, turn off the power switch and unplug the power cord before you resume work inside the case.

After you are finished . . .

☐ 19. Put away your tools.

☐ 20. Document any changes you made to a system or its components in the site installation notebook.

Figure 9-7   Hardware installation safety precautions

Typical Operating System and Network Installation Steps

After a hardware installation is completed, the next steps may involve the related tasks of installing and configuring an operating system and a network connection.

Operating System Installation

Support specialists do not always install operating systems. Most preassembled computer systems have an operating system already installed on the hard drive. In situations that do require support specialists to install an operating system, most are supplied on a CD or DVD. Some vendors provide operating system updates, patches, service packs, and special drivers that users can download from a Web site. In cases where support specialists install identical operating system configurations on a large number of machines, an image of the system can be written on a removable hard drive or optical media. Alternately, images or updates for an operating system on computers that are connected to a network can usually be installed on a large number of machines via the network server.

The installation process is usually not complicated, but it can take an hour or more from beginning to end. The steps to install operating system software might include partitioning the hard disk, installing the operating system software and any necessary device drivers, and installing the network operating system client. After the operating system and network client have been configured for the hardware peripherals and to meet site-specific standards, support specialists perform updates and install other necessary software, including virus checkers, screen savers, and security and utility software.

Many PCs use a version of the Windows operating system, which reduces the need to install special device drivers. For the most part, Windows automatically recognizes devices that conform to Plug and Play standards. In these cases, Windows installs a default driver for devices it recognizes during the boot process. However, recent versions of Windows may not recognize some older peripheral devices and device drivers may need to be installed manually in those cases, if they are available. Each peripheral vendor's Web site should be checked to see if an updated device driver is available for download, because bugs may have been discovered in earlier versions or performance enhancements may have been introduced. Installers of Macintosh systems usually have an easier task, because the Mac OS automatically recognizes most peripheral devices; however, some peripheral devices are sold which require specialized device drivers for the Mac OS.

Experienced installers know that incompatibility between hardware, operating systems, and device drivers can cause many hours of lost time during installations. These installers check system requirements and vendor Web sites prior to installation to reduce the probability that time will be lost due to incompatible components.

ON THE WEB

To learn more about device drivers and how to check versions and problems with device drivers, read an article on PCAuthorities' Web site (**www.pcauthorities.com/drivers/device-drivers-explained**).

Several vendors provide a free scan of device drivers on a user's PC, report out-of-date drivers, and provide access to a database of updated device drivers for a paid registration. One example is Driver Guide's DriverScan (**www.driverguidetoolkit.com**).

Vendor manuals are a good source of specific information about how to install an operating system. However, the process has been highly automated in recent releases, so little printed documentation may be available. User manuals may be included on distribution CDs, or on a vendor Web site. Trade publications also cover how to install and configure popular operating systems.

ON THE WEB

To view the steps Microsoft recommends to install Windows Vista, visit **support.microsoft.com/kb/918884**.

To learn about installing Linux operating systems, visit **www.linux.org/docs/beginner/install.html**.

Network Installation

Network connectivity is implemented with a combination of hardware, software, and operating procedures. The role of a support specialist in network installation is primarily concerned with the client or user workstation components. A support specialist may perform tasks such as:

- Install client software

- Configure network connectivity

- Perform network administrative tasks:

    - Administer user accounts (login IDs and passwords)

    - Grant rights to access network resources such as application software, disk space, peripheral devices, and shared printers

    - Perform periodic server media backups

    - Monitor network performance

    - Monitor network security

    - Report problems to the network support staff

In situations where a support staff has primary network installation and configuration responsibility, such as in a small organization, a network vendor or consultant often provides assistance with network server installation and configuration details.

Figure 9-8 is a checklist installers can use as a starting point when installing an operating system and network connection.

**Operating System and
Network Installation Checklist**

PRELIMINARY STEPS (as necessary)

☐ Make backup copy of existing operating system (if applicable)

☐ Make backup copy of any user data files (if applicable)

☐ Run FDISK to partition hard drive (if necessary)

BASIC INSTALLATION

☐ Install operating system software

☐ Install device drivers required by peripherals

☐ Configure operating system and startup files (consistent with organization standards)

☐ Modify startup and configuration files

OPTIONAL INSTALLATION

☐ Install and configure antivirus, media backup, utilities, security software, and screen savers

DIAL-UP NETWORK INSTALLATION

☐ Verify that modem hardware is operational

☐ Configure dial-up networking client and communication protocols

☐ Test dial-up network connectivity

NETWORK CLIENT INSTALLATION

☐ Verify that network hardware connection is operational

☐ Install client software on workstation

☐ Modify startup files to connect to network

☐ Log on to network server

☐ Download any additional required network software

☐ Configure client software

☐ Test network connectivity

NETWORK ADMINISTRATION

☐ Create the user account and initial password

☐ Grant user rights to access shared network resources, such as network drives, printers, and shared folders

COMPLETE INSTALLATION

☐ Update operating system and network configuration information, node addresses, and startup file modifications in site management notebook

Figure 9-8   Operating system and network installation checklist

The steps to install and configure network software are specific to each type of network and each user's specific needs. For installation of a standalone system, the steps related to network connectivity can be skipped. A typical network installation involves many of the steps described in Figure 9-8. A network administrator often builds a disk or optical media image that contains preconfigured network client software so it can be copied easily to a computer during installation. Vendor manuals and trade books are available that describe the details of specific network client software installation.

Typical Steps to Install Application Software

Before installing an application software package, a support specialist needs to verify that the software is compatible with the hardware and network on which it will be installed. Ideally the application software's compatibility with the hardware and network should be verified before any software is purchased. Before support specialists install any software, they should determine the following:

- The CPU types the software runs on

- The amount of memory the software requires

- The amount of disk drive space the software requires for a full installation

- Whether the software is compatible with hardware peripherals

- Whether the software operates in a networked environment compatible with the user's

Software vendors usually distribute application software on **distribution media**, such as CDs or DVDs. However, application software packages are often available to download, in compressed format, from a network server or the Internet. Before any application software is downloaded from the Internet, a support specialist should consider the available connection speed. When a user has a slow dial-up connection to the Internet, a large software package (larger than a few megabytes) can sometimes be downloaded on another system that has a broadband link to the Internet. Then the software can be transported on a USB drive, optical media, or via a local area network connection to the user's computer, where it can be installed. Because application programs often automatically update registry and configuration files maintained by the operating system, application software packages should be installed directly on the computer on which they will be used. Problems can arise when an attempt is made to install a program by simply copying its image from another computer, which bypasses the steps to update the system registry with information about the program.

Whatever the distribution media, the installation steps for most application packages are generally simpler than they were several years ago. Most packages auto-install after the user double-clicks an install icon. Most computers are equipped with a CD or DVD drive that has an Autoplay feature enabled. In these cases, a system can usually recognize that media containing a software installation has been inserted in the drive, and it will automatically begin the installation process. In other cases, the My Computer tool in the Windows operating system can be used to examine the installation media for a setup.exe or install.exe program.

During the installation of some software, it is advisable to disable the security features on a PC such as anti-virus programs and firewalls that could prevent a successful installation. As a precaution, the PC can be disconnected from the Internet during the time that the security software is disabled.

Immediately before installing a new program, all open data files and programs should be closed to make sure that operational programs do not interfere with the installation process. Prior to installing a large application on a system with limited disk space, an installer may want to perform a hard disk defragmentation to ensure that an application's image will be written on contiguous disk blocks (which increases execution speed). The first step in an application software installation is often the execution of an installation utility program, such as InstallShield. The install utility guides the installer through the process and provides prompts about available user options. An example of a topic frequently covered during installations is whether the user wants a shortcut icon to run the program placed on the desktop, in the system tray, or on the quick launch toolbar.

As you saw in Figure 4-3, the most common software installation options allow a user to select from among the following choices:

- **Express installation**—Sometimes called a typical or common installation; an express installation installs the most frequently used program functions and features as determined by the manufacturer, and asks the fewest questions during installation.

- **Custom installation**—Sometimes called an expert or special installation; a custom installation lets a user select specific components or features to install. A custom installation will require an installer to answer more questions than in an express installation.

- **Minimal installation**—Sometimes called a notebook or space-saver installation; a minimal installation installs the fewest functions and features for users with little free hard drive space available.

- **Full installation**—Sometimes called a maximum or complete installation; a full installation installs all program functions and features, asks few questions, and takes the maximum amount of disk space and time.

It is a good idea to ask each end user about the type of installation required to meet his or her needs. However, users are generally not familiar with the terms *express* or *minimal* and may not understand the implications of the various installation choices. A support specialist may need to translate these options into lists of specific features for an end user (i.e., what features will and will not be available for each installation choice). Users often need specific software functions or features that are not included in a minimal installation.

Support specialists are also responsible for verifying that a user has the appropriate software licenses to permit an authorized installation. Some organizations maintain a software license database that needs to be updated as part of the installation process. Installing application software may also include installing organization-specific options, document templates, style sheets, macros, or device drivers.

After installation, a support specialist should test the software and make sure it runs properly. Figure 9-9 shows a sample checklist that installers can use to guide software installations.

Application Software Installation Checklist

PRELIMINARY STEPS
❏ Close all open applications
❏ Make backup copies of any user data files that could be affected by the installation process
INSTALLATION
❏ Install standard application software packages (such as an office suite)
　❏ Express　❏ Custom　❏ Minimal　❏ Full
❏ Install and configure e-mail and Web browser applications
❏ Install special-purpose software (such as accounting, marketing, manufacturing, or other organization-specific applications). Reboot system as needed after each installation.
❏ Install any device drivers required by application software. Reboot system as needed after each installation.
❏ Configure application software to meet the user's needs and conform to organization standards
　❏ Adaptive options: _____
❏ Create desktop shortcuts to applications or add to startup menu as appropriate
❏ Add any organization-specific templates or style sheets for word processing or spreadsheets
❏ Reboot system
❏ Test all application software
COMPLETE INSTALLATION
❏ Fill out software configuration sheets in site management notebook
❏ File software licenses in site management notebook
❏ Register software with vendor (via mail-in card or online registration)
❏ Verify that user knows how to start the application
❏ Verify that the user is satisfied with the installation and knows how to get help if needed

Figure 9-9　Application software installation checklist

420

Typical Installation Wrap-Up Tasks

The previous sections described common steps and procedures to install hardware, operating system, network, and application software. Depending on the kind of installation and on organizational policy, a support specialist (or an end user) might undertake several additional steps. These are steps in which an installer documents software settings, backs up critical files, creates rescue disks, fills out warranty and registration cards, documents installation problems, addresses ergonomic concerns, and makes sure the user will be able to operate the system effectively. Support specialists can also perform "housekeeping" tasks such as storing documentation and disposing of shipping containers. Some of these tasks can be described as facilities management or installation documentation tasks, whereas other activities involve some end-user orientation or training. Most installers think of these as "wrap-up tasks," because they are generally performed at the end of an installation.

Keep in mind that an installation doesn't end as soon as the hardware or software is installed. Support specialists who install or upgrade a system should always check with each user to make sure they can operate the new system correctly, or know where to get the training they need. Review any new equipment with users; ensure that they can start, operate, and shut it down properly. Then, alert end users to training opportunities and alternatives. Finally, verify that the end user is satisfied with the installation and that his or her questions were answered. The ultimate measure of any installation procedure is the answer to the question: "Is the user 100% satisfied?"

Figure 9-10 shows a checklist for some of these wrap-up tasks. Not every step in the checklist applies to every installation. The tasks vary depending on the type of installation and the needs of each user.

Wrap-up Checklist

HOUSEKEEPING

❏ Store or recycle shipping containers

SECURITY

❏ Make backup copies of registry, configuration, and startup files

❏ Create bootable rescue or boot disk and store in site notebook

USER ORIENTATION

❏ Check system with user for any ergonomic problems

❏ Brief user on basic system operation

    ❏ Walk through system startup procedures

    ❏ Provide network user ID and password

    ❏ Provide reference sheets to document common operating system and application software tasks

    ❏ Describe antivirus, backup, and security procedures

    ❏ Review printer operation, paper loading, and cartridge or ribbon change procedures

    ❏ Go over operating procedures for peripherals

    ❏ Walk through system shutdown procedures

❏ Brief user on:

    ❏ Organization policies regarding acceptable computer use and abuse

    ❏ Importance of not consuming food and beverages around computer equipment

    ❏ Preventive maintenance procedures

    ❏ User support and help desk contacts

❏ Discuss training needs and opportunities with user

SITE MANAGEMENT NOTEBOOK

❏ Document system configuration (configuration printouts, startup file settings) and file in site management notebook

❏ Complete warranty and registration cards or online registration procedures

❏ Document any installation problems or special configuration specifications in site management notebook

❏ Store user and system documentation in convenient place

❏ Store software distribution media, drivers and backups

COMPLETION

❏ Verify that user is satisfied with installation

Figure 9-10 Installation wrap-up checklist

Installing systems is often a smooth and relatively error- and stress-free process that serves its main purpose—to get a user's system up and running as soon as possible. Occasionally, a system installation can become frustrating for both the installer and the end user because an unexpected incompatibility or defective hardware or software can suddenly terminate an installation before it is complete. In some instances, installers may have to uninstall or reinstall components to get them to work correctly. Installers must be sure that they plan carefully for each installation, have the appropriate tools, follow step-by-step procedures, and are alert to the issues and potential problems that each installation can present. Although proper advanced planning does not guarantee a smooth and successful installation, poor planning almost always guarantees the opposite.

Ongoing Site Management Responsibilities

Even after an installer has completed all the checklists in this chapter and repacked his or her tool kit, ongoing administrative and support responsibilities continue in order to keep users productive. Those who support end users are likely to encounter user site management challenges, such as those listed in Figure 9-11.

- Media backup
- Security problems and challenges
- Disaster and contingency planning
- Other site management activities
  - Preventive maintenance
  - Computer supplies
  - Recycling computers and peripherals

Figure 9-11   Typical ongoing user site management responsibilities

In addition to procedures that back up media on a server or workstation, support specialists should encourage users to make effective use of automatic backup procedures in application software packages. Many word processor and spreadsheet programs, for example, can be configured so that the current document or worksheet is saved periodically on a local hard drive or network drive.

Media Backup

A **media backup** is produced by copying the files and folders of software and data from a PC's hard disk onto a separate medium, to preserve them in case the original data is damaged or accidentally deleted. Media backups on a network system can significantly reduce site management costs and problems. In many network environments, an administrator can schedule automated backups of server software applications and user file space. And because network servers often operate 24 hours a day, 7 days a week, media backups can be scheduled at times when the load on a system is at its lightest, such as at night or on weekends. The storage media on a server which is accessible via an office network also provides convenient storage space and a method for users to back up any data files stored on their individual hard drives. For example, a backup software utility on an individual user's system can access the server hard drive as a backup medium so that the user does not need to manually back up his or her system using magnetic or optical backup media.

Chapter 12 includes a description of media backup utility software that support specialists can use to help with this user site management responsibility.

Finally, while regular backups of important files should be made, documented procedures also should be available in the event a user needs to restore files from backup media. **File restoration** is a procedure to copy one or more files from backup media to the original or a replacement disk when data or programs have been erased or destroyed—the opposite of a file backup operation. File restorations are necessary when a hard disk drive fails or when a user accidentally deletes one or more files and needs to recover them. A support staff member may be assigned the responsibility of restoring backup files based on requests from users. The file restore procedure often involves using the same backup utility program that made the backup, only in restore mode. In all media backup situations, periodic tests of file restore operations should be conducted to verify that backup media is viable and restore procedures work as designed.

In large organizations, the file restoration procedure can pose a security problem. Users are normally permitted to restore only files that they themselves created or for which they have user rights. Users need special permission to restore a file that is owned by another user.

Security Problems and Challenges

Access security in a network environment is usually a more significant concern than on a standalone PC. Users (both authorized and unauthorized) can potentially access data and resources anywhere on a network, and sometimes from outside the network. However, network operating systems provide additional security features that are often more sophisticated and reliable than those available on a standalone PC. A network administrator plays a key role in the control of access to network facilities, because the administrator controls the user account management process.

Security problems can be classified based on the origin of the threat (internal or external) and on the kind of threat (electronic or physical):

- Electronic threats arise from attempts to breach the information or resources in a computer system.

- Physical threats arise from attempts to damage or disrupt computer facilities.

- Internal threats arise from inside an organization, including employees.

- External threats arise from outside an organization, including clients, hackers, and the public.

Electronic Threats to Security

The list of potential security problems that affect computer facilities from external sources via electronic or remote access is long and grows every year, but the most common sources of problems include:

Chapter 12 includes a description of security utilities that support specialists can use to help with this user site management challenge.

- Proliferation of virus software, including worms and viruses that overload networks and deny service to legitimate traffic

- Spam e-mail attacks on network servers and end-user computers

- Attempts by unauthorized users to gain access to or control over computers and information

- Operating system software vulnerabilities that permit unauthorized access due to bugs in distributed software

- Proliferation of malware software that spies on the habits and behavior of end users or targets users for pop-up advertisements

- Lack of secure data transmission using encryption features

To deal with threats from electronic access, useful tools such as passwords, antivirus software, Internet firewalls, utility software, callback modems, and other online security measures are common precautions in installations of every size.

Physical Threats to Security

Physical access tools are designed to reduce threats from both unauthorized access and sabotage. Computer facilities are often a target of people looking to commit theft. They are also targets of workers or the public who are disgruntled with technology or with the way they have been treated by a bureaucracy (of which computer systems are a visible symbol). To address physical threats, computer facilities that have a large investment in equipment in a central location take steps to limit physical access to their facilities. Access management tools that are used to prevent information and equipment loss include:

- Keypad entry locks

- Identification badges and ID cards that function like entry keys

- **Biometric readers** (hardware devices that can uniquely identify a user through analysis of eye patterns, hand geometry, fingerprints, or voice and signature recognition)

In very small facilities, locked doors are the primary means to control physical access to computer facilities.

- Motion sensors and heat-detection devices

- Camera systems to monitor facilities

- Reception desks

- Metal detectors

- Physical barriers (walls and windows)

ON THE WEB

In an era of identity theft, the field of biometric access controls is becoming increasingly important. To learn more about the basics of this technology, read an introduction to the topic by Bryan Feltin, *"Information Assurance Using Biometrics,"* available as a Word document at **www.giac.org/practical/Bryan_Feltin_GSEC.doc**, or view a video tutorial at **www.biometrics.dod.mil/Bio101/Default.aspx**.

ON THE WEB

Support staff who have major responsibilities for security are the target audience for two print publications that address security concerns. *SC Magazine* is available for subscription at **www.scmagazineus.com**. *CSO*, a resource for security executives, is available for subscription at **www.csoonline.com**. Both publications are available free to qualified professionals who have security responsibilities.

While many kinds of threats to computer facility security are intentional, other threats come in the form of natural disasters and accidents.

Disaster and contingency planning

Support specialists cannot prevent events such as power failures, floods, fires, storms, earthquakes, terrorist attacks, and sabotage from affecting computer services. But they can help plan to manage the consequences of unpredictable events by using risk management strategies. **Risk management** is the use of strategies and tools to reduce the threat to an organization from uncontrollable disasters or accidents and to help the organization recover from a disaster, with minimal financial impact or customer service loss.

- **Insurance**—An organization can purchase **business interruption insurance**, which helps offset the cost of returning an organization to normal operation after an unforeseen event occurs.

- **Inspections**—Organizations can obtain an **engineering inspection** to help identify the potential for damage to computer equipment

A disaster/contingency plan is effective only if workers are aware of its existence and are trained in its procedures. Support specialists responsible for disaster planning should find the most effective way to communicate these plans to workers to ensure that recovery procedures can and will be carried out.

426

and facilities due to natural disasters and accidents. An engineering inspection report may recommend that an organization modify building structures or recommend detection devices, such as fire alarms and moisture sensors.

- **Media Backups**—Media backups of important data and programs are a critical component of any disaster/contingency plan. Media backups may be stored at a separate facility from the primary work location, so that data can be replaced in the event of a major disaster such as a fire.

- **Disaster/Contingency Plans**—A disaster/contingency plan is a useful planning tool for both large and small computer installations. A **disaster/contingency plan** is a document that describes various activities that will occur if a computer facility experiences a temporary disruption of service. Disaster plans often address such events as fires, earthquakes, power outages, water damage, and sabotage. An effective plan should answer the question: "What specific steps will our organization take in the event a disaster occurs?"

ON THE WEB

Computing and Network Services at the University of Toronto has developed an outline for organizations that want to prepare a disaster recovery plan. Their guidelines, checklists, and eight-step action plan emphasize the importance of business continuity. See the guidelines at **www.utoronto.ca/security/documentation/business_continuity/dis_rec_plan.htm**.

An example of a disaster/contingency plan prepared at Adams State College is available at **www2.adams.edu/administration/computing/dr-plan100206.pdf**.

Other Site Management Activities

User support specialists who support internal workers may also be asked questions about or have responsibilities that include preventive PC maintenance, acquiring computer supplies, and recycling used computer systems and components.

Preventive Maintenance

Although most personal computer equipment is primarily electronic and does not require a great deal of preventive maintenance, some moving parts do benefit from periodic attention. **Preventive maintenance** involves using tools and procedures to reduce the likelihood of computer component failure and expensive repair costs. Preventive maintenance steps focus on cleaning and adjusting equipment to prolong its useful life and enhance operational efficiency.

System Unit

Most components inside a system unit either cannot be maintained by an end user or do not require preventive maintenance. However, in a dusty environment, the life of a PC can be increased by periodically vacuuming the inside of the case to reduce dust buildup on the components. A low intake vacuum cleaner with an antistatic plastic (not metallic) nozzle is preferable to cans of compressed air, which tend to blow dust around, rather than sweep it up. Use of a standard shop vac should be avoided. After vacuuming inside a case, compressed air can be used while the vacuum cleaner is running to remove any residual dust. The system unit case and other plastic or painted parts can be cleaned with isopropyl alcohol and a lint-free or microfiber cloth, or with pretreated wipes designed for that purpose.

Prior to removing the case on a PC for any reason, turn off the power and unplug the electrical supply as a precaution.

Disk Drives

For the most part, hard drives, CD and DVD devices, and removable drives do not include user-serviceable components; when these devices fail, they are replaced, rather than repaired. Check the manufacturer's Web site for troubleshooting options or refer problems to a qualified technician.

Printers

The biggest enemies of most printers are paper dust and ink buildup. Even printer paper that looks clean can attract and carry dust particles. A good preventive maintenance strategy for printers is to use a non-static vacuum cleaner to clean out the dust periodically. The insides of a printer should also be kept free of ink and toner spills, because these chemicals attract dust particles. Toner should be cleaned up with a vacuum designed for PC use that is equipped with a toner filter if available.

Keyboards

Vacuum a keyboard or spray it with compressed air periodically to remove dust and dirt particles from between the keys. A buildup of dust can make the keys stick or wear out the mechanism that makes contact with the membranes in the keyboard. Dirty keyboard keys can be cleaned with a lint-free cloth moistened with isopropyl alcohol.

For especially dirty keyboards, a small brush, such as a toothbrush, dipped in isopropyl alcohol can be an effective cleaner.

428

Mouse/Trackball Parts

Both the rubber ball inside an older mouse or trackball and the mouse case can become dusty and grimy with use. In order to clean the mouse, unplug it and remove the rubber ball by twisting or pushing on the plastic restrainer in the direction indicated by the arrow on the underside of the mouse. Remove the ball; clean it, the metal contacts inside the mouse cavity, and the mouse case with isopropyl alcohol and a lint-free cloth. Then reassemble the mouse and plug it in.

The case and glides on an optical (laser) mouse can also be cleaned with isopropyl alcohol and a cloth, but avoid using excess chemicals around the optical eye opening.

Display Screen

Preventive maintenance on a CRT or LCD monitor is limited primarily to external cleaning and adjustment. There are no user-serviceable parts inside a monitor.

Clean dust and smudges on a computer screen regularly with a special pretreated cloth designed for that purpose, with a microfiber cloth, or with isopropyl alcohol and a lint-free cloth.

ON THE WEB

To view a video on preventive PC maintenance, visit **reviews. cnet.com/4520-11319_7-6240575-1.html?tag=nav**.

For more information on preventive maintenance, visit **www. pcguide.com/care/pm.htm**.

Preventive maintenance can extend the useful life of many components in a PC system. Support specialists can often help users understand important maintenance steps to increase both the life expectancy of the PC and its operating efficiency.

Computer Supplies

Another user site management task that often gets assigned to support specialists is the purchase or recommendation of computer supplies. Alternately, support specialists may be asked for advice about where to find specific supplies or where to get the best prices on them. Sources of supplies range from local office supply stores to electronics specialty stores to mail-order companies to suppliers that do business primarily on the Internet.

ON THE WEB

Vendors that specialize in selling computer and office supplies on the Internet include:

Vendor	URL
Amazon.com	**www.amazon.com**
Cheap Office Supplies	**www.cheapofficesupplies.com**
Clean Sweep Supply	**www.cleansweepsupply.com/pages/category0003.html**
Global Computer	**www.globalcomputer.com**
Keysan	**www.keysan.com/indh1034.htm**
Office Depot	**www.officedepot.com**
Office Max	**www.officemax.com**
Quill Office Supplies	**www.quill.com**
Staples	**www.staples.com**

Local computer supply stores can be found in the Yellow Pages of most telephone directories under the headings *Computers – Supplies & Parts* and *Office Supplies*.

Managing the Recycling of Computers, Peripherals, and Supplies

Any organization with a turnover in computer equipment faces the challenge of how to dispose of used systems and peripherals. Most organizations practice a hand-me-down strategy, in which users who receive new computers and peripherals pass their older systems to other users; one user's obsolete computer may be another user's upgrade. In other situations, obsolete computers and peripherals may be donated to schools, religious groups, charities, or other nonprofit organizations; however, very obsolete equipment should probably be recycled.

ON THE WEB

Before a computer system is handed down or donated, the hard disk drive should be removed and destroyed, or should be erased with a special utility program, to protect the confidentiality of personal or corporate data. A free utility for this purpose is Darik's Boot and Nuke program, available at **dban.sourceforge.net**.

ON THE WEB

The EPA's Web site lists links to community and vendor programs that recycle used computer and electronic parts at **www.epa.gov/epawaste/conserve/materials/ecycling/donate.htm**.

Direct disposal of used computer equipment into a garbage landfill should be avoided, and is illegal in many areas. Some recycling organizations take processing units, monitors, and printers for the salvage value of the raw materials, such as metals, although many charge a nominal fee to dispose of electronic equipment.

In addition to computers and peripherals, some types of supplies are recyclable. Printer paper is an obvious example. Ink-jet and laser printer cartridges can be mailed to a recycler to be remanufactured and refilled. Postage-paid mailing envelopes for empty cartridges are available in many large office and computer supply stores and online; many of these retailers will also accept used ink and toner cartridges in-store.

Chapter Summary

- The basic steps for installing a computer system include site preparation, hardware installation and configuration, operating system and network installation and configuration, installation and configuration of application software, and wrap-up tasks.

- During the site preparation step, support specialists deal with several issues, including:

  - Locating the computer system and devising strategies to conserve space

  - Ergonomic concerns, including ways to adapt the computer system and work environment to maximize user comfort, productivity, safety, and health

  - Power requirements, which address the need to provide a convenient and reliable electric power supply

  - Connectivity issues, which deal with network and telephone access

- Air conditioning, which is usually not a concern for standalone personal computers, but is an issue in offices and training facilities

- Lighting problems, which are the source of several productivity and ergonomic concerns

- Fire-suppression precautions

- One of the secondary goals of the system installation process is to collect a notebook of information about the computer system. A site management notebook is a convenient way to organize information that support specialists may need in the future to operate, diagnose, troubleshoot, restore, reconfigure, upgrade, and repair a system.

- Tools needed to work with computer hardware include a variety of screwdrivers, a nut driver, pliers, a parts-picker, a pocketknife, a small parts container, a mirror, isopropyl alcohol, a lint-free cloth or foam-tipped brush, an antistatic wrist strap, cable ties, compressed air or a vacuum cleaner, a circuit tester, and a multimeter (VOM).

- Installation of hardware and related peripherals includes unpacking the system, connecting power and signal cables, installing any upgrades, and testing the system. Installing an operating system and setting up network connectivity includes installing the software and device drivers if needed, configuring various options and startup files, and installing network client software. Application software installation usually involves a choice of the kind of installation: express, custom, minimal, or full. Support specialists may also install organization-specific utilities, templates, macros, or style sheets.

- The final steps in the installation process include briefing the user on various operational aspects of the system and other activities that wrap up the installation. These steps often include updates to information in the site management notebook. The wrap-up tasks also include a transition into the user training process. The ultimate installation question is: "Is the user 100% satisfied?"

- Support specialists are often asked to manage or provide advice on other aspects of users' ongoing activities, including media backups, security threats, disaster and contingency planning, preventive PC maintenance, purchasing computer supplies, and recycling computers.

Key Terms

assistive devices—Computer peripherals and software that adapt a computer system so that users with various physical limitations can be more productive.

biometric reader—A computer hardware device that can uniquely identify a user through analysis of eye patterns, hand geometry, fingerprints, or voice and signature recognition.

business interruption insurance—A type of business insurance policy that helps offset the cost of returning an organization to normal operation after an unforeseen event, such as a natural disaster or accident.

carpal tunnel syndrome—A common form of repetitive strain injury that affects wrists and fingers.

custom installation—A software installation option that lets the installer select which components and features to install; also called an expert or special installation.

disaster/contingency plan—A document that describes various activities that will occur if a computer facility experiences a temporary disruption of service; disaster plans often address such events as fires, earthquakes, power outages, water damage, and sabotage.

distribution media—Media, such as CDs, DVDs, and Internet downloads, which contain the original copies of operating system, network, or application software.

downtime—A measure of the number of hours (per week or month) that a computer system is unavailable for use because of power failures or other problems.

engineering inspection—A study by an engineering firm to help identify the potential for damage to computer equipment and facilities due to natural disasters or accidents.

ergonomics—The study of how to design computer systems (both hardware and software) and lay out workspaces to minimize health problems and maximize worker safety, productivity, comfort, and job satisfaction.

express installation—A software installation option that installs only the most frequently used functions and features as determined by the manufacturer; also called a typical or common installation.

file restoration—A procedure to copy one or more files from backup media to the original or a replacement disk when data or programs have been erased or destroyed; the opposite of a media backup operation.

footprint—The amount of desktop space a system unit occupies; measured in square inches (length of case × width of case).

full installation—A software installation option that installs all program functions and features; usually requires the most disk space of any installation type; also called a maximum or complete installation.

media backups—The process of copying files and folders of software and data from a PC's hard disk onto a separate medium to preserve them in case the original is damaged; media backups are commonly written on magnetic disks or tapes, or on optical media.

minimal installation—A software installation option that installs the fewest functions and features possible to minimize the system resources required to run the software; also called a notebook or space-saver installation.

power conditioner—An electrical device installed between a computer and its power source; it draws in electrical power, makes sure that the frequency, voltage, and waveform are within acceptable specifications, and then outputs clean power to the computer system.

preventive maintenance—Tools and procedures used to reduce the likelihood of computer component failure and expensive repair costs; preventive maintenance steps focus on cleaning and adjusting equipment to prolong its useful life and enhance operational efficiency.

repetitive strain injury—A physical problem that results from continuous use of joints in a limited range of motion; symptoms include swelling, numbness, tingling, and stiffness of joints.

risk management—The use of strategies and tools to reduce the threat to an organization from uncontrollable disasters and to help the organization recover from a disaster, with minimal financial impact or customer service loss.

site management notebook—A binder that consolidates important information about a computer system's hardware, operating system, network, and application software configurations, and facilities management information in one location; contains information needed to upgrade, maintain, restore, diagnose, or repair the system.

surge suppressor (surge protector)—A power strip that includes a protective circuit to help prevent damage to computer equipment due to electrical power surges and spikes.

uninterruptible power supply (UPS)—An electrical device that includes power conditioning circuits and a battery backup to supply electricity during power outages of short duration.

uptime—A measure of the number of hours when a computer system is operational; compare to downtime.

Check Your Understanding

Answers to Check Your Understanding questions are found in Appendix A.

1. The purpose of a pre-installation site visit is to:

   a. anticipate possible installation problems

   b. get acquainted with the user

   c. train the user

   d. complete a wrap-up checklist

2. The length times the width of a computer case is called its
   _____.

3. True or False? A keyboard placed on a regular height office desk (30") can cause user discomfort because the angle of the user's wrists at the keyboard is unnatural.

4. The display screen connected to a computer system should be located so a user looks:

   a. up slightly

   b. straight ahead

   c. down slightly

   d. any of these positions is okay

5. _____ deals with how to design computer equipment and workspaces to minimize health problems and maximize worker safety, productivity, and job satisfaction.

6. True or False? Wrist and finger pain is usually the result of a mouse that needs maintenance.

7. True or False? Most computer hardware components function well, even if the quality of electrical power is very poor.

8. A(n) _____ is an electrical device that permits a user to power on a computer system with one switch.

9. True or False? To calculate the air conditioning requirements for computer equipment, an HVAC specialist considers the heat generated by both the computer equipment and its users.

10. Before a computer is plugged into an outlet for the first time, the outlet should be checked:

    a. by a licensed electrician

    b. with an LED tester

    c. by the local electric utility

    d. all of these

11. A light source that may flicker at the same rate as a CRT display screen is a(n):

    a. incandescent light

    b. fluorescent light

    c. LED light

    d. halogen light

12. True or False? Support specialists may need to add to or delete from site installation checklists like those in the chapter because user and support needs change over time.

13. A site management notebook is especially useful in:

    a. a home computer installation

    b. a standalone computer installed in an office

    c. multiple systems installed in an office or training facility

    d. none of these

14. An antistatic wrist strap is designed to:

    a. protect the safety of a support technician

    b. reduce the risk of damage to computer components

    c. reduce the risk of fire due to a static spark

    d. reduce the risk of shock if the computer is not unplugged

15. _____ is an industry standard that helps the Windows operating system automatically recognize the configuration and operating characteristics of many hardware devices.

16. True or False? A support specialist who installs an application software package must edit the system registry and configuration files manually before the software will operate correctly.

17. A software _____ is required to ensure that a software package can be legally installed on a system.

18. A(n) _____ tries to answer the question: "What steps will an organization take in the event an emergency occurs?"

19. Which of the following electrical devices contains a battery backup?

    a. a PC power supply

    b. a power conditioner

    c. a surge suppressor

    d. an uninterruptible power supply

20. True or false? An end user who encounters a malfunctioning CRT monitor should be encouraged by a support specialist to remove the case to check the fuse.

Discussion Questions

1. Who should perform a basic computer system installation, an end user or a support specialist? Discuss the pros and cons of each before you make a decision.

2. Do you agree or disagree with this statement? "Because they are portable, notebooks are very flexible and do not create the same ergonomic problems as desktop computers." Explain your position.

3. What kind of support specialist would need a simple, basic hardware tool kit described in this chapter? What kind of support specialist would need a more complete tool kit? Would a support specialist under any circumstances need a soldering gun?

4. Are computer ergonomics primarily an employee concern or a management concern? Explain your reasoning.

5. A user support specialist said, about end users, "I can't be responsible for users who don't back up their data files. It's their problem if they lose data due to a disk crash." Do you agree or disagree with the statement? Explain your position.

6. Which do you think poses greater problems for a network support specialist: the cables required in a wired network or the security problems associated with a wireless network? What are some common tools for dealing with each problem?

Hands-On Activities

Activity 9-1

Modify an installation checklist. Choose one of the installation checklists in this chapter. Based on your personal experience, what steps would you add to the checklist? What steps would you omit? If you have access to a machine-readable version of the checklist you selected, make the modifications you recommend.

Activity 9-2

Design an ergonomic checklist. Based on the description of ergonomic issues described in this chapter and the Web resources relating to computer ergonomics, design a checklist like the ones in this chapter that could be used by a support specialist to evaluate an end user's work area for possible ergonomic problems. Compare your checklist with your colleagues. Use their ideas to improve your checklist, or come up with a single, combined checklist that represents the group's consensus.

Activity 9-3

Perform an ergonomic analysis. Use the ergonomic design checklist you developed in Activity 9-2 to conduct an ergonomic analysis of your home, office, or school computer site. List any problems with the site you identified based on the ergonomic issues described in this chapter. As a support specialist, what recommendations would you make to address the ergonomic problems you identified? If possible, compare your findings with that of your colleagues. Write a summary of your recommendations.

Activity 9-4

Locate ergonomic products and prices. Find two mail-order or online catalogs for computer equipment or supplies, such as TigerDirect, PC Mall, PC Connection, CDW, Staples, Office Depot, or Global Computer Supplies. Look at the computer supplies sold. What products are available to address specific ergonomic problems such as those described in this chapter? Make a list of at least five examples of ergonomic products and their price ranges. Are some ergonomic products more cost-effective than others? Explain your answer.

Activity 9-5

Prepare a configuration report for a PC. Use *Belarc Advisor*, the *Sandra* utility, or the System Information Tool (msinfo32), described in this chapter, to prepare a configuration report for a PC to which you have access.

- List the major categories of information reported by the software.

- Describe any configuration information you would like to see included in the report.

- Did any of the configuration information surprise you?

- Find the hardware requirements for the next version of Windows. Highlight the configuration information on the report that indicates whether or not the PC will support the next version of Windows.

Activity 9-6

Analyze computer tool kit contents. Find a mail-order or online catalog for computer equipment or supplies (see Activity 9-4 for suggestions) that sells tool kits for working on computer hardware. How many tool kits does the supplier sell? What is the price range? Pick one of the tool kits and describe how the contents of the kit differ from the list of tools in this chapter. Write a list of the tools you would want to add to the kit and explain why you would add each tool.

Activity 9-7

Outline a site management notebook. Write a detailed table of contents for a site management notebook. Think about the best way to organize the site information so a support specialist who needs to find information about a specific system quickly can locate the information easily.

Activity 9-8

Observe a system installation. Find a facility at your organization or school where you can observe or participate in the installation of a typical system. Make a list of the installation steps you observe. Be sure to ask about steps you don't understand, and find out why they are necessary. Describe how the steps you observed differ from those listed in this chapter.

Activity 9-9

Update configuration checklists. Checklists of hardware and software configurations, such as those included in this chapter, can quickly become outdated as hardware and software technology changes. Review the hardware and software configuration checklists in this chapter. Select one of the checklists and update it based on changes in technology since the lists were created for this book; you should also incorporate your own ideas into the checklist. You can find the original versions of the checklists in this chapter on this book's Web site (**www.CUS4e.com**).

Activity 9-10

Define technical terms. The hardware and software configuration checklists in this chapter contain some technical material and product descriptions. Depending on your previous experience in the computer field, you may not have encountered some of the technical terms, product names, and specifications used in the chapter. Make a list of any technical words used in the chapter that are unfamiliar to you or that you want to know more about. Select five terms to research further. Use the Webopedia Web site at **webopedia.internet.com/Hardware** and the PC Guide Web site at **www.pcguide.com** to find definitions of the terms you'd like to know more about. Do these resources agree on the definitions?

Activity 9-11

Locate local recycling options. Use the EPA Web site at **www.epa.gov/epawaste/conserve/materials/ecycling/donate.htm** to find local recycling centers that specialize in computer and electronic components. Prepare a list that you could hand to end users who inquire about the local options. Include any agencies that may be looking for donations of used computers. Create a list of items that can be recycled as well as those than can't, along with any fees charged.

Activity 9-12

Research out-of-date device drivers. Download and install DriverScan at the Driver Guide's Web site at **www.driverguidetoolkit.com**, or a similar program. Run a scan for out-of-date drivers on a PC to which you have access. Prepare a brief report of the results of the scan. (You do not need to actually update the drivers' DriverScan identifies, unless you want to.) Compare your results with your work or school colleagues. Were their results similar to yours? Select one obsolete device driver from your report and find the vendor's Web site where a new version can be downloaded.

Activity 9-13

Work with electrical values. A formula used frequently by electricians is: watts = volts × amps. (Alternately, amps = watts/volts.) Assume an installer determines that a dedicated electrical circuit has a capacity of 15 amps and the computer and peripherals connected to the circuit are currently rated at up to 1000 watts. At best, how much spare capacity does the electrical circuit have? Would it be possible to add a printer that operates at 100 watts without overloading the circuit? Develop a simple spreadsheet to make this calculation for you.

Activity 9-14

Write a disaster/contingency plan. Review the materials in this chapter on disaster/contingency planning. Prepare a contingency plan for a typical home computer installation or another installation you have responsibility for. Your plan should:

1. Identify any important risks to the ongoing operation of the installation (how likely is each risk you identified?).

2. Describe any applicable insurance that would cover replacement costs if the installation was damaged, stolen, or destroyed.

3. Identify any security vulnerability or security devices (including detectors and alarms) that apply to the installation.

4. Describe the location of media backups (including both on-site and off-site backups), how frequently backups are created, and restoration procedures.

5. Outline the major steps necessary to get the installation operational again after any kind of disaster.

Activity 9-15

Inventory printers on a network. As a network administrator in a job with a new company, you attend a meeting in which a manager asks, "How many printers do we have in this company?" You answer that you don't know the number, but will find out. After the meeting, you discover that no one else really knows the number of printers, which models the company owns, or where they are located. Write a memo to the manager that explains how you will go about finding this information and what tools you will use. (*Based on an activity suggested by Ron Koci, Madison Area Technical College.*)

Case Projects

1. Windows Vista Installation for Brianna Mishovsky's Training Facility

Brianna Mishovsky is the training coordinator for a large national insurance company. The company has recently agreed to purchase a new software package that will substantially increase worker productivity in its Claims Processing department. The new software represents a major change for the company, and it is scheduled to come online in a month. The implementation schedule presents problems for Brianna's training group because several weeklong training sessions on the use of the new software must be scheduled to accommodate all the workers in the Claims Processing department. To meet the need for additional training classes for workers, Brianna has to install computers in a training room where none exist now.

Brianna has purchased 20 refurbished computer systems that can be used for the training activity, but they do not currently have an operating system installed (the hard drives were replaced with larger drives). Brianna learned that the new claims processing software is designed to run on Windows Vista.

You will assist Brianna with the installation of Windows Vista on the 20 training systems. Your first task is to prepare an installation procedure for installing Vista on the training machines. First, research the steps in the Windows Vista installation procedure. (If possible, go through an actual Vista installation to identify the steps in the procedure, the key decision points, and the installation options available.) Next, write a first draft of the installation procedure for the Vista installation. As you work on your draft, make a list of some questions you will need to ask Brianna to clarify how she wants Vista configured on the training machines. Brianna has asked you to make the procedure steps brief, but as complete as possible. Write a draft of the Vista installation procedure steps and prepare a list of questions for Brianna that you need answered before you can polish your draft.

2. The UPS and Downs of Electrical Power at Cascade University

Mary Ann Lacy, a training facility coordinator at Cascade University, plans to install a new network server for her training facility. Mary Ann has been advised by the electric utility that provides power to Cascade University that she probably also needs to install an uninterruptible power supply (UPS) for the server she plans to install. Mary Ann likes the idea that a UPS would help protect the university's investment in server hardware and reduce user frustration if a power outage occurs. She wants your help with the UPS part of the installation project.

The consultant at the electric utility mentioned that articles online and in computer periodicals sometimes describe UPS equipment. Many organizations that sell UPS devices for computers have Web pages that describe their products. The consultant pointed Mary Ann to an online tutorial on UPS devices at the PC911 Web site, **www.pcnineoneone.com/howto/ups1.html**. The consultant also recommended an article on UPS devices on PC Guide's Web site at

www.pcguide.com/ref/power/ext/ups, and a UPS tutorial at **www. falconups.com/pdf-04-2004/sbs_ups_tutorial.pdf**.

Mary Ann would like you to (1) learn about some of the important features to consider when purchasing and installing a UPS, and (2) write a one- to two-page summary of the issues the university needs to consider in the purchase and installation of a UPS for its new network server.

3. Utility Software to Automate System Installation Tasks

Suppose you work as a user support specialist for an engineering company, and you receive the following e-mail:

From: Ayaka

To: User Support

Date: 28-Aug-2009

Subject: Installation tasks

I am concerned about the amount of time our support group spends with system installations for new employees and the occasional errors that occur in the process when we omit a step or enter the wrong information. I would like to try to automate some of the manual system installation procedures we currently use. I am thinking, for example, about the process of installing various software packages and network client software on engineering workstations. I'd like to find a utility program that would allow us to define an installation script.

By the way, would such a utility also permit our users to write a short script to define hot keys and hot strings of text? If so, we could reduce the amount of repetitive key entry work users have to do, for example, to enter a standard phrase or paragraph into an e-mail message or a document.

Thanks very much for your help with this task.

Go to the AutoHotKey Web site at **www.autohotkey.com.** Download the program to your computer. Study the installation and configuration options for this program. Then write an installation checklist that describes how to obtain, install, and configure the program. Write your checklist so that other support specialists who work with Ayaka can follow the steps. Also provide an example of how an end user can write a short script to enter their name, department, e-mail address, and telephone number whenever they press a predefined key.

4. Installation Troubleshooting at North Jetty Manufacturing

North Jetty Manufacturing company makes windows and doors for local building contractors. Several of North Jetty's workers have received new computers in recent weeks. They need your advice about how to deal with the problems described below:

1. **Jose Fonseca, production scheduler**—the desk space for his workstation is very limited.

2. **Ralph Emerson, accounting specialist**—because of carpeting, static electricity is a problem in the office area where Ralph's computer was installed.

3. **Anna Liu, marketing database coordinator**—reports eyestrain, headaches, back strain, and sore wrists.

4. **Roberta Green, employee benefits coordinator**—has to squint at the display screen in the computer late in the afternoon because the windows in her office face west and the sun shines in.

5. **Mary Pat Schaeffer, Webmaster**—wants to minimize the number of power switches required to turn on her computer and peripherals (system unit, display screen, printer, and scanner).

6. **Lou Campanelli, shipping and receiving**—installation is in an unusually dusty shop environment.

Write a memo to Holguer Vasconez, CEO at North Jetty Manufacturing, that recommends how you would deal with each of these specific problem areas.

CHAPTER 10

Training Computer Users

In this chapter, you will learn about:

- ◎ Goals of training activities
- ◎ Steps in the training process
- ◎ How to plan a training session
- ◎ How to prepare a training session
- ◎ How to present a training module
- ◎ How to progress toward higher-quality training

Most organizations find that providing user support is expensive. As a result, many organizations try to make end users as self-reliant as possible in order to reduce the need for support activities. Every problem that end users can solve by themselves is one fewer problem the support group must resolve. Every question end users can answer on their own further reduces the burden on the support group. Ultimately, user self-reliance shrinks an organization's total support costs.

Training is one of the most effective ways to make users self-reliant. A Chinese proverb says, "Give a person a fish and you provide a meal; teach a person to fish and you provide food for life." That principle certainly applies to the relationship between an end user and a user support center: "Answer a question for a user and you have solved a problem; teach users to find their own answers and you have solved many problems."

Many support specialists who work with internal users spend a significant amount time on training-related activities. Some training occurs in formal classes, and much more occurs during one-on-one interactions. Many people who have been primarily on the receiving end of the training process are often surprised at the amount of work that goes into a successful training activity. This chapter takes you step-by-step through the training process. It describes how to plan a training session as well as how to prepare, present, and evaluate training materials. The end-of-chapter materials are designed to help you think further about the training process and give you an opportunity to plan, prepare, present, and evaluate your own training activities.

What Is Training?

Training is a teaching and learning process that aims to build skills that are immediately useful to the trainees. Sometimes the terms *training* and *education* are used interchangeably. Although training and education are related, the terms sometimes mean different things.

Education is a teaching and learning process that aims to provide conceptual understanding and long-term thinking skills. Especially in introductory courses, the goal of education is to build a basic vocabulary and understanding of general principles. In education, teachers commonly test learners' understanding by measuring their ability to explain concepts and principles. The effects of education are intended to be long lasting.

Training focuses on performing activities and building expertise that will be immediately useful. Trainers often test the success of a training session by measuring a learner's ability to perform a task. Although the results of training may be long lasting, a worker might be trained to perform a task that she or he will do only once or a few times.

People sometimes associate education with a school environment and training with an industrial or organizational environment. However, some schools, such as vocational-technical schools and community colleges, have a mission that specifically emphasizes training. Furthermore, education often occurs outside a school environment, because skills training is usually based on a firm foundation of conceptual knowledge. For example, workers need basic vocabulary and computer operating principles before they can become skilled users. The ability to troubleshoot and solve problems is often closely related to one's understanding of computers and one's facility for applying general knowledge to a specific task. Although this chapter focuses primarily on user training, it assumes that all training is based on a solid foundation of vocabulary and concepts.

ON THE WEB

Educators and trainers often use a specialized vocabulary. Donald Clark has prepared an online glossary of vocabulary used in the training field. See his Web site at **www.nwlink. com/~donclark/hrd/glossary.html**.

The Training Process

Trainers can use a four-step process to successfully teach users. The four Ps of the training process are listed in Figure 10-1. In the planning step, the trainer gathers information about the objectives of the training. In the preparation step, a trainer gathers and prepares materials and organizes them into modules. In the presentation step, a trainer presents the training modules to end users, who then help evaluate the training process in the progress step.

- Step 1. Plan the training
- Step 2. Prepare the training
- Step 3. Present the training
- Step 4. Progress toward higher-quality user training

Figure 10-1   Steps in the training process

Step 1: Plan the Training

Experienced trainers know that planning is essential to a successful training activity. Trainers must learn who the trainees will be, what the trainees need to know, what skill levels the trainees need to achieve as a result of the training, and what their current skill levels are. Once trainers have this background information, they can set learning and performance objectives.

Determine the Trainees' Backgrounds

Perhaps the most obvious detail that a trainer needs to understand is who the trainees are. Are they children, young people, adults, or seniors? Adult workers who need specific job-related training usually require different content and training techniques than younger users or schoolchildren. Workers are often highly motivated to learn new skills because they already understand the benefits of applying new technology to their jobs and careers. Adults bring their personal work experiences to a training session, which can be very useful because a trainer can build on prior experiences and use analogies and metaphors to introduce new material. For example, a trainer might point out that an unfamiliar software feature or procedure is similar to one in a program the users already know. Although not all adult workers are equally motivated, the characteristics of adult learners can often be used to good advantage in a training situation. Adults are usually better able to form generalizations based on examples, and to articulate what they do and do not understand. In addition, adult trainees are often less willing to put up with an ineffective trainer than are younger trainees.

Trainers should be aware that some trainees do not attend training voluntarily, but rather do so as a job requirement. Required attendance can affect a trainee's motivation level. In these cases, a trainer may have to spend extra time and effort to convince attendees of the training's benefits and find creative ways to engage the trainees in order to overcome their initial resistance to being there.

Determine the Trainees' Content Needs

Once a trainer knows who the trainees are, the next step is to ascertain what the trainees need to know, which may require some research. A trainer usually tries to discover the kinds of jobs or tasks users will be asked to perform, what specific skills they will need, and how expert the trainees need to be at these skills. Trainers can sometimes locate information about the job, task, or skill objectives in workers' position descriptions. In other cases, trainers must interview the workers or their supervisors (or both) to determine the training objectives. For example, a trainer who prepares a session on building Access databases may discover that the trainees really need to learn how to prepare reports based on data in existing databases. Specifically, the trainer may discover that the trainees already know how to use basic features of the Access Report Wizard, and now need an introduction to custom reports.

Determine the Skill Levels Trainees Need

After trainers define the required content, they need to determine the skill level the trainees need to obtain. To determine an appropriate target skill level, a trainer should have a basic understanding of skill levels, and how they are classified. One way to classify skill levels in education and training is:

1. Conceptual level—an ability to use basic vocabulary

2. Understanding level—an ability to explain concepts

3. Skills level—an ability to perform a basic task

4. Expertise level—an ability to perform a task effectively and efficiently

In this skill classification, the first two levels, concepts and understanding, are conceptual. A training activity often begins with vocabulary: trainees learn to use the language necessary to communicate with others about the topic. They need to know the meanings of the words others use to exchange information about a subject. Then trainees can begin to build an understanding of how things work, why things work (or don't work) the way they do, and the relationships between things. Once trainees understand new material at a conceptual level, they can build a mental model of how things work and explain it to others. Analogies are especially useful during the vocabulary and conceptual learning steps. For example, a trainer could explain that a computed field in a database is like (analogous to) a formula in a spreadsheet cell.

Once trainees have a conceptual understanding, they can move on to building skills and abilities to perform tasks. At the skill-building level (level 3 above), users learn the steps to perform a basic task. Basic tasks may take a while to learn, and trainees may not get them exactly right at first. Trainees need to develop an ability to perform a task at a basic level before they can become proficient. Then, trainees can work on building speed, accuracy, and expertise. For example, trainees with word-processing expertise not only can embed a graphic object in a document (a basic ability or skill), they can do so quickly and without prompting; they can also easily control the placement, size, and design of the result.

Based on these four levels of conceptual knowledge and skills, a trainer can define the vocabulary and level of understanding trainees need, the basic tasks trainees need to be able to perform, and how much expertise the trainees need to develop.

Determine What Trainees Already Know

Successful trainers also establish what trainees already know, so they do not waste learners' time. For adult trainees, training should begin with a brief review of how the training material fits with what they already know, in order to establish a context for the training; the training should then move quickly to new material. One way to gauge what trainees already know is to interview several workers or their supervisors about the trainees' backgrounds and current skill levels. Another strategy is to administer a short pretest to determine more precisely the trainees' baseline skill levels.

If a wide disparity in backgrounds exists among a group of trainees, a trainer runs the risk of covering introductory material too quickly for some and too slowly for others. Both novices and more advanced users may be equally dissatisfied because the training is not targeted at the level they need. When trainees have different interests or ability levels, trainers can provide background materials or arrange a special introductory session or activity before the actual training session begins to help less-experienced users feel more comfortable with the basic vocabulary and concepts. For example, prior to a training session on Microsoft Word, the trainer should make sure that trainees who participate have basic keyboarding, mouse, and Windows skills; otherwise, they will struggle with the Word training and slow down other learners with their questions.

Even with extra preparation to bring novice users up to the class level, trainers almost always find that a group of trainees has a range of skill and interest levels. Trainers must find an "average" level of instruction that addresses the needs of as many trainees as possible. Trainers handle this in different ways. Some trainers aim to teach to the average level of a class, with occasional asides to give extra explanations for those below the average as well as some more in-depth material to challenge those above the average. Other trainers target the level of instruction somewhat below the class average level; they believe a somewhat slower pace for a training session is preferable to leaving

As industry certification tests become more widespread, training session pretests that attempt to measure what a trainee already knows will become more common. Online tests are a good way to gauge what a trainee "brings to the table."

half the trainees behind with a quicker pace. Practice and experience are the best teachers in handling this classic training challenge.

When planning a training program for an audience with a wide variety of skill levels and job functions, a trainer should try to focus on materials and examples that are common to a wide group of users. For example, a session on basic word-processing skills for a divergent group of trainees (such as department heads, administrative assistants, and engineers) might focus on the skills needed to produce basic office communications such as memos or simple correspondence, rather than technical reports.

If you have an opportunity to talk with veteran trainers, ask them about their experiences with cultural differences and benefit from their observations.

Many training groups bring not only a variety of skill levels, but also a diverse range of cultural and language backgrounds. A trainer needs to recognize these situations and be sensitive to the audience's needs. For example, if some learners are nonnative English speakers, avoid idioms and jargon, and use vocabulary that is as straightforward as possible. A trainer also needs to be sensitive to cultural mores. For example, in many cultures, touching another's arm in a friendly way, as one might do to motivate a colleague or a trainee in the United States, is considered too familiar and is unacceptable behavior for a trainer. Learn to observe trainees' body language as a guide to what behaviors are acceptable to trainees.

Armed with a knowledge of who the trainees are, what they know, and what they need to know, trainers can plan a training session. At this point, trainers often find it useful to ask, "How do I effectively move the trainees from where they are now to where they need to be?"

Define the Training Objectives

In the final planning step, trainers should specify the learning and performance objectives for the training. A **learning objective** is a statement of the knowledge and skills trainees need to learn. To determine learning objectives, trainers answer the question, "What do the trainees need to learn?" For example, a learning objective for this chapter is: *Be able to explain the activities that occur during each of the main steps in the training process.*

A **performance objective** is a statement of what tasks the trainees should be able to perform at the end of a training session. To determine performance objectives, trainers answer the question, "What should trainees be able to do as a result of this training activity?" For example, a performance objective for this chapter is: *Plan and present a successful training session.*

The best performance objectives are measurable: they specify how well the trainees need to be able to perform a task. A training session on search engines, for example, might include a performance objective such as: *Use the Google search engine to locate a specific piece of information on the Web within five minutes.* Training objectives (both learning and performance objectives) should begin with an action verb, which makes them easier to evaluate later on. Avoid training objectives that begin with the words *understand* or *know*, because *understanding* and *knowing* can be difficult to measure or evaluate. Better verbs include *plan, describe, explain, perform, evaluate, analyze, repair,* or *prepare.* Be as specific as possible about the tasks learners will be able to perform after the training.

ON THE WEB

To learn more about how to design training sessions with specific performance outcomes, consult a book by Ruth Stiehl, *The Outcomes Primer: Reconstructing the College Curriculum, Third Edition* (Corvallis, Oregon: The Learning Organization, 2008). Although Stiehl's book is aimed at college instructors, the learning-centered performance outcomes she advocates are equally useful in planning technology training sessions. To learn more about Stiehl's approach, visit **www.outcomesnet.com/OUTCOMES_PRIMER/outcomes_primer.html**.

Trainers often summarize the results of the planning steps described above in a goal statement. Identify the concepts, understanding, abilities, skills objectives, and learning and performance objectives in the training plan shown in Figure 10-2.

451

Windows Vista Introduction
Training Objectives

Goal: Provide workers who are new computer users with an introduction to the Windows Vista environment.

Audience: Computer users who have little or no previous experience with Windows Vista

Prerequisites: Trainees should be able to use a keyboard and mouse, and have a basic understanding of computer vocabulary and concepts.

Methods: The training will include hands-on experience with basic Windows Vista operations to give trainees the ability to use the Windows Vista user interface. Exercises will include mouse operations; window management; and use of the Start Menu, the Search tool, and the Recycle Bin. With practice, trainees should be able to perform basic Windows Vista tasks with little help or prompting.

Learning and Performance Outcomes: At the end of the training, trainees will know enough about the Windows Vista operating system that they will be able to perform basic tasks such as the following:

- Start and shut down a PC.
- Open and close windows.
- Manipulate a mouse to right-click, left-click, and drag.
- Use navigation aids, such as the menu bar, scroll bar, and toolbar icons.
- Start an application program.
- Create, move, and delete folders and subfolders.
- Store, move, delete, and use files and the My Documents folder.
- Use a printer in the Windows environment.
- Locate and manage files and folders.
- Use the Windows Vista help system.

The session will introduce terms used frequently in the Windows Vista environment, including: desktop, window, menu, icon, shortcut, file, folder, path, dialog box, cursor, mouse buttons, and Recycle Bin. The training will not provide a complete understanding of the organization and operation of Windows Vista, but will focus on using Windows Vista to run applications as well as using Search and My Computer to manage files and storage space. Because the training session is intended to be short, it will not attempt to build skills or expertise in the use of Windows Vista beyond a basic level.

Performance Measures: Trainees should be able to define 70 percent of common terms in a simple test. Trainees should be able to demonstrate an ability to use the Start Menu to run applications as well as the ability to use My Computer and the Recycle Bin to locate and manage files.

Figure 10-2   A sample training plan for Windows Vista

Notice that the training plan is short and describes the objectives in general terms. It does not describe *how* the training will be presented (for example, self-guided tutorial, classroom demonstration, face-to-face tutorial, televised demonstration, or Web-based training) or list specific topics (for example, which "basic My Computer operations" will be covered). The details of training topics, methods, and organization occur during the second step: training preparation.

A ROLE-PLAYING SCENARIO

In Case Project 4 at the end of this chapter, Andrew Nussbaum asks you and Randy, another user support specialist, to prepare a training module for users in a company that will be converting from Office 2003 to Office 2007 in the next few weeks. Here is a transcript of an interview with Andrew conducted by Randy. If possible, have fellow students or coworkers play the parts of Andrew and Randy, and then evaluate the interview.

ANDREW: I'm pleased that you agreed to help prepare one of the training modules for the Office 2003 to 2007 conversion project.

RANDY: Well, I have some questions about the project before I get started.

ANDREW: Okay, what questions do you have?

RANDY: First, I understand the trainees need to know how to use the new ribbon menu interface in 2007. What experience with Office 2003 do these trainees have?

ANDREW: The trainees are all experienced 2003 users. We expect about 20 of them for the training session. The training does not need to cover features of Office 2007 products such as Word and Excel. What they need to know is how to find the features and functions they are familiar with in Office 2003 in the new version of Office.

RANDY: Is the purpose of this training to get them to a level where they are comfortable and productive with the Office 2007 ribbon menu?

ANDREW: No, I think that is too ambitious a goal for one training session. I think we need to introduce them to the look and feel of the new menu interface, perhaps with a brief demo of the 2007 versions of Word and Excel. Just so they know what to expect. Then, perhaps we need to do a PowerPoint slide show that says, for example, if you know what formatting option you would use in Office 2003, here is where you can find it on the ribbon menus.

RANDY: Would a handout or reference sheet for each package (Word, Excel, etc.) that they could take away from the training be useful?

ANDREW: Yes, I think that would be a great idea.

RANDY: Maybe I can find some materials online that cover the correspondence between Office 2003 menus and the Office 2007 versions. If I can find something, I could adapt it for our needs. How will we know if the training session has been successful?

ANDREW: These are all experienced Office suite users, and this is primarily a "get acquainted with 2007" session, so I don't think a hands-on test is necessary. What I would suggest is that you give them a challenge problem or two and see if they can solve it. And leave plenty of time to answer their questions, and maybe give them a short training-evaluation questionnaire to let them say whether the training session and materials met their needs.

RANDY: Okay, I'll see if we have an evaluation form we've used before that I can modify for this training session. Thanks very much for helping me get started on this assignment.

Can you think of other questions Randy should have asked Andrew in order to be able to plan and prepare a training module for the Office 2007 ribbon menu interface? At what points in the interview should Randy have probed with follow-up questions to clarify Andrew's answers? How would you evaluate the success of the interview from Randy's perspective? From Andrew's perspective?

Step 2: Prepare for the Training

During the preparation step, a trainer develops more detail about the specific topics that will be covered and how these topics will be organized in a sequence. This step also addresses the types of training methods and how the training will be accomplished.

Specify Which Topics Will Be Covered

Based on the learning and performance objectives defined in Step 1, a trainer decides next which topics to cover. Even with very clear learning and performance objectives, deciding on specific training content may not be easy.

Most trainers do not start from scratch, however. They begin by brainstorming a long list of possible topics. Usually a preliminary list comes from several sources, including a trainer's knowledge of what is important, the learning and performance objectives defined in Step 1, and topics covered by other trainers and writers. In order to reduce the cost of training preparation, trainers should review topics covered by other trainers in existing training materials for ideas on topics to include.

While trainers should never simply copy verbatim training ideas, topics, and examples from other sources, neither should trainers feel that they must start from scratch when preparing for each training session. The process of selecting specific topics from among the preliminary list is like setting priorities. When considering the list of possible topics, a trainer tries to select topics that are most useful to trainees. Consequently, the decision about what *not* to cover is just as important as the decision about what to cover. Most trainees prefer a session that devotes adequate time to fewer topics instead of a rush job that tries to cram two hours of material into one hour. Good trainers prefer to include a little less material rather than too much.

Organize the Topics

Training topics should be organized to begin with lower-level skills and progress to higher-level skills. Introduce concepts and vocabulary terms first, followed by explanations of concepts in order to enhance trainee understanding. Then focus on building basic skills and abilities. Finally, use exercises to build expertise. Following this strategy, a template for a training session might look like the following:

1. Introduce the trainer

2. Review previous topics

3. Introduce the new topic

4. Establish motivation for the new material

5. Present the new material

   - Concepts

   - Explanations

6. Perform training activities

   - Teach basic skills and abilities

   - Build skills and develop expertise

7. Summarize and review the main points

8. Describe next steps and resources

9. Obtain evaluation and feedback

In Step 4 of the training outline, a trainer establishes motivation by reviewing with the trainees why they are there and what they will be able to do by the end of the training. Establishing motivation early in a training session is important because trainees who understand the need for the training and its objectives are more likely to participate in the training activities.

Trainees remember better how to perform tasks they have heard about and executed more than once. Recall the adage, "First, tell them what you're going to tell them. Second, tell them. Third, tell them what you told them." While this advice, if taken too literally, could lead to overly repetitive training sessions, it underlines the importance of introducing (Step 3 above), presenting (Steps 5 and 6), and summarizing (Step 7) the training material.

Step 8 in the outline, in which a trainer describes the where to go from here, is an opportunity to point out additional information and resources, to recommend other training opportunities that logically build on this one, or to suggest how to build additional expertise, if that is a user's goal.

Select an Effective Training Format

Training occurs in a variety of formats, depending on the type of training, its objectives, the needs of the trainees, and the available facilities. Each format has advantages and disadvantages. The most common training formats are:

- Classes (15–25 trainees)
- Small groups (12 or fewer trainees)
- One-to-one training
- Self-guided tutorials

Classes

Classroom training is usually more cost effective than other formats because the ratio of trainees to trainers is high. A single trainer can instruct a large group of trainees, sometimes in a special training facility that includes a computer projection system, an overhead projector, audiovisual equipment, and possibly computer workstations for hands-on activities. Classroom training can also take advantage of the **social learning** that takes place during interactions among trainees.

What is an ideal training class size? No one class size is appropriate for every situation. Some introductory materials, vocabulary, concepts, demonstrations, and explanations can be presented in very large training groups. However, training that includes a substantial hands-on component, especially training designed to teach basic skills, should take place in sessions no larger than 15 to 25 trainees. Large classes do not permit individual instructor attention when trainees need assistance. If a training session will exceed 25 trainees, try to arrange for additional trainers or experienced users to mingle among trainees to assist when help is needed. Another factor that influences the class size that a trainer can reasonably handle is the skill level of the trainees: more highly skilled trainees usually require less individual attention than beginners.

Some trainees don't perform as well in large training group settings, however, because they are uncomfortable asking questions or asking for help in a large group. Furthermore, if a trainer stops to help a couple of trainees, the rest of the trainees may be left idle. If some trainees learn at a slower pace than others, they are either left behind or they slow down the rest of the session. With practice, trainers can learn to effectively handle a large group in a classroom environment, present material at a comfortable pace for nearly everyone, and provide adequate feedback to trainees.

Small Groups

Trainees in a small group format of up to 12 trainees have an advantage over classroom sessions in that they may receive more individual assistance. Small group training also permits more interactions among trainees as well as social learning. However, the lower the number of trainees per each trainer, the higher the cost will be per trainee.

One-to-One Training

One-to-one training is the ultimate small group, which offers the most effective format for many trainees. A trainer can closely monitor a trainee's learning curve and provide help and feedback in a timely way. **On-the-job training** is a form of one-to-one training in which a work colleague or supervisor plays the role of coach and mentor to a new employee. On-the-job training ranges from informal coaching while performing a task to a more formal apprenticeship or internship relationship.

Obviously, the cost of one-to-one training is higher than other formats. Then, too, social learning among peers is rarely possible in one-to-one training. One-to-one training is a very flexible training format for both trainer and trainee. However, the advantages of informality and flexibility should not be an invitation to provide a poorly planned or executed training session.

In reality, many user support workers are always in "training mode." Many of the interactions support staff members have with end users are directly or indirectly educational. This discussion of one-to-one training focused on more formal training situations rather than the informal training opportunities that can occur every day. However, many of the principles of formal training, such as awareness of differences in learning styles, also apply to informal training situations.

Self-Guided Tutorials

Self-guided **tutorials** permit trainees to work through an interactive learning session at their own pace. Self-guided training, in which each trainee works alone without a trainer, would appear to be the most cost-effective training format because once the materials have been prepared, there is no trainer cost. Trainees can cover material at an individualized pace. However, in self-guided tutorial programs a trainee may not be able to obtain the assistance and feedback they need. Self-guided training and very large class sessions are similar training formats in this respect. If help can be provided when needed during self-guided training (a possible role for a user support center), then self-guided tutorials can be among the most effective learning and cost-effective training formats.

How Learners Learn

To select an effective training method, a trainer needs to consider how trainees learn. A **learning style** is the way an individual learns most effectively. Trainers who take into account learning style differences recognize that individual trainees perceive and process information in different ways. Not every trainee has the same learning style. Learners do not all learn in the same way or at the same pace. While trainees can learn something from almost any training method, each trainee has a preferred learning style. Some learners are self-motivated and self-reliant. Others need prodding and the structure and motivation that a formal training session can provide. Some workers learn concepts easily; others need examples to understand a concept thoroughly. Some trainees learn most effectively working alone; others benefit from working in a group.

Three common learning styles are listed below:

- **Visual learner**—A trainee who learns most effectively by seeing new material, reading about it, working through a self-guided tutorial, looking at a picture or a chart, or watching a demonstration or a video.

- **Auditory learner**—A trainee who learns most effectively by listening to someone talk through the new material.

- **Experiential learner**—A trainee who learns most effectively by performing a task (also called a kinesthetic learner).

Trainers believe that the most effective learning methods are those that are targeted at two or more of these learning styles, such as interactive, multimedia presentations.

ON THE WEB

For more information about learning styles, including descriptions of visual, auditory, and experiential learners, visit a Web site sponsored by the Canadian government at **www. jobsetc.gc.ca/pieces.jsp?category_id=325&lang=e**.

Take an online survey to learn more about your predominant learning style using a Diablo Valley College Web site at **www. metamath.com/lsweb/dvclearn.htm**, or the Paragon Learning Style Inventory (PLSI) at **www.oswego.edu/Candl/ plsi/index.html**. The PLSI relates learning styles to the Myers-Briggs MBTI personality types you learned about in Chapter 2.

Another Web resource on learning styles is **www.learning-styles-online.com**.

In general, information retention and learning performance improve with activity and repetition. Figure 10-3 shows several learning methods and how they relate to retention.

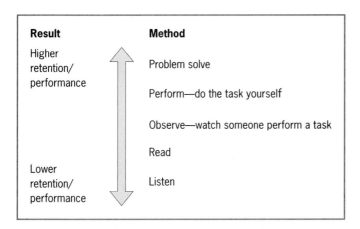

Figure 10-3   Learning methods and retention

Training methods toward the top of the continuum in Figure 10-3 increase the likelihood that information presented will be retained and that job skill performance will improve. In other words, the more that trainees are active participants in the learning process—rather than passive recipients of information—the better they will retain

 To understand the relationship between learning methods and retention, think about the different learning outcomes that would result if you simply read this book from cover to cover versus both reading each chapter and completing several of the end-of-chapter projects.

information. The continuum in Figure 10-3 is based on a popular approach to learning called Bloom's Taxonomy. Benjamin Bloom described six major categories of cognitive skills, ranging from simple to complex behaviors:

1. Knowledge—ability to remember facts or information (can describe, identify, list, or recognize data or information)
   Example: Read and quote from a help desk incident-handling database.

2. Comprehension—ability to understand meaning (can summarize, paraphrase, interpret, or explain information)
   Example: Paraphrase a help desk problem incident in an agent's own words.

3. Application—ability to use information in a new situation (can evaluate, solve, demonstrate, or apply what was learned to a problem in a work environment)
   Example: Use information in a help desk database to resolve a new and different problem incident.

4. Analysis—ability to break down information into understandable parts (can separate, contrast, troubleshoot, or draw inferences based on facts and information)
   Example: Use multiple pieces of information in a help desk database to troubleshoot a problem incident.

5. Synthesis—ability to reconstruct a new pattern or meaning from facts and data (can reorganize, categorize, integrate, or compile data into information)
   Example: Rewrite information in a help desk database to make it clearer and more understandable.

6. Evaluation—ability to judge ideas or information (can critique, interpret, select, or defend methods or procedures)
   Example: Review incidents in a help desk database to identify those that remain relevant and need to be retained and those that are obsolete and can be archived.

Based on Bloom's Taxonomy from simple to complex cognitive skills, what conclusion do you reach about the effectiveness of classroom education experiences based almost entirely on listening to lectures and reading a textbook?

ON THE WEB

To learn more about Bloom's Taxonomy of cognitive skills, see **krummefamily.org/guides/bloom.html**. The site includes links to additional Web resources and printed materials.

Learning is often a social phenomenon. The trainer-trainee relationship is a human relationship, as is the trainee-trainee relationship. Learning from peers in a group can augment the training process and is also a good way to build teamwork skills. The ability to work with a team is excellent practice for today's business world, where the size and complexity of projects often require group effort and expertise.

ON THE WEB

For more information on the benefits of peer learning, read an article by Alice Christudason at **www.cdtl.nus.edu.sg/ success/sl37.htm**.

Select Delivery Methods for the Training Materials

When a trainer decides how to present training materials, they can consider a number of alternative delivery methods. A **delivery method** is a choice among several instructional technologies, media, or approaches to presenting information. Most presentations use one or a combination of the delivery methods listed in Figure 10-4; these methods are described in more detail in the paragraphs that follow.

- Lecture method
- Reading assignments
- Online reading assignments
- Group discussion
- Visual aids
- Multimedia materials
- Handouts and reference sheets
- Product demonstrations
- Tutorials
- Hands-on activities
- Case studies
- Role playing
- Collaborative or group learning
- Computer-based training (CBT)
- Web-based training (WBT)

Figure 10-4 Commonly used training delivery methods

Lecture Method

The lecture method is a familiar way to communicate information from an instructor to a learner. It makes effective use of an instructor's time, which is one reason it remains popular in higher education. However, the learner's role is often very passive, which is why some experts question the effectiveness of this method. Lectures can often be used effectively in combination with other delivery methods to introduce topics and materials, motivate trainees, and guide trainees toward a useful learning experience.

Reading Assignments

Some trainers believe that reading is preferable to lectures because a trainee is more actively involved in the learning process. Reading a textbook, trade book, or vendor manual is probably an effective way to define vocabulary and explain concepts. However, a trainer needs to select materials carefully so that the amount of assigned reading is reasonable given the time available. Materials should be selected to match the reading ability of the trainees. Some textbook and trade book materials are written at too high a reading level for trainees to understand easily.

Trade books may cover materials thoroughly but often are not appropriate for use in training sessions. Because trade books are usually designed for professionals in a field, they are less trainee-friendly; they frequently lack such features as learning objectives, chapter summaries, glossaries, comprehension self-tests, and hands-on activities or projects that are often needed by both trainers and learners.

Vendor manuals usually seem very authoritative because product manufacturers publish them. However, vendor manuals vary considerably in quality. Some are well organized and well written; others are so poorly written that they actually hinder effective learning. Vendor manuals are often prepared as reference manuals, rather than as tutorials that guide learners through an effective step-by-step learning process.

In addition to giving trainees specific reading assignments, trainers should encourage users to access a variety of supplementary resource materials. Point trainees to high-quality supplementary materials and ensure that they know how to use them effectively.

Online Reading Assignments

An increasing number of hardware and software vendors provide online tutorials and help systems with their products. Online reading assignments can be an effective training-delivery method. Some vendors include help systems embedded in software; others provide materials on a CD or on the Web. Online materials today tend to be better designed and written than many printed vendor manuals, which are becoming scarcer as vendors try to save on production costs. Furthermore, online materials with hyperlinks are interactive so that users can search for the information they need, which promotes more effective learning. However, anyone who has spent considerable time searching a CD or the Web for information knows that not all online information is equally accessible, useful, or even accurate. Some users have difficulty reading lengthy documents online, especially if the resolution of their display screens is low. And, of course, online documents are not as portable as printed materials.

ON THE WEB

For an example of an online tutorial that also provides a print option, see Microsoft's tutorial on PowerPoint at **www. microsoft.com/education/ppt2003tutorial.mspx#EPE**.

Group Discussion

For some types of training, group discussion is an improvement over the lecture method because trainees are more actively engaged. Group discussion is most effective for sharing experiences, as in user needs assessment training, help-desk incident-handling procedures, discussing design issues in desktop publishing, or dealing with ethical issues. Beginning trainers are sometimes reluctant to use group discussion as a training method because they fear they will lose control of a training session. However, many experienced trainers have learned that group discussions are often one of the most effective approaches to training.

Visual Aids

Visual aids are a popular supplement to lectures and readings because they take advantage of the adage that "a picture is worth a thousand words." Pictures, charts, diagrams, and other images are useful training aids because most trainees tend to retain visual information better than information they have only heard or read (as noted in Figure 10-3). Visual aids should be large enough to be visible to everyone in an audience. The most effective visual aids have simple designs with judicious use of color and fonts for emphasis.

 Visual aids are an important component of many presentations. Appendix C in this book is devoted to the design of visual presentation aids.

464

ON THE WEB

For guidelines on the preparation and use of visual aids, consult a Web site developed by the U.S. Occupational Safety and Health Administration (OSHA), called "Presenting Effective Presentations with Visual Aids" at **www.osha.gov/ doc/outreachtraining/htmlfiles/traintec.html**.

Multimedia Materials

Visual aids are effective presentation tools, and multimedia materials can be even more effective learning aids. **Multimedia materials** are a combination of text, still images, animation, and sound. Each form of media can reinforce other forms to provide a powerful presentation, which increases the amount of material learned, as well as the ability to recall material at a later time. However, the cost to develop effective multimedia materials is greater than the cost of many other delivery methods. The cost may be especially prohibitive for a one-time training session, but affordable when spread over multiple sessions.

ON THE WEB

To see an example of a multimedia presentation, view a tutorial on how to build a basic Web site on the Virtual Training Company's Web site at **www.vtc.com/products/How-To-Build-A-Basic-Website-Tutorials.htm**. Or choose one of VTC's other multimedia presentations from their extensive library. Select topics in the first three modules to view a free demonstration of a multimedia approach to training.

The demonstration tutorials require QuickTime or Flash Player (either is a free download); a PC equipped with a sound card and speakers or a headset is generally required for multimedia presentations.

Handouts and Reference Sheets

Training sessions are, by their nature, generally a one-time event. When users return to their workstations, time passes, and they often forget important parts of the training. Training sessions, especially short ones, are more effective if they include printed materials users can take with them. Handouts and reference sheets should contain enough information that users can recall important facts or steps in a procedure. They should not contain extensive detail, or trainees will be less likely to use them. When a trainer prepares a handout or reference sheet, simplicity is more important than comprehensiveness.

465

ON THE WEB

For an example of a reference sheet designed for end users who already know HTML, but need a short list of available tags, go to **www.webmonkey.com/reference/HTML_Cheatsheet**.

An example of a helpful reference sheet of commands for the UNIX operating system on University of Washington computers can be found at **www.washington.edu/computing/unix/ unixqr.html**.

Product Demonstrations

Although hands-on use of an actual software or hardware product during a training session is usually desirable, lack of equipment, insufficient copies of software, inadequate training time, or other logistical problems sometimes dictate that the training include only a product demonstration. LCD or DLP projectors, which feature liquid crystal display (LCD) or digital light processing (DLP) projection technology, have improved so dramatically that even a large group of 50 to 75 trainees can effectively "look over the shoulder" of a trainer demonstrating an operating system or application software package. The cost of many LCD and DLP projectors has dropped from $6000–$8000 to $2000–$3000 in recent years, and many basic models are available for $500–$1000, so these units are more affordable for training facilities even in small organizations.

ON THE WEB

To learn more about the role of LCD and DLP projectors in product demonstrations and other training activities, visit the portable projector buyer's guide at the Projector Central Web site, **www.projectorcentral.com/buyers_guide.cfm**.

A demonstration of a computer product should be carefully paced. A trainer must not overwhelm trainees by going so fast that the audience cannot follow or understand the material. The pace of a demonstration is especially important in a GUI (graphical user interface) environment, in which a trainer can point and click so rapidly that trainees may be unable to follow the sequence of steps in a procedure. Experienced trainers learn to pause between mouse clicks to give each trainee's eyes and brain an opportunity to assimilate the procedure. They talk through a procedure to add verbal explanations to the visual display and give adequate time for each trainee to absorb the sequence of steps.

Tutorials

Tutorials are one of the most effective ways for computer users to learn how to perform basic tasks. Tutorials are most effective for trainees who are self-motivated. Trainees who lack motivation to learn new materials often benefit from more structured training methods, such as classroom lectures or group activities.

In some tutorials, trainees use the actual hardware or software products they are learning about as they step through the tutorial. Other onscreen tutorials merely simulate hardware or software products. In either case, trainees have an opportunity to learn new materials in an environment that is very close to the one they will use when the training is completed.

ON THE WEB

For an example of an online tutorial, view a Purdue University tutorial titled "Evaluating Internet Sources & Sites" at **www.lib. purdue.edu/ugrl/staff/sharkey/interneteval**. Note the overall organization of the tutorial, the effective use of hypertext links, and the table of contents feature for experienced users.

Many trainees like the self-guided nature of tutorials as well as the opportunity to repeat difficult lessons or take a refresher course. Although the cost to develop an effective tutorial is very high, once it is developed, hundreds or thousands of users can benefit from it at little additional cost per user.

Hands-On Activities

Because task performance leads to skill development and better information retention, hands-on activities are an especially effective delivery method for many kinds of computer training. Hands-on activities (sometimes called lab exercises) and practice projects let trainees try out what they have learned, build skills and expertise, and learn to become independent users. Well-designed activities can be a significant step toward user self-reliance.

Hands-on activities and projects should begin with easier tasks and gradually progress to more difficult ones so that trainees can experience initial success before trying more complex tasks and projects. Trainees should receive immediate feedback during hands-on activities, because unlearning a skill is difficult, even if it's an incorrect or counterproductive way to perform a task. For example, many new users meticulously tap the arrow keys to move the cursor across an entire line of text to the end when a single keystroke or mouse click would accomplish the same result.

Case Studies

Larger hands-on or teamwork projects, sometimes called case studies, are designed to encourage trainees to make the transition from the artificial environment of the training room to the realities of the business world. Usually based on real business situations, case studies are a popular teaching method in higher education because they simulate the kinds of experiences learners will encounter on the job. Case studies are usually more involved than a simple step-by-step, hands-on activity or a small project and require trainees to apply and integrate the skills they have learned. The Case Projects at the end of the chapters in this book are examples of this integrative method of skill building.

ON THE WEB

The case study method was originally developed at Harvard Business School, and is now widely used in higher education. To learn more about the goals of the case study method and how to benefit from them, visit **www.uiweb.uidaho.edu/ag/agecon/391/casestudmeth.html**.

Role Playing

A common teaching strategy for effective communication and customer service skills is **role playing**, in which trainees participate in a rehearsal of a work environment situation. Role playing permits trainees to try out their skills in a situation in which trainees can at various times take the roles of trainer, trainee, client, support provider,

The role-playing scenarios in each chapter of this book are designed to give readers an opportunity to experience role playing as a learning method.

project leader, or project team member. Although a role-playing situation might be artificial, it can allow trainees to build skills and experience some of the emotions of a particular situation before confronting something similar in their work environment. Some people love role-playing activities; others are less comfortable participating. The latter group may benefit from being an observer at first, and participating by giving feedback to others in the role-playing activity. Role playing can be an effective way to build actual experience with skills required as a support agent and as a trainer.

ON THE WEB

For a description of some benefits and tips for role-playing activities, see **www.businessballs.com/roleplayinggames.htm**.

Collaborative or Group Learning

Collaborative learning is learning that occurs in a group. Collaborative (or cooperative) learning activities may include group discussions, hands-on activities for work teams, group problem solving, role playing, or participation in a joint case study team. Once called group learning, collaborative learning is based on the experience that learning is often a social activity and that trainees can learn a great deal from other trainees independent of the trainer. Collaborative learning challenges obsolete learning models that say all useful information must flow from a trainer to trainees. The roles of trainer and trainee blur in a collaborative environment. In many collaborative learning environments, the trainer is a facilitator who can also be a learner in a joint learning experience.

ON THE WEB

A Web site devoted to collaborative learning is hosted by the University of Wisconsin-Madison at **www.wcer.wisc.edu/ archive/CL1/CL/doingcl/DCL1.asp**. The site includes descriptions and examples of collaborative learning activities, such as "Think – Pair – Share."

Computer-Based Training

A growth industry in the technical training field is computer-based training. **Computer-based training (CBT)** includes tutorials, multimedia presentations, product demonstrations, and hands-on activities that use a computer as an automated training system. Some CBT systems provide features that handle administrative tasks, such as registering trainees, controlling access to course materials, presenting information, assessing trainee learning, and monitoring trainee progress. Most CBT products today are distributed on CDs, but older systems used audiocassettes and videotapes as delivery media. CBT training can be cost effective for large groups, but high-quality, instructionally sound CBT materials are usually very expensive to develop. Existing CBT products vary considerably in quality from very poor to excellent. An important role for trainers is to help evaluate the suitability, quality, and effectiveness of CBT materials. Because trainees can learn at their own pace and repeat difficult material, CBT is an increasingly popular delivery method among trainees.

Web-Based Training

A recent development in automated training systems is use of the Web as a delivery vehicle. **Web-based training (WBT)** is very similar to computer-based training, except that the Internet replaces CDs or videotapes as the delivery medium. Because the development cost can be spread over many trainees, WBT allows low-cost training modules to be readily available anywhere in the world. Web-based materials are also easier to update when changes need to be made, and because the delivery vehicle is a browser, WBT presents fewer compatibility issues across hardware and operating system platforms. Unfortunately, quality control is sometimes missing in the development of Web-based materials. User support staff members who are responsible for providing training should preview and evaluate prospective WBT training modules for quality, relevance, and cost-effectiveness. Many education and training institutions use WBT to deliver distance learning in an effective way.

ON THE WEB

To experience an example of a WBT training lesson, try one of the sample lessons available on the DigitalThink Web site at **www.digitalthink.com/els/samplers.html**.

Does the popularity of self-guided training materials such as online tutorials, computer-based training, and Web-based training mean human trainers are obsolete? Will human trainers eventually be replaced by computer technology? Probably not. Although a delivery system revolution is currently under way in the training industry, the trainer's role will likely not disappear. Trainers can contribute their wealth of experience in ways that self-guided training materials cannot. And trainers add a social element so important in collaborative learning. In many organizations, training continues to be a responsibility of the user support group, even though the popularity of various training delivery methods changes over time. However, the training role will surely change. In the future, trainers will likely spend relatively more of their time to:

- Assess the training needs of workers

- Plan and design training programs

- Evaluate and recommend training materials from among those already available

- Motivate trainees

- Help trainees make transitions between modules

- Assess training performance and effectiveness

- Assist trainees when individual attention is needed

These are not tasks that automated CBT or WBT delivery systems can perform very well, if at all. Future trainers are less likely to develop and present training materials, except where specialized materials are needed for small training audiences. The mass market for user training will undoubtedly be satisfied in part by automated training delivery systems.

ON THE WEB

For another perspective on trends in training and worker development, read the article "Trends in Training and Development" by Sandy Dutkowsky at **careers. stateuniversity.com/pages/852/Trends-in-Training-Development.html**.

Develop Specific Training Materials

Most trainers do not prepare lectures, reading materials, demonstrations, tutorials, and other materials from scratch for every training session they develop. Successful trainers rely heavily on existing material in vendor manuals, trade books, industry training packages, and other resources. Why reinvent the wheel if good ideas are already available? Examples of successful training materials used elsewhere can provide a good starting point as trainers develop their own materials. However, trainers should respect copyrighted material and avoid copying verbatim from a single source. Successful trainers also try to relate the training topics to the trainees' specific interests, and develop examples that trainees are likely to encounter in their own work. Imagine, for instance, the differences in examples that could be used to teach Web search engine basics to a group of accountants versus a group of product design engineers.

 Use Web searches to locate examples of training materials that can be tailored to meet the specific needs of a group of trainees. For example, to locate introductory materials for training on Excel 2007, enter a keyword search such as: "introduction tutorial guide excel 2007."

471

Design Training Evaluation Methods

The final task in training preparation is **assessment**, which measures whether the training activities have met the intended learning and performance goals. Trainers should plan two separate assessment activities during the preparation: trainee assessment and trainer assessment.

Trainee assessment provides feedback to the trainees on how well they met the learning objectives. Feedback can be in the form of a test or quiz that covers concepts and vocabulary. Trainee feedback can also include hand-on activities, exercises, or projects that use a computer to perform a task that measures mastery of the performance objectives.

Trainer assessment is feedback to the trainer on his or her instruction. Trainees' performance on quizzes, tests, and hands-on activities also provides feedback to the trainer. If trainees don't do very well on the tests and hands-on activities, however, does that say more about the performance of the trainee or the trainer? Test results actually provide feedback to both trainees and trainers. Trainers should analyze the results of tests, quizzes, hands-on activities, and exercises to see where trainees succeeded and where they didn't. Armed with that knowledge, trainers can adjust training modules to improve the results of future training activities.

Trainer evaluation forms are another way for trainers to obtain feedback on their performance. Evaluation forms provide an opportunity for trainees to comment on the strengths and areas that need improvement in the training session. Figure 10-5 shows a sample training evaluation form that can be filled out by both the trainee and the trainer (as a kind of self-evaluation).

Training Evaluation

☐ Trainer: _____   ☐ Trainee: _____

Place a check mark (✓) in the column that represents your reaction to each statement.

	Agree	Somewhat Agree	Somewhat Disagree	Disagree	Does Not Apply
1. The objectives of the training were clear.					
2. Terms used in the training were defined.					
3. The training was organized in a step-by-step approach.					
4. The training included useful examples.					
5. The trainer made effective use of time, and the pace was about right.					
6. Training aids were useful.					
7. Overall, the training was done well.					

What was the best part of the training?

What could be improved?

Figure 10-5 A sample training evaluation form

A common practice is to assign weights of 5 points for "Agree," 4 points for "Somewhat Agree," and so on, and then calculate an average score for a trainer for each item on the Training Evaluation form in Figure 10-5. To analyze feedback on evaluation forms, trainers should look for patterns of responses instead of occasional very high or low scores. Although trainees may not agree in their responses to all questions, look for items that receive lower ratings from many trainees. Trainers should pay particular attention to these items, because they identify the most obvious ways to improve the training activity. Some trainers dislike trainee evaluations because they feel that trainees are not qualified to evaluate trainers. However, most trainers consider trainee evaluations an important source of feedback. Professional trainers or support staff who do a lot of training also rely on peer evaluations from other experienced trainers or work colleagues to identify problem areas and make constructive suggestions for improving their performance as a trainer.

Training evaluation is a useful tool to help trainers constantly improve their skills at planning, preparing, and presenting training sessions. An evaluation strategy should be designed during the training preparation phase.

Step 3: Present the Training

The training presentation should follow the structure the trainer planned during Step 2. If a trainer has done a good job in the planning and preparation steps, the actual presentation of the training is likely to be effective and satisfying to both the trainer and the trainees. Figure 10-6 lists the top 10 training presentation guidelines that you should observe in your role as a trainer. These guidelines are described in the paragraphs below.

1. Practice the presentation
2. Arrive early to check out the facility
3. Don't read notes and PowerPoint slides verbatim
4. Don't try to cover too much material
5. Teach the most important skills
6. Use humor sparingly
7. Pause for comprehension checks
8. Monitor the training environment
9. Provide frequent breaks
10. Obtain professional feedback

Figure 10-6   Training presentation guidelines

Practice the Presentation

Most trainers find it helps to practice a training session with one or more colleagues to evaluate materials and identify problem areas prior to the actual training session. Some trainers call this practice session a **beta test run**, a term borrowed from software beta tests, in which companies distribute prereleases of their software to potential users and ask them to note any problems they find as they work. A training beta test gives a trainer feedback from a neutral perspective. With a beta test run, you learn how the materials work, whether the topics can be delivered in the allotted time, if transitions between topics are smooth, and whether overhead slides, PowerPoint slides, and handouts are effective.

474

Arrive Early to Check Out the Facility

If you are presenting a training session at an unfamiliar site, find out in advance who the facilities manager is and how that person can be contacted in case of problems.

A trainer should arrive at the training facility early enough to check out the physical environment. Experienced trainers always do a dry run to make sure their equipment works (including trainer and trainee computers, projection and overhead equipment, lights, sound, and other aspects of the training environment). Make sure participants can see you and your materials from everywhere in the room. You may need to reconfigure the room setup, such as the table and chair layout or the equipment location, so that it meets your needs and is more comfortable for trainees.

Don't Read Notes or PowerPoint Slides

If you have prepared detailed notes to use during the training, avoid reading them or reciting lengthy materials from memory. Have a general familiarity with what you want to say and use your own words to present the material in a conversational manner. Most successful trainers find that using an outline is more effective than writing out or memorizing what they want to cover. Reading material on an overhead or PointPoint slide verbatim is an insult to the intelligence of the audience and one of the fastest ways to put trainees to sleep. The admonition against reading slides verbatim has even earned its own reproach among trainers: "Death by PowerPoint."

Don't Try to Cover Too Much Material

One strategy successful trainers use is to prioritize topics and examples prior to a training session. With a clear understanding of the priority of topics, a trainer can quickly cut less important material if necessary due to time constraints.

Trainers who have too much material for the allotted time should eliminate some less important topics and cover the rest thoroughly. When a trainer tries to review or cover too much material, they often rush through it, which results in training that is not well paced; this can make it difficult for trainees to keep up. Similarly, don't let trainees' questions force you too far from the planned material. Although trainee questions should be answered immediately if possible, experienced trainers make notes of user questions that aren't directly relevant and answer them, if time is available, at the end of the presentation, or they give pointers to places where trainees can find more information themselves.

Teach the Most Important Skills

When trainers know a piece of hardware or a software package thoroughly, they are sometimes tempted to augment the training with **bells and whistles,** or features of hardware or software that may be interesting but that are not frequently used, especially by beginning users. Bells and whistles might impress the audience, but they often distract from the primary training objectives. They may even confuse new users who are struggling to understand what is important among all the new material with which they are presented. Remember to focus on the needs of the learners, not on the trainer's ego.

Use Humor Sparingly

Humor during a training session can make the session more enjoyable for trainees, but trainers should be careful about the amount and type of humor they use. The best humor is self-directed because it shows trainees you are human. Ridicule, which is humor directed at someone else, is never acceptable. Avoid making negative comments about vendor products, even in jest. If you are a naturally humorous person, you may need to rein in your talent and recognize the important difference between training and entertainment. Some trainers, mindful that the trainees will evaluate them, cross the line between training and entertainment. Use humor effectively, but recognize that the tradeoff between short-term entertainment and long-term training results should err on the side of training.

Pause for Comprehension Checks

During a presentation, pause periodically to gauge whether trainees are following the material. Many trainers plan in advance to break at predetermined points for a few "quick check" questions. Use a variety of question styles, including direct questions about the material that has been covered (such as, "What keys would I press to select this text?"), open-ended questions (such as, "What is the fastest way to locate a file using Windows Explorer?"), or group questions (such as, "Get together with your group and take five minutes to list what you think are the most useful features of the grammar checker."). Periodic comprehension questions will help keep trainees alert and involved because they know they might be called on to discuss what was covered.

Monitor the Training Environment

A trainer should always keep an eye on the training environment to make sure that users are comfortable and focused on the training. Is the room temperature too hot or too cold? Is the room too noisy

A corollary to teaching the most important skills is to teach a single way to accomplish a task. For example, if a task can be accomplished with a keyboard shortcut, a menu option, a function key, and a toolbar icon, trainees rarely need to be shown every possible method. Trainees will be less confused if a trainer demonstrates and sticks to one method.

because a door or window is open? Learn to read your audience. Watch for signs that tell you whether trainees are uncomfortable or interested, bored or attentive. Successful trainers often check their perception with the trainees: "It seems like a lot of noise is coming from the hallway. Can you all hear the presentation?" or, "Can those in the last row see the screen?"

Provide Frequent Breaks

In a lengthy session, recognize that trainees can become tired, which can affect their concentration. Plan the training to include frequent breaks. Trainers usually find that more frequent short stretch breaks are preferable to a few long breaks. A good guideline is to schedule a break after about 45 minutes, and every 30 to 45 minutes thereafter.

Obtain Professional Feedback

After a new trainer gets some initial experience with the training process, a professional evaluation from other trainers is often helpful. Colleagues can frequently spot even very small mannerisms that may be distracting to trainees. Another excellent training improvement tool is to videotape a training session. Although a videotape of your own training session can be difficult to watch, all trainers can learn something from the experience that will improve their training proficiency.

For more information on presenting successful training sessions, see Stephani Gerberding's book, *The Accidental Technology Trainer* (Medford, NJ: Information Today, 2007). Or see Terrance Keys's book, *How to be a Successful Technical Trainer: Core Skills for Instructor Certification* (McGraw-Hill Osborne Media, 2000), which is geared to CompTIA's Certified Technical Trainer certification exam.

Step 4: Progress Toward Higher-Quality User Training

The final step in the approach to user training described in this chapter is perhaps the most important. After each training session, a trainer should review the feedback and evaluate his or her performance. Trainers can then modify their presentation style or training materials if necessary to correct any problem areas they identify. Professional trainers and especially user support staff who do occasional training sessions are always on the lookout for ways to continually progress toward providing higher-quality user training.

Inputs to a trainer's efforts to improve training quality include: the results of training beta tests with colleagues as trainees; the results of performance tests of trainees; feedback on the training session from trainees; the observations of colleagues who observe a training session; and evaluation of videotape recordings of training sessions. Each of these tools provides useful information to a trainer who wants to improve the quality of their training sessions. For example, an analysis of which questions on a quiz or which steps in a hands-on exercise caused trainees the most difficulty can point to needed revisions in the training materials for subsequent training sessions. Or perhaps the real problem is that some test questions or exercises aren't very good measures of trainee performance. In either case, a trainer should look for clues that modifications to the training materials need to be made.

Another aspect of training materials that should be evaluated whenever a training session will be repeated is the currency of technical materials. Because hardware, software, networks, and operational procedures change frequently, technical details and training materials that were prepared just a few weeks or months ago may be out of date today. Don't assume that the screens, icons, keyboard shortcuts, and program features that worked in version 2 of a software package will work the same in version 3. Review all topics, procedures, slides, demonstrations, handouts, reference sheets, and other training materials prior to the next presentation.

ON THE WEB

Trainers and support specialists who are interested in improving the quality of their training should take advantage of the many useful training resources on the Web. To get started, review the training resources listed in Table 10-1. While not all resources are specifically targeted at technology training, all are useful resources for those who want pointers to improve their training courses as well as their performance as a trainer. Many of these sites have links to other resources.

Resource	URL
ItrainOnline's *Topic-Specific Resources for Trainers*	**www.itrainonline.org/itrainonline/english/ trainers_topics.shtml**
The United States Navy's *Train the Trainer Guide*	**www.au.af.mil/au/awc/awcgate/edref/ traingde.htm**
IntraHealth International's *Learning for Performance* (a health-oriented Web site with some useful down-loadable resources)	**www.intrahealth.org/lfp/tools.html**
British Columbia Public Service Agency's *Facilitator's Train-the-Trainer Handbook*	**www.bcpublicservice.ca/learning/ sotellme/ttt/tttintro.htm**
The Bob Pike Group's collection of training articles	**www.bobpikegroup.com/articles. asp?columnid=2746**
I-Tech's *Training Toolkit* developed by the Universities of Washington and California for HIV/AIDS trainers in the Caribbean (includes useful checklist and resource downloads)	**www.go2itech.org/HTML/TT06/ toolkit.html**

Table 10-1   Training resources

In addition to the training tools described in this chapter, trainers who have primary responsibility for a training program in a large organization may want to investigate a learning management system. A **learning management system** (LMS) is a software tool that automates many tasks associated with running a training program. Learning management systems feature:

- Authoring tools (especially for Web-based interactive multimedia training sessions)

- Training session management, including facilities, equipment, and trainee scheduling

- Trainer access to libraries of instructional and reference materials and media

- Trainee testing and exam management

- Trainee progress tracking and record keeping, including skills and certification databases

Learning management systems are usually not appropriate for an organization that conducts only occasional, small training sessions. They are targeted at organizations that make a substantial ongoing commitment to worker training and career development, and need help with program administrative and instructional tasks.

ON THE WEB

To learn more about learning management systems, read a white paper on open source LMS software at **www.epic. co.uk/content/news/oct_07/whitepaper.pdf**. The paper discusses the features of learning management systems, including Moodle (**moodle.org**), which is a popular system in many universities and community colleges.

Finally, remember that the goal of all training is to meet users' needs and help them become more self-reliant, which reduces an organization's overall user support costs.

Chapter Summary

- Training is an important part of user support, because it makes users more self-reliant. A well-trained user is more productive and less likely to need support services than one who has not been adequately trained. Training must be based on a solid foundation of vocabulary and concepts.

- The training process is a four-step approach:

  - **Step 1. Planning**—This step identifies who the trainees are, what they need to know or be able to do as a result of the training, the background of the trainees, the level of skills the trainees need to obtain, and the specific learning or performance objectives for the training. Plans should address several levels of training skills, including concepts (vocabulary), understanding (explanatory ability), skills (basic task performance), and expertise (highly skilled performance).

  - **Step 2. Preparation**—Preparation for training answers questions such as: Which specific topics will be covered and how will they be organized? What training format will be most effective (classroom, small group, one-to-one, or self-guided)? How will the training be delivered (alternatives include lectures, readings, discussion, visual aids and media, handouts, demonstrations, tutorials, hands-on activities, case studies, role playing, group learning, and automated learning systems like CBT and WBT)? How will the trainee and the trainer be evaluated?

- **Step 3. Presentation**—A successful training presentation depends on adequate planning and preparation. Ten guidelines are included in the chapter to help new trainers make more effective presentations.

- **Step 4. Progress**—Evaluation of training sessions is an important way trainers improve their skills as trainers and continually progress toward providing higher-quality presentations.

- Organizations that operate an extensive training program for end users often invest in a learning management system to automate many instructional and administrative tasks.

Key Terms

assessment—Process that measures whether training activities have met the intended learning goals; two common assessment activities are trainee assessment and trainer assessment.

auditory learner—A trainee who learns most effectively by listening to someone talk through new material.

bells and whistles—Features of hardware or software that may be interesting to include in training materials but that are not used frequently, especially by beginning users.

beta test run—A practice training session to evaluate materials and identify problems; a dry run without an audience.

collaborative learning—Learning that occurs in a group; can include group discussions, collective hands-on activities, group problem solving, role playing, or participation in a joint case study team.

computer-based training (CBT)—An automated training system in which learners use a computer system; includes tutorials, multimedia presentations, product demonstrations, and hands-on activities.

delivery method—An instructional technology, media, or approach to presenting information or training materials, such as a lecture, group discussion, hands-on activity, or computer-based tutorial.

education—A teaching and learning process that aims to provide conceptual understanding and long-term thinking skills; the goal is to provide basic vocabulary and understanding of general principles.

experiential learner—A trainee who learns most effectively by performing a task (also called a kinesthetic learner).

learning objective—A statement of the knowledge or a skill trainees need to learn.

learning management system (LMS)—A software tool that automates many tasks associated with running a training program.

learning style—The way an individual learns most effectively.

multimedia material—A combination of text, still images, animation, and sound used as part of a presentation.

on-the-job training—A type of one-to-one training in which a work colleague or supervisor plays the role of coach and mentor to a new employee; may include informal coaching or a more formal apprenticeship or internship.

performance objective—A statement of a task trainees should be able to perform at the end of a training activity; objectives should be measurable, and usually start with an action verb, such as *plan, change, describe, explain, perform, evaluate, analyze, repair,* or *prepare*.

role playing—A training delivery method in which trainees participate in a rehearsal or practice of a simulated work environment situation by taking the roles of users, support staff, trainers, and trainees.

social learning—Knowledge or job skills that are learned during interactions among trainees in a classroom or collaborative learning environment.

training—A teaching and learning process that aims to build skills that are immediately useful to trainees; focuses on performing tasks and building expertise; can be short term and is often tested by measuring a learner's ability to perform specific tasks.

tutorial—An interactive learning technique in which a trainee works through learning tasks step-by-step, usually at their own pace.

visual learner—A trainee who learns most effectively by seeing new material, by reading it, working through a self-guided tutorial, looking at a picture or a chart, or watching a demonstration or video.

Web-based training (WBT)—A form of computer-based training in which the Web replaces CDs or videotapes as the delivery medium; highly interactive and available wherever Internet access is available.

Check Your Understanding

Answers to Check Your Understanding questions are found in Appendix A.

1. True or False? A goal of end-user training is to make users as self-reliant as possible in order to reduce their need for support.

2. True or False? Training is a teaching and learning process that aims to provide conceptual understanding and long-term thinking skills.

3. _____ is a skill level in which a trainee has gone beyond basic skills to be able to perform a task effectively and efficiently.

4. Which one of the following is not a step in the training process described in this chapter?

    a. plan

    b. present

    c. perform

    d. progress

5. True or False? The best performance objectives for a training session specify how well a trainee needs to be able to perform a task.

6. True or False? Experienced trainers agree that most trainees learn best by watching a demonstration.

7. Which of the following skill levels deals with performing a task effectively and efficiently?

    a. concepts and understanding

    b. basic skills

    c. expertise

    d. all of these

8. In the classification of skill levels listed below, what is the sequence in which the skills are usually built?
   (1) basic skills, (2) concepts, (3) expertise, (4) understanding

    a. 1 – 2 – 3 – 4

    b. 2 – 4 – 1 – 3

    c. 1 – 4 – 2 – 3

    d. 2 – 1 – 3 – 4

9. _____ materials combine text, images, animation, and sound in a training delivery system.

10. True or False? Due to the popularity of self-guided training materials and online interactive training delivery systems, the role of support specialists as trainers is likely to disappear in the next few years.

11. Which of the following training environments is generally the most cost-effective because the ratio of trainees to trainers is highest?

   a. classes

   b. small groups/teams

   c. one-to-one training

   d. role playing

12. Which of the following learning methods results in the highest retention and trainee performance?

   a. listen

   b. read

   c. observe

   d. problem solve

13. True or False? Trainers often discover that more short breaks during a training session are preferable to fewer long breaks.

14. Which statement accurately describes the costs associated with computer-based delivery methods?

   a. The development cost is high, but the cost per user is low.

   b. The development cost is high, and the cost per user is high.

   c. The development cost is low, but the cost per user is high.

   d. The development cost is low, and the cost per user is low.

15. Printed material designed to be taken away by trainees from a training session to refresh a user's memory is called

   _____.

16. True or False? Effective trainers often cover bells and whistle features in a software package to pique trainees' interests.

17. Which of these assessment tools is aimed primarily at evaluating a trainer's effectiveness?

   a. quizzes

   b. tests

   c. hands-on activities

   d. training evaluation surveys

18. _____ is a training approach that matches the needs of each individual trainee with an information-acquisition strategy in order to achieve the most effective training results.

19. _____ is an activity in which trainees participate in a rehearsal or practice of a simulated work environment situation.

20. True or False? A first-time trainer should read notes and slides to trainees in order to avoid making a mistake or omitting important material.

Discussion Questions

1. Why does education generally rely so heavily on the lecture method in courses? Is the reliance on lectures appropriate? What are effective alternatives to the lecture method in training environments?

2. Do you think trainees have the knowledge and perspective to effectively evaluate the performance of a trainer? Explain why or why not.

3. How will the availability of high-quality training materials on the Web affect the need for user support workers to provide training as part of the user support role?

4. Can visual aids actually detract from learner understanding in a training activity? Give some examples to support your viewpoint.

5. Do the advantages of one-to-one or on-the-job training outweigh the added costs to train a new employee using these methods? Explain your reasoning.

6. What are some ways to make role-playing activities more useful as a training activity for user support workers?

Hands-On Activities

Activity 10-1

Analyze trainee backgrounds. Suppose you are assigned to prepare an introductory training module on a scripting language, such as JavaScript or VBScript. Develop a brief questionnaire to use with your classmates or work colleagues to learn about their background knowledge and experience for such a training session. Analyze their responses to your questionnaire. Do they all have similar experience and interest levels? Are they from diverse backgrounds? What problems would differences in education or experience among your classmates or colleagues pose for a trainer who is planning a training module on scripting for the group? Write a one-page summary of your analysis and findings about how the background of your classmates or colleagues would prepare them for a training activity on scripting.

Activity 10-2

Analyze learning levels. Choose a software package you know well, such as Windows Vista, a Microsoft Office application, or a Web browser. For the package you select, show that you understand the four skill levels introduced in the chapter. Provide one or two examples of:

1. The definition of an important *concept* or vocabulary term

2. An *explanation* of the concept or vocabulary term that aids in understanding it

3. A *skill* or task related to the concept that a user should be able to perform at a basic level

4. A measure of *expertise* that a highly skilled user would be expected to perform

Activity 10-3

Write measurable performance objectives. Suppose that a trainer has identified as a general goal for a training module, "Able to format printed output according to a specification sheet." First, rewrite this goal statement so that it specifies a measurable performance objective. Then, write three additional measurable performance objectives for printing in an application program.

Activity 10-4

Research and discuss resources for training materials. Discuss this statement with a small group of coworkers or classmates: "Using existing materials from a vendor's user manual, textbook, or trade book as a source of training ideas violates the original author's copyright, and therefore should never be done." If you need more information on copyrighted materials, use a search engine to locate information online or study the University of Texas tutorial on copyrights at **www.lib.utsystem.edu/copyright**. Write a summary of your reaction to the statement after your discussion with your colleagues. Note any points of disagreement among members of your group.

Activity 10-5

Compare training formats. Do you personally prefer classroom training, small group sessions, one-to-one training, or self-guided tutorials? Why? Are there circumstances in which you feel a one-to-one training format is more effective than another? Interview two or three classmates or coworkers and get their answers to these questions. Write a summary that compares your response to the responses of those whom you interviewed.

Activity 10-6

Evaluate CBT or WBT materials. Locate a training module that uses computer-based or Web-based training. (This chapter lists several examples.) The module you select can be a video, a CD, or a Web site. Try out the CBT or WBT approach, either alone or with a group of colleagues. Write a critique of the module. How well does it achieve its goals? What improvements would you suggest to the author? What are the advantages and disadvantages of CBT or WBT delivery systems for training modules in the subject area?

Activity 10-7

Analyze training evaluation forms. List some additional aspects of training that could be evaluated in the training evaluation form in Figure 10-5. Locate a training evaluation or assessment form used at your school or workplace, or examine an evaluation form on the Web, such as the ones at **it.toolbox.com/blogs/enterprise-solutions/ training-course-evaluation-form-template-instructorled-29507** or **www-group.slac.stanford.edu/esh/forms/train_class_ evaluation.doc**.

Compare the form you found with the one in Figure 10-5. Describe the similarities. What are the major differences? Describe the changes you would make to improve the evaluation form in Figure 10-5 based on your research.

Activity 10-8

Develop training guidelines. Based on your personal experiences as a trainee or student (a recipient of training), describe some common mistakes you have observed trainers or instructors make that you would add to the suggestions for trainers listed in Figure 10-6. Which of the guidelines in the chapter or ones you added do you think will be the most difficult for you when you lead a training activity?

Activity 10-9

Experience a learning management system. Moodle is a popular Web-based learning management system used in many higher education institutions in the United States. You can take a sample course to get a flavor of Moodle as a learning management system at **e-subjects.co.uk/course/view.php?id=19** or **moodle.sbc.edu/course/view.php?id=313**. Explore one or more of the sample courses and make a list of at least five features in Moodle that a trainer would find useful when preparing training for end users. Include your own reaction to this method of training.

Case Projects

1. Learn About Learning Styles

Barbara A. Soloman and Richard M. Felder at North Carolina State University have researched different learning styles. They created an instrument to assess learning styles on four dimensions:

* Active/reflective
* Sensing/intuitive
* Visual/verbal
* Sequential/global

Find out more about each of these learning styles at their Web site: **www.engr.ncsu.edu/learningstyles/ilsweb.html**. Answer their Index of Learning Styles (ILS) questionnaire (there are no right or wrong answers) to learn more about your preferred learning style. Compare your scores on the ILS questionnaire with the scores of three coworkers or classmates. Write a summary of the results you observed and what the results mean for you as a trainee. In your summary, answer the question: "Does any one of the training methods described in this chapter meet the needs of all the different learning styles that Felder and Soloman describe on their Web site?" Explain why or why not.

2. Design a Training Module

Choose a topic on which you could train others. Plan, prepare, and present a training module on the topic. Examples of possible topics include:

* How to do a mail merge in a word processor
* How to install a CD or DVD drive in a PC
* How to use a switchboard in Microsoft Access

- How to use one or more of the basic features of a help desk software package, such as HelpSTAR, BMC Remedy, HEAT, HelpTrac, or Spiceworks (see Chapter 5 for ideas)

- How to use advanced features of an online search engine to perform more effective searches

- How to use the Mac OS (aimed at Windows users)

- How to write simple scripts using the Windows Script Host

- How to import tabular data from the Web into a Microsoft Excel worksheet

The training module you prepare should include all of the following elements:

PLANNING

1. Analyze job skills required
2. Analyze the trainees
3. Assess the needs of the trainees
4. Set training objectives

PREPARATION

5. Select and organize training content
6. Select training methods, techniques, and aids
7. Prepare training module
8. Decide how to evaluate training

PRESENTATION

9. Present training module
10. Evaluate the training

PROGRESS

11. Review and revise training materials and methods, as necessary

First, work on a plan for a sample training module for your topic. Cover Steps 1 through 6 and 8 in planning and preparation first. For some of these steps, such as analyzing the trainees, your instructor may give you some background information or ask you to make some assumptions. Work with other class members to brainstorm topic priorities. What could be included and what could be omitted from your training module?

Next, based on the results of brainstorming with class members, work independently to prepare a 20- to 30-minute training module for one-to-one delivery (Step 7). The module should include a hands-on component, a short quiz, and time for a brief evaluation.

Then, present your training module (Step 9) to another class member. At the end of the training session, both the trainer and the trainee should fill out a short evaluation (for the trainer it will be a self-evaluation). Use the evaluation form from this chapter, the one you produced in Activity 10-7, or write one of your own specifically for this training activity. Then reverse roles, so your partner can present his or her training module to you. (If you are working alone, ask a friend or colleague to help you evaluate your training module as a training beta test.)

When your training beta test is finished, write a short summary of what you learned from the experience that would improve the training module, or your presentation of it, the next time you present it. If possible, after you have refined the quality of your training module, present it to your entire class or work team. Use the evaluation form you prepared for the beta test to get feedback from your colleagues.

3. Present Someone Else's Training Module

In corporate training, a trainer is often provided with preplanned and prepackaged training materials to present. Repeat presentation Steps 9 through 11 from Case 2, *Design a Training Module*, using the training materials a classmate has planned and prepared. After the training activity, provide feedback to the original developer about what worked well and what could be improved.

4. A Training Module for Office 2007 Users

Andrew Nussbaum is the Director of Training Services. The company where Andrew works is planning to convert from Office 2003 to Office 2007 in the next few weeks. Andrew would like to offer a training session for about 20 experienced Office 2003 users to acquaint them with the changes to the user interface they will encounter when they convert to Office 2007. Andrew has asked you and Randy, another user support specialist, to design one training module for Office users. You may select the Office 2007 program of your choosing. Then plan and prepare a training module on the Office 2007 ribbon menu for the program you selected. Assume the trainees are already acquainted with the features of the software features in Office. *(The Role-Playing Scenario in this chapter relates an interview between Andrew and Randy, your coworker on the project, which will give you additional background information for this case.)*

The training module you prepare should include all the following elements:

PLANNING (make assumptions where necessary)

1. Analyze job skills required

2. Analyze the trainees

3. Assess the needs of the trainees

4. Set training objectives

PREPARATION

5. Select and organize training content

6. Select training methods, techniques, and aids

7. Prepare training module

8. Decide how to evaluate the training

Write a brief description of your plan to address Steps 1 through 6 and 8 above. Then prepare training materials (Step 7 above) you would use to introduce users to the Office 2007 ribbon menu for the program you selected. One objective is to answer the trainees' question, "If I know how to accomplish a task in Office 2003, where will I find the comparable tool in Office 2007?" Develop training materials that could be presented by another trainer. Create a PowerPoint slide presentation and any handouts you believe would be useful during the training activity.

5. Design a Facility for the Office 2007 Training

Review the information in Case Project 4. Draw or describe an ideal room configuration for this training session. Show or describe the location of chairs, tables, presentation equipment, computers, and a whiteboard or flip charts. If it is available, use Visio, Dia (an open source alternative to Visio, available at **dia-installer.de/index_en.html**), a CAD program, or similar software to prepare your training room design.

CHAPTER 11

Writing for End Users

In this chapter, you will learn about:

- ◎ Types of end-user documentation
- ◎ How technical writing differs from other writing
- ◎ How technical documents are organized
- ◎ How to plan effective user documentation
- ◎ The technical writing process
- ◎ Effective use of formats
- ◎ Strategies for technical writing
- ◎ Common problems in technical writing
- ◎ Tools used for technical writing
- ◎ How to evaluate documentation

Most effective training sessions make use of written materials, including handouts, quick reference sheets, and other documents that users can take back to their work area for reference. In addition to documents used in training sessions, online documentation such as help systems, assistants (wizards), Web pages, FAQs (frequently asked questions), e-mail messages, and README files are a popular way for vendors and support groups to communicate essential information effectively to end users.

The creation of any document targeted for end users, whether printed or online, requires at least basic technical writing skills. The goal of technical writing is to produce documents that effectively and efficiently communicate information that a reader needs. **Documentation** is any form of written communication intended to provide user support information to end users. Good documentation saves users time; poor documentation can cost users time and reduce their productivity. This chapter provides a brief overview of several important topics in technical writing, including strategies for writing user documentation and pointers for writing successfully on technical subjects in a user support position.

Types of User Documentation

Members of a user support staff may be asked to produce written materials in a variety of situations. Although technical writing can have several purposes and can appear in very different formats, all documentation must clearly communicate a message. Figure 11-1 lists the common types of documentation, which are described below.

● Brochures and flyers	● E-mail and chat messages
● Newsletters	● Web pages
● Handouts and training aids	● Proposals, letters, and memos
● User guides, handbooks, and manuals	● Procedural and operational documentation
● Online help systems	● Troubleshooting guides

Figure 11-1   Types of user documentation

Brochures and Flyers

Brochures and flyers often promote various computer-related activities, such as staff training sessions, computer fairs, hardware and software product demonstrations, and talks by guest speakers. These documents are primarily promotional and are intended to catch the reader's eye and "sell" the event. Because support staff members are often involved in organizing these kinds of events, they may need to create informational advertisements for them. To speed delivery and reduce paper use and postage costs, many support groups now send advertisements for events via e-mail or post announcements on an organizational intranet or Web portal.

Newsletters

Newsletters are an important way many support groups communicate with users. Support staff can use desktop publishing or word-processing software to create newsletters with embedded images such as diagrams, pictures, icons, and charts. User support newsletters are especially popular for large organizations in which the support staff does not come in direct contact with most employees on a regular basis. An increasing number of organizations now deliver newsletters online to their employees and customers.

ON THE WEB

For an example of an online newsletter resource targeted to the support industry, visit the TechRepublic Web site at **techrepublic.com**. Sign up to check out one or more of their e-newsletters. Although TechRepublic newsletters are written by a variety of writers, they generally provide good examples of technical writing.

For more information about publishing an online newsletter, visit the Web site of eBook Crossroads at **www.ebookcrossroads. com/newsletter-publishing.html**. The site includes links to several resources for newsletter publishers.

Handouts and Training Aids

Handouts and training aids are primarily intended to summarize and promote recall of material covered in a training session. They may also be distributed online or via a computer documentation library of frequently asked questions. Printed handouts of PowerPoint slides with space for trainees to take notes next to each slide are common training aids. These documents are usually short and address a single topic.

User Guides, Handbooks, and Manuals

User guides, handbooks, and computer manuals are more formal examples of written documentation. For some support groups, these documents can be tens or hundreds of pages long, and are often printed in book format or as a PDF (portable document format). They supplement vendor documentation and trade books with information specific to an organization or computer facility. For example, an organization may issue a user handbook detailing what computer facilities and services are available to workers, including how to access them, how to obtain software to connect to the organization's VPN (virtual private network), ground rules for computer use and abuse, and how to get system support. In educational institutions, IT departments may publish similar guides for students, faculty, and administrators. Even very small organizations may find a printed user guide an effective way to communicate basic information to new employees and those who are only occasional users.

Software developers and hardware vendors publish a variety of user guides and computer manuals that describe how to install and use their products. These manuals may be organized in a **tutorial format**, which guides a user step-by-step through the features of a program, with frequently used features covered first. Other manuals may be organized in a **reference format**, which pulls together all the information on a specific topic in a single page, section, or chapter.

A tutorial format is convenient for new users, because it emphasizes the natural sequence of steps, beginning with the simplest tasks. Features are introduced as users need them for a particular task. Information about printing, for example, may be scattered throughout a tutorial manual, as various printing features and options are introduced. Basic printing features might be explained early, and more advanced or seldom-used features covered later. For experienced users, a reference format is often more useful, because all the information on printing, including a description of all available options, is usually located in a single section or chapter within the manual. Some manuals combine tutorials with a reference guide to address the needs of both types of users.

Online Help Systems

Online help systems and software assistants (wizards) are common features in software packages. They are sometimes supplied on CDs, which customers can use for self-training. In other cases, help modules are embedded in a software product and are installed at the same time as the software itself. Some online help systems are well written and can effectively rival or replace printed manuals as a source of well-organized and accurate information. Writing online documentation is an art, however, because the information must be presented succinctly. Printed training materials are usually organized sequentially with less concern about the length of each section. In online documentation, individual topics should be broken up into shorter sections that can appear on a single screen page; readers are not likely to spend time searching for information on a Web site where the text appears on one very long page rather than on shorter pages divided by topic.

Hypertext links and index searches in online documents are powerful tools to help users jump quickly to needed information. A hypertext link is a highlighted word or phrase in a document that acts as a pointer to additional information. When a user clicks a link, the software displays more detailed information about the word or phrase. An index search permits a user to enter a word or phrase of interest; the software then searches the document and displays detailed information about the topic.

The Windows Help system illustrates the use of hypertext links and index searches and includes several examples of interactive help systems called troubleshooters. To access the troubleshooters, click the **Start** button, and then click **Help** in the Windows XP Start menu, click the **Contents** tab, click **Troubleshooting**, and then click a troubleshooter to open a page of information. In Windows Vista, click the **Start** button, click **Help and Support** in the Start menu, and then click the **Troubleshooting** icon to view a variety of troubleshooting tips.

Despite the increasing popularity and convenience of online documentation, some users prefer print media when they need to read large amounts of information. Printed information is often easier to read for long periods, and it can be read even when a computer is not available. Depending on the quality and resolution of the display screen and the room lighting, lengthy online documents may be difficult to read. Some end users need extra time to feel comfortable with online documentation and to change their preference for printed materials.

E-Mail and Chat Messages

The ability to communicate effectively via e-mail and instant messaging (chat) is an important writing skill for user support specialists, especially those who work at a help desk that communicates primarily with online users. Some support organizations have switched their primary method of communication with end users from telephone to e-mail and chat. In these cases, support specialists who honed their verbal skills at the expense of their writing skills may find that they need to update their skills. E-mail and chat messages may appear to be less formal methods of communication. However, e-mail and chat messages from a help desk staff project an image of an organization and should reflect good technical writing skills.

Dashing off a few disorganized phrases with typos and spelling and grammatical errors in an e-mail message or chat exchange can give the recipient a poor impression. Writing a careful response to an end user via e-mail helps a support agent to organize his or her thoughts and provides an opportunity to review and revise a response before it is sent. Although internal e-mail messages may be less formal than messages intended for recipients outside an organization, even these project an image of the sender. Remember that once you have sent an e-mail message, you have no control over where it may be forwarded. Supervisors may review and evaluate the quality of support e-mail and chat messages as one measure of an agent's communication skills and promotability.

ON THE WEB

Support staff who correspond frequently via e-mail and instant messaging need to understand some basic guidelines called netiquette. A useful resource is Kaitlin Duck Sherwood's *A Beginner's Guide to Effective Email* at **webfoot.com/advice/email.top.php**.

The OWL (Online Writing Lab) at Purdue University also provides very useful suggestions on e-mail etiquette at **owl.english.purdue.edu/owl/resource/636/01**.

Web Pages

Because many written materials end up on the Web, the ability to write for that medium is important for support workers. Web pages need to be organized and written so that users can quickly locate information. Because a Web site may be accessible to the general public, the image of an organization is at stake. Think about how long you typically stay at a Web site that is poorly organized, contains incorrect information, or provides broken links (URLs that point to inactive Web pages). In general, materials designed for Web access should be very short, with hypertext links that lead readers to additional information. Web-based materials must be well written because Web users often do not have the patience to wade through a long document to find the information they need. They tend to skim quickly and then click a link to another site. Another challenge for support agents who maintain Web sites is to keep information accurate and up to date. Obsolete or inaccurate support information is often worse than no information.

ON THE WEB

You can sometimes learn useful information from studying bad examples. To find Web sites that users have nominated as among the worst on the entire Internet, go to **www.worstoftheweb.com**. The site features an archive of nominated sites and a commentary by three pundits about what makes each one so bad.

On a more positive note, check out an interactive tutorial on Web site design on the University of Albany Library's Web site at **library.albany.edu/imc/webdesign/#how**.

Proposals, Letters, and Memos

Support staff members need to be able to write clear and effective proposals, reports, letters, memos, and other business documents. Support specialists who perform needs assessments for end users or departments frequently need to present the results of their investigations in the form of a proposal or report. In addition, support staff often need to write letters, memos, and other correspondence to colleagues, end users (both inside and outside an organization), and supervisors. The ability to write standard business documents is a basic user support communication skill.

Procedural and Operational Documentation

Procedural and operational documentation includes procedure steps and checklists, usually intended for internal use. The descriptions of the steps to install hardware and software in Chapter 9 are examples of technical procedural documentation. Even for internal documents such as these, technical writing skills are essential. Procedural and operational documentation that is unclear, poorly organized, or incorrect costs staff time, results in errors, and increases user frustration. Clear, well-organized documents communicate information efficiently and reflect well on the writer and the support organization.

Many support specialists who have never thought of themselves as writers enjoy the challenge of writing procedural and operational documentation that is accurate and easy to follow.

Troubleshooting Guides

User support staff members often write troubleshooting guides to help other workers solve problems. Common examples of trouble-shooting guides include:

- A problem-solving chapter in a user guide
- An FAQ page for a Web site
- A script to handle a specific type of problem incident
- A problem report in a help desk knowledge base

Although this type of documentation is often for internal use, it must be clear, concise, and well written.

ON THE WEB

An example of a troubleshooting guide in PDF can be viewed at **www.qualitynet.net/documents/homewifiug.pdf**.

Each type of technical writing described above is a form of support documentation. They have more similarities than differences. The following sections discuss the similarities, including how technical writing in general differs from other types of writing.

How Technical Writing Differs from Other Writing

Technical writing is different from other types of writing—such as personal letters, research papers, or novels—in terms of the type of information communicated as well as the goals, style, and organization of the documents.

Technical Writing Style

Technical writing typically follows specific style guidelines. The goal of these guidelines is to help technical writers create documents that are clear, accurate, and accessible to most users. Keep in mind the following points as you write documentation:

- Technical writing uses short, declarative sentences, short phrases, and lists—instead of long sentences with unnecessary words or phrases. In general, short, simple sentences are preferable to long sentences. A simple sentence has one subject and one verb, and expresses a complete idea. Compound sentences often contain *and* or *but* as a connector and include two subjects and two verbs, and express two complete thoughts. Most technical writing is based on simple and compound sentences. Avoid run-on sentences and overly complex sentence structures with multiple clauses and modifiers. Compare these examples:

  - **Simple sentence:** *Parentheses let you control how Excel uses operators in a formula.*

  - **Compound sentence:** *Parentheses let you control how Excel uses arithmetic operators in a formula, and parentheses also make equations easier to read or revise.*

  - **Run-on sentence:** *If you specify an uneven number of parentheses in a formula or a pair of parentheses that don't match, Excel displays the message, "Parentheses do not match or Error in Formula," and this highlights the location of the mistake which you can correct on the formula bar.*

- Technical writing starts with the most important point at the beginning of a section or topic rather than at the end, as in other types of writing. The goal of technical writing is not to build suspense or work toward a punch line, but to communicate information as clearly and effectively as possible and help a reader make transitions between topics.

- Technical writing often communicates step-by-step sequences of events or tasks. The writing style and format used can help readers understand the sequence. For example, a sequence of steps should be listed in the order the users would perform the steps. Compare the following:

Example 1: *Click the Margin option in Page Setup under the File menu.*

Example 2: *In the File menu, click Page Setup, and then click the Margin option.*

In the first example, the actions appear in reverse order to how they are actually performed. A user must read to the end of the sentence before they learn what action to perform first. The second example is preferable because the actions are listed in the

 Some writers believe that simple sentences are not as interesting as more complex ones; however, the purpose of technical writing is not to entertain, but to communicate understandable information vital to the reader's productivity. Also, not all readers have good reading skills; they may have a reading disability (such as dyslexia), or English may be their second language. To communicate effectively with the largest number of readers, keep sentences simple.

order in which they are performed. When steps in a procedure or task must be performed in a specific sequence, a numbered list can emphasize the sequence. When information has no required order, a bulleted list is more appropriate.

- Technical writing should be concise, but not cryptic. Concise writing is short, but covers the essential information a user needs. Readers of technical documents usually want to open a document, find what they need to know, and get back to work. If they have to spend unnecessary time searching for buried information, their productivity is reduced. To include more detailed information, add **pointers**, or cross-references to the location where a user can find more information. In online documents, hypertext links effectively move a user from general to more specific information on a topic.

- The goal of technical writing is not to entertain readers with humor or call attention to the writer's personality or preferences. Humor in a technical document is likely to be misunderstood by some readers, especially those who are new to a topic or for whom English is a second language. The writer's personal preferences should be clearly labeled as such, enabling readers to quickly identify possible sources of bias.

Good technical writing follows these guidelines to ensure that users get the help they need from a document. If users cannot locate the information they need, the result is a higher volume of calls to the support group, or a higher level of user frustration.

How Technical Documents Are Organized

Two common ways to organize technical documents are sequentially and hierarchically. **Sequential organization** follows a step-by-step approach whereby information is arranged in the order in which the steps are executed. Procedural documents usually follow a sequential organization. **Hierarchical organization** flows from top to bottom, and information is arranged from general to specific. Online help systems often use a hierarchical organization.

Most successful technical documents use a combination of sequential and hierarchical organization strategies, depending on the material to be communicated, the medium of communication, and the users' needs. A common organization for a technical document is:

- **Introduction**
  - Purpose of document
  - Who are the intended readers of the document
  - Why read the document

- **Body**
  - Specific task steps
  - Common problems users encounter
- **Summary**
  - Pointers to additional information

The overall organization is hierarchical. At the top level, the general sections are: Introduction, Body, and Summary. The body in this example includes "task steps," which are sequential.

The introduction begins by addressing three questions. First, what is the purpose of this document? Second, who is the intended audience? Third, why would anyone want to read this? In other words, readers are told up front what information they will get from reading this document. Technical writers should answer these three questions early in order to save time for those readers for whom a document is *not* intended. Even a short piece of writing, such as an FAQ or an e-mail message, should state its purpose in the first or second sentence.

The body of a technical document should include explanatory material. Most readers want a short explanation to help them understand why something works, what result should be expected, or why the information is important. Often, technical writers include a brief explanation of what the hardware or software is capable of and how it can help readers in their work. The explanation is often followed by a detailed description of the sequential steps necessary to perform a task. Finally, the body should briefly describe common problems users are likely to encounter and how to recover from them. The summary should be brief—review the main points and the results achieved, and direct the reader to where additional information can be accessed.

Some technical writers are tempted to include as much information as they can in a document. The writer may digress from the main points to cover material that may be of interest to only a few readers, is not critical, or is very technical. Omit less critical information or place this material in an appendix or attachment. Include a pointer to the appendix in the body, so that interested readers will know where to find it.

Document Planning

The steps writers follow to plan user documentation projects are very similar to those that trainers follow to plan training sessions. As in training, planning is essential to produce high-quality documents, regardless of their length or purpose. Most planning involves determining the characteristics of the audience and its needs, as listed in Figure 11-2.

- Who is the target audience?
- What does the audience already know?
- What does the audience need to know?
- What do you want the audience to be able to do when they finish reading the document?
- What medium will be used to transmit the document to its audience?

Figure 11-2   Information needed for documentation planning

Asking these questions helps prepare technical writers to create useful, well-targeted documents.

Who Is the Target Audience?

The question about the target audience is often intended to pinpoint the readers' level of technical expertise. To write a task description for new users requires different assumptions and techniques than writing for more experienced, technically sophisticated users. The audience definition should also include an estimate of their reading level. Most newspapers, for example, are written at an eighth or ninth grade reading level, which is a good level to strive for in computer documents targeted to a general audience of end users. Most word processors include a tool to measure the approximate reading level (readability index) of a document.

The readability index for this chapter is 10th–11th grade level.

ON THE WEB

To quickly check the reading level of a document, visit the Web site **www.online-utility.org/english/readability_test_ and_improve.jsp**. Cut and paste text from the document into the Window and click the **Process text** button to view the results. Note that the popular readability indexes do not always agree on the readability level of a document because they use different algorithms, but they provide a general indication of the level at which a document is written.

What Does the Audience Already Know?

To determine who the audience is, a technical writer should attempt to find out the readers' backgrounds, including what they already know. A statement in the introduction about what the writer assumes the readers know can help readers make an informed decision about whether the material is intended for them—whether it covers things they already know or whether it covers technical information that is beyond their ability to understand.

Example: *The information in this reference sheet is for PowerPoint users who have a basic understanding of presentation software concepts and need a reference tool for the most frequently used features in PowerPoint.*

When writing for readers who need to know a specific procedure, assessing what skills they already have is sometimes difficult. In some situations, a technical writer may be able to assess skills using a questionnaire. Because a questionnaire is not always feasible, cover the most basic skills first, but with appropriate section headings so that more skilled users can easily skip to what they need to know.

What Does the Audience Need to Know?

Answering this question is a critical step in technical writing because it helps a writer define the purpose of the document. As with training, the purpose of technical documentation should be to move readers from what they already know to what they need to know. The purpose of a document should be stated early, within the first few sentences.

What Do You Want the Audience to Be Able to Do?

A technical writer should know what specific tasks she or he wants the audience to perform after they read the document. A task focus gives direction to the writing and helps users know when they have successfully mastered the information. Although some documents are intended for general information purposes only, most are aimed at getting a reader to a point at which they can make a decision or perform a specific task.

What Medium Will Be Used to Transmit the Document to Its Audience?

The medium that will be used to transmit a document to its audience should be determined before the document is written. Common media types include print format and online format. Although some

503

documents are written for either or both media, printed documents are often longer and therefore need transitions between topics and levels of information to help readers know where they are in the hierarchy of information. Online documents should be shorter, but can include hyperlinks and other pointers to help readers navigate quickly to the desired information or to additional information. The computer industry has experienced a transition from primarily printed documentation several years ago to almost entirely Web-based or optical media documentation today.

The Technical Writing Process

After document writers have defined the audience, purpose, and medium for a document, they can then begin to write the document itself. Many writers use a seven-step process shown in Figure 11-3 to write a document.

1. Generate a list of important ideas or features to be covered.

2. Organize the list into a logical, hierarchical sequence to form an outline.

3. Expand the outline into a first draft.

4. Edit the draft one or more times for clarity.

5. Arrange for an outside review of the document.

6. Revise the draft into its final form.

7. Proofread the final document.

Figure 11-3   The technical writing process

Good technical writing follows this process. A writer may be tempted to take shortcuts because of time constraints, but once a document is published, especially in a print medium, there is often little opportunity to change it. Even very experienced writers would never consider releasing a first draft to end users. They realize that the entire seven-step process is critical to producing quality documents.

Step 1: Generate an Idea List

Some writers use a word processor to generate a list of ideas; others use paper and pencil. At this stage, a writer **brainstorms** to generate as many topics as they can think of that might be useful to readers. Some potential topics become major topics, others become minor topics, and some are discarded. While brainstorming, the strategy is to exclude nothing; after brainstorming, the idea list can be prioritized, reorganized, and pared down to essentials.

Step 2: Organize the List into an Outline

Once writers have a topic list that includes everything they want to cover, they organize the topics into a logical order to form an outline. Most writers don't settle on a final organizational structure on the first attempt. Flexibility is important during the early organizational steps; writers often cut and paste to try out different sequences of ideas. Most word processors have an outlining feature that makes it easy to rearrange topics, to promote some in importance to major topics and demote others. As writers begin to create an outline, other topics may come to mind that can be added. The most important question an outline answers is "In what order does the reader need to know this information?" Cover the essential information, including qualifiers or assumptions, first.

ON THE WEB

The Outline View feature in Microsoft Word (an alternative to the more familiar normal and print views), lets a writer focus on the overall structure or outline of a document. To view a short tutorial on using Outline View, visit **www.brighthub.com/computing/windows-platform/articles/26077.aspx**.

Step 3: Expand the Outline into a First Draft

After creating an initial outline and checking it for logical flow, expand the outline into a first draft by explaining each point in the outline. When writing the first draft, a writer often uses the features described below to make their documents readable and understandable. Although many techniques help produce understandable documentation, these four are basic.

Paragraphs with Topic Sentences

A document should be organized into paragraphs, and each paragraph should cover a different aspect of the topic. Each paragraph should have a topic sentence to introduce the topic in general terms. After the topic sentence, develop other sentences in each paragraph

506

Identify the topic sentence in each paragraph in this section of the chapter. Does each topic sentence tell you what the paragraph is about? Are some topic sentences better than others?

with details that support or expand on the topic sentence. When writing Web-based documents and e-mail messages, the number of paragraphs on a page or in a message should be small: one or a few.

Transitions

Use transitional words and phrases such as *for example, therefore,* and *as a result* to help show a reader the relationship of one sentence to another. Other transitions useful for steps in a procedure are *first, second, next, then,* and *finally.* Transitions help readers keep track of where they are in a sequential organization. Numbered and bulleted lists also help show organization and transitions.

Defined Terms

Good technical writers always define the terms they use. To introduce readers to a new term, define it clearly and boldface the term in the sentence that defines it, as you have seen in this book. When defining terms, be careful not to define a term using the term itself; use a synonym instead.

Formats

Writers use format features to help readers understand the organization of information. Different sized headings, for example, help clarify the overall structure. Many writers use italic type for emphasis, although emphasis should be used sparingly. Bulleted or numbered lists are useful to alert a reader to the structure of a long section.

A document's structure helps guide readers through the parts of a document. After a technical writer determines the basic structure of a document, he or she adds formats to communicate the structure to readers. The following list focuses on useful formatting tools that you can incorporate in your own writing.

Although changes in font, case, indentation, centering, and other format features can help clarify the structure of a document, some writers get carried away with the power of a word processor. Two fonts can be useful to help a reader deal with different types of material. But too many different fonts or too much boldface or italics can be a distraction.

- **Style elements**—When a document is organized into chapters or modules, different fonts, font sizes, boldface, capitalization, centering, indentation, underlines, bullets, and numbering help a reader understand the structure. These design elements help the reader to understand what is more or less important and help the reader identify where each topic begins and ends. They answer questions such as, "If I am not interested in this section, where do I skip to start reading again so I don't miss anything?"

- **Format consistency**—Format consistency is important. Use a consistent format for headings, paragraphs, and tables. Style sheets and templates in popular word processors can help make consistent formatting easier. For technical manuals or other materials that will receive widespread commercial distribution, hardware and software organizations and publishers often hire a graphic designer to create a design for the interior of a document. For many smaller projects, however, preformatted templates, which are often created by professional designers and included with word-processing programs, are sufficient.

- **Lists and tables**—When a writer needs to present a sequence of information, a bulleted or numbered list or a table is often more understandable than a long narrative passage. Lists and tables permit readers to quickly locate the information they need; users often find it very difficult to locate information in a long narrative passage. Lists are most effective when they support a generalization or summarize information presented in narrative text.

Step 4: Edit the Draft

After expanding an outline into the first draft, read and edit it. Most writers read through and edit a draft more than once, looking for particular problems on each pass. One edit pass rarely catches all the different types of problems.

One edit pass is often used to delete extra words in order to tighten the text because a goal of technical writing is to be brief. Consider, for example, the following short paragraph:

Let's spend a bit more time discussing the relationship between the automatic call distribution (ACD) system and other help desk systems. Only the more sophisticated ACDs include interfaces to other devices now, but it's clearly the wave of the future, not to mention a productivity enhancer.

The following version eliminates extraneous words while maintaining the meaning:

Let's discuss the relationship between the automatic call distribution (ACD) system and other help desk systems. Currently, only sophisticated ACDs can connect to other devices. However, future models will have connectivity to enhance user productivity.

Eliminating extra words takes some practice, but is beneficial because tighter prose takes less time to read. Eliminate words that are not critical to understanding your meaning.

A second edit pass that many writers perform is a format consistency check. The purpose of a **format consistency check** is to make sure that the fonts of headings and subheadings, indentation, centering, boldface, italics, and underlining are used consistently throughout a document. Check to see that these format features are not overused. Remember that the purpose of formats is to help readers understand the structure of the document, not to show off all the features of document-processing software. Format features should guide a reader through a document without hindering understanding or becoming a distraction.

A third edit pass is a technical accuracy check. During a **technical accuracy check**, a writer tests any procedure or technical steps in a document by performing the steps with the hardware or software. The purpose of a technical accuracy check is to eliminate any errors in step-by-step instructions or other technical information. If a document has been written about a beta or other prerelease version of hardware or software, an accuracy check should be performed with the final version of the product. Check URLs to make sure addresses are spelled correctly and that the URLs still point to active sites. If a document includes screenshots to illustrate the result of steps in a procedure, each screenshot should be verified against the software to make sure it reflects the latest version of the software.

Step 5: Get an Outside Review

An outside review is a like a second opinion. Another pair of eyes can often raise questions, spot inconsistencies, find unclear meanings, identify poor writing techniques, and locate other problems that a writer cannot see. Getting outside criticism can be surprising, especially because writers who spend a lot of time on their first draft are often satisfied that it is just about perfect. Criticism can be especially painful if a reviewer doesn't share the same writing style and approach as the writer. But a second perspective on any written document is important, especially for documents that will be widely distributed. An outside review serves the same purpose as a beta test of a training module. Over time, writers learn to set aside the natural defensiveness they may feel about their work and realize that a reviewer represents the potential target audience. Most writers would rather a reviewer point out problems in the writing stage than for readers to do so after publication.

Step 6: Revise the Draft

After a writer edits a draft and gets feedback, he or she revises it to incorporate suggestions and corrections. If a writer is a perfectionist, one of the challenges in the writing process is to know when to stop revising. Although edit passes can serve a useful purpose up to a point, a writer must learn when to stop. Fortunately for many technical writers, publication deadlines dictate when they are finished. After a few revisions, additional edit passes may result in very small incremental improvements in a document. At the end of each edit pass, a writer should ask whether the last pass resulted in a substantial improvement, or whether the improvements were only marginal; if they didn't significantly enhance the readability or accuracy of the document, then it is time to stop.

Step 7: Proofread the Document

After writing, editing, and revising a document, writers should proofread it one last time to make sure that no small errors remain. Sometimes another person, possibly a professional proofreader, copy editor, or a work colleague can perform this task. Most technical writing benefits greatly from another proofreader's perspective. Proofreaders look for a variety of common errors, including:

- **Inconsistent capitalization and punctuation**—Are proper nouns capitalized consistently? Are words capitalized that shouldn't be? Are commas used consistently in sentences, in lists, and within large numbers?

- **Inconsistent font use**—Are headings the correct font and size? Is the body text in the same font throughout the document?

- **Extra spaces between words and sentences**—Is the number of spaces after each sentence consistent? (Most typeset books and many desktop-published documents use only one space after periods.) Is there a single space between words?

- **Incorrect page breaks**—Are all the page breaks in logical locations? Should any page breaks be adjusted to eliminate orphaned sentences (a situation in which the first or last sentence in a paragraph or list is on a separate page from the remainder of the paragraph or list)?

The seven steps in the technical writing process help both new and experienced document writers ensure that their work is both well organized and understandable.

You can use a word processor to search for two spaces and replace each occurrence with one space.

If a document will eventually be typeset or transferred to desktop publishing software, page breaks are not a concern because the length of a typeset page usually differs from a page created with word-processing software.

ON THE WEB

The Web contains a wealth of useful resources for beginning and experienced technical writers. For example, David A. McMurrey, a professor at Austin Community College, provides a complete online technical writing textbook at **www.io.com/~hcexres/textbook**. To learn more about guidelines for the use of formatting tools, click topics in the table of contents under *Document Design*.

A brief tutorial on writing user guides can be found at **www.klariti.com/technical-writing/User-Guides-Tutorial.shtml**.

Technical Writing Strategies

Although you may not have written technical documents before, you have probably used a manual, online help, or some other form of documentation. Based on your experience, you probably already have some opinions on what makes good or bad technical writing, and what has or has not been effective at addressing your needs as a reader and end user. Some technical writing is a pleasure to read because it is well organized and important information is presented clearly and concisely. If you analyze successful documents, some common strategies and approaches stand out.

Analogies

Technical writers often use analogies to explain new material. An **analogy** is a comparison between an unfamiliar concept and a familiar one; an analogy highlights the similarities between things. For example, writers often use the analogy of an office filing system to explain the hierarchical structure of computer media; they draw a parallel between the information stored manually in an office filing system and the information stored electronically in a computer filing system (e.g., a hard disk is like a filing cabinet). Analogies are useful because they relate something most users are familiar with, such as an office filing system, to something they need to understand.

Repetition

Technical writers often use repetition for emphasis. Repetition is also a training strategy you encountered in Chapter 10. In both technical documents and user training, a useful strategy is to introduce a topic, explain it, and then summarize it. Repetition helps users learn new material and recall it later. However, excessive use of repetition can unnecessarily lengthen a document without contributing to its usefulness.

Consistent Word Use

Technical writers try to use words consistently. In creative writing, writers are taught to look for synonyms to avoid overuse of certain words and to inject variety in written work. In technical writing, however, consistent use of words can contribute to the reader's understanding. To vary word use unnecessarily may cause the reader to question whether different words signal a subtle difference in meaning. For example, a writer may use synonyms such as *CD*, *CD-ROM*, *compact disc*, and *optical disk* interchangeably to refer to the same thing, which can confuse readers. Technical writing is often clearer when one word among synonyms is selected and used throughout a document.

Many organizations maintain a **style sheet** that lists their preferences for common terms so that all writers use the same terminology. Sometimes a style sheet is a simple list of preferred terms and spelling conventions. In other cases, a style sheet can be a lengthy document that lists not only terms and spelling conventions but also preferred grammatical structures, product name usage conventions, and the like. Figure 11-4 shows a sample page from a publisher's style sheet.

Style Sheet   *Page 3*

Item	Comments
check box (not checkbox)	
check mark	
checkbook	
choose	Do not use in steps
click (not "click on")	
click and drag (v.)	
click in	Use when positioning a pointer "in" a text box or placing the insertion point "in" a specific area
clip-art (adj.)	clip-art image, clip-art library
click-drag technique	
ClipArt	when referring specifically to Microsoft ClipArt Gallery

Figure 11-4   Page from a style sheet

ON THE WEB

English Teaching Forum, a quarterly journal published by the U.S. Department of State for teachers of English, maintains an online style sheet to describe how writers should prepare documents for publication by their organization. For an example of a style sheet, see its Web site at **exchanges. state.gov/englishteaching/forum/style-sheet.html**.

Parallel Structure

The concept of parallel structure is important in technical writing. **Parallel structure** is a writing strategy in which similar items are treated consistently throughout a document. Consistent formats for titles, headings, and subheadings are one application of parallel structure, as are consistent verb tenses and parts of speech. Parallel structure is also important in bulleted lists, as shown in Figure 11-5.

Problems with parallel structure	Revision to use parallel structure
Consider the following ways to measure help desk performance:	Consider the following ways to measure help desk performance:
• first: volume of calls	• call volume
• next: time it takes to respond	• call response time
• resolution time	• call resolution time
• how many calls are backlogged	• call backlog
• call aging	• call aging time

Figure 11-5   Parallel structure in a bulleted list

In Figure 11-5, note that the items on the left side of the figure are not worded in the same way. The list on the right shows one way to rewrite the list using parallel structure; all the terms are nouns, and the phrasing is similar. In a parallel list structure, each item in the list should make a complete sentence when used with the phrase that introduces the list.

Consistent Verb Tense

Technical writers generally use a consistent verb tense throughout a document. Present tense is often preferable in technical writing unless the topic is something that clearly happened in the past. Consider the following examples:

Example 1: *After you have powered up your computer and booted into Windows, the network connection wizard is used to establish a network connection.*

Example 2: *First, power up your computer and boot into Windows. Then use the network connection wizard to establish a network connection.*

The first example uses the past tense unnecessarily. The second example uses the present tense, which leads the reader through the actions. Past tense may be appropriate in a problem description to indicate actions a user performed because the actions did occur in the past.

Common Technical Writing Problems

Technical writers learn from experience to avoid common problems so that their writing is clearer, more understandable, and easier to read. Figure 11-6 lists 10 common problems to avoid.

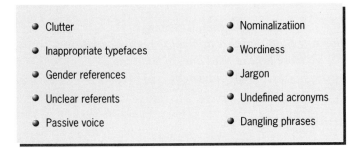

- Clutter
- Inappropriate typefaces
- Gender references
- Unclear referents
- Passive voice
- Nominalizatiion
- Wordiness
- Jargon
- Undefined acronyms
- Dangling phrases

Figure 11-6   Common technical writing problems

Clutter

The availability of powerful word processors and desktop publishing software means that even novice writers can produce very professional-looking results. However, all writers need to be careful not to include too many distracting design elements. Just because graphics, clip art, shading, word art, borders, and neon printer colors can be easily included does not mean that you should use all of them. Add graphics to illustrate or highlight an important point, not just for decoration. Apply formatting sparingly and consistently, and only when it helps readers locate information or understand the subject. A user document with simple formatting is often more effective than one with too many format features.

The most successful documents are those that include considerable white space where readers can rest their eyes. Leave reasonable margins at the top, bottom, and sides of pages; insert spaces between paragraphs; and use a font that is large enough to be readable. The body text font size should be at least ten points or larger; don't reduce the size of a font just to fit material that is too long in the space allocated to it. Rather, edit for conciseness.

Most body text should be left-aligned. Large passages of centered text are difficult to read, as is **justified text**, which is aligned at both the right and left margins. Justified text, also called block-justified, sometimes contains large white spaces between words that can make text difficult to read. For example, which of these passages is easier to read?

This paragraph is left-aligned to illustrate how easily the reader's eye moves from word to word. This justification style is recommended for the body of most documents because it enhances readability.

This paragraph is block-justified to illustrate that it is more difficult to read a passage when software inserts additional spaces between words. This approach creates an artificial block style with text that extends to the right and left margins.

This paragraph is centered to illustrate that it is more difficult to read, and it takes more time to read lines of text that differ in length.

Inappropriate Typefaces

For most readers, serif typefaces are easier to read than sans serif. **Serif typefaces** include serifs, fine lines that project from the top and bottom of a font's letters. These lines lead the eye from letter to letter across the line. The font you are reading now is called Warnock Pro, which is a serif font. **Sans serif typefaces** do not have the serifs (*sans* is French for *without*). Sans serif typefaces are often used for titles and headings, whereas serif typefaces are frequently used for body text.

Most word processors include several **specialty typefaces** that are intended for special uses, such as invitations, brochures, or flyers. Script fonts fall into this category. Specialty typefaces are interesting and fun, but you should save them for informal use. Figure 11-7 shows a serif font, a sans serif font, and a specialty font. Which do you think is easiest to read?

This is an example of a 12-point serif typeface called Goudy Old Style.

This is an example of a 12-point sans serif typeface called Arial.

This is an example of a 14-point script typeface called Brush Script.

Figure 11-7   Font readability examples

Gender References

In recent years, the use of gender-related pronouns has decreased. *He*, *she*, *him*, and *her* are often replaced with gender-neutral words, such as *they*, *their*, and *it*. This change in style means that writers sometimes use a plural pronoun where they might have previously used a singular pronoun. You can also use the phrase *he or she* (the order is sometimes reversed). Some writers use the combined form *s/he*, but this solution is usually not preferred because it is less common and more difficult to read. Others writers alternate between *he* and *she*—a strategy that can confuse a reader. Choose one of these strategies to use consistently, but try to avoid gender-related words, unless they clearly fit.

Gender-neutral words include *staff* instead of *manpower*, and *staffed* instead of *manned*. Use *chair* or *chairperson* instead of *chairman* (unless Chairman is an official title). But be consistent: don't refer to a male as a *chairman* and a female as a *chair*; instead, refer to both genders as a *chair*. Use *supervisor* rather than *foreman*. Can you think of other common examples? It takes some practice to use gender-neutral language, but the result is often clearer and less offensive than the alternatives.

Unclear Referents

Another common problem in technical writing is the use of unclear or missing referents. A **referent** is a concrete word or concept that is designated by another word. Words such as *this*, *that*, *it*, and *they* are common words used to designate referents. Consider this example:

Windows and the Office Suite use pull-down context menus. They are good examples of the power of the GUI interface.

The word *they* at the start of the second sentence designates or refers to a concept in the previous sentence. But does the writer mean that Windows and the Office Suite are examples of the power of the GUI interface, or that pull-down context menus are good examples? The concrete referent of *they* is not clear. To clarify the second sentence, replace *they* with the intended referent:

Windows and the Office Suite use pull-down context menus. Both software packages are good examples of the power of the GUI interface.

Passive Voice

Good technical writing uses the active voice instead of the passive voice whenever possible. With **active voice**, the subject of a sentence *performs* the action indicated by the verb; the subject is an actor.

With **passive voice**, the subject of a sentence *receives* the action indicated by the verb; the subject is not acting. In some sentences written in the passive voice, the real subject is missing. Consider this example:

The new operating system was installed on Friday.

In this example, the subject (*operating system*) does not perform the action (*was installed*), but is the recipient of the action. Passive voice is often used to avoid naming the real subject of a sentence, as in the classic example of passive voice: "Mistakes were made." The sentence below is much stronger in active voice:

A support specialist installed the new operating system on Friday.

In this revision, the subject (*support specialist*) performs the action (*installed*). Although some technical writers prefer passive voice because it makes the writing seem more objective, others avoid passive voice whenever possible because it can give text a stilted, awkward tone (few people talk in passive voice), and is often unclear. Active voice makes text livelier and more interesting. Compare the examples in Table 11-1 and see how much easier the active voice sentences are to understand.

Résumés are often more interesting and convey an action-orientation when they are written primarily in active voice rather than passive voice. The grammar checkers in some word processors alert writers to excessive use of passive voice.

Passive Voice	Active Voice
The text is highlighted by clicking the bold button.	Highlight the text by clicking the bold button.
The USB drive gets inserted into an available USB slot.	Insert the USB drive into an available slot.
The file is read from the disk.	The computer reads the file from the disk.
Touching the disk media should be avoided.	Avoid touching the disk media.

Table 11-1　Active versus passive voice

Nominalization

Nominalization is the use of *–tion, –ing, -ment* and other word endings to create nouns out of verbs. In general, avoid nominalization; verbs are easier to understand. Table 11-2 shows examples of sentences using nominalization as well as their improved forms.

Nominalization	Improved Form
Development of a JavaScript module will take three weeks.	The project team will develop a JavaScript module in three weeks.
Perform an installation of the printer driver.	Install the printer driver.
The configuration of the system should take about an hour.	The system takes about an hour to configure.

Table 11-2 Nominalization examples

Wordiness

Wordiness can lead to long sentences and hinder understanding. Avoid unnecessary words; find the shortest way to state your ideas. Table 11-3 presents several examples of how to reduce unnecessary words.

Wordy	Concise
Call customer support to raise questions about the problem you are having.	Call customer support to ask about the problem.
Prior to the actual installation of the system . . .	Before installing the system . . .
Before making an attempt to install the card . . .	Before installing the card . . .
Put the computer in a location where it will not be in danger of being harmed by anyone who might be passing by.	Locate the computer where passersby will not accidentally damage it.

Table 11-3 Reducing wordiness

To make text easier to read, use short words whenever possible. Replace long words such as *approximately* with a shorter word that means the same thing, such as *about*; replace *utilize* with *use,* and try *document* instead of *documentation.* Can you think of other examples?

Jargon

Computer technology often intimidates new users because of the amount of jargon used to describe and discuss it. Avoid the use of **jargon**, words understood only by those experienced in a field. Instead, use simple, direct words that anyone can understand, unless the target audience will clearly understand the jargon. For example, technical writers may write about the *cold boot process* for a computer system. However, in documents for new users, use a term like *start-up process* or *power-on step* instead.

If you must use jargon terms, define them first so that you and the reader share a common understanding of the vocabulary. Writers often include a glossary at the end of a chapter or book, much like the key terms list at the end of the chapters in this book.

Undefined Acronyms

Like jargon, an **acronym**—a word formed from the initial letters of words in a phrase—can make technical writing difficult to understand. For example, *I/O* is an acronym for *input/output*; *RAM* is an acronym for *random access memory*. Writers should define the meaning of each acronym for a reader, unless the target audience will obviously understand the acronym. Even for advanced audiences, err on the safe side and define each acronym. The first time an acronym is used, spell out the words that the acronym represents, and then include the acronym in parentheses:

Three main types of random access memory (RAM) are in common use today: SDRAM (Synchronous Dynamic RAM), DDR-SDRAM (Double Data Rate SDRAM), and RDRAM (RAMBUS Dynamic RAM). Of the three, DDR-SDRAM is dominant in today's market.

Another effective strategy is to include acronyms in a glossary or a key terms list.

Dangling Modifiers

A **dangling modifier** is a few words (or even a single word) at the beginning or end of a sentence that add little to the meaning of the sentence other than to make it longer. Sometimes, dangling modifiers can make a sentence unclear and confusing.

Example 1: *The Accounting Department is eager to begin training on QuickBooks, generally.*

Example 2: *Generally, the Accounting Department is eager to begin training on QuickBooks.*

Example 3: *Mohammed turned on the LCD projector, but the image did not appear, as everyone noticed.*

Example 4: *After trying several troubleshooting approaches, the problem remained unsolved.*

Either eliminate the dangling phrase, if it makes little difference to the meaning of the sentence, or look for a way to include it in the sentence.

Revision of examples 1 and 2: *The Accounting Department is generally eager to begin training on QuickBooks.*

Revision of example 3: *When Mohammed turned on the LCD projector, everyone noticed that the image did not appear.*

Revision of example 4: *Mohammed tried several troubleshooting approaches, but the problem remained unsolved.*

This list of potential writing problems is long, and we've only covered a few common mistakes. However, many technical writers find that with practice and experience, they become adept at avoiding these problems.

ON THE WEB

Paul Brians, an English professor at Washington State University, has compiled a list of common mistakes in language use. See his Web site at **www.wsu.edu/~brians/errors**.

Also see Western Washington University Professor Gene Myers's list of writing errors to avoid at **www.ac.wwu. edu/~gmyers/writeerr.html**.

A ROLE-PLAYING SCENARIO

The role-playing activity in this chapter is in the form of writing a response to an e-mail from a user, Erin, in the Accounting Department where you work. Your task is to prepare a response to Erin's e-mail.

From: *Erin@Accounting.SPI.com*

To: *UserSupport@IT.SPI.com*

My computer has been running slower and slower recently. One of my coworkers in Accounting said I probably need to check my computer for something called a key logger. I know nothing about that. How can I learn how to check my PC for a key logger? Could they slow my machine down? Where can I get a program that checks for a key logger? How do I know if this will even help?

Write an e-mail response to Erin from UserSupport @IT.SPI.com. Make your response an example of a well-written e-mail message.

Then compare your response with that of your colleagues or coworkers. Based on what you learned from the comparison, how would you improve your response to Erin?

Technical Writing Tools

Many word processors include tools that support staff can use to develop useful user documentation. These include:

- An outline tool to help organize work

- A spell checker to identify and correct spelling errors

- A custom dictionary to spell-check jargon words, acronyms, and technical terms

- A thesaurus to help find a word that exactly expresses a concept

- A grammar checker to recommend changes in wording to improve readability

- A readability index to measure the level of difficulty for the audience

- Desktop publishing features to help writers produce professional-looking documents

Even with all these built-in software tools, a good collegiate dictionary is also a useful tool, because spell checkers don't know the meaning of words. Be on the lookout for good examples of well-written documents. Be critical of documents you read. Ask yourself what makes a document or message useful and easy to read, and by the same token, what makes one difficult to understand and use.

ON THE WEB

One of the classic books on writing clearly in English is *The Elements of Style* by William Strunk, Jr. and E. B. White (4th edition: Longman, 1999). An earlier online version of this entire book is available on the Bartleby.com Web site at **www.bartleby.com/141**. Many writers think of *The Elements of Style* as the bible of written communication.

Microsoft publishes the *Microsoft Manual of Style for Technical Publications* (3rd edition: Microsoft Press, 2004). Another popular online resource is the *Chicago Manual of Style* at **www.chicagomanualofstyle.org**.

Documentation Evaluation Criteria

All technical writers have personal preferences and writing styles. Although writers may disagree on specific style issues, the ultimate measure of user documentation is whether it effectively and efficiently communicates information the reader needs. For technical writers, *effectively* means readers get the correct information they need to master a topic or to perform a task. *Efficiently* means readers do not have to spend extra time searching for information or reading through irrelevant material to find what they need.

Four general criteria can be used as a checklist to evaluate written documents:

- Content
    - Is the information relevant?
    - Is the information timely and accurate?
    - Is the coverage of the topic complete?
- Organization
    - Is the information easy to locate?
    - Are transitions between topics identifiable?
    - Can the user get in and out quickly with the right answer?
- Format
    - Does the layout help guide the reader?
    - Is the format consistent?
- Mechanics
    - Are words spelled correctly?
    - Is it grammatically correct?
    - Is the writing style effective?

As you plan, write, review, and revise your writing, think about how it measures up to these criteria. The principles and practices you learned in this chapter apply to all the forms of documentation a user support specialist creates. Regardless of a document's intended use, the purpose remains the same: clear communication that addresses readers' needs by giving them concise information they can use.

 The hands-on activities and case projects at the end of this chapter are designed to give you an opportunity to use the guidelines presented in this chapter in your own writing. The activities and projects are important parts of the chapter and will help you develop your writing skills.

Chapter Summary

- User support staff are frequently assigned technical writing tasks to produce brochures, flyers, newsletters, handouts, training aids, user guides, computer manuals, online help files, e-mail and chat messages, Web pages, proposals, memos, operating procedure documentation, and troubleshooting guides.

- The goal of technical writing is to produce documents that effectively and efficiently communicate information needed by the reader.

- A technical writing task begins by defining the characteristics of the target audience, including their background and reading level. Each document should be planned with a clear understanding of what the writer wants the reader to be able to do after reading it.

- In technical documents, short words and sentences are preferable to long ones. Information should be organized so that it is easy to locate. The purpose of a document and its intended audience should be clearly stated so each reader can decide at the beginning whether to read the document.

- The process of technical writing includes organizing ideas and topics into an outline and expanding the outline into a first draft. Edit passes through a document are intended to eliminate extra words, tighten prose, and check for format consistency and technical accuracy. A review by another person is a useful check to improve a document before the final revision.

- The layout of a document should help a reader understand the organization, know what is important, and be aware when transitions between topics occur. Formatting should be used consistently to enhance the information presented, not detract from it.

- Successful technical writers use strategies such as analogies, repetition, consistent word use, and parallel structure to help the audience understand the material.

- Common problems to avoid in technical documents include clutter, inappropriate typefaces, gender references, unclear referents, and passive voice. Other common problems are nominalization, wordiness, jargon, undefined acronyms, and dangling modifiers.

- Several software tools, including an outline tool, spell checker, thesaurus, grammar checker, and desktop publishing features are available to help technical writers produce well-organized, accurate, and professional-looking documentation.

- Writers use four criteria—review, organize, format, and mechanics—to evaluate a technical document.

Key Terms

acronym—A word formed from the initial letters of words in a phrase; for example, *CPU* is an acronym for *central processing unit*; define acronyms to ensure readers' understanding.

active voice—A sentence in which the subject performs the action indicated by the verb; for example: *Mary will present a tutorial on Excel macros on Monday;* compare to passive voice.

analogy—A comparison between an unfamiliar concept and a familiar one; an analogy highlights the similarities between things; for example, the CPU in a computer system is analogous to an office calculator in a manual system.

brainstorm—A method used to generate a list of potential ideas or topics; the brainstormed list is then prioritized and pared down, as needed.

dangling modifier—A few words (or a single word) at the beginning or end of a sentence that add little to the meaning of the sentence.

documentation—Written communication intended to provide user support information to end users; can be printed or online; includes brochures, flyers, newsletters, handouts, training aids, user guides, handbooks, manuals, online help systems, proposals, letters, memos, e-mail and chat messages, procedural and operational documentation, Web pages, and troubleshooting guides.

format consistency check—An edit pass through a draft document in which a writer checks to make sure that the headings and subheadings fonts, indentation, centering, boldface, italics, underlining, and other format elements are used consistently throughout a document.

hierarchical organization—A document organization style that flows from top to bottom; information is arranged from general to specific; online help systems are an example.

jargon—Words that are understood only by those experienced in a field; for example, *hacker* is jargon, whereas *unauthorized user* is more general; define jargon words to ensure that readers understand them.

justified text—A document or paragraph format in which the text is extended to both the right and left margins; commonly used in books and newspapers, but can be difficult to read.

nominalization—The use of *–tion, –ing, -ment* and other word endings to create nouns; for example, *Capitalization can be performed with the Change Case command* could be rewritten to avoid nominalization as: *To capitalize words, use the Change Case command.*

parallel structure—A writing strategy in which similar items are treated consistently throughout a document; examples include consistent verb tenses and consistent phrasing in lists.

passive voice—A sentence in which the subject of a sentence *receives* the action indicated by the verb; for example, *The documentation was prepared by me* is in passive voice, whereas *I prepared the documentation* is in active voice.

pointer—A cross-reference in a document indicating where a user can find more information on a topic; often used in technical writing to reduce the size of a document by including directions to appendices, attachments, exhibits, figures, tables, and other related materials.

reference format—A documentation style that pulls together all the information on a specific topic in a single page, section, or chapter; compare to tutorial format.

referent—A concrete word or concept that is designated by another word; for example, in *Before you insert a CD, inspect it for scratches*, the word *CD* is the referent of *it*; avoid pronouns such as *it*, *them*, and *their* when the referent is unclear.

sans serif typeface—A style of type that does not have fine lines (serifs) added to each character; often used in titles and headings; compare with serif typeface.

sequential organization—A document organization style that follows a step-by-step approach whereby information is arranged in the order in which the steps are executed; procedural and operational documents are examples.

serif typeface—A style of type in which each character includes fine lines (called serifs) that project from the top and bottom of each letter; serifs lead the reader's eye from letter to letter across the line, improving readability; compare with sans serif typeface.

specialty typeface—A style of type that is intended for special uses, such as invitations, brochures, or flyers; draws attention to text, although it makes general text more difficult to read; script typefaces are an example.

style sheet—A list of common terms, formats, and writing conventions that describes the preferred use and spelling of a documentation department or organization so that writers use consistent terminology and formats.

technical accuracy check—An edit pass through a draft in which a writer tests any procedural or technical steps in a document by performing the steps with the hardware or software; helps reduce errors in step-by-step instructions or other technical information.

tutorial format—A documentation style that guides a user step-by-step through the features of a program with frequently used features covered first; compare to reference format.

Check Your Understanding

Answers to Check Your Understanding questions are found in Appendix A.

1. True or False? The primary goal of technical writing is to entertain readers and hold their interest.

2. A(n) _____ is a short document primarily intended to summarize material covered in a training session and promote recall.

3. True or False? All users prefer online documentation to printed documentation because access to the information needed is easier.

4. Documentation that is organized as a step-by-step introduction to the features of a computer program is called a:

    a. reference manual

    b. technical manual

    c. tutorial manual

    d. troubleshooting manual

5. True or False? Effectively written user documents should result in a lower volume of user support calls and e-mails.

6. Which of the following forms of documentation often contain hyperlinks to related topics?

    a. online help systems

    b. newsletters

    c. e-mail messages

    d. troubleshooting guides

7. True or False? Good technical documents should provide a reader with everything they would ever want to know about a topic.

8. A(n) _____ is an attempt to relate something a reader may be familiar with to something they need to know about.

9. What is the correct sequence of the following steps in the technical writing process?
(1) proofread the document; (2) generate a list of ideas; (3) arrange for an outside reviewer; (4) write a first draft

   a. 1 – 2 – 3 – 4

   b. 2 – 4 – 3 – 1

   c. 4 – 2 – 1 – 3

   d. 2 – 1 – 4 – 3

10. True or False? An outside review of a technical document serves the same purpose as a beta test of a software package.

11. True or False? Changes in case, font, indentation, and centering are format elements used to help the reader of a document understand its structure.

12. Which of the following words or phrases is least descriptive of the information on a Web page?

   a. complete

   b. concise

   c. includes pointers to other information

   d. well organized

13. True or False? A technical writer should use the same word to refer to an object or a concept throughout a document rather than a variety of different words that are synonyms.

14. A reading level that is appropriate for most technical documentation is _____.

   a. 5th grade

   b. 8th grade

   c. 12th grade

   d. college level

15. Whether to use the form 'Plug-n-Play' or 'Plug-and-Play' in a document would likely be specified in a(n) _____.

16. True or False? The following example illustrates good parallel structure:

    1. *Move the mouse pointer to the button of your choice.*

    2. *Next, click the button on the mouse.*

    3. *You then click on "OK."*

17. To avoid jargon, a technical writer might substitute a word(s) such as _____ for *head crash* in the following sentence: *Users frequently lose their data when there is a head crash on the file server.*

18. _____ is a method used to generate a list of potential ideas or topics to include in a document.

19. A document organization style in which all the information on a topic is pulled together in one place is called:

    a. reference format

    b. hierarchical format

    c. tutorial format

    d. sequential format

20. A(n) _____ is a list of common terms and writing conventions specifying spelling and usage preferences to insure consistency in an organization.

Discussion Questions

1. "Because e-mail and chat messages are less formal methods of communication, good technical writing skills are less important for these messages." Do you agree or disagree with this statement? Explain why.

2. In order to avoid using gender-related pronouns, some writers use a plural pronoun with a singular subject. For example: *A technical writer should choose their words carefully.* Other alternatives are: *A technical writer should choose his or her words carefully*; and, *Technical writers should choose their words carefully.* Which format do you prefer? Discuss these alternatives and other ways around this writing challenge.

3. All professions use technical jargon terms and acronyms. Professionals such as health care workers, accountants, and lawyers can frequently be difficult to understand. Why should the computer field be any different?

4. Discuss some ways to determine whether the target audience for a document will understand various acronyms and jargon terms. Brainstorm some effective ways to deal with these terms if a writer is not sure whether the audience will understand them.

5. "If one purpose of a flyer is to advertise an event, a writer should use as many design elements (fonts, bold, italic, underlining, color, shading, clip art) as possible to attract attention to the flyer." Do you agree or disagree with this statement? Explain your position.

6. "If a technical writer has a choice of reading levels for a document (as measured by a readability index), it is preferable to aim the reading level a little too high, rather than a little too low and risk insulting the intelligence of your readers." Explain your position on this statement.

Hands-On Activities

Activity 11-1

Revise existing documents. The following sentences and paragraphs highlight some of the problems you learned about in this chapter. Use what you have learned to rewrite the examples to make them clear and readable.

1. From a one-page notice informing employees which machines they can use in a training facility:

   Employees should be well advised that they should use only the first row of machines, the HP PCs. All other machines are used only for classes for training new users. If an employee doesn't do this, he will be asked to leave the training room.

2. From an e-mail message sent to all employees of a law firm advising them to be alert for a new virus:

   This virus has been known to cause the destruction of files, and it is very important that you perform a search of your hard drive to try and attempt eradication of it using the search feature. Search for .EDT file extensions and delete them. Then the problem will be solved.

3. From an instruction sheet that an instructor will hand out during a training session on a new e-mail package; this passage explains the capabilities of the package to users who have never used e-mail before:

E-mail messages are stored on a central server, and you download it every time you open one, in effect. You can save it to a local disk if you want to keep it.

4. From a booklet that a user support department will distribute to employees of an insurance organization to explain the capabilities of a new software claims management package:

This is a new type of CMS (claims management software) that every adjuster, regardless of his level, will benefit from, greatly. This claims management software can: (1) organize claims information, (2) be used while you are on the telephone, (3) do reports by claim type, and (4) for generation of summary claims information.

Activity 11-2

Write and compare procedural documentation. Write an explanation of the steps required to insert a USB flash drive into a USB port. Your explanation should be aimed at a person who has never used a computer before.

Exchange explanations with a classmate or coworker and critique each other's draft. Did you include enough information for the user to insert the USB flash drive correctly? Is your explanation complete, or did you leave out important information about the steps? Did you include extra information that wasn't necessary?

Find an inexperienced user to test your document. Have that person use your document without any assistance to see if he or she can perform the task using only your written documentation. Revise your instructions based on the peer and user feedback you receive.

Activity 11-3

Revise procedure documentation. The instructions below are intended to describe the steps for running a defragmentation utility under Windows. Your task is to revise the document following the guidelines in this chapter so that it is a good example of technical writing.

*These instructions will run the Windows defragmenter program, which is named **defrag.exe,** once a week on Friday afternoon at 6PM. Of course, you can change the schedule to whatever time you desire.*

1. Click on **Add a Scheduled Task** from the **Scheduled Tasks Wizzard**, which you can find in the **Control Panel**.

2. Click **Next** and the user will see a list of programs he can schedule.

3. Note that the **defragger.exe** does not appear, so click on **Browse**.

4. Browse lets you find defrag.exe in this path: **C:\Windows\System32\defrag.exe**. Click on **Open**.

5. Next, please give the task Wizzard the name of the task, such as **defrag** and then set up the schedule.

6. When you click on **Weekly** and **Next**.

7. Type in the start time, which is **6:00 PM** and click the box for **Friday**.

8. Windows will ask you what user name and password to use to login the defragger.

9. You are done.

Activity 11-4

Revise a textbook paragraph. The following document is an excerpt from a computer textbook. It contains examples of many of the common problems described in this chapter. (The line numbers are for your convenience to identify and refer to problems).

First, go through the document and note the problems that you find with it. If you are working as part of a project group, compare your list of problems with others to see where group members agree and disagree. Second, rewrite the document to correct the problems you identified. Your rewrite should make the document as clear and as easy to understand as possible. Your instructor may be able to provide you with a copy of the document in machine-readable form.

1. *MANAGING FOLDERS AND DISKS*
2.
3. *Introduction*
4.
5. *There are many types of storage media today. Hard disks are the most*
6. *common. It is the best of all the possible ways to save data. A hard*

7.   *drive is divided into various folders so that files can be*
8.   *saved to them. Definitely, this is the most efficient way to manage a large*
9.   *number of files stored on a disk.*
10.
11.   *Various commands, especially those dealing with disks and*
12.   *directories, produce lots of computer numbers. To get a handle*
13.   *on computer numbers, you need to get the big picture on bits, bytes,*
14.   *megabytes, and gigabytes.*
15.   *A computer may seem intelligent, but essentially it can "understand"*
16.   *only whether power is on or not. To issue an instruction to a computer,*
17.   *we need to go by 1 (on) or 0 (off). The two digits of 1 and 0 are the*
18.   *foundation of binary (base 2) math. Binary math is based on bits, which*
19.   *is a contraction of two words—binary digit. One bit can have the*
20.   *value of either 1 or 0. Bits get a little large to move around, so*
21.   *programmers combine 8 bits together to form a byte. Bytes can increase*
22.   *in number: 1 byte can store a 1; 1 KB (kilobyte) is the same as 1024; 1 MB*
23.   *(megabyte) is 1048576; and 1073742824 equals 1 GB. So, when you*
24.   *hear that a disk has a 40 GB capacity, it can store $40 \times 1074742824 =$*
25.   *42989712960 bytes.*
26.
27.   *Formatting of Disks*
28.
29.   *When you create a file you need to store it on a hard disc. Before that,*
30.   *it must be properly prepared to receive information (formatted). If you*
31.   *have used a disk and it has some space on it, you can not follow this section.*
32.
33.   *While it was being formatted, the disk was divided into a number of*
34.   *concentric rings or tracks. Each track was separated into a number of*
35.   *sectors. Each sector stored 512 bytes. A higher capacity disk contains*
36.   *more tracks and sectors; that is how they stored more data, for your*
37.   *information.*

Activity 11-5

Experiment with format and font variations. Select a short description of a simple computer task, such as the procedure for inserting a USB flash drive into a USB port from Activity 11-2. The description should include at least two headings and some procedural steps. Format the document in three ways, using font and style variations. Show the three versions to three classmates or colleagues. Ask them to choose which one is easiest to read and then to explain their preferences. Write a short summary of their responses and describe the conclusions you reached about document formatting from this activity.

Activity 11-6

Evaluate and rewrite a document. Find a piece of computer documentation, a memo, or other technical writing that you wrote prior to reading this chapter. It should be at least one page and contain two or more paragraphs. Apply the concepts and ideas you have learned in this chapter to critique the document; revise it to correct any problems you discovered.

If the word processor you use has a readability index feature, check the reading level of your revised document. Then revise the document to lower its readability index by at least one grade level (for example, if your rewritten document is at 10th grade level, modify the document until the readability index is at a 9th grade level).

Have a classmate or coworker review your work and make suggestions. Do you agree with her or his suggestions? Explain why or why not. Use the suggestions to revise your work.

Activity 11-7

Evaluate online documentation. Visit a Microsoft Web site that displays information about the accessibility features in Internet Explorer 8, at **www.microsoft.com/enable/products/ie8/default.aspx**.

Analyze and critique the Web site based on the information you have learned in this chapter. Remember that the target audience for this site is made up of users who have physical limitations that might affect their ability to use Web browser software. Write a one-page summary of your evaluation, with recommendations on how you would improve the documentation. Include in your analysis how the Web site document meets or doesn't meet the four evaluation criteria described in this chapter.

Activity 11-8

Revise a section in this chapter. The last section in this chapter, *Documentation Evaluation Criteria*, describes four criteria a writer can use to evaluate technical writing. Apply what you have learned about technical writing in this chapter to this section.

- With three or four of your colleagues, critique this section of the chapter.

- Apply the criteria described in this section to the section itself. What are the strengths of the section? What improvements could be made?

- Based on your evaluation, write an evaluation and describe how you would modify the section for the next edition of this book.

Case Projects

1. Web Search Guide for Sergio Escobar

Sergio Escobar is the supervisor of a computer facility used by trainees in a job retraining program. The computer facility has 18 Macintosh systems, which are used by the trainees to improve their job skills and to aid them in their job search efforts. The Macs' software includes a résumé-preparation program that is very popular with the trainees. Sergio has recently connected the Macs to a network to provide Internet access. However, the trainees he serves do not have good Web search skills, and many are frustrated that they cannot find useful employment information on the Web.

Sergio posted a few URLs for various local and regional job banks, but he knows that information online changes daily. He also knows that if trainees knew how, they could use the Web to research organizations in preparation for job interviews. As a support specialist, you are assigned to work with Sergio to prepare some basic documentation for the trainees on how to do information searches on the Web. Use the search engine you are most familiar with for this case project.

Create a short "Guide to Web Searches" document that Sergio can give to users of the facility he supervises. The document should include a description of how to use a search engine, instructions on how to enter a search term and how to narrow a search, and helpful Web search strategies. It should include some examples that relate to job search strategies. The document should be self-contained and designed for use outside a classroom environment. Use the online documentation published by one or more organizations that provide Web search engines as a resource.

If you work in a group with other workers or students, post several examples of group members' documents and let each member nominate the Guide they think best meets the four criteria for good documents discussed in the chapter.

2. Orientation Guide for The Career School

As a user support specialist for a computer lab at The Career School, you have been assigned the task of developing a lab orientation guide aimed at new students who use the facility. Prepare a one-sheet (two pages printed back to back) summary of information for new users of the lab. You can use the policies of a lab environment you are familiar with, such as a lab at your school or workplace. First, describe who uses the lab. Orient your guide to those users.

Your orientation guide can include basic information about lab operating policies and procedures, instructions on logging in and out of the network, how to access popular software packages, printing procedures, use of resource materials, and other general or technical information you think should be included. You may want to include short sections with information aimed at students in specific courses or training sessions.

For ideas on topics you may want to include, think about what information a new student or trainee would want to know. For inspiration, go to the lab and look at the postings on bulletin boards, whiteboards, walls, doors, machines, and tables. Rely on your own experience as a user or as a lab assistant. One of the goals of this writing project is to replace as much of the verbal instructions given by lab staff and as many printed signs as possible with an information sheet that the lab staff can distribute to new users.

3. Templates for Rocky Mountain Consultants

Erica Allan is the supervisor of documentation for Rocky Mountain Consultants, a firm that provides consulting services to engineering organizations. She recently received a request from several departments at Rocky Mountain to design a memo form that each department can adopt and use as their standard memo format. Erica wants to accommodate each department, but is short of staff she can assign to the project. Erica also feels strongly that it would be more useful to give each department the tools it needs to develop its own memo template, rather than designing a template for each department.

Erica wants you to develop an instructional document aimed at word-processor users that describes the procedure to create a simple template. (Use whichever word processor you have access to for this project.) Although each department wants a different and distinctive memo format, Erica suggests you use a simple memo like the one shown in Figure 11-8 as an example. Describe the fonts and format features to create a template that looks as much like the example as you can. Your document should include the steps a user would take to create and store a template for the memo in the figure. Prepare a document titled "How to Prepare a Simple Memo Template" that describes the process to users at Rocky Mountain Consultants.

Rocky Mountain Consultants
Document Preparation Department

MEMO

To:

From:

Copy:

Date:

Subject:

Figure 11-8   Sample memo format

4. Cartridge Recycling at Re-Nu-Cartridge

Elma McDonald works in the Production department at Re-Nu-Cartridge, a local company that refills ink and toner cartridges for computer printers. Elma's job is to clean and inspect inkjet and toner cartridges before they are refilled. With the equipment at Re-Nu-Cartridge, Elma can clean several types of common cartridges. However, the company does not have the facilities to clean all types of cartridges, especially less common ones. Several of Re-Nu-Cartridge's environmentally responsible corporate customers have asked Elma for information about how to recycle cartridges that Re-Nu-Cartridge can't refill.

Elma would like you to use the Web to research companies that recycle ink and toner cartridges. See if you can find more than one company that offers a cartridge recycling service. Based on your research, write a set of instructions for recycling cartridges. Your documentation should be targeted at employees of Re-Nu-Cartridge's customers (but would probably be useful to anyone who uses printer cartridges). The information sheet should include how to package and ship used cartridges to recycle service centers, which cartridges the recyclers will take, where to send the cartridges, what the service costs (if anything), a description of the benefits of using a cartridge recycle service, and any other information someone would need to use the recycle services. Follow the guidelines for good technical writing in this chapter to make the recycling instruction sheet an example of your best professional documentation.

5. Describe a support problem you solved.

Chapter 4 includes descriptions of common support problems, some of which are based on actual reports by support specialists who solved the problems. Your task in this assignment is to write a descriptive report, similar to those in Chapter 4, of a support incident or situation that you worked on and resolved. Your report should describe the situation, the end user(s), the problem you solved, the method and steps you took to solve the problem, and what you learned from the experience. Make your report an example of your best professional technical writing—write your report as if you were preparing it to include in the next edition of this textbook. If you do this exercise as part of a class or training assignment, share your report with others so they can benefit from your problem-solving and writing experience.

CHAPTER 12

A User Support Utility Tool Kit

In this chapter, you will learn about:

◎ Software utilities and information resources used by support specialists

◎ Categories of common user support utilities

◎ Some useful support utilities

User support specialists use a variety of software, information resources, and tools to perform their assigned tasks. Some tools are software utilities that help diagnose and resolve problems encountered by users. Other tools are information resources which support specialists use to locate information about common problems or about products and services. Yet another category consists of tools support workers use to help users prevent common problems, including threats to security and invasion of privacy. These tools also include utilities designed to increase the productivity of support specialists.

This concluding chapter returns to the problem-solving process discussed in Chapters 3 and 4 and provides a beginning tool kit to tackle many of the user support problems described in those chapters. The following sections cover several software utilities and information tools that can help user support workers to do their jobs—with a focus on common tools that many support specialists find useful in their work. In some cases, the software described may be most useful to support specialists. In other cases, the software could be recommended for use by users to solve problems common to end user behavior. The chapter will not cover the much larger categories of applications and personal productivity software aimed at end users.

 The utilities presented in this chapter were selected based on the author's experience, recommendations of colleagues, lists of highly rated utilities, and online reviews. Table 7-2 in Chapter 7 lists several industry publications that publish reviews of software, including support utilities.

Introduction to Utility Software and Information Resources

The tools described in this chapter are representative of various utility software and information resources categories. Their inclusion in the chapter is not intended as a recommendation or an endorsement, and in no case should a utility be used without a clear understanding of its effects on a PC. In many cases, other utilities and resources perform similar tasks or provide comparable information, and some alternatives to those described in detail are listed. Details about specific products and services discussed in this chapter, including their costs and features, may change as providers update their offerings.

Many of the utilities listed in this chapter are open source, freeware, or shareware with free trial options. Open source or shareware products frequently provide features and functions similar to commercial software. However, especially in an educational or training environment, the opportunity for readers to get a variety of experiences with free or low-cost products is important. That does not mean commercial products are less desirable. Readers can expect to encounter commercial versions of utility software on the job. In fact, many of the vendors of free versions of software utilities also sell enhanced business versions with additional features or functionality.

Some of these resources are specifically designated for personal rather than commercial use. Observe any restrictions on use before downloading or accessing any of these resources. Open source, freeware, and shareware should not require payment, except for continued use after a trial period. However, vendors of utility software often require users to register prior to downloading their software. Unfortunately, some vendors use free product registrations as a way to accumulate and sell lists of e-mail addresses to their business partners or third parties. Users who register to download software should check the vendor's **privacy policy**, the **end-user license agreement (EULA)**, and information explaining any **opt-in check boxes** on each registration form to determine whether registration implies an agreement to receive e-mail offers. Some users maintain a separate e-mail address to use specifically for product registrations in order to avoid receiving spam e-mail offers at their primary e-mail address.

Several caveats about the use of utility software are summarized in Figure 12-1.

Before downloading and using any software utilities, be aware that:

- Information about specific utilities, including features, costs, download instructions, and documentation, often changes from version to version; check online software specifications and reviews for changes and suitability before downloading or purchasing any utility.

- Open source, freeware, and shareware utilities may not include all the functionality and features of their better-known, commercial counterparts.

- Some vendors who offer a trial or demonstration version of a software utility disable some features or enforce other limitations, including use limited to a specific time period; for example, a "free" utility that scans a PC for problems may repair the problems only in a paid version.

- Some vendors who offer free versions may limit their use to noncommercial, personal use. Use by nonprofit organizations, corporations, educational institutions, and government agencies may fall under a commercial license for which there is a fee.

- Vendors who offer both free and commercial versions of utilities encourage users to buy their commercial versions in a variety of obvious and less-than-obvious ways, including advertisements on their Web sites or during the operation of a utility and sometimes misleading links to download commercial versions.

- Web sites which advertise "free download" do not necessarily mean use of the software is free (only that it doesn't cost anything to download the software).

- While most utility software vendors are reputable and up-front about their use of registration information, some use various methods, including opt-in checks boxes to allow them to accumulate and sell registration information to third parties; often the details of these methods are buried in privacy policies and end-user license agreements (EULAs).

- Not all software utilities run on every version of an operating system. Check the system requirements for hardware and software prerequisites for each utility.

- Utilities that modify the setting or contents of a system (such as performance-enhancement settings or Registry and disk cleaners) should be used with caution and only after backing up the parts of a system that will be modified so that settings or content can be recovered in case of a malfunction.

- Some organizations, agencies, and educational institutions do not permit unauthorized software to be downloaded, installed, and used in a network environment in which security and support issues are common. Learn about restrictions on the use of utility software in your environment.

Figure 12-1 Warnings about utility software

The discussion of the various software utilities in this chapter is intended to provide a brief description of some popular and affordable tools and information resources that a reader can use to begin to build a tool kit to help solve a variety of user support problems. Many of the tools described below are useful primarily to agents who provide support for internal end users in a face-to-face or on-site environment.

Categories of Utility Software Tools

The variety of available utility software tools mirrors the variety of tasks performed by support agents in positions that support internal end users. Figure 12-2 lists the categories of support tools described in this chapter. In some cases, the utilities described may not be useful to all agents. For example, a support specialist who has primarily application software or training support responsibilities may not have immediate use for utilities to diagnose operating system configuration problems. However, most support agents change jobs and responsibilities from time to time. Support agents are also computer users themselves, and may find the tools in some categories, while not directly useful in their work, of interest as they make software recommendations or maintain their own computers, or those of family, friends, and colleagues.

Throughout this chapter, some technical terms that may be unfamiliar are highlighted with bold text. These terms are defined in the Key Terms section at the end of the chapter, rather than in the chapter text or figures.

541

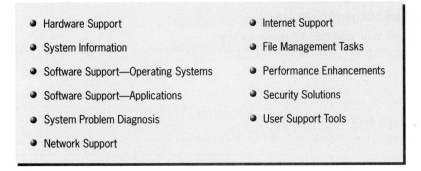

- Hardware Support
- System Information
- Software Support—Operating Systems
- Software Support—Applications
- System Problem Diagnosis
- Network Support
- Internet Support
- File Management Tasks
- Performance Enhancements
- Security Solutions
- User Support Tools

Figure 12-2   Categories of support utilities

Hardware Support

Tools to help support agents solve hardware problems include tools that **stress test** hardware during a burn-in period, update drivers for peripheral devices, and test a PC's hardware components.

- Figure 12-3 describes a tool that helps evaluate hardware reliability and stability during a burn-in period. These tools are of use to support specialists who assemble or install hardware systems.

- Figure 12-4 describes a utility that can be used to find and download updated device drivers.

- Figure 12-5 describes a utility that performs diagnostic tests of hard disk drives to evaluate the likelihood of drive failure.

- Figure 12-6 describes a utility that tests internal RAM to identify problems caused by memory modules that may need to be replaced.

Each utility is described in this chapter on a standard form, like the one in Figure 12-3. The form includes information about each utility's purpose, features, download information, other alternatives, and when available, pointers to documentation and other information.

Utilities in the System Problem Diagnosis and Performance Enhancement categories also perform related tests on hardware components.

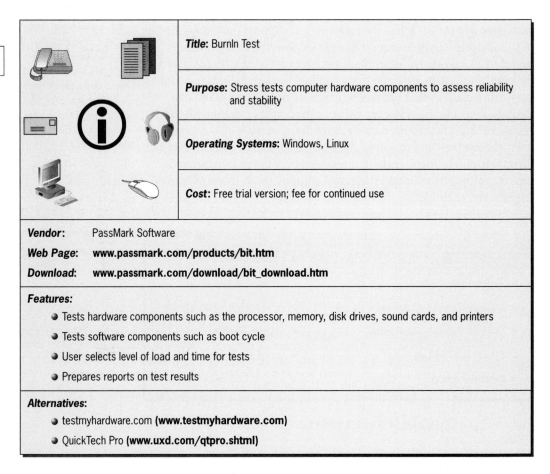

Title: BurnIn Test
Purpose: Stress tests computer hardware components to assess reliability and stability
Operating Systems: Windows, Linux
Cost: Free trial version; fee for continued use

Vendor:	PassMark Software
Web Page:	www.passmark.com/products/bit.htm
Download:	www.passmark.com/download/bit_download.htm

Features:
- Tests hardware components such as the processor, memory, disk drives, sound cards, and printers
- Tests software components such as boot cycle
- User selects level of load and time for tests
- Prepares reports on test results

Alternatives:
- testmyhardware.com (**www.testmyhardware.com**)
- QuickTech Pro (**www.uxd.com/qtpro.shtml**)

Figure 12-3   Utilities that stress test a PC during a burn-in period

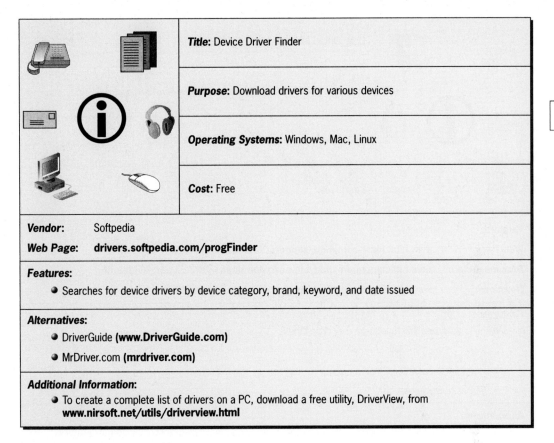

	Title: Device Driver Finder
	Purpose: Download drivers for various devices
	Operating Systems: Windows, Mac, Linux
	Cost: Free

Vendor: Softpedia

Web Page: **drivers.softpedia.com/progFinder**

Features:
- Searches for device drivers by device category, brand, keyword, and date issued

Alternatives:
- DriverGuide (**www.DriverGuide.com**)
- MrDriver.com (**mrdriver.com**)

Additional Information:
- To create a complete list of drivers on a PC, download a free utility, DriverView, from **www.nirsoft.net/utils/driverview.html**

Figure 12-4 Resources to help locate and download updated device drivers

		Title: Drive Fitness Test
		Purpose: Performs test routine on IDE, SATA, and SCSI drives
		Operating Systems: Windows, Linux
		Cost: Free

Vendor:	Hitachi
Web Page:	www.hitachigst.com/hdd/support/download.htm#DFT
Documentation:	www.hitachigst.com/hdd/support/downloads/Dft32_User_Guide.pdf
Download:	www.hitachigst.com/hdd/support/download.htm#DFT

Features:
- Tests, analyzes, and reports on disk drive fitness
- Works on many models of drives (see documentation for exceptions)
- User selects operational mode: quick test, full scan, or stress exerciser
- Creates bootable test disk

Alternatives:
- Seagate's SeaTools for Windows **(www.seagate.com/www/en-us/support/downloads/seatools)**
- Panterasoft's HDD Health **(www.panterasoft.com)**

Figure 12-5   Utility tools to test hard disk drive devices

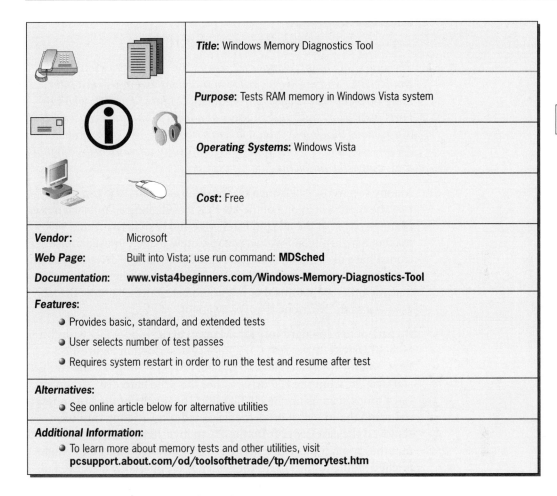

	Title: Windows Memory Diagnostics Tool
	Purpose: Tests RAM memory in Windows Vista system
	Operating Systems: Windows Vista
	Cost: Free

Vendor: Microsoft

Web Page: Built into Vista; use run command: **MDSched**

Documentation: **www.vista4beginners.com/Windows-Memory-Diagnostics-Tool**

Features:
- Provides basic, standard, and extended tests
- User selects number of test passes
- Requires system restart in order to run the test and resume after test

Alternatives:
- See online article below for alternative utilities

Additional Information:
- To learn more about memory tests and other utilities, visit
pcsupport.about.com/od/toolsofthetrade/tp/memorytest.htm

Figure 12-6   Utility tools to test internal memory

CASE STUDY: Utilities for User Support Tasks

The case study in this chapter illustrates the use of utility software to troubleshoot and resolve a variety of problems end users encounter every day. The case is based on Manuela "Manny" Fuentes, who supports instructors and student users at a local community college. Throughout the chapter, you will learn about the variety of problems Manny encounters in her work and how utility software helps diagnose and resolve the problems.

Manny received a call from a teaching lab assistant who reported that the hard disk in one of the lab PCs was making an unusual noise. Manny arrived at the lab and listened to the hard drive, which was making a high-pitched whine. Manny knew that an unusual noise from a hard disk can be one of the first signs that the drive may be on the verge of failure. She asked the lab assistant whether the PC exhibited any other symptoms that might indicate a drive failure. The lab assistant said, "No, none that I'm aware of."

As part of her standard tool kit, Manny carries a boot CD with the Hitachi Drive Fitness Test (DFT) utility described in Figure 12-5. First, Manny made a change to the PC's BIOS settings so she could start the PC from the CD drive rather than the hard drive. Then she ran a quick scan using the DFT utility. The results of the fitness test indicated that the disk drive media tested okay. Manny carefully removed the case cover from the PC to investigate further and found that the case fan was extremely hot. She eventually traced the high-pitched whine to the fan motor, which was apparently about to fail. Using the DFT utility, Manny was able to test and eliminate the disk drive as the source of the noise, and ordered a replacement fan for the PC.

System Information

Tools to help support agents locate information about a system include those that search a PC and report on configuration information and utilities that monitor and prepare a log of activities during a system's start-up process.

- Figure 12-7 describes a tool that prepares reports on installed hardware, software, and configuration information. These reports are useful additions to a site installation notebook, described in Chapter 9.

- Figure 12-8 describes a utility that monitors the start-up process and lists device drivers and system services identified during start-up.

Utilities in the System Problem Diagnosis and Performance Enhancements categories also report configuration information.

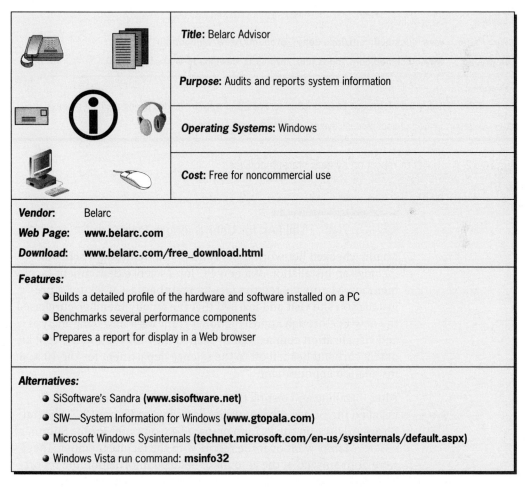

| **Title:** Belarc Advisor |
| **Purpose:** Audits and reports system information |
| **Operating Systems:** Windows |
| **Cost:** Free for noncommercial use |

Vendor:	Belarc
Web Page:	**www.belarc.com**
Download:	**www.belarc.com/free_download.html**

Features:

- Builds a detailed profile of the hardware and software installed on a PC
- Benchmarks several performance components
- Prepares a report for display in a Web browser

Alternatives:

- SiSoftware's Sandra (**www.sisoftware.net**)
- SIW—System Information for Windows (**www.gtopala.com**)
- Microsoft Windows Sysinternals (**technet.microsoft.com/en-us/sysinternals/default.aspx**)
- Windows Vista run command: **msinfo32**

Figure 12-7   Utility tools to report on system configuration information

	Title: WinBootInfo
	Purpose: Monitors and reports on start-up activities
	Operating Systems: Windows
	Cost: Free 30-day trial; $15 to continue use

Vendor: Green Vantage

Web Page: www.clockmod.com/index.php?/products/view/winbootinfo_1.0

Download: www.clockmod.com/index.php?/products/downloads/winbootinfo_1.0

Features:

  ● Provides detailed information about drivers, services, and software loaded during the boot process

  ● Reports timing of boot process events

Figure 12-8   Utility to report on system start-up activities

CASE STUDY: Utilities for User Support Tasks

Manny checked her work orders and found that today's schedule includes an installation of a new PC for a science department faculty member. Manny visited the faculty member last week for a pre-installation site visit and learned that the faculty member purchased the new PC through an instructional grant for a new data-analysis and visualization course. Manny loaded the new PC and her tool kit onto a cart and headed off to the science department for the 10 A.M. installation appointment.

After installing and testing the new PC, Manny downloaded and installed the Belarc Advisor utility described in Figure 12-7. She ran Belarc Advisor on the PC and prepared a Computer Profile Summary report. Manny went over the report with the faculty member. They were both amazed at the amount of detailed information the report included on hardware devices, the operating system, and software installed. The faculty member noted that a specialized data-analysis program he wanted for the curriculum project was not listed among the installed software. Manny asked whether he had the installation disk for the software. Since he did, Manny installed the package and re-ran Belarc Advisor. Manny included the updated Belarc profile summary report in the site installation notebook in case questions arose in the future about the original configuration of the new PC.

Software Support—Operating Systems

Tools to help support agents diagnose problems with operating systems software include utilities that permit an agent to modify the programs that are loaded during system start-up, utilities that delete unused and obsolete information out of the Windows Registry, an information resource that describes utilities and commands that can be entered into the **Windows command-line** interface, a procedure to prepare a Windows **recovery disk** to start up an inoperative system, and a variety of other Windows utilities.

- Figure 12-9 describes a tool to identify and modify the list of software that gets launched automatically during system start-up.

- Figure 12-10 describes a utility that cleans debris from a system Registry to improve its efficiency.

- Figure 12-11 shows a report from Comodo's Registry Cleaner, which checks for several common Registry problems.

- Figure 12-12 describes a utility tool to perform Registry management tasks, including editing Registry keys and values.

- Figure 12-13 describes a resource with information on Windows command-line utilities (sometimes still referred to as DOS commands or utilities).

- Figure 12-14 describes a tool to create a Windows recovery disk, which can be used to start up a system that has an inoperative hard drive or a corrupted operating system.

Utilities in the System Problem Diagnosis, Software Support—Applications, and File Management categories also contain tools that help manage operating system tasks.

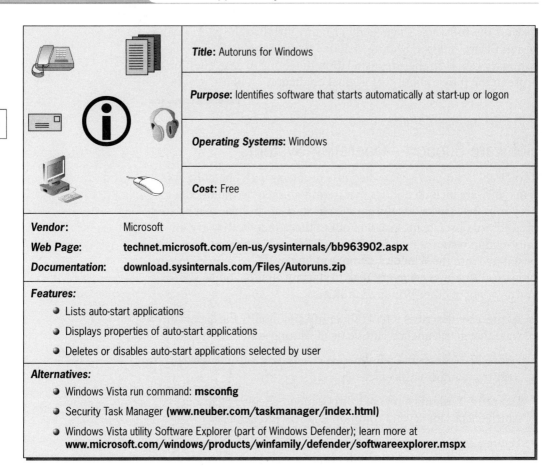

Figure 12-9   Autoruns utility to manage Windows start-up software

Title: System Cleaner/Registry Cleaner

Purpose: Suite of utilities that deletes obsolete and corrupted information from Windows Registry and frees up disk space

Operating Systems: Windows

Cost: Free

Vendor:	Comodo Group
Web Page:	www.comodo.com/index.html
Documentation:	system-cleaner.comodo.com/Comodo_System_Cleaner_User_Guide.pdf
Download:	system-cleaner.comodo.com/download.html

Features:

- Deletes Windows Registry entries that are no longer needed
- Optimizes Windows Registry for improved performance
- Reduces system crashes caused by invalid Registry entries
- Deletes temporary and unused files left behind during software installations and removals, as well as those created during regular use
- Provides system configuration information
- Allows user control over start-up programs

Alternatives:

- Eusing Registry Cleaner (**www.eusing.com/free_registry_cleaner/registry_cleaner.htm**)
- Wise Registry Cleaner (**www.wisecleaner.com**)
- Glary Registry Repair (**www.glarysoft.com/registry-repair**)
- Several commercial Registry cleaners are available; some perform free Registry scans, but require payment to clean problems identified during the scan

Additional Information:

- Read reviews of commercial Registry cleaner utilities at **www.downloadatoz.com/registry-cleaner-reviews**

Figure 12-10   Utility tools to clean and repair Windows Registry

551

552

Figure 12-11 Comodo's Registry Cleaner checks several common Registry problems

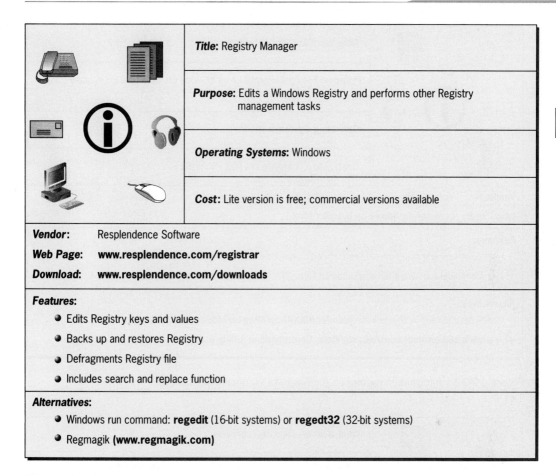

	Title: Registry Manager
	Purpose: Edits a Windows Registry and performs other Registry management tasks
	Operating Systems: Windows
	Cost: Lite version is free; commercial versions available

Vendor: Resplendence Software

Web Page: **www.resplendence.com/registrar**

Download: **www.resplendence.com/downloads**

Features:

- Edits Registry keys and values
- Backs up and restores Registry
- Defragments Registry file
- Includes search and replace function

Alternatives:

- Windows run command: **regedit** (16-bit systems) or **regedt32** (32-bit systems)
- Regmagik **(www.regmagik.com)**

Figure 12-12   Utility tools to edit and manage Windows Registry database

	Title: Windows Vista commands
	Purpose: Provides information on entering commands in the Windows Vista command-line interface
	Operating Systems: Windows
	Cost: Free (commands are built into Vista)

Vendor: Victor Laurie

Web Page: commandwindows.com/index.html

Features:
- Describes command-line utilities that can be run from the Windows command-line prompt
- Command lines are often used in batch files

Alternatives:
- Hidden Utilities in XP and Vista (camtech2000.net/Pages/hidden_utilities.htm)
- www.codeproject.com/KB/vb/Vista_Commandline_Utility.aspx

Figure 12-13   Information resources for Windows command-line utilities

	Title: Windows Vista Recovery Disk
	Purpose: Downloads an image of a Windows Vista bootable recovery disk that can be used to recover inoperable systems
	Operating Systems: Windows
	Cost: Free

Vendor: NeoSmart Technologies

Web Page: neosmart.net

Documentation: neosmart.net/wiki/display/G/NeoSmart+Technologies+Guides

Download: neosmart.net/blog/2008/windows-vista-recovery-disc-download

Features:
- Downloads an **ISO image** of a bootable Windows Vista system recovery disk
- Provides instructions on how to burn the ISO image onto a CD
- Provides several recovery tools, including system start-up, restore, memory diagnostics, and Windows command prompt

Figure 12-14   Utility to create a Windows system recovery disk

CASE STUDY: Utilities for User Support Tasks

Manny and her coworkers use a PC in the support team office as a test bed for nonstandard software that needs to be downloaded, tested, and checked for viruses and compatibility with the college's network. Recently Manny's coworkers have complained that the operation of the PC has slowed considerably. Since Manny has a break in her schedule today, she decided to perform some standard maintenance operations on the test bed PC to see if she could improve its performance.

She first did a hard disk backup, which is standard procedure among the support team members prior to any maintenance work. Then she ran the Uninstaller utility described in Figure 12-17, a disk cleanup utility, CCleaner, which is described later in the chapter in Figure 12-31, and she defragged the drive using Defraggler, described in Figure 12-32. Finally, Manny felt that, since the machine was used to install and test software packages, it was likely that the Registry contained a lot of temporary, obsolete, and invalid entries. She ran the Comodo System Cleaner (which includes Registry Cleaner) described in Figure 12-10. The Registry Cleaner gave her the option of backing up the Registry before the scan, which she accepted as a precaution. Then Manny ran a scan on the test bed PC's Registry. Registry Cleaner identified 455 problem entries across several of the categories. She clicked a button to Fix the Registry Problems.

When the work was completed, Manny noticed that the Registry Cleaner also includes a feature to examine Start Up programs. She knew that if the software packages that had been tested on the machine in the past were still loading into memory at start-up, the machine would probably boot slowly. Manny looked at the Start Up entries in the Comodo software and identified several programs that no longer needed to be loaded when the system was started. She deleted these. One entry in the Start Up list was RtHDVcpl.exe. Manny was unsure whether it was still needed or not. She did a Web search for RtHDVcpl.exe and learned that it is valid software that installs components of RealTek's audio system, so she left the program in the Start Up list.

Manny was able to use several utilities, including a Registry Cleaner, to improve the performance of the test bed machine.

Software Support—Applications

Tools to help support agents manage applications software include those that help inventory software installed on PC systems and verify the existence of authorized **software licenses**, utilities that report on the update status of software, and those that perform tasks to uninstall a software package.

- Figure 12-15 describes a utility that **audits** installed software on a PC to help verify that only licensed software is in use.

- Figure 12-16 describes a utility that reports on the **patch status** of installed software and assists with obtaining updates when needed.

- Figure 12-17 describes a utility tool to help uninstall software when the Add/Delete Programs tool in Windows does not do a thorough job.

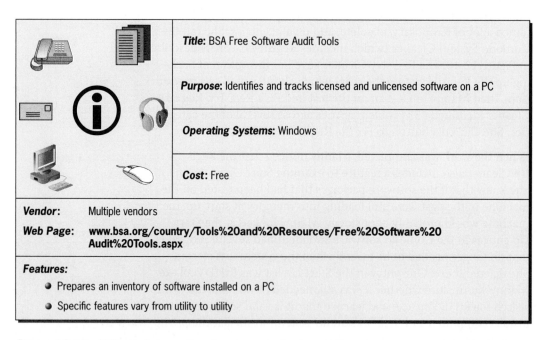

Title: BSA Free Software Audit Tools

Purpose: Identifies and tracks licensed and unlicensed software on a PC

Operating Systems: Windows

Cost: Free

Vendor: Multiple vendors

Web Page: www.bsa.org/country/Tools%20and%20Resources/Free%20Software%20Audit%20Tools.aspx

Features:
- Prepares an inventory of software installed on a PC
- Specific features vary from utility to utility

Figure 12-15 Utility tools to audit and manage applications software

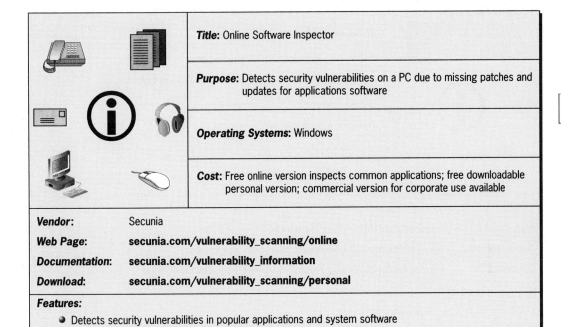

	Title: Online Software Inspector
	Purpose: Detects security vulnerabilities on a PC due to missing patches and updates for applications software
	Operating Systems: Windows
	Cost: Free online version inspects common applications; free downloadable personal version; commercial version for corporate use available

Vendor:	Secunia
Web Page:	secunia.com/vulnerability_scanning/online
Documentation:	secunia.com/vulnerability_information
Download:	secunia.com/vulnerability_scanning/personal

Features:

- Detects security vulnerabilities in popular applications and system software
- Verifies that Microsoft patches are installed
- Suggests patches to install to update system

Figure 12-16   Utility to report on the patch status of applications and system software

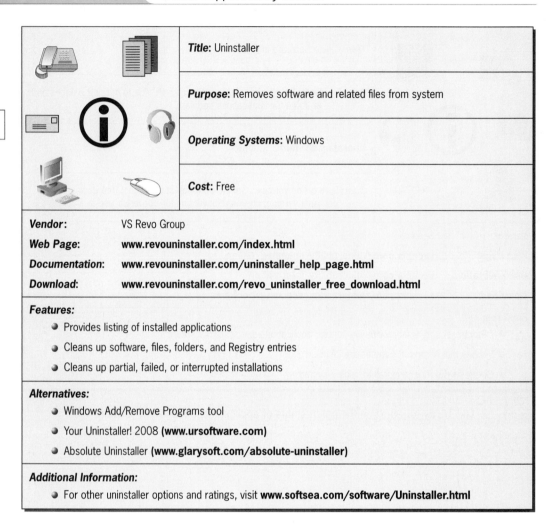

	Title: Uninstaller
	Purpose: Removes software and related files from system
	Operating Systems: Windows
	Cost: Free

Vendor:	VS Revo Group
Web Page:	**www.revouninstaller.com/index.html**
Documentation:	**www.revouninstaller.com/uninstaller_help_page.html**
Download:	**www.revouninstaller.com/revo_uninstaller_free_download.html**

Features:
- Provides listing of installed applications
- Cleans up software, files, folders, and Registry entries
- Cleans up partial, failed, or interrupted installations

Alternatives:
- Windows Add/Remove Programs tool
- Your Uninstaller! 2008 **(www.ursoftware.com)**
- Absolute Uninstaller **(www.glarysoft.com/absolute-uninstaller)**

Additional Information:
- For other uninstaller options and ratings, visit **www.softsea.com/software/Uninstaller.html**

Figure 12-17   Utilities to complete software uninstall tasks

System Problem Diagnosis

In addition to individual utilities that help support agents diagnose problems involving hardware, operating systems, and applications software, suites that bundle several utility tools are also available.

- Figure 12-18 describes a diagnostic tool to find, analyze, and, in some cases, repair hardware and software problems in computer systems.

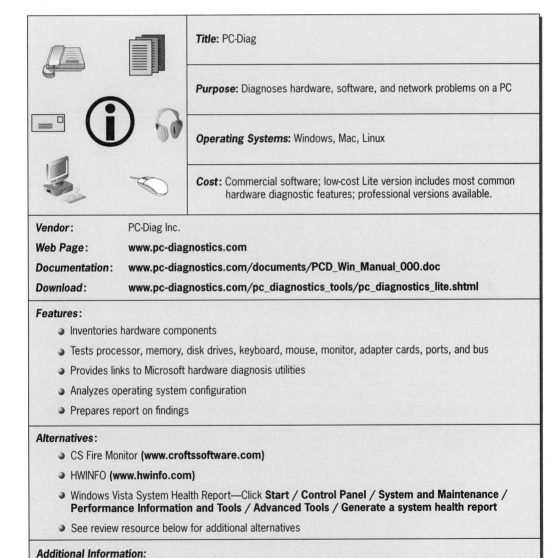

	Title: PC-Diag
	Purpose: Diagnoses hardware, software, and network problems on a PC
	Operating Systems: Windows, Mac, Linux
	Cost: Commercial software; low-cost Lite version includes most common hardware diagnostic features; professional versions available.

Vendor: PC-Diag Inc.

Web Page: www.pc-diagnostics.com

Documentation: www.pc-diagnostics.com/documents/PCD_Win_Manual_000.doc

Download: www.pc-diagnostics.com/pc_diagnostics_tools/pc_diagnostics_lite.shtml

Features:
- Inventories hardware components
- Tests processor, memory, disk drives, keyboard, mouse, monitor, adapter cards, ports, and bus
- Provides links to Microsoft hardware diagnosis utilities
- Analyzes operating system configuration
- Prepares report on findings

Alternatives:
- CS Fire Monitor (**www.croftssoftware.com**)
- HWINFO (**www.hwinfo.com**)
- Windows Vista System Health Report—Click **Start / Control Panel / System and Maintenance / Performance Information and Tools / Advanced Tools / Generate a system health report**
- See review resource below for additional alternatives

Additional Information:
- Read a review of diagnostic software utilities at **pc-system-utilities-software-review.toptenreviews.com**

Figure 12-18 Utilities to analyze and diagnose PC system problems

- Figure 12-19 shows sample output from Windows Vista Reliability and Performance Monitor that helps identify problems in PC systems.

- Figure 12-20 describes a utility suite that bundles several of the utility tools described individually in this chapter into an integrated suite of related tools.

Individual utilities in the Hardware Support, Software Support—Operating Systems, Software Support—Applications, and Network Support categories perform similar tasks.

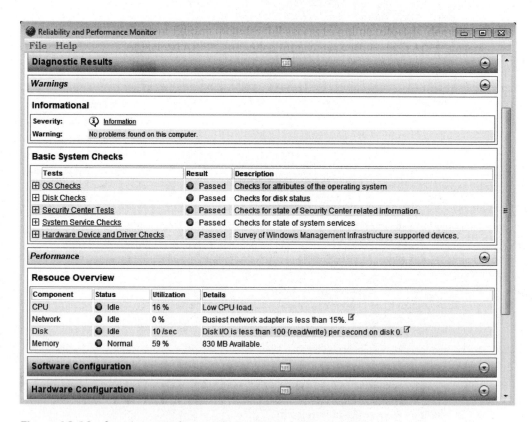

Figure 12-19   Sample output from a Windows Vista System Health Report

Title: WinUtilities Suite	
Purpose: Combines several software utilities to provide system information, utility, and repair functions	
Operating Systems: Windows	
Cost: Commercial versions available for personal, home, and business use	

Vendor: YL Software

Web Page: **www.ylcomputing.com**

Documentation: **www.ylcomputing.com/content/blogcategory/5/36**

Download: **www.ylcomputing.com/content/view/12/31**

Features:

- Tools include: file undelete, disk cleaner, duplicate file finder, secure file eraser, Registry cleaner, Registry backup and restore, start-up file manager, history cleaner, memory optimizer, system information, uninstall manager, task scheduler, and Windows utilities launcher

Alternatives:

- jv16 Power Tools **(www.macecraft.com)**
- SystemSuite **(www.avanquest.com/USA/pc-utilities/anti-virus-anti-spyware/complete-packages/System_Suite_Professional.html)**
- Norton SystemWorks **(www.symantec.com/norton/systemworks-basic-edition)**
- Wopti Utilities **(download.cnet.com/windows/wopti-technologies/3260-20_4-6306435.html)**
- System Mechanic **(www.iolo.com)**

Additional Information:

- For a review of several Windows utility suites, see **www.pcmag.com/article2/0,1759,1812056,00.asp**

Figure 12-20   Description of suites of utility software to perform a range of support tasks

---

CASE STUDY: Utilities for User Support Tasks

Manny's support team has adopted a goal for the current year to be more proactive in anticipating problems with end-user systems. They have decided to recommend that users in the college periodically run a diagnostic utility program to help identify any possible hardware, software configuration, or network performance problems. The team's plan is to e-mail the college's user base a monthly reminder to run a System Health Report, which is part of the Windows Vista operating system, and an example of a diagnostic utility. The e-mail reminders will invite users to report to the support team any problems identified on the System Health Report, especially if any of the warnings in the Basic System Checks and Resource Overview sections of the Diagnostic Results window (shown Figure 12-19) are red. The full report includes an analysis of the network, as well as the PC's software and hardware configurations (CPU, disk, and memory); the report also includes various performance statistics. At the end of the year, the support team plans to evaluate whether the monthly reminders and the Windows Vista diagnostic utility tool have improved the group's ability to anticipate users' PC problems.

Network Support

Tools to help support agents diagnose problems with computer networks include tools to trace and locate the source of network outages, as well as those designed to monitor network performance. Since poor performance can indicate problems with the hardware, software, or configuration settings of a network, many network utilities monitor performance, detect **service faults**, and perform other diagnostic functions. Network utilities often provide administrators with a convenient **dashboard** of performance statistics and fault alerts.

- Figure 12-21 describes a tool to monitor network performance and help identify **throughput bottlenecks** as well as other problems.

- Figure 12-22 describes a utility tool to diagnose and troubleshoot network operation to identify faults in network infrastructure.

Utilities in the Internet Support and Security Solutions categories
address other network management tasks.

	Title: GNetWatch
	Purpose: Monitors and reports on network performance
	Operating Systems: Windows, Mac, Linux
	Cost: Free

Vendor:	Alexandre Fenyo
Web Page:	gnetwatch.sourceforge.net
Documentation:	gnetwatch.sourceforge.net/doc.html
Download:	gnetwatch.sourceforge.net/download.html

Features:
- Monitors and reports on network system performance
- Displays network performance graphically
- Updates performance data every few seconds

Alternatives:
- OpenSMART (opensmart.sourceforge.net)
- GroundWork Monitor (www.groundworkopensource.com/products)
- NetMeter (www.hootech.com/NetMeter)
- Network Monitoring Utility (www.nimsoft.com/solutions/network-monitoring/index.a1.php)
- SNM—System and Network Monitor (snm.sourceforge.net)

Additional Information:
- For a listing of free and low-cost network performance and monitoring tools, visit
  www.manageengine.com/products/opmanager/network-monitoring-tool.html

Figure 12-21   Utilities to monitor and report network performance

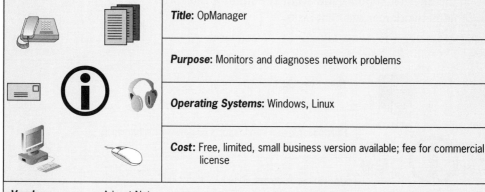

Title: OpManager	
Purpose: Monitors and diagnoses network problems	
Operating Systems: Windows, Linux	
Cost: Free, limited, small business version available; fee for commercial license	

Vendor:	Advent Net
Web Page:	www.manageengine.com/products/opmanager/download.html
Documentation:	www.manageengine.com/products/opmanager/documents.html#helpdocs
Download:	www.manageengine.com/products/opmanager/download-free.html

Features:

- Automates network device discovery and mapping
- Monitors network traffic and throughput
- Monitors server operation and performance
- Detects network faults and generates alarms
- Provides a customizable report dashboard

Alternatives:

- PCS Network Tools (**www.learnxgroup.com/software/software.html**)
- OpUtils (**www.manageengine.com/products/oputils**)
- Total Network Monitor (**www.softinventive.com/products/total-network-monitor**)
- Splunk (**www.splunk.com**)

Additional Information:

To learn more about network monitoring tools, visit:

- **www.slac.stanford.edu/xorg/nmtf/nmtf-tools.html**
- **support.3com.com/infodeli/tools/netmgt/tncsunix/product/091500/c1ovrvw.htm**

Figure 12-22   Utility tools to diagnose and troubleshoot network operation problems

CASE STUDY: Utilities for User Support Tasks

One afternoon, Manny received a call from an end user in the college's business department who stated that her PC was operational but that she was suddenly unable to access the Internet. She had been able to use the Internet earlier that morning. Manny's support group runs OpManager, a utility described in Figure 12-22, to monitor and diagnose network problems. Manny's first thought was to check OpManager to see whether any network problems had been identified. She looked at the OpManager dashboard, and noted that none of the network devices on the business department's side of the gateway were responding to pings. The network appeared to be down in the entire business department building. The phone would soon be ringing off the hook.

Manny contacted one of her support colleagues, Randy, who was in the vicinity of the business department. After discussing several options, Manny suggested that Randy go to the network equipment closet in the business department office and reboot the gateway to see whether that would make a difference. Manny continued to monitor OpManager and noted that when Randy restarted the business department gateway, the PCs in the department began to respond to OpManager's pings. Manny called the faculty member back to verify that her PC was able to access the Internet and to thank her for the call. She also made an entry in the support team's problem database to record the incident in case further problems with the gateway device were reported.

Internet Support

Tools to help support agents monitor and identify problems with Internet use include utilities to test and report on Internet connection bandwidths as well as those that identify potential security problems due to Internet connectivity.

- Figure 12-23 describes a tool to test a PC's Internet connection bandwidth, including download and upload speeds.

- Figure 12-24 describes a utility tool to identify possible connectivity **vulnerabilities** due to an external Internet device's ability to penetrate a connected PC.

Utilities in the Security Solutions category address other Internet challenges.

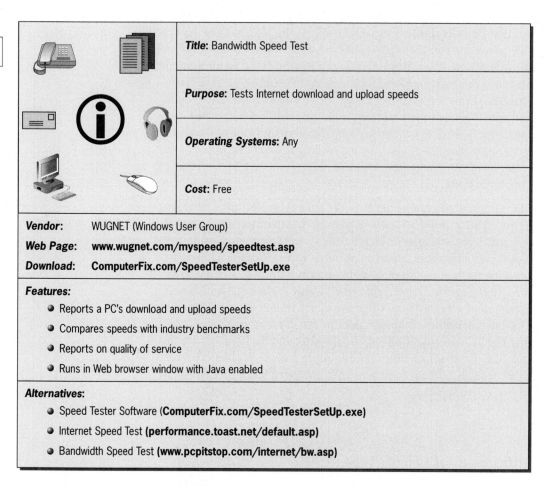

	Title: Bandwidth Speed Test
	Purpose: Tests Internet download and upload speeds
	Operating Systems: Any
	Cost: Free

Vendor:	WUGNET (Windows User Group)
Web Page:	**www.wugnet.com/myspeed/speedtest.asp**
Download:	**ComputerFix.com/SpeedTesterSetUp.exe**

Features:
- Reports a PC's download and upload speeds
- Compares speeds with industry benchmarks
- Reports on quality of service
- Runs in Web browser window with Java enabled

Alternatives:
- Speed Tester Software (**ComputerFix.com/SpeedTesterSetUp.exe**)
- Internet Speed Test (**performance.toast.net/default.asp**)
- Bandwidth Speed Test (**www.pcpitstop.com/internet/bw.asp**)

Figure 12-23 Utility tools to test the speed of a PC's connection to the Internet

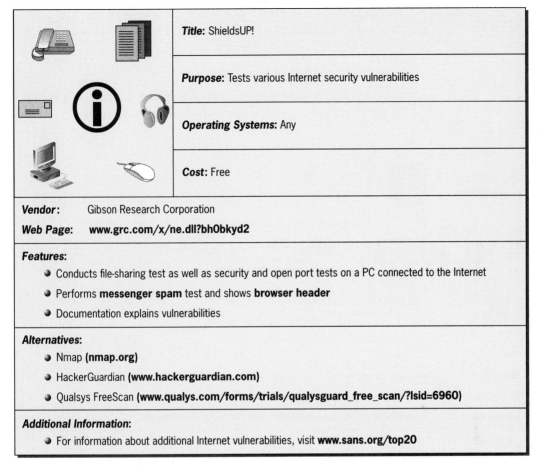

	Title: ShieldsUP!
	Purpose: Tests various Internet security vulnerabilities
	Operating Systems: Any
	Cost: Free

Vendor: Gibson Research Corporation

Web Page: www.grc.com/x/ne.dll?bh0bkyd2

Features:
- Conducts file-sharing test as well as security and open port tests on a PC connected to the Internet
- Performs **messenger spam** test and shows **browser header**
- Documentation explains vulnerabilities

Alternatives:
- Nmap **(nmap.org)**
- HackerGuardian **(www.hackerguardian.com)**
- Qualsys FreeScan **(www.qualys.com/forms/trials/qualysguard_free_scan/?lsid=6960)**

Additional Information:
- For information about additional Internet vulnerabilities, visit **www.sans.org/top20**

Figure 12-24   Utility to test and identify vulnerabilities in a PC's Internet connection

File Management Tasks

Tools to help support agents manage files and folders on a PC include utilities to back up disk media, back up disk media to an Internet service, convert files from one format to another, and recover files that were accidentally deleted.

- Figure 12-25 describes a utility to back up files and folders from a disk to another local or network device, such as a hard drive, optical disk, removable disk, or USB drive. Backups can be scheduled to run on a predefined schedule.

- Figure 12-26 describes an Internet service that provides file and folder backup storage on an Internet server. Backups can be scheduled to run automatically.

- Figure 12-27 describes a tool to convert a file from one format to another; for example, .jpg format to .tiff format.

- Figure 12-28 describes a utility tool that attempts to recover deleted files from disk media.

Utilities in the Hardware Support and Software Support—Operating Systems categories provide related file management tools.

	Title: GFI Backup
	Purpose: Backs up disk files and folders onto alternate media
	Operating Systems: Windows
	Cost: Free Home Edition available

Vendor: GFI Software

Web Page: www.gfi.com/backup-hm

Documentation: support.gfi.com/support.asp?pii=71&lcode=en

Download: www.gfi.com/downloads/register.aspx?pid=bkuphm&lid=en

Features:

- Backs up to internal, external, and removable hard drives, as well as network drives, USB, CD, and DVD drives
- User selects files and folders for backup
- Performs incremental and differential backups
- User schedules times for automatic backups
- Optionally encrypts backup files for security

Alternatives:

- Cobian Backup (www.educ.umu.se/~cobian/cobianbackup.htm)
- FileHamster (www.mogware.com/FileHamster)

Additional Information:

- To read reviews of several backup utilities, visit www.pcmag.com/article2/0,2817,2278661,00.asp

Figure 12-25 Utility software to perform media backups onto other local media

	Title: Online Backup
	Purpose: Backs up user files and folders to Internet server
	Operating Systems: Windows, Mac
	Cost: Free for basic-level service, which includes 2 GB storage space; commercial levels provide larger storage space

Vendor:	Pro Softnet Corporation
Web Page:	**www.idrive.com**
Documentation:	**www.idrive.com/online-backup-resources.htm**
Download:	**www.idrive.com/online-backup-download.htm**

Features:

- Provides automatic, scheduled backups of selected files and folders
- Encrypts backup files for security
- Retains multiple versions of files
- User chooses between incremental and continuous backup options
- Backup files accessible via any Internet connection

Alternatives:

- Mozy (**Mozy.com**)
- Carbonite (**Carbonite.com**)

Additional Information:

- For additional information about online backups and reviews of vendors, visit **www.backupreview.info**

Figure 12-26   Services that provide for media backups onto an Internet server

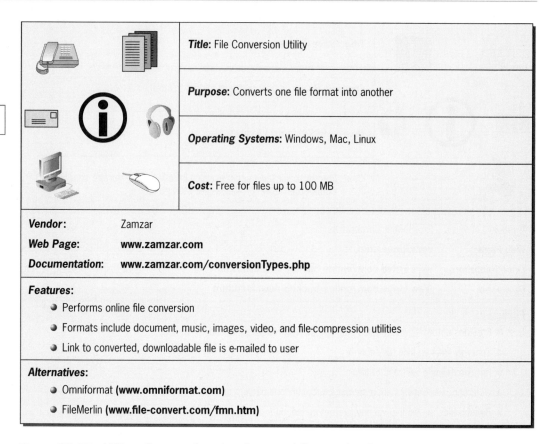

| **Title:** File Conversion Utility |
| **Purpose:** Converts one file format into another |
| **Operating Systems:** Windows, Mac, Linux |
| **Cost:** Free for files up to 100 MB |

Vendor: Zamzar

Web Page: **www.zamzar.com**

Documentation: **www.zamzar.com/conversionTypes.php**

Features:

- Performs online file conversion
- Formats include document, music, images, video, and file-compression utilities
- Link to converted, downloadable file is e-mailed to user

Alternatives:

- Omniformat (**www.omniformat.com**)
- FileMerlin (**www.file-convert.com/fmn.htm**)

Figure 12-27   Utility software and services to convert files to other formats

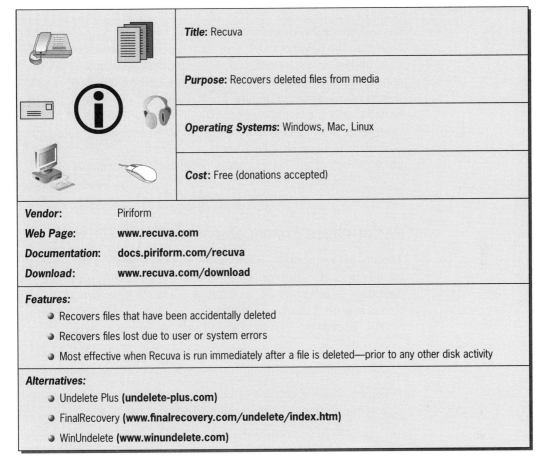

	Title: Recuva
	Purpose: Recovers deleted files from media
	Operating Systems: Windows, Mac, Linux
	Cost: Free (donations accepted)

Vendor:	Piriform
Web Page:	www.recuva.com
Documentation:	docs.piriform.com/recuva
Download:	www.recuva.com/download

Features:
- Recovers files that have been accidentally deleted
- Recovers files lost due to user or system errors
- Most effective when Recuva is run immediately after a file is deleted—prior to any other disk activity

Alternatives:
- Undelete Plus (undelete-plus.com)
- FinalRecovery (www.finalrecovery.com/undelete/index.htm)
- WinUndelete (www.winundelete.com)

Figure 12-28   Utilities to recover deleted files

CASE STUDY: Utilities for User Support Tasks

A student with a USB flash drive in hand approached the walk-in help desk while Manny was on duty. The student was obviously upset and explained that he had been working on a spreadsheet assignment for an accounting class. The spreadsheet was open on the USB drive when the PC he was using in the teaching lab mysteriously power cycled. After the PC restarted, the student discovered that the spreadsheet file had disappeared from the USB drive and several hours of work had been wiped out. The student reported that he had searched the drive, but could not locate the missing spreadsheet file. Manny asked whether the student had written any files on the USB drive since the incident. The answer was, "No way!"

Manny then suggested that they try to recover the file using Recuva, a file undelete utility described in Figure 12-28. They plugged the USB drive into the help desk's PC and started Recuva. It searched the USB drive and located several files and file fragments, a couple of which appeared to be versions of the missing spreadsheet file. Recuva was able to reconstruct the missing file and the student was delighted to find that only the last few edits to the accounting assignment had not been saved in the recovered file. He promised to save multiple copies of spreadsheets on alternate media in the future, and asked if he could obtain a copy of the Recuva utility program for his personal use.

Performance Enhancements

Tools to help support agents monitor and improve PC performance include utilities to benchmark a PC's performance, adjust the configuration settings on a PC to improve operational performance, erase files to free up disk space, and defragment disk space to reduce the number of disk accesses to read and write programs and data.

- Figure 12-29 describes a utility that evaluates and benchmarks a PC's operating speed against other systems or known standards.

- Figure 12-30 describes a software tool that adjusts the configuration and settings of a PC to optimize performance.

- Figure 12-31 describes a tool that erases temporary, unused, damaged, obsolete, and archived files from a PC's disk drive in order to free up disk space. A disk cleanup operation is a procedure support agents often perform prior to defragmenting a drive.

- Figure 12-32 describes a utility tool that defragments disk space to reduce the number of input/output operations required to read or write a file. Defragmented disks often perform better than those whose files are heavily fragmented.

Utilities in the Hardware Support and System Problem Diagnosis categories provide related performance-enhancement tasks.

	Title: Performance Test
	Purpose: Evaluates and benchmarks PC performance against other systems and standards
	Operating Systems: Windows
	Cost: 30-day free trial; fee for continued use

Vendor: Passmark
Web Page: www.passmark.com/products/pt.htm
Download: www.passmark.com/download/pt_download.htm

Features:
- Performs several speed tests
- Compares and rates performance results against similar systems
- Tests processor, memory, graphics, disk, and CD/DVD
- User selects report options

Alternatives:
- Bapco's SYSmark (**www.bapco.com**)
- Hans Niekus' System Analyzer (**www.sysanalyser.com**)

Figure 12-29   Utilities to benchmark PC operating speeds

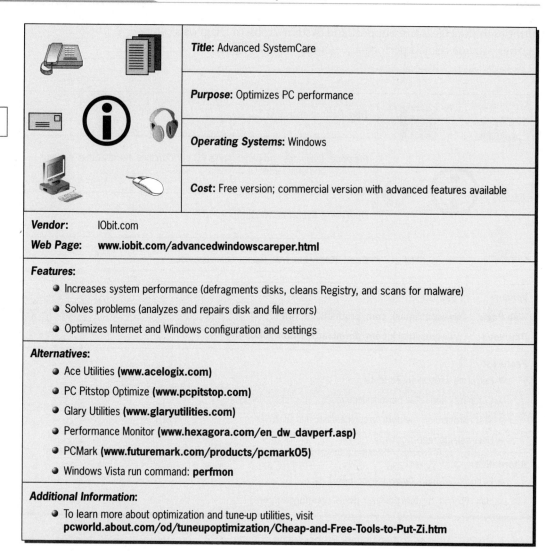

	Title: Advanced SystemCare
	Purpose: Optimizes PC performance
	Operating Systems: Windows
	Cost: Free version; commercial version with advanced features available

Vendor: IObit.com

Web Page: www.iobit.com/advancedwindowscareper.html

Features:
- Increases system performance (defragments disks, cleans Registry, and scans for malware)
- Solves problems (analyzes and repairs disk and file errors)
- Optimizes Internet and Windows configuration and settings

Alternatives:
- Ace Utilities (**www.acelogix.com**)
- PC Pitstop Optimize (**www.pcpitstop.com**)
- Glary Utilities (**www.glaryutilities.com**)
- Performance Monitor (**www.hexagora.com/en_dw_davperf.asp**)
- PCMark (**www.futuremark.com/products/pcmark05**)
- Windows Vista run command: **perfmon**

Additional Information:
- To learn more about optimization and tune-up utilities, visit
  pcworld.about.com/od/tuneupoptimization/Cheap-and-Free-Tools-to-Put-Zi.htm

Figure 12-30   Software tools to increase system performance

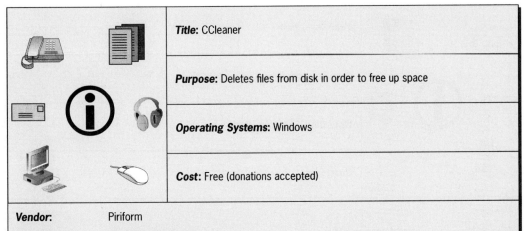

	Title: CCleaner
	Purpose: Deletes files from disk in order to free up space
	Operating Systems: Windows
	Cost: Free (donations accepted)

Vendor: Piriform
Web Page: **www.ccleaner.com**
Documentation: **docs.piriform.com/ccleaner**
Download: **www.ccleaner.com/download**

Features:

- Deletes temporary and unused files left behind by Windows, Web browsers, and application programs
- Deletes file fragments, Clipboard images, and recycle bin files
- Deletes obsolete Registry entries
- Improves system performance

Alternatives:

- EasyCleaner (**personal.inet.fi/business/toniarts/ecleane.htm**)
- Wise Disk Cleaner Pro (**free-disk-cleaner.wisecleaner.com**)
- HackCleaner (**hackcleaner.en.softonic.com**)
- Windows run command: **cleanmgr**

Figure 12-31   Utility tools to clean disk space of unused files

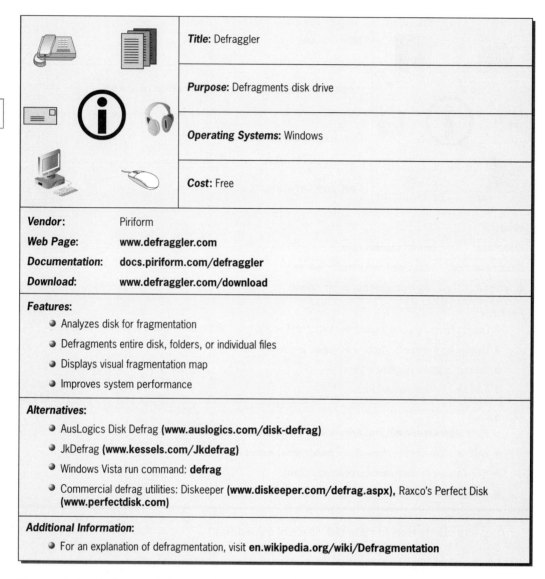

	Title: Defraggler
	Purpose: Defragments disk drive
	Operating Systems: Windows
	Cost: Free

Vendor:	Piriform
Web Page:	**www.defraggler.com**
Documentation:	**docs.piriform.com/defraggler**
Download:	**www.defraggler.com/download**

Features:

- Analyzes disk for fragmentation
- Defragments entire disk, folders, or individual files
- Displays visual fragmentation map
- Improves system performance

Alternatives:

- AusLogics Disk Defrag (**www.auslogics.com/disk-defrag**)
- JkDefrag (**www.kessels.com/Jkdefrag**)
- Windows Vista run command: **defrag**
- Commercial defrag utilities: Diskeeper (**www.diskeeper.com/defrag.aspx**), Raxco's Perfect Disk (**www.perfectdisk.com**)

Additional Information:

- For an explanation of defragmentation, visit **en.wikipedia.org/wiki/Defragmentation**

Figure 12-32   Utilities to defragment disk space

CASE STUDY: Utilities for User Support Tasks

Manny was asked to serve on a college-wide committee that was established to develop a recommendation for a standard PC, which the college would purchase for its use and sell to students through the bookstore during the next two years. On the selection committee, Manny was appointed to a hardware benchmark subcommittee. Manny had previously used a PassMark utility to evaluate hardware for purchase and suggested that the benchmark subcommittee use the software, described in Figure 12-29, to rate the three machines they were asked to evaluate. Manny ran PassMark's Performance Test on each of the three machines and compared each to a standard model PC with an Intel Celeron CPU. When presenting the results to the subcommittee, Manny noted that PassMark's Performance Test benchmarks several very specific aspects of a computer's operation, but that she had recorded only the summary results in a spreadsheet, shown in Table 12-1.

Component	System A	System B	System C	Benchmark
CPU	930.8	624.0	900.8	227.1
Graphics	156.3	137.7	143.2	112.7
Memory	383.5	225.8	401.6	157.9
Disk	256.5	263.1	223.8	197.8
Overall	393.5	292.2	345.0	162.8

Table 12-1 Summary results of benchmarking test

Using the raw data from PassMark's Performance Test utility in Table 12-1, Manny and the members of the hardware benchmark subcommittee compared the strengths and weaknesses of each machine.

Which system do you think they recommended, based on the results of the hardware benchmark? Why?

Security Solutions

Tools to help support agents provide end users with Internet security solutions include utilities to protect against viruses, spyware, firewall penetration, and rootkit violations, as well as tools to evaluate the strength of user passwords and utilities to securely erase files from a hard drive.

- Figure 12-33 describes a utility that scans hard drive memory, incoming and outgoing e-mail messages, attachments, data files, and Internet pages for viruses.

- Figure 12-34 describes a software tool that scans a PC's memory and media for spyware and other malware that could compromise the identity, privacy, or confidentiality of an end user and affect PC performance.

- Figure 12-35 describes a tool to monitor **firewall** breaches and identify software that requests an open port to the Internet, which may serve as a target for Internet security attacks.

578

- Figure 12-36 describes a utility to detect hidden files and folders, which may indicate the presence of **rootkit** software on a PC.

- Figure 12-37 describes a utility tool to evaluate the strength of a user's password and make suggestions on how to improve passwords so they are less susceptible to **password guessers**.

- Figure 12-38 provides an example of a utility that performs a **secure erase** operation (also called a file shred or destructive delete operation) on files, folders, or an entire drive. These utilities are useful for protecting confidential information before a PC is recycled, donated, or handed down to another user.

Utilities in the Network Support, Internet Support, and System Problem Diagnosis categories provide related security solutions.

Computer viruses are now a part of almost every end user's vocabulary and the news media often report on some of the new potential threats that attract user and media attention. Virus hoaxes are also common—users receive what appears to be an authentic e-mail warning them about a possible virus problem on their computer. Figure 12-33 includes a pointer to a Symantec Web site where information about virus hoaxes can be found.

ON THE WEB

Microsoft maintains a Web site devoted to security problems and information about tools to enhance the security of its software products; visit the site at **www.microsoft.com/ security**. Microsoft offers a software tool, Microsoft Baseline Security Analyzer (MBSA), to analyze a Windows system for security vulnerabilities; MBSA can be downloaded from **support.microsoft.com/kb/895660**.

Title: avast! Antivirus
Purpose: Protects a PC against viruses and other malware
Operating Systems: Windows, Mac, Linux
Cost: Free for home use; discounts available for government, nonprofit, educational use; professional version available for commercial use

Vendor:	ALWIL Software
Web Page:	**www.avast.com/eng/avast_4_home.html**
Documentation:	**download670.avast.com/files/manuals/user-manual-home-eng.pdf**
Download:	**www.avast.com/eng/download-avast-home.html**

Features:

- Protects against operating system and applications software viruses
- Protects against spyware and rootkit violations
- Updates threats database automatically every day
- Requires annual registration

Alternatives:

- AVG Technologies AVG **(free.avg.com)**
- Avira AntiVir **(www.free-av.com)**
- Commercial antivirus software available from
  - Norton AntiVirus **(www.symantec.com/norton/antivirus)**
  - McAfee **(home.mcafee.com/Default.aspx)**
  - Trend Micro AntiVirus + AntiSpyware **(us.trendmicro.com/us/products/personal/antivirus-plus-anti-spyware)**
  - Kaspersky Anti-Virus **(usa.kaspersky.com/products_services/anti-virus.php)**
  - F-Secure Anti-Virus **(www.f-secure.com/en_US/products/home-office/antivirus/index.html)**
  - Sophos **(www.sophos.com/products/small-business)**

Additional Information:

- Read reviews of free antivirus software at **www.free-antivirus.info**
- To learn more about **virus hoaxes**, visit the Symantec Antivirus Center's hoax pages at **www.symantec.com/business/security_response/threatexplorer/risks/hoaxes.jsp**

Figure 12-33   Antivirus software tools

Title: Ad-Aware	
Purpose: Searches and deletes spyware software such as key loggers, adware, spyware, and hijackers	
Operating Systems: Windows	
Cost: Free for home and personal use (donations accepted); commercial versions available with advanced features	

Vendor:	Lavasoft
Web Page:	www.lavasoft.com/products/ad_aware_free.php
Documentation:	www.lavasoft.com/support/supportcenter/tutorial_movie_5.php
Download:	www.lavasoft.com/single/trialpay.php

Features:

- Scans disks for spyware
- Deletes or quarantines spyware upon user command
- Continuously monitors for real-time changes
- Updates spyware database automatically

Alternatives:

- Malwarebytes (**malwarebytes.org**)
- Spybot—Search & Destroy (**www.safer-networking.org/en/index.html**)
- Microsoft Windows Defender (**www.microsoft.com/windows/products/winfamily/defender/ default.mspx**)
- Spyware Terminator (**www.spywareterminator.com**)

Additional Information:

- Read reviews of commercial antispyware products at **anti-spyware-review.toptenreviews.com**
- Read review of free antispyware products at **www.pcworld.com/downloads/collection/collid, 1347-order,1-c,downloads/files.html**

Figure 12-34   Tools to protect against spyware and other malware

Title: Internet Security	
Purpose: Provides firewall and antivirus security features	
Operating Systems: Windows	
Cost: Free; commercial version has advanced features	

Vendor: Comodo

Web Page: **personalfirewall.comodo.com**

Documentation: **support.comodo.com/index.php?_m=downloads&_a=viewdownload&**
                     downloaditemid=35&nav=0

Download: **personalfirewall.comodo.com/download_firewall.html**

Features:

- User selects firewall and/or antivirus utilities to be installed
- Prevents unknown software from executing
- Learns user behavior to personalize security alerts
- Updates protection database automatically

Alternatives:

- ZoneAlarm (**www.zonealarm.com/security/en-us/zonealarm-pc-security-free-firewall.htm**)
- Online Armor Free (**www.tallemu.com/free-firewall-protection-software.html**)

Additional Information:

For reviews of firewall and security software, visit

- **www.consumercompare.org/internet_security_software/index.php**
- **www.pcmag.com/article2/0,2817,2333448,00.asp**

Figure 12-35   Firewall software utilities

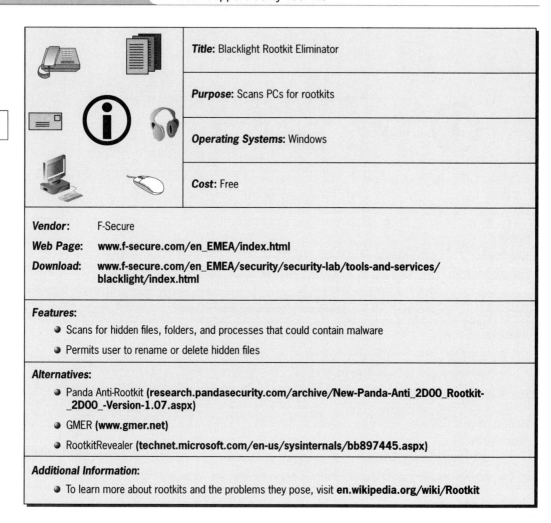

	Title: Blacklight Rootkit Eliminator
	Purpose: Scans PCs for rootkits
	Operating Systems: Windows
	Cost: Free

Vendor: F-Secure

Web Page: www.f-secure.com/en_EMEA/index.html

Download: www.f-secure.com/en_EMEA/security/security-lab/tools-and-services/
             blacklight/index.html

Features:

- Scans for hidden files, folders, and processes that could contain malware
- Permits user to rename or delete hidden files

Alternatives:

- Panda Anti-Rootkit (research.pandasecurity.com/archive/New-Panda-Anti_2DOO_Rootkit-_2DOO_-Version-1.07.aspx)
- GMER (www.gmer.net)
- RootkitRevealer (technet.microsoft.com/en-us/sysinternals/bb897445.aspx)

Additional Information:

- To learn more about rootkits and the problems they pose, visit en.wikipedia.org/wiki/Rootkit

Figure 12-36   Utilities to scan PCs for evidence of rootkits

	Title: Password Meter
	Purpose: Evaluates the strength of passwords
	Operating Systems: Any
	Cost: Free

Vendor:	GNU Public License (Free Software Foundation)
Web Page:	**www.passwordmeter.com**
Download:	**www.passwordemeter.com/pwd_meter.zip**

Features:
- Provides instant check of password strength on Web site
- Recommends mixture of uppercase and lowercase letters, digits, and special characters
- Adds and deducts points based on visible criteria

Alternatives:
- Secure Passwords (**www.securepasswords.net/site/TestPassword.html**)

Additional Information:
- To locate lost user passwords on a PC, use a password cracker utility such as John the Ripper (**www.openwall.com/john**)
- To add a password checker to a Web site, visit **tools.devshed.com/webmaster-tools/password-strength**

Figure 12-37   Tools that evaluate the strength of user passwords

	Title: Darik's Boot and Nuke (DBAN)
	Purpose: Erases contents of disk media before PC recycling
	Operating Systems: Windows, Mac, Linux
	Cost: Free

Vendor:	Darik Horn
Web Page:	www.dban.org
Documentation:	www.dban.org/documentation
Download:	www.dban.org/download

Features:

- Creates a boot disk (floppy, CD/DVD, or USB drive)
- Performs a secure bulk erasure of all files, folders, and directories
- Protects against disclosure of personal and confidential information when a computer is recycled, sold, or handed down to another user

Alternatives:

- Active @ Kill Disk (www.killdisk.com)
- Hard Disk Erasing Utility (hard-disk-erasing-utility.findmysoft.com)
- File Shredder (www.fileshredder.org)

Additional Information:

- To learn more about hard disk erase utilities, read an article at blogs.zdnet.com/storage/?p=129
- Several file-deletion utilities are reviewed at www.thefreecountry.com/security/securedelete.shtml

Figure 12-38   Software to protect a user's information with a secure media erase

CASE STUDY: Utilities for User Support Tasks

The support group at the college receives many questions about passwords. Manny and her team usually recommend a utility such as Password Meter, described in Figure 12-37, to help users evaluate the security of their passwords. Manny always warns users about the dangers of using a password that is easy to guess.

A faculty member reported that he was taught in school to use a long word that is easy to remember and then drop all the vowels to form the password. For example, "elephant" (easy to remember) becomes *lphnt* as a password. However, when Manny asked the user to enter *lphnt* into Password Meter, the resulting score was 7%. Manny suggested that the user add some digits to the letters, so the user tried *lphnt1988* and received a score of 48%. In an attempt to obtain a perfect score, Manny suggested he capitalize the first letter: *Lphnt1988*, which received a score of 76%. Then the user added a special character (!) between the letters and digits and received a score of 96% for *Lphnt!1988*. Manny suggested that, with this example in mind, and Password Meter as a tool, the user build a password that gets a Very Strong rating. The support group at the college includes a link to Password Meter (**www.passwordmeter.com**) on their Web site.

User Support Tools

Tools to help support agents perform their work include utilities that manage help desk operations and those that enable remote access to an end user's PC to diagnose and troubleshoot problems. Help desk software is covered in detail in Chapter 5 and in Appendix B, and will not be described further here.

- Figure 12-39 describes a utility that permits a support specialist to access a user's PC to perform diagnostic tests, troubleshoot problems, install software, and configure settings without the need for a face-to-face visit to the user's work site. Some utilities use the Internet as a remote access medium; others use a local area network, such as a virtual private network to enable communication between a help desk agent and a user. Remote access is an especially useful productivity tool when users are geographically dispersed.

Many utilities in other categories in this chapter are also designed to make support staff and end users more productive.

586

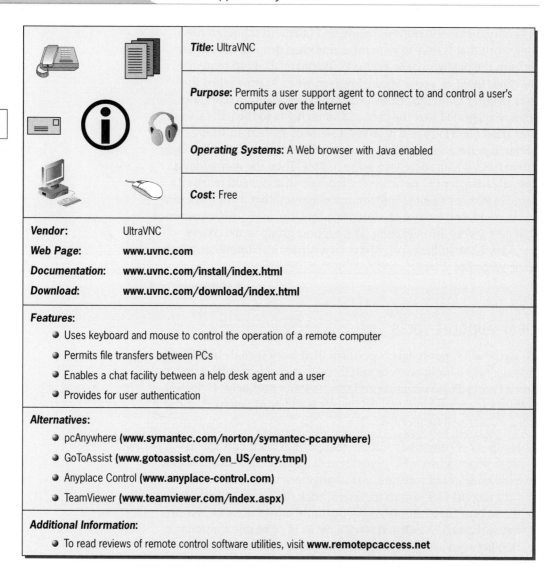

	Title: UltraVNC
	Purpose: Permits a user support agent to connect to and control a user's computer over the Internet
	Operating Systems: A Web browser with Java enabled
	Cost: Free

Vendor:	UltraVNC
Web Page:	**www.uvnc.com**
Documentation:	**www.uvnc.com/install/index.html**
Download:	**www.uvnc.com/download/index.html**

Features:

- Uses keyboard and mouse to control the operation of a remote computer
- Permits file transfers between PCs
- Enables a chat facility between a help desk agent and a user
- Provides for user authentication

Alternatives:

- pcAnywhere **(www.symantec.com/norton/symantec-pcanywhere)**
- GoToAssist **(www.gotoassist.com/en_US/entry.tmpl)**
- Anyplace Control **(www.anyplace-control.com)**
- TeamViewer **(www.teamviewer.com/index.aspx)**

Additional Information:

- To read reviews of remote control software utilities, visit **www.remotepcaccess.net**

Figure 12-39   Remote access software to control a user's PC over a network

The software tools described in this chapter are intended as examples for readers to evaluate for possible inclusion in a support specialist tool kit of useful utilities and information resources that can be applied to diagnose and solve user problems and increase the productivity of support workers. The utilities described here should be considered a starting point, from which each support worker will begin an investigation and evaluation of various tools based on their job description. Each support worker will add, delete, and replace tools and resources as new or better tools are discovered, or as job responsibilities change over time. Table 12-2 summarizes the tools in the utility tool kit described in this chapter.

Utility Category	Utility Name	Purpose	Fig. #
Hardware Support	BurnIn Test	Stress tests hardware to assess reliability and stability	12-3
	Device Driver Finder	Downloads drivers for hardware devices	12-4
	Drive Fitness Test	Performs test routine to evaluate IDE, SATA, and SCSI hard disk drives	12-5
	Windows Memory Diagnostics Tool	Tests RAM memory in Windows Vista	12-6
System Information	Belarc Advisor	Audits and reports system configuration information	12-7
	WinBootInfo	Monitors and reports on system start-up activities	12-8
Software Support— Operating Systems	Autoruns for Windows	Identifies software that starts automatically at start-up or logon	12-9
	System Cleaner	Deletes obsolete and corrupted information from Windows Registry	12-10
	Registry Manager	Edits Registry keys and values and performs other Registry management tasks	12-12
	Windows Vista commands	Provides information resources on entering commands in the Windows Vista command-line interface	12-13
	Windows Vista Recovery Disk	Downloads an image of a bootable recovery disk to recover inoperable systems	12-14
Software Support— Applications	BSA Free Software Audit Tools	Identifies and tracks licensed and unlicensed software on a PC	12-15

Table 12-2 Summary of utility software tools described in this chapter *(continues)*

(continued)

Utility Category	Utility Name	Purpose	Fig. #
	Online Software Inspector	Detects security vulnerabilities on a PC due to missing patches	12-16
	Uninstaller	Removes software and related files from a PC	12-17
System Problem Diagnosis	PC-Diag	Diagnoses hardware, software, and network problems on a PC	12-18
	WinUtilities Suite	Combines several software utilities to provide system information, diagnosis, and repair functions	12-20
Network Support	GNetWatch	Monitors and reports on network performance problems	12-21
	OpManager	Monitors and diagnoses network problems	12-22
Internet Support	Bandwidth Speed Test	Tests Internet download and upload speeds	12-23
	ShieldsUP!	Tests various Internet security vulnerabilities	12-24
File Management Tasks	GFI Backup	Backs up disk files and folders onto alternate media	12-25
	Online Backup	Backs up user files and folders to an Internet server	12-26
	File Conversion Utility	Converts one file format into another	12-27
	Recuva	Recovers deleted files from media	12-28
Performance Enhancements	Performance Test	Evaluates and benchmarks PC performance against other systems and standards	12-29
	Advanced SystemCare	Optimizes PC performance	12-30
	CCleaner	Deletes files from disk in order to free up space	12-31
	Defraggler	Defragments files and folders to make disk accesses more efficient	12-32
Security Solutions	avast! Antivirus	Protects a PC against viruses and other malware	12-33
	Ad-Aware	Searches for and deletes spyware software	12-34
	Internet Security	Provides firewall and antivirus security features	12-35
	Blacklight Rootkit Eliminator	Scans PCs for rootkits	12-36
	Password Meter	Evaluates the strength of passwords	12-37
	Darik's Boot and Nuke (DBAN)	Securely erases files on disk media before PC recycling	12-38
User Support	UltraVNC	Provides remote access to a user's PC for support tasks	12-39

Table 12-2 Summary of utility software tools described in this chapter

A ROLE-PLAYING SCENARIO

This scenario is based on situations in which working support specialists regularly participate in meeting and discussions.

Your role-playing assignment is to participate in a panel discussion with three or four of your work or school colleagues. The group should begin by selecting a position description for an actual help desk or user support position. You could use a position description included in Chapter 1 or one in use at your organization.

The panel should develop a list of the top five utility tools a worker in the position the group selected would probably find most useful in performing their job duties. The panel should start by giving each participant a few minutes to nominate their personal top five utilities. (The nominated utilities do not need to come from those discussed in this chapter.) Then the panel should discuss the pros and cons of each utility that was nominated. Try to reach a consensus on the panel's top five.

The companion Web site for this book, **www. CUS4e.com**, contains updates and further suggestions to augment the information in this chapter. The Web site also includes a link to the author's e-mail address, where readers are invited to send recommendations for useful support utilities for publication on the Web site.

Chapter Summary

- User support specialists employ a variety of software tools and information resources to perform their work responsibilities. As with all tools, care must be exercised by support specialists to ensure that only appropriate, up-to-date, tested, and authorized tools are downloaded and used. The tools in this chapter are examples of those commonly available.

- Categories of user support tools include utilities to resolve hardware problems, provide system information, configure and troubleshoot operating system and applications software, diagnose system and network problems, test and identify Internet connection speeds and vulnerabilities, manage files and disks, provide solutions to security threats, and increase the productivity of support specialists.

Key Terms

audit—A process to determine which software versions are installed on a PC or on a network server; an audit may be conducted for inventory purposes (asset management), to gauge compliance with the terms of a software license or EULA, or to identify use of unauthorized software by an end user.

590

browser header—Identification information about a user's PC which is sent to an Internet server by a Web browser whenever a request for information is transmitted; results in a potential vulnerability related to Internet connectivity.

dashboard—A real-time display of statistical performance information and service fault alerts in a visual, graphical format; a network administrator may view a dashboard on a monitor that reports the performance of the network operation and sounds an alarm or alert during a service interruption.

end-user license agreement (EULA)—A legal contract between a vendor and a user that governs the use of a software package or information service; in order to use a software package, an end user must agree to the terms of the license agreement; EULAs often state that an end user does not own a software package, but is allowed to use it following the terms and conditions of the agreement.

firewall—Hardware or software designed to intercept and prevent unauthorized attempts to access a computer system from an external network, such as the Internet (*see also* **vulnerabilities**).

ISO image—An archive file format that contains software modules in a form that can be burned (copied) onto a CD or DVD; the ISO format is based on industry specifications of the International Standards Organization and is often used to distribute software for installation on a PC.

messenger spam—An attack that uses a common network communication service to broadcast multiple and continuous messages to users, each of which opens a pop-up window on a user's screen and requires a user response.

opt-in check box—An input form on a Web site that permits a user to agree to specified services and provisions (a check box to accept the terms of an EULA is a common example); check box responses are not always prominently displayed and may default to a positive agreement to accept a service (periodic e-mail ads, for example) or even a subscription to a fee-based service, unless a user unchecks the box.

password guesser—Software that attempts to discover a user's online password either by making repeated, obvious guesses based on the user's name, address, and other known information, or by using a brute force guessing method which employs repeated tries of words in a dictionary or database of common passwords.

patch status—An evaluation of whether all current updates have been downloaded and applied to a software package to fix one or more known bugs; includes an evaluation of service packs, security fixes, and feature releases.

privacy policy—A statement describing how an organization collects, maintains, and uses information provided by and about its customers or users; a privacy policy may authorize certain uses of information—such as its sale to a business partner or other third parties.

recovery disk—A disk medium that contains software images to reinstall, repair, or restore an operating system on a PC's hard drive to its original condition; most recovery disks are optical media and are designed to start a PC when an installed operating system has been damaged or corrupted.

rootkit—Malware that permits viruses and spyware to be installed on a user's PC without their knowledge or consent; rootkits are activated during a system's start-up process and may capture keystrokes and mouse clicks; they are difficult to detect because rootkit files and folders are hidden from normal view.

secure erase—An operation that obliterates data in disk files and folders by repeatedly writing random bit patterns on disk media; often used before a PC is recycled, donated, or handed down to another user to erase sensitive personal or corporate information.

service fault—An interruption of service in a network environment; may appear as a performance degradation or as a complete disruption of normal service; a server crash or an inoperative network device (such as a router or gateway) are common causes of service faults.

software license—A legal contract between a vendor and a user that governs the use of a software package or information service; a user is provided with a license to use a software package according to the terms and conditions of the license agreement by paying a fee (for commercial software) or agreeing to the terms of an end-user license agreement (for freeware, open source, or trial shareware); the license may be in the form of a purchase receipt, an online registration with e-mail confirmation, or a product activation key.

stress test—A repetitive operation performed to evaluate the ability of a PC system to operate at peak efficiency for a defined time period under a maximum processing load; a burn-in test of new hardware components is an example of one use of a stress-test.

throughput bottleneck—An interruption of normal network traffic that reduces or halts the flow of data on a network; common bottlenecks include heavy packet volumes, external denial-of-service attacks, huge volumes of spam e-mails, processor or memory overload, and contention for disk accesses.

vulnerabilities—Any weakness in a system that is connected to the Internet or other network that permits an attacker to violate the integrity of the system; common vulnerabilities include the transmission of viruses, spyware, and other executable code and scripts; open firewall ports that permit external access; software design flaws that open a back door into a system; and security breaches such as easily guessed passwords.

Windows command-line interface—A mechanism for accepting keyboard commands entered by a user at a command-line prompt—as an alternative to the Windows GUI interface; the Windows Run command window is one method to access the command-line interface in Windows; early versions of Microsoft operating systems used text command strings exclusively.

ON THE WEB

Definitions of many of the technical terms used in the chapter can be found in one of these resources:

- **www.webopedia.com**
- **www.wikipedia.org**
- **whatis.com**
- **whatis.techtarget.com**
- **www.netlingo.com**

Check Your Understanding

Answers to Check Your Understanding questions are found in Appendix A.

1. A system problem diagnosis utility suite is designed to identify problems with:

    a. hardware

    b. applications software

    c. operating system software

    d. all of these

2. True or False? Disk fragmentation indicates that a PC's hard drive may be about to fail.

3. True or False? Open source, freeware, and shareware utilities are not commercial products.

4. A(n) _____ is a legal contract between a vendor and a user that governs the use of a software package, such as a utility.

5. True or False? A software utility advertised as a "free download" is freeware that can be used without paying a license fee.

6. A software utility tool of primary use to a support specialist who assembles or installs hardware systems is:

    a. a network performance monitor

    b. a software audit tool

    c. a file backup utility

    d. a burn-in utility

7. Which category of utility tools prepares documentation that would likely be included in a site installation notebook?

    a. System Information

    b. Rootkit

    c. Bandwidth Tester

    d. Network Support

8. Which of these actions should be performed on a PC prior to using a Windows Registry edit utility?

    a. Defragment the hard drive

    b. Back up the Registry onto a hard drive

    c. Temporarily disable the system's firewall

    d. Verify that the system patch status is up-to-date

9. A type of utility tool that can modify which software is launched automatically at system start-up is:

    a. a benchmark utility

    b. an autoruns utility

    c. an audit utility

    d. a bootinfo utility

10. True or False? Versions of Windows operating systems after Windows 2000 no longer have a command-line prompt feature.

11. True or False? A dashboard is a display of network performance information and fault warnings that a network administrator uses to monitor network operation.

12. A(n) _____ tool is a utility that inventories the software versions that are installed on a PC to determine compliance with licensing agreements.

13. True or False? A PC may be vulnerable to attacks from the Internet if some patches have not yet been downloaded and installed.

14. A type of software utility designed to clean up a failed software installation is:

   a. an undelete utility

   b. a disk clean utility

   c. an uninstaller utility

   d. a diagnostic utility

15. List two examples of common network bottlenecks that utility software tools might be able to detect.

16. True or False? Before a user recycles a PC, he or she must physically destroy the hard disk drive in order to obliterate sensitive personal information.

17. A backup utility can write copies of important data files and folders on:

   a. an internal hard disk drive

   b. a network server's disk drive

   c. an Internet server's disk drive

   d. any of these

18. A(n) _____ utility rewrites all the files and folders on a disk drive so they are stored in contiguous blocks in order to improve disk performance.

19. A(n) _____ is software that can attach itself to other software or to disk media and cause harm to the programs and data stored in a computer.

20. List three activities that can be performed by a system tune-up utility to improve system performance.

21. True or False? A firewall is hardware or software designed to prevent unauthorized attempts to penetrate a computer system from outside a network.

Discussion Questions

1. An experienced user support specialist made the following statement: "I'm not very interested in PC performance tools. It is not our job to be concerned about the operational performance of our PCs. That is the users' responsibility." Explain why you agree or disagree with the statement.

2. What do you think is the motivation of computer hackers who write virus programs and disseminate them, or who spam other users with unwanted e-mail messages? Are their motives understandable to you? Are they justified?

3. If you have previous experience with utility software, describe the pros and cons of free, open source software utilities versus commercial versions of tools that perform similar tasks. In your view, should a for-profit business enterprise ever use free, open source utilities? Why or why not?

4. Which utility tools described in this chapter should be scheduled to run on a user's PC on a regular basis? Which should be run only as the need arises? Compare your answers to these questions with your colleagues' answers.

5. Based on what you know and have read about security software, do you believe it is ever possible to completely protect the data files, programs, and confidential information on a user's PC from malicious attacks from external threats, such as those launched via the Internet? Explain your viewpoint on the effectiveness of security software.

6. "When I download software, I always check the 'I agree' box on an end-user license agreement or software license. Who needs to read all that legal mumbo-jumbo, anyway?" Do you agree or disagree with this statement? If you disagree, how would you respond to it?

Hands-On Activities

Activity 12-1

Add a utility to the list of those described in the chapter. Based on your personal experience with user PCs, add a utility tool to the list of examples described in the chapter. The tool you describe could be one with which you have personal experience, or one that addresses a support need that the existing tools don't address adequately. In which category does the tool you selected fit best? Prepare a form like those used in this chapter to describe the tool you selected.

Activity 12-2

Get experience with a utility tool. Select a utility described in this chapter. If possible, download and install the utility. Learn about its operation and features. Then write a short report on your experiences. Describe the tool you investigated in terms of ease of use, purpose and features, performance in the tasks for which it is designed, and any difficulties or surprises you encountered in its use. Compare your experiences with your fellow students or work colleagues.

Activity 12-3

Compare the features of two utility tools. Examine the features of one utility tool described in this chapter. The one you select to examine could be one you used in another activity. Then, from the *Alternatives* section for that utility, pick another tool that performs similar tasks. Use a features checklist to compare the features of both tools. Briefly explain which utility you prefer and why.

Activity 12-4

Make a Windows Recovery Disk. For a PC to which you have authorized access, make a Windows recovery disk following the procedures in the Windows Vista Recovery Disk tool description (see Figure 12-14). Demonstrate the use of the recovery disk to a small group of your colleagues.

Activity 12-5

Evaluate user passwords. Ask each of several colleagues to think up two or three passwords (the passwords should not be ones they currently use, but could be ones they have used in the past). Use the Password Meter utility described in the chapter (see Figure 12-37) to evaluate each password suggested by the group. Which passwords received the highest score in Password Meter? Which ones received the lowest score? Explain why. Design an information sheet that could be given to end users with some guidelines on creating effective passwords. Include on the information sheet instructions on how to use Password Meter.

Activity 12-6

Audit the software on a PC. Download and install one of the audit tools described on the BSA Web site listed in the chapter (see Figure 12-15). Perform an audit of the software on a PC to which you have authorized access. Prepare a summary report on the installed software. Describe any surprises that the audit software identified. Was the audit utility able to properly identify all of the software on the PC? Explain why or why not.

Activity 12-7

Recover a deleted file. Download and install a utility tool that claims to be able to undelete files which were accidentally deleted (see Figure 12-28). Prepare a practice file on a USB drive if one is available; otherwise use the hard disk drive, but set up a separate folder for your experiment. Delete the file (make sure it is not the only copy of the file if it contains data you need to keep). Before you perform any other file management tasks on the same disk, use the undelete utility tool to try to recover the deleted file. Did the undelete utility perform as advertised? Why or why not? Write a brief report on your experiment and your experience with the undelete utility.

Activity 12-8

Add a feature to print a directory listing. Support specialists frequently need to print a directory listing of the files in a folder on a disk. Recent versions of Windows do not include a feature to easily obtain a printout of a directory listing. Research whether a utility tool is available to print a directory listing. If so, describe the steps to download and install a solution to this problem. Is there more than one way to provide this capability?

Activity 12-9

Research a computer virus warning. A user received the following text in an e-mail message:

Subject: Virus Alert

Importance: High

If anyone receives mail entitled: PENPAL GREETINGS! please delete it WITHOUT reading it. Below is a little explanation of the message, and what it would do to your PC if you were to read the message. If you have any questions or concerns please contact SAF-IA Info Office on 697-5059.

This is a warning for all Internet users—there is a dangerous virus propagating across the Internet through an e-mail message entitled "PENPAL GREETINGS!" DO NOT DOWNLOAD ANY MESSAGE ENTITLED "PENPAL GREETINGS!"

This message appears to be a friendly letter asking you if you are interested in a pen pal, but by the time you read this letter, it is too late. The "Trojan horse" virus will have already infected the boot sector of your hard drive, destroying all of the data present. It is a self-replicating virus, and once the message is read, it will AUTOMATICALLY forward itself to anyone whose e-mail address is present in YOUR mailbox!

This virus will DESTROY your hard drive, and holds the potential to DESTROY the hard drive of anyone whose mail is in your inbox, and whose mail is in their inbox, and so on. If this virus remains unchecked, it has the potential to do a great deal of DAMAGE to computer networks worldwide!!!!

Please, delete the message entitled "PENPAL GREETINGS!" as soon as you see it! And pass this message along to all of your friends and relatives, and the other readers of the newsgroups and mailing lists which you are on, so that they are not hurt by this dangerous virus!!!

The end user wants to know what he should do if he receives an e-mail with a subject PENPAL GREETINGS! Please research the problem (see Figure 12-33), and write a response to the user.

Activity 12-10

Perform a disk clean operation. On a PC to which you have authorized access, use a system information utility of your choosing to discover the amount of free space available on the hard disk drive (see Figure 12-31). Then use the disk cleanup utility to free up disk space by deleting files that are no longer needed. Use the system information utility to again measure the amount of free space on the cleaned disk. How much free space was gained by the procedure?

Write a brief report on the results of the disk clean operation, including a description of the options the tool offers a user. In addition, explain any options you would not advise a typical user to choose, and explain why. If possible, perform another disk cleanup operation with a different utility (perhaps the Windows built-in disk cleaning tool). Did the second tool free up any additional disk space? Explain which tool you would recommend for use by end users.

Activity 12-11

Benchmark a PC's Internet connection. Use the Bandwidth Speed Test tool described in this chapter (see Figure 12-23) or a similar tool to run benchmark tests on the download and upload speeds on a PC to which you have access. Run the test at least 10 times at different times of the day on the same computer. Keep a record of the results of the bandwidth test in a spreadsheet program.

Are the test results consistent? Explain why, or why not. Use the spreadsheet to analyze the download and upload speeds and quality of service ratings. Find the range (high and low) for each measure. Also compute the average download, upload, and quality of service measures. How much variation in the times did you observe? Use the chart feature in the spreadsheet program to prepare a graph to illustrate your results.

Activity 12-12

Locate forgotten user passwords on a PC. Download and install a password cracker utility, such as John the Ripper (see Figure 12-37). Run the utility only on a PC to which you have authorized access. Prepare a brief report on the features of John the Ripper and describe the type of user passwords it was able to recover. Explain any concerns you have about the use of password cracker utilities.

Activity 12-13

Get experience with a suite of utility tools. Advanced SystemCare is a package of several utility programs that perform a variety of diagnosis, maintenance, optimization, and repair functions (see Figure 12-30). Download and install Advanced SystemCare on a PC to which you have authorized access. Learn about its features.

Prepare a document designed for end users that describes each function available in Advanced SystemCare, including the utility's features and why an end user would want to use it. Finally, list any utility functions that are not currently included in Advanced SystemCare that you would like to see added in the next version.

Case Projects

1. Content Filtering Software for the Library

Some organizations that provide public Internet access, such as schools, libraries, and churches, may want to make sure that Web pages displayed or downloaded from the Internet have appropriate content for their clients, including young children. As a user support specialist at the local library, you need to learn about software utility programs that are available to filter Internet content. Research this category and then write a memo to the head librarian that explains how content filtering software works. In your memo, describe the pros and cons of using content filter utilities as a tool in a library.

2. Preventive Maintenance Checklist for BizNet Systems

Kai Edmonds is a manager of client support services for BizNet Computer Systems, a vendor that sells computer networks to small organizations. She is aware that a number of BizNet's customers have very little experience with the tasks associated with keeping a network system up and running. Kai spends considerable time on the telephone answering questions. The top three kinds of questions she gets related to:

- Security threats
- Media backups
- Disk performance

Kai thinks BizNet needs a document to provide to its customers when they take delivery of their office network. The document Kai has in mind would address the three concerns she hears most often from customers. Assume that BizNet sells Windows desktop clients that are attached to a Windows or Novell NetWare server (or make any other assumptions that are consistent with the kind of network environment with which you are familiar).

First, develop a preventive maintenance checklist of tasks that a small business organization could use to manage their systems for maximum performance and reliability.

Next, if time permits, Kai would like to expand the checklist to provide clients with a brief explanation of how to perform each step on the checklist. If time is short, your instructor or trainer may ask you to pick one of the three categories above to work on.

As you write your preventive maintenance checklist and explanation of how to perform each step, remember that BizNet clients are not computer professionals.

3. How to Manage Spam E-Mail at Columbia Watercraft

Columbia Watercraft is a manufacturing and distribution facility for fiberglass pleasure boats. Several workers at Columbia who have Internet access on their desktop computers have complained recently in a computer user's group meeting about the amount of unwanted e-mail they receive. CEO Lucy Falk wants you to research some ways to deal with the excessive number of unwanted e-mail messages as a way to improve worker productivity—the fewer the spam e-mail messages received, the less time Columbia's workers have to spend reading and deleting them.

First, research whether any spam management tools exist in the e-mail system that Columbia uses, which happens to be the same e-mail software you use.

Second, research whether any software utility programs are available at no or low cost that Columbia's workers could use to help filter out spam e-mail messages.

Write a one- to two-page document targeted at end users at Columbia Watercraft that responds to their need to reduce or eliminate spam messages.

4. Prepare a Training Session on a Utility Tool for Your Colleagues

Select a utility tool with which you have experience. You might choose a tool you learned about in another activity in this chapter. Prepare a 20-minute training session on the use of the utility you select. Design the training as if the target audience is a group of user support workers or trainees, such as your school or work colleagues. Your training session could include elements such as:

- An explanation of the purpose and major features of the tool

- A demonstration of its use

- A description of any problems you encountered while using the tool

- Your personal evaluation of how useful the tool would be to support workers

- A handout on the steps to use the tool in support situations

Use the ideas you learned about in Chapter 10 to prepare and present your training session, either in a one-to-one environment or to a larger group of your colleagues.

Answers to Check Your Understanding Questions

This appendix lists the answers to the end-of-chapter Check Your Understanding questions.

Chapter 1	Chapter 2
1. True	1. True
2. d. all of these	2. personal communication style
3. environment, software use, features used, relationship	3. a. incident greeting
4. Information Technology (IT), Information Services (IS)	4. d. Therapeutic
5. d. 1990s	5. a. Discriminative
6. b. worker in an organization	6. c. talk to fill awkward silences
7. False	7. eye contact, gestures, distance, voice quality
8. Ergonomics	8. True
9. c. an invasion of privacy	9. False
10. graphical user interface (GUI)	10. c. We
11. True	11. b. the support agent's own words
12. True	12. True
13. d. any of the above	13. False
14. c. Outsourcing uses expertise a company may not have	14. greet a caller, transfer a call, terminate a call
15. True	15. True
16. needs analysis, needs assessment	16. c. Agree to any demand a client makes
17. Support standards	17. d. Never admit that you are not sure
18. c. operates a large-scale computer	18. False
19. documentation, user manual	19. False
20. knowledge, skills, and abilities (KSAs)	20. organization, format
21. d. chat session	

Chapter 3

1. d. All of these are difficult problems.
2. False
3. False
4. b. active listening
5. b. critical thinking
6. decision making
7. False
8. Escalation
9. metacognition
10. probe
11. c. knowledge base
12. True
13. a. Look for a simple, obvious fix
14. d. an opportunity to look at other alternatives
15. "You don't see any text or colors displayed on your display monitor?"
16. contradiction
17. b. verification
18. False
19. virtual private network (VPN)
20. variables

Chapter 4

1. False
2. a burn-in test
3. a. at the time a component is purchased and installed
4. False
5. c. hard disk drive
6. d. configuration problem
7. conflict
8. False
9. d. new version
10. workaround
11. False
12. False
13. c. both hardware and software problems
14. True
15. Quick start behavior
16. Written reminder note, save password in operating system, reference sheet, script, checklist
17. False
18. d. a service pack
19. a. incompatible
20. Automatic update

Chapter 5

1. True
2. c. **level 1**: incident screener; **level 2**: product specialist; **level 3**: technical support; **level 4**: support manager
3. Incident or call management
4. False
5. c. 1 – 3 – 4 – 2
6. False
7. b. a problem
8. a. first in, first out (FIFO)
9. d. escalation
10. queue
11. False
12. True
13. False
14. automatic call distributor (ACD)

Chapter 6

1. True
2. False
3. b. justify the value and expense of help desk services
4. False
5. b. help desk fees for services
6. performance appraisal
7. d. an Erlang
8. True
9. True
10. False
11. a. adaptive test
12. b. behavioral question
13. code of ethical conduct
14. d. a nondirected question

Chapter 5 *(continued)*

15. False
16. False
17. Job stress
18. end users; help desk agents, support managers
19. c. on a support Web site
20. Changes in off-shore outsourcing; employer demand for certified workers; acceptance of telecommuting work style; industry best practices; pressure to reduce support costs; Web support portals; quantitative metrics, resources for security; help desk software integration.
21. a. a set of industry best practices
22. True

Chapter 6 *(continued)*

15. Noisy interview environment; interruptions; multiple interviews; overly technical questions
16. a. increase
17. Best practices
18. a. a user satisfaction survey
19. d. abandonment rate
20. professional association

Chapter 7

1. False
2. True
3. Product standards
4. False
5. Acceptable use policies
6. Trial, evaluation, demonstration
7. False
8. False
9. benchmark
10. d. weighted point method
11. request for proposal (RFP)
12. b. industry standard products
13. b. B – D – A – C
14. Subjective criteria
15. True
16. d. any of these
17. extraneous variable
18. c. user preferences
19. Vendor literature, market information, Web sites and user manuals; demonstration and evaluation products; product review articles; industry expert opinion; colleague opinion
20. True

Chapter 8

1. False
2. d. purchase
3. False
4. c. technological feasibility
5. True
6. d. 4 – 3 – 1 – 2
7. True
8. True
9. Build-versus-buy decision
10. c. model
11. deliverable
12. True
13. False
14. True
15. b. operating costs
16. project plan, charter
17. Flowchart
18. True
19. d. predecessor task
20. d. all of the above

Chapter 9

1. a. anticipate possible installation problems
2. footprint
3. True
4. c. down slightly
5. Ergonomics
6. False
7. False
8. power strip, surge suppressor
9. True
10. b. with an LED tester
11. b. fluorescent light
12. True
13. c. multiple systems installed in an office or training facility
14. b. reduce the risk of damage to computer components
15. Plug and Play
16. False
17. license
18. disaster recovery, contingency plan
19. d. an uninterruptible power supply (UPS)
20. False

Chapter 10

1. True
2. False
3. Expertise or expert
4. c. perform
5. True
6. False
7. c. expertise
8. b. 2 – 4 – 1 – 3
9. Multimedia
10. False
11. a. classes
12. d. problem solve
13. True
14. a. The development cost is high, but the cost per user is low.
15. handouts, reference sheets
16. False
17. d. training evaluation surveys
18. Learning styles
19. Role-play, role-playing
20. False

Chapter 11

1. False
2. reference sheet, handout
3. False
4. c. tutorial manual
5. False
6. a. online help systems
7. False
8. analogy
9. b. 2 – 4 – 3 – 1
10. True
11. True
12. a. complete
13. True
14. c. 12th grade

Chapter 12

1. d. all of these
2. False
3. False
4. license agreement, software license
5. False
6. d. a burn-in utility
7. a. System Information
8. b. Back up the Registry onto a hard drive
9. b. an autoruns utility
10. False
11. True
12. audit
13. True
14. c. an uninstaller utility

Chapter 11 *(continued)*

15. style sheet
16. False
17. drive error, disk error
18. Brainstorming
19. a. reference format
20. style sheet

Chapter 12 *(continued)*

15. Heavy packet volumes, external denial-of-service attacks, processor or memory overload, contention for disk accesses
16. False
17. d. any of these
18. defrag, defragmentation
19. virus
20. Defragment disks, clean Registry, manage startup applications, analyze and repair disk and file errors, optimize Windows configuration and settings
21. True

HelpSTAR®*2008*
Student Edition

In this appendix, you will learn about:

◎ The features of a commercial help desk software package

◎ How to install HelpSTAR*2008* on a PC

◎ How several organizations use HelpSTAR*2008*

◎ How to access HelpSTAR*2008*'s online tutorials and demonstrations

◎ How to use some basic features of HelpSTAR*2008*

The purpose of this appendix is to give you some hands-on experience with a commercial help desk software package similar to those you might encounter in a help desk position. Chapter 5 provided an overview of help desk software tools and the HelpSTAR^{2008} package. This appendix contains additional information about HelpSTAR^{2008} software and provides you with an opportunity to get experience using the software.

A CD packaged with this book includes the HelpSTAR^{2008} Student Edition software, a product of Help Desk Technology International Corporation. The Student Edition is a 180-day trial version of the Help-STAR^{2008} commercial edition. The trial period should give you a good opportunity to learn as much as you would like about the product. The Student Edition includes full access to online tutorials, demonstrations of HelpSTAR^{2008}, and video interviews with HelpSTAR^{2008}'s users.

ON THE WEB

Additional educational resources for HelpSTAR^{2008} are located at **edu.helpstar.com**. The site has been designed to support the academic community with Web-based tutorials, demos, and forums.

Install HelpSTAR^{2008} Student Edition

To install the Student Edition of HelpSTAR^{2008}, you must have:

- HelpSTAR^{2008} Student Edition installation CD (packaged with this book)
- Windows XP or Vista operating system
- Windows Installer version 3.1 or later
- Minimum of 1 gigabyte of RAM
- Approximately 1 gigabyte of disk space available
- Internet access (broadband connection)

If you reinstall HelpSTAR^{2008} in order to start over with the original sample database, the reinstallation process will only take about 10 minutes, because .NET and SQL do not have to be installed. This procedure deletes any changes you made to the sample database.

The installation process takes approximately 20 to 30 minutes, depending on the speed of the PC on which HelpSTAR^{2008} will be installed. During the installation, in addition to HelpSTAR^{2008}, two software packages will be loaded onto the PC (unless they are already installed): Microsoft's .NET framework version 3.5 SP1 and Microsoft's SQL Server 2005 Express edition. The .NET framework contains a support library of software that HelpSTAR^{2008} needs to operate. SQL Server is the database software in which HelpSTAR^{2008} information is stored.

To install HelpSTAR^{2008}, follow these steps:

1. Insert the HelpSTAR^{2008} CD into the CD/DVD drive.

2. Click **My Computer** or **Computer** (depending on your operating system). This step may be unnecessary if the CD Auto-Play feature is activated on the PC.

3. The CD should appear in **My Computer** as "HelpSTAR2008SE."

4. Double-click the **HelpSTAR2008SE** CD icon; a welcome screen for the Student Edition is displayed.

5. InstallShield guides you through the installation process (see Chapters 4 and 9 for more information about installation utilities).

6. The License Agreement for HelpSTAR^{2008} Student Edition is displayed. Read the license agreement carefully. Paragraph 1 says that the Student Edition is limited to 180 days for the purpose of testing and evaluation. Paragraph 3 indicates that you can install and use the software on more than one PC, such as a school or work system and a home system.

7. InstallShield copies HelpSTAR^{2008} to the C:\Program Files\ HelpSTAR Student Edition\ directory. In addition to Help-STAR^{2008}, the .NET and SQL Server packages are installed.

8. InstallShield configures the HelpSTAR^{2008} package. In the Student Edition, the user is a help desk support representative named Beth Markham, and Beth's password is *helpstar*.

9. When the installation and configuration process is completed, a login screen for Beth Markham will be displayed. Click the **Login** button to view HelpSTAR^{2008}'s home page.

10. HelpSTAR^{2008} installs a shortcut to the program on the PC's desktop. The executable program is named WinI.exe in the \HelpSTAR Student Edition\ directory created in Step 7 above.

The Student Edition of HelpSTAR^{2008} does not include technical support for installation or operational problems. In case of problems, please do not contact Help Desk Technology International Corporation, the author, or the publisher, Course Technology (Cengage Learning); contact your instructor about any installation or operational problems.

HelpSTAR^{2008} Home Page

Launch HelpSTAR^{2008} by double-clicking the program icon. The initial screen shows the login screen, with Beth Markham's name and password ("helpstar") already entered. Click the **Login** button to display the HelpSTAR^{2008} home page, shown in Figure B-1. The home page contains:

- **Ribbon menu interface**—A ribbon menu appears across the top of the home page; this menu style will be familiar to anyone who has used programs in the Microsoft Office 2007 Suite.

- **HelpSTAR^{2008} shortcuts**—On the left side of the home page, eight icons are displayed; these are shortcuts to several of the most popular tools in HelpSTAR^{2008}.

- **Find panel**—The Find panel is in the center of the screen; it accesses HelpSTAR^{2008} database search options.

- **A/V Resources**—On the right side of the home page are links to several A/V resources on HelpSTAR^{2008}'s Web site. These include CBT tutorials, interviews with users, and product demonstrations.

- **Support Rep's status**—At the bottom of the home page is a status summary bar. Figure B-1 shows the home page with the status bar for help desk support representative Beth Markham with links to various alerts, messages, reminders, and queues that are part of Beth's HelpSTAR^{2008} desktop workspace. Beth's workspace consists of all the HelpSTAR^{2008} facilities and services to which she has authorized access.

Figure B-1   HelpSTAR^{2008} Student Edition home page

Getting Started Learning About HelpSTAR²⁰⁰⁸

The Student Edition of HelpSTAR²⁰⁰⁸ includes a variety of online audio/visual tutorial information to help you get started learning about the software. These resources are accessed via the A/V Resources icons on the HelpSTAR²⁰⁰⁸ home page. Because the A/V Resources are data intensive, they should be accessed on a high-speed, broadband Internet connection.

ON THE WEB

You do not have to install HelpSTAR²⁰⁰⁸ to view the online product information. Follow these links:

- Client Interviews: **edu.helpstar.com/se/ClientInterview. asp**

- Feature Demos: **edu.helpstar.com/Learn.asp?MKTCode= 198411004**

- Computer-Based Training tutorials: **edu.helpstar.com/se/ Computerbasedtraining.asp**

You can also access additional information on the HelpSTAR²⁰⁰⁸ Web site by using the following links:

- HelpSTAR²⁰⁰⁸ Help file: **help.helpstar.com/HelpSTAR_2008. htm**

- User Forums: **forums.helpstar.com/login.aspx? Educational=true**

Client Interviews

To learn why other help desk managers chose HelpSTAR²⁰⁰⁸ software and how it is used in a variety of business, educational, and government organizations, click the **Client Interviews** icon. This link takes you to HelpSTAR²⁰⁰⁸'s Web site where you can use a Web browser to view user video testimonials. The interviews of help desk workers and network technicians provide several help desk support reps' perspectives on using the software. To return to the HelpSTAR²⁰⁰⁸ home page, close the browser window.

Feature Demos

The A/V resources pane also includes a link to product demonstration videos that describe HelpSTAR^{2008} product features. The **Feature Demos** Web page contains the following product demonstrations:

- HelpSTAR^{2008}'s Interface
- Business Rules
- Auto Discovery
- Email Inbox
- End-user Web Portal
- User-Defined Fields
- Project Templates
- Memo Templates
- Reports
- Mail Sentry
- Dashboards
- Active Directory
- Reminders

The material in these product demos includes descriptions of how HelpSTAR^{2008} solves a variety of help desk and user support problems. This material is covered in greater depth in the tutorials described below.

The HelpSTAR^{2008} tutorials are viewed with Adobe Flash Player software. The controls to play, pause, move forward or backward, control the volume, etc., are similar to the controls on many interactive software programs. Hover the mouse pointer over a control icon to learn its purpose.

Computer-Based Training

The computer-based training (CBT) tutorials are the best place to begin learning how HelpSTAR^{2008} operates. To view a tutorial on a HelpSTAR^{2008} topic, click the **Computer-Based Training** icon. The CBT tutorials are described in Figure B-2; the tutorials marked with an asterisk are the recommended place to begin for those just getting started with HelpSTAR^{2008}. Other topics are more advanced.

CBT Tutorial Title	Topics Covered

HelpSTAR Home Page*	**Home Page** Shortcuts
	• HelpSTAR messages
	   • Alerts
	   • Reminders (follow-ups)
	   • Quick Messages (internal instant messaging)
	• My Workspace
	   • Support Rep's current service request work-in-progress
	   • Support Rep's service request queue
	• My Custom Views
	   • Customize a Support Rep's workspace view
	• Audit My Workstation
	   • Prepare a detailed report on a workstation's configuration
	• Scheduled/Overdue Requests
	   • Service Requests that require attention
	• Email Inbox
	   • Link to send and receive e-mail messages
	• Dashboards
	   • Performance information
	• Learn HelpSTAR
	   • Link to online tutorials
	Find Panel
	• Search for and locate users, equipment, and solutions
	Message Board—replaced by A/V Resources in Student Edition

HelpSTAR Interface: The Ribbon*	Ribbon structure • Tabs • Groups • Tasks

Figure B-2   HelpSTAR^{2008} CBT tutorials *(continues)*

(continued)

HelpSTAR Interface: HelpSTAR button*	HelpSTAR button functions • Frequently used tasks • Open windows • Recent service requests • My User Options (configuration settings)

HelpSTAR Views*	Common views in HelpSTAR
	• A view is a list of service requests
	    • My Workspace—current service requests
	    • History—previous service requests
	    • Timesheet—how long a support rep has worked on a request
	• A view is defined by:
	    • Selection query (criteria)
	    • Display options
	        • Line item grid (listing of service requests)
	        • Preview pane (details of service requests)
	            • Transactions
	            • Properties
	            • Attachments
	        • Project pane
	        • Queue pane

Evolution of Priority/Skill-based Queuing*	How HelpSTAR's service request queuing system evolved to blend priorities with support rep skills

Service Request Basics*	Types of information in a service request
	• Management data (properties)—how each task will be carried out
	• Documentation—details about activities performed (including attachments)
	• Communication—messages about task-related activities
	    • Alerts
	    • Reminders
	    • Emails
	    • Quick Messages

Figure B-2   HelpSTAR^{2008} CBT tutorials *(continues)*

(continued)

Service Request Details	Anatomy of a service request
	• Management data (properties)
	    • General information—identification
	    • Importance—priority
	    • Scheduling—deadlines
	    • Current location
	        • In-service—current tasks
	        • Queue folders—future requests
	        • Dispatch—unassigned requests
	    • Asset/Discovered Item
	• Documentation
	    • Memo—an entry in a service request
	    • Attachment—supporting documentation
	• Communication
	    • E-mail messages
	    • Reminders
	    • Quick Messages (internal communications)

Response Service Level Management	How business rules in HelpSTAR manage service levels to automatically respond to service requests
	• Business rule uses
	    • Automatic routing of requests
	    • Service level management
	    • End user communication
	• How to create a business rule
	• E-mail templates

Resolution Service Level Management	How business rules in HelpSTAR manage service levels to help automate the resolution of service requests
	• Business rule uses
	    • Automatic routing of requests
	    • Service level management
	    • End user communication
	• How to create a business rule
	• E-mail templates

Figure B-2 HelpSTAR[2008] CBT tutorials *(continues)*

(continued)

ITIL Configuration Management*	Configuration management deals with assets (computer equipment, software, furniture, etc.)
	
	● How to enter a new asset
	● How to find assets with the Asset Explorer
	● Methods to allocate an asset
	    ● Right-click
	    ● Drag and drop
	    ● Change properties
	● Asset properties
	    ● Location
	    ● Service request history
	    ● Specifications
	    ● Configuration
	● Auto discovery (network environment)
	    ● Scheduled automatic scans
	    ● Document discovered hardware and software
	    ● License compliance

Business Rules	Uses of business rules in HelpSTAR ● Automatic routing of requests ● End-user communication ● Service level management Types of business rules ● Condition-based rules (queries) ● E-mail-based rules Business rule design view ● General—characteristics and run frequency (when?) ● Conditions—selection criteria (what?) ● Workflow—processing steps (how?) ● Notification—communication (who?)
Projects	How HelpSTAR facilitates management of projects

Figure B-2   HelpSTAR*2008* CBT tutorials

HelpSTAR*2008* Terminology

Part of learning a new software package is adapting to its vocabulary. Some HelpSTAR*2008* terminology is similar to key terms defined elsewhere in this book; other terms are unique to HelpSTAR*2008*. In addition to these key terms, HelpSTAR*2008* provides a glossary of terms as part of its online help system. To access the glossary within the software, press the **F1** function key and click the **Glossary** button. Figure B-3 is a brief list of key terms and their definitions that you are likely to encounter as you use HelpSTAR^{2008}.

---

alert—A message to a support rep generated by HelpSTAR, by an event that occurs (such as a request being closed), or by the application of a business rule.

asset—An item, such as a PC, server, network gateway, or software package.

auto discovery—A tool to scan the hardware and software on a network to locate new or unauthorized devices or audit for compliance with the terms of software license agreements.

best solution—HelpSTAR's knowledgebase of resolved service requests and support articles.

business rule—An if-then rule used to automate tasks in HelpSTAR; when a condition has been met (such as when a service request with a critical priority is not handled within 30 minutes), an action is triggered (such as the service request is escalated or an e-mail is sent).

configuration management—A collection of tools to record the details of various technology assets such as their purchase information, specifications, physical location, allocation to users or departments, or service request history.

dashboard—A brief management report (statistics and charts) on the performance of a help desk.

find panel—HelpSTAR^{2008}'s search tool.

history—A record of previous information (such as requests) relating to a user, department, asset, or service request.

home page—HelpSTAR^{2008}'s opening page, with ribbon menu options and shortcuts to common tasks.

line item grid—A list of service requests or details on a report.

preview pane—A view that displays properties and recent updates of service requests.

project—A predefined procedure or sequence of steps to accomplish an objective; a software installation on a PC or information entered into HelpSTAR^{2008} for a new employee are examples of projects.

query—Criteria used to search for or filter (select) information in a database.

quick message—Similar to an instant message; uses HelpSTAR^{2008} software to initiate, receive, and respond to the message.

reminder—A message, initiated by a user, an agent, or a manager, to prompt a user to take some action, such as make a follow-up phone call.

ribbon—HelpSTAR^{2008}'s user interface of menus, buttons, and tool icons at the top of each window.

service level agreement—A contract between end users and a service provider which defines a specified level of help desk services; for example, an SLA may specify maximum help desk response and resolution times. Provisions of a service level agreement are often defined as business rules in HelpSTAR^{2008}.

service request—An incident, phone call, or e-mail from a user to a help desk or service facility.

support rep—A help desk agent or user support specialist who handles service requests.

template—A predefined form or memo.

timesheet—A tool for collecting data on the time a support rep spends working on a service request; used as billing or performance data.

view—A list of a support rep's service requests. A view can be customized to display requests by priority, time received, department, or other criteria.

workflow—A process during which a service request passes through various stages (sometimes called a life cycle) from receipt to dispatch, prioritization, assignment, escalation, resolution, documentation, and finally to termination; similar to the steps in incident management.

workspace—A support rep's work area. Workspace will display a list of service requests and HelpSTAR^{2008} features that are available to a support rep.

Figure B-3   Key terms used in HelpSTAR^{2008} software and tutorials

A Case Study Using HelpSTAR^{2008}

Lakspur Technologies is a high-tech company with offices in New York and Miami. The New York office has several departments, including management, administration, sales, human resources, and IT (including network, security, and technical support). George Friedman is a product engineer from the Miami office who is being transferred to the New York office. George is the first of several product engineers who will be transferred to New York. Beth Markham is a support rep who works in the technical support department at Lakspur's New York office. Beth needs to enter information about George into the HelpSTAR^{2008} system.

This case study assumes you have installed HelpSTAR^{2008}. The Student Edition of HelpSTAR^{2008} is distributed with a sample database which includes a few users, assets, service requests, solutions, and other information that will be used in the case study.

The case study does not detail each keystroke or mouse click. It assumes that you are generally familiar with the use of the Windows GUI interface and that you have viewed several of the tutorials described above.

Step 1: Start HelpSTAR^{2008}

In HelpSTAR^{2008}, users often find they have multiple windows open. Any time you want to return to the HelpSTAR^{2008} home page, click the **Close** button in the top-right corner to close the top window, or click the **HelpSTAR^{2008} Student Edition** button on the Windows taskbar.

1. Double-click the **HelpSTAR^{2008}** icon on your desktop and log in as Beth Markham.

Step 2: Enter a New Department

Since George is the first Engineering department employee in New York, Beth needs to add Engineering as a department into HelpSTAR^{2008}'s database.

- On HelpSTAR^{2008}'s ribbon menu, click the **Setup/Administration** tab.

- In the *Manage* group of tasks, click the **Departments** task button.

- In the *Departments* menu, click the **Add New** option.

- In the *New Department* window, enter "Engineering" as a new department.

- Then click the **Save** icon in the top-left corner of the *New Department* window (next to the HelpSTAR^{2008} icon) to update the list of departments and exit from the *New Department* window.

- To verify that the Engineering department has been added, click the **Departments** task button again.

- In the *Departments* menu, click the **Manage Existing** option, and confirm that Engineering is now in the list of departments.

To delete a department from the *Manage Existing* list, right-click its name and click **De-Activate**.

619

Step 3: Enter a New User

To add George Friedman as a new user in HelpSTAR^{2008}, follow these steps:

- On the ribbon menu, click the **Setup/Administration** tab

- In the *Manage* group of tasks, click the **Users** task button

- Then click the **Add New** option

- In the *New User* window, click the **Main** tab

- Enter the following information about George Friedman:
  - *Name:* "George Friedman"
  - Click the **Internal User** option button
  - In the *Department* pull-down list, click **Engineering**
  - *Telephone*: "906-222-3321" *Ext:* "777"
  - *Location:* "New York"

- Then click the **Logins/Email** tab and perform the following steps to establish George's password and e-mail address:
  - *Logins section:* Click the **Enabled** radio button; in the *Password* field, enter "George777"; reenter the password to confirm it.
  - *Email section*: Click the **Enabled** radio button; in the *Email Address* field, enter "gfriedman@lakspur.net".
  - Click the **Save** icon in the top-left corner of the *New User* window (next to the HelpSTAR^{2008} icon) to update the list of users. When HelpSTAR^{2008} asks about adding another user, click **No**.

- Leave other fields in the *New User* window blank and, when asked about adding privileges for George, click the **No** button.

- Verify that George has been added as a user:
  - On the ribbon menu, in the *Manage* group, click the **Departments** task button. Click the **Manage Existing** option button.
  - On the Department list, double-click **Engineering** and confirm that George is listed as a user in Engineering.

To delete a user from the list, right-click their name and choose **De-Activate**.

- On the *Engineering* department list, click the link to George's name to display the information about George shown in Figure B-4.

- Close all open windows, except the Home page.

Figure B-4 HelpSTAR*2008* entry for user George Friedman

Step 4: Add an Asset

George brought his laptop computer with him from the Miami office. Beth needs to add information about George's laptop to HelpSTAR*2008*'s asset database for Lakspur.

- On the ribbon menu, click the **Setup/Administration** tab

- In the *Manage* group of tasks, click the **Assets** task button

- Click the **Add New** option

- Enter the following information about George's laptop:

  - In the *Asset Type* field, use the pull-down list to select **Workstation**

  - *Name:* "Dell Latitude D630"

  - *ID Tag:* "D73124"

  - *Serial Number:* "D211XL62607-9"

- In the *Allocated to* field, use the pull-down list to select **User**; in the user list; double-click **George Friedman**.

- In the *Product* field, use the pull-down list to select **Dell Laptop**.

- In the *Vendor* field, use the pull-down list to select **Dell Inc.**

- *Cost:* "749"

- *Acquisition Date:* "4/15/09"

- *Memo:* "George brought his Dell laptop from Miami when he transferred to New York."

- Leave the other fields blank. Figure B-5 shows the completed entry for George's laptop. Click the **Save** button, and then click **OK** to add the asset.

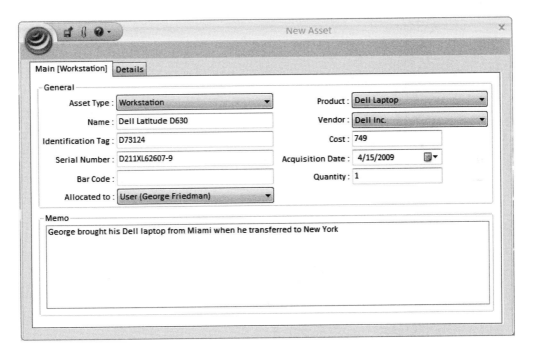

Figure B-5   HelpSTAR[2008] entry for Dell laptop

- Verify that George's laptop has been added as an asset:

  - In the *Manage* group of tasks, click the **Users** task button again.

  - Click the **Manage Existing** option.

  - Then double-click **George Friedman** and confirm that the Dell laptop is an asset assigned to George Friedman. (Since it is a link, you can click **Dell laptop** to view details of this asset.)

To delete an asset from the *Manage Existing* list, right-click its name and choose **De-Activate**.

Step 5: Enter a Service Request

George called Beth later the same day to say that he is getting settled into his New York office, but is having difficulty connecting his Dell Laptop to the Lakspur network. He reports that his laptop cannot find a wireless network to connect to. Beth explained to George that the New York office is still using wired Ethernet connections to their office network. She asked if George has an Ethernet cable to use to connect. He doesn't. So Beth entered a service request ticket and told George that either she or another support rep would bring one to his office and show him where to connect it.

- On HelpSTAR²⁰⁰⁸'s ribbon menu, click the **Service Request** tab

- In the *New* group of tasks, click the **Request** task.

- Enter the following information about George's service request:

    Main [Tech Support Request] tab

    General Information section:

    - In the *Request Type* field, use the pull-down menu to select **Tech Support Request**

    - In the *Requester* field, click **Find User** and double-click **George Friedman** in the list of users

    - In the *Category* field, click the plus (+) sign in front of **Network Support** and click **Cabling & Connectivity**

    - *Title:* "Needs Ethernet cable to connect"

    Importance section:

    - *User Urgency:* Select **High**

    Scheduling section:

    - *Due By:* Select **ASAP** (as soon as possible)

    Current location: Dispatch

    Asset/Discovered Item:

    - Search for: "Dell laptop"; when HelpSTAR²⁰⁰⁸ presents the list of all Dell laptops, click the one listed for George Friedman in Engineering, and then click **OK**.

    Memo field:

    - Enter: "George needs a 12 foot Ethernet cable to connect his laptop to the Internet."

When you have completed these steps, the service request will look like the example in Figure B-6.

Figure B-6 HelpSTAR*2008* entry for a new service request

If you try to save the new service request at this point, HelpSTAR*2008* will notify you that the *Error Number* and *Error Message* on the **Tech Details** tab are required fields.

- Select the **Tech Details** tab
  - *Error Number:* "NA" (NA here means "not applicable")
  - *Error Message:* "NA"

When you fill out any HelpSTAR*2008* form, such as the new service request form, you can choose one of several ways to save the record in HelpSTAR*2008*'s database:

- Click the **Close** button in the top-right corner of the open window; then click **Yes** to save.

- With the window open, press **ALT+F4** on the keyboard; then click **Yes** to save.

- With the window open, press **CTRL+S** on the keyboard.

- Click the **HelpSTAR²⁰⁰⁸ button** in the top-left corner of the home page window; in the list of open windows (in the right column), click the **Close** button; then click **Yes** to save.

Step 6: Assign a Service Request to a Support Rep

A little later, Beth is headed in the direction of George's office to perform another task, so she checks on the status of George's request for an Ethernet cable.

- From HelpSTAR²⁰⁰⁸'s home page, click the **Service Request** tab; then in the *Workbench* group, click the **Workspace** task.

- In the left pane, note that Beth can select whether the *Workspace List* (in the right pane) shows service requests *In Dispatch, In Service,* or *In Queue*

  - *In Dispatch* displays service requests that are not yet assigned to a support rep.

  - *In Service* displays service requests that Beth is currently working on.

  - *In Queue* displays service requests that are assigned to Beth as future tasks.

- Click **In Dispatch** to see whether George's request has been assigned to a support rep.

- Since it is still *In Dispatch*, double-click the service request line for George's request to display the details.

- To move George's request from *In Dispatch* to Beth's queue (which assigns the request to Beth), on the ribbon interface click the **Home** tab and select the **My Service** option in the *Move To* group. Click **Save** to save changes to the service request.

When these steps are completed, George Friedman's service request for an Ethernet cable is reassigned from *In Dispatch* to Beth Markham's queue (see Figure B-7). From the *Move To* group, Beth can move a pending service request to herself (*My Service*), to another queue, to another support rep's queue, or back to *In Dispatch;* she can also choose to *Close* it. Whether a support rep can perform some or all of these assignment tasks depends on the privileges set for that agent. For example, senior support reps can be assigned privileges that entry-level agents don't have, and supervisors or team leaders can be assigned an even wider array of privileges.

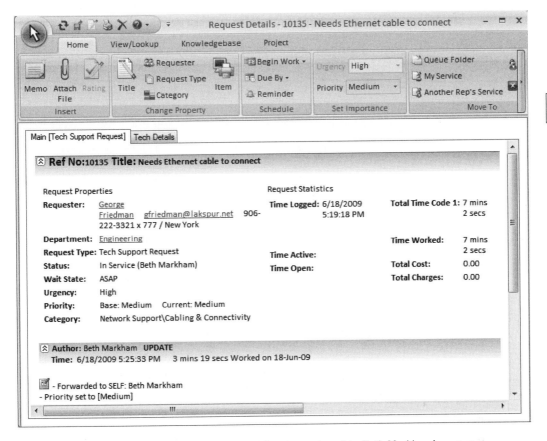

Figure B-7 George Friedman's service request is now assigned to Beth Markham's queue

Step 7: Close a Service Request

Beth delivered an Ethernet cable to George and got him connected to the New York office network. When she returned to her office, she closed the service request.

- From HelpSTAR*2008*'s home page, click the **My Workspace** short-cut on the left side of the page. In the left pane, click **In Service**. Find George's service request.

- Right-click George's request, and select **Update Request**.

- In the *memo* field, write a notation: "Delivered cable to George and got him connected"; then click the **Save** icon, or press **CTRL+S** to save the memo.

- Right-click George's request for an Ethernet cable, and select **Close Request**.

Step 8: Find a Service Request

Beth would like to verify that the HelpSTAR^{2008} record for George's service request was completed. She uses the *Find* panel to locate the service request.

- On HelpSTAR^{2008}'s home page, use the *Find* panel in the center of the page. In the *Search In* box, use the pull-down list to select **User**.

- In the *Search For* box, enter "George" and click the **Search** button.

The list of all users whose name includes "George" is displayed (there may be only one in the sample database).

- Click **George Friedman** in the listing.

- In the ribbon menu, use the *History* group of tasks and click **User** to view the service requests for George.

- In the *Date Range* field, use the pull-down list to select a predefined time period, or enter a specific date range and click **OK**.

- On the *Request History* page, double-click the entry for the Ethernet cable request and view the request details to verify that they were recorded correctly.

The *Find panel* permits very flexible searches for HelpSTAR^{2008} objects in its database, such as service requests (by number, title, or category), users, departments, companies, assets, or support reps.

Step 9: Find a Solution to a Problem

Beth was the agent assigned to the Help Desk hotline phone when she received a call from George Friedman in Engineering. George thanked her again for bringing the Ethernet cable to connect him to the network. He reported, however, that when he attempted to print an e-mail message, someone in the human resources department called to tell him that his message had printed on a printer in their department. George asked Beth how to change his computer's settings so that his documents would be sent to a printer closer to his office. Beth followed Step 5 above to enter a service request for George's printing problem. Then she searched HelpSTAR^{2008}'s Best Solutions database for information about printing problems that sounded similar to the one George had encountered.

- On HelpSTAR^{2008}'s home page, use the *Find* panel in the center of the page. In the *Search In* box, use the drop-down list to select **Best Solution**.

- In the *Search For* box, enter "printer" and click the **Search** button.

The list of solutions in which the word *printer* appears in the title or as a keyword is displayed.

- Double-click solution **ID = 5** (**Change Default Printer**) in the listing to display the Best Solution entry, as shown in Figure B-8.

Beth used the information from the Best Solution to guide George through changing the default printer on his laptop to one near his office.

Figure B-8 Best Solution knowledge base entry in HelpSTAR[2008] for George's printer problem

Step 10: Escalate a Service Request

Beth noticed that the Alert button was flashing on her workspace status bar at the bottom of the HelpSTAR[2008] interface. She clicked the Alert button to view her current alerts. One alert caught her eye—Ref# 10128, a request from Malcom Worthington II that he is having problems with his virtual private network (VPN) connection. Beth checked the Best Solutions database, but found no entries that referred to VPN problems. Beth knew that Jeff Allen would normally take this kind of service request, since Jeff is the VPN expert on the Network Support team.

- To move request 10128 into Jeff Allen's queue, double-click the listing for 10128.

- In the ribbon menu, use the *Move To* group and click **Another Rep's Service**.

- Double-click **Jeff Allen** in the listing of support reps.

Note that service request Ref# 10128 is now in Jeff Allen's queue. Beth was able to move a request from *In Dispatch* to Jeff Allen's queue because that privilege is assigned to her in HelpSTAR^{2008}'s user database.

- To verify the current status of a service request by number, use the *Find* panel on HelpSTAR^{2008}'s home page. In the *Search In* box, use the pull-down list to select **Request #**.

- In the *Search For* box, enter "10128," and click the **Search** button.

Step 11: Draft a New Best Solution

Beth's supervisor at Lakspur asked her to write a new Best Solution in HelpSTAR^{2008}'s knowledge management system on how to use HelpSTAR^{2008}'s online help system. Beth briefly reviewed the features of the help system and then wrote a draft of an article for a Best Solution.

- On HelpSTAR^{2008}'s ribbon menu, click the **Knowledge Management** tab. In the *New* group, click the **Best Solution** task.

- Enter a *Title* for the Best Solution: "HelpSTAR help system."

- In the Category pull-down list, select **Tech Support**; within the Tech Support category, select the subcategory **Training**. (To expand any category that is collapsed, click the plus (+) sign in front of the category name.)

- In the Keywords box, click the **Add** button to the right. At the top of the Keywords box, click the **New** icon (the key symbol), or press **CTRL+N**.

- Enter the keyword "HelpSTAR" and click **OK**.

- From the *Available Keywords* list in the left pane, click **HelpSTAR** and click the **Add** button.

- Repeat these steps to add two other keywords: "online" and "help."

- When you have added "HelpSTAR", "online", and "help" as keywords for this Best Solution, click **Save**.

- In the *Problem Description* box, enter: "Support Reps need to be able to use HelpSTAR's online help system to locate information about features."

- In the *Resolution* box, enter the following text:

"To access HelpSTAR's online help system, click the question mark button next to the HelpSTAR button, or press F1.

On the help system page, which is displayed in your Web browser, click the Contents tab at the top of the page to view the table of contents in the left pane.

The help topics that are most relevant to beginning support reps are:

- *A Brief Lesson in How HelpSTAR works*

- *HelpSTAR Home Page*

- *Service Request*

- *Configuration Management*

- *Knowledge Management*

The help system's Search tab is also useful and the Glossary tab can provide definitions of unfamiliar terms."

- Click the **Save** button at the bottom of the window to save the Best Solution draft.

Use the *Find* panel on the home page to locate the Best Solution.

- In the *Search In* box, use the drop-down list to select **Best Solution**.

- In the *Search For* box, enter "help" and click the **Search** button.

The draft Best Solution that Beth wrote is shown in Figure B-9. Note that Find can locate the Best Solution you wrote using the keyword "help," but it cannot locate the same solution using "glossary," even though "glossary" appears in the Best Solution text.

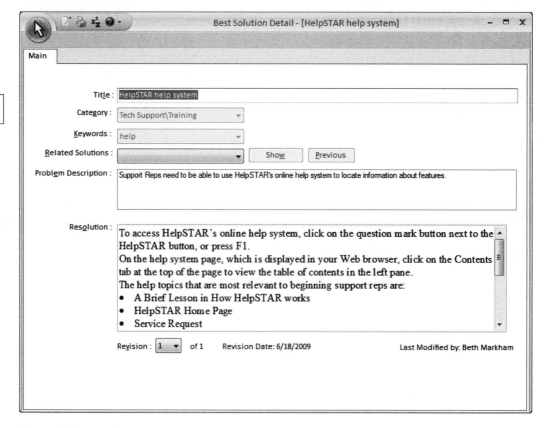

Figure B-9 Best Solution knowledge base draft article on HelpSTAR[2008]'s help system

Step 12: Update a Service Request

Beth noticed that one of the service requests in the *In Dispatch* queue reported a printing problem. Since she regularly deals with this kind of problem, Beth looked at the service request and responded to it.

- On HelpSTAR[2008]'s home page, click the **My Workspace** icon on the left side of the page.

- Locate and double-click service request 10133 from Tim Thomas in Human Resources.

- In the *Insert* group on the ribbon interface, click **Memo**.

- In the *Create a New Memo* window, enter the following:

"Tim -

In most cases, if you power off the printer and then turn it back on, the computer will re-establish the connection with the printer.

Please call me if this doesn't fix the problem.

Beth"

Click the **OK** button in the top-left corner to add this response as a memo to Tim's service request, as shown in Figure B-10.

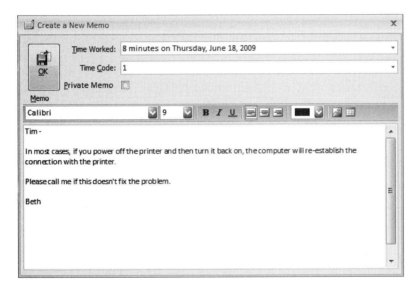

Figure B-10 Memo Beth added to Tim's service request #10133 on printer problems

Step 13: Set a Reminder

Beth wanted to call Tim later to verify that he had been able to fix the printer problem. She used HelpSTAR^{2008}'s reminder system to help her remember to make the call.

- On HelpSTAR^{2008}'s home page, click the **My Workspace** shortcut. Then double-click service request #10133 to make it active.

- In the *Schedule* group, click the **Reminder** task.

- In the *Reminder* window, click in the box to send the reminder to *Myself.*

- In the *Settings* section, use the drop-down list to set the time to **5 minutes**, or set a time of your choosing a few minutes in the future (as a test of this feature).

- In the *Memo* box, enter: "Call Tim re: printer problem" and click **Save**.

Check the *Reminder* icon on her workspace bar at the bottom of the HelpSTAR[2008] window in a few minutes to verify that Beth received the reminder you set. The *Reminder* icon should flash to indicate a reminder is waiting for attention.

- Click the **Reminder** icon to view the reminder, or click the **HelpSTAR Messages** shortcut on the left side of the home page.

- Locate the reminder message in the list. To delete the reminder, in the *Reminder Actions* group, click the **Dismiss** task option.

Step 14: Create a Standard Report

Beth would like to view a listing of the Best Solution topics currently included in Lakspur's knowledge database. The listing of topics is pre-defined as a standard report in HelpSTAR[2008]. To access the report, follow these steps:

- On HelpSTAR[2008]'s home page, click the **Service Request** tab and find the *Data Analysis* group. Click the **Reports** task.

- On the *Reports* ribbon menu, locate the *Listing* group and click **Best Solution**.

- In the *Reports List* pane on the left, click **Best Solutions**.

The report of current Best Solution topics is displayed. Click the ➤ button at the top of the report window to view subsequent pages. Does the online help system topic that you added in Step 11 appear in the list?

Step 15: Create a Query Report

Beth wants to verify that she has responded to all of the previous reminders she received and dismissed. In order to list her reminders, Beth uses the data-analysis tools in HelpSTAR[2008] to construct a query and prepare a listing or report of all reminders she previously read and dismissed.

- On HelpSTAR[2008]'s home page, click the **Service Request** tab and find the *Data Analysis* group. Click **Queries**, and then click **Create New**.

- In the *Query Designer* window, locate the *Request Field Selection* in the left pane. Begin with all boxes in the list of fields unchecked, except the box in front of the *Service Request* field. Verify that no design criteria are listed in the *Design and Preview* pane on the right.

- Then, check the boxes in front of *Ref#* and *Title*. These two fields should now appear in the *Design and Preview* pane on the right.

- In the *Request Field Selection* list, click the plus (+) sign in front of *Reminder* to expand that group of fields, and click to check the box in front of *Dismiss*. Verify that there are now three fields listed in the *Design and Preview* pane.

- In the *Design and Preview* pane, click the **Design Query** tab. Then click the *Dismiss* criteria line to select that field. Click the **Criteria…** link on the right end of the line to display the *Selection Criteria* window.

- In the *Selection Criteria* window, verify that the *Selection Type* radio button is set to *AND* and the *Criteria* is set to *Dismiss Equal to Yes*. Click the **Add** button to define the criteria, and then click **OK**. Verify that the criteria *Selection* column for the *Dismiss* field now contains the criteria *Dismiss Equal to Yes*.

- Do not define selection criteria for *Ref#* and *Title* (these fields will simply be displayed on the query results). Click the **Preview Query Results** tab to see a list of dismissed service requests. Note the service requests listed for which Beth previously dismissed reminders.

Once Beth has prepared the criteria for this database query report, she can save the query to run it again in the future, print a report of the query results, or export the query results to Excel.

Step 16: Display a Performance Dashboard

Beth wants to quickly check on the performance of Lakspur's user support team. HelpSTAR[2008] includes a dashboard feature, which displays a customizable, one-page summary of various performance indicators. (Because the sample database is small, these statistics are for illustration only.)

- On HelpSTAR[2008]'s home page, click the **Dashboard** shortcut on the left of the page.

- In the dashboard display, Beth noticed in the lower-right corner that Human Resources produced the largest number of service requests. Click the HR bar to drill-down to the list of requests from that department.

These tutorial activities emphasize common and frequent tasks support reps perform in HelpSTAR[2008] every day. However, HelpSTAR[2008] is an extensive software package with many capabilities for help desks and other applications. These tutorial steps have just scratched the surface of the software's capabilities. We have not covered many useful features, such as purchase order processing, business rules to automate HelpSTAR^{2008} tasks and communications, links to e-mail and pagers, user-defined fields to customize HelpSTAR^{2008}, advanced data analysis and reporting features, and use of HelpSTAR^{2008} as a Web portal. Make good use of the 180-day student edition to explore these and other features of the software. Many support organizations use HelpSTAR^{2008} or a similar package to automate help desk recordkeeping.

Hands-On Activities

Activity B-1

Add another new user. Follow the steps in the tutorial above to add another user, Rahim Waleed, to the Engineering Department. Rahim just transferred from the Miami office.

Enter the following information about Rahim:

Main tab

    Name: Rahim Waleed

    Internal User

    Department: Engineering

    Telephone: 906-222-3321 *Ext:* 778

    Location: New York

Logins/Email tab

    Logins: Enabled; set password to: Rahim778

    Email: Enabled; set address to: rwaleed@lakspur.net

Leave other fields blank and don't add privileges for Rahim at this time.

Verify that Rahim has been added as a user. If this activity is for a class assignment, display and print Rahim's user information.

Activity B-2

Enter a service request. Follow the steps in the tutorial above to add a service request for Rahim.

Enter the following information about Rahim's service request:

Main tab

    General Information section:

        Request Type: Tech Support Request

        Requester: Rahim Waleed

        Category: Technical Support\Software\Installation

        Title: Would like to have MS Office 2007 installed

    Importance section

        User Urgency: Low

    Scheduling section

        Due By: ASAP

    Current location

        Dispatch

    Tech Details tab

        Error Number: NA

        Error Message: NA

Verify that the service request has been entered correctly. If this activity is for a class assignment, display and print the service request.

Activity B-3

Find a service request. Use the *Find* panel on HelpSTAR^{2008}'s home page to locate the service request you created in Activity B-2 (or use any other service request in the database as an example). Write short descriptions for three different ways you can find a service request using HelpSTAR^{2008}'s *Find* search tool. Which of the three methods is easiest for you?

Activity B-4

Enter a new vendor/manufacturer. Search the Web to locate contact information for user support at Toshiba USA, which supplies laptop computers to Lakspur Technologies. Use the *Setup/Administration* tab on HelpSTAR^{2008}'s ribbon menu to enter information into the database for Toshiba. Verify that the vendor contact information has been entered correctly. If this activity is for a class assignment, display and print the vendor information for Toshiba USA.

Activity B-5

Find the service request categories that are defined for Lakspur Technologies. Locate a list of the service request categories currently defined in HelpSTAR*2008*. Add a new category under *Tech Support\ Software* for service requests that are related to *Engineering* software. Verify that the new category for *Engineering* software has been added to the service request category list. If you enter a new service request now, does *Tech Support\Software\Engineering* appear as a category in the *General Information* section? If this activity is for a class assignment, display and print the list of *Tech Support* categories and subcategories.

Activity B-6

Add an attachment to a service request. Use HelpSTAR*2008*'s help system to research how to add an attachment to a service request. Then use the service request from Rahim in Activity B-2 (or any other service request) to add an attachment.

- Verify that the attachment has been added to the service request. If this activity is for a class assignment, display and print the service request to show that the attachment was added.

- Write a short description of the steps in HelpSTAR*2008* to add an attachment to a service request. Write your description so that other new HelpSTAR*2008* support reps could follow the procedure.

Activity B-7

Write a draft of a Best Solution. Follow the procedure in tutorial Step 11 above to write a Best Solution for a technical support problem with which you are familiar. The problem could be one you wrote about for an end-of-chapter activity earlier in this book. Your Best Solution should describe the problem and how you solved it.

Which keywords did you use to describe the best solution you wrote about? What is the difference between a draft best solution and a published one? If this activity is for a class assignment, display and print the best solution report you prepared.

Activity B-8

Audit the hardware and software on your workstation. Use the *Audit My Workstation* shortcut on HelpSTAR*2008*'s home page to prepare a report on the hardware and software for the PC you are using. Write a brief report that describes the kinds of information available on the audit report. If this activity is for a class assignment, display and print the Summary page of the audit for your workstation.

Does HelpSTAR*2008* remember the audit information for your PC? If so, how can you redisplay the information after the original audit report is closed?

Activity B-9

Prepare a report based on a query. Follow the procedure described in tutorial Step 15 above to prepare a query report listing the *Ref#* and *Title* for all service requests for which the *Current Priority* is equal to *Critical*. List the reference numbers for the service requests that are currently defined as critical.

To which support reps are the critical service requests assigned? How would you find out using the query tool? Why do you think there are so many support reps assigned to 10128?

Case Projects

1. Create a Help Desk Solution for Willamette Planning.

Willamette Planning is a local company that performs urban planning and land use studies for local business and government agencies. It has a small research and design department as well as a management team. Willamette Planning relies heavily on computer technology, and expects to grow; therefore, they hired Beth Markham as a help desk support rep, and have decided to adopt HelpSTAR[2008] as a help desk platform.

Your task in this assignment is to play the role of Beth Markham and set up HelpSTAR[2008] for Willamette Planning. Use the information in the table below (you may make any reasonable assumptions or use any fictitious information you feel is appropriate for the purposes of this case study).

User	Department	Ext	E-Mail	Workstation	ID
Aaron Rupp	Management	10	a.rupp@wp.net	Toshiba Laptop	WS0018
Chris North	Management	14	c.north@wp.net	Toshiba Laptop	WS0023
Rakhi Windsor	Design	11	r.windsor@wp.net	Dell Laptop	WS0019
Walter Willis	Design	12	w.willis@wp.net	Dell Laptop	WS0020
Chris Green	Design	13	c.green@wp.net	Dell Laptop	WS0021
Beth Markham	Help Desk	15	b.markham@wp.net	Toshiba Laptop	WS0022

Enter the following service requests into HelpSTAR[2008].

User	Service Request
Chris Green	I am unable to connect to the server from my workstation (WS0021).
Chris Green	I need to install the latest version (9.3) of the GIS software package.
Aaron Rupp	I can no longer print from my workstation.
Rakhi Windsor	The battery in my laptop now lasts less than 60 minutes when I am out of the office.

Prepare a report that lists the open service requests by user.

Challenge activity: Since Beth Markham is currently the only help desk support rep at Willamette Planning, research how to write a HelpSTAR*2008* business rule that automatically assigns service requests from *In Dispatch* to *In Queue* for Beth.

2. Perform a Feasibility Study for a Help Desk.

If you work or volunteer at a help desk, training lab facility, or instructional computer lab, assemble a small group of your colleagues to work as an assessment team to perform a feasibility study to implement HelpSTAR*2008* in your facility. You may want to view some of the client videos available on HelpSTAR*2008*'s home page to learn more about how various organizations use HelpSTAR*2008*. For additional background information, download and read a HelpSTAR*2008* Evaluator's Guide at **www.helpstar.com/quickeval/quickEvalGuide.pdf**, which contains an overview of HelpSTAR*2008* features.

Use your team's knowledge of the operation of your facility to prepare a feasibility study that addresses these issues:

1. Which features in HelpSTAR*2008* could be used to implement a help desk or instructional lab service request tool in your facility? Your team should use its knowledge of your facility and consider features in HelpSTAR*2008* for problem management, knowledge management, asset management, purchase order processing, and data analysis and reporting.

2. Which features in HelpSTAR*2008* would probably not be of immediate use in your facility, and why not?

3. Review the material on feasibility studies in Chapter 8 in this book. Include a section in your report that briefly evaluates economic, operational, technological, and timeline feasibility.

4. Conclude your report with a recommendation to the management of your facility about whether HelpSTAR*2008* is a suitable help desk package for your facility.

User Support Presentations and Meetings

In this appendix, you will learn about:

◎ How to design and develop effective presentations

◎ How to prepare for and participate in effective support worker team meetings

Two aspects of work as a support specialist are introduced in this appendix. First, support workers often need to develop presentations. Some presentations, such as user training modules and reports on the findings and recommendations of a needs assessment project, are aimed at end users. Other presentations, such as training sessions for other support workers, or progress reports on special projects, are aimed at support colleagues or managers. In all of these examples, the goal of a support specialist is to prepare an effective, professional presentation of information for end users and work colleagues.

Second, support workers are often participants in or conveners of meetings. These meetings may include end users, work colleagues, or managers. The purpose of a meeting may be to gather or report on information related to special project work, or a periodic team meeting to discuss and make decisions about the activities of a support work group. In every meeting in which a support worker participates, the goal is to be an effective contributor, whether in the role of meeting convener or participant.

The purpose of this appendix is to describe some ways in which a support specialist can improve their performance as a presentation preparer and presenter, or as a meeting convener or participant.

Introduction to Presentation Software

This appendix focuses on presentation software used as a tool to design and deliver effective presentations. For many support workers, Microsoft PowerPoint is the presentation software tool of choice, if for no other reason than it is installed and available in so many training and work environments. However, several other good presentation software tools are available, including some products that can be used at no cost. Popular examples include Zoho Show, Google Docs presentations, and OpenOffice Impress. Corel's WordPerfect Office Suite includes a tool with many of PowerPoint's features named Corel Presentations, which is only available as part of the Corel Suite.

ON THE WEB

For information about free and open source presentation tools, which offer varying degrees of compatibility with PowerPoint, visit one or more of these sites:

- **show.zoho.com**—Zoho's Show is a Web-based presentation tool (free registration required).

(continues)

(continued)

- **docs.google.com**—Google's presentations is a Web-based tool (free registration required).

- **www.openoffice.org/product/impress.html**—Impress is a presentation tool that can be downloaded and installed without charge on a PC as part of the OpenOffice suite.

The purpose of this appendix is to provide information about how to design an effective presentation, rather than to serve as a user's manual or tutorial on presentation software. Tutorial introductions and other learning resources on these tools are available elsewhere, as described in Figure C-1. To learn the basic features of presentation software tools, start with a PowerPoint tutorial since Zoho Show,

Presentation Tool	Learning Resources
Microsoft PowerPoint	▫ **homepage.cs.uri.edu/tutorials/csc101/powerpoint/ppt.html**; brief introduction ▫ **oregonstate.edu/instruction/ed596/ppoint/pphome.htm**; brief introduction ▫ **www.guidesandtutorials.com/powerpoint-tutorial.html**; in-depth coverage of 2003 version ▫ **www.fgcu.edu/support/office2007/ppt/index.asp**; covers 2007 version ▫ David Beskeen, *Microsoft Office PowerPoint 2007 – Illustrated Introductory* (Course Technology, 2008); an edition covering the 2003 version is also available by the same author
Zoho Show	▫ **www.readwriteweb.com/archives/zoho_show_20_launches.php** ▫ Nancy Connor, *Zoho 4 Everyone* (Que, 2009); one chapter on Show in a book that covers several Zoho tools
Google Docs presentations	▫ **www.googletutor.com/2007/09/18/the-new-google-presentation-app** ▫ Steve Holzner, *Google Docs 4 Everyone* (Que, 2009); two chapters on Google presentations in a book covering several Google Docs tools
OpenOffice Impress	▫ **www.learnopenoffice.org/contents.htm** ▫ **presentationsoft.about.com/od/openofficeimpress/tp/071021openoffice_beginguide.htm** ▫ OOoAuthorsTeam, *OpenOffice.org 3 IMPRESS Guide* (CreateSpace, 2009); also available online at **documentation.openoffice.org/manuals/userguide3/0500IG3-ImpressGuideOOo3.pdf**

Figure C-1   Tutorials on selected presentation software tools

Google Docs presentations, and OpenOffice Impress have many of the same features as PowerPoint (all three can also read and write PowerPoint .PPT slideshow files).

Steps to Design and Develop a Presentation

Most support workers follow a sequence of basic steps when they design and develop a presentation. These steps are summarized in Figure C-2.

Plan the presentation
  1. Define the audience, topic, and purpose
  2. Learn about the presentation location and delivery media
  3. Outline the major points

Design the presentation
  4. Select a slide design
  5. Select a slide background and color scheme

Create the individual slides
  6. Choose a slide layout
  7. Prepare the text for each slide
  8. Add other objects to selected slides, such as sound, photos, charts, tables, movies, maps, and diagrams

Organize the slides into a slideshow
  9. Decide on the sequence of slides
  10. Add transitions or animation

Generate handout materials
  11. Create speaker notes
  12. Create handouts

Present the presentation

Figure C-2 Basic steps to design and prepare a presentation

As with other lists of steps in this textbook, the set of steps in Figure C-2 should be considered a starting point, to which a support specialist will add, subtract, and modify as the specifics of a presentation warrant. The sections that follow provide guidelines for each of these steps.

Plan the Presentation

Step 1: Define the Audience, Topic, and Purpose

The chapters on training (Chapter 10) and technical writing (Chapter 11) emphasized the importance of (1) identifying the target audience, (2) clarifying the topic, and (3) focusing on the purpose of a presentation. These admonitions apply equally to planning a presentation.

Characteristics of the audience that need to be identified include whether they are novice end users, sophisticated computer users, user support staff, or managers. The technical experience of the audience makes a difference in the amount of technical detail, jargon terms, and acronyms that can be used in a presentation.

Without a clear definition of the presentation topic, a presenter may create slides which contain materials that stray from the central point. The topic definition should also identify what the presentation will *not* cover, as a way to focus on the central topic. A good presenter prepares each slide with an important question in mind: "What information do I want the audience to take away from viewing this slide?"

Finally, a presenter should define the purpose of the presentation—whether to inform, convince, or entertain. Since most user support presentations are not primarily entertainment, the choice is usually between an informational presentation (such as a training module) and one that tries to convince the audience to take some action or reach a decision (such as a recommendation at the conclusion of a user needs assessment project). Related to the purpose of a presentation is the question of whether the presentation will be presented one time (which perhaps requires less preparation) or at several events, such as product information presentations. Presentations that are offered on more than one occasion or that will be available for an extended period on the Web may require more time and effort to polish. In any case, a presentation represents both the presenter and the organization, and it should be the most professional product that can be prepared in the time allocated to it.

Step 2: Learn About the Presentation Location and Delivery Media

During the presentation planning stage, a preparer should identify the location where the presentation will be delivered. It is also important to identify the equipment that will be available to host the presentation. Location is important: will the presentation room be brightly lit or dimly lit? In brightly lit rooms, darker slides can be used for visibility, but lighter slides should be used in a dimly lit room.

Some presentations occur in a meeting room equipped with a computer, projector, and screen. If a computer-equipped meeting room is available, does the projector include a handheld remote unit that can control the computer's mouse? Is the projector or computer enabled for sound? Or, lacking a computer projection system, will the presentation need to be printed on overhead slides for an older projection system?

Other presentations are targeted for audience access via the Web or as printed handouts. If Web access is the delivery medium, will sound or animation or both be used to augment the informational slides? If a presentation will be distributed as a printed handout, will the material include color pages, black and white, or grayscale? How many printed pages can be included in the handout?

Step 3: Outline the Major Points

With a clear definition of a presentation's audience, topic, purpose, location, and delivery medium, a preparer can begin to outline the major points in a presentation. Each major point will probably translate into one or more slides.

 Chapter 11 on writing end user documents contains additional suggestions for developing an outline of a presentation.

It is probably not too early to mention a mistake that many first-time presenters make. Remember that in most presentations, a slideshow is a visual presentation method that should augment and emphasize a presenter's verbal message. Rarely should a slideshow presentation contain all the information the audience members need. Except in stand-alone slideshows designed for presentation at tradeshows or on the Web, the presenter is the star of the show. Slides containing too much detail that the audience needs to read or which make excessive use of format features (such as color, fonts, animation, and photos) may distract from the presenter and from the central message of the presentation.

Design the Presentation

Step 4: Select a Slide Design

Presentation software packages include a large number of predefined slide themes, sometimes called slide masters or templates, from which a preparer can choose. The purpose of a standard master slide design is to give the slideshow a consistent, professional appearance. Generally, simpler master slide designs that do not distract from the information content are more effective than flashy designs (unless the target audience is younger people who may prefer colorful, creative designs). Many of the format features on a master slide can be modified to create a custom appearance that can be part of a presenter's unique signature.

Other slide design elements are optional, and probably best omitted, unless there are specific reasons for their inclusion. Footers fall into this category—they should not be included in a slide master design just because the feature to create them is available in the presentation software. A slide number may be a useful tool to keep the presenter on track. A copyright notice is useful when the material is proprietary. Other footer features should be used judiciously.

Step 5: Select a Slide Background and Color Scheme

The background and color scheme, font selection, and other aspects of a slide's appearance can either contribute to or detract from the effectiveness of a presentation. Avoid using a photo or a pattern as a slide background; they tend to overshadow the information content on a slide. Plain backgrounds or ones with simple logos or designs are preferable. Muted colors are often more effective than bright hues. Simpler fonts (ones that avoid handwriting, scripts, stylized, and medieval fonts) keep the focus on the content.

The selection of design and format elements is an important decision every presenter makes. When in doubt, get a second opinion. Show some design candidates to a few colleagues you trust and get their feedback.

The general design principle here is that anything that draws attention away from the central message on a slide will detract the attention of audience members. As a presenter, do you want the audience to remember how unusual or fancy your slides were, or remember the message you want to communicate?

Create the Presentation Slides

Step 6: Choose a Slide Layout

Slide layouts give a presenter control over the arrangement of information on each slide. A slide layout is a combination of one or more of (1) a title, (2) contents, (3) objects, and (4) optional footer. Presentation software provides a variety of slide layout options. Each slide layout contains placeholders—a blank space such as a textbox to which a presenter will add some content, as shown in Figure C-3. Some placeholders are intended to hold titles for the slideshow or major sections within it; others provide space for text information. Some placeholders are designed to present comparisons between two or more side-by-side placeholders. Still other placeholders are arranged to include media objects, such as photos, tables, charts, sound, video clips, diagrams, and maps.

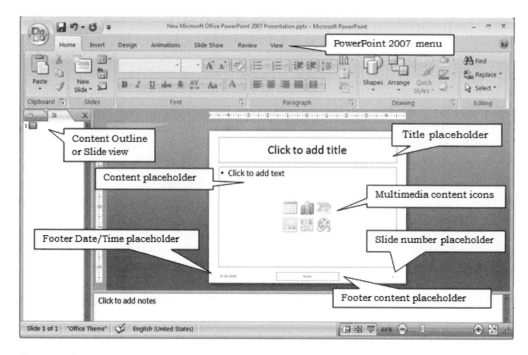

Figure C-3 PowerPoint 2007 slide layout with content placeholders

Slide layouts that use several of these layout elements (or placeholders) should be used with care. Audience members must take time to read a title, text contents, and view other media objects when several design elements are included on a single slide. During the time an audience member is absorbing all of the information content on a slide, they are not focusing their attention on you, the presenter. Is that your goal?

Step 7: Prepare the Text for Each Slide

If you find yourself continually reducing the font size on a slide in order to make information fit in the space, you've probably included too many points. Split a slide when the information becomes too large to fit.

Most slides consist of at least some text information. Here are some guidelines for the preparation of text:

- Keep text information short; avoid lengthy passages. Information items can be a word or a phrase, rather than a complete sentence. Let white space be the dominant feature of each slide. (A presenter should use complete sentences, but the slides don't necessarily have to if they really are supplemental to the presenter.)

- If a title or phrase extends over more than a single line, help the viewer by using natural breaking points between the lines. Use the title of this chapter as an example and consider various ways to break the title into two lines.

- Keep the number of bullets on a slide to a reasonable number (three to four points is plenty—never more than seven); avoid large numbers of lengthy points.

- When they view a slide, audience members notice *differences*. Changes in font sizes, different font colors, changes from normal to bold or italic, and differences in alignment or spacing all invite the audience to ask why there are differences and what the differences mean. Avoid differences for variety's sake, or changes just to make the text fit in the content space.

- To highlight important content on a slide, use a different font size or color, or use the drawing toolbar to add a callout or textbox. But don't overdo the use of these elements to call attention to important content—an audience will tire of looking at information, all of which appears to be of special importance. In other words, use differences in design elements to help your audience figure out what is really important.

- Vary the length of each slide's information content. Avoid creating several slides in a sequence, all of which use the same slide layout and have the same number and lengths of points or bulleted items.

- Always check the spelling of the content of a slideshow, and if possible, ask a colleague to proofread the slide content. A proofreader who is not a subject matter expert can often help identify gaps in content as well as mechanical problems.

Step 8: Add Other Objects to Selected Slides, Such as Sound, Photos, Charts, Tables, Movies, Maps, and Diagrams

Multimedia objects can certainly add interest to a slideshow. However, many beginning presenters make the mistake of thinking that each slide must contain something of interest beyond its text content. When used sparingly, multimedia objects embedded in a slideshow presentation can highlight important information and add information to supplement that provided by the presenter. Photos, graphics, sound, color, clipart, and other attention-getting devices are most effective at the beginning of a presentation to grab attention; they can be a distraction if used extensively in the heart of the message.

An exception to this guideline is slideshows that are specifically designed to be stand-alone presentations, such as those intended for the Web. Stand-alone slideshows can often benefit from more multimedia material because, without a presenter, the slideshow must carry the entire weight of the presentation.

Especially when adding sound, photos, movie clips, and other multi-media materials to a slideshow, a presenter must observe copyright laws, as well as cite the source of materials that are not the presenter's own work.

ON THE WEB

Guy Kawasaki, a venture capitalist, formulated a 10-20-30 rule for slide design. You can view a short video clip of Guy discussing his rule at **www.youtube.com/watch?v=liQLdRkOZiw**.

Organize the Slides into a Slideshow

Step 9: Decide on the Sequence of Slides

Presentation tools permit a designer to copy, move, and delete slides easily using a slide sorter or other tools. As part of the normal editing process, it is often necessary to move slides around, split some, and combine others.

Step 10: Add Transitions or Animation

 Presenters should avoid transitions between bulleted items on a slide, where the presenter must click to reveal each new bulleted item. Let audience members view the slide's entire contents, and avoid the distraction of transitions between bullets.

Use of slide transitions and animation is tricky. Often, nothing is wrong with a transition that simply replaces a slide with the next one in sequence with little or no transition between them. This guideline follows the principle that the mechanical features of a slideshow should not detract from the information content. However, some presenters use simple transitions, such as a rapid fade, to add interest to the presentation. If so, keep the transitions simple, smooth, and consistent throughout the slideshow—in a word: unobtrusive. If an audience member is wondering from which direction the next slide will fly in, or whether the presenter has an even trickier dissolve planned for a future slide, they are likely not focusing on the message.

Generate Handout Materials

Step 11: Create Speaker Notes

Most presentation packages include a feature to add speaker notes to a slide. These notes do not appear during a presentation or in handout materials, but are reminders to the presenter to discuss additional information or ask the audience a question to see whether they are following the presentation.

Step 12: Create Handouts

Because training sessions, project team reports, and other presentations are usually one-time events, many presenters choose to prepare and distribute handouts of the slideshow to participants. Handouts can consist of a reduced-size version of each slide and, optionally, space for audience members to take notes next to each slide.

Present the Presentation

Presenters may want to review the suggestions for trainers in Chapter 10, especially the 10 guidelines listed in Figure 10-6 and described on the pages that follow the figure. These suggestions apply equally to any presentation in which a slideshow is featured. If you have followed the discussion in this appendix, you know that successful presenters design slideshow materials that are simple, rather than elaborate; that are short, rather than lengthy; and that supplement the presenter, rather than steal the show. Figure C-4 contains some additional tips on slideshow presentations.

- Stand to one side of the screen instead of directly in front of it; don't cross in front of the screen to switch sides.
- Face the audience; don't turn your back to the audience to read what is on a slide.
- Don't insult the intelligence of your audience by reading either the content of your slides or the speaker's notes. Use your slides as an outline of your presentation.
- Give audience members time to read and study each slide, especially one with a lot of material or an image. A pause in the presentation is preferable to talking while the audience is trying to read.
- Use your abilities as a presenter, rather than elaborate slides, to make your presentation interesting. Make eye contact with your audience. Use your hands and arms to gesture to your slides for emphasis (rather than standing stiffly).
- Don't use a laser pointer unless the speaker's position is naturally in the back of the room, behind the audience. Use hands and arms to point to slide information instead of a pointer.
- Avoid the temptation to deliver your presentation as rapidly as possible in order to be finished quickly. It is preferable to speak too slowly than to speak too fast.
- Don't sound like a *presenter*. A presenter in this context speaks in a stilted, rapid, professional voice. Better to aim for the kind of relaxed, conversational speech you would use around a water cooler than to sound too much like a scripted, professional presenter.
- When not using your hands for gesturing, practice letting them hang naturally at your side, or folded in front. Don't put your hands in your pocket, or fold them in back.
- Review the guidelines for training session presentations in Chapter 10.

Figure C-4   Tips on slideshow presentations

In summary, the most important aspects of a presentation are, in order:

1. The audience

2. The information content of the presentation

3. The presenter

4. The contents of each slide

5. The layout or arrangement of each slide

6. The design elements and format features of the slideshow

Don't let numbers 5 and 6 in this list overwhelm the first three items. With this list of priorities in mind, and based on the discussion in this appendix, compare the two example slides in Figure C-5. Which do you think is the most effective slide to cover the material in the first part of this appendix? Which guidelines in this appendix are violated in each slide?

Figure C-5   Alternate slide designs covering the first part of this appendix
(*continues*)

(continued)

Figure C-5   Alternate slide designs covering the first part of this appendix

ON THE WEB

To view a collection of slides that illustrate several poorly designed slides along with suggested improvements, visit **www.slideshare.net/garr/sample-slides-by-garr-reynolds**.

Figure C-6 lists some additional resources for presenters

- Rice University has prepared a PowerPoint slideshow on *Using PowerPoint to Design Effective Presentations;* view the slideshow at **www.owlnet.rice.edu/~cainproj/presenting.ppt**
- Use a checklist of PowerPoint Presentation Advice by Mike Splane at **www.cob.sjsu.edu/splane_m/PresentationTips.htm**
- The University of Connecticut provides *Guidelines for Developing PowerPoint Lectures* at **library.uchc.edu/copyright/docs/guidelines.pdf**
- The Association for Education and Rehabilitation of the Blind and Visually Impaired offers advice on preparation of PowerPoint materials with assistive strategies at **www.aerbvi.org/downloads/8/0/06%20AER%20PowerPoint%20Guidelines.doc**
- Rick Altman, *Why Most PowerPoint Presentations Suck—And How You Can Make Them Better* (Harvest Books, 2007)
- Garr Reynolds, *Presentation Zen: Simple Ideas on Presentation Design and Delivery* (New Rider's Press, 2008)
- Edward R. Tufte, *The Cognitive Style of PowerPoint: Pitching Out Corrupts Within, Second Edition* (Graphics Press, 2006)

Figure C-6   Additional resources for presentation presenters

Improving User Support Meeting Performance

Like many professional workers, user support workers often do not like to attend meetings. However, meetings with end users and support team colleagues are common in many support situations. Meetings are frequently necessary to obtain information from a group of users, such as when a support specialist interviews users as part of a needs assessment project. Similarly, the results of a needs assessment project are often presented to users and managers at a meeting. Support specialists often meet as a team to discuss operational issues, such as how to support a new product or new version of an existing product. And special project teams may meet periodically to assess progress on a project or troubleshoot problems that have arisen. Some groups of support staff, such as team leaders, may meet regularly to discuss operational or personnel issues within a support department.

The challenge for support workers, of course, is to make meetings as productive for team members as possible. Professionals who study meetings held in corporations, nonprofit organizations, government agencies, and educational institutions provide many suggestions for improving the productivity of attendees and the usefulness of meetings. The purpose of this section of the appendix is to offer some strategies and tools for productive meetings.

Figure C-7 lists some strategies and tools for successful meetings.

 Some organizations, in an attempt to encourage short, productive meetings, have designed meeting rooms where participants stand at 4-foot-high tables during a meeting. The tables permit participants to take notes, but few meetings where participants must stand are likely to last very long.

- Avoid regularly scheduled meetings
- Focus the purpose of a meeting
- Prepare a meeting agenda
- Prepare meeting materials
- Refine the list of attendees
- Define the roles of attendees
- Manage meeting time
- Manage the agenda
- Manage interruptions and distractions
- Prepare meeting minutes

Figure C-7   Strategies and tools for effective meetings

Avoid Regularly Scheduled Meetings

Meetings that are scheduled on a periodic basis frequently pose challenges. Often these meetings lack a purpose; rather they occur simply because the meeting time popped up on attendees' calendars. Productive meetings are those that occur for a specific purpose, as you will see below, rather than because they are driven by a calendar.

Focus the Purpose of a Meeting

Less productive meetings are those that have agenda items such as: call to order, approval of minutes, approval of a financial report, announcements, additions to the agenda, routine project status reports, refreshment breaks, discussion of new topics, topics for the next meeting, for-the-good-of-the-order announcements, set the next meeting time, and adjournment. Notice that few of these agenda items contribute directly to the productivity of the attendees; some only add to the length of the meeting and to the poor reputation meetings often have.

 Under normal circumstances, a meeting should not be so long that a mid-meeting break is required.

The primary purpose of any meeting should be to enable participants to perform tasks that cannot be accomplished individually or in smaller work teams. In most cases, meetings should be designed to brainstorm ideas; analyze the pros and cons of alternatives; reach a consensus, decision, or recommendation; and assign follow-up action tasks to attendees. Here are some specific ways to help focus the purpose of a meeting and improve its usefulness:

- Distribute minutes of the previous meeting via e-mail and ask for any suggested corrections or additions via e-mail.

- Make announcements via e-mail (eliminate this agenda item).

- Do not permit additions to a meeting's preset agenda (set aside worthwhile new topics for a follow-up meeting).

- Solicit suggested agenda topics for the next meeting via e-mail.

- Assign the task of setting a next meeting date and time to the convener, use a calendaring system, or use a free, Web-based tool such as **www.doodle.com**.

- Reduce or eliminate social activities, refreshments, routine reports, good-of-the-order announcements, corporate bragging, rumors, gossip, etc.

The measure of each item on a meeting's agenda should be: is this a task which must be accomplished at this meeting, or can this task be accomplished in some other way that uses fewer resources?

Prepare a Meeting Agenda

An agenda is a description of a meeting that answers basic *when, where, who,* and *what is the purpose* of the meeting questions. A meeting that does not have a preset agenda is an open invitation to one that will last too long and wander off topic. A meeting's convener can prepare an agenda based on e-mailed topic suggestions received from participants. But the convener should filter suggested topics by considering whether there are other ways to deal with a topic besides using time and resources in a meeting. Figure C-8 describes an example outline of the agenda of a typical meeting.

Meeting agenda example outline

1. Date of meeting
2. Time of meeting
3. Location of meeting
4. Attendees list (based on topics to be discussed)
5. Primary Roles
   - Coordinator
   - Recorder
   - Time keeper
6. Project status reports (focus on problems to be resolved)
7. New topics
   - Brainstorming (idea generation)
   - Pros and cons (analysis)
   - Decisions (consensus model)
   - Action items (task assignments)
8. Review of assignments
9. Lessons learned
10. Next meeting
    - Date
    - Time
    - Location
    - Agenda items

Figure C-8   Outline of typical meeting agenda

Many items on the agenda outline in Figure C-8 are self-explanatory or will be described in greater detail below. Item 9, "Lessons learned," can be used to provide an opportunity for meeting participants to share whether problems identified in project status reports or in the discussion of new topics reveal any conclusions about what has been learned by participants or by the organization that should be recorded in the meeting summary. This is a short topic, but one that can contribute to an organization's knowledge about itself and how it operates.

Prepare Meeting Materials

In addition to the preparation and distribution of an agenda, as well as a summary of the previous meeting, other pre-meeting activities include distribution of materials participants will use as the basis for discussion of new topics. Each participant should commit to read and study the background materials prior to the meeting so that valuable time is not spent reading reports, drafts of proposals, problem descriptions, and so on. Meetings go faster and are more productive when participants come to a meeting prepared for the agenda with relevant issues already identified for agenda items.

Refine the List of Attendees

Attending a meeting at which your presence is not required is a very unproductive use of your time. One role of a meeting convener is to make sure the list of attendees includes those whose participation is needed to address the decision items, but does not include people who are not required, or are only tangentially required, to make decisions about the topics under discussion.

Define the Roles of Attendees

There are at least four important roles in any meeting, as described in Table C-1.

 Organizations that take meeting productivity very seriously may bring in certain participants only for the portion of the meeting for which they are needed; they then let them go on with other activities.

Role	Responsibilities
Convener (also called chair, coordinator, or facilitator)	• Collect and filter topics to narrow agenda • Prepare list of attendees and identify roles • Prepare and distribute meeting agenda • Allocate time for topic discussion • Start the meeting on time • Follow the preset agenda • Coordinate targeted discussion of topics • Encourage participation • Help participants identify when a consensus has been reached • Identify topics for next meeting
Recorder (also called secretary or recording secretary)	• Prepare and distribute a summary of decisions made and lessons learned
Timekeeper	• Monitor time allocated for topic discussion • Alert convener and participants when time is exceeded
Participants	• Contribute suggested agenda items • Read summary of previous meeting for errors and omissions • Read distributed, preset agenda • Study background materials to prepare for discussion • Identify issues that need attention for each topic • Arrive on time and ready to begin meeting • Engage in active listening • Participate in discussions and decisions • Move the discussion toward a consensus on a decision • Avoid grandstanding, bragging, rumors, and gossip • Contribute to lessons learned • Read summary of meeting • Follow up on assigned tasks

Table C-1   Roles of meeting participants

Many meeting participants assume that the most important role in any meeting is that of convener. It's an important role; however, count the number of responsibilities in Table C-1 for the convener and for the participants. Who has the longest list of responsibilities?

Manage Meeting Time

Managing meeting time to increase productivity is a joint responsibility. The convener obviously has a responsibility to follow the preset agenda, keep the discussion on topic, quickly identify when the discussion gets off-topic, encourage participation, and help the participants identify when a consensus on a topic or decision has been reached. As noted in Table C-1, some groups use a timekeeper to monitor the time spent on each topic and to alert the convener and participants when the time allocated has been reached. (By consensus, consideration of a topic whose allocated time has expired can continue for a short period—but the timekeeper helps by saying, "Time has come to wrap up this topic.") Meeting participants can help to manage meeting time by arriving on time, preparing well for the discussion, participating in the discussion, and helping to move the discussion toward a consensus.

Some groups rotate convener responsibilities (perhaps monthly or quarterly); rotating leadership gives every participant an opportunity to develop their meeting planning, participation, and leadership skills. Serving in the role of convener often gives attendees a new perspective on meeting mechanics that helps them be better participants.

657

Manage the Agenda

Managing the agenda is also a joint responsibility, which begins when participants contribute agenda items to the convener for consideration. It requires a commitment from participants that they will refrain from getting off-topic, monopolizing the discussion, grandstanding, bragging, and other unproductive meeting behaviors. Grandstanding occurs when participants offer opinions on issues, whether or not they have anything important or new to contribute. One way to identify a tendency to grandstand is when a participant expresses a belief (perhaps to him or herself), "I haven't said anything for awhile—it is time to make myself heard."

When meeting participants recognize a topic or aspect of a problem that is off-the-point, the person taking the minutes should make a note to suggest the topic for a future meeting.

Manage Interruptions and Distractions

Interruptions and distractions in meetings are another form of unproductive participation. Interruptions are sometimes tolerated simply because they become part of an organizational meeting culture. Interruptions can occur when a work colleague enters a meeting room to talk with a participant on a topic that "just can't wait," when a cell phone goes off during a meeting, or when a participant with a laptop receives an urgent e-mail message. Productive meetings occur when participants commit to help the convener and the group reduce or eliminate interruptions and distractions; with a group effort, these behaviors can be discouraged

A convener can help reduce cell phone and pager interruptions by reminding participants to turn off electronic devices at the start of a meeting.

Prepare Meeting Minutes

One of the onerous jobs associated with meetings is that of the recorder. No one wants to "take minutes." The job is considered onerous partly because meeting minutes are misunderstood or misused in many situations. The term "minutes" itself implies a blow-by-blow

Serving as a meeting recorder is an excellent way for a support specialist to build their technical writing skills and to use the writing tools you learned in Chapter 11. Capturing the results of a one-hour meeting on a single sheet of paper takes skill—a skill worth building, and one your colleagues will appreciate and admire.

account of everything that happened during each *minute* of a meeting. No wonder few want the recorder job, or want to read the resulting lengthy minutes, for that matter.

Meeting minutes are more appropriately titled a meeting summary because in most cases (legal discussions are an important exception), a summary of decisions made and lessons learned is the appropriate content of meeting minutes. Effective minutes do not relate all aspects of the discussion of a topic. Their purpose is to briefly record decisions made and lessons learned. Minutes can simply state when, where, who, what was decided, what follow-up assignments were made, and what lessons were learned. The most effective meeting summaries are less than a page. That's about all anyone wants to read, anyway.

This appendix has described some guidelines designed to encourage effective and productive meetings. Meetings serve many purposes for an organization beyond simply providing a vehicle for decision making. Many meetings include a team-building, collegiality, motivational, or social dimension that was not adequately described above. Organizational culture determines which guidelines in this appendix are followed to the letter, and which get a reduced emphasis. The point of these guidelines is to increase the effectiveness of meetings for participants and organizations and to present some lessons learned from those who have sought ways to make many kinds of meetings more productive. Use these guidelines to influence the meeting culture where you attend school or work.

Figure C-9 provides some additional resources for meeting participants.

- Download and read a manual on *The Makings of a Good Meeting* at **www.dcn.davis.ca.us/go/kjwolf/manual.html**
- Read an article by Nick McCormick, *Effective Meeting Management: 12 Tips to Improve Meeting Productivity* at **ezinearticles.com/?Effective-Meeting-Management:—12-Tips-to-Improve-Meeting-Productivity&id=406722**
- Find other useful suggestions on meetings at **www.entrepreneur.com/tradejournals/article/162620693.html**
- Participate in a tutorial on meetings at **www.wikieducator.org/Introductory_Course_on_Organising_Meetings:_Tutorial_Structure**
- Glenn M. Parker, *Meeting Excellence: 33 Tools to Lead Meetings that Get Results* (Jossey-Bass, 2006)
- Dee Kelsey, *Great Meetings! Great Results* (Hanson Park Press, 2004)
- Shri L. Henkel, *Successful Meetings: How to Plan, Prepare, and Execute Top-Notch Business Meetings* (Atlantic Publishing Company, 2007)

Figure C-9   Resources for effective meetings

Hands-On Activities

Activity C-1

Examine poorly designed slides along with some suggested improvements. Garr Reynolds has written and presented extensively on slideshow design. He assembled a collection of slides that illustrate poor design. For each slide, he provides a version to show how the slide could be improved to communicate more effectively. View the collection at **www.slideshare.net/garr/sample-slides-by-garr-reynolds**. Select several of the slides in the Reynolds collection. Using guidelines from this appendix, or based on your own experience, write a paragraph that describes the difference between the poor example and Reynolds' version.

Activity C-2

Critique an example slideshow. The Web has thousands of examples of slideshows that can be used to learn about the differences between good and poor slideshow design. An example intended to promote a discussion of slideshow design is at **www.shkaminski. com/Classes/Samples/haitema.pdf**. Assemble a small group of work or school colleagues to view and critique the slideshow. Although the example is not related to user support, it provides an opportunity to apply what you have learned in this chapter and in your previous experience. Be sure to understand the stated purpose of the slideshow, which is included on the first slide, before you begin your critique. Prepare a brief report on your conclusions.

Activity C-3

Evaluate examples of meetings. View four short examples of meetings on YouTube listed below. As you view each video clip, make a list of guidelines to increase meeting productivity.

- *How Not to Conduct a Meeting*: **www.youtube.com/ watch?v=KRk4DHF8sr8**

- *No Bull*: **www.youtube.com/watch?v=u5MoWq-5xrM**

- *Meeting from Hell*: **www.youtube.com/watch?v=xQW1fEwYZVA**

- *How to Avoid Meetings that Suck*: **www.youtube.com/ watch?v=BVHIMxW6D8w&NR=1**

Prepare a short report on guidelines you can use to make meetings more productive. Better yet, design and prepare a short slideshow of your guidelines suitable to present to your colleagues.

Activity C-4

Prepare and conduct a meeting on project meetings. If you belong to a project group or team at work or school, prepare and conduct a meeting on how to make meetings of the group more useful. Develop an agenda and a list of attendees; assign the roles of convener, recorder, and timekeeper. The primary purpose of the meeting is to identify some lessons learned and best practices for future meetings of the group. Use the meeting as an example of a well-run meeting. Use the minutes of the meeting to record the group's lessons learned and best practices for future meetings.

Activity C-5

Use activities in previous chapters to get more experience with presentations and meetings. Several hands-on activities and case projects in prior chapters provide an opportunity to get additional experience with presentations and meeting productivity tools. Some of these end-of-chapter exercises ask you to make presentations on various topics. Other exercises ask you to organize or participate in a meeting. Use the table below to locate one or more exercises that you can build upon to further develop your presentation and meeting skills.

Presentation Exercises

Chapter	Exercise	Activity
1	Case 1	Prepare a slide presentation to present the results of the total cost of ownership of a PC.
4	Case 1	Prepare a slide presentation to communicate information about Internet error messages.
4	Case 3	Prepare a slideshow on a topic related to problem-solving.
5	Activity 5-8	Prepare a slideshow for support staff on job stresses.
6	Case 3	Prepare a slide presentation on employee retention strategies.
8	Activity 8-3	Prepare a slideshow that explains the costs and benefits of a home PC.
9	Activity 9-11	Prepare a slideshow on local recycling options.
10	Cases 2 & 4	Prepare a slide presentation as part of a training activity.

Meeting Exercises

Chapter	Exercise	Activity
7	Activity 7-6	Prepare an agenda for a meeting to set product standards.
8	Case 1	Participate in a meeting to perform a feasibility study.

Index

Note: Page numbers in boldface indicate key terms.

A

abandonment rate
    described, **253**
    performance statistics
        and, 253–254
acceptable use guidelines, **315**
Access (Microsoft), 266,
    357. *See also* Office
    (Microsoft)
accessibility issues, 387,
    394–395
ACD (automated call
    distributor) systems
    described, **226–227**
    performance statistics
        and, 254
acronyms, avoiding
    undefined, 518
active listening, **109–110**.
    See also communication
adaptive test, **271**
administration, cost of, 12–13
administrators, network,
    169–170, 172–175
air conditioning, 400
American Staffing
    Association, 20
Americans with Disabilities
    Act, 387
analogies
    analyzing, **106**
    described, **510**
animations, for slide shows, 648

antistatic wrist strap, 409
antivirus software, 180, 418,
    578, 581, 589. *See also*
    viruses
apologies, 71, 72
Apple Computer, 266, 289.
    See also Macintosh
applicants
    interviewing, 259–262
    screening, 259
application(s). *See also*
    software; *specific*
    software
    development backlog, **5**, 42
    software, **13–16**
archive, **207**
archived files, erasing, 572, 575
assessment, of training
    activities, **471**
asset management, 216
assistive devices, **394–395**
attachments, 13
attendees, of meetings. *See*
    also meetings
    list of, refining, 655
    role of, defining, 655–656
audiences
    knowledge of,
        determining, 503
    for presentations, 642–643,
        644, 647, 650
    reading levels of, checking,
        502, 520

    selecting the best medium
        for, 503–504
    technical writing and, 502
auditory learner, **458–459**.
    See also learning
audits, of software, **556**
authentication procedure, **201**
automated call distributor
    systems. *See* ACD
    (automated call
    distributor) systems

B

back pain, 391, 393
backup(s)
    battery, 398–399
    described, **422**
    disaster planning and, 426
    utilities and, 555, 567–572
bandwidth, 565–566
battery backups, 398–399
Belarc Advisor, 547,
    548–549, 587
bells and whistles, use of the
    term, **475**
benchmark(s)
    certifications as, 269
    described, **298–299**
    product evaluation and,
        298–300
    utilities and, 572–573, 577
best practices, for help desks,
    208–209

beta test run, **473–474**, 477
biometric readers, **424–425**
BIOS (Basic Input/Output
    System), 128
Bjorseth, Lilliam D., 60
blogs, **84**, 90, 157
Bloom, Benjamin, 460
Bloom's Taxonomy, 460
Boolean operators, 118
bottlenecks, throughput, **562**
brainstorms, **504–505**
broadband Internet, 399, 417,
    608, 611
brochures, 492–493
brokerage transaction
    software, 15
browsers
    described, **13–14**
    graphics and, 182–183
bugs, **163–165**
bulleted lists, 512
Bureau of Labor Statistics
    (BLS), 20, 272–273
burn-in tests, **156**
business interruption
    insurance, **425**

C
cable ties, 409
CAD (computer-aided
    design), 11
call(s). *See also* help desks;
    telephones
    accounting, 227
    centers, 25
    lost, reporting, 227
    management, **199–207**
    monitoring, 227
capitalization, 509
carpal tunnel syndrome,
    19, 43, 392–393
case studies, 467
CBT (computer-based
    training), **469–470**,
    611, 612–616
central processing units.
    See CPUs (central
    processing units)
CEOs (chief executive
    officers), 57

certification(s)
    benefits of, 269
    described, **265–272**
    exam preparation, 270–272
    formal education, 265
    help desk, 268
    industry-standard, 267
    programs, 268–269
    user support, 268–269
    vendor-specific, 266–267
chairs, adjustment of,
    388–392, 394
change management, best
    practices for, 208
charts
    flowchart, **356**
    Gantt, **364–366**
    I-P-O, **356–357**
    needs assessment and,
        356–357
    presentations and, 647–648
    training and, 458
chat
    described, **25**, 28–29, 43
    writing skills and, 495–496
check boxes, 539
checklists, **114–116**
Chicago Manual of Style, 520
CIOs (chief information
    officers), 291
circuit(s)
    amperage, 396
    shared, 396
    testers, **409**
Cisco, 86, 204, 266
Clark, Donald, 446
classroom training, 456–457.
    See also training
client(s). *See also* users
    difficult, **77–82**
    external, 197
    feedback, **217**
    information databases, 214
    internal, 197
    satisfaction, 87–88
    services, comprehensive,
        87–88
    surveys, 87–88, 255
client-friendly Web sites,
    83–87

Client Outsource, 27
cloud computing, 231–233
code of ethics, **274–275**. *See
    also* ethics
color
    font, 647
    schemes, for slides, 645
communication. *See also*
    technical writing
    importance of, to customer
        service, 56–67
    listening and, **109–110**
    nonverbal, 65–66, 69
    resources, for help
        desks, 215
    style, 65, **67–68**
    troubleshooting and, 108,
        109–110
community colleges, 308–312
compatibility issues, 152–153,
    158–161, 290–291
competitors, products used
    by, 298
comprehension checks, in
    training sessions, 475
compressed air, 409, 427
computer(s). *See also* end-user
    computers
    crime, **17–18**
    facilities management, **31**
    telephony, **226–228**
computer-based training. *See*
    CBT (computer-based
    training)
configuration
    examining, 125, 127
    hardware, **153–155**
    information, access to,
        214–215
    management, best practices
        for, 208
    restoring, 125, 132
conflicts, **160**
contacts, professional,
    118–121
contingency planning,
    425–426
contradictions, analyzing, **106**
Control Panel, 157
Convergys, 26

cost(s)
acquisition, **352**
administration, 12–13
of alternatives, 352
center operation, **256**
continued pressure to
reduce, 235
facilities, 12–13
ISP fees, 11–12
operating, **352**
overhead, 12–13
of supplies, 11
cost-benefit analysis, 346,
352–353
CPUs (central processing
units), 6, 10, 417, 577
crash courses, **270**
creativity
critical thinking and,
106–108
described, **107**
credit-card processing,
178–180
criteria, for documentation, 521
critical
path, **366**
thinking, **106–108**
CRM (customer relationship
management), 15, **236**
cubicles, physical layout of,
209–210
customer relationship
management. *See* CRM
(customer relationship
management)
customer service. *See also* help
desks; support; users
comprehensive, 87–88
ethic, **57**, 58, 85
responding effectively,
63–64
skills overview, 55–91
Czegel, Barbara, 251

D

dangling modifiers,
518–520
dashboards
described, **225**, 562, 564
HelpSTAR and, 633–634

database(s). *See also*
knowledge bases
certification, 272, 478
client information, 214
customization of, 217
FAQ, 86
management software, **14**
data-collection instruments,
353–356
Davis, Jeff, 58
decentralized computing, 4
DecideRight, 305
decision(s). *See also* decision
making
build-versus-buy, **347–349**
criteria, 336–338
phase, 330–371
decision making. *See also*
decisions
described, **108**
tools, for product
evaluation, 296–308
Defense Department, 75
defragmentation utilities, 572,
576
deliverables, **350–351**
delivery methods, for training
materials, **461–470**
Department of Agriculture
(USDA), 34
design software, 15
desktop publishing software,
14–15
device drivers, 413–414, 543,
547. *See also* Device
Manager
Device Manager, 157, 176. *See
also* device drivers
diagnostic tools, 108, **122–124**,
157, 215. *See also* remote
access diagnostic tools
diagrams, 356–357, 367,
647–648
disabled individuals. *See*
accessibility issues
disaster planning, **425–426**
Digisoft, 116
Digital Subscriber Line.
See DSL
DIP switches, 153–154

direct observation, 355–356
disk drives, maintenance of, 427
disk space, freeing up, 572, 575
display screens. *See* monitors
distributed computing, **7**
distribution media, **417**
DLP (digital light processing)
projectors, 465–466
documentation. *See also*
documents; technical
writing
cluttered designs and,
513–514
described, **492**
evaluation criteria for, 521
installation, 403–407
KSAs for, 36
needs assessment and, 353
operational, 497–498
outlines, 505–507
planning, 501–504
preparation of, 31
procedural, 497–498
site management, 403–407
types of, 492–498
documents. *See also*
documentation;
technical writing
complete, characteristics
of, 170
format of, evaluating,
506–508, 521
grammar checking, 86, 496,
516, 520, 521
organizing, 500–501
PDF (Portable Document
Format), 493, 498
reading levels of, checking,
502, 520
spell checking, 86, 496, 520,
521, 647
Doodle Web site, 653
downtime, **398**
drivers, 413–414, 543, 547. *See
also* Device Manager
Drucker, Peter, 5
DSL (Digital Subscriber Line),
399
dual-boot systems, 160
Dutokowsky, Sandy, 470

E

eBay, 18
economic
    feasibility, **336**
    recession, 20
EDI (electronic data
    interchange), 178–180
education, use of the term,
    445–446. *See also*
    training
educational software, 15
electrical
    power requirements,
        396–399
    tape, 409
e-mail
    announcing meetings
        by, 653
    asynchronous character
        of, 229
    computer crime and, 17
    described, **13**
    ListServs and, **120**
    security and, 19, 424
    spam, 424
    support vendors and, 121
    viruses and, 19
    Web-based support and,
        229–230
    writing skills and,
        495–496, 501
empathy, **61–63**, 90
employment. *See also*
    hiring; jobs
    agencies, 20–21
    statistics, 272–273
end user. *See* end-user
    computers; users
end-user computer(s). *See also*
    computers; end-user
    computing
    installation, 384–418
    location of, 387–395
    managing, 384–433
    power requirements,
        396–399
    recycling, 429–430
    site preparation for, 386–407
end-user computing. *See also*
    end-user computers

described, **2**
historical changes in, 2–7
end-user license agreements.
    See EULA (end-user
    license agreements)
engineering
    inspections, **425–426**
    software, 15
English, fluency in, 36
enterprise application
    software, **15**
enterprise resource planning.
    See ERP (enterprise
    resource planning)
entertainment software, **15**
EPA (Environmental
    Protection Agency),
    401, 430
Erlang calculator, **257**
ergonomics, 172, 210
    assistive devices and,
        394–395
    carpal tunnel syndrome
        and, **19**, 43, 392–393
    chairs and, 388–392, 394
    described, **19**, 390–391
    eyestrain and, 392, 393
    installation and, 387–390
    keyboards and, 388,
        391–395
    lighting and, 400
ERP (enterprise resource
    planning), 15
escalation, of incidents, **122**,
    205–206
ethics, **57–58**, 85, 274–275
EULA (end-user license
    agreements), **539**, 540
Excel (Microsoft), 36, 181,
    266, 357
Executive Blueprints, 110
experiential learners, **458–459**.
    See also learning
explanations, **113**
eyestrain, 392, 393
e-zines, **294**

F

Facebook, 83
facilities, cost of, 12–13

FAQs (Frequently Asked
    Questions), 64, 83–86.
    See also questions
    newsgroups and, 120
    writing, 498, 501
feasibility
    economic, **336**
    operational, **336**
    studies, **336–337**
    technological, **336**
    timeline, **336**
file(s)
    archived, erasing, 572, 575
    formats, conversion
        between, 568, 570
    hidden, detecting, 577
    management utilities,
        567–572, 588
    recovering/restoring, **423**,
        568, 571–572
File Transfer Protocol.
    See FTP (File Transfer
    Protocol)
fire suppression, 401–403
firewalls, **577**, 581
flashlights, 408
flowcharts, **356**
flyers, **492–493**
foam-tipped brush, 408
focus groups, **355**
fonts. *See also* text
    color, 647
    consistent use of, in
        documentation, 509
    for presentations, 647
footprints, of computers,
    386–387
footrests, 392, 394
forms
    customization of, 217
    input, **353–354**
    output, **353**
forums, 84, 91, 119–120, 157
fraud, 17
freeware, 161, 549–550
Frequently Asked Questions.
    See FAQs (Frequently
    Asked Questions)
FTP (File Transfer Protocol), 15
furniture, 388–392, 407

G

Gantt charts, **364–366**
gender-neutral language, 515
glossary, of terms, 616–617
goal(s)
    goal-directed diagnostic
        questions, asking,
        71, 72
    needs assessment and,
        334–336
    project, **359–360**
    states, **105–106**
Google, 118, 120, 174, 451,
    640–642
grammar checking, 86, 496,
    516, 520, 521
graphic(s)
    benchmarks and, 577
    browsers and, 182–183
    JPEG, 568
    software, **14**
    TIFF, 184, 568
greetings, sincere, 63–64, 69
group(s)
    discussions, 463
    focus, **355**
    learning (collaborative
        learning), 457, 468
GUI (graphical user interface)
    described, **6–7**, 43
    training and, 466

H

hackers, 423
handbooks, writing, 493
handouts, 464–465, 477,
    493, 648–649
hands-on activities, for
    training, 466–467, 471
Hanks, Jim, 210
hardware. *See also specific
        types*
    compatibility issues,
        152–153
    configuration, 153–155
    evaluating, 29–30
    installation, 152–153, 155,
        169, 408–412
    maintenance, 10–11
    malfunctions, 155–157

problems, overview of,
    152–157
rebates, 171
troubleshooting, 123,
    152–157, 174,
    541–546, 587
upgrades, 10–11, 344
utilities, 541–546, 587
Harvard Business Review, 57
Harvard Business School, 467
headaches, 392, 393
headsets, 210
health problems, *See*
    ergonomics
Help and Support Center,
    117, 157
help desk(s). *See also* customer
        service; incidents;
        support management
    best practices, **208–209**
    careers, information on, 37
    certifications, 268
    described, **24–25**, 28–29,
        197–199
    end user tools, 218–220
    job stress and, 210–213
    managerial concerns for,
        251–265
    operations overview,
        196–240
    position descriptions,
        32–35
    software/tools, 213–226
    staffing, overview of,
        257–265
    technology, 213–226
    trends, 230–236
    work areas, physical layout
        of, 209–210
Help Desk Institute, 268, 274
Help Desk Technology
    International
    Corporation, 609
help systems
    described, **117**
    Microsoft Windows, 117,
        157, 494
    writing, 493–494
HelpSTAR
    adding assets with, 620–621

adding users with, 619–620
A/V resources, 610–612
case study, 618–634
client interviews, 611
creating reports with,
    632–633
described, **221–226**
displaying dashboards with,
    633–634
drafting best solutions with,
    628–630
entering new departments
    with, 618–619
finding solutions with,
    626–627
handling service requests
    with, 622–628,
    630–631
home page, 609–610
installation, 608–609
learning about, 611–617
login, 609–610
overview, 607–634
performance statistics
    and, 254
setting reminders with,
    631–632
shortcuts, 610, 613
starting, 618
terminology, 616–617
tutorials, 611, 612,
    613–617
hidden files, detecting, 577
hiring, 20, 259–262, 355–356.
    See also employment
histograms, 254
honesty, 71, 72
Honolulu Community College,
    308–312
horizontal market
    applications, **297–298**
hotlines, 25, 28–29. *See also*
    calls; telephones
HTML (HyperText Markup
    Language)
    described, **14**
    reference sheet, 405
human resources
    departments, 259
humor, use of, 475

HVAC (heating, ventilating, and air conditioning) systems, 400
hypothese(s)
　critical thinking and, 106–108
　described, **107**
　sequential/iterative approaches to, 103
　testing, 125, **130–132**

I

IBM (International Business Machines), 229, 289, 290
ID badges, 424
idea lists, generating, 504–505
identify theft, 425
images. *See* graphics
incident(s)
　archiving, **207**
　assigning, 204–205
　automated management of, 217
　closing, **206**
　difficult, strategies for, 77–82
　escalating, **122**, 205–206
　that "get off track," 78, 79–80
　logging, **201–202**, 214
　management, **70–74**, 199–208
　prescreening, **200**
　prioritizing, **203–204**
　resolution, **206**
　screening, **200**, 203
　tracking, 205–206, 214
incompatible computer components, **153**
India, 20, 233
industry
　industry-specific software, **15**
　standard products, **297–298**
information. *See also* IT (Information Technology)
　forgotten, 169–170
　identifying sources of, 341–342
　inadequate, 168–169

needs assessment and, 341–342
　product-related, 214, 293–296
　troubleshooting resources, 29, 108, 113–140, 214–215
Information Technology Infrastructure Library. *See* ITIL (Information Technology Infrastructure Library)
input forms, **353–354**
inspections, engineering, **425–426**
installation
　custom, **418**, 419
　of end-user computers, 384–417
　express, **418**, 419
　full, **418**, 419
　hardware, 152–153, 155, 169, 408–412
　HelpSTAR, 608–609
　minimal, **418**, 419
　overview, 30–31, 385–386
　quick start behavior and, 169
　site preparation before, 386–407
　software, **158–161**, 417–422
　wrap-up tasks, 420–422
insurance, business interruption, **425**
intangible benefits, **353**
interfaces, customization of, 217
Internet. *See also* browsers; ISPs (Internet Service Providers); networks; Web sites
　broadband, 399, 417, 608, 611
　history of, 3
　illegal use of, 18
interviews, 259–262, 355–356, 611
intranets, **230**
inventories, 341
investigation phase, 332, **333**
IS (Information Systems), 7
isopropyl alcohol, 408, 427, 428

ISPs (Internet Service Providers)
　costs of, 11–12
　installation and, 399
　modems and, 177–178
　needs assessment and, 332
IT (Information Technology)
　code of ethics for, 274–275
　described, **7**
　needs assessment and, 340
　personality types and, 76–77
　product evaluation and, 291
　responsibility, user support as an, 25–26
　screening applicants and, 259
　software development and, 32
　specialists, position descriptions for, 34–35
　workers, demand for, 20
iterative processes, 103–104
ITIL (Information Technology Infrastructure Library), **208–209**, 235
IVR (interactive voice response) systems, **227–228**

J

jargon, 517–518
job(s). *See also* employment
　market, 20, 32, 272–273
　position descriptions, **32–35**, 257–259
　salaries, 21, 276
　stress, **210–213**
Jones, Thomas O., 57
JPEG (Joint Photographic Experts Group) format, 568

K

keyboard(s)
　ergonomics and, 388, 391–395
　maintenance of, 427
　troubleshooting, 156–157
　users mistakes and, 166–167
keystroke loggers, 166
kinesthetic learning. *See* experiential learners

Kline, John A., 60
knowledge and skills test, **259**
knowledge bases. *See also*
    databases
    described, **116–118,** 215
    support vendors and, 121
knowledge workers
    described, **5**
    productivity of,
        measurement of, 16
KSAs (knowledge, skills, and
    abilities)
    described, **35–38**
    position descriptions and,
        258–259
    screening applicants
        and, 259
Kuwasaki, Guy, 648

L
laptop computers, 388
LCD projectors, 465–466
learners. *See also* learning
    auditory, **458–459**
    experiential, **458–459**
    visual, **458–459**
learning. *See also* learners;
    training
    collaborative, **468**
    continuous, 133, 134
    social, **456**
    styles, **458–461**
learning management system.
    See LMS (learning
    management system)
lecture method, 462
leg pain, 392, 393
legal issues, regarding RFPs,
    305–306
letters, writing, 497
license agreements, 539, 540, 609
lighting, appropriate, 400–401
lint-free cloth, 408, 428
Linux, 267, 414
list(s)
    bulleted, 512
    idea, generating, 504–505
    parallel structure and, 512
    technical writing and,
        504–505, 507, 512

listening, active, **109–110.** *See
    also* communication
ListServs, 120
LMS (learning management
    system), **478,** 479. *See
    also* learning
log(s)
    described, **355**
    incident, **201–202,** 214
    needs assessment and, 355
    problem, **355**
login, with HelpSTAR, 609–610

M
Macintosh, 168, 310, 312
    certifications, 266
    installation, 413
malware, 166, 424
    described, **180**
    security utilities and, 577
managers
    described, **39–40**
    interviews with, 341
    needs assessment and, 339,
        341, 358–367
    role of, identifying, 339
manuals, writing, 493, 506
maps, use of, in presentations,
    647–648
MBTI (Myers-Briggs Type
    Indicator), **74–77**
McMurrey, David A., 509
media backups, **422.** *See also*
    backups
medical software, 15
meeting(s)
    agendas, preparing/managing,
        654–655, 657
    attendees, defining the role
        of, 655–656
    interruptions/distractions,
        647
    materials, preparing, 655
    minutes, 653, 657–658
    overview, 639–660
    purpose of, focusing on, 653
    regularly scheduled,
        avoiding, 653
    rooms, learning about,
        643–644

successful, strategies/tools
    for, 652–658
time, managing, 656–657
memory
    benchmarks and, 577
    compatibility problems
        and, 153
    HelpSTAR and, 608
    performance problems
        and, 166
    security utilities and, 577
    testing, 541–542, 545
    upgrades, 10
memos, writing, 497
mental models, 106–108
mental modes, **107**
metacognition
    critical thinking and,
        106–108
    described, **107–108**
microcomputers, **5–6,** 44
microfiber cloth, 409, 428
Microsoft
    Accessibility Update, 395
    certifications, 266, 268, 269
    security resources, 578
Microsoft Access, 266, 357
Microsoft Excel, 36, 181,
    266, 357
*Microsoft Manual of
    Style for Technical
    Publications,* 520
Microsoft Office, 258, 266. *See
    also specific applications*
    needs assessment and,
        360, 364
    support standards and, 318
    training and, 453–454
Microsoft Outlook, 266
Microsoft PowerPoint, 36,
    110, 266. *See also*
    presentations; slides
    described, **640–641**
    technical writing and, 503
    training and, 474, 493
Microsoft Press, 116
Microsoft SQL Server,
    608, 609
Microsoft Visio, 342
Microsoft Visual Basic, 357

Microsoft Windows, 36, 180.
    See also PCs (personal
    computers)
    Add/Delete Programs tool,
        556, 558
    certifications, 266
    command-line, **549**
    compatibility problems and,
        153, 159–160
    configuration and,
        162–163, 407
    Ease of Access Center, 167
    Help system, 117, 157, 494
    HelpSTAR and, 608–609, 618
    installation and, 413–414
    Live Mail, 363–366
    position descriptions
        and, 258
    Registry, 124, 162–163,
        549–554
    SIT (System Information
        Tool), 407
    support standards and,
        317, 318
    training and, 452–453
    troubleshooting
        Web sites, 174
    utilities and, 549–562,
        587–588
Microsoft Word, 36, 162,
    266, 290
    Outline View feature, 505
    training and, 453–454
mirror, use of, for hardware
    installation, 408
mission statements, **252–253**
models
    of existing systems,
        342–343
    mental, 106–108
    of proposed solutions,
        346–347
modems, 177–178
module replacement strategy,
    125, **129–130**
monitors
    assistive devices and,
        394–395
    location of, 389–394
    maintenance of, 428

Moore's Law, 6
motherboards, 182
mouse
    ergonomics and, 388, 394
    maintenance of, 428
movies, use of, in
        presentations, 647–648.
        See also video
multilevel support model,
    198–199
multimedia materials
    described, **464**
    for presentations,
        647–658
    for training, 464
multimeters, **409**
My Computer, 609
Myers-Briggs Type Indicator.
        See MBTI (Myers-Briggs
        Type Indicator)
MySpace, 83

N
neck pain, 391
needs analysis, 306, 349–358
    described, **30**
    steps and tasks, 333–349
needs assessment
    decision criteria and,
        336–338
    investigating alternatives,
        344–345
    modeling existing systems,
        342–343
    organizational goals and,
        334–336
    overview, 330–371
    stakeholders and, 339–341
    tools, 349–358
.NET Framework (Microsoft),
    608, 609
network(s). *See also* Internet;
        Web sites
    access, installation of, 399,
        413–417
    administrators, 169–170,
        172–175
    computing, era of, 7
    diagnostic tools, 124
    nonresponsive, 181–182

problems, overview, 152,
    172–175
products, evaluating, 29–30
support utilities, 562–565, 588
technicians, **39**
newsgroups, **120–121**
newsletters, **493**
niche (vertical) markets
    applications, **298**
    needs assessment and, 344
Nickols, Fred, 106
nominalization, **516–517**
notebook computers, 388
notes, reading, 474
Novell, 266
nut drivers, 408

O
objective(s)
    evaluation criteria, **299**
    learning, **450**
    performance, **450–451**
Office (Microsoft), 258,
    266. *See also specific
    applications*
    needs assessment and,
        360, 364
    support standards and, 318
    training and, 453–454
open source software
    described, **161**
    utilities, 549–550
OpenOffice Impress, 640–642
operating system(s). *See also*
        Linux; Macintosh;
        Windows (Microsoft);
        systems
    installation, 413–417
    problems, 152, **172**
    utilities, 587
opt-in check boxes, **549**
organization
    hierarchical, **500**
    sequential, **500**
orientations, for new staff,
    263–264
OSHA (Occupational
    Safety and Health
    Administration), 387,
    395, 464

OSI (Open Source Initiative), 161
Outlook (Microsoft), 266
output forms, **353**
outsourcing
changes in, 233
described, **26–27**
service management and, 216–217
overflow routing, 227
overhead, cost of, 12–13

P

page breaks, 509
parallel structure, **512**
paraphrasing, **110**
parts-picker, 408
PassMark, 156, 576–577
password(s)
forgotten, 169–170
guessers, **578**, 583–584
site management and, 424
troubleshooting and, 130–132
patches
described, **163**
obtaining, 164–165
status of, **556**, 557
patience, 133, 230
pauses, in training sessions, 475
payroll systems, 297
PCs (personal computers).
See also Windows (Microsoft)
declining cost of, 5–6
history of, 2–7
installation and, 413–417
maintenance of, 10–11
needs assessment and, 358
optimizing the performance of, 572, 573–574
product evaluation and, 289–291
security and, 423–425
support standards for, 310–312, 317
upgrades, 10–11
PDF (Portable Document Format), 493, 498

peer support, **22–23**
performance. *See also* performance statistics
appraisals, **264–265**
enhancement utilities, 588
metrics, 235
problems with software, **165–166**
performance statistics. *See also* performance
described, **253–254**
performance appraisals and, 264–265
peripheral devices. *See also* *specific devices*
described, **10**, 44
recycling, 429–430
personality types, 74–77, 108, 133–135
PERT diagrams, 367
photographs. *See* graphics
PINs (personal identification numbers), 169–170
piracy, software, **18**
planning
contingency, **425–426**
disaster, **425–426**
documentation, 501–504
enterprise resource (ERP), 15
presentations, 642–645
project, **360–361**
software, **14**
training, 447–454
pliers, 408
Plug and Play standards, **154–155**
pocketknife, 408
pointers, **500**
portals
described, **235**
increased use of, 235
position descriptions, **32–35**, 257–259
power
conditioners, **397**, 398
devices, specialized, 397–399

requirements, 396–399
stability, 396–397
PowerPoint (Microsoft), 36, 110, 266. *See also* presentations; slides
described, 640–641
technical writing and, 503
training and, 474, 493
predecessor tasks, **365**
preparation phase, 332, **333**
presentation(s). *See also* PowerPoint (Microsoft); slides
delivery media, 643–644
designing/developing, 642–651
location, learning about, 643–644
multimedia elements in, 647–648
outlining major points, 644
overview, 639–660
planning, 642–645
software, 640–641
tips for, 649–651
preventive maintenance, **426–429**
printer(s)
location of, 389
maintenance of, 427
problems, 115–116, 128–129
testing, 299–300
priority codes, **203–204**
privacy. *See also* security
invasions of, **18**
policies, **539**
security utilities and, 577
probes
described, **111–112**
scripts and, 114
problem(s). *See also* problem solving; troubleshooting
clear definition of, 338–339
common, overview of, 151–187
needs assessment and, 338–339
replicating, 125, **126**
state, **105**

problem solving. *See also* problems; troubleshooting
  best practices, 208
  critical thinking and, 106–108
  described, **105**
  developing your own approach to, 135–136
  handling common problems, 151–187
  iterative processes and, 103–104
  models, 105–106
  processes, applying, 175–184
  sequential, 103–104
  skills overview, 105–106
  strategies, 108, 124–136
procedures, training in, provision of, 31
product(s). *See also* product standards
  compatibility problems, 290–291
  demonstrations, 465–466
  evaluation, 29–30, **288–308**
  ID numbers, 201
  information, links to, 214
  order entry capabilities, 215–216
  purchasing the wrong, 167–168
  registrations, 540
  returns, 168
  selecting, 291–308
product standard(s). *See also* products
  committee, **313**
  described, **289–291**
  development of, 313–315
  implementation of, 316–318
productivity software, advent of inexpensive, 6
professional associations, **273–274**
profit center operation, **256**
programmers, 39
project(s). *See also* project management

charters, **350–351**
definition, **359–360**
goals, **359–360**
implementation, **361–362**
monitoring, **362**
plans, **360–361**
risk factors, **361**
special, **357–367**
tasks, **360**
termination, **362–364**
project management. *See also* projects
  described, **359–367**
  software, 14, **364–367**
project managers, 40
proofreading, 509, 647
proposals, writing, 497
prototype software, **357–358**
punctuation, 509
purpose, of presentations, 642–643, 644

Q

quantitative metrics, widespread use of, 235
query reports, 632–633
question(s). *See also* FAQs (Frequently Asked Questions)
  behavioral, 259, **260**
  critical, **112–113**
  directed, **259**
  goal-directed diagnostic, asking, 71, 72
  illegal, **261**
  interview, 259
  needs assessment and, 355, 357–358
  non-directed, **259**
  scenarios, **260–261**
  troubleshooting and, 112–113
queues
  ACD systems and, 227
  described, **204**
  performance statistics and, 254
quick start behavior, **169**
QuickBooks, 203

R

RAM (random access memory), 608. *See also* memory
reading assignments, 462–463
README files, 157, 159
rebates, 171
rebooting, 126, 182, 203
recession, 20
recovery disks, **549**, 554
recycling, 429–430
reference sheets, 464–465
referents, **515**
release management, best practices for, 208
Registry, 124, 162–163, 549–554
reminders, setting, 631–632
remote access diagnostic tools. *See also* diagnostic tools
  described, **122–123**, 585–586, 588
  increased use of, 231, 232–233
repair tools, 122–124
repetitive strain injuries, **392–395**
replicating problems, 125, **126**
report(s)
  creating, 632
  customization of, 217
  HelpSTAR and, 632–633
  needs assessment and, 341
  problem, 498
  query, 632–633
  standard, 632
  statistical, 217–218
  writing, 498
RFP (requests for proposal), **305–307**
Ribbon menu, 610, 618
risk factors, **361**
risk management, **425–426**
Ritts, Vicki, 67
RMA (return Merchandise Authorization), 168
role playing
  described, **467**
  training through, 467–468
root cause analysis, 125, **127–128**

rootkit software, **578**, 582
routing, overflow, 227
RSS (Really Simple Syndication), **121**

S

salaries, 21, 276
Sapphire Technologies, 32–34
Sasser, W. E., Jr., 57
satellite television, 399
scheduling software, **14**
scope creep, **362**
screwdriver set, 408
script(s)
    appropriate use of, 64
    described, **64**, 114–116
    troubleshooting and, 114–116
search engines, 120–121, 175. *See also* Google
    described, **118**
    problem solving and, 157
secure erase operation, **578**, 584
security. *See also* malware; passwords; privacy; viruses
    e-mail and, 19, 424
    firewalls, **577**, 581
    forgotten information and, 170
    increased resources devoted to, 236
    installation and, 418
    physical threats to, 424
    site management and, 423–425
    specialists, 40
    spyware and, 18, 166, 577, 580
    utilities and, 565–567, 577–585, 588
self-reliance, 71, **73–74**
self-study courses, **270**
sentence(s)
    compound, 499
    run-on, 499
    simple, 499
    spaces between, 509
serial numbers, 201
servers, 182, 608, 609

service faults, **562**
service management, 216–217
service packs, **164**
service requests
    assigning, to support reps, 624–625
    closing, 625
    entering, 622–624
    escalating, 627–628
    finding, 626
    updating, 630–631
shareware
    described, **160**, 161
    utilities, 549–550
Sherwood, Kaitlin D., 496
SIT (System Information Tool), 407
site management notebook, **403–407**
skill level, of end users, 8
SLAs (service level agreements), 217
slide(s). *See also* PowerPoint (Microsoft); presentations
    backgrounds, 645
    choosing a layout for, 645–646
    color schemes, 645
    contents, 645–646
    creating, 645–648
    design, 644–645, 650–651
    footers, 645
    objects, 645, 647–648
    organizing, 648–649
    preparing text for, 646–647
    titles, 645
    transitions/animations, 648
small parts container, 408
social learning, **456**, 461. *See also* learning
software. *See also* applications; *specific software*
    bugs, **163–165**
    compatibility issues, 158–161
    configuration, 162–163
    customization, 217
    developers, 39
    development projects, 31–32

    evaluating, 29–30, **295–296**
    installation, **158–161**, 417–422
    licenses, **556**
    new releases, **164**
    overview, 11
    platforms, virtualization of, 231, 232
    problems, 158–166, 174
    rebates, 171
    specific use of, classifying end users by, 8
    support utilities, 549–558, 587
    upgrades, 11, **164**, 344
solution(s)
    looking for simple, 125–126
    optimal, **346**
    proposed, models of, 346–347
sound(s)
    operating system, loss of, 175–176
    use of, in presentations, 647–648
spam, 424
speaker notes, 648–649
spell checking, 86, 496, 520, 521, 647
spreadsheet software, **14**
spyware, 18, 166, 577, 580
SQL Server (Microsoft), 608, 609
stakeholders
    described, **339**
    identifying the roles of, 339–341
statistical information, 217–218, 235
Stein, James, 67
Stiehl, Ruth, 451
stress
    management, 210–213
    tests, **541–542**
    tolerance assessment, **261**
Strunk, William, Jr., 520
style sheets, 506–507, **511**
subjective evaluation criteria, **307–308**
Sun Microsystems, 256

supplies
location of, in the
workplace, 389
maintaining, 428–429
purchasing, 428–429
recycling, 429–430
support. *See also* help desks;
customer service;
support management
analysts, 340
centers, **25**
described, 21–27
as an IT responsibility, 25–26
outsourced, **26–27**
as a profession, 272–276
services, **27–38**
standards, **30**, 308–318
support management. *See also*
support
certification and, 265–272
interviewing applicants,
259–262
managerial concerns for,
251–265
overview, 250–279
performance statistics and,
253–254
support utilities. *See* utilities
surge suppressors, **398**
system(s). *See also* operating
systems
information utilities,
546–548, 587
problem diagnosis utilities,
559–562, 588
start-up, 546–550
unit, 387–388, 410–412, 427
viewing, as groups of
subsystems, 125,
128–129

T

tables, 507, 647–648
target audiences
knowledge of, determining,
503
for presentations, 642–643,
644, 647, 650
reading levels of, checking,
502, 520

selecting the best medium
for, 503–504
technical writing and, 502
TCO (total cost of ownership), **13**
technical accuracy check, **508**
technical support. *See also*
help desks; support;
support management;
user support workers
described, **21–22**
needs assessment and, 340
technical writers, **40**. *See also*
technical writing
technical writing. *See also*
documentation
editing drafts, 507–508
first drafts, 505–507
formats for, 506–507
getting outside reviews, 508
organizing documents,
500–501
problems, common, 513–520
process, 504–509
revising drafts, 508
specific nature of, 498–501
strategies, 510–513
style sheets, 506–507, **511**
tools, 520
telecommuting, **234–235**
telephone(s). *See also* calls
communication, challenges
specific to, 68–70
headsets, 210
hotlines, **25**, 28–29
installation of, 399
telephony, **226–228**
television service, 399
testing
adaptive, **271**
beta, **473–474**, 477
burn-in, **156**
circuits, **409**
hypotheses, 125, **130–132**
knowledge and skills, **259**
MBTI (Myers-Briggs Type
Indicator), **74–77**
memory, 541–542, 545
printers, 299–300
stress, **541–542**
training and, 471, 478

text. *See also* documentation;
fonts; technical writing;
typeface
justified, 513–514
for presentations, preparing,
646–647
thank you, saying, 71, 73
theft, of resources, 18
TIFF (Tagged Information File
Format), 184, 568
time management tools, **216**
timelines, feasibility, **336**
topics, for presentations,
642–643, 644
trackballs, 428
trade
books, 116, 462
periodicals, **116–117**, 135,
294, 344
trainee(s). *See also* training
backgrounds of,
determining, 447, 449
content needs of, 447–448
knowledge of, determining,
449–450
skill levels of, 448–449
trainers, **40**
training. *See also* learning;
trainees
breaks in, providing, 476
described, **445–446**
environment, monitoring,
475–476
evaluation methods,
designing, 471–473
facilities, setting up, 474
formats, effective, 456–458
higher-quality, progressing
toward, 476–479
inadequate, 168–169, 210, 212
materials, **461–470**, 471
objectives, defining,
450–454
obtaining feedback
regarding, 476
ongoing, 264
on-the-job, **457**
overview, 31, 444–481
planning, 447–454
preparation for, 454–473